THE NATIONAL PARKS FISHING GUIDE

"*The National Parks Fishing Guide* is the most complete work ever on this subject. Every traveling angler should have it."
—Bernard "Lefty" Krey, outdoors writer

"I've benefited extensively from *The National Parks Fishing Guide* and plan to use it as a standard research volume whenever I schedule a fishing trip to one of our national parks."
—Gerald Almy, Hunting and Fishing Editor, *Sports Afield Magazine*

"*The National Parks Fishing Guide* will save thousands of anglers millions of hours by aiding them to easily find the best angling in all of our national parks. The information Mr. Gartner provides is accurate, concise and timely. Fishermen contemplating a trip to any national park should have this book."
—Harry W. Murray, author of *Fly Fishing in the Shenandoah National Park*

THE NATIONAL PARKS FISHING GUIDE

ROBERT GARTNER

Chester, Connecticut

Library of Congress Cataloging-in-Publication Data

Gartner, Robert H.
The national parks fishing guide / by Robert H. Gartner. — 1st ed.
p. cm.
ISBN 0-87106-493-6
1. Fishing—United States—Guide-books.
2. National parks and reserves—United States—Guide-books. I. Title.
SH463.G37 1990
799.1'0973—dc20 89-77348
CIP

Produced by Menasha Ridge Press
Design by Deborah Wong
Manufactured in the United States of America
First Edition/First Printing

DEDICATION

This book is dedicated to my father, Hank, and my brother, Bill, who taught me how to fish and who remain my favorite fishing partners. And to my wife, Sally, and daughter, Amy. Sally, for her continuing enthusiasm and support for my various projects, and Amy, my future fishing partner.

• CONTENTS

• AUTHOR'S NOTE

To ensure the accuracy of this book, the report for each park has been reviewed by either someone on the park staff or someone with the appropriate state fish commission (or both). In most cases, I have not mentioned or recommended guides or tackle shops by name or listed the prices of recommended reference materials. My reasoning is that both people and prices change too frequently and such information is quickly outdated. I hope this book will save you time by providing the basic information, but further effort is required on your part.

• PREFACE

Ask someone to name a national park and nine times out of ten the person will say Yellowstone. Ask people who love to fish what national park they would like to fish and the usual answer is Yellowstone. Yellowstone was the first national park in the United States (designated in 1872) and is probably the most famous national park in the world.

The National Park System comprises 355 protected areas in 49 states, the District of Columbia, Guam, Puerto Rico, Saipan, and the Virgin Islands. The parklands range from the vast wilderness of Alaska's national parks to the birthplaces and homes of former presidents. The National Park Service (NPS), an agency in the Department of Interior, manages this system.

Of the 355 park service units, 125 provide fishing opportunities. Fishing is a major attraction in only a few parks. Usually the natural beauty of a park or its historical significance is the main attraction. In the majority of parks, fishing is a secondary activity, meaning that it is not promoted but is available to those who are interested.

Everyone knows about the wealth of riches that Yellowstone provides for fishing, but how many know about the large rainbow trout found in the Colorado River flowing through the canyon in Grand Canyon National Park? Another example is Valley Forge National Historical Park in Pennsylvania, the site of the Continental Army's winter encampment during 1777–78. It now features trout fishing in Valley Creek, which runs through the park.

Glacier National Park is very popular for backpacking and fishing because of its large number of high-country lakes. The fallacy of the high country is that although the lakes are beautiful, some are also barren of fish. Thousands of hours are wasted every year casting flies and lures in fishless waters. This book details the parks with high-country areas and will help put an end to the myth that all high-country lakes are teeming with fish that have never seen a hook and will bite anything.

The National Parks Fishing Guide is not only for the serious fisherman, but also for the family vacation planner for whom fishing is not the primary reason to visit the park. This book describes the fishable areas of the National Park System. This is not a how-to book with instructions in fishing techniques, but rather a where-to guide providing basic information required for fishing. One can never have too much information when traveling to a new area.

Every National Park Service area that provides fishing is listed by state. Not all the states are included. For example, although Idaho is a fishing paradise, the two NPS units in Idaho are Craters of the Moon National Monument and Nez Perce National Historical Park, neither of which offers fishing. Idaho has large tracts of federal land with great fishing; this land, however, is located either in national forests managed by the U.S. Forest Service in the Department of Agriculture or is public domain land managed by the Bureau of Land Management (BLM) in the Department of Interior.

Other states omitted because their national parks do not provide fishing are Connecticut, Delaware, Illinois, Iowa, New Hampshire, Rhode Island, and Vermont. Delaware is the only state without a unit of the national park system.

• ACKNOWLEDGMENTS

Unfortunately, space does not allow me to mention by name all my friends and National Park Service and state fisheries people who supplied information, reviewed sections of this book, or provided photographs. Their generous assistance was invaluable. I would like to especially thank Bob Gallagher for his help with the research; Stan Young for his editing help; Dan Cutrona and Tim Krasnansky for their fine map work; Karl Esser for his technical advice; and Tom DuRant of the National Park Service Historic Photographic Collection (Springfield, Virginia) for his help in locating photographs.

THE NATIONAL PARKS FISHING GUIDE

• HOW TO USE THIS BOOK and Other Useful Information

The National Parks Fishing Guide is designed to provide information for each park and to list other sources of information that will make a fishing trip to the park more enjoyable and productive.

Outdoor writer Byron Dalyrmple wrote a two-part article in *Fly Fisherman* (1977, Vol.8, Nos. 2,3) entitled "Trips Without Tears," which extolled the common-sense methods of proper planning and acquiring as much knowledge as possible about an area. If money is going to be spent traveling to and fishing a new area, it makes sense to spend some time researching the area. A few phone calls or letters can supply information about weather conditions, water conditions, fly hatches, or whatever information is necessary to ensure a successful trip. This book will provide the basic information as well as explain where to write and whom to contact for more details.

The information provided for each park that has fishing is:

1. A brief description of each park. Numerous books have already been written describing the national parks.
2. How to get there.
3. A description of the fishing.
4. A general map of the park (where appropriate).
5. Whether a fishing license is needed.
6. A brief description of camping.
7. A list of the necessary topographical maps or nautical charts.
8. The park address and phone number.
9. The address and phone number of the nearest chamber of commerce that can provide a list of accommodations, guides, and available services.
10. Sources of additional information about the park or area that will be helpful for fishing.

State and park fishing regulations are constantly changing, are often very lengthy, and so were not included. Contact the park or state for current regulations.

As a starting point, write to the individual park, addressing the letter to the Superintendent. They have short brochures that include the most up-to-date maps (especially trail maps) and information about the climate and clothing recommendations, lists of area concessions and accommodations and, most important, fishing information and special park regulations. Also, ask for a list of publications regarding fishing in the park.

One final note about requesting information: Try to be as specific as possible. If it is camping in the back country that is of interest, don't just ask whether camping facilities are available in the park; ask about back-country camping and whether permits are required. If the area of interest is a specific river in Montana, write to the Montana Department of Fish, Wildlife, and Parks and ask about that stream rather than about fishing in Montana.

National Park Classifications

Units of the National Park System have a variety of titles. These include such designations as national park, national monument, national battlefield, and national seashore. Despite the name differences, all are federally owned and managed by the government to preserve their scenic, historical, or wildlife values. Most of the titles are self-explanatory. Throughout this book, the generic term "park" is used to encompass the various titles. Brief definitions of the most common titles are:

National Park (NP)—generally covers a large area containing a variety of resources, usually chosen for its natural scenic and scientific values. Yellowstone in Wyoming/Montana/Idaho and Everglades in Florida are prime examples.

National Monument (NM)—generally covers a smaller area than a national park and does not have as great a diversity of attractions. For example, Dinosaur National Monument in Colorado/Utah is an area of archeological significance.

National Seashore (NS)/National Lakeshore (NL)—protects offshore islands and coastal areas and offers water-oriented recreation. National lakeshores include freshwater areas such as Sleeping Bear Dunes in Michigan; National seashores include saltwater areas such as Point Reyes in California.

National Historic Park (NHP)—an area preserving the location of an event or activity important to our heritage. The Chesapeake and Ohio Canal (C&O Canal) is an example; it runs through parts of Maryland, West Virginia, and the District of Columbia.

National Historic Site (NHS)—similar to a national historic park but is usually smaller. One example is the Lyndon B. Johnson Natural Historic Site in Texas, which preserves the former president's birthplace, home, and ranch.

A wide variety of titles have been used for areas associated with military history: national military park (NMP), national battlefield park (NBP), national battlefield site (NBS), and national battlefield (NB). National monuments and national historical parks may also include features associated with military history.

National Memorial (NMem)—areas that are primarily commemorative and are associated with an nationally significant individual or event. Wright Brothers National Memorial in North Carolina and Lincoln Memorial in Washington D.C. are examples.

National Recreation Area (NRA)—an area or facility set aside for recreational use. It may include major areas in urban centers. Examples are Lake Chelan NRA in Washington, a natural area, and Golden Gate NRA in San Francisco, an urban area.

National River (NR) and Wild and Scenic River (WSR)—free-flowing waterways and the land along their shores (usually a one-quarter-mile-wide corridor of land on each side of the river). Buffalo River in Arkansas is a national river and the Obed River in Tennessee is a wild and scenic river.

National Preserve (NPr)—an area set aside for the protection of certain natural resources. Big Cypress in Florida and Big Thicket in Texas were the first national preserves.

National Parkway (NPKY)—a scenic roadway designed for leisurely driving. The Blue Ridge Parkway in Virginia and North Carolina is representative of the parkways.

Park Fees and Discounts

Many parks have entrance fees ranging from $1.00 per person to $10.00 per vehicle. In addition, there may be recreation fees for camping, boat launching, parking, and special use permits such as off-road vehicle (ORV) permits. These fees are subject to change each year.

Discounts available to park users are:

1. *Golden Eagle Pass*—costs $25 per year and allows free entrance to the national parks. It can be obtained in person at the parks that charge entrance fees or by mailing a check or money order, payable to the National Park Service, Public Inquiries Office, P.O. Box 37127, Washington, D.C., 20013-7127.

2. *Golden Age Passport*—is a free lifetime entrance pass to all the national parks available to U.S. residents age 62 or older. The holder is entitled to a 50 percent discount on recreation fees.
3. *Golden Access Passport*—is a free lifetime entrance pass to all the national parks for U.S. residents who are permanently blind, disabled, or otherwise handicapped. The person must be receiving federal benefits or be eligible for such benefits as a result of the disability.

These special passports pertain to any federal recreation area where fees are charged. Applications for the Golden Age and Golden Access passports must be made in person by those eligible, from the parks where they are used, from the regional offices of the National Park Service (listed in Appendix 4), or from the above address for the Golden Eagle Passport.

Fees for privately operated concession facilities within parks are collected by the concessioners and are not federal recreation use fees. Concession fees are not covered by any of the three passports.

Camping

There are 108 areas in the national park system that provide camping facilities. In this book, 74 have camping facilities. Most campsites are available on a first come, first served basis and cannot be reserved.

Eleven parks are so popular that reservations are required for certain campgrounds. These parks are:

1. Grand Canyon in Arizona
2. Yosemite in California
3. Sequoia/Kings Canyon in California
4. Rocky Mountain in Colorado
5. Shenandoah in Virginia
6. Great Smoky Mountains in Tennessee and North Carolina
7. Cape Hatteras in North Carolina
8. Acadia in Maine
9. Yellowstone in Wyoming/Montana/Idaho
10. Joshua Tree in California
11. Whiskeytown in California

Reservations for the summer camping season can be made through Ticketron, a nationwide ticket agency, no earlier than eight weeks in advance. They can be made in person at any one of approximately six hundred nationwide Ticketron walk-in outlets or by mail from: Ticketron, Dept. R, 401 Hackensack Avenue, Hackensack, NJ, 07601.

By mail, allow about six weeks. A walk-in reservation can be made up to the day before expected campground use. Reservations cannot be made by phone. A brochure on campground reservations that explains the Ticketron system is available from: National Park Service, Public Inquiries Office, P.O. Box 37127, Washington, D.C., 20013-7127.

Many parks offering back-country camping, such as Glacier in Montana, require free back-country use and fire permits. Usually these can be obtained at park headquarters, ranger stations, or visitor centers upon arrival. In some parks, the number of permits is limited to avoid overcrowding, so one should inquire to determine if a reservation is necessary.

The best source of information is a small book entitled *The National Parks Camping Guide*, available for $3.50 from: Superintendent of Documents, U.S. Government Printing Office, Washington, D.C., 20402. The stock number is 024-005-01028-9. Payment by check or money order should be made payable to the Superintendent of Documents. This book is updated regularly and lists camping facilities in the parks and explains the NPS camping policies, types of campgrounds, and fees.

In addition, most bookstores carry campground and trailer park guides for specific regions of the U.S. as well as for the entire country. These guides include public and private campgrounds near the parks and may be useful in case park campgrounds are full or nonexistent.

Maps

Wherever you go, you will need maps. Most parks have a brochure—obtainable by mail or at the entrance to the park—containing a park map. The park map may suffice for smaller parks but may be inadequate for larger parks where more detail is required to find fishing and hiking locations.

Topographic Maps

The main source of topo maps is the U.S. Geological Survey (USGS). The USGS has mapped each state and publishes an index for each state showing how the state is divided into map quadrangles (quad sheets). The state index maps are free and are an essential aid in ordering the proper maps.

Index maps and quad sheets can be obtained from the USGS at two locations. Maps of the areas east of the Mississippi River, including Minnesota, Puerto Rico, and the Virgin Islands, may be ordered from: Branch of Distribution, U.S. Geological Survey, 1200 South Eads Street, Arlington, VA, 22202.

Topographic maps and a compass are essential for finding back-country lakes and streams. *—National Park Service photo by Fred Mang Jr.*

Maps of the areas west of the Mississippi River, including Alaska, Hawaii, Louisiana, American Samoa and Guam, are obtainable from: Branch of Distribution, U.S. Geological Survey, Box 25286, Federal Center, Denver, CO, 80225.

Included in each state index map is a list of dealers in that state who stock and sell the USGS maps. Dealer prices are usually a bit higher than USGS prices, but dealers provide the convenience of instant availability and through them it is possible to examine a map before buying it. The index also lists libraries that maintain reference files of the USGS maps. These files are usually in major city and college libraries.

The USGS has also mapped a number of parks and sells a single, complete park map, in addition to the quad sheets for the park. Although a complete park map is at a smaller scale than individual quad sheets, it may be adequate and will cost far less than several quad sheets. A list of individual park maps is available from the USGS.

The price as of 1990 for the 7.5-minute quad sheets (scale 1:24,500) and the 15-minute quads (scale 1:62,500) is $2.50 per sheet. An individual park map is $4.00.

Nautical Charts

Nautical charts are invaluable for anyone fishing offshore along either coast or the Great Lakes. Chart features include the coastline, topography, dangers, soundings, buoys and beacons, radio and radar stations, and other navigational aids.

Although nautical charts are listed for the coastal and Great Lakes parks, it would be beneficial to order the Nautical Chart Catalogs from the address below. The free catalogs are similar to the state index for the topographic maps and they also include lists of additional navigational maps and a list of dealers in each state.

Nautical charts vary in price and can be ordered from: Distribution Division (OA/C44), National Ocean Survey, Riverdale, MD, 20737; phone: (301) 436-6990.

Catalogs of interest for fishing are:

1. *Nautical Chart Catalog #1*—Atlantic and Gulf coasts, including Puerto Rico and the Virgin Islands.
2. *Nautical Chart Catalog #2*—Pacific Coast, including Hawaii, Guam, and the Samoa Islands.
3. *Nautical Chart Catalog #3*—Alaska, including the Aleutian Islands.
4. *Nautical Chart Catalog #4*—Great Lakes and adjacent waterways.

U.S./ Canadian Map Service The U.S./Canadian Map Service is a private company that has researched and coordinated the availability of all maps and charts produced by the federal, state, and provincial governments of the United States and Canada and by private map makers. The Map Service offers USGS topographical maps along with raised-relief maps, oceanographic charts, and special interest maps.

These maps cost a bit more and there is a charge for each state index; however the added cost may be offset by faster service. Unlike government agencies, the Map Service will accept phone orders and charge cards. The address for inquiries or phone orders is: U.S./ Canadian Map Service, Box 249, Neenah, WI, 54956; phone: (414) 731-0101.

Other Maps Various private companies publish maps useful for fishing, such as hydrographic (contour) maps of individual lakes. These maps are listed in the discussions of each park.

High-Country Lakes

Eleven parks in the west contain numerous high-country lakes. Lakes that are situated at an elevation higher than 8,000 feet are considered high-country lakes. Some of these lakes are barren of fish even though they may have been stocked at one time. Barren lakes occur because: 1) waterfalls prevent fish from entering the lake; 2) they may freeze up during the winter; or 3) they may lack the necessary nutrients to support fish. The water in many high-country lakes is almost pure and contains few nutrients, without which fish will be stunted. It is a good idea, therefore, to keep in mind that the best fishing may be in lakes at lower elevations.

This book provides as much information as possible about the high-country lakes in the 11 parks, but cannot detail every lake in each park because of the large number of lakes involved and because information is often lacking.

When planning a trip into the high country, plan a route and select the lakes that may be fished along the route. Contact the park and inquire about the fishing potential of the lakes along the route. Don't assume that fish are everywhere in the high country.

For example, in Glacier National Park, fish stocking was stopped in the late 1960s. Current park service policy is to manage waters to protect native species and the natural food chain. Many lakes in Glacier that were once stocked are now marginal fisheries or have reverted to their natural barren state. Unless you do some checking beforehand, you may be wasting your time on fishless waters.

Also be aware that high-country lakes have very short seasons. They may be ice-free for only two or three months and these periods may not coincide with your trip. Don't hike back into an area only to find the lake frozen; do some checking ahead of time. Finally, these lakes are often fragile ecosystems and keeping a mess of fish could do permanent damage to the fishery stocks of the lake. Keep only enough to eat and release the rest.

• ALABAMA

Horseshoe Bend National Military Park

Horseshoe Bend NMP is located on the Tallapoosa River at the place where, on March 27, 1814, Andrew Jackson led a military force of Tennessee frontiersmen that defeated the Creek Indians who were allied with the British. The defeat broke the Creeks' power in the southeastern United States and Creek lands comprising three-fifths of the present State of Alabama and one-fifth of Georgia were added to the United States and opened for settlement.

Access Located in east central Alabama (Tallapoosa County), the park is on Alabama Highway 49, 12 miles north of Dadeville and 18 miles northeast of Alexander City via Newsite.

Fishing The Tallapoosa River flows for 3.5 miles through the park and contains a wide variety of sport fish species, including bass, bream, crappie, catfish, and carp. Spotted bass fishing is especially good.

The area from Alabama Highway 49 at Horseshoe Bend to the headwaters of Lake Martin at Irwin Shoals is a fine area to float fish for spotted bass. This is a beautiful stretch of river with many shoals. It is also a good stretch for flathead catfish. In the spring, white bass and large striped bass are caught near Irwin Shoals. Upstream from the park are fewer shoals and more deep water with a mixture of largemouth and spotted bass.

The abundant tree tops, stumps, and brush in the water provide good areas to fish, as do the head and tail areas of the shoals. The most popular lures are the standard crankbaits, spinnerbaits, and plastic worms.

The construction of Harris Dam and Reservoir upstream from the park has affected river fishing. The flows can be quite variable depending on whether the turbines are running at Harris Dam. There may be plenty of water or very little. When the turbines are running, the river can be floated with little trouble. The best times for floating are summer and fall. Canoes or flat-bottom johnboats with motors of less than 10 horsepower are recommended, since the river is riddled with large boulders and ledge rock exposures.

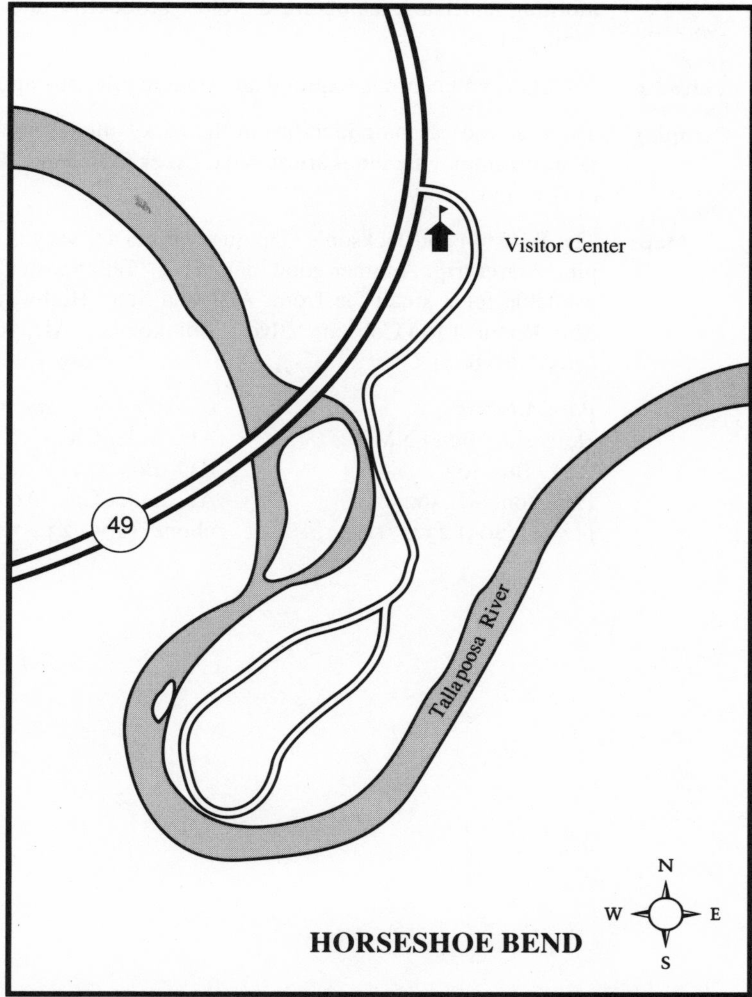

The river is readily accessible from the park's boat ramp on the south side of the Highway 49 bridge. When floating from Highway 49 to the headwaters of Lake Martin (Irwin Shoals), access is available at the mouth of Jaybird Creek via a dirt road along the east side of the river. The float trip is about 6 miles.

Fishing pressure ranges from light during the summer and winter months to moderate during the spring and fall. Summer use is light because of the uncomfortably high temperature and humidity. Early morning and late evening are the most productive and comfortable fishing times.

License An Alabama license is required and state regulations apply.

Camping There are no camping facilities in the park, only a picnic area. The nearest camping facilities are at Wind Creek State Park, 6 miles south of Alexander City.

Maps The Buttston and Jackson's Gap quad sheets are very useful in planning a river trip. Another good map is the "Tallapoosa County Map" available for a small fee from: Alabama State Highway Dept., c/o Map Room, 1409 Coliseum Blvd., Montgomery, AL, 36130; phone: (205) 261-6071.

Park Address
Horseshoe Bend NMP
Rt.1, Box 103
Daviston, AL 36256
phone: (205) 234-7111

Chamber of Commerce
Alexander City C.C.
P.O. Box 229
Alexander City, AL 35010
phone: (205) 234-3461

• ALASKA

Every superlative applied to fishing has been used to describe fishing in Alaska. It is so great that writer Homer Circle has stated: "Every fisherman owes himself a trip to Alaska." Fishing in Alaska is largely a fly-in operation. Visitors typically spend a week or longer at a lodge or camp and are flown to a different area each day, or charter a plane and have the pilot fly them to an area and pick them up at a specified time.

Alaska fishing in general is legendary, but when traveling to Alaska strictly for the fishing, Glacier Bay, Katmai, Gates of the Arctic, and Lake Clark among the national parks and preserves are most noteworthy. A few of the lakes and rivers in the parks are on the itinerary of the lodge operators, but by and large, the really great fishing is not on parklands, except for Katmai National Park and Preserve, which has top rainbow trout and salmon waters.

One of the problems in detailing the resources of Alaska is the state's vast size. Large parts of Alaska have not been inventoried to determine exactly what is there. This is especially true of the national parks and preserves, which embrace some of the state's most inaccessible and primitive lands.

When most of the parks were established in 1980 by the Alaska National Interest Lands Conservation Act, one of the first priorities of the newly hired park staff was to inventory the resources. This is an ongoing process and progress has been slow because of the limited number of park personnel and the huge size of the areas.

Planning a do-it-yourself trip to Alaska can be a logistical nightmare. My advice for fishing Alaska is to book the entire trip through a guide service or lodge. Choose a section of the state to fish or a species to catch (one area may be better for steelhead while another is tops for king salmon) and write for information. Costs for one week will range from $1,500 to $4,000 depending on destination and season. Alaska lodges and guide services advertise in most of the major outdoor magazines. Either write directly to the lodges or send for a copy of *Worlds of Alaska and Canada's Yukon* from: Alaska State Division of Tourism, Pouch E, Juneau, AK, 99811; phone: (907)465-2010.

For those who prefer do-it-yourself trips, a good aid is *The Mile-*

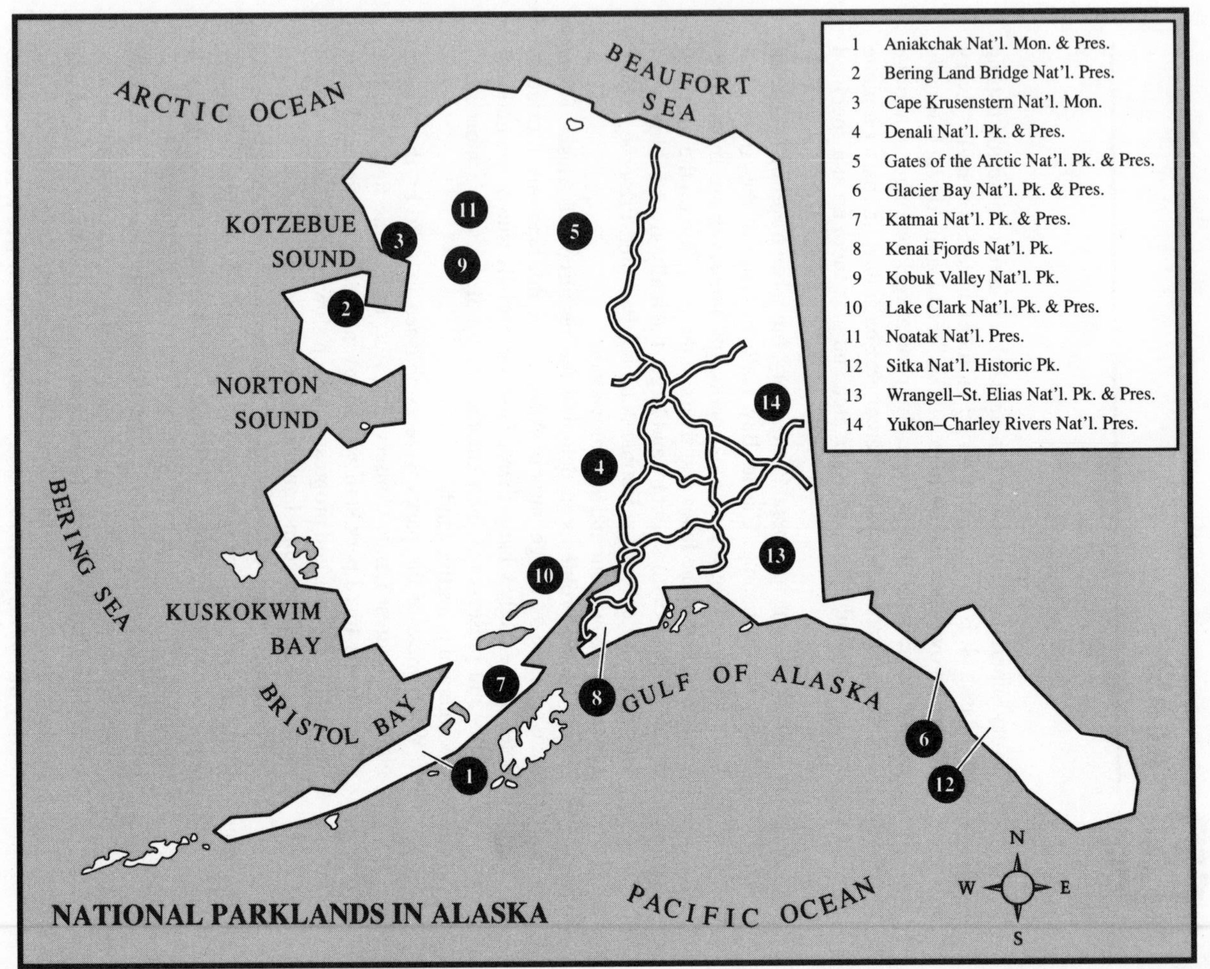

NATIONAL PARKLANDS IN ALASKA

post, a comprehensive travel guide to Alaska and the north including a large-scale, color map of Alaska entitled "Milepost Plan-a-Trip Map." *The Milepost* is updated yearly and is available from Alaska Northwest Publishing Company, 130 Second Avenue South, Edmonds, WA, 98020; phone: (206) 774-4111. The map can be purchased separately.

Another excellent information source is *Alaska's Parklands* by Nancy Simmerman. This book is a complete guide to all federal and state parks, forests, preserves, etc. The book is published by: The Mountaineers, 306 Second Avenue West, Seattle, WA, 98119. The toll-free number is: 1-800-553-4453.

A successful fishing trip to Alaska will take considerable planning and research, not to mention a substantial bankroll. Don't scrimp on the planning or research. A thorough effort here will save money, eliminate costly surprises, and help ensure a dream trip with lifetime memories.

Aniakchak National Monument and Preserve

Located on the Alaska Peninsula in southwestern Alaska, Aniakchak is one of Alaska's most remote national park areas. The park contains a huge collapsed volcano with a caldera 6 miles in diameter and walls up to 2,000 feet high. Few people other than natives and scientists have explored the park.

Access Access is by scheduled airlines from Anchorage to Meshik (Port Heiden). The park is 10 miles from Meshik. Access into the park is by floatplane or foot; there are no roads or trails leading there. Foot access from Port Heiden is across moist tundra and is tough going but not impossible.

Fishing The Aniakchak River, a designated wild-and-scenic river, originates from Surprise Lake within the caldera and flows eastward for 27 miles to the Pacific Ocean. The river is shallow and rocky with low falls as it drops at a rate of 60 feet per mile for the first 15 miles after flowing out of the lake. This upper river is floatable by raft but is considered hazardous because of protruding and submerged rocks that can damage or upset a raft. The lower 12 miles slowly meander through flatland to Aniakchak Bay.

The Aniakchak is one of the very few rivers on the Pacific side of the Alaska Peninsula supporting good runs of sockeye salmon. The sockeye runs start in June. Larger runs of pink and chum salmon begin in July.

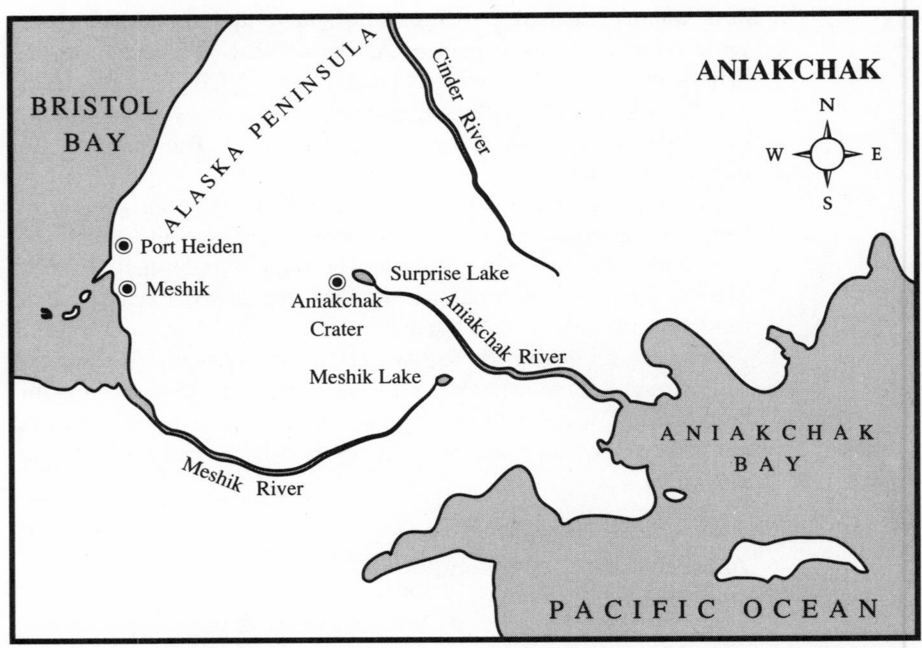

Other major rivers in the park are the Meshik and the Cinder. Both contain Dolly Varden trout, as well as hosting runs of king, sockeye, silver, and chum salmon, with the addition of pink salmon in the Meshik. The Meshik River is floatable (from Meshik Lake) in a small raft but several portages may be required around shallow rocky sections.

The Aniakchak area has some of the stormiest weather to be found anywhere. It can make aircraft access difficult and access into the caldera is frequently impossible because of clouds and very strong downdrafts. Plan for cold, wet weather and don't be surprised if your pickup is delayed due to the changing weather. Remember too, that an equipment failure or accident may have far more serious consequences here than in a less remote area.

License An Alaska fishing license is required.

Camping Camping is unrestricted in the park but a back-country permit is required from the park office at King Salmon. For safety reasons, leave a copy of your itinerary with the park office. A lodge has recently opened on nearby Paint Creek.

Maps Topographic maps for the park in the 1:250,000 series are: Bristol

Bay, Chignik, Sutwick Island, and Ugashik. Maps just for the river in the 1:63,360 series are Chignik D-1, and Sutwick Island D-5 and D-6.

Park Address
Aniakchak NMP
c/o Katmai NPP
P.O. Box 7
King Salmon, AK 99613
phone: (907) 246-3305

Bering Land Bridge National Preserve

The Bering Land Bridge was a bridge of land used by humans, plants, and animals to migrate from Asia to North America more than ten thousand years ago. The bridge is now overlain by the Bering Sea and Strait, and the Chukchi Sea. The park totals 2,767,520 acres and is totally undeveloped. Its main attractions are an abundant variety of flora and wildlife. The Eskimos continue to use the area for subsistence hunting and fishing.

Access The park lies just below the Arctic Circle on the Seward Peninsula in northwest Alaska between Kotzebue and Nome and is almost totally isolated. There are no roads and the only access is by plane from Nome or Kotzebue.

Fishing The park includes a number of clear streams and lakes that can provide excellent fishing for salmon, char, and grayling. However, much remains to be learned about the area's fish and fishing.

Grayling seem to be common throughout the park. They are abundant in Imuruk Lake, its largest body of water. Grayling fishing is reportedly very good when the lake is quiet, but frequent winds restrict fishing. The least cisco (whitefish family) is also found in the lake.

The Serpentine and Inmachuk rivers and Hot Springs Creek contain grayling and arctic char. Dolly Varden are also found in the park.

All five species of Pacific salmon occur outside the park in the Seward Peninsula area, but their distribution in the park is unknown. Pink and chum salmon are thought to use park waters.

Northern pike are found in the park's Kuzitrin and Noxapaga rivers, while cisco inhabit the Devil Mountain Lakes and the Killeak Lakes. Generally, the rivers and streams have good populations of aquatic insects, which indicates an adequate food supply.

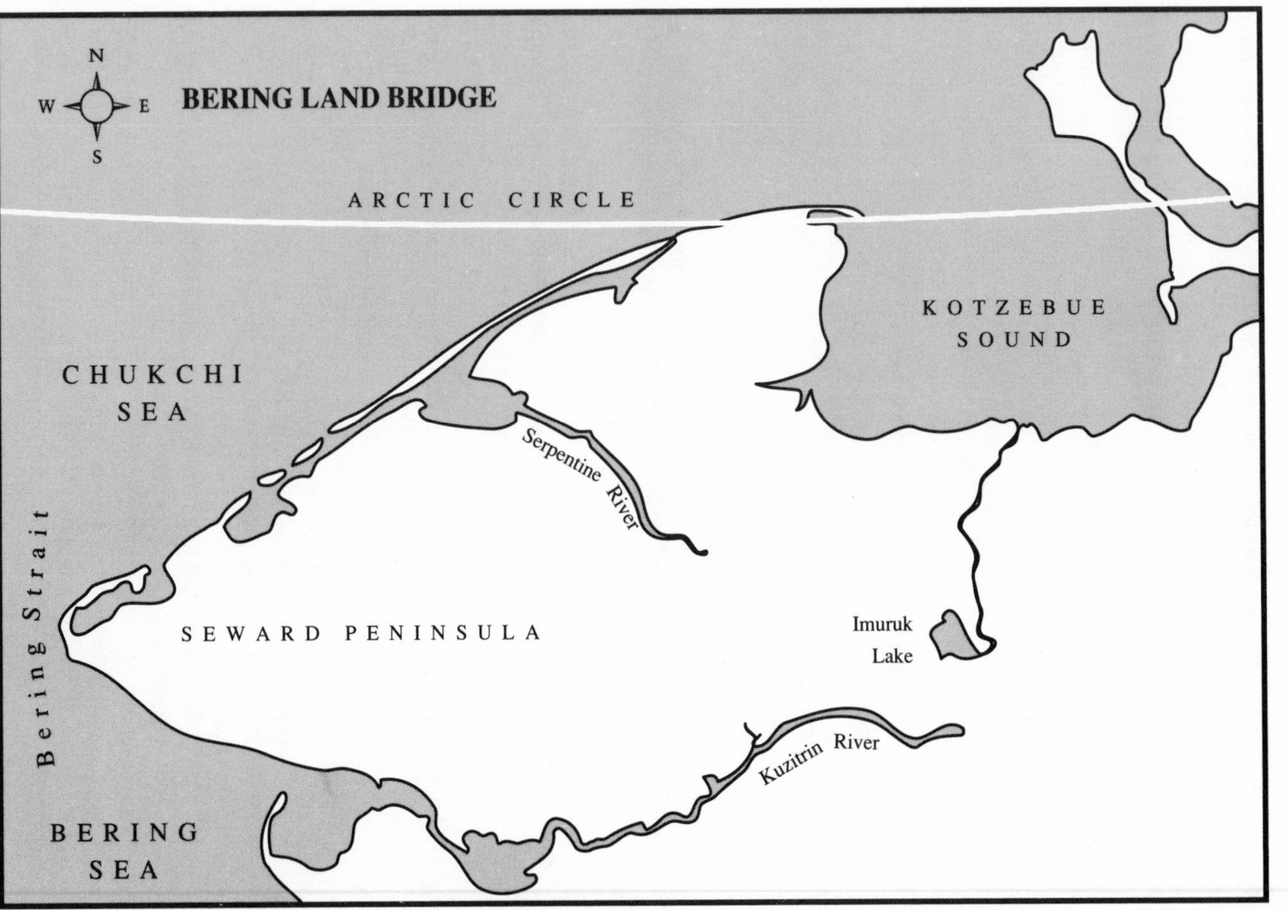
N
W
E
S
BERING LAND BRIDGE
ARCTIC CIRCLE
KOTZEBUE SOUND
CHUKCHI SEA
Serpentine River
Bering Strait
SEWARD PENINSULA
Imuruk Lake
Kuzitrin River
BERING SEA

No local guides or outfitters operate in the park. You will have to provide everything. Fishing, river floating, boating, and canoeing opportunities are there if the logistical problems can be solved.

License An Alaska fishing license is required.

Camping Camping is permitted anywhere on public lands. Wood for campfires is scarce. There are extensive private lands in the area, mostly along the coast. Do not camp on the private lands. There are no accommodations in the park or the Eskimo villages. The nearest lodging and meals are at Kotzebue and Nome.

Maps After reading all of the above, if you still wish to visit the park, refer to the following USGS maps in the 1:250,000 series: Bendeleben, Kotzebue, Shishmaref, and Teller.

Park Address
Bering Land Bridge NP
P.O. Box 220
Nome, AK 99762
phone: (907) 443-2522

Chamber of Commerce
Nome C.C.
P.O. Box 251
Nome, AK 99762
phone: (907) 443-5535

Cape Krusenstern National Monument

Cape Krusenstern National Monument is in northwestern Alaska and borders the Chukchi Sea and Kotzebue Sound, north of the Arctic Circle. It encompasses 560,000 acres and is archeologically important because the beach ridges along the Chukchi Sea contain artifacts of every major cultural period of arctic prehistory. The area is important to local Eskimos for subsistence hunting and fishing. The park is totally undeveloped.

Access Northwestern Alaska is inaccessible by road. Daily commercial flights serve Kotzebue from Anchorage and Fairbanks. From Kotzebue, access to the park is by chartered plane or chartered boat.

Fishing Little is known about the park's waters. Most visitors are chiefly interested in backpacking or camping.

A series of inland lagoons and ponds contain grayling, arctic char, and whitefish. Rabbit Creek, in the northern part of the park, offers fine fishing for grayling and Dolly Varden. The Noatak River, to the east of the park, has plentiful chum salmon, grayling, Dolly Varden, and arctic char.

The Wulik River, immediately north of the park, is rated as the best arctic char river in Alaska. There is a lodge on the river and charter

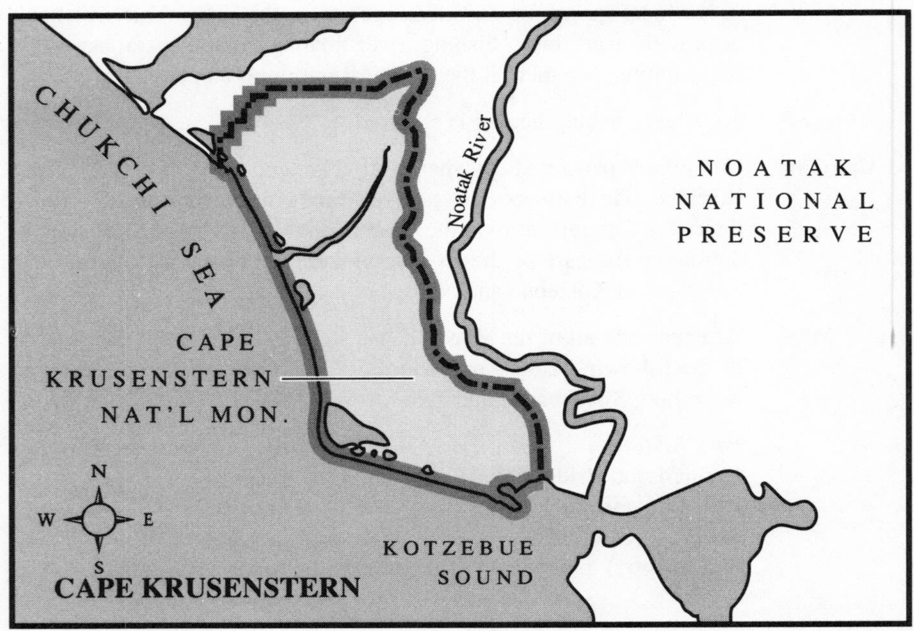

flights can be arranged from Kotzebue. Char fishing is best from July into September.

License An Alaska fishing license is required.

Camping There are no facilities, trails, or services in the park. Camping is permitted anywhere on public land, but firewood is scarce. Be sure not to camp on private land.

Maps These topographic maps in the 1:250,000 series will be needed: Kotzebue and Noatak.

Park Address
Cape Krusenstern NM
P.O. Box 1029
Kotzebue, AK 99752
phone: (907) 442-3890

Denali (Mount McKinley) National Park and Preserve

Denali National Park was created by the 1980 Alaska National Interest Lands Conservation Act. The boundary of former Mount McKinley

National Park was enlarged by 4 million acres and the area was redesignated as Denali National Park. Denali is the ancient Athapascan Indian name for North America's loftiest mountain, meaning "the high one." Although the park name changed, Mount McKinley remains named for William McKinley, 25th president of the United States.

Denali typifies Alaska's character as one of the last great wilderness areas in the world. The park is studded with mountains, glaciers, hundreds of small lakes and rivers, and abundant and varied wildlife for which it is famous.

Access Denali is in south central Alaska, approximately 240 miles north of Anchorage and 120 miles south of Fairbanks. Alaska Highway 3 connects the two cities and runs along the park's eastern boundary.

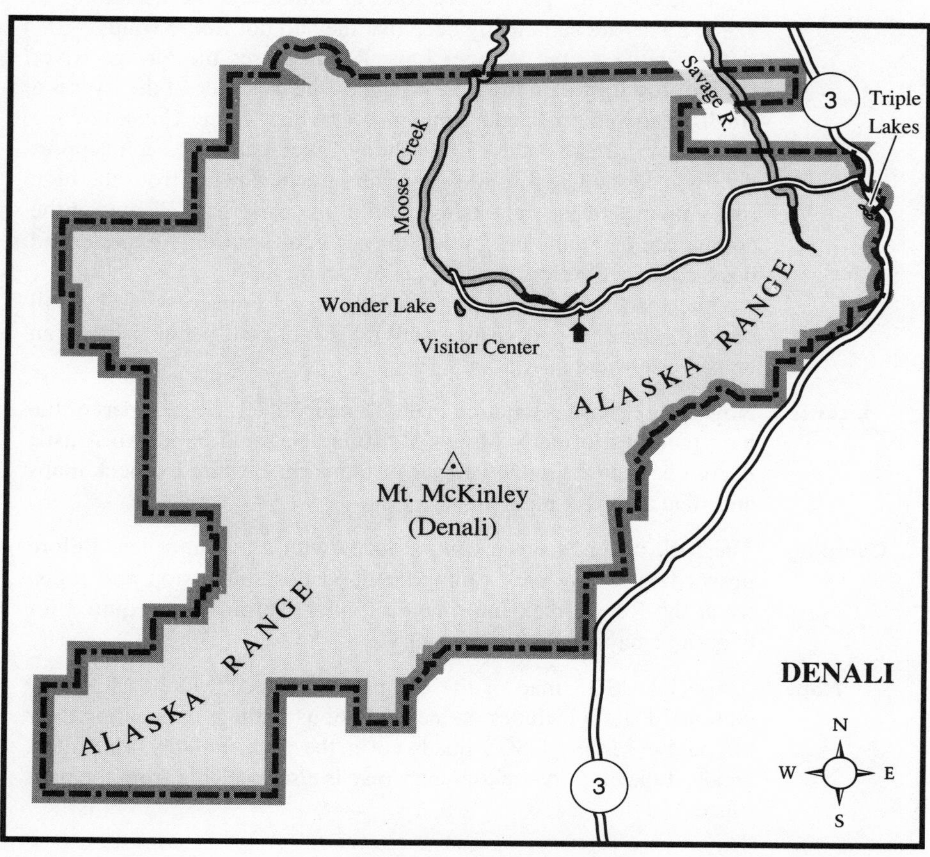

Air, bus, and train transportation is also available. The park brochure contains a good description of the various means of access.

Fishing Fishing opportunities in the park are limited and fishing is considered poor by Alaska standards. Fishing is generally confined to arctic grayling, although lake trout also exist in some of the park's accessible waters.

The park valleys are choked with millions of tons of glacier-gouged gravel and silt, and glacial runoff keeps most park waters in a constantly milk-colored, silt-laden condition that fish find intolerable.

Wonder Lake contains lake trout. Boating is permitted although there are no rental boats and motors are not allowed. To the east of Wonder Lake is Moose Creek with good grayling fishing in its upper reaches.

Near the park entrance are the Triple Lakes (also known as the Yanert Lakes), which contain a population of small grayling. Many of the lakes in the park freeze solid in winter and are fishless. The Triple Lakes are sufficiently deep that they do not freeze solid.

At mile 14.5, the Wonder Lake Road crosses the Savage River Bridge. Just upstream from the bridge on the west side of the river is a small clear-water tributary containing grayling. Stony Creek flowing out of Bergh Lake and its Little Stony Creek tributary each support grayling. Stony Creek is a clear-water stream flowing from the high rocky ravines of the mountains south of the park road. Fishing at the confluence of Stony and Little Stony is good, but only experienced back-country travelers should plan to fish there.

Other park waters also have fish but they are inaccessible by trail or road. Overall, park fishing activity is minimal; better fishing can be had elsewhere in Alaska.

License No fishing license is required in the Denali Wilderness, the part of the park that was formerly Mount McKinley National Park. An Alaska license is required in the balance of the park. Be sure to check maps and state and park regulations.

Camping The park contains seven campgrounds with 230 campsites. Before proceeding to any park campground, visitors must stop and register at the Riley Creek Information Center. Permits are required for overnight stays in the back country.

Maps A special USGS map of the old park (entitled "Mount McKinley National Park") includes the new additions without delineating their boundaries. Many USGS quads cover the park, notably McKinley, Healy, Talkeetna. A back-country map is also available from the park office.

Park Address
Denali National Park and Preserve
P.O. Box 9
Denali Park, AK 99755
phone: (907) 683-2294

Additional Information The park can send a list of publications available from the Alaska Natural History Association.

Gates of the Arctic National Park and Preserve

Located in north central Alaska in the Brooks Range, Gates of the Arctic is considered to be America's ultimate wilderness. The park is characterized by rugged mountains with deep glacial valleys and contains six designated wild rivers. Additionally, this immense park (8,472,665 acres) is a haven for wildlife, particularly arctic caribou, grizzly bear, Dall sheep, and wolf.

Access Most access is by chartered aircraft from the town of Bettles, 40 miles south of the park. Scheduled airlines operate from Fairbanks to Bettles and to Anaktuvuk Pass. Another access is from the rigorous North Slope Haul Road (Dalton Highway) which skirts the park's eastern boundary near the town of Wiseman. Most of the road is open to public use from June 1 to September 1.

Fishing Fishing in the park is very good with arctic char, grayling, lake trout, Dolly Varden, northern pike, sheefish, and salmon providing the sport in park waters. Gates of the Arctic is a true wilderness in that it is relatively inaccessible and unexplored. Travel within the park is limited to floating the rivers or backpacking during the summer.

Because of the size of the park, many of the park waters are unfished. Park management prefers to emphasize a sense of discovery for fishermen rather than recommend particular rivers or lakes. Much of the fishing is concentrated along the six designated wild rivers. These rivers, Tinayguk, John, Alatna, Kobuk, Noatak, and the North Fork of the Koyukuk, combine fine fishing with unsurpassed wilderness.

Grayling is the most widespread sport fish in the park and is found in nearly all permanent water courses and larger lakes. The Killik and Anaktuvuk rivers are particularly good for arctic char, while sheefish run in the Alatna and Kobuk rivers in the fall.

Fishing in the Kobuk River is described in the section on Kobuk

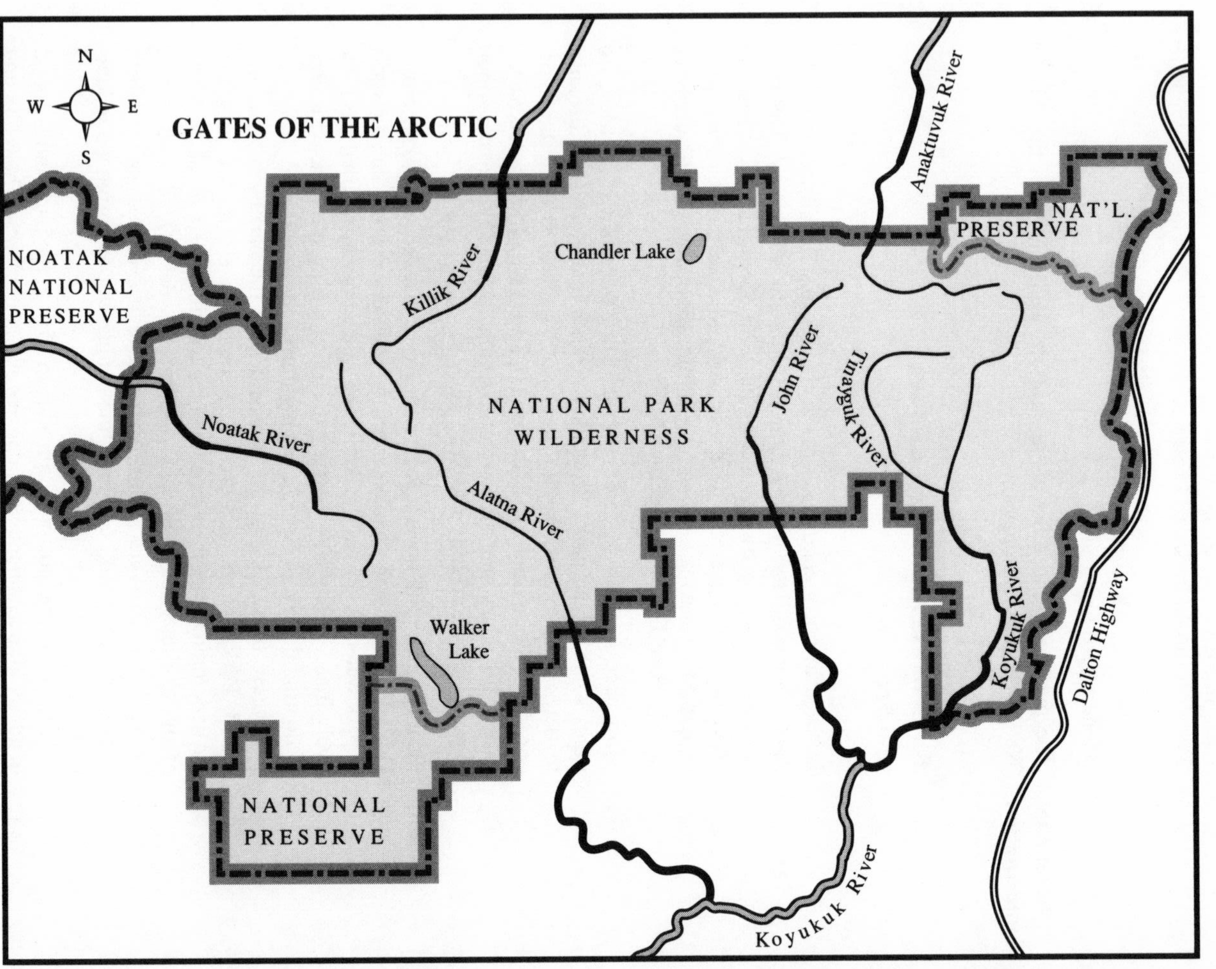

N
W
E
S
GATES OF THE ARCTIC
NOATAK NATIONAL PRESERVE
Chandler Lake
Killik River
Anaktuvuk River
NAT'L. PRESERVE
NATIONAL PARK WILDERNESS
Noatak River
John River
Tinayguk River
Alatna River
Walker Lake
Koyukuk River
Dalton Highway
NATIONAL PRESERVE
Koyukuk River

Valley National Park. The Kobuk originates near Walker Lake in Gates of the Arctic and is a popular float stream with only two major sets of rapids below the Walker Lake outlet. The Kobuk River has resident populations of grayling and arctic char along with fall runs of sheefish and chum salmon.

Lake trout are found in most of the bigger lakes and attain large sizes from the absence of fishing pressure. Because of the deep, cold water, lake trout roam the shallows during the summer and are accessible from shore. Lakes to try are Walker, Wild, Narvak, Chandler, and Selby. Northern pike are also prevalent in the lakes and in the backwaters of some rivers.

Fishing activity starts in mid to late June, after spring runoff and the lakes thaw, and continues into early September, depending on weather conditions. Outfitter and guide services offering a variety of fishing and floating options are available in Fairbanks and Bettles.

It is not hard to catch a lot of large fish in park waters. This is a result of minimal fishing pressure rather than the productivity of the waters, which is very low. Fish grow very slowly in arctic waters and there is a very real danger that heavy fishing pressure could damage the fish populations. It would be wise to practice catch-and-release in the park, keeping only the smaller fish to eat.

The Kobuk River is popular for float trips.—*National Park Service*

License An Alaska fishing license is required.

Camping Camping is allowed anywhere on public land in the park but there are no facilities.

Maps Topographic maps for the park in the 1:250,000 series are: Ambler River, Chandalar, Chandler Lake, Hughes, Killik River, Philip Smith Mountains, Survey Pass, and Wiseman. For river floating, look at the USGS map index for Alaska and order the quad sheets for the river of your interest. The park can send an information sheet about the topographic maps needed for exploring the park.

Park Address
Gates of the Arctic NPP
P.O. Box 74680
Fairbanks, AK 99707
phone: (907) 456-0281

Glacier Bay National Park and Preserve

Glacier Bay, in southeastern Alaska, features glaciers in every stage of their development. In addition to the glaciers, the park also includes a heavily forested coastline with miles of beaches and a large variety of animals including whales, brown and black bears, seals, eagles, and mountain goats. Mount Fairweather, the highest peak in southeastern Alaska, is also located there.

Access Glacier Bay is approximately 60 miles northwest of Juneau. There are no roads to the park and access is by regularly scheduled planes or boats (tour boats or charter boats). The visitor season is from mid-May through mid-September.

Fishing Glacier Bay boasts excellent fishing for king (chinook), silver (coho), and pink (humpback) salmon and for the largest sport fish in Alaska, the Pacific halibut. Most of the fishing in the park is saltwater fishing. The freshwater areas are remote and rarely visited.

King salmon, the largest of all the salmon, run from late May until mid-July and again from mid-August through September. These huge fish range from 15 to 60 pounds and larger.

The silver and pink salmon move through the bay in scattered schools on their way to spawn in the rivers. The peak time is from the end of July through September. The Dry Bay area and Alsek and East Alsek rivers in the northwest portion of the park are very good areas for salmon and Dolly Varden trout.

The best fishing in the Glacier Bay portion of the park is from

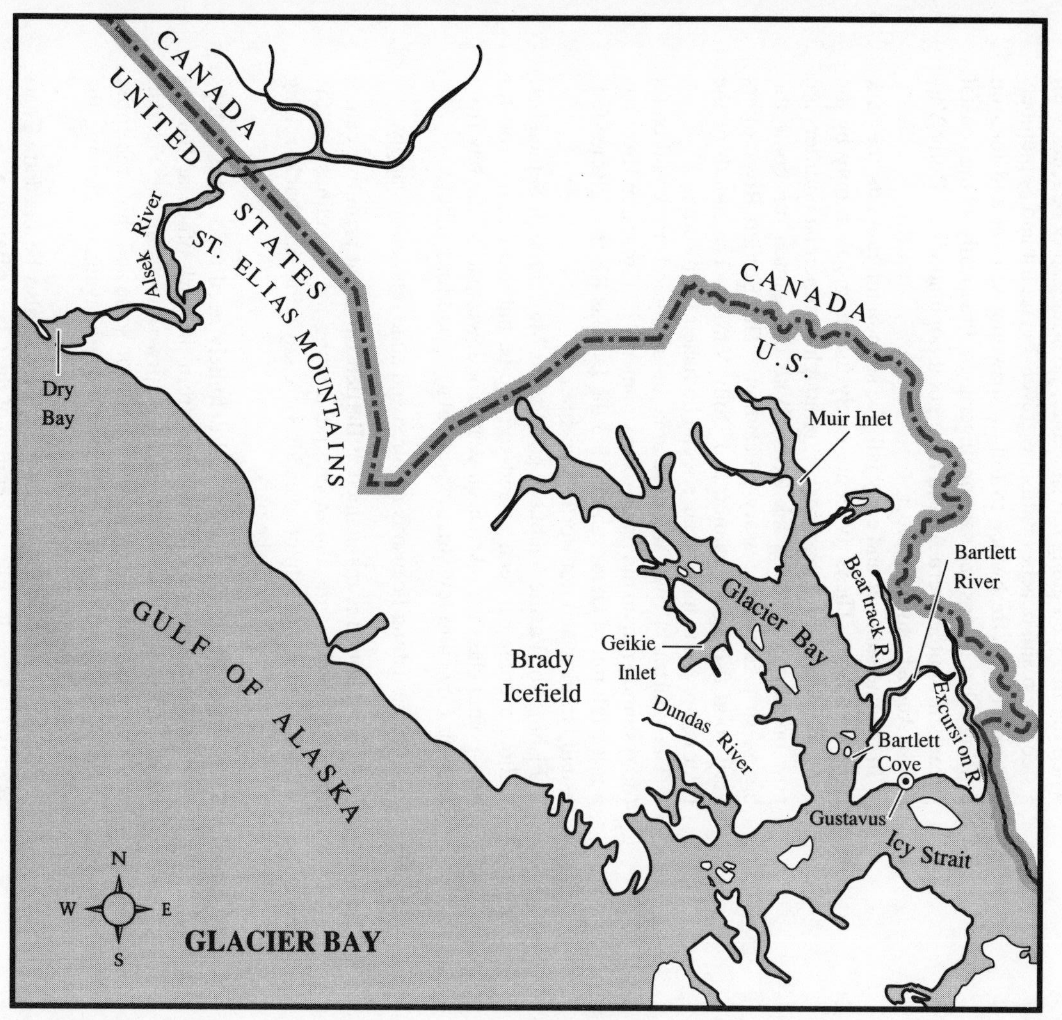

CANADA
UNITED STATES
Alsek River
ST. ELIAS MOUNTAINS
Dry Bay
CANADA
U.S.
Muir Inlet
Bear track R.
Bartlett River
Glacier Bay
Geikie Inlet
Brady Icefield
Dundas River
Excursi on R.
Bartlett Cove
Gustavus
Icy Strait
GULF OF ALASKA
N
W
E
S
GLACIER BAY

Geikie Inlet south to Icy Strait. Salmon are found around prominent land points where the tidal currents are strong and swift.

Saltwater fishing for Dolly Varden is good from May through July when the fish feed along the shoreline, favoring sandy beaches with a steep drop and beaches with fine gravel. In August and September, they move into freshwater to follow spawning salmon and feed on drifting salmon eggs and salmon fingerlings. Practically all the coastal streams in southeastern Alaska have good populations of Dolly Varden in August and September.

In the late summer and early fall, the salmon migrate into the park rivers to spawn. These rivers are rarely fished and then only by the occasional kayaker or backpacker, although commercial outfitters are now operating on the Alsek River. With the salmon run come the bears, so take the necessary precautions. The Bartlett River offers very good fishing for salmon and Dolly Varden. The mouth of the river is a popular spot because it can be fished from shore.

The Beartrack River and cove area are also good. Pink and chum (dog) salmon run up the river in the summer. The Excursion River has a large fall run of chum salmon, but the Dundas River is glacier-fed, usually murky, and not worth your time.

Fishing for Pacific halibut is good from May through September. Halibut average between 25 and 50 pounds, but many in the 100-to-200-pound class are taken each year. The lower part of the bay from Bartlett Cove into Icy Strait is particularly good for halibut.

License An Alaska fishing license is required and state regulations apply.

Camping One campground is maintained at Bartlett Cove but primitive camping opportunities are almost unlimited along the shorelines, on the islands, and in the alpine meadows. A kayaking and backpacking guide is available from the park.

Maps Travelers to the back country will definitely need topo maps. Maps covering the park may be obtained from the park office at Bartlett Cove. The maps needed are: Mount Fairweather, Juneau, Yakutat, and Skagway. These maps have a 1:250,000 scale and show the entire park. A set of 16 smaller-scale topo maps is available showing the entire shoreline of the park.

Nautical charts #17300 and #17318 will also be needed. Chart #17319 is a small-craft pocket map of the Glacier Bay area.

Park Address
Glacier Bay NPP
Gustavus, AK 99826
phone: (907) 697-3341

Chamber of Commerce
Juneau Visitor Center
134 Third Street
Juneau, AK 99801
phone: (907) 586-2201

Additional Information The Glacier Bay Lodge at Bartlett Cove operates from Memorial Day to late September. Fishing charters are available through the lodge. During the season, write to: Glacier Bay Lodge, Gustavus, AK, 99826; phone: (907) 697-3221. The remainder of the year, write to: Glacier Bay Lodge Inc., 1500 Metropolitan Park Building, Seattle, WA, 98101; phone: 1-800-426-0600 (toll free).

Glacier Bay is popular with recreational boaters. At the present time, boat access to the bay is limited. Entry is by permit only from June 1 through August 31. This limited-entry system is due to a recent decline in the number of humpback whales using Glacier Bay.

Because humpback whales are an endangered species, motor vessels are required to operate in a manner that would prevent any possible harm to the whales. Boats are required to remain at least one-quarter mile away from the whales and are not to pursue a whale within one-half mile. Permits for entry may be reserved by writing or phoning the park (address and phone above) not more than 60 days in advance of the requested entry date.

Katmai National Park and Preserve

Katmai is in southwestern Alaska at the beginning of the Alaska Peninsula, about 250 miles southwest of Anchorage. Katmai was originally established as a national monument in 1918 to preserve a scenic region known as the Valley of Ten Thousand Smokes because of its once active thermal geysers. In 1980, the park name was changed from "Monument" to "National Park and Preserve."

Katmai is famous for the major sockeye (red) salmon runs in the Naknek and Alagnak River drainages and for the bears that come to feed on the spawning salmon. Katmai is the largest brown bear sanctuary in the United States.

Access Katmai is essentially a roadless area. There is an unimproved road from the town of King Salmon to the western boundary. There is daily air service from Anchorage to King Salmon. From King Salmon, float planes are available to the park interior and to the four lodges in the park.

Fishing Katmai is one of the finest fishing areas in existence. The park is renowned for superb rainbow trout fishing and attracts fishing enthusiasts from around the world. It is a vast wilderness in which chains of lakes and rivers are open pathways to and from the sea. To the north is world-famous Bristol Bay, and to the south is the Shelikof Strait. Park waters contain salmon, char, grayling, lake trout, Dolly Varden, northern pike, and trophy rainbow trout. The entire region, including

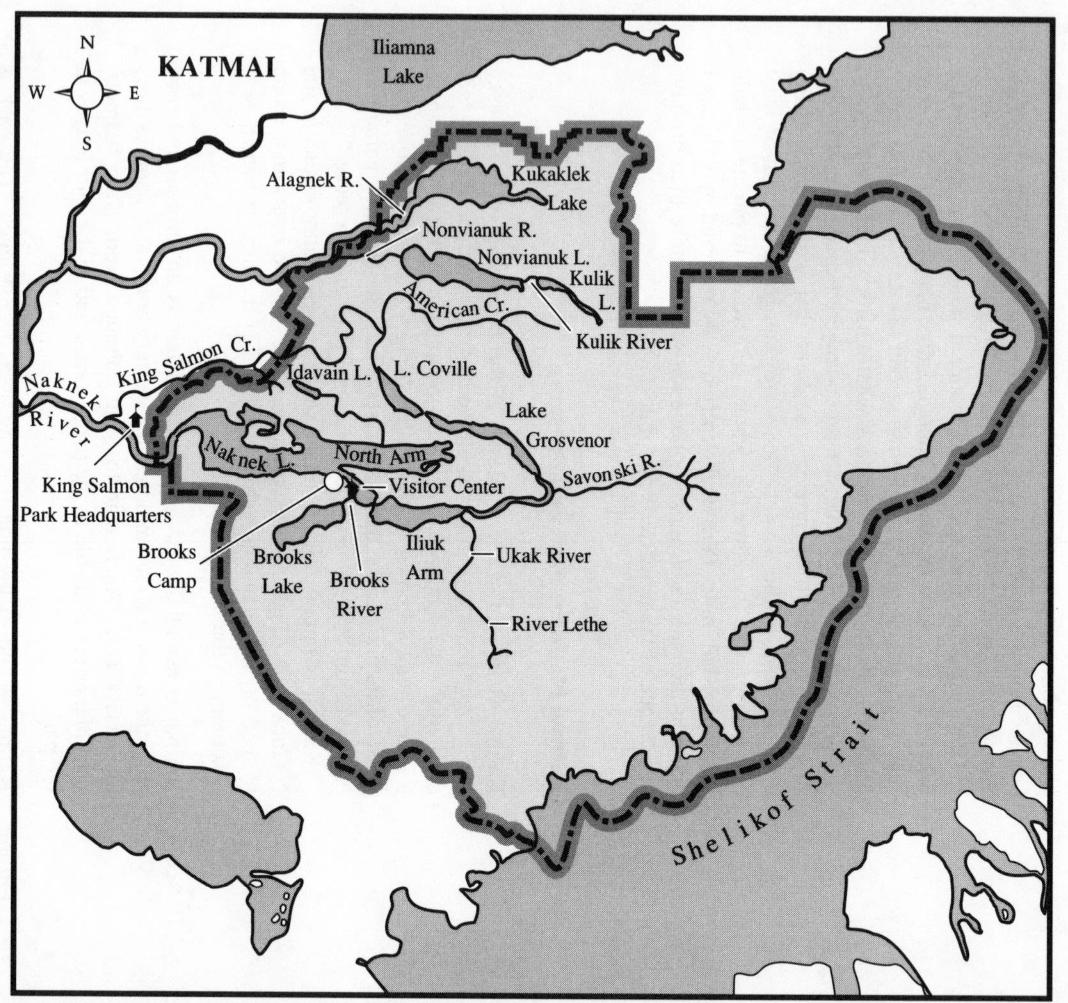
KATMAI
N
W
E
S
Iliamna Lake
Alagnek R.
Kukaklek Lake
Nonvianuk R.
Nonvianuk L.
Kulik L.
American Cr.
Kulik River
King Salmon Cr.
Idavain L.
L. Coville
Lake Grosvenor
Naknek River
Naknek L.
North Arm
Visitor Center
Savonski R.
King Salmon Park Headquarters
Brooks Camp
Brooks Lake
Brooks River
Iliuk Arm
Ukak River
River Lethe
Shelikof Strait

the park, Bristol Bay, Lake Clark National Park and Preserve, Iliamna Lakes area, and Wood River–Tikchik Lake is the greatest sport fishing region in the world. Lodges, guides, and outfitters are available throughout the region.

Many trophy trout are taken from park waters, with the heaviest fishing pressure occurring along the 1-mile Brooks River, the upper 3.5 miles of the Naknek River, and in the Bay of Islands section of Naknek Lake. Below is a general summary of park waters.

Brooks River Probably the most famous fishery in the park is the Brooks River. This easily waded, short (1-mile) river connects Brooks Lake with the Iliuk Arm of Naknek Lake and hosts a resident population of rainbow trout in the 2-to-4-pound range, with much larger rainbows appearing in the fall. Special regulations, including a flies-only stipulation, are designed to protect this magnificent fishery.

The season opens in early June and the first two weeks offer outstanding fishing for the rainbows. Favored patterns are smolt imitations, sculpin flies, Skunks, and Woolly Buggers. Large schools of sockeye salmon move into the river to spawn in late June to early July. This invasion dampens trout activity and brings the bears out in force to feast. Thousands of sockeye line the shallow waters of the Brooks. Rainbows follow the salmon and feed on stray salmon eggs. Salmon egg imitations such as the Polar Shrimp, Babine Special, and the Glo-Bug are the favored flies.

A word of caution is in order about bears. Large numbers of brown bears prowl the stream all summer and the angler needs to be alert and prepared for close encounters. The park staff has prepared a special information handout about bears, entitled *Fishing Among the Bears on Brooks River*.

Brooks Camp and Lodge is the headquarters for fishing on the river. It is the largest camp in Katmai and the jumping-off point for trips into the park. Brooks Lodge closes right after Labor Day because of the excessive number of bears and generally because the coming winter forces the lodge utilities to shut down.

Naknek River The Naknek River is famous for trophy-size rainbow trout. It flows west out of Naknek Lake for 3 miles before leaving the park and passing through the town of King Salmon and on to Bristol Bay. Fishing is especially good for rainbow trout between the lake outlet and in the Naknek River rapids, a 5-mile stretch of river just beyond the park boundary. This upper stretch abounds with rainbows in the 3-to-5-pound range. The larger rainbows, from 8 to 15 pounds, hit best in late May, early June, and September.

The river also receives a good run of sockeye salmon in August and

September. King salmon constitute a major sport fishery below the town of King Salmon, particularly near the mouth of King Salmon Creek, which enters the river just below town. The first strong run of king salmon appears in the middle of June.

Humpback (pink) salmon are taken throughout the river and its tributaries in even-numbered years. The pinks are usually small, rarely exceeding 5 pounds, and are popular because they readily strike lures and flies. The Naknek also contains arctic char, Dolly Varden, and grayling. Wherever there is fast water, there is grayling. They can be taken on egg flies or dry flies.

Naknek Lake With 240 square miles, Naknek Lake is the fourth largest lake in Alaska. The lake is very good for northern pike, lake trout, and rainbow trout. The three arms of the main lake: Northwest Bay, Iliuk Arm, and North Bay including Bay of Islands, are all excellent fishing areas. The Bay of Islands area regularly produces rainbows over 10 pounds. The east end of Iliuk Arm should be avoided because the Savonoski River dumps glacial silt and volcanic ash into the lake there.

The lake can be extremely dangerous to boaters because sudden winds whip the water into a sea of whitecaps. Fishing from shore can be good although most midsummer angling is by trolling. The shoreline is rocky but there is enough room for walking and casting.

Alagnak River The Alagnak is a designated wild-and-scenic river flowing from Kukaklek Lake outside the park. The Nonvianuk River flows from Nonvianuk Lake into the Alagnak. Float trips on the Alagnak start at Nonvianuk Lake and float down to the Alagnak. The Alagnak, from Kukaklek Lake to the confluence with the Nonvianuk, is too rocky and shallow to float and includes an 8-foot waterfall that is difficult to portage.

Both rivers have excellent fishing, containing good numbers of rainbow trout, arctic char, and grayling in the fast water, and northern pike in the slacker water. In addition, the five kinds of salmon occur at different times of the year, with sockeyes being the most common. King salmon fishing is best from mid-June through July, chum salmon in early July, and silver salmon from late July to mid-September. In September, the really large rainbow trout move out of the lakes into the rivers, but often the smaller resident rainbows reach 7 pounds.

The Nonvianuk River tributary is best in June and September. The same flies listed under the Brooks River are recommended. One fly-fishing tip is to carry fast sinking line in order to be able to get the flies deep enough in fast water.

American River About 20 miles north of the Brooks River, the American River lies isolated, accessible by plane or by boat from the Grosvenor Lodge. This crystal clear river contains large rainbows, arctic char, and Dolly Varden and has a small run of sockeyes. The Grosvenor Lodge is also the headquarters for fishing Coville and Grosvenor lakes.

Kulik River The Kulik River is similar to the Brooks River. It is a short river connecting Nonvianuk and Kulik lakes and contains rainbow in the 2-to-3-pound range, with larger rainbow available in the fall when sockeyes invade the river to spawn. Kulik Lodge on Nonvianuk Lake is the headquarters for fishing the Kulik River.

Other Waters Nonvianuk, Coville, Kulik, and Grosvenor lakes are all excellent for rainbows and lake trout. Don't bother with the Savonoski, Ukak, or Lethe rivers, or Ikagluik Creek, which flow into the east end of the Iliuk Arm of Naknek Lake. They are all silt-laden from glacial runoff.

Idavain Lake provides good fishing for arctic char. An impassable waterfall below the lake prevents entry by sockeyes and other migratory species. King Salmon Creek, south of the town of King Salmon, has a bit of everything and is worth checking. Practically all clear-water streams support fish, usually rainbow trout and grayling, and many are used by sockeye salmon for spawning.

One final note about bears. They are prevalent throughout the park, especially when the salmon are spawning. Always be careful to avoid bear encounters. Read the park literature and stay off the well-worn bear paths along the rivers. Be sure not to leave fish or other food where a bear can get it. Don't teach bears that humans are a source of food.

License An Alaska fishing license is required. Be sure to check special park regulations, since some waters are closed to protect spawning fish and the Brooks River is a flies-only fishing area. Catch-and-release fishing for rainbow trout is strongly encouraged, particularly on the Brooks and Naknek rivers and the Bay of Islands. A 1983 creel census showed that of the approximately ten thousand rainbow trout caught in park waters, fewer than three hundred were kept.

Camping Camping in the park is unrestricted although back-country permits are required and can be obtained at park headquarters at King Salmon or at Brooks Camp. There is a developed campground at Brooks River.

Maps When fishing near one of the lodges, topographic maps may not be necessary, and the park brochure map is adequate. If you plan a back-country trip, the maps for the park in the 1:250,000 series are: Afognak, Iliamna, Karluk, Mount Katmai, and Naknek.

Park Address
Katmai NPP
P.O. Box 7
King Salmon, AK 99613
phone: (907) 246-3305

Additional Information Information concerning Brooks Lodge or "Anglers Paradise," consisting of Kulik Lodge and Grosvenor Camp, may be obtained by writing to: Katmailand Inc., 4700 Aircraft Dr., Anchorage, AK, 99502; phone: (907) 243-5448.

The March 1979 issue of *Fly Fisherman* (Vol.10, No.3) contains an excellent in-depth article by Lani Waller on fishing Katmai. Entitled "Alaska's Katmai Rainbows," the article discusses park waters, tactics, clothing, bears, weather, and related subjects. Anyone heading to Katmai should make an effort to read this article. Check with fly-fishing friends or libraries for this back issue.

The best guide to the park is *Exploring Katmai National Monument* by Alaska Travel Publications. The guide was written in 1974 and although it does not cover the 1978 additions to the park, it still contains much applicable fishing information. Contact the park for a publication list from the Alaska Natural History Association.

Fly Patterns of Alaska by the Alaska Flyfishers is a small, spiral bound book of 136 fly patterns that would be helpful to anyone fly-fishing in Alaska. The book is available from Frank Amato Publications, P.O. Box 02112, Portland, OR, 97202; phone: (503) 236-2305.

Kenai Fjords National Park

Kenai Fjords encompasses a coastal mountain system on the southeastern side of the Kenai Peninsula. The park is a land of ice and rock dominated by the Harding Icefield, one of four major icecaps in the United States. Glaciers radiate out in all directions from the ice field. When the glaciers recede and are replaced by ocean, fjords are created.

Access The park is in south central Alaska. Seward is the nearest city and boat or floatplane charters are available to the park from Seward. The park is also accessible from a road up the Resurrection River valley off the Seward Highway.

Fishing Fishing on the Kenai Peninsula is very good; however, fishing in the park is minimal since most streams are of glacial origin and do not

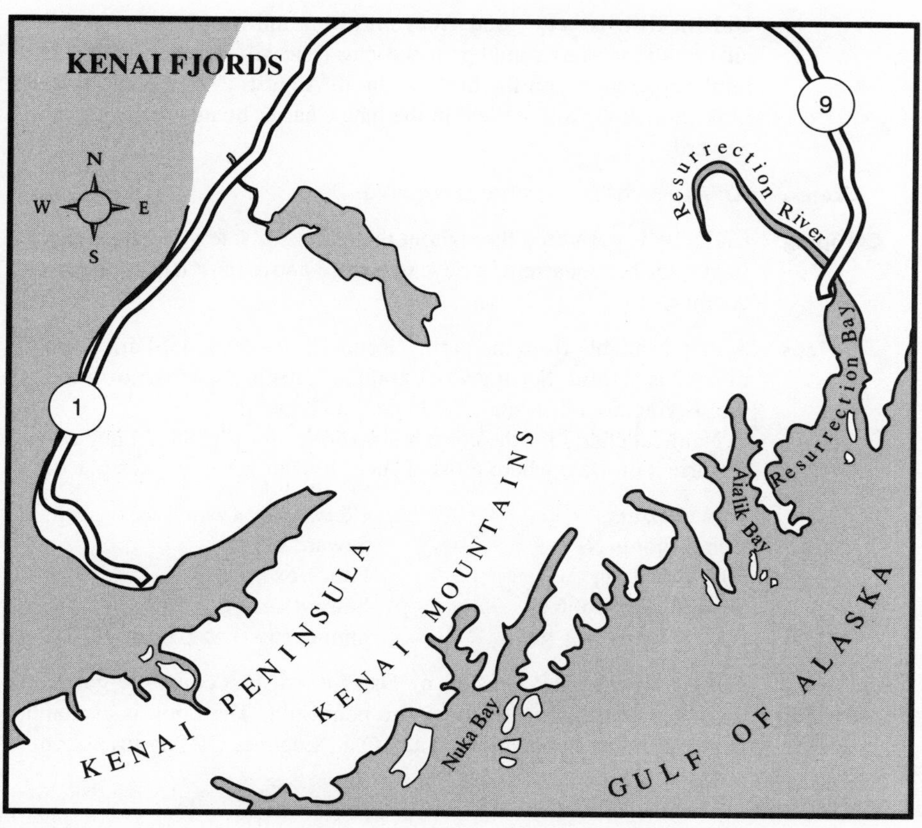

support fish populations. Access to park waters is difficult compared to other areas on the peninsula.

Fish within the park include Dolly Varden, rainbow trout, and silver, red, pink, and chum salmon. Saltwater fish in the Kenai Fjords include salmon, halibut, lingcod, and rockfish.

Little is known about the freshwater fishery on the south coast. The evidence available indicates that few lakes or streams contain fish. Most streams are not named. There are a handful of these unnamed and unfished small streams that support excellent silver and pink salmon runs in season. An adventurous person (with money) might be interested in exploring these streams. Along the south coast, red salmon can be found in Delight and Desire lakes and the streams that flow from these lakes. Pink, silver, and chum salmon are known to spawn in Nuka Bay.

Resurrection Bay is a popular area for saltwater fishing because it is sheltered and provides good fishing. Bottom fishing for lingcod and rockfish is very good from mid-May until mid-July when the silver salmon start running in the bay. The silver run usually lasts until September with the best fishing in August. A few chinook and pink salmon are also caught in the bay. Charter boats are available in Seward.

License An Alaska fishing license is required.

Camping Camping is permitted throughout the park. For safety reasons, check in at park headquarters in Seward before and after a trip to the back country.

Maps A map available from the park, "Kenai Fjords National Park Topography," is helpful. Separate topographic maps in the 1:250,000 series are: Blying Sound, Kenai, Seldovia, and Seward.

Nautical charts for the coast are #16681 and #16682. They cover Resurrection Bay, where most of the saltwater activity takes place.

Park Address
Kenai Fjords NP
P.O. Box 1727
Seward, AK 99664
phone: (907) 224-3874

Chamber of Commerce
Seward C.C.
P.O. Box 749
Seward, AK 99664
phone: (907) 224-8051

Additional Information *Fishing the Kenai Peninsula,* by Dan Sisson, is a complete guide to the lakes and streams of the entire peninsula. The book is available from: Windsor Publications, 1425 Oak, Eugene, OR, 97401; phone: (503) 345-1151.

Kobuk Valley National Park

North of the Arctic Circle in northwestern Alaska and east of Kotzebue, Kobuk Valley National Park lies between the Baird Mountains to the north and the Waring Mountains to the south. Kobuk Valley is a collage of landscapes including sand dunes, meandering rivers, and ridges offering scenic views across the boreal forest and tundra east to the Brooks Range.

Wildlife abounds in the park and the valley is also a major junction of the North American and Asiatic migratory bird flyways. The park is undeveloped. The most common method of visiting it and enjoying the beautiful scenery is by floating the Kobuk River.

Access The upper Kobuk River can be reached by charter flights from Kotzebue, Ambler, Bettles, or Fairbanks. Folding boats or rubber rafts are practical for flying in, and the villages of Ambler, upstream from

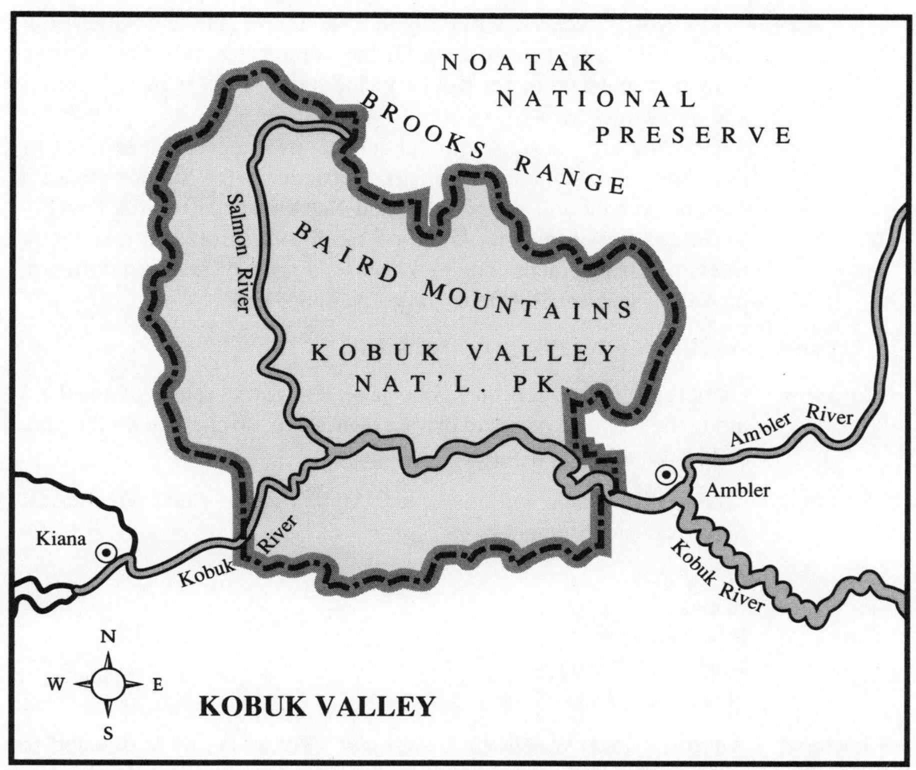

the park, and Kiana and Noorvik, downstream from the park, have charter planes and boat service available.

Fishing The Kobuk River is the main fishing attraction in the park. This large, unusually clear river flows placidly through the park. As mentioned above, floating the Kobuk is the most common method of visiting the park. The Kobuk is loaded with approximately 23 species of fish, which are an important food source for the local people. It is an excellent river for fishing but is not heavily used for sport fishing. Grayling, chum salmon, arctic char, Dolly Varden, whitefish, northern pike, and sheefish—the so-called tarpon of the north—are abundant.

The sheefish is a large predatory fish found only in the far north that rivals the arctic char as a sport fish and as table fare. As well as being a great sport fish, the sheefish is the single most important fish species to the Eskimo villagers along the Kobuk River. The Kobuk contains the largest specimens in Alaska and fish in the 40-to-50-pound range are not uncommon.

The Kobuk receives a run of chum salmon in July and August but there is very little sport fishing for the salmon. Chum salmon spawn in many tributaries of the Kobuk including the Kallarichuk, Salmon, and Tutuksuk rivers.

Grayling are prevalent throughout the area and found in most of the clear water streams in the park, particularly the Salmon River, a designated wild-and-scenic river, and its tributary, the Kitlik River.

Guided float trips are offered on the Kobuk River and other park rivers by arrangement. The park can send a list of licensed outfitters providing services in Kobuk Valley National Park.

License An Alaska fishing license is required.

Camping Camping is permitted on public land. However, much of the land along the Kobuk River is in private ownership, so check with the park staff beforehand to avoid trespassing.

Maps These USGS maps will be needed: Ambler River, Baird Mountains, Selawick, and Shungnak.

Park Address
Kobuk Valley NP
P.O. Box 1029
Kotzebue, AK 99752
phone: (907) 442-3890

Additional Information An entire issue of *Alaska Geographic* (Vol.8, No.3) is devoted to the Kotzebue Basin. It provides a detailed description of the area including some good fishing information about the Kobuk and Salmon rivers. Contact: The Alaska Geographic Society, Box 93370, Anchorage, AK, 99509; phone: (907) 258-2515.

Lake Clark National Park and Preserve

Often described as the Alaskan Alps, Lake Clark National Park and Preserve is in south central Alaska, just west of Cook Inlet and north of Katmai. The park is characterized by diversity, not surprisingly, since it encompasses 3,653,000 acres of mountains, lakes, rivers, and woodlands to provide a broad array of magnificent scenery.

Access Access is by floatplane from Anchorage, Soldotna, Iliamna, and Kenai. The park is about a one-hour flight from Anchorage. There are no roads to the park.

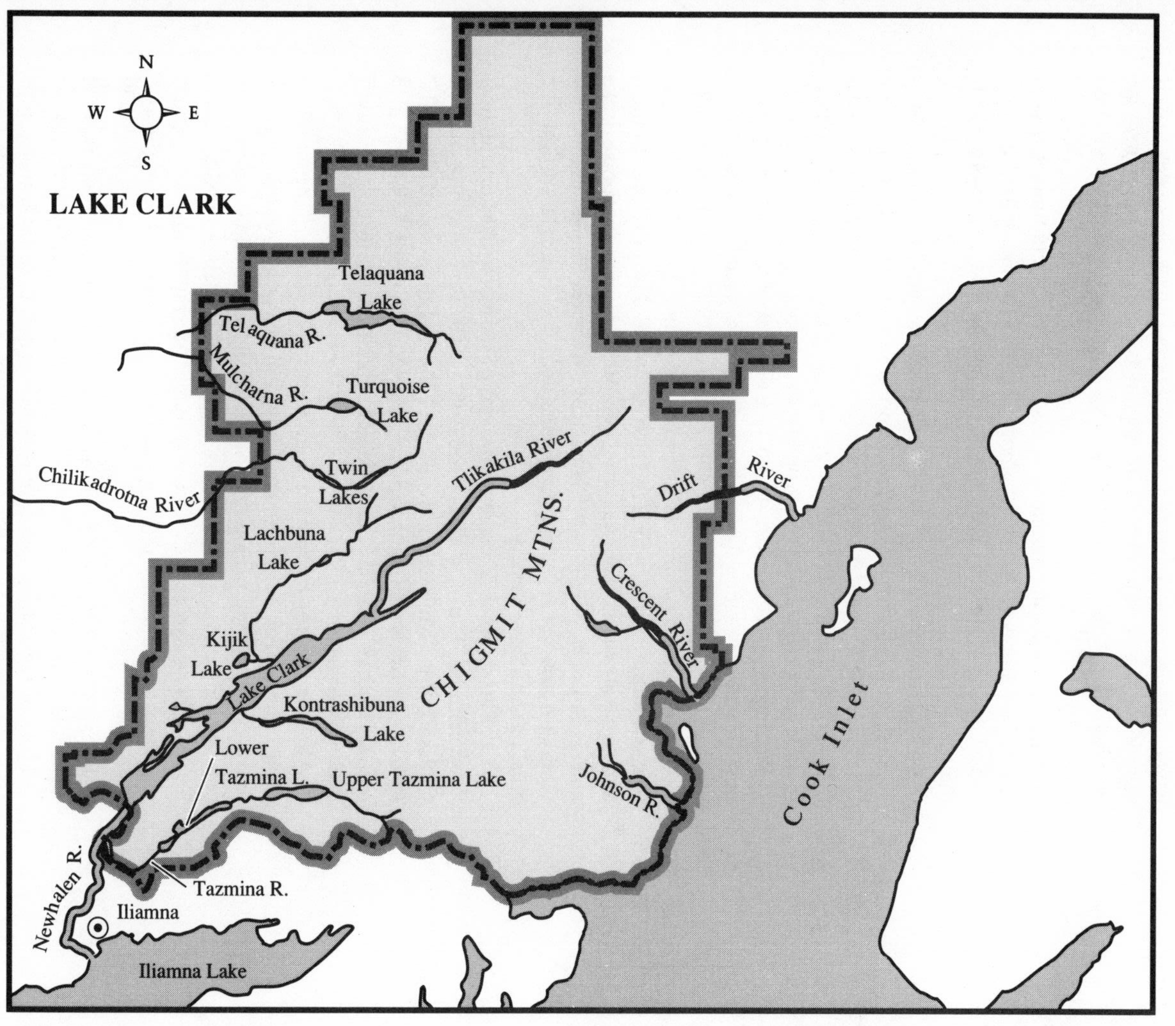
N
W
E
S
LAKE CLARK
Telaquana Lake
Tel aquana R.
Mulchatna R.
Turquoise Lake
Twin Lakes
Chilikadrotna River
Tlikakila River
Drift River
Lachbuna Lake
CHIGMIT MTNS.
Crescent River
Kijik Lake
Lake Clark
Kontrashibuna Lake
Lower Tazmina L.
Upper Tazmina Lake
Johnson R.
Cook Inlet
Newhalen R.
Tazmina R.
Iliamna
Iliamna Lake

Fishing Lake Clark National Park and Preserve is part of the famous Kvichak River drainage, which hosts the largest populations of sockeye (red) salmon in the world. The entire region is justifiably renowned for outstanding fishing, and Lake Clark National Park and Preserve is no exception.

Within the park are numerous lakes and rivers, including three designated wild-and-scenic rivers, most of which offer excellent fishing. Lake Clark itself is the sixth largest freshwater lake in Alaska and is the focal point of the park.

Fishing in the park is for salmon, rainbow and lake trout, Dolly Varden, grayling, arctic char, and northern pike. Most lakes contain lake trout, Dolly Varden, and grayling, while most nonglacial streams offer good grayling fishing. Many of the park's lakes and streams include important spawning grounds for salmon.

Fishing is good in most of the lakes and streams that drain west into Bristol Bay since these waters are less affected by glacial runoff than the shorter streams flowing east to Cook Inlet. Lakes Clark, Kontrashibuna, Tazmina, Kijik, Lachbuna, and the Tlikakila, Current, Chulitna, Kijik, and Newhalen rivers all drain to Lake Iliamna and then down the Kvichak River to Bristol Bay. Turquoise Lake and Twin Lakes flow into the Nushagak River via the Mulchatna and Chilikadrotna rivers, while Telaquana and Two Lakes drain into the Kuskokwim River system.

All of these waters receive migrations of spawning salmon and host good fishing. The best rivers for trout, char, and grayling are the Chilikadrotna, Mulchatna, Kijik, and the Tazmina below the falls. Rivers east of the Chigmit Mountains drain into Cook Inlet and also receive runs of salmon, but their silty condition from glacial runoff discourages fishing.

All five species of salmon spawn in park waters. The chinook (king) salmon run begins in early June and peaks in late June, just as the sockeye salmon run begins. Sockeye and chum (dog) salmon run concurrently and are usually over by late July when the coho (silver) runs begin. Coho runs continue through August. Humpback (pink) salmon run biannually in even years and go from mid-June through mid-August.

Pike are an overlooked sport fish in the park. The lower sections of Lake Clark, especially the Chulitna Bay area, are loaded with pike.

Most of the fishing pressure is concentrated in the southwest portion of the park around the Newhalen River, which connects Clark and Iliamna lakes and supports a resident population of trophy rainbow trout. Fishing pressure is only light to moderate throughout the rest of the park. Lake Clark in the southwest has very good fishing and lodges around the lake cater to visitors who come to fish.

A typical Tazmina River rainbow trout.—*Bill Horn*

There are too many rivers and lakes in the park to review each one individually. Because 99 percent of the people fishing in the park will be with guides and outfitters, you can count on their knowledge of the locations with the best fishing.

License An Alaska license is required. Be sure to check Alaska fishing regulations because streams in the Kvichak River drainage are designated as trophy-fish waters with special regulations.

Camping Camping is unrestricted in the park, but developed public facilities are nonexistent.

Maps Topographic maps for the park in the 1:250,000 series are: Lime Hills, Lake Clark, Iliamna, Kenai, Seldovia, and Tyonek.

Park Address
Lake Clark NPP
701 C St., Box 61
Anchorage, AK 99513
phone: (907) 271-3751

Additional Information The park can send a business directory that lists the businesses servicing Lake Clark, including fishing lodges within and outside the park, and outfitters specializing in float trips. Also ask for the booklet, *Alaska Float Trips,* which describes some of the rivers in the area along with fishing information.

Noatak National Preserve

Noatak National Preserve is in northwestern Alaska and features the Noatak River basin, the most extensive undeveloped river valley in the United States. Ringed by mountains, the Noatak River basin is a vast primitive area characterized by its pristine condition, outstanding scenery, and abundant wildlife. The park abuts Gates of the Arctic National Park and Preserve on the east and Kobuk Valley National Park on the south.

Access There is no road access to the area. Charter flights to the upper Noatak River are available from the town of Bettles and the lower Noatak River is accessible by charter from Kotzebue.

Fishing The Noatak River originates in Gates of the Arctic National Park and Preserve and flows west for more than 400 miles to Kotzebue Sound. Part of the river is designated as wild and scenic. The river is totally remote and rarely fished. The small community of Noatak (population approximately 250) is the only settlement along the river's entire course. A float trip from the Noatak headwaters to the sound takes three to four weeks.

Fish are abundant in the Noatak River. Arctic char, grayling, Dolly Varden, northern pike, whitefish, and chum salmon are taken throughout the Noatak.

The Noatak supports the most northerly major run of chum salmon on the western coast of North America. The run extends from July to September, peaking in late July. Although most of the spawning takes place in the lower Noatak below the mouth of its principal tributary, the Kelly River, some salmon are known to run 300 miles upstream to the Cutler River. Fishing opportunities are sparse above the Cutler River. The Squirrel River, south of the Noatak, also has a major annual run of chum salmon.

Accompanying the salmon are major runs of arctic char in the Noatak and Kelly rivers, and in other tributary streams such as the Eli and Cutler. Some larger and deeper lakes, such as Feniak, Desperation, and Matcharak contain lake trout, and northern pike are prevalent in many rivers and lakes in the region where water depth is adequate to prevent winter kill.

A trip down the Noatak River requires extensive planning. A few guides and outfitters work out of Kotzebue. Outfitters at Bettles will fly canoes to the upper Noatak.

License An Alaska fishing license is required.

Camping Camping is permitted throughout the park but there are no accommodations or campgrounds. There are numerous private lands along the

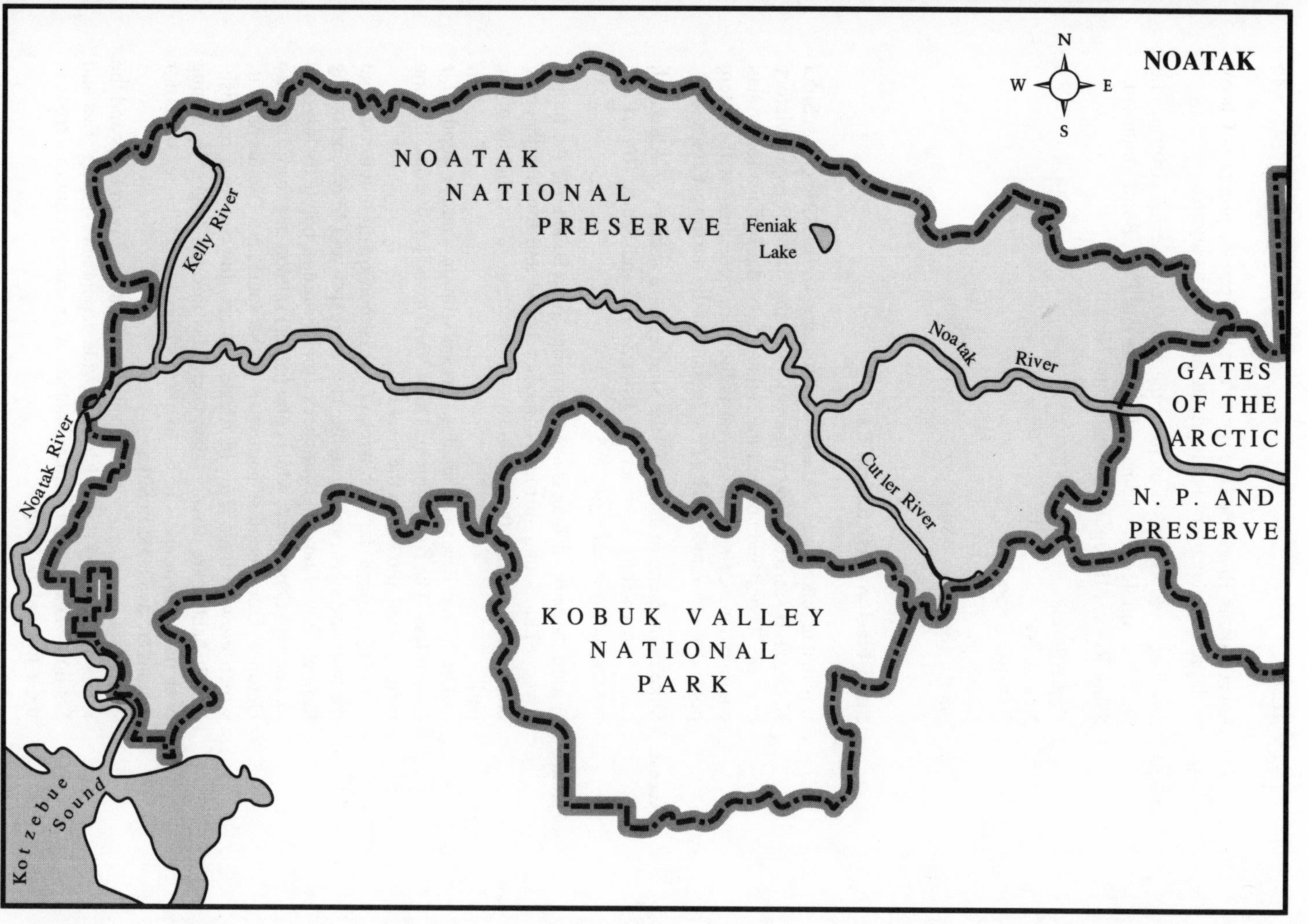
NOATAK
N
W
E
S
NOATAK NATIONAL PRESERVE
Feniak Lake
Kelly River
Noatak River
Noatak River
Cutler River
GATES OF THE ARCTIC N. P. AND PRESERVE
KOBUK VALLEY NATIONAL PARK
Kotzebue Sound

lower Noatak River. Be sure not to camp on private property. Check with park headquarters about private property locations.

Maps Small-scale topographic maps in the 1:250,000 series covering the park are: Ambler River, Survey Pass, Howard Pass, Baird Mountains, Killik River, Misheguk Mountain, and Noatak.

Park Address
Noatak NP
P.O. Box 1029
Kotzebue, AK 99752
phone: (907) 442-3890

Sitka National Historical Park

Located in Sitka, one of Alaska's most scenic and historic cities, Sitka National Historical Park commemorates the 1804 Russian victory over the Tlingit Indians and the resistance of the Indians to Russian colonization. Of special interest is the park collection of the totem poles that are a trademark of the Indians of the northwest coast.

Access Sitka is on Baranof Island in the southeastern section of Alaska. It can be reached by ferry service from Seattle and Prince Rupert and is serviced by Alaska Airlines.

Fishing Within the park, fishing is available from Sitka Sound and the Indian River. Sitka Sound surrounds Baranof Island and touches the park on two sides, while the Indian River flows through the middle of the park.

The Indian River is a shallow stream with an average depth of 1 foot or less. The river contains Dolly Varden and a few trout. Salmon fishing is not allowed in the river.

In Sitka Sound, large chinook (king) salmon are present throughout the year and start running up the rivers in April and May, continuing through July. Runs of Humpback (pink) salmon begin in July and extend into September, while coho (silver) salmon last from July into October. Other popular game fish in the sound are Pacific halibut, which grow to huge sizes in Alaska waters, lingcod, and rockfish. Pacific halibut are usually taken from May through August by fishing over flat bottom areas in 60 to 180 feet of water. Charter boats for fishing are available in Sitka.

Baranof Island is a popular fishing destination. Fly-in lakes and the rivers and streams on the island provide dependable fishing. Eva and Salmon lakes on the island are noted for producing cutthroat trout in the 1-to-2-pound range.

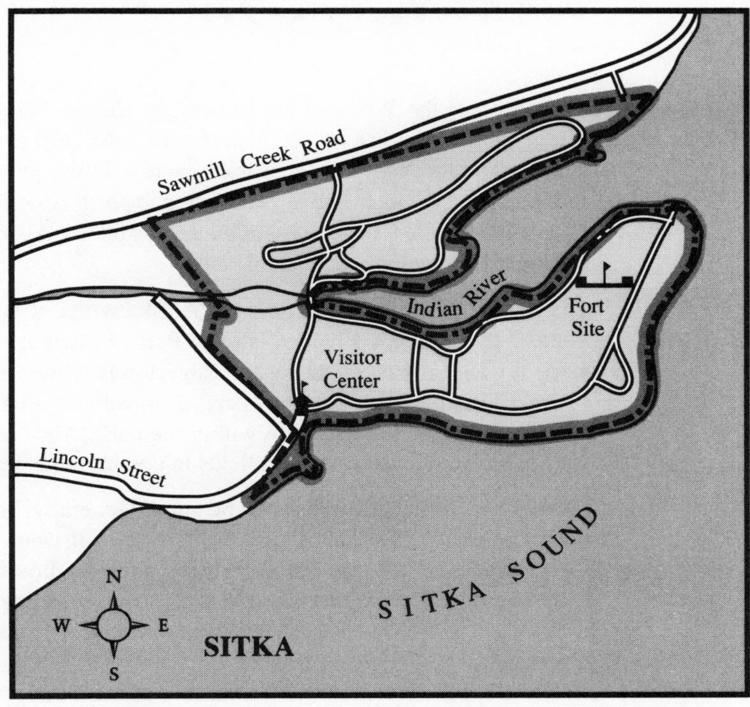

The U.S. Forest Service maintains a series of trails on the island and rents cabins in the wilderness on a reservation basis. Some of the cabins are accessible on foot, others by plane. The price of the cabins is very reasonable.

License An Alaska license is required for both fresh and saltwater fishing.

Camping There are no camping facilities at the park but camping is available in nearby Tongass National Forest.

Maps Nautical charts #17324 and #17326 will cover most of Sitka Sound. Chart #17325 covers a small portion of the sound.

Park Address
Sitka NHP
P.O. Box 738
Sitka, AK 99835
phone: (907) 747-6281

Chamber of Commerce
Greater Sitka C. C.
P.O. Box 638
Sitka, AK 99835
phone: (907) 747-8604

Additional Information For information on Forest Service cabins, write to: Forest Supervisor, Tongass National Forest, Chatham Area, 204 Siginaka Way, Sitka, AK, 99835; phone: (907) 747-6671.

Wrangell–St. Elias National Park and Preserve

Composed of the Wrangell Mountains and the St. Elias Mountains, Wrangell–St. Elias is a vast domain (8,331,406 acres) of rock and ice, peaks and valleys, rivers, meadows, and wildlife. Within this preserve is found the most active glacial area in north America, including Malaspina Glacier, the continent's largest glacier. Also located here is Mount Wrangell, an active volcano.

Access The park is in eastern south-central Alaska where it is bordered on the east by Canada's Kluane National Park. Principal road access is along the Richardson Highway and Edgerton Highway from Glennallen to Chitina. In the northern part, a gravel secondary road leads to Nabesna, a small settlement within the park. Air charters into the park are available from landing fields in communities near the park.

Fishing Fishing in certain park waters can be good. Generally, however, sport fishing is marginal because most streams are silt laden from glacial melt, with heavy flows in the summer and low flows in the winter. Other than the Copper River system, stream fishing is limited to a few clear-water streams in the Beaver Creek and Hanagita River drainages.

The Copper River, along the west side of the park, is a broad river loaded with glacial silt. The upper river is bordered by the Glenn Highway and easily accessible. The Copper receives major runs of sockeye (red) salmon and a smaller run of chinook (king) salmon, along with coho (silver), humpback (pink), and chum (dog) salmon. Sockeye, which spawn in clear lakes and outlet streams in the Wrangells, are most abundant in June and July, while the king salmon run from May into July. Some recreational fishing in the park centers on the sockeye runs in the Copper River.

The Beaver Creek system is north of White River on the northeastern side of the park near the Canadian border. Numerous small, clear-water streams in this area support grayling. Also in the area are Ptarmigan, Rock, and Braye lakes, which contain lake trout, grayling, and lingcod and are reached by floatplane.

The Hanagita River is south of the Chitina River Valley in the eastern Chugach Mountains. A tributary of the Chitina River, the Hanagita and its Tebay River tributary are two of the major clear-water streams in the park. Each river drains a lake of the same name and offers excellent fishing for rainbow trout and grayling. The Tebay lakes, especially, provide good fishing for rainbows in the 12-to-18-inch range. The Hanagita River also receives a small steelhead run.

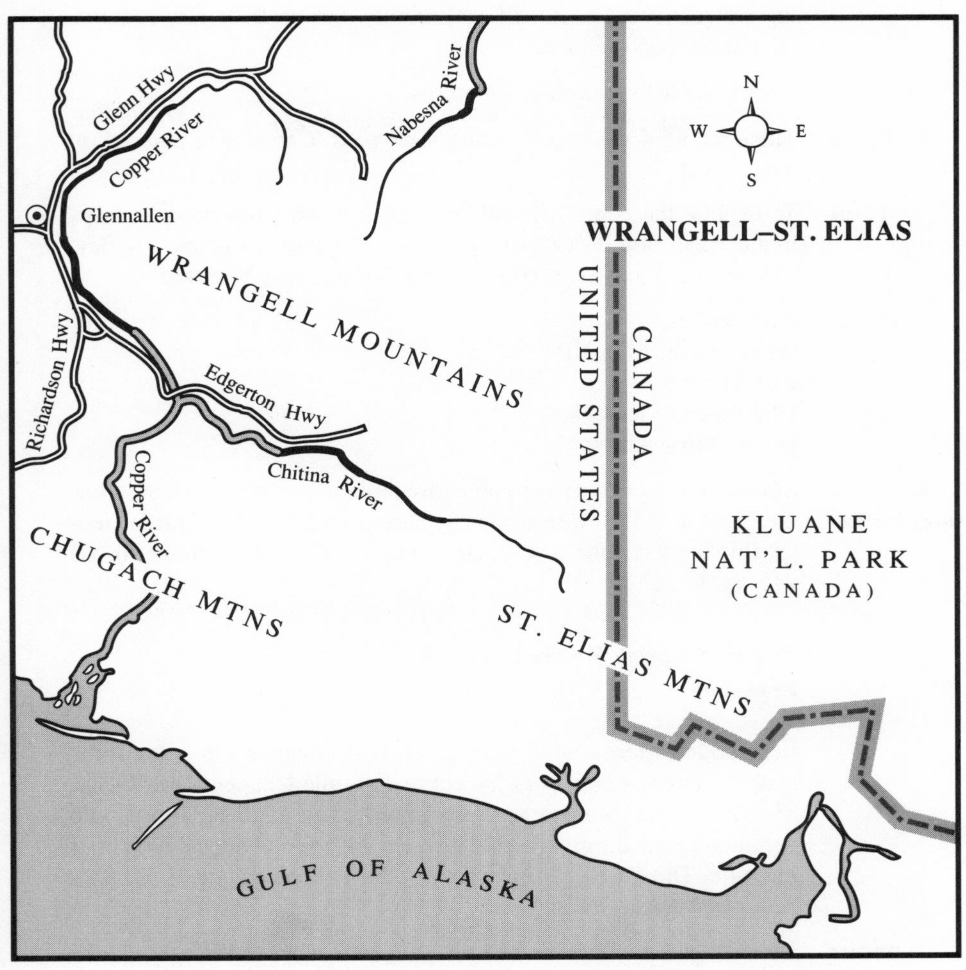

Other lakes in the Chitina Valley and Hanagita drainage also contain rainbow trout and grayling. Both the rivers and lakes are lightly fished because of the difficulty of access. A small number of fly-in visitors come to fish the area.

Additional park lakes that contain trout and grayling are Tanada, Copper, Jack, Long, and Strelna. Tanada Lake can be reached by all-terrain vehicles from Nabesna Road. There is a lodge operating on Tanada Lake. Jack, Long, and Strelna lakes are located along the Nabesna and Chitina-McCarthy roads and receive heavy fishing pressure because of their accessibility. Strelna Lake also contains landlocked coho salmon.

License An Alaska fishing license is required.

Camping There are no developed facilities in the park. Camping is allowed on public lands.

Maps To explore the park, you will need the following topographic maps in the 1:250,000 series: Bering Glacier, Cordova, Gulkana, Icy Bay, McCarthy, Mount St. Elias, Nabesna, Valdez, and Yakutat.

Park Address
Wrangell–St. Elias NP
P.O. Box 29
Glennallen, AK 99588
phone: (907) 822-5235

Additional Information *Alaska Geographic* devoted an entire issue to the Wrangell–St. Elias area (Vol.8, No.1). Copies may be purchased from: The Alaska Geographic Society, Box 93370, Anchorage, AK, 99509; phone: (907) 258-2515.

Yukon–Charley Rivers National Preserve

Located in eastern central Alaska, this park contains 128 miles of the historic Yukon River, plus the entire 118-mile Charley River basin. The Yukon was a major transportation artery of trade, travel, and communication during the gold rush era and the early development of the state. The Charley is a tributary of the Yukon and one of Alaska's best white-water rivers.

Access The two communities nearest the park are Eagle, to the east via the Taylor Highway, and Circle, to the northwest via the Steese Highway. Access to the park from both towns is by boat on the Yukon River, traveling downstream from Eagle and upstream from Circle, or by air. Both towns have scheduled air service, air taxis, and charter boats. Currently, helicopters and bush pilots provide charter service to the Charley River.

Fishing The Yukon and Charley rivers in the park receive little sport-fishing pressure. Fishing is incidental to other recreational activities and is generally limited to the clear-running tributaries of the Yukon.

The Yukon is a huge river. Its size is hard to grasp without actually seeing it. Very little sport fishing occurs in the Yukon because it remains heavily silted into October from upstream glacial runoff.

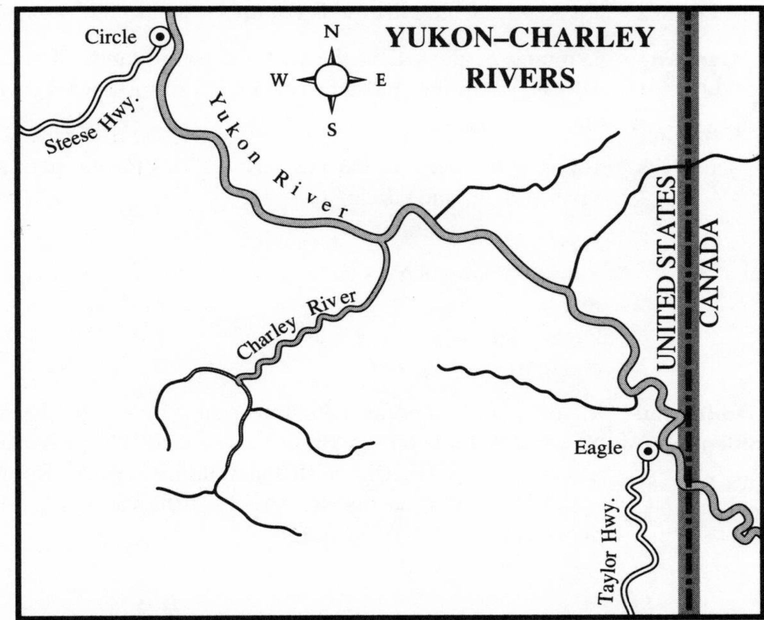

Good fishing for grayling and some salmon is available in every clear tributary of the Yukon.

The Charley is a designated wild-and-scenic river, and is accessible only by fly-in. Because of its white-water qualities, the Charley is more popular for kayaking than for fishing.

Grayling are common in both rivers and most of the tributaries of the Charley contain grayling. Northern pike are common in backwater sections of the Yukon and in parts of the Charley near the mouth. Sheefish and whitefish are also found in the Yukon.

King and chum salmon are common in the Yukon during the summer as they work their way upstream to spawning grounds. They are taken by Alaskan residents who fish for subsistence using nets and fish wheels, but rarely taken by sport fishers because of the silty water. They are most readily caught in the clear side-streams.

The best time to float and fish the area is during the summer. The ice breaks up in mid-May. A float trip from Eagle to Circle takes from five to ten days, depending on time spent on side trips up tributary streams. Floating beyond Circle takes you into the Yukon Flats National Wildlife Refuge. Beyond Circle, the only way out is by plane. Guided floats and fishing trips can be arranged in Eagle or Circle.

License An Alaska fishing license is required.

Camping Camping is allowed in the park on public lands. There are no developed facilities. Floaters usually camp on open beaches or river bars.

Maps Topographic maps in the 1:250,000 series for the park are: Charley River, Eagle, and Circle.

Park Address
Yukon–Charley Rivers NP
Box 64
Eagle, AK 99738
phone: (907) 547-2233

Additional Information If you plan to continue floating past Circle into the Yukon Flats National Wildlife Refuge, information on the refuge is available from: Yukon Flats NWF, U.S. Fish and Wildlife Service, Room 226, Federal Bldg. and Courthouse, 101 Twelfth Avenue, Fairbanks, AK, 99701; phone: (907) 456-0440.

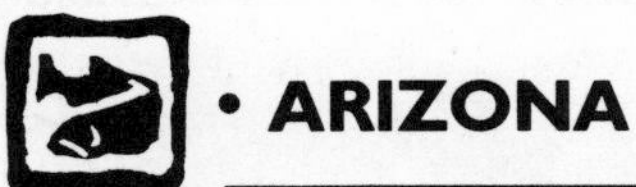

• ARIZONA

Glen Canyon National Recreation Area

Lake Powell, formed by Glen Canyon Dam on the Colorado River, is one of the best and most popular fisheries in the U.S. Known as the Jewel of the Colorado, Lake Powell is an immense, 186-mile-long reservoir with 1,900 miles of shoreline containing hundreds of vividly colored canyons. Just as popular is the Lees Ferry section of the Colorado River, which extends downstream from the dam to Lees Ferry.

Although most of the activities at Glen Canyon NRA are water related, hundreds of archeological sites are located in the park as well as some important historic sites related to the pioneer settlement of the area. Another outstanding feature is Rainbow Bridge National Monument, the largest known natural-stone arch in the world. Rainbow Bridge can be reached by boating up Forbidden Canyon and walking a short distance.

Access Glen Canyon NRA is in southeastern Utah (Kane, Garfield, and San Juan counties) and northern Arizona (Coconino County). The majority of Lake Powell is in Utah, while the Glen Canyon Dam and the Lees Ferry section of the Colorado River is in Arizona.

The southern portion of the park is the most accessible and is intersected by U.S. 89 through Page, Arizona. The only other road crossing the park is at Hite Crossing along Utah 95 on the north end of the lake.

A ferry connects Bullfrog Basin Marina with Halls Crossing Marina linking Utah State highways 276 and 263.

Fishing Glen Canyon NRA offers two separate types of fishing: 1) cold-water river fishing for large rainbow trout on the Colorado River below Glen Canyon Dam; and 2) predominantly warm-water fishing in Lake Powell for striped bass, walleye, largemouth bass, and black crappie.

Colorado River The Colorado River below the dam is a trophy trout fishery. Large trout thrive in the 45-to-50-degree water released from Lake Powell. Rainbow trout in the 8-to-10-pound range are possible, and even larger fish exist. Brook and cutthroat trout are also present in the river but do not attain the size of the rainbows.

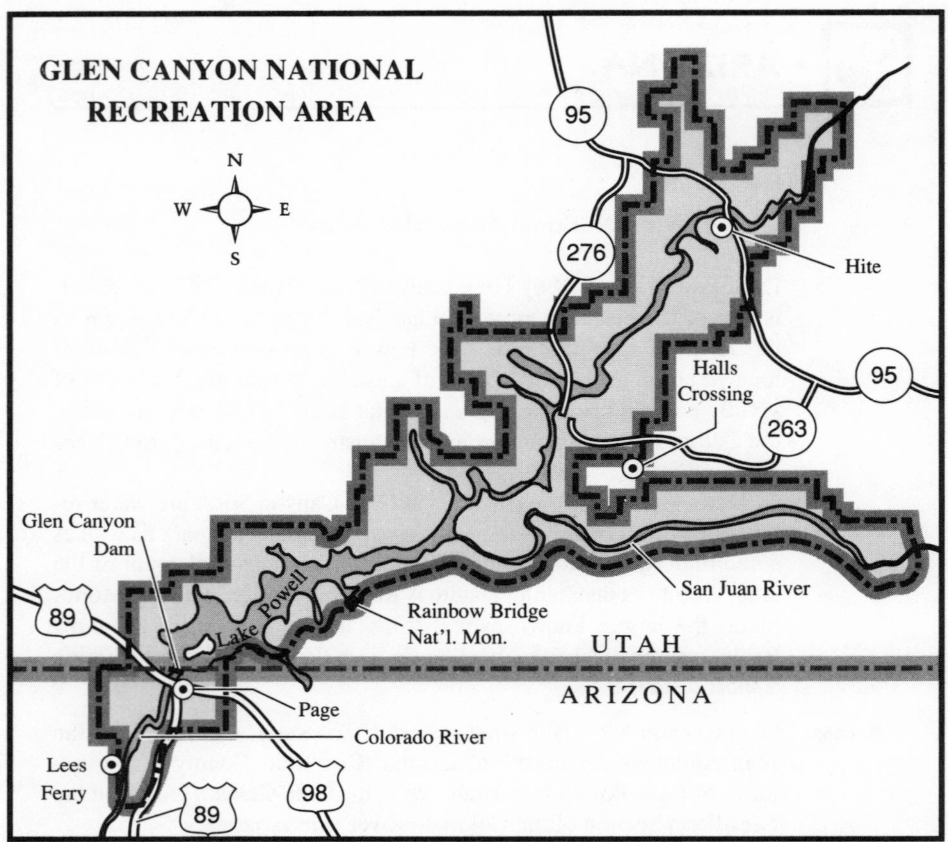

Prior to the construction of Glen Canyon Dam, this section of the Colorado River flowed red-brown as it carried a half-million tons of silt a day. Only carp, catfish, suckers, and Colorado squawfish could survive in its waters. Once the dam was completed and Lake Powell formed, the silt settled out in the deep lake, resulting in clear, cold, and pure water releases. Trout now abound where they never could have existed before.

Trout fishing is excellent for 15 miles downstream from the dam to Lees Ferry, the only access area. Lees Ferry is also the start of the float trips through the Grand Canyon further downstream. A boat ramp and campground are located at Lees Ferry. The usual way to fish the river is to launch a boat and motor upstream to the dam and then drift back downstream. Normal current flow is approximately 7 mph, so a motor of at least 25 horsepower is recommended. The park service also recommends a minimum boat length of 16 feet, along with an extra prop and motor pins. Because of the coldness and swiftness of the Colorado, boaters should wear a life jacket at all times when on the river.

Water levels are raised and lowered to meet power demands so a constant watch must be maintained for large rocks and obstructions just below the surface. If you are wading, be aware that the water can rise at any time and take the proper precautions. At low water, you may have to get out and pull the boat upstream in places, but this inconvenience is offset by the fact that fishing is better in low water.

Drifting downstream from the dam, you can stop at the numerous sand and gravel bars and wade fish the riffles and pools, or choose to drift through the deep holes. The bigger trout tend to hug the bottoms of the deep holes. During high flows, fishing the eddies is productive. Without a boat, only 2 miles (upstream from Lees Ferry) of this 15-mile section are accessible by foot, because of sheer canyon walls.

Below Lees Ferry, fishing is good only to the junction of the Paria River, approximately a mile downstream, where silt and mud again discolor the Colorado River. However, this section of river is best for wading as you fly-fish. In low water, most of this downstream stretch can be waded. I've had success by being on the water at dawn and getting in four or five hours of fishing before the water came up.

Good fishing is available year-round but the best time is from late summer through fall and early winter. If you want trophy fish, try the river from November through early March, when large rainbow trout come upstream from Lake Mead to spawn on the gravel bars below Glen Canyon Dam.

Spinners, plastic jigs, bait, and flies are all popular lures. The river is loaded with freshwater shrimp, so for fly-fishing any shrimp pattern or Woolly Worm is good, particularly a black Woolly Worm with fluorescent-orange hackles and a green Woolly Worm with a red tail. San Juan Worms in fluorescent colors (orange and pink are good) and large streamers such as the Zonker or black Woolly Bugger are also productive. Because this is a tail water, midges are prevalent and often hatch in the early morning when the sun hits the water.

When wading, use a dead-drift technique with a weighted fly and a strike indicator. If the fly is picking up moss about half the time, you are fishing at the correct depth. When floating the river and drifting through the deep holes, use high-density sinking lines and large, heavily weighted flies such as black Woolly Worms or Woolly Buggers to reach the large trout holding on the bottom.

The Marble Canyon Lodge, located at the entrance road junction to Lees Ferry, is a motel and restaurant with a small store attached. The store stocks the fly patterns needed for Lees Ferry.

Lake Powell Lake Powell is a fishing paradise, but the sheer size of it can frustrate and intimidate newcomers. Lake Powell consists of a deep, clear lower lake section, and is fed upstream by the San Juan, Escalante, and Colorado rivers. The endless canyons and 1,900 miles of shoreline provide a wealth of good fish habitat. Despite this wealth of habitat, there is much unproductive water that doesn't hold fish. Keep moving if you don't find fish. When you find fish, try to put together a pattern. Keep working toward developing a fishing pattern until you have consistent success. Unless you are very experienced at fishing, consider hiring a guide for the first day or two to learn where the fish are located and how to properly fish the lake.

Striped bass, walleye, largemouth bass, and black crappie are the most abundant species and the ones that attract the crowds at Lake Powell. In addition, there are rainbow trout, catfish, bluegills, and an occasional large northern pike or brown trout.

Smallmouth bass were introduced in 1984 and are a well-established and exciting species to fish. Smallmouth are doing very well in Lake Powell and may in the future be the prime attraction of this fishery. They locate near rocky ledges and points along the main river channel. Try jigs, plastic worms, and crayfish imitations. Some of the better smallmouth areas are Warm Creek Bay and Wahweap and Zahn bays.

Largemouth bass, averaging 2 to 5 pounds, are found throughout the lake and were formerly the most popular game fish in Lake Powell. Striped bass now lead in popularity.

Some of the best bass fishing occurs during spawning in April through June when bass are in the coves and canyons in shallow water. Prior to spawning, in February and March, try fishing in slick-rock canyons. Find a high, sandstone slick-rock wall and flip plastic jigs or worms right next to the wall on the sunny side. The sun reflecting off these walls warms the adjacent water a few degrees higher than the surrounding water. Bass seek out this warmer water and hold tight to the canyon wall.

In the early summer, when the water is cool, bass are near shallow rocks. As summer progresses and the water warms, bass move deeper until they find the thermocline.

During the summer and winter, bass move toward the main channel and locate near underwater rocks and points along the channel. During summer, bass gravitate to any available structure. They usually hold deep (20 to 60 feet) during the day, but rise toward the surface at dawn and twilight to feed. Rocks are the usual structure in the lake and bass locate near them, attracted by the crayfish hiding under the rocks or the small panfish that hide near the rocks.

Rocky structures also provide shade, which hide bass and allow them to ambush their prey. One cannot overemphasize the attraction of shade on this clear-water lake. The fish will constantly move to find shade and those fishing should follow suit. In the upstream sections of the lake, look for stained water and floating debris as the primary fish-holding cover.

In the fall, starting in late September when the water begins to cool, bass move back into the coves into shallower water to feed on crayfish and bluegills, their main forage base.

Proven bass techniques require light lines and finesse lures. Slim plastic worms free-lined against the canyon walls and crevices are effective, as are flipping jigs and plastic worms and casting spinnerbaits into stained water.

Black crappie grow to large sizes and also spawn in the spring, with March through May being the most productive months. Find bottoms with rock or brush piles and you'll find crappie. In the spring, large schools of crappie mass together in the back ends of canyons. During the winter and summer, the crappie often suspend over deep water and are harder to find. Your typical marabou and curly-tail jigs work well, as do minnow imitations. Live minnows are illegal on the lake.

Striped bass were first introduced in the lake in 1974 and have thrived in the deep-water environment. Stripers are now the most abundant game species in the lake. They run in large schools, feeding mostly at night on threadfin shad and are seen boiling the surface in feeding frenzies. During the day, stripers prefer deep water where spoons, deep-diving plugs, and frozen anchovies are productive. They are consistently caught from late August through October when they are running. The preferred method is to cast floating crankbaits from a boat or shore. They are a schooling fish and once you find the school, one after another can be taken.

Prior to the introduction of striped bass, the lake contained a good population of rainbow trout in the 3-to-6-pound class. Trout fishing is now declining. Rainbows are found throughout the lake but the largest concentration is found in the deep channel behind the dam where the water is deeper than 500 feet. Spawning occurs from mid-January through March and fishing from shore can be good. Wahweap Bay is rated as one of the better areas.

Walleye are considered a native fish in the lake. While most other species were introduced, walleyes moved down from the tributaries to establish themselves. Typically, walleyes seek out deep water over gravel or rubble and feed at night. They are found throughout the lake but good populations are present in Red Canyon, Good Hope Bay, Bullfrog Bay, and Padre Bay.

Walleyes spawn in shallow water over gravel, rubble, or boulders, from January through March. May and June are top months for walleyes. Likely areas to try are rubble-rock shorelines or shoals and the points near tributaries along the main lake channel. Plastic grubs and jigs, about one-quarter-ounce size in smoke or sparkle colors, fished slow and deep work well, as do deep-running diving lures in chartreuse or rainbow.

The other game species are channel catfish, northern pike, and bluegill. Channel catfish are plentiful and found mainly in shallow water in stream-fed canyons where the inflowing roiled water and brush provide prime habitat. Pike may show up now and then but they are most often found during spring, spawning in shallow, weedy areas. Bluegills occur throughout the lake.

It is suggested that you fish from a boat (17 to 20 feet long with a deep V-shaped hull) carrying a large gas tank or take an extra tank. The lake is large and there are few marinas for refueling.

License On Lake Powell, you will need either an Arizona or Utah license. As of 1990, the Arizona license was considerably cheaper for both residents and non-residents. In addition to the license, you must also purchase a special Colorado River stamp ($8.00 as of 1990) that validates your license for both states, allowing you to fish anywhere on the lake. The Colorado River downstream from the dam is entirely within Arizona and requires an Arizona license.

Camping The four park service campgrounds around the lake offer a total of 365 spaces, the largest being Wahweap with 208 spaces. There are also three concession-operated campgrounds with an additional 182 spaces. There is a park service campground at Lees Ferry with 65 spaces. The campgrounds are open all year. Back-country camping is allowed throughout much of the park on a first-come, first-served basis. A back-country permit is required only for the Escalante Canyon area. Back-country camping usually consists of boaters camping along the shore.

Maps The best map of the Lake Powell and Lees Ferry area is the "Stan Jones Boating and Exploring MAP of Lake Powell and Its Canyons." It is available for $4 postpaid from Stan Jones, P.O. Box 955, Page, AZ, 86040; phone: (602) 645-2636. The Stan Jones map is not a contour fishing map, but a map of the lake that provides the topography of the surrounding area along with fishing information and historical notes.

Contour fishing maps are available from the Fish-N-Map Company, 8535 West 79th Ave., Arvada, CO, 80005; phone: (303) 421-5994. The map called "Lake Powell North" covers the northern half of the lake including the Escalante Arm and the "Lake Powell South" map covers the rest of the lake.

There is also a special USGS topographic map of the area entitled "Glen Canyon National Recreation Area."

Park Address
Glen Canyon NRA
P.O. Box 1507
Page, Arizona 86040
phone: (602) 645-2471

Chamber of Commerce
Page/Lake Powell C.C.
P.O. Box 233
Page, AZ 86040
phone: (602) 645-2741

Additional Information The January 1989 issue of *In Fisherman* (book #82) contains a very detailed article about walleye fishing on Lake Powell. The article, "Walleyes from a Canyon," by Doug Stange and Gregg Myer, contains maps and photographs illustrating seasonal locations and patterns of walleyes and recommends the appropriate fishing technique. Copies of *In Fisherman* are available from: *In Fisherman*, P.O. Box 999, Brainerd, MN, 56401; phone: (218) 829-1648.

Houseboating on Lake Powell, by Bob Hirsch, is a comprehensive source of information about Lake Powell that would be useful to anyone interested in fishing there. The book is available for $7.95 postpaid from: P.O. Box 644, Cave Creek, AZ, 85331.

Lees Ferry is a two-hour round trip from Page, Arizona, the nearest town. Rather than drive back and forth, visitors can use the Marble Canyon Lodge as a convenient base for fishing Lees Ferry. The lodge has a fine restaurant. For reservations, contact: Marble Canyon Lodge, Box 1, Marble Canyon, AZ, 86036; phone: (602) 355-2225.

Colorado River flow rate and water release information is available from the Bureau of Reclamation office at Glen Canyon Dam. Phone: (602) 645-2481 from 7:00 A.M. to 3:30 P.M..

Grand Canyon National Park

"Grand" is inadequate to describe the greatest gorge in the world. Awesome and magnificent come close. President Theodore Roosevelt described it best as "the one great sight which every American should see."

Cut by the erosive force of the Colorado River to depths greater than a mile, the Grand Canyon's immense variety of formations displays an open record of geological history as far back as 2,000 million years.

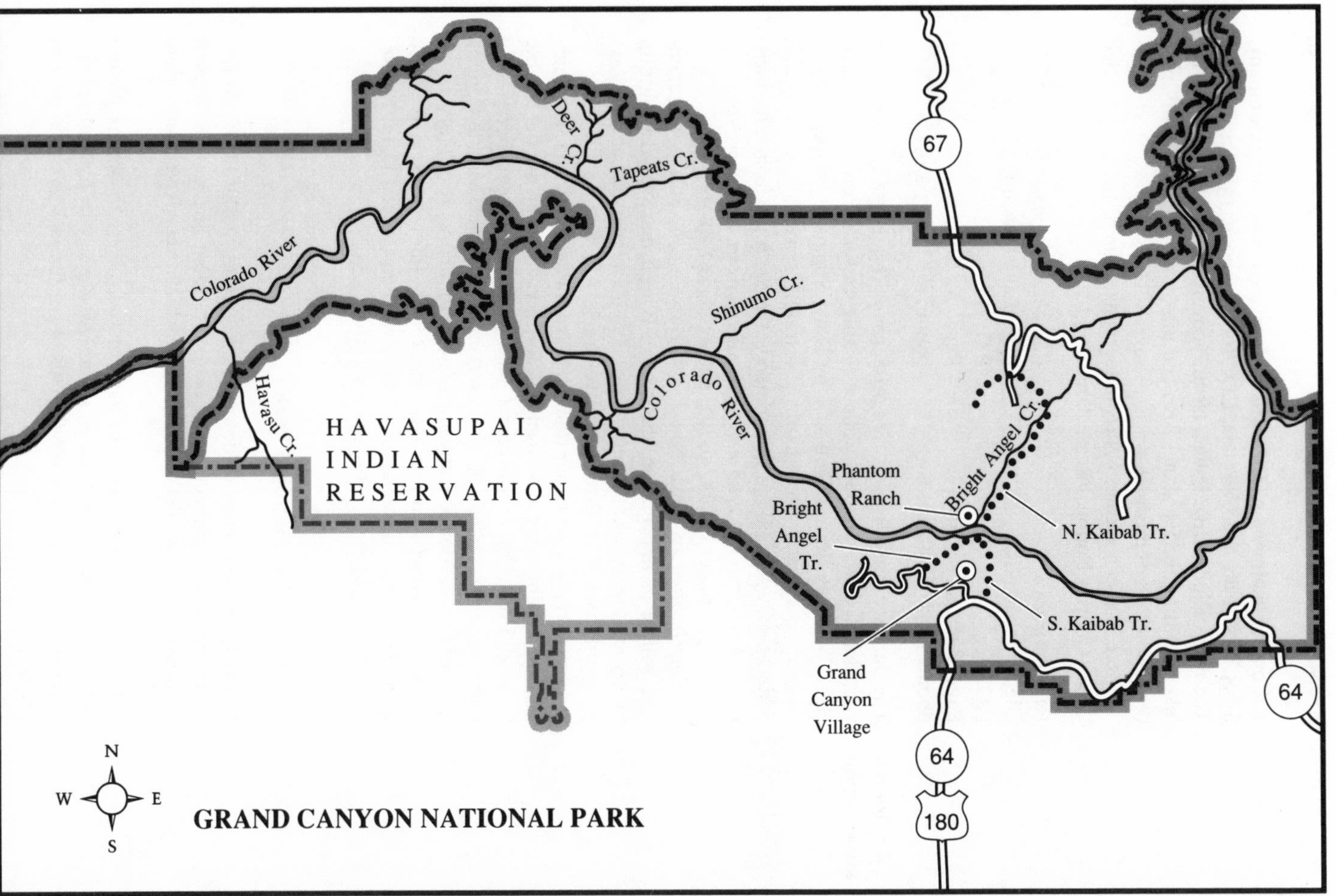
Colorado River
Deer Cr.
Tapeats Cr.
67
Shinumo Cr.
Havasu Cr.
Colorado River
HAVASUPAI
INDIAN
RESERVATION
Bright Angel Cr.
Phantom Ranch
Bright Angel Tr.
N. Kaibab Tr.
S. Kaibab Tr.
Grand Canyon Village
64
64
180
N
W
E
S
GRAND CANYON NATIONAL PARK

Access The park is in northwestern Arizona (Mohave and Coconino counties). Two main areas have been developed for viewing the canyon, the North Rim and the South Rim. They are 9 miles apart straight across, but 214 miles apart by road.

To reach the North Rim, take Arizona Highway 67 south from Jacobs Lake for 33 miles to the park entrance. Bright Angel Point on the North Rim is 13 miles further on the park road.

The South Rim can be reached by U.S. 180 and Arizona Highway 64 from Flagstaff to Grand Canyon Village (82 miles) or by U.S. 89 and Arizona Highway 64 (108 miles). The South Rim is open all year; the North Rim is open only from mid-May to mid-October.

Fishing All the fishing activity is on the Colorado River and tributary creeks at the bottom of the canyon. This area is known as the inner canyon and is accessible by trail from either rim or from the river.

Very large rainbow trout in the Colorado River at the bottom of the canyon await those willing to hike into and out of the canyon. Trout in the 10-pound range are not uncommon.

The fishery in the Grand Canyon is merely a downstream extension of the fine fishing in the Colorado River below Glen Canyon Dam, as described in the section on Glen Canyon National Recreation Area. The damming of the river by Glen Canyon Dam stopped the daily load of 500,000 tons of silt that flowed through the canyon, changed the water color from muddy red to turquoise, and provided water temperatures in the 45-to-55-degree range, ideal for trout.

Rainbow, brown, brook, and cutthroat trout have been planted in the river by the state, along with bait fish and freshwater shrimp as forage for the trout. The trout grow quickly in this cold-water environment with shrimp as their main food source. Your best chance of catching a large rainbow is to use a large lure. Countdown Rapalas in sizes 11 and 13 are popular, as are size-3 Mepps spinners in silver or brass.

For fly-fishing, large streamers, although difficult to cast, are the best bet. Patterns such as Zonkers, black Woolly Buggers, and Matukas (olive and black) are good. Freshwater shrimp imitations also excel.

The curse of fishing the canyon is the green moss that always seems to be afloat on the water. The time spent cleaning equipment is aggravating, but the reward could be the fish of a lifetime.

Because so many "fish of a lifetime" are being caught, fishing in the Grand Canyon has received national publicity in the last few years. The long and difficult two-way hike still discourages all but the most determined. Actually, the hike isn't as bad as its reputation and the trails are well maintained. From the North Rim, the hike along the North Kaibab Trail is 14.2 miles. From the South Rim, Bright Angel Trail to the river is 7.8 miles and the South Kaibab Trail is 6.4 miles. A pamphlet entitled *Hiking the Bright Angel and Kaibab Trails* is available from the park.

At the bottom of the canyon is Phantom Ranch, where overnight accommodations and dining are available on a reservation basis. Campgrounds are also available, but reservations and back-country camping permits are required.

Only short sections of the river are accessible by these trails. Another way to fish the river is to take a commercial float trip through the canyon. These trips vary in length and price. A list of river-running concessioners licensed by the park service is available from the park. If you are primarily interested in fishing, make sure you select an outfitter who specializes in fishing trips rather than rafting or sightseeing trips.

Some of the best fishing is found in the side streams flowing into the canyon. The cold, clear inlets of many of these streams provide a haven for brook and cutthroat trout in addition to rainbows. Streams such as Tapeats, Deer, Shinumo, and Havasu are accessible from the river and are worth investigating. Bright Angel Creek can also be good, but it receives heavy fishing pressure because of its proximity to trail ends.

License An Arizona fishing license is required and state regulations apply. Be sure to check the regulations relating to the Colorado River system.

Camping The North Rim Campground has 82 spaces and is open seasonally on a first-come, first-served basis. On the South Rim, Mather Campground at Grand Canyon Village has 327 spaces and is operated on a reservation basis by Ticketron. Desert View Campground has 50 spaces and is located one-half mile west of the east entrance.

Three campgrounds in the inner canyon—Bright Angel (Phantom Ranch); Cottonwood (North Kaibab Trail); and Indian Gardens (Bright Angel Trail)—are of primary interest for fishing. These campgrounds require overnight permits, and advance reservations are usually necessary. For details on trails, campgrounds, and permits, write to: Back-country Reservation Office, P.O. Box 129, Grand Canyon, AZ, 86023.

Reservations for Phantom Ranch, from April 1 through October 31 and for holiday periods, should be made at least six months in advance to: Reservations Department, Grand Canyon National Park Lodges, Grand Canyon, AZ 86023; phone: (602) 638-2401.

The park can provide a brochure entitled *Accommodations and Services in Grand Canyon National Park*.

Maps A special USGS park map, "Grand Canyon National Park and Vicinity," is the best bet, since it shows all the maintained trails.

Park Address
Grand Canyon National Park
P.O. Box 129
Grand Canyon, AZ 86023
phone: (602) 638-7888

Chambers of Commerce

Flagstaff C.C.
101 W. Santa Fe
Flagstaff, AZ 86001
phone: (602) 774-4505

Page/Lake Powell C.C.
P.O. Box 233
Page, AZ 86040
phone: (602) 645-2741

Additional Information The Grand Canyon Natural History Association has an interesting list of publications that may be helpful. The Association also sells park maps. Write: Grand Canyon Natural History Association, P.O. Box 399, Grand Canyon, AZ, 86023; phone: (602) 638-7774.

• ARKANSAS

Arkansas Post National Memorial

Arkansas Post was the oldest settlement in Arkansas and the site of the first European settlement in the lower Mississippi Valley. During its history, French, Spanish, Confederate, and U.S. flags flew over the various forts and settlements that occupied the site. Today there are few visible remains.

Access The park is in eastern Arkansas (Arkansas County) on the banks of the Arkansas River between the towns of Gillett and Dumas. It is on Arkansas Highway 169 off U.S. 165, about 7 miles south of Gillett.

Fishing Fishing is popular in the park along the banks of the Arkansas River. The catch is mixed and may include largemouth bass, crappie, catfish, sauger, gar, and bream. From December through February, sauger gather to spawn below the dams on the Arkansas River. Nearby, Dam #2 is a local hot spot during the sauger run.

There is a small, 7.5-acre lake in the park that provides surprisingly good fishing. A largemouth bass weighing 9.5 pounds was once taken from the lake. Crappie, catfish, and bream also inhabit the lake.

License An Arkansas fishing license is required.

Camping None within the park.

Maps The park brochure map is sufficient.

Park Address
Arkansas Post NM
Route 1, Box 16
Gillett, AR 72055
phone: (501) 548-2432

Chamber of Commerce
Dumas C.C.
P.O. Box 431
Dumas, AR 71639
phone: (501) 382-5447

Buffalo National River

Nestled in the Arkansas Ozarks, the timeless Buffalo River is one of the few remaining free-flowing rivers in the lower 48 states. The river flows for 150 miles (132 miles are in the park) through the highest

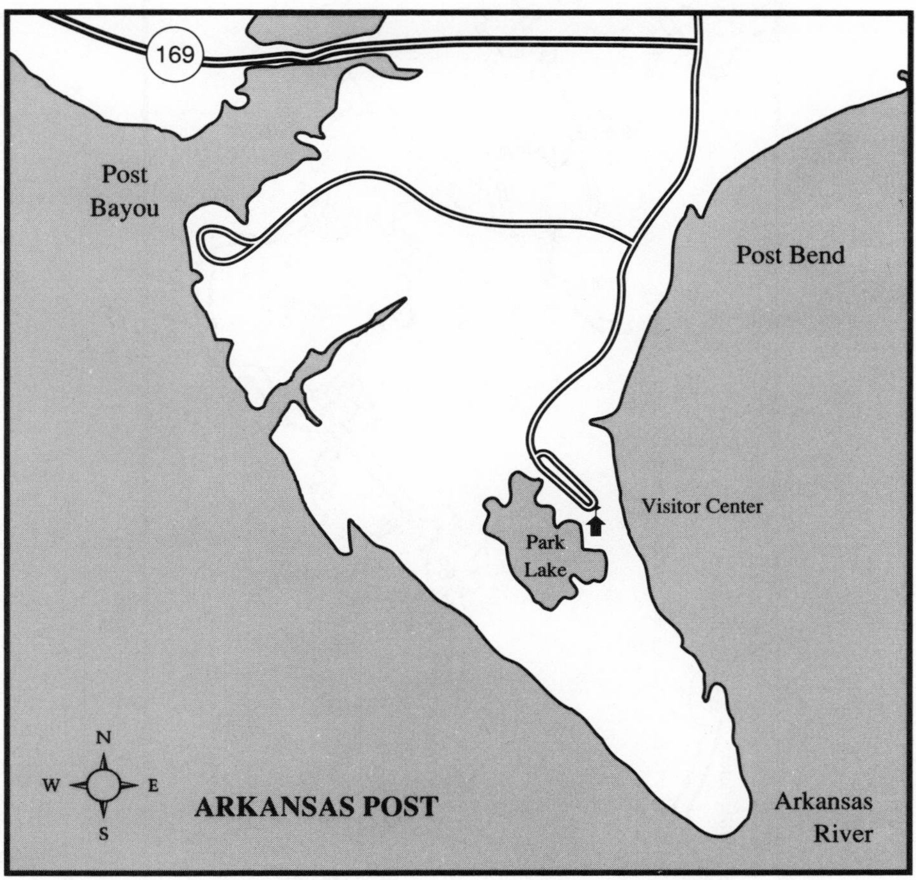

bluffs in the Ozarks to its terminus in the White River. The Buffalo River has long been popular with canoeists because of its endless supply of picturesque scenery.

Access Located in north central Arkansas (Newton, Searcy, Baxter, and Marion counties), the Buffalo River's major access points are: State Highway (SH) 21 at Boxley; SH 43 at Steel Creek; SH 7 at Pruitt; SH 123 at Carver; U.S. 65 at Silver Hill; and SH 14 and SH 268 at Buffalo Point. Other access points via gravel roads are noted on the river map in the park brochure.

Fishing The Buffalo River has been acclaimed as a classic smallmouth-bass river. Its cool, unpolluted waters also support large populations of

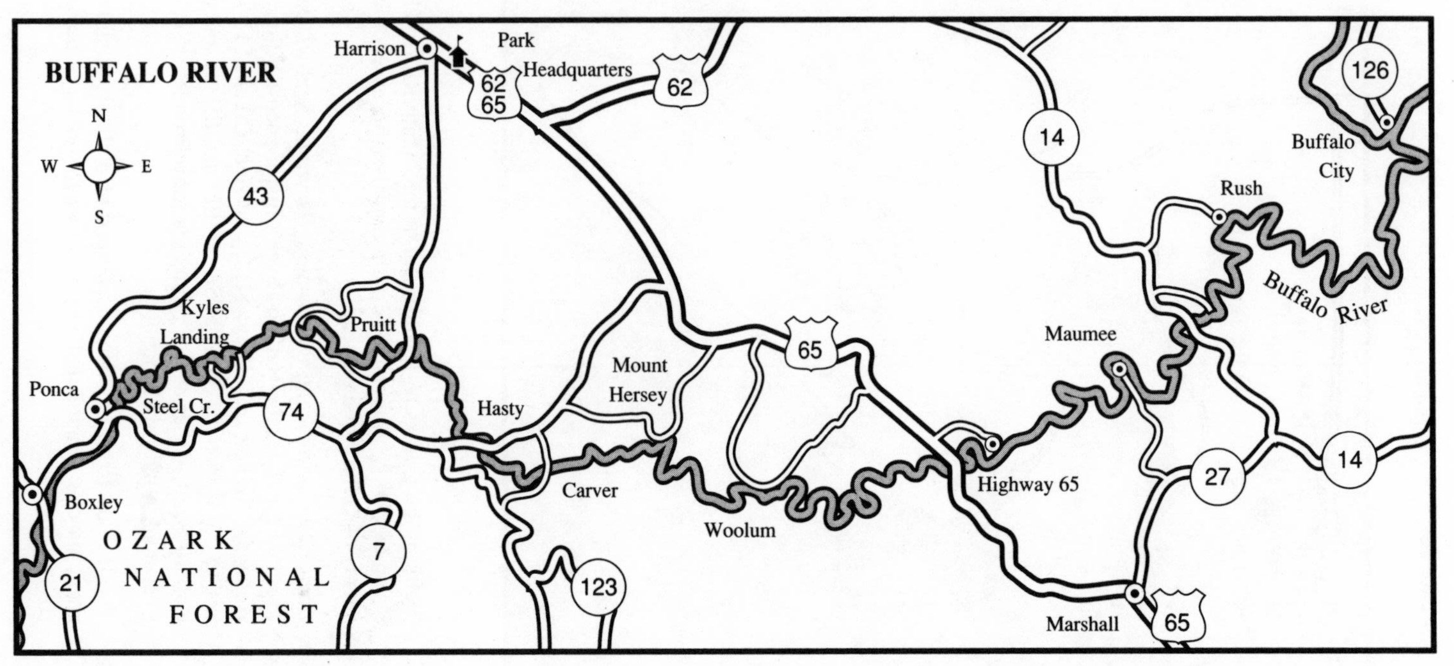
BUFFALO RIVER
N
W
E
S
Harrison
Park
Headquarters
62
65
62
43
14
126
Buffalo
City
Rush
Buffalo River
Kyles
Landing
Pruitt
Ponca
Steel Cr.
74
Hasty
Mount
Hersey
65
Maumee
Carver
Woolum
Highway 65
27
14
Boxley
OZARK
NATIONAL
FOREST
21
7
123
Marshall
65

rock bass and panfish, along with some catfish, largemouth bass, and spotted bass (also known as Kentucky bass). On the lower Buffalo, from the town of Rush to the White River, an occasional rainbow or brown trout is found. Both browns and rainbows inhabit the White River and move up into the Buffalo during late fall to early spring.

Prime fishing time is during April, May, and June. After June, the fishing slows down as the river gets extremely clear and flows diminish in the upper river. As the fishing slows, it may be worthwhile to fish some of the feeder streams such as Big Creek, Richland Creek, and Little Buffalo River, or to fish at night when temperatures are cooler and fish are more actively feeding.

The traditional way to fish the Buffalo and other Ozark streams is float fishing from a johnboat. Fishing from a canoe is also popular, especially on the upstream sections, but the long (20 feet) johnboats are always in evidence. Guided float trips using johnboats are available for most stretches of the river. These floats can vary from one-day to overnight camping trips. A list of canoe and johnboat concessioners is available from the park.

It is essential to check the river conditions before you start your

The Buffalo River is a favorite with canoeists and fishermen.—*National Park Service photo by Fred Mang Jr.*

trip. The lower river, east of U.S. Highway 65, is usually floatable all year. The upper river down to U.S. 65 is usually very low by late summer. If early fall rains come, floating the upper river may resume in September and October. Information on river levels and floating conditions is available by calling park headquarters after 8:00 A.M., Monday through Friday: (501) 741-5443.

License An Arkansas fishing license is required, plus a trout stamp if you plan to keep any trout.

Camping There is a major campground of 107 spaces at Buffalo Point. Rental cabins are also available seasonally from a concessioner. For advance cabin reservations, contact: Buffalo Point Concession, HCR 66, Box 388, Yellville, Arkansas 72687; phone: (501) 449-6206.

Twelve primitive campgrounds also provide excellent places from which to begin or end a float trip. Camping is permitted on gravel bars along the river but you must be alert to weather conditions. Heavy or prolonged rainstorms in the area can rapidly raise water levels and quickly inundate gravel bars and other low areas along the river.

Maps The park brochure contains a good map showing river access areas, camping areas, and the river distances between starting and ending points. The Corps of Engineers also distributes a good river map, which is free. Contact: U.S. Army Corps of Engineers, Little Rock District, Public Affairs Office, P.O. Box 867, Little Rock, Arkansas, 72203; phone: (501) 378-5551.

Both the park and the Corps maps show roads and access areas. For more details, quad sheets will be necessary. The names of the 15 quad sheets for the entire river are: Big Flat, Boxley, Buffalo City, Cozahome, Eula, Hasty, Jasper, Marshall, Maumee, Mount Judea, Osage SW, Ponca, Rea Valley, Snowball, and Western Grove.

At $2.50 a sheet, the best bet is to get a state index and only order the maps for the section of river that you plan to float. Various other guides and maps are also available at park headquarters in Harrison or at the Pruitt and Buffalo Point ranger stations.

Park Address
Buffalo National River
P.O. Box 1173
Harrison, AR 72602
phone: (501) 741-5443

Chamber of Commerce
Harrison C.C.
P.O. Box 939
Harrison, AR 72602-0939
phone: (501) 741-2659

• CALIFORNIA

Cabrillo National Monument

Cabrillo National Monument commemorates the discovery of the California coast in 1542 by Portuguese explorer Juan Rodriguez Cabrillo, who was the first explorer to visit the shores of present-day California and Oregon.

The monument is popular for its outstanding seascapes and, in mid-December to mid-February, as an observation point for watching gray whales during their annual migration to Baja California from the Arctic.

Access Located on Point Loma, about 10 miles from downtown San Diego, Cabrillo is easily reached by driving southwest from San Diego on Rosecrans Street, turning right on Canon Street, left on Catalina Boulevard, and then through the gates of the U.S. Navy Ocean System Center.

Fishing The Point Loma section of the California coast is characterized by upland cliffs and rocky shorelines. Consequently, the only fishing in the monument is from the cliffs and rocks along the west coast. Access requires sure footing and caution because of eroded and steep sandstone cliffs.

Species commonly caught are opaleye, halfmoon, surfperch (black, shiner, walleye, and pile), kelp bass, cabezon, an occasional sargo, and rockfish (kelp, grass, and brown). Opaleye, rockfish, and halfmoon are available all year but opaleye fishing is best in the spring.

The fishing area is in an intertidal preserve, one of the best in California, and consequently only sport fish may be taken from the area and no invertebrates may be taken or used for bait.

Fishing pressure in the park is light, although the area is locally popular. The fishing area is open from 9:00 A.M. to 4:30 P.M. daily.

Offshore, the Point Loma kelp beds are a major fishing ground for bonito, yellowtail, barracuda, giant sea bass, rockfish, sheepshead, kelp bass, and white croaker. Charter and party boats to the kelp beds are available in nearby Mission Bay and San Diego Bay.

During late spring and summer, as waters near the shore warm up, fishing intensifies for kelp bass and migratory species such as Cali-

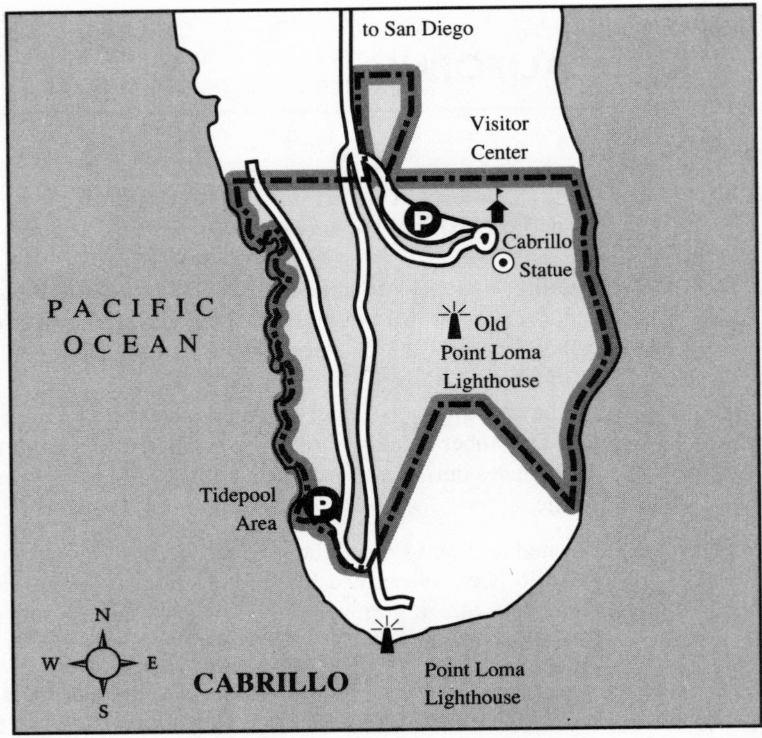

fornia barracuda and yellowtail. Fishing for migratory species tapers off in the fall as the waters cool. During the winter months, much of the fishing effort is for local varieties of rockfish and bonito and mackerel, when available.

License A California fishing license is required and state regulations apply.

Camping Although there are no camping facilities in the monument, private campgrounds are available nearby.

Maps Topographic maps are not necessary. The second parking lot as you come in from the north on Cabrillo Road is the best staging area for fishing. For taking your own boat offshore, nautical chart #18772 should be used.

Park Address
Cabrillo NM
P.O. Box 6670
San Diego, CA 92106
phone: (619) 293-5450

Chamber of Commerce
San Diego C.C.
110 West C. St., Suite 1600
San Diego, CA 92101
phone: (619) 232-0124

Additional Information Because San Diego is a major metropolitan area, there is a wide variety of tackle shops and charter boat services that can provide current fishing information. A list can be obtained from the Chamber of Commerce.

Channel Islands National Park

The Channel Islands, off the coast of southern California, consist of eight islands. In 1980, five of these islands, Anacapa, Santa Barbara, San Miguel, Santa Cruz, and Santa Rosa, were set aside as Channel Islands National Park. The two largest islands, Santa Cruz and Santa Rosa, are private property as well as being part of the park. Future plans call for certain portions of Santa Cruz and all of Santa Rosa to be acquired by the federal government.

These islands have long been of interest for their recreational opportunities and biological diversity. The waters for 6 miles around the islands were designated as a national marine sanctuary in recognition of their rich marine environment.

Access You can get to the islands by public transportation from many southern California ports or by private boat. Contact the park for up-to-date transportation information. A permit is needed to go to San Miguel Island. There is a park brochure that describes access to the various islands and the park also distributes an information sheet concerning landing and camping on the islands.

Fishing Fishing is very popular in the waters surrounding the islands as well as in the Santa Barbara Channel. Sheepshead, rockfish, kelp bass, lingcod, and barracuda are commonly caught. Fishing is from private boat or from charter boats, which are available at many points along the coast.

The shorelines of the islands are predominantly rocky and the islands are surrounded by kelp beds of varying size. The kelp provides excellent habitat for fish, allowing them to feed, reproduce, and hide from predators.

The two western islands, San Miguel and Santa Rosa, receive the least fishing pressure because of their distance from the mainland and the fact that weather, wind, and sea conditions are usually more severe there than around islands nearer the mainland. Each island is briefly reviewed below.

Anacapa Island Anacapa, closest island to the mainland (11 miles), receives heavy fishing pressure. Fishing is particularly good around this island for kelp bass, black sea bass, and canary rockfish. In the

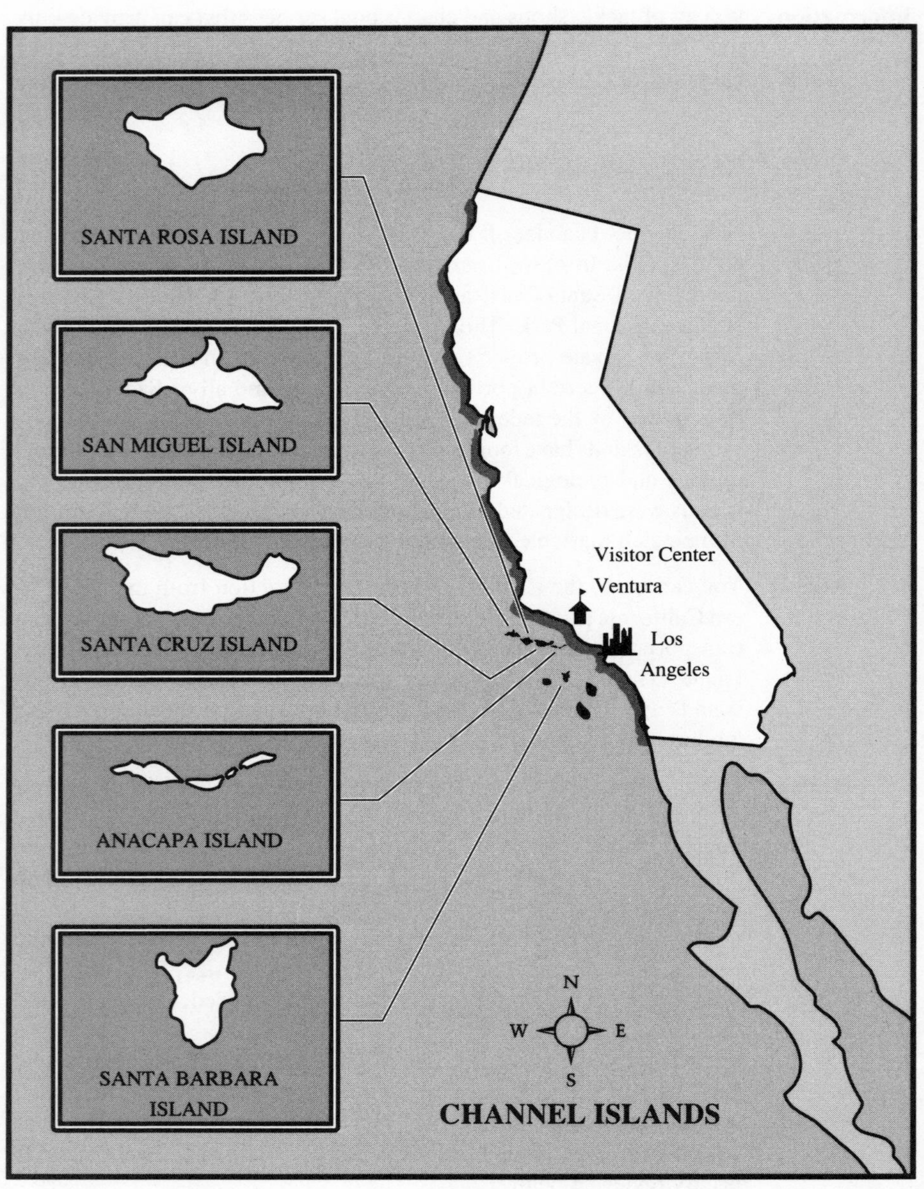
SANTA ROSA ISLAND
SAN MIGUEL ISLAND
SANTA CRUZ ISLAND
ANACAPA ISLAND
SANTA BARBARA ISLAND
Visitor Center
Ventura
Los Angeles
N
W
E
S
CHANNEL ISLANDS

summer, people fishing here occasionally catch barracuda and yellowtail. In the fall, the area south of the island is noted for broadbill swordfish and striped marlin.

Santa Barbara Santa Barbara is a small island (640 acres) almost entirely surrounded by cliffs. The island is noted for its dense and extensive kelp beds, especially along the north side. Rockfish, kelp bass, and sheepshead are caught around the island.

San Miguel San Miguel is the westernmost island and probably receives the least fishing pressure. Although the coastline is predominantly rocky, there are some sandy beaches at scattered points. One of the largest seal and sea lion rookeries is found on a beach at the west end, but state regulations restrict boats from approaching too closely. Lingcod, kelp bass, rockfish, and halibut predominate.

Santa Rosa Santa Rosa has rocky shorelines along the northwest and southwest sides. The southwest shore is particularly good for rockfish and kelp bass while the southeast is noted for halibut. Other fish taken are lingcod, sea bass, and an occasional bluefin tuna.

Santa Cruz The largest of the Channel Islands, Santa Cruz receives heavy fishing pressure. Rockfish are caught all around the island. The southeast side is protected from westerly winds and is usually a productive area for rockfish, yellowtail, and bonito. Bluefin tuna are found off the southwest end during the summer.

License A California fishing license is required. The waters for 1 nautical mile around San Miguel, Santa Barbara, and Anacapa islands have been designated as a California State Ecological Reserve, so be sure to check the current regulations.

Camping Primitive camping is available on Anacapa and Santa Barbara islands with a permit from park headquarters. Camping on San Miguel, Santa Cruz, and Santa Rosa is not permitted.

Maps For fishing or boating around the islands, you will need nautical charts #18720 and #18727. Additional charts of smaller scale that may be helpful are #18728, #18729, and #18756.

Park Address
Channel Islands NP
1901 Spinnaker Drive
Ventura, CA 93001
phone: (805) 644-8157

Chambers of Commerce

Port Hueneme C.C.
220 N. Market St.
P.O. Box 465
Port Hueneme, CA 93041
phone: (805) 488-2023

Channel Islands C.C.
3886 W. Channel Islands Blvd.
Oxnard, CA 93030
phone: (805) 985-2244

Devils Postpile National Monument

Devils Postpile is a mass of columnar basalt stones, 40 to 60 feet high, resembling a giant pipe organ. This geological oddity is the remnant of a million-year-old volcanic eruption.

Access The park is in Madera County, southeast of Yosemite National Park. Devils Postpile is reached by a 16-mile drive on a paved road from U.S. 395.

Fishing The Middle Fork of the San Joaquin River, featuring "wild" trout, traverses the entire length of the park. The river contains brook, brown, and rainbow trout. Fish in park waters are considered wild because the river within the park is not stocked by the state. The California Department of Fish and Game stocks trout at numerous sites upstream from the park but apparently few of these specimens make it downstream to park waters.

Fishing is considered very good in the park and brown trout as long as 27 inches have been taken from the deeper pools. The San Joaquin has many types of water, including broad, low-gradient meanders, scattered pools, fast-flowing rapids, cascades, and falls. Three small creeks enter within or near the park. They are King Creek, Boundary Creek, and an unnamed creek from Red's Meadow.

License A California fishing license is required.

Camping One developed campground (24 spaces) near the park ranger station is open approximately from June 15 to October 15, depending on the weather. More camping is available in nearby Inyo National Forest.

Maps The park brochure map showing the maintained trails to the river should be sufficient.

Park Address

Devils Postpile NM
c/o Sequoia–Kings Canyon NP
Three Rivers, CA 93271
phone: (714) 934-2289

Chamber of Commerce

Madera District C.C.
P.O. Box 307
Madera, CA 93639
phone: (209) 673-3563

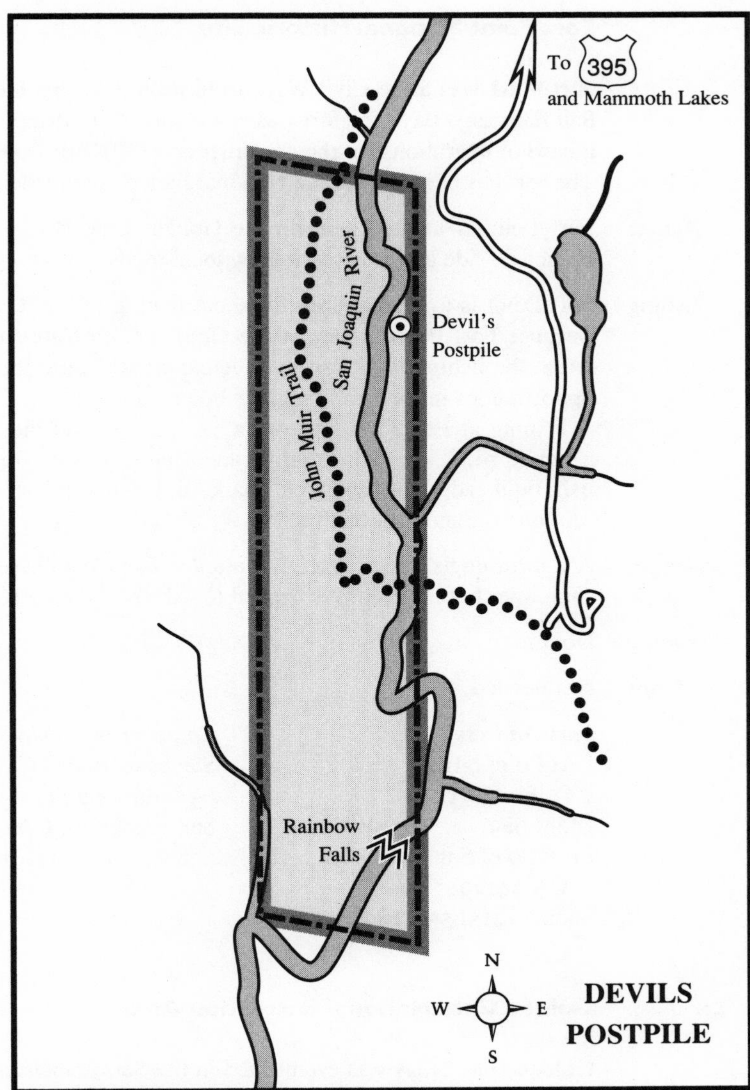

Additional Information Information and maps for Inyo National Forest are available from: Forest Supervisor, Inyo National Forest, 873 North Main St., Bishop, CA, 93514; phone: (619) 873-5841.

Fort Point National Historic Site

Fort Point was a pre-Civil War fortification guarding the entrance to San Francisco Bay. The fort was abandoned in 1886 and later used as a base of operations for the construction of the Golden Gate Bridge. The fort has been part of the National Park System since 1970.

Access Fort Point is located beneath the Golden Gate Bridge on the San Francisco side and is accessible by local roads.

Fishing Fort Point is a popular spot for shore fishing in San Francisco Bay. Because Fort Point is part of the Golden Gate National Recreation Area, the fishing report on that recreation area describes the fishing opportunities in the San Francisco Bay area.

Fishing at Fort Point is from a sea wall around the fort or from a public pier. The fish usually caught here include flounder, kingfish, bullhead, stingray, perch, shark, and an occasional striped bass, salmon, sturgeon, or halibut.

License A California fishing license is required to fish from the sea wall or the shoreline, but no license is needed to fish from the pier.

Camping None.

Maps Not needed.

Park Address
Fort Point NHS
P.O. Box 29333
Bldg. 989
Presidio of San Francisco,
CA 94129
phone: (415) 556-1693

Chamber of Commerce
San Francisco C.C.
65 California St.
San Francisco, CA 94104
phone: (415) 392-4511

Golden Gate National Recreation Area

Golden Gate NRA was established in the San Francisco Bay area as one of the first major urban parks created for the purpose of locating parks near the places where people live and work. The park is made up of many scattered areas and combines spectacular scenery and natural qualities with historic interests. Golden Gate embraces 26,000 acres of ocean beaches, marshes, redwood forests, and lagoons.

Access The park includes areas in San Francisco (northern San Mateo County) and in Marin County, north of San Francisco, across the Golden Gate Bridge. Public transportation is available to the various parts of the

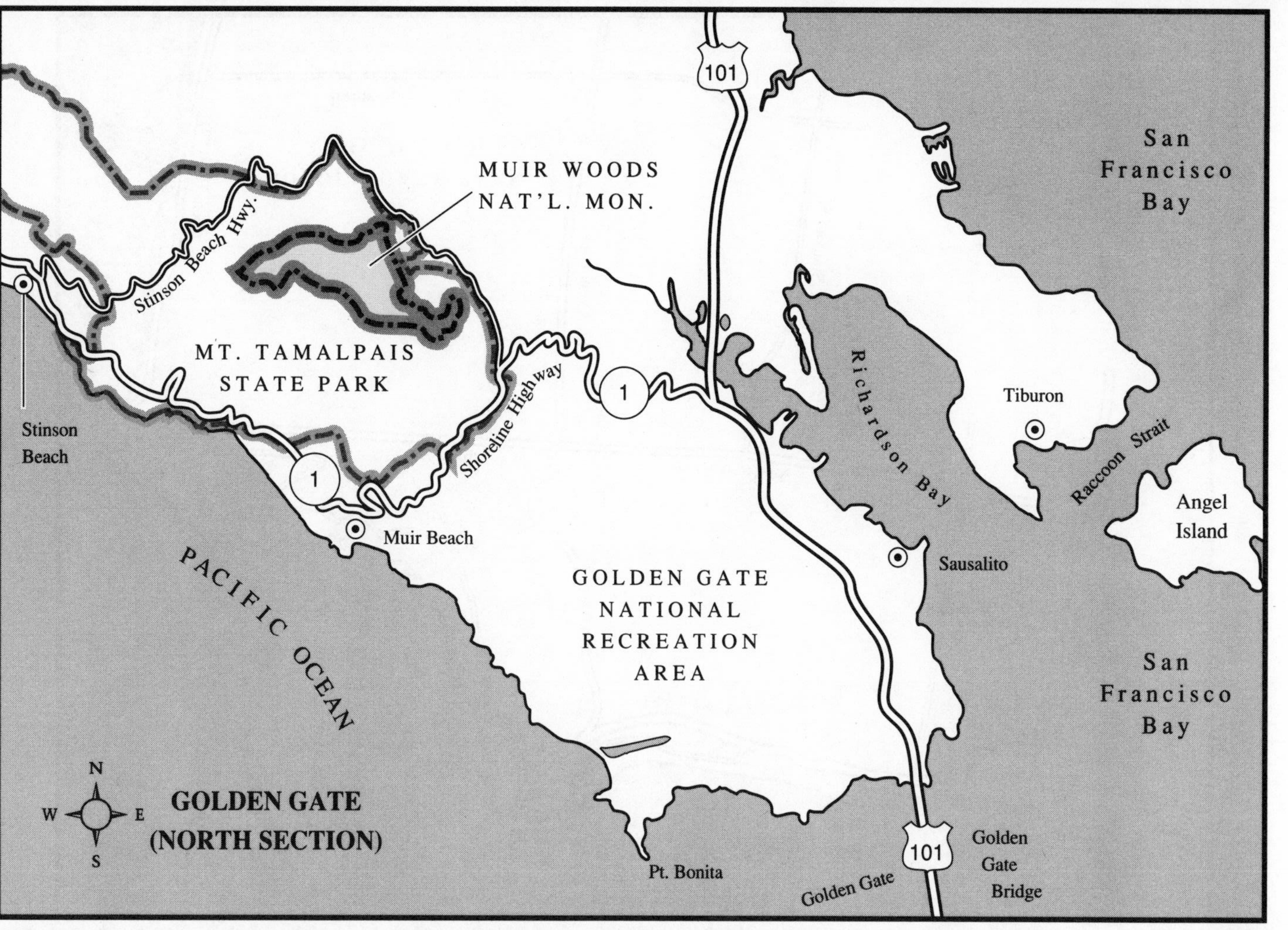
101
San Francisco Bay
MUIR WOODS NAT'L. MON.
Stinson Beach Hwy.
MT. TAMALPAIS STATE PARK
Shoreline Highway
1
1
Richardson Bay
Tiburon
Raccoon Strait
Angel Island
Stinson Beach
Muir Beach
Sausalito
PACIFIC OCEAN
GOLDEN GATE NATIONAL RECREATION AREA
San Francisco Bay
N
W
E
S
GOLDEN GATE
(NORTH SECTION)
Pt. Bonita
101
Golden Gate
Golden Gate Bridge

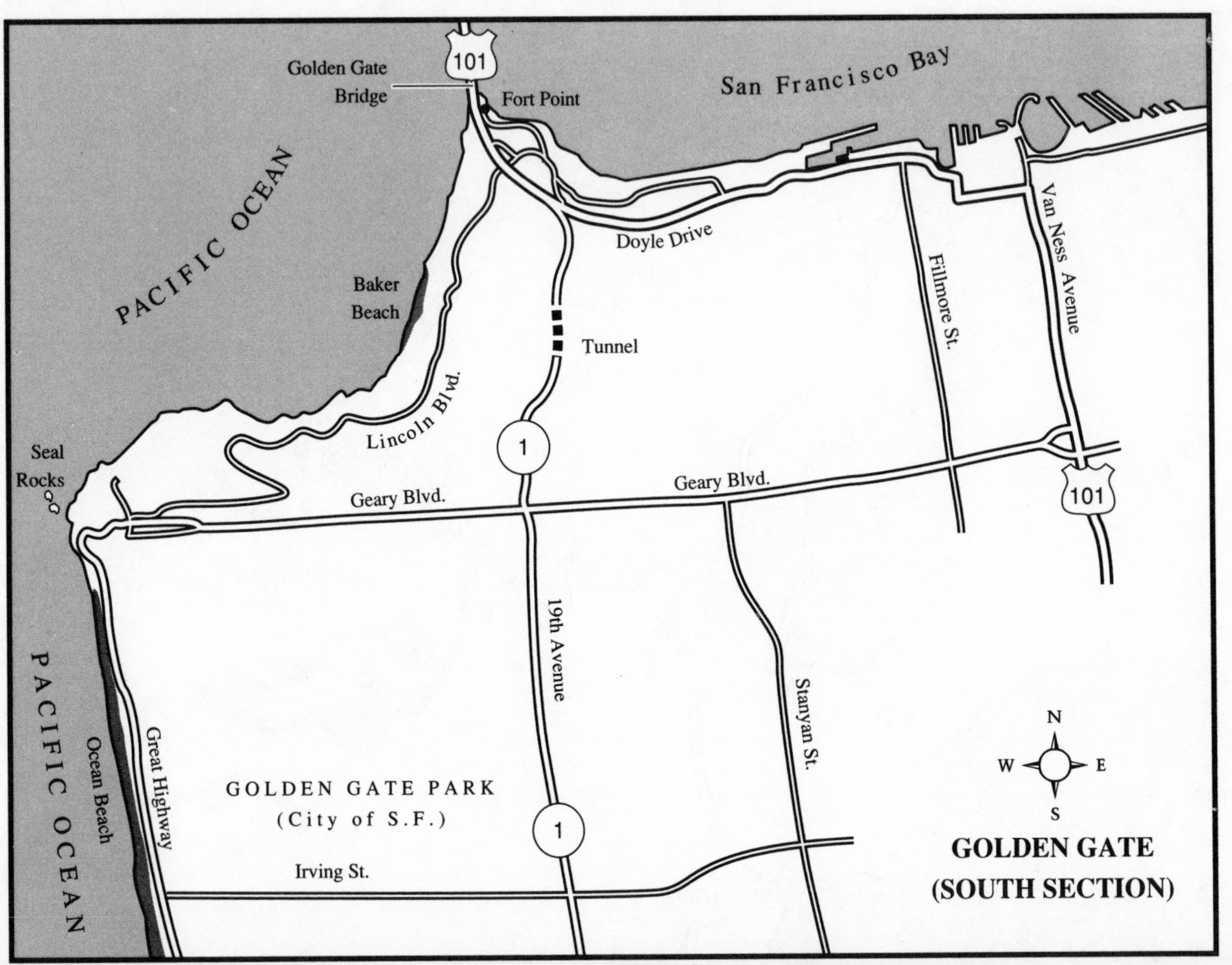
Golden Gate
Bridge
101
Fort Point
San Francisco Bay
PACIFIC OCEAN
Baker
Beach
Doyle Drive
Tunnel
Fillmore St.
Van Ness Avenue
Lincoln Blvd.
1
Seal
Rocks
Geary Blvd.
Geary Blvd.
101
19th Avenue
Stanyan St.
PACIFIC OCEAN
Ocean Beach
Great Highway
GOLDEN GATE PARK
(City of S.F.)
1
Irving St.
N
W
E
S
GOLDEN GATE
(SOUTH SECTION)

park. The Shoreline Highway (California 1) crosses parts of the park. Ferries go to Alcatraz Island. A very good description of the various areas and access to them is contained in the park brochure.

Fishing Striped bass and chinook salmon are the most popular sport fish in the San Francisco Bay area. There are a variety of other popular saltwater and estuarine fish in the bay, including white sturgeon, but the stripers and the chinook head the list.

San Francisco Bay is a major sport fishing area. Charter and party boats and rental skiffs are available throughout the year out of numerous marinas and basins. Reservations are usually necessary, especially during the salmon runs.

Most of the salmon fishing occurs in the ocean beyond the Golden Gate Bridge. Major runs occur in the spring and fall. The most productive salmon areas are far offshore near the Farallon Islands. Some skiff fishing for salmon takes place in the late summer off Stinson and Muir beaches to the north, but skiff fishing can be dangerous in rough weather. An occasional chinook or coho salmon is caught in the bay.

San Francisco Bay is also the domain of the striped bass. Large schools of stripers move into the bay in May after spawning in the San Joaquin and Sacramento rivers. By June, the bay is alive with stripers heading for the ocean and their summer feeding grounds where, feeding heavily on schools of anchovies and surf smelt, they grow quickly. In September, the stripers follow the anchovies back into the bay. Fish that began the summer weighing 15 to 20 pounds now weigh 25 to 40 pounds and more.

October, when schools of stripers range throughout the bay, has long been the best month to catch these fish. When the winter rains begin, the fish begin migrating back to the river delta areas in preparation for spawning in the spring. Throughout the winter and spring, stripers may be caught in the San Joaquin and Sacramento rivers and their delta areas.

Surf fishing for striped bass is also popular outside the Golden Gate. Along Highway 1, from Pacifica to the Golden Gate, the coastline is mostly sandy beaches. The heaviest runs of stripers occur in the surf along these beaches in July, August, and September before the fish head back into the bay. Bakers Beach near the Golden Gate Bridge is one of the most popular and heavily fished areas.

In Marin County north of Golden Gate Bridge, very little shore fishing takes place along the rocky coast north to Stinson Beach. The rugged nature of the coast, its inaccessibility, and private ownership discourage most fishing; however, striped bass are occasionally caught during the summer and fall in sandy coves.

Although the striped bass and chinook salmon get the lion's share of attention, San Francisco Bay has other popular game fish. Sturgeon are hard to catch but highly prized. Sharks, skates, and rays are common, starry flounder are abundant, and there is an assortment of surfperch. The surfperch are usually caught from the shore or piers. Shore fishing is popular and can be productive, but patience is required.

License If you fish from shore or surf, a California fishing license is required. No license is required to fish from public piers. Be sure to check the regulations and seasons for striped bass and other game fish.

Camping The Marin County portion of the park contains two group campsites and three back-country camping areas. Camping reservations may be obtained through the Marin Headlands Visitor Center Bldg., 1050, Fort Cronkhite, Sausalito, CA, 94965; phone: (415) 331-1540. Mount Tamalpais State Park also has camping and there are private campgrounds along Highway 1.

Maps The park brochure contains a good map. Topographic maps are not necessary since the fishing activity centers on the bay and the ocean. Nautical chart #18649 ("San Francisco Entrance") may be helpful if you have your own boat.

Park Address
Golden Gate NRA
Building 201, Fort Mason
San Francisco, CA 94123
phone: (415) 556-0560

Chambers of Commerce

San Francisco C.C.
465 California St.
San Francisco, CA 94104
phone: (415) 392-4511

Marin County C.C.
30 N. San Pedro Rd.
No. 150
San Rafael, CA 94903
phone: (415) 472-7470

Additional Information Wilderness Press publishes a book entitled *Guide to the Golden Gate National Recreation Area*. This is not a fishing book but a directory of all the attractions at Golden Gate NRA. Wilderness Press has also published other bay area books. For their catalog and prices, contact: Wilderness Press, 2440 Bancroft Way, Berkeley, CA, 94704; phone: (415) 843-8080.

Lassen Volcanic National Park

Lassen is a 106,000-acre expanse of mountains, forests, and lakes, dominated by Lassen Peak, a dormant volcano. The park also contains an extinct volcano and active hot springs. The last volcanic activity occurred over a seven-year period from 1914 to 1921. The park is rich in plant and animal life and is very popular with hikers.

Access The park is in northeastern California (Lassen, Shasta, Pluma, and Tehama counties). It is reached from the north and south via California Highway 89 and from the east and west by California Highway 36 and Highway 44.

Fishing Lassen is similar to other parks with a large number of high-country lakes. It appears to be a fishing paradise, but in truth the fishing is only mediocre. There are approximately 50 lakes in the park but only about 16 contain fish. Brook, brown, and rainbow trout are found in park waters. The park staff reports that the fishing is only fair to poor.

The following lakes and streams contain fish. Trout reproduction is marginal in some of the lakes. Before heading into the back country, check with a park ranger to determine the current fish-producing status of a specific lake.

B, brook trout; **BN,** brown trout; **R,** rainbow trout.

Bathtub Lake(s)—**B**
Butte Lake—**R**
Crystal Lake—**R**
Dream Lake—**B**
Hat Lake—**B**
Horseshoe Lake—**B,R**
Juniper Lake—**R**
Manzanita Lake—**BN,R**
Rainbow Lake—**R**
Reflection Lake—**R**
Ridge Lake—**B**
Shadow Lake—**B**
Snag Lake—**R**
Summit Lake—**B,R**
Terrace Lake—**B**
Upper Twin Lake—**R**
Hot Springs Creek—**R**
Kings Creek—**R**

Note: Manzanita, Reflection, and Summit lakes are located along the main park road, and Dream, Juniper, Crystal, and Butte lakes are readily accessible by trail. As can be expected, these lakes receive the heaviest fishing pressure. One of the best known fishing spots is Hat Creek, which originates in the park. A stretch of Hat Creek outside of the park is managed as a wild trout fishery by the state and attracts statewide attention.

License A California fishing license is required. Check the park regulations; some waters may be closed to fishing.

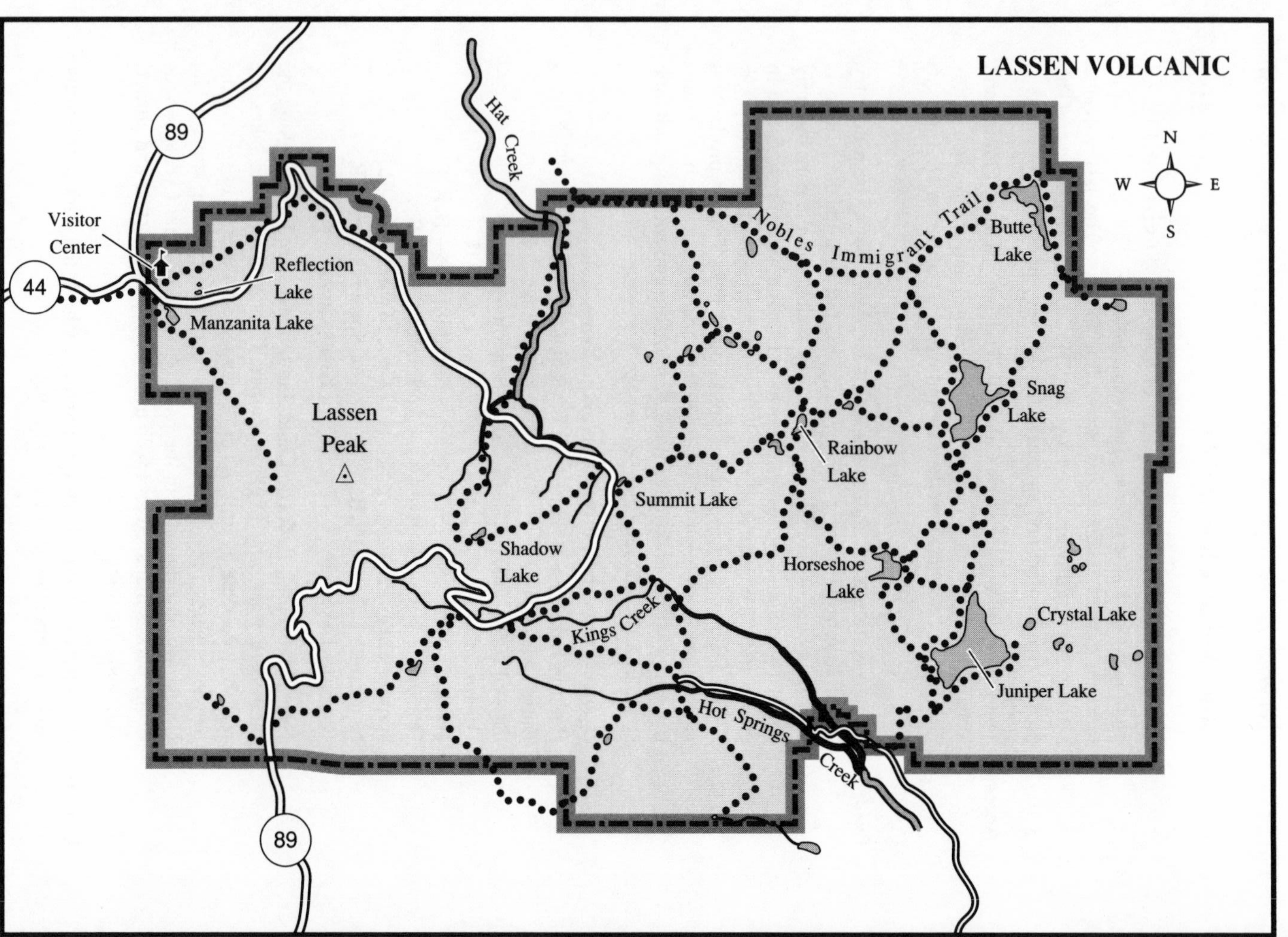
LASSEN VOLCANIC
N
W
E
S
Hat Creek
89
Visitor Center
44
Reflection Lake
Manzanita Lake
Nobles Immigrant Trail
Butte Lake
Snag Lake
Lassen Peak
Rainbow Lake
Summit Lake
Shadow Lake
Horseshoe Lake
Kings Creek
Crystal Lake
Juniper Lake
Hot Springs Creek
89

Camping There are eight campgrounds in the park with a total of 470 spaces. Camping in the back country requires a permit.

Maps There is a special USGS map of the park, "Lassen Volcanic National Park and Vicinity."

Park Address
Lassen Volcanic NP
P.O. Box 100
Mineral, CA 96063-0100
phone: (916) 595-4444

Chamber of Commerce
Lassen County C.C.
P.O. Box 338
Susanville, CA 96130
phone: (916) 257-4323

Additional Information A guide to the park, *Lassen Volcanic National Park and Vicinity,* by Jeffrey P. Schaffer, is available from Wilderness Press. The book mainly describes hiking trails but also covers botany, geology, area facilities, and includes one page on fishing. Contact: Wilderness Press, 2440 Bancroft Way, Berkeley, CA, 94704; phone: (415) 843-8080.

Point Reyes National Seashore

Point Reyes is a peninsula park containing 66,000 acres of long beaches, sand dunes, forested ridges, and cliffs. Sir Francis Drake is believed to have stopped at Point Reyes in 1579 and Drakes Bay is named after him. The park is noted for its many miles of hiking trails. Its more than 300 species of birds and 56 species of mammals are popular with bird and wildlife watchers.

Access The park is in Marin County, approximately 35 miles north of San Francisco, and is most easily reached by taking Sir Francis Drake Boulevard from U.S. Highway 101 to State Route 1. Park headquarters and the visitor center are on Bear Valley Road just north of Olema.

Fishing Both saltwater and freshwater fishing are available at Point Reyes. Drakes Bay, the beach area along the coast, and Tomales Bay are all popular and productive areas for saltwater fishing. Freshwater fishing opportunities are limited within the park and are generally rated as fair.

A number of small streams within the park contain small rainbow trout but they rarely attain legal size. During the winter months, salmon and steelhead use some of the park streams for spawning, but the streams are closed to fishing at that time.

Prior to the establishment of the park, a few ponds were planted with rainbow trout but the pond environment is only marginal for

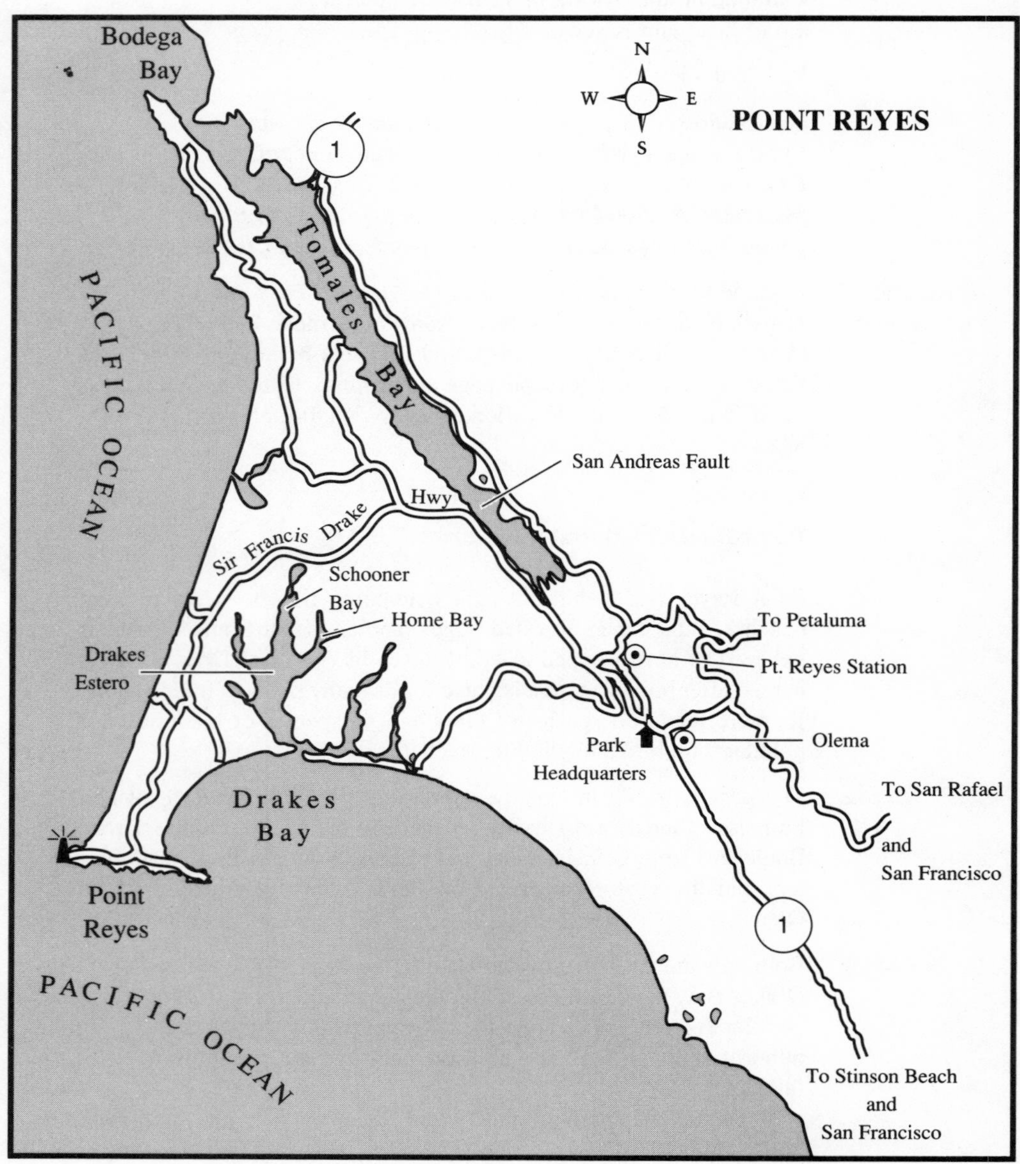
Bodega Bay
N
W
E
S
POINT REYES
1
Tomales Bay
PACIFIC OCEAN
San Andreas Fault
Hwy
Sir Francis Drake
Schooner Bay
Home Bay
To Petaluma
Drakes Estero
Pt. Reyes Station
Park Headquarters
Olema
To San Rafael and San Francisco
Drakes Bay
Point Reyes
1
PACIFIC OCEAN
To Stinson Beach and San Francisco

trout and there has been no effort to restock these ponds. Muddy Hollow Pond produces trout in the 6-to-10-inch range. This pond is near a trail head and is subjected to heavy fishing pressure. Trout in the 12-inch range have been taken in Lower Muddy Hollow Pond, but effective fishing there requires a boat. There is no indication that the other ponds in the park are still producing.

Saltwater fishing is much better. The Drakes Bay area contains chinook salmon in April and May and again from July to mid-October. The beach inside the bay is usually good for surfperch.

Surf fishing is good along the sandy beaches of the Point Reyes Peninsula for calico, redtail, and surfperch. March through June are the best months for surfperch. Offshore are 27-fathom reefs that are popular for rockfish. Lingcod, cabezon, and an occasional chinook salmon are also caught there.

Tomales Bay has a bit of everything. Chinook salmon are in the bay all year, particularly around the entrance. However, the entrance is very dangerous for small boats because unexpected waves can easily capsize a boat. Coho salmon are found in the lower bay from September through November, and steelhead move into Papermill Creek to spawn from November to February. Striped bass are found in the southern part of the bay during summer.

California halibut provide good action from June to October, along with the usual assortment of surfperch, turbot, rockfish, rays, and sharks. The sharks are especially plentiful.

Party boats operate out of Bodega Harbor, north of the park, and Dillon Beach, east of Tomales Point. Fishing from skiffs or small boats is not advisable outside Tomales Bay. The beaches in the park are pounded by heavy surf, particularly the Point Reyes beaches and McClures Beach, so caution should be observed when fishing.

License A California fishing license is required.

Camping Hike-in camping is permitted at four locations along the trail system. The Coast Campsite has 14 sites, while Sky and Glen campsites each have 12 sites. Wildcat Group Camp has 7 sites that accommodate 20 persons each. Back-country permits are required and should be requested in advance to reserve a campsite. Private campgrounds are located on State Route 1 near Olema.

Maps The park brochure includes a good general map and shows the park trails. Detailed trail maps are available at the visitor centers. Topographic maps are recommended if you plan extensive exploring. There is a special USGS map of the park, entitled "Point Reyes National Seashore and Vicinity."

For offshore fishing, nautical charts #18647 (Drakes Bay) and #18643 (Bodega and Tomales Bay) are helpful.

Park Address
Point Reyes NS
Point Reyes, CA 94956
phone: (415) 663-8522

Chamber of Commerce
Marin County C.C.
30 N. San Pedro Rd.
No. 150
San Rafael, CA 94903
phone: (415) 472-7470

Redwood National Park

Redwood National Park was established in 1968 to preserve prime examples of coastal redwood forest. The redwoods of the Pacific Coast are the world's tallest trees and may live to be 2,000 years old. To protect additional redwood groves from logging and land-use destruction, Congress expanded the park in 1978 by adding 48,000 acres to the original 58,000 acres.

There are four *state* parks within the national park boundaries: Jedediah Smith, Del Norte Coast, Gold Bluffs Beach, and Prairie Creek.

Access The park stretches along California's north coast (Humboldt and Del Norte counties) from about 30 miles north of Eureka to just below the Oregon border. U.S. 101 runs north and south through the park. U.S. 199 enters the north end of the park from the east.

Fishing Sport fishing is a major industry in northern California and anglers use the area extensively. Short sections of two of California's best steelhead rivers, the Klamath and the Smith, flow through the park and are popular fishing spots. Surf fishing is also popular along the park's ocean beaches and a number of freshwater lagoons and ponds contain rainbow trout. Most fishing actually occurs adjacent to the park rather than within park boundaries.

Aside from the Klamath and Smith rivers, park streams are not noted for their fishing. However, many rivers and ocean areas surrounding the park are famous for their salmon and steelhead catches. The best fishing occurs in the fall and winter months when salmon and steelhead return to the rivers to spawn.

Saltwater Fishing Sand dunes and beaches are prevalent along the coast of the park and surf fishing is popular for redtail surfperch. The surfperch are abundant and available all year, although spring and early summer are the best times. Surf smelt and a related smelt, locally known as night fish,

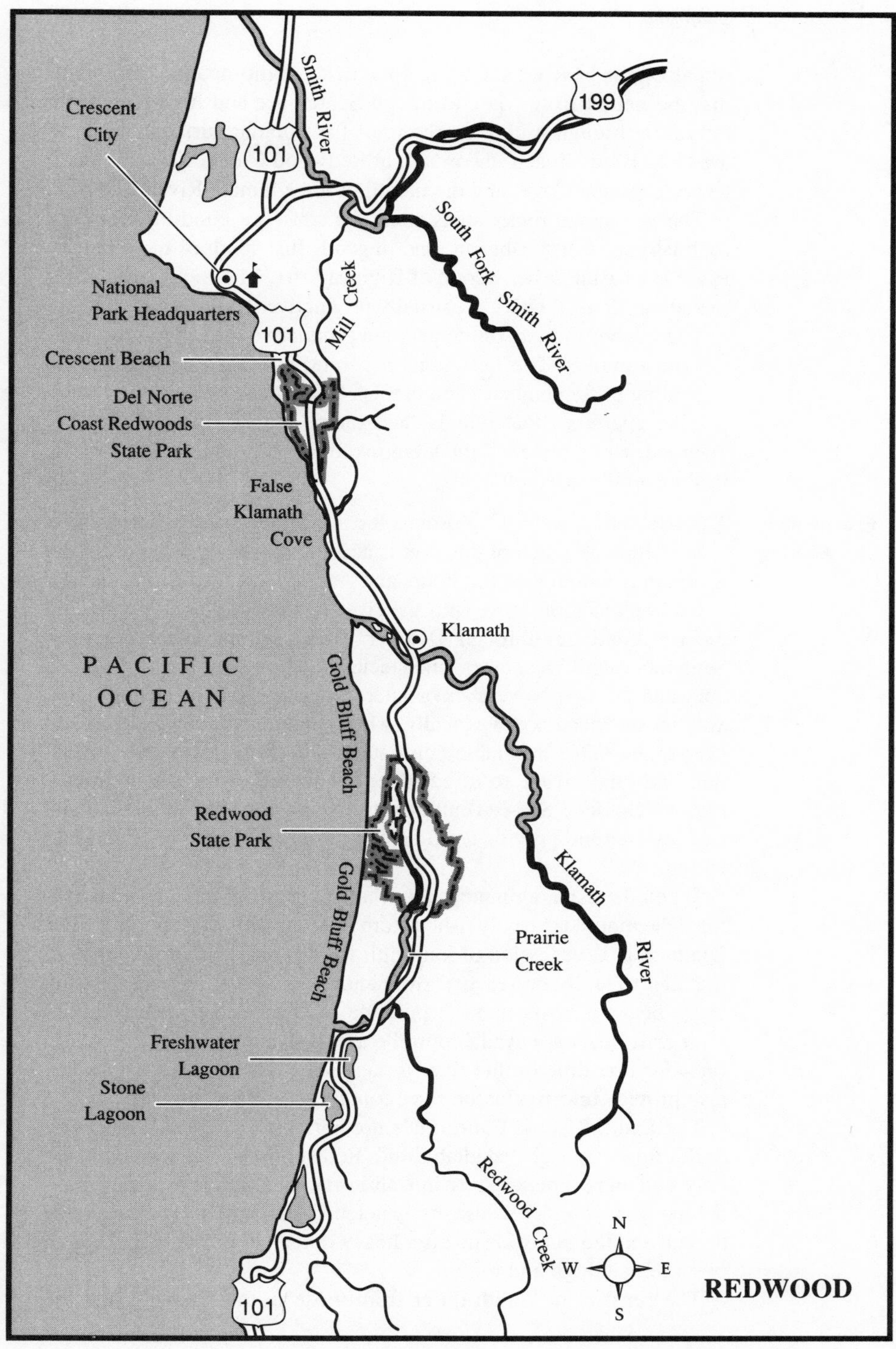

Crescent City
101
Smith River
199
South Fork Smith River
Mill Creek
National Park Headquarters
101
Crescent Beach
Del Norte Coast Redwoods State Park
False Klamath Cove
Klamath
PACIFIC OCEAN
Gold Bluff Beach
Redwood State Park
Gold Bluff Beach
Klamath River
Prairie Creek
Freshwater Lagoon
Stone Lagoon
Redwood Creek
N
W
E
S
101
REDWOOD

run along the beaches and bring out crowds of dip-netters. Surf smelt may be netted from March through September and night fish from February through mid-May. Some of the popular surf-fishing areas are Gold Bluffs Beach, the mouth of Redwood Creek, False Klamath Cove, Crescent Cove, and the mouth of the Klamath River.

The occasional rocky areas along the coast are good locations for rockfish, sea trout, cabezon, and lingcod. Just south of the Klamath River is Coastal Drive, a loop of Highway 101. The rocky promontories along Coastal Drive are usually productive fishing areas.

The offshore waters of the park are productive for salmon throughout the summer. The best salmon fishing is from mid-May to the beginning of September when the fish begin to move into the rivers. Fishing charters, boat rentals, and ramps are available at Eureka, Trinidad, and Crescent City. Chinook and coho salmon are taken by trolling a mile or so offshore.

Freshwater Fishing

The Klamath River is California's top steelhead and chinook salmon river. Although much of the river is accessible, only the mouth of the Klamath is within the park boundary.

Chinook salmon move into the river in mid-July and August and the run continues through October. Coho salmon run from mid-September until December, and steelhead begin their run in July and continue through November or later depending on river conditions. Smaller steelhead, known locally as half-pounders, are in the Klamath year-round. They resemble adult steelhead, but are sexually immature and range from 10 to 22 inches. The main runs are in August through October. Sea-run cutthroat trout enter the river in late fall and early winter and provide good fishing throughout the winter and into spring.

When the fish are running, the Klamath is crowded with folks fishing. The mouth is heavily fished from skiffs and by shore anglers. The Klamath is a succession of long riffles and rapids with holding pools that can't readily be reached from shore; most fish are caught from boats because boats make it possible to cover more water. Guides with drift boats are available in the area—using one of these guides for your first time on the river is suggested. Local tackle shops can also provide information on river conditions and techniques.

The Smith River is California's northernmost steelhead river. The Smith flows through Jedediah Smith Redwoods State Park and is the only undammed major river in California. The Smith provides good fishing year-round because its watershed has not been extensively logged and it quickly clears after heavy rains. Other rivers in the area often remain high and roily.

The runs in the Smith differ from those in the Klamath and the chinook salmon run is not as heavy in the Smith. Again, fishing is very heavy at the mouth. Chinook are best from September through December, coho in October and November, and steelhead in December and January. The fall and winter steelhead average 5 pounds, but are often larger with some fish of 20 pounds and more. In the park section of the Smith, you can catch cutthroat and rainbow trout in the spring and summer, salmon in the fall, and steelhead in the winter.

Redwood Creek receives some salmon and steelhead, but the stream bed has become heavily silted as a result of extensive logging within the watershed. The park is in the process of rehabilitating Redwood Creek and its tributaries to provide a better habitat for fish.

Mill Creek flows through Del Norte Coast Redwoods State Park and also has good fishing all year. Early-season fishing is mainly for rainbow and cutthroat trout, while chinook salmon spawn in the fall.

The state stocks several areas within the park boundaries with trout every year. They are Espa Lagoon in Prairie Creek Redwoods State Park, Freshwater Lagoon, which is bisected by the park boundary, and Lagoon Creek.

Big Lagoon and Stone Lagoon, located a few miles south of the park boundary, offer excellent fishing. They occasionally break open to the sea during high water and then salmon and steelhead may move into the lagoons. These lagoons contain a freshwater/saltwater mixture and numerous marine fish, such as flounder, exist along with the rainbow and cutthroat trout. Steelhead and salmon migrate upstream of the lagoons to spawn in tributary creeks in the spring and fall.

License A California license is required for both fresh- and saltwater fishing. Be sure to check the regulations governing salmon and steelhead.

Camping The park service operates three walk-in campgrounds with 30 total sites and a back-country campsite at Redwood Creek. Each of the four state parks within the national park boundaries provides camping facilities. California is on a centralized system for camping reservations, and reservations are usually necessary in the summer. To reserve space, contact: Mistix, P.O. Box 85705, San Diego, CA, 92138-5705; phone: (619) 452-1950 or toll free (in-state only) 1-800-444-7275. Nearby state parks and national forests also have camping facilities.

Maps The park brochure map or a highway map is recommended for most fishing. If topographic maps are needed, they can be obtained at the park headquarters, which carries the ten topographic maps needed to cover most of the park. Nautical chart #18600 covers the offshore waters.

Park Address	*Chamber of Commerce*
Redwood National Park	Crescent City C.C.
1111 Second Street	P.O. Box 246
Crescent City, CA 95531	Crescent City, CA 95531
phone: (707) 464-6101	phone: (707) 464–174

Sequoia National Park and Kings Canyon National Park

Sequoia and Kings Canyon national parks are two distinct parks that are adjacent to each other in the Sierra Nevada mountains of California. Their combined 846,989 acres are administered as one park.

Sequoia National Park, the southernmost park, was established to protect the giant sequoia groves, which are more abundant here than anywhere on earth. Also in the park is Mount Whitney, the highest mountain in the contiguous United States.

Kings Canyon was designated a national park because of its rugged canyons and high granite mountains. It also contains healthy stands of giant sequoia trees and boasts the highest canyon wall in America, the 8,300-foot, sheer wall from the South Fork of Kings River to the top of Spanish Mountain.

Both parks and the surrounding national forests in the Sierra Nevadas are interlaced with miles of back-country trails and are a major attraction to hikers and backpackers.

Access Both parks are in central California (Fresno and Tulare counties). The main access is from the west via California Highway 180 from Fresno to Kings Canyon. From the south, California Highway 198 from Visalia enters Sequoia. California Highway 395 parallels the Sierra Crest on the east side of the park.

Fishing Both parks are dotted with lakes and streams that can provide good trout fishing. Very few of these waters have been inventoried and many are now barren of fish even though they may have been stocked in the past. In general, all the lakes are in the high country and those supporting fish will contain primarily rainbow, brook, and golden trout. The streams in the lower elevations hold predominantly brown and rainbow trout.

Rivers The South Fork of the San Joaquin River and the Middle and South Forks of the Kings River in Kings Canyon National Park along with the Kern River and the Kaweah River (including its numerous forks) in Sequoia National Park, are all excellent trout streams. Fishing is usually best in the spring and fall on these main rivers.

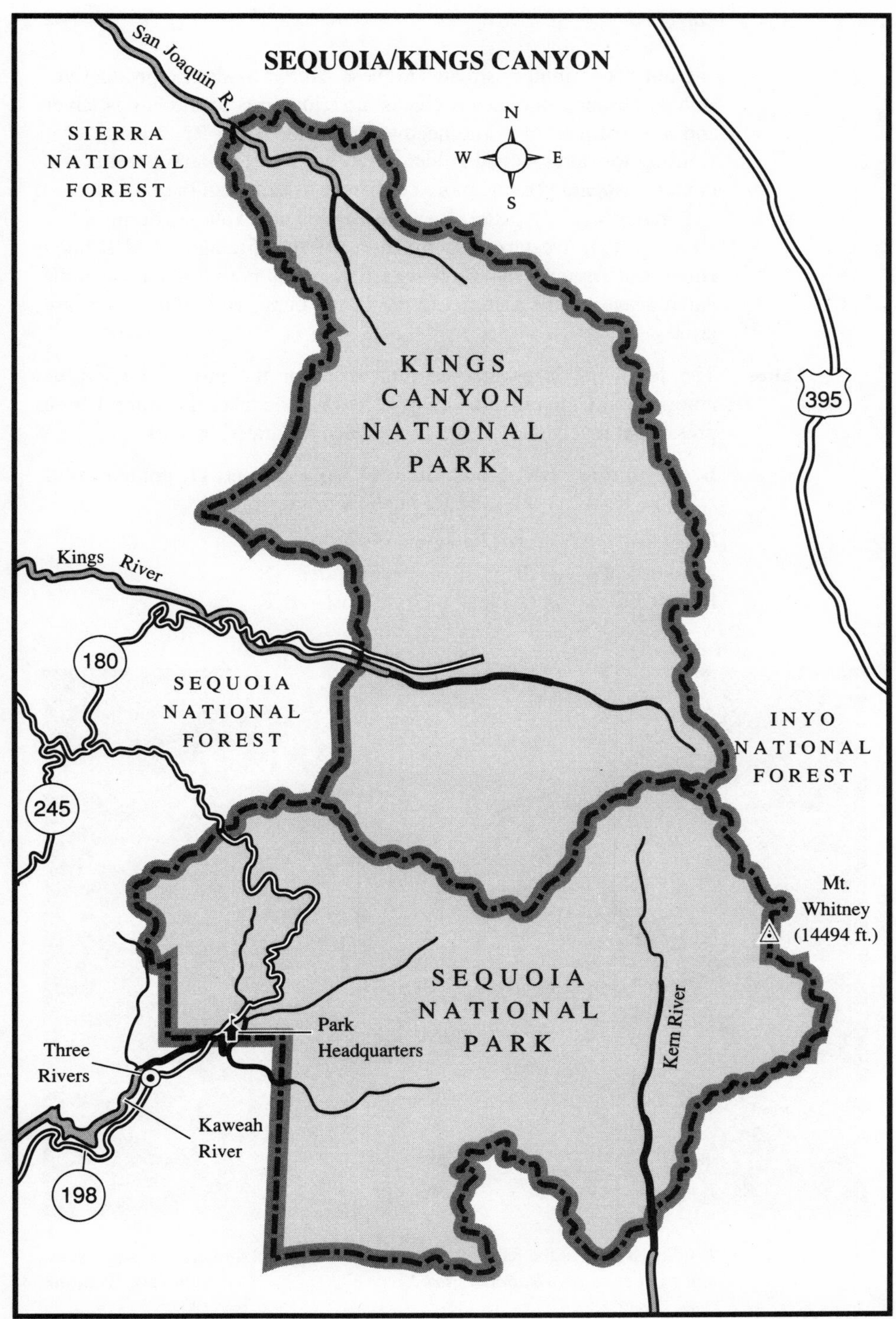
SEQUOIA/KINGS CANYON
San Joaquin R.
N
W
E
S
SIERRA NATIONAL FOREST
KINGS CANYON NATIONAL PARK
395
Kings River
180
SEQUOIA NATIONAL FOREST
245
INYO NATIONAL FOREST
Mt. Whitney (14494 ft.)
SEQUOIA NATIONAL PARK
Kern River
Park Headquarters
Three Rivers
Kaweah River
198

Numerous tributary streams to these rivers can also be productive. Bubbs, Granite, and Lewis creeks are tributaries to the Kings River and are worth trying. The headwaters of the Kern River can be rewarding for rainbow and golden trout. Most of the park streams will contain fish and provide more consistent fishing than the lakes.

Popular local fly patterns are the Adams and Yellow Humpy (dry; sizes 12–18), Western Coachman (wet; 10–16), and Gold Ribbed Hares Ear (nymph; 8–16). Kings River is famous for large caddis hatches and caddis patterns in the larva, pupa, and adult stages are good.

Lakes The following lakes are recommended for the more adventurous among you. Generally, the more accessible the lake, the more fishing pressure it receives. The lakes have been separated by park.

B, brook trout; **BN,** brown trout; **G,** golden trout; **H,** golden trout/rainbow trout hybrids; and **R,** rainbow trout.

Kings Canyon National Park

Amphitheater—**H,R**
Barrett Lakes—**R** (Lake #3-G)
Ladder—**R**
Lost—**B,R**

The South Fork of the Kings River in Kings Canyon National Park is an excellent trout stream.—*National Park Service photo by M. Woodbridge Williams*

Bench—**BN,R**
Beville—**B**
Big Bird—**B**
Big Brewer—**R**
Big Pine—**R**
Blue Canyon Lakes 1–7—**R**
Darwin Lakes 1,2,3—**G**
Double-Eleven-O—**G,H,R**
Dragon—**B**
Dumbbell Lakes 2,3,4—**R**
Dusy Basin Lakes 1 through 6 —**G,H,R**
Evolution—**G**
Ferguson Lakes 1,2—**R**
Glacier Lakes 1,2—**G,H**
Golden Bear—**G,H,R**
Granite—**B**
Horseshoe Lakes 1,2,3—**R**
Josephine—**R**
Marion Peak Lakes 1,3,4—**R**
Martha—**G,H,R**
McGee Lakes 1,1W,2,3,4—**G**
Mount Goddard—**R**
Mount Pinchot 2—**B**
Palisade 1,2—**G,H,R**
Rainbow 1—**R**
Ranger 2—**R**
Seville—**B,R**
Sixty Lakes 1,2,3,8—**G,H,R**
Sphinx Lakes 1,6,8,9—**R**
State Lakes 1—**G,H,R**
Tunemah 2—**R**
Vidette Lakes 1,3—**R**
Vidette Lake 2—**G,H,R**
Volcanic Lakes 1,3W—**G,H,R**
Volcanic Lakes 2,4,5,7E, 7W,10—**R**
Woods—**B**

Sequoia National Park

Ansel—**R**
Aster—**B**
Blossom Lakes 1,2,3,4—**B**
Emerald—**B**
Hitchcock 1—**G,H,R**
Little 1—**B**
Little Moose—**B**
Moose—**B**
Mosquito Lakes 1 through 5—**B**
Pear—**B**
Summit—**B**
Tamarack—**G,H,R**
Twin Lakes 1,2—**B**
Wallace Lake—**B**

Both parks have well-developed trail systems that allow access to park waters and connect to the surrounding national forests. Access to off-trail lakes by pack and saddle horse may be restricted. Check with the park before planning a trip.

License A California license is required and state regulations apply. Check also for special park regulations as some park waters may be closed for research or management purposes.

Camping Kings Canyon has seven developed campgrounds with a total of 727 spaces. Only one campground (Azalea) is open all year. Sequoia has six developed campgrounds (405 spaces) and three primitive campgrounds (72 spaces). Three campgrounds are open all year in Sequoia. Permits are required for back-country camping.

Maps A special USGS map, "Sequoia and Kings Canyon National Park and Vicinity," covers the entire park. Also, a total of 15 separate quadrangle maps cover the park. All the maps are available from: Sequoia Natural History Association, Ash Mountain P.O. Box 10, Three Rivers, CA, 93271; phone: (209) 565-3341. Ask for their list of park publications.

Park Address	*Chamber of Commerce*
Sequoia/Kings Canyon NP	Visalia C.C.
Three Rivers, CA 93271	720 W. Mineral King
phone: (209) 565-3341	Visalia, CA, 93291
	phone: (209) 734-5876

Additional Information *The Sierra Trout Guide,* by Ralph Cutter, contains a wealth of information about trout fishing in the Sierra Nevadas. The book discusses the history of Sierra trout and their management, fly hatches, and a county-by-county chart of trout lakes, including the elevation and the required USGS topographic map for each lake. The book is available from: Frank Amato Publications, Box 02112, Portland, OR, 97202; phone: (503) 236-2305.

Both parks are surrounded by national forests, which contain unlimited fishing opportunities. To the east and south is Inyo National Forest; to the west is Sierra National Forest; to the west and south is Sequoia National Forest. An area of special interest for fishing is the Golden Trout Wilderness Area in Sequoia and Inyo national forests. Maps and information on each forest are available from: Regional Forester, U.S. Forest Service, Pacific Southwest Region, 630 Sansome St., San Francisco, CA, 94111; phone: (415) 556-0122.

Whiskeytown-Shasta-Trinity National Recreation Area

Whiskeytown, Shasta, and Clair Engle (Trinity) are three large impoundments in northern California built by the Bureau of Reclamation to store and regulate water as part of California's Central Valley Project. The National Park Service manages the Whiskeytown area, while the U.S. Forest Service manages Shasta Lake and Clair Engle Lake (Trinity). Whiskeytown Lake is on Clear Creek, a tributary of the Sacramento River.

Access The Whiskeytown area is in north central California (Shasta County) about 10 miles west of Redding. Access is by California Highway 299, which connects with Interstate 5 at Redding.

Fishing Whiskeytown Lake is a 3,220-acre impoundment containing brook, brown, and rainbow trout; largemouth and smallmouth bass; and

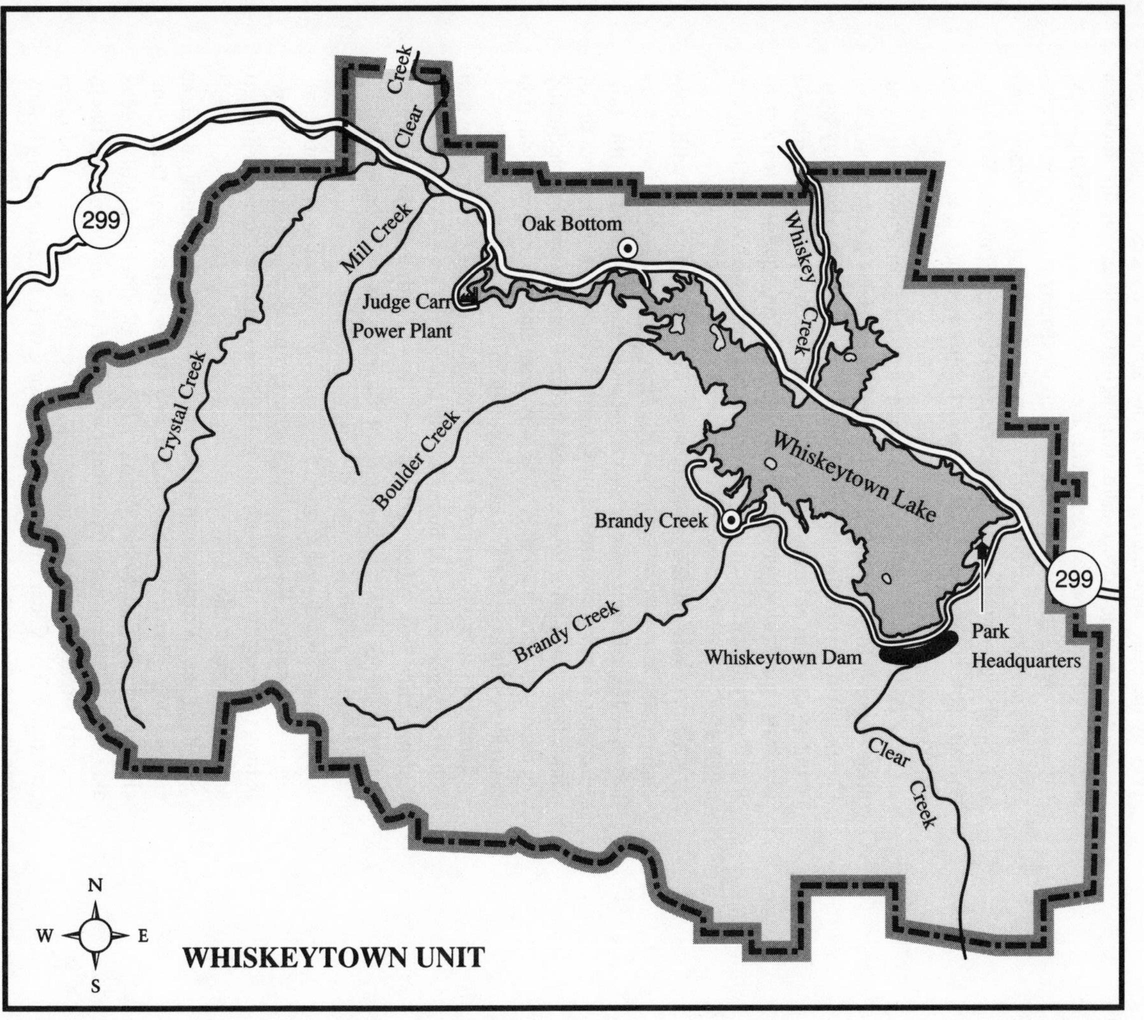
Clear Creek
299
Mill Creek
Oak Bottom
Whiskey Creek
Judge Carr Power Plant
Crystal Creek
Boulder Creek
Whiskeytown Lake
Brandy Creek
299
Brandy Creek
Park Headquarters
Whiskeytown Dam
Clear Creek
N
W
E
S
WHISKEYTOWN UNIT

kokanee salmon, crappie, bluegill, and catfish. Trout are stocked each year by the state and managed on a put-and-take basis.

Whiskeytown is a deep, cold, nonfluctuating reservoir that lacks an effective forage base for game fish. Because of this forage deficiency, the lake offers little potential for becoming trophy trout water. Therefore, the state stocks trout yearly for immediate harvest. Planted trout achieve little growth in the lake. Despite these limitations, Whiskeytown is still considered to have good fishing because it is so heavily stocked.

Most of the trout fishing takes place near the Carr Powerhouse, an area popular for shore fishing. The powerhouse is located on Clear Creek northwest of the main lake and is accessible by Highway 299. Trout stocked in all areas of the lake are attracted to the powerhouse tail water and quickly migrate to that area. Consequently, trout fishing is only marginal in the main lake regardless of where trout are stocked.

Kokanee salmon are a deep-water fish. Boat fishing with specialized trolling equipment generally brings good catches from May through July. Fishing from shore yields a few kokanee in the fall, when the fish concentrate below Carr Powerhouse or at the mouths of major tributaries prior to spawning. Kokanee are stocked periodically because spawning habitat is generally poor and natural reproduction contributes little to the kokanee population.

Largemouth bass are rarely taken. Much of the lake is too deep and cold for largemouth, although they do inhabit the protected coves that warm earlier than other parts of the lake. Smallmouth bass inhabit the exposed rocky shoreline areas of the main lake and are especially fond of rocky points.

The state introduced spotted bass in 1981. Apparently that planting was successful because the bass have reproduced. Generally, bass fishing is more effective with a boat because shoreline access is limited around the main lake.

Within the Whiskeytown area, rainbow trout are found in Clear Creek, both above the lake and below the Whiskeytown Dam, and also in Brandy Creek and Whiskey Creek. Boulder and Mill creeks also have a few rainbow trout that moved in from the lake. The backcountry streams are rarely fished because of their small size and inaccessibility. The Clear Creek sections, along with Brandy and Whiskey creeks, are the best bets.

Marinas with rental boats are located at Oak Bottom and at Brandy Creek.

License A California fishing license is required. The lake is open to fishing all year. Check the state regulations for sizes and bag limits.

Camping There are three campgrounds in the park: Brandy Creek (37 spaces for self-contained RV's), Oak Bottom (155 spaces), and Dry Creek, for group camping. Oak Bottom is on the Ticketron system.

Maps The park brochure map shows road access points but doesn't contain any lake contour information. Oak Bottom Marina has prepared a fishing map of the lake. Although not a contour map, it shows a variety of bottom structures and orientation points. The map is free from: Oak Bottom Marina, P.O. Box 197, Whiskeytown, CA, 96095; phone: (916) 359-2269.

Park Address
Whiskeytown NRA
P.O. Box 188
Whiskeytown, CA 96095
phone: (916) 241-6584

Chamber of Commerce
Shasta Dam Area C.C.
P.O. Box 1368
Central Valley, CA 96019
phone: (916) 275-8862

Additional Information For information on Shasta and Clair Engle lakes, contact: Forest Supervisor, Shasta/Trinity National Forest, USDA Forest Service, 2400 Washington Ave., Redding, CA, 96001; phone: (916) 246-5222.

Yosemite National Park

Yosemite, one of the most beautiful national parks in the world, is considered one of the crown jewels of our national park system. The park features giant sequoias, alpine meadows, high waterfalls, miles of trails, and 13,000-foot mountains in the Sierra Nevada range.

Yosemite is a very popular vacation area and consequently, one of the most crowded parks during the summer. It is crowded in the sense that most of the people are congregated in the developed sections of the park. Yosemite is so large (1,200 square miles) that one can easily find solitude in the back-country wilderness sections.

Access Yosemite is in east central California, in Madera, Mariposa, and Tuolumne (Twa-la-mee) counties, approximately four to five hours from San Francisco and five to six hours from Los Angeles. The park is reached by California State Highways 120, 140, and 41.

Fishing Yosemite National Park is dotted with lakes and streams throughout. Despite all this water, the park offers only average fishing. There are 268 lakes in the park and 165 of these are barren of fish. There are also 58 permanent streams, with a combined length of 770 miles, that support trout. Of the streams, the Tuolumne and Merced rivers are the best known and both are very good trout streams. Generally, the better fishing is in the lakes and streams at the lower elevations.

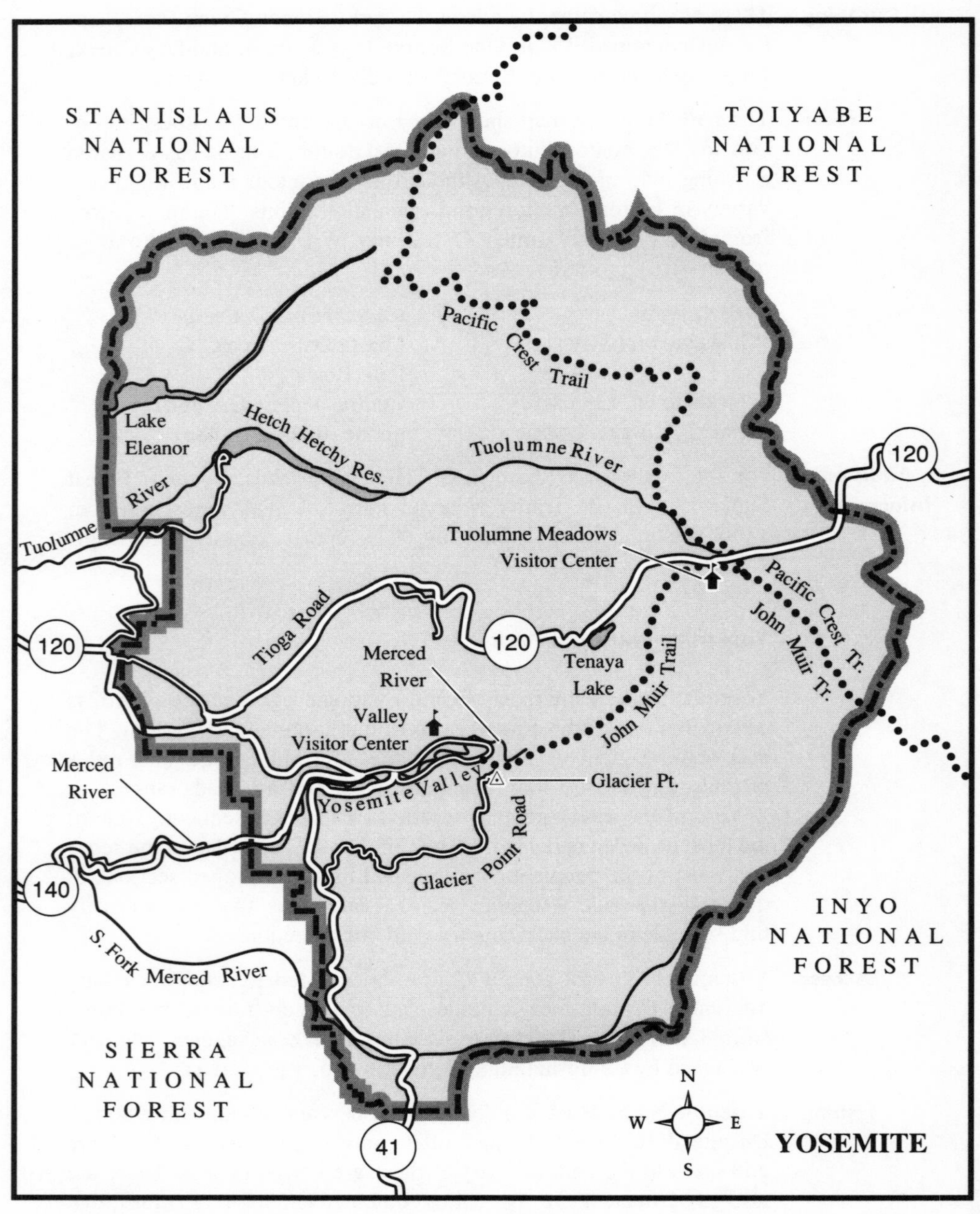
STANISLAUS NATIONAL FOREST
TOIYABE NATIONAL FOREST
Pacific Crest Trail
Lake Eleanor
Hetch Hetchy Res.
Tuolumne River
120
River
Tuolumne
Tuolumne Meadows Visitor Center
Pacific Crest Tr.
John Muir Tr.
Tioga Road
120
120
Merced River
Tenaya Lake
John Muir Trail
Valley Visitor Center
Merced River
Yosemite Valley
Glacier Pt.
Glacier Point Road
140
S. Fork Merced River
INYO NATIONAL FOREST
SIERRA NATIONAL FOREST
N
W
E
S
YOSEMITE
41

Lakes Most of the higher elevation lakes in the park are barren. Lake fishing is usually best right after the ice leaves the lakes (usually by July 15) and again in the fall (September and October). August fishing is poor because the fish seek the deeper, cooler water to avoid the warm surface temperatures. Early morning and evening are the best times to fish during the warmest part of the summer.

Lakes close to Highway 120 and along popular trails are heavily fished. Only Hetch Hetchy Reservoir and Tenaya Lake can be reached by car. All the other lakes require a hike. Boats, rafts, or canoes are allowed only on Merced, Tenaya, May, Many Island, Benson, Tilden, Kibbie, and Twin lakes, but motors are prohibited.

Listed below are the park lakes known to contain fish.

B, brook trout; **BN,** brown trout; **G,** golden trout; and **R,** rainbow trout.

Northwestern back country (includes Hetch Hetchy area)

Bearup—**R**
Benson—**B,R**
Branigan (Lower)—**R**
Dorothy—**R**
Edyth—**R**
Lake Eleanor—**R**
Fawn—**R**
Grant (Upper and Lower)—**R**
Harden—**R**
Lake Eleanor—**R**
Hetch Hetchy Reservoir —**B,BN,R**
Irving Bright—**R**
Kibbie—**R**
Laurel—**R**
Snow—**B,R**
Spotted Fawn—**R**
Swamp—**B**
Table—**R**
Ten Lakes 1,5,6—**R**
Ten Lakes 2,3,4—**B,R**
Tilden—**G,R**
Lake Vernon—**R**
Wilmer—**R**

Northeastern back country

Doe—**R**
Mary—**G**
Mattie—**B**
Mattie (Little)—**B**
McCabe (Lower and Middle) —**R**
McCabe (Upper)—**B,R**
Neall—**R**
Return—**B**
Rodgers—**R**
Roosevelt—**R**
Shepherd—**R**
Smedberg—**R**
Tallulah—**R**
Twin (Upper and Lower)—**R**
Virginia—**B**

Tuolumne Meadows area

Bernice—**B**
Boothe—**B**
Budd—**B**
Cathedral (Lower)—**B,R**
Matthes—**B**
May—**B,R**
Mildred—**B**
Nelson—**B**

Cathedral (Upper)—**B**
Echo—**B**
Elizabeth—**B**
Emeric—**B,R**
Evelyn—**R**
Fletcher—**B**
Gallison—**B**
Gaylor (Lower, Middle, Upper) —**B**
Granite (Lower and Upper)—**B**
Helen—**B**
Ireland—**B**
Kuna—**B**
Lukens—**R**
Polly Dome (Lower and Middle) —**R**
Polly Dome—**B,R**
Reymann—**B**
Skelton (Lower and Upper)—**B**
Spillway—**B,R**
Sunrise (Lower and Middle) —**B,R**
Sunrise (Upper)—**B**
Tenaya—**B,R**
Townsley—**B**
Vogelsang—**B**
Young (Lower, Middle, Upper) —**B**

Southeastern back country

Adair—**G**
Babcock—**B**
Breeze—**R**
Chain (Lower and Middle) —**B,R**
Chain (Upper)—**R**
Dog—**B,R**
Edna (Lower)—**R**
Florence (Lower and Upper) —**R**
Givens—**B**
Grayling—**R**
Harriet—**R**
Harriet #2, #3—**R**
Hoover (North, South, West) —**B**
Isberg Pass—**R**
Merced—**B,BN,R**
Edna—**R**
Minnow—**B**
Ottoway (Lower)—**R**
Washburn—**B,R**

Southwestern back country

Buena Vista—**B**
Chilnualna (Lower, Middle, Upper)—**B**
Edson—**R**
Hart—**R**
Johnson—**R**
Ostrander—**B,R**
Royal Arch—**B,R**

Rivers The Tuolumne and Merced rivers are both fine trout fisheries. The Tuolumne holds good-sized rainbow and brown trout in its upper stretches above Hetch Hetchy Reservoir and also below the reservoir where it can be reached by a park road. The river is very popular near Tuolumne Meadows where it is easily accessible. The Lyell Fork, a tributary of the Tuolumne, is also worth trying.

The Merced River and its forks offer excellent fishing all through the summer and into winter. Inside the park, east of Yosemite Village, the Merced features long, placid pools and good, dry fly-fishing. This section of the Merced is crowded during the summer with float tubes and rubber rafts. Fishing is limited to the early morning and evening. West of Yosemite Village, the river features rocky runs and rapids, no crowds, and good fishing. Caddis flies predominate until the cooler fall weather brings out the mayfly hatches. Much of the river is accessible by road from the Arch Rock entrance to the Yosemite Valley area.

Small streams run throughout the park and can provide fair fishing. Streams flowing out of lakes will usually contain fish if the lakes contain fish. Again, avoid the high-country streams. Some of the better streams are Rancheria Creek and Eleanor Creek in the northwest, Bridalveil Creek in the southwest, and Fletcher Creek in the southeast.

Successful fly patterns for park waters include dry flies such as the Elk-hair caddis, Adams, and Dark Cahill. The Gold-Ribbed Hares Ear nymph is a must. Also carry caddis larva and pupa imitations (especially green) and wet Renegades.

License A California fishing license and the appropriate license stamps are required. Park and state fishing regulations are identical except that live bait is not permitted in the park.

Camping Yosemite has 15 campgrounds totaling 1,785 spaces. In addition, there are group campgrounds and back-country sites. The Upper River, Lower River, Upper Pines, North Pines, and Lower Pines campgrounds are on the Ticketron reservation system. These campgrounds are all located in Yosemite Valley. Permits are required for overnight stays in the back country.

The park overflows with campers during the summer, and weekends are especially crowded. The chances of getting an unreserved camping spot are better if you arrive during the week rather than the weekend. Camping is also available outside the park in private campgrounds but these also fill up quickly.

Maps The park brochure map is a good general location map. The best map for the back country is the topographic map, titled "Yosemite National Park and Vicinity," available from: Wilderness Press, 2440 Bancroft Way, Berkeley, CA, 94704; phone: (415) 843-8080.

This map contains a wealth of information about camping, hiking, backpacking, and weather, along with an index of all the park's features including lakes and streams. It will cost a bit more than a similar USGS map, but the amount of solid information makes it worth the added expense.

Park Address
Yosemite NP
P.O. Box 577
Yosemite National Park,
CA 95389
phone: (209) 372-0200

Chamber of Commerce
Mariposa County C.C.
P.O. Box 425
Mariposa, CA 95338
phone: (209) 966-2456

Additional Information See the Additional Information section for Sequoia/Kings Canyon parks. Of particular interest for Yosemite is Ralph Cutter's *Sierra Trout Guide*; also note the address for Forest Service information. Yosemite National is surrounded by national forests (Inyo, Toiyabe, Sierra, and Stanislaus), which offer many other fishing and camping options.

Another helpful book is *Yosemite National Park: A Natural History Guide to Yosemite and Its Trails*, by Jeffrey Schaffer. The book discusses all aspects of the park and describes the trails and hikes throughout the park. It is available from Wilderness Press at the address provided above in the Maps section.

• COLORADO

Black Canyon of the Gunnison National Monument

This national monument protects one of the deepest and narrowest canyons in North America. At the bottom of the canyon is the Gunnison River which has carved a gorge as deep as 2,700 feet through base rock. Black Canyon is about 53 miles long but only the deepest and most spectacular 12 miles lie within the monument.

Access The park is in west central Colorado (Montrose County). It is possible to drive to both the north and south rims of the canyon. The south rim is 11 miles from Montrose, and can be reached by traveling via U.S 50 east for 6 miles then Colorado 347 north for 5 miles. The north rim is 14 miles from Crawford off Colorado 92, just east of Crawford. At the park, there is a road along each rim.

Fishing The Gunnison River is the only body of water in the monument and it is full of good-sized (1 to 2 pounds and larger) brown and rainbow trout. The Black Canyon stretch of river lies downstream from Crystal Dam (part of Curecanti National Recreation Area) and the cold-water flows from the dam have nurtured an excellent fishery for wild trout.

Colorado has instituted a program for designating and managing selected streams and rivers as Gold Medal fisheries. The program encourages the management of rivers for wild trout and large trout. The entire length of the Gunnison in the monument area is designated as Gold Medal water and is subject to special regulations. Part of the regulations restrict fishing to artificial flies and lures.

Standard spinning lures should produce good results. Popular fly patterns include stonefly nymphs (sizes 6–10), caddis larva patterns in cream, olive, or yellow (sizes 12–16), Hopper patterns, Adams, and Elk Hair Caddis (12–16) and Blue-Winged Olives (16–20).

That's the good news. The bad news is climbing down to the river. Get in good physical condition and be prepared to hike. Several primitive trails lead into the canyon; however, a special back-country permit is required. Permits can be obtained at the Gunnison Point Visitor Center along the south rim or at the NPS Montrose office, Hwy. 50 east in Montrose, or you may register at the north rim upon entering.

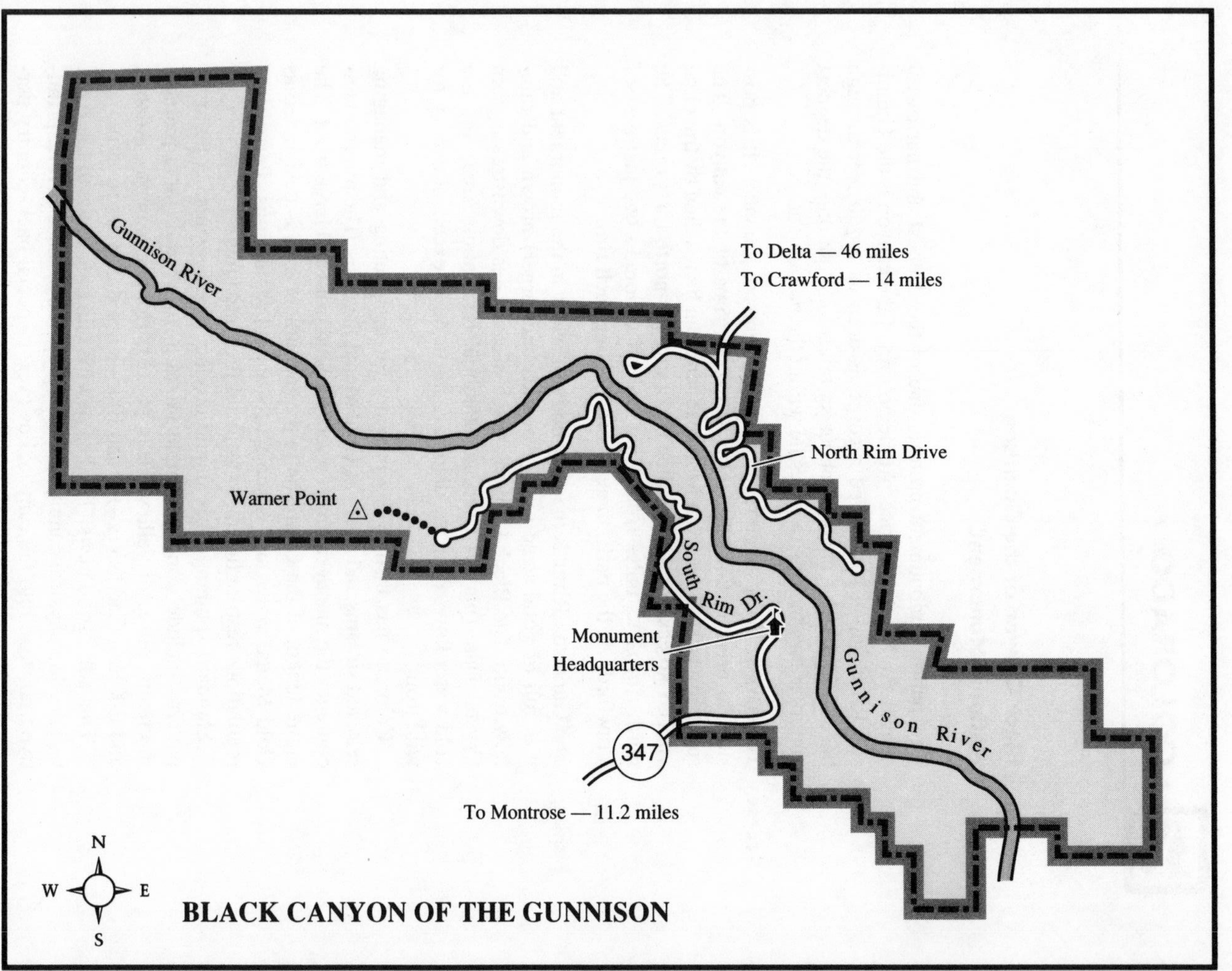

BLACK CANYON OF THE GUNNISON

Warner Point is considered the best fishing and camping area in the park. When camping in the canyon, remember that you are below Crystal Dam; camp far enough from the water to allow for a 6-foot river rise during the night.

License A Colorado fishing license is required. Also be sure to check the regulations for Gold Medal waters.

Camping There are 116 sites in two campgrounds. The campground on the south rim campground has 102 sites and the campground on the north rim has 14 sites. Camping in the canyon requires a permit. The nearest KOA campground and motels are in Montrose.

Maps Topo maps would be of little value. However, the quads covering the monument portion of the river are Grizzly Ridge and Red Rock. There is also a special USGS map of the entire park, entitled "Black Canyon of the Gunnison National Monument."

Park Address
Black Canyon of the Gunnison NM
P.O. Box 1648
Montrose, CO 81402
phone: (303) 249-7036

Chamber of Commerce
Montrose County C.C.
550 N. Townsend
Montrose, CO 81401
phone: (303) 249-5515

Additional Information Ask for the "Colorado Fishing Map" and a copy of the *Gold Medal Water Regulations* from: Colorado Division of Wildlife, Dept. Natural Resources, 6060 Broadway, Denver, CO, 80216; phone: (303) 297-1192.

Also very informative, especially for the trail descriptions, is an excellent guidebook entitled *The Black Canyon of the Gunnison,* by John Dolson. It is available from: Pruett Publishing Company, 2928 Pearl St., Boulder, CO, 80301; phone: (303) 449-4919.

Curecanti National Recreation Area

Curecanti NRA is comprised of three reservoirs in the deep canyons of the Gunnison River. The three reservoirs, Blue Mesa, Morrow Point, and Crystal, are part of the Colorado River Storage Project. Blue Mesa Lake is the largest body of water in Colorado. Curecanti NRA is named for Ute Indian Chief Curicata, who roamed and hunted the Colorado territory. Adjacent to the park's west boundary is the Black Canyon of the Gunnison National Monument.

Access The park is in west central Colorado (Gunnison and Montrose counties). U.S. 50, a major east-west transcontinental route, parallels the

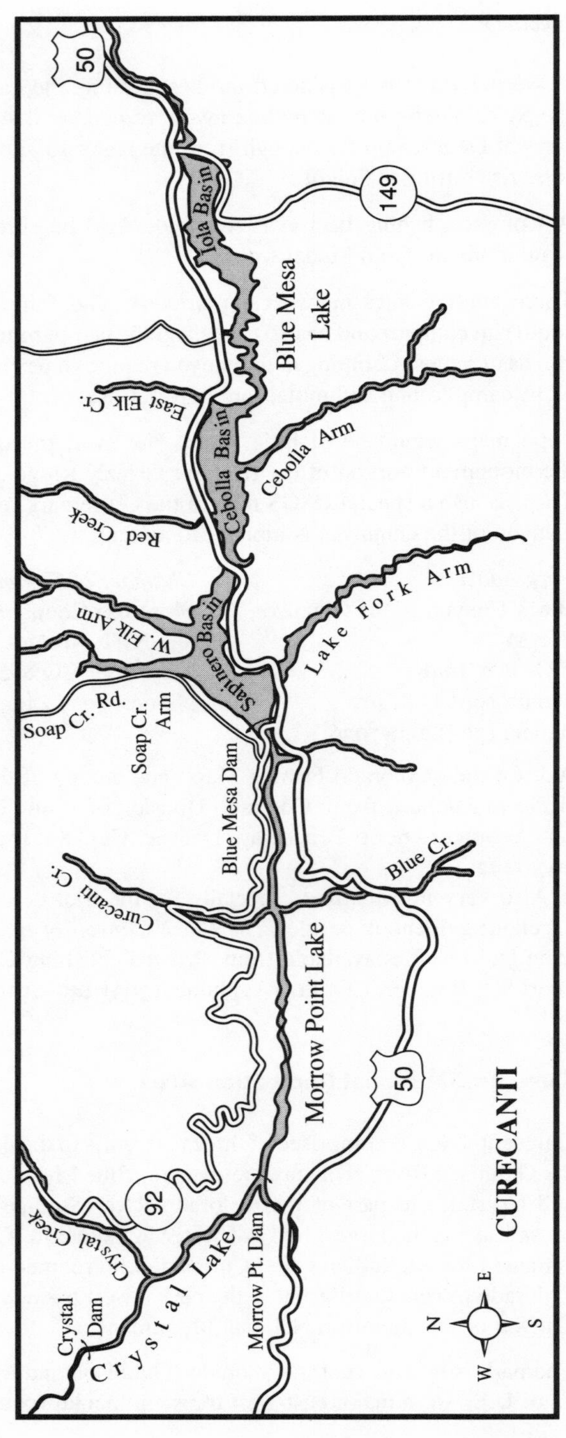
50
149
Iola Basin
Blue Mesa Lake
East Elk Cr.
Cebolla Basin
Cebolla Arm
Red Creek
W. Elk Arm
Sapinero Basin
Lake Fork Arm
Soap Cr. Rd.
Soap Cr. Arm
Blue Mesa Dam
Curecanti Cr.
Blue Cr.
Morrow Point Lake
50
CURECANTI
92
Crystal Creek
Crystal Dam
Crystal Lake
Morrow Pt. Dam
N
E
S
W

length of Blue Mesa Lake. Colorado Highway 92 parallels Morrow Point Lake and part of Crystal Lake on the north side. The nearest towns are Gunnison, about 4 miles east of the park boundary, and Montrose, 14 miles southwest of the western portion of the park.

Fishing Fishing activity centers around Blue Mesa Lake, which is easily accessible and has boat ramps and two marinas with boat rentals. Morrow Point and Crystal lakes are accessible by trail; boats must be hand carried to these lakes. All three lakes contain kokanee salmon, brown, rainbow, and lake trout (also known as mackinaw trout). A portion of the Gunnison River upstream from Blue Mesa Lake is also within the park and accessible along U.S. 50.

Blue Mesa Lake As mentioned, Blue Mesa Lake is the largest body of water in Colorado. The lake is 20 miles long with 90 miles of shoreline. Blue Mesa receives very heavy pressure from both boat and shore fishing. The lake is divided into three large and distinct basins. From the east, they are: Iola, Cebolla, and Sapinero Basins. There are three boat ramps and two marinas (Lake Fork and Elk Creek) providing rentals and guides.

Blue Mesa is heavily stocked by the state with salmon and trout, with rainbow trout being the mainstay of the fishery. Shore fishing is best in the spring and fall when the fish are often close to the shoreline. Creek inlets also are usually productive areas, and one popular area is the east end of Iola Basin where the Gunnison River flows into the basin. Deep trolling is popular along the submerged river channel along the major arms of the lake and near Blue Mesa Dam.

The kokanee salmon are usually found in 30 to 70 feet of water. Kokanee prefer cool water and generally occupy greater depths than the browns and rainbows. In the spring and fall, the kokanee feed in the upper 20 feet of open water. Kokanee are school fish, so after catching one, you should concentrate on that area. In October, the kokanee run out of the lake up the Gunnison River to spawn.

Lake trout are found in relatively shallow water after ice-out in the spring and again in the fall. Most of the year, lake trout are deep along rocky ledges and reefs. Fishing for rainbow trout holds up throughout the year but is best in the spring when the fish congregate near the inlets in anticipation of spawning.

Brown trout are frequently caught in the early spring and summer near shore, usually very early in the morning or in the evening. In the fall, the browns enter some of the tributary streams to spawn. In mid-September, they move out of the lake into the Gunnison River and at that time good fishing is available in park waters off U.S. 50.

Blue Mesa is also a popular lake for ice fishing from December until the fishing tapers off in March. Park rangers check on ice conditions weekly and a call to the park office can tell you what to expect.

Tributaries of the lake are Beaver, Coal, East Elk, West Elk, Willow, Red, Soap, and Steuben creeks on the north and Cebolla Creek and Lake Fork of the Gunnison River on the south. Generally these streams are small and brushy, difficult to get to, and have fair fishing for brook and rainbow trout. Soap Creek is the most accessible off Soap Creek Road near the Blue Mesa Dam.

Morrow Point Lake Morrow Point Lake, in the canyon below Blue Mesa Lake, is 11 miles long and as deep as 400 feet. Morrow Point is accessible only by the Pine Creek Trail on the south side, just below Blue Mesa Dam off U.S. 50. The trail is three-fourths of a mile long and private boats must be carried to the lake.

The lake is in a canyon with steep walls, so a boat is required for fishing. Because of the difficult access, this lake receives very little fishing pressure and contains some large fish. Tributaries, Curecanti Creek on the north and Blue Creek on the south, provide fair fishing for brook and rainbow trout.

Crystal Lake Crystal Lake is approximately 6 miles long and is similar to Morrow Point Lake in difficulty of access. It is a steeply walled canyon lake that is lightly fished. Access is below Morrow Point Dam and small boats can be carried to the water. Fishing with a guide is advised because the water level fluctuates appreciably and it can be difficult to get out of the lake if the water level drops. A strong motor is recommended to come upstream against the current from water releases at Morrow Point.

A fishing trip to both Morrow Point Lake and Crystal Lake requires advance planning, and guides are recommended for a first trip. Information and guides are available from Elk Creek Marina on Blue Mesa Lake (phone: (303) 641-0707).

License A Colorado fishing license is required.

Camping Camping is available at nine sites with a total of 409 spaces.

Maps The park brochure map is sufficient, but a contour map of Blue Mesa Lake is available from Fish-N-Map, 8535 W. 79th Ave., Arvada, CO, 80005; phone: (303) 421-5994.

Park Address
Curecanti NRA
102 Elk Creek
Gunnison, CO 81230
phone: (303) 641-2337

Chamber of Commerce
Gunnison County C.C.
500 E. Tomichi Ave.
P.O. Box 36
Gunnison, CO 81230
phone: (303) 641-1501

Dinosaur National Monument

Dinosaur National Monument is an ancient burial ground containing large deposits of petrified dinosaur, crocodile, and turtle skeletons. At the quarry, visitors may watch park technicians at work with jackhammers, chisels, and ice picks, cutting away at the rock to expose the fossilized bones.

Dinosaur is a large park (211,000 acres) with very little development. This very rugged country features the deep canyons of the Green and Yampa rivers, popular with white-water boaters.

Access The park is located along the northern part of the Utah/Colorado state line (Uintah County, Utah; Moffat County, Colorado). Access is off U.S. 40 near Jensen, Utah and Dinosaur, Colorado.

Fishing Fishing in the park is for catfish in the Green and Yampa rivers and brown and rainbow trout in Jones Hole Creek on the Utah side. Most fishing, however, is centered on the nationally famous Flaming Gorge Reservoir upstream from the park in Utah and Wyoming. Flaming Gorge has received national attention for yielding huge brown trout in the 20-to-30-pound range.

The Green River was dammed to form Flaming Gorge Reservoir. Below the dam, the river provides good trout fishing down to the park. Just above the northern park boundary is Browns Park National Wildlife Refuge, which offers some good fishing for rainbow trout.

The Green and Yampa rivers in the park are popular with boaters and receive little fishing pressure because of the lack of access. The Yampa often runs high and roily and is a favorite with boaters. It is fair for channel catfish.

The Green River is cleaner and faster because it is affected by water releases from the dam upstream. There may be a few trout in the river in the Gates of Lodore area at the northern boundary, but the majority of visitors within the park are white-water boaters. The Yampa flows into the Green at Echo Park and fishing is good for catfish at that confluence and further downstream on the Green.

The best fishing in the park is at Jones Hole Creek in Utah. The unpaved road to Jones Hole Creek can be reached from Utah Highway 44, north of Vernal; at the end of the road is a federal fish hatchery. Stopping at Vernal or Jensen for directions would probably be a good idea. The creek is populated with browns and rainbows in the 15-inch range. Below the hatchery, a hiking trail follows the creek for 4 miles to its confluence with the Green River at Whirlpool Canyon.

Guided raft trips of various lengths are available along both the Green and Yampa rivers. The park has a list of river concessioners

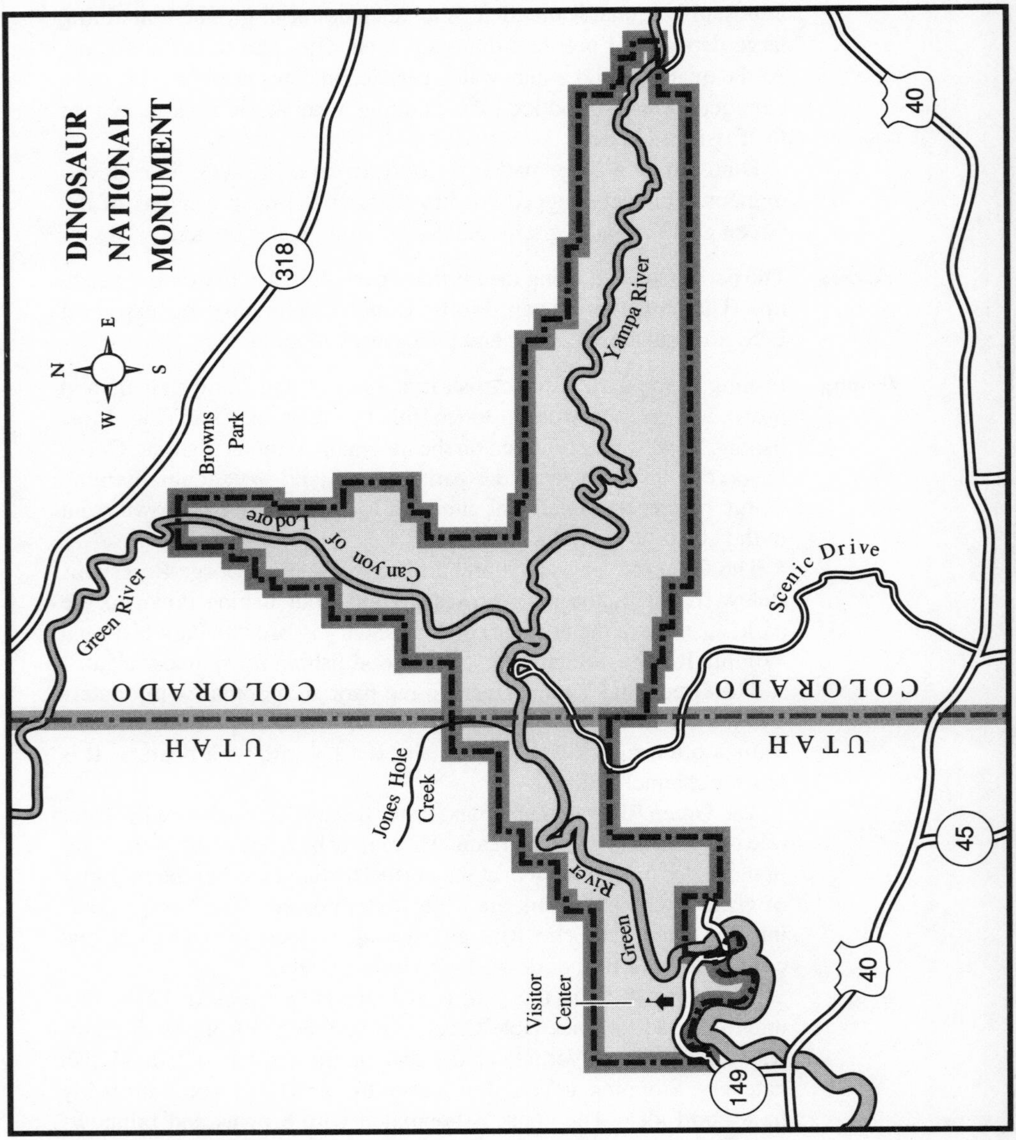

DINOSAUR
NATIONAL
MONUMENT

N
W
E
S

Green River
Browns Park
318
UTAH
COLORADO
Canyon of Lodore
Jones Hole Creek
Visitor Center
Green River
Yampa River
149
UTAH
COLORADO
Scenic Drive
40
45
40

authorized by the park service to provide guided river trips within Dinosaur National Monument. The best trout fishing trip, however, is outside the park, from Flaming Gorge Dam down to Browns Park National Wildlife Refuge.

License You will need either a Utah or a Colorado fishing license, depending on where you fish.

Camping There are two improved campgrounds, Green River (99 spaces) and Split Mountain (35 spaces), and four primitive campgrounds at Echo Park (15 spaces), Rainbow Park (2 spaces), Gates of Lodore (17 spaces), and Deerlodge Park (10 spaces). Camping along the river is also allowed with a permit.

Maps There is a special USGS map of the park, "Dinosaur National Monument," although fishing in the park won't require topographic maps. Fishing on the rivers is from a raft or at the access points shown on the park brochure map. A road leads to Jones Hole Creek and a trail runs along the creek. The park provides an information sheet on the road to Jones Hole along with a road and hiking trail map for Jones Hole Creek.

Park Address	*Chamber of Commerce*
Dinosaur NM	Vernal Area C.C.
P.O. Box 210	50 E. Main
Dinosaur, CO 81610	Vernal, UT 84078
phone: (303) 374-2216	phone: (801) 789-1352

Additional Information The *Dinosaur River Guide*, by Laura Evans and Buzz Belknap, is a good guide, with maps to both the Green and Yampa rivers. It doesn't contain much fishing information because it was written mainly for river runners, but its river descriptions, mileage markers, and historical information, and numerous photographs will certainly come in handy. Contact: Westwater Books, P.O. Box 2560, Evergreen, CO, 80439; phone: (303) 674-5410.

The U.S. Forest Service administers Flaming Gorge National Recreation Area as part of Ashley National Forest. A one-half-inch-scale map of Ashley National Forest costs $2 and is available from: Forest Supervisor, Ashley National Forest, 335 North Vernal Avenue, Vernal, UT, 84078; phone: (801) 789-1181.

Information on Browns Park National Wildlife Refuge may be obtained from: Browns Park NWR, 1318 Highway 318, Maybell, CO, 81640; phone: (303) 365-3613.

Great Sand Dunes National Monument

Great Sand Dunes is the home of North America's tallest sand dunes. Nestled against the Sangre de Christo Mountains, the dunes have been deposited by the winds over a period of many thousands of years. The dunes will always be subject to the vagaries of nature and the dune surfaces change with each succeeding wind.

Access The park is 32 miles northeast of Alamosa (Saguache and Alamosa counties). It can be reached by U.S. 160 or Colorado 150 from the south, or from Colorado 17 and County Six Mile Lane from the west.

Fishing Fishing is very limited in the park. The two major streams that flow into the park are Sand Creek and Medano Creek. Sand Creek is intermittent within the park, although it is a year-round stream in its upper reaches outside the park. Sand Creek contains small brook and cutthroat trout but is seldom fished because of its inaccessibility.

Below its junction with Castle Creek, Medano Creek is also intermittent, though it maintains a constant flow in its upper reaches. Medano Creek is a brushy, swift stream holding small brown and brook trout. The brown trout are found primarily above the junction with Little Medano Creek, which also contains brown trout. Neither Medano nor Little Medano receive much fishing pressure because of the difficult access.

For both Medano and Sand creeks, the fishing is better outside and upstream from the park. Future proposals of the Colorado Division of Wildlife call for the removal of brown and brook trout from the Medano drainage and the reestablishment of the native Rio Grande cutthroat trout.

License A Colorado fishing license is required.

Camping Pinyon Flats Campground (88 spaces) operates from April through October. Back-country camping is available. Permits are required and may be obtained at the visitor center.

Maps Topographic maps aren't necessary; the map on the park brochure should suffice. There is also a special USGS map of the park, "Great Sand Dunes National Monument."

Park Address
Great Sand Dunes NM
11500 Highway 150
Mosca, CO 81146
phone: (719) 378-2312

Chamber of Commerce
Alamosa County C.C.
Cole Park
Alamosa, CO 81101
phone: (719) 589-3681

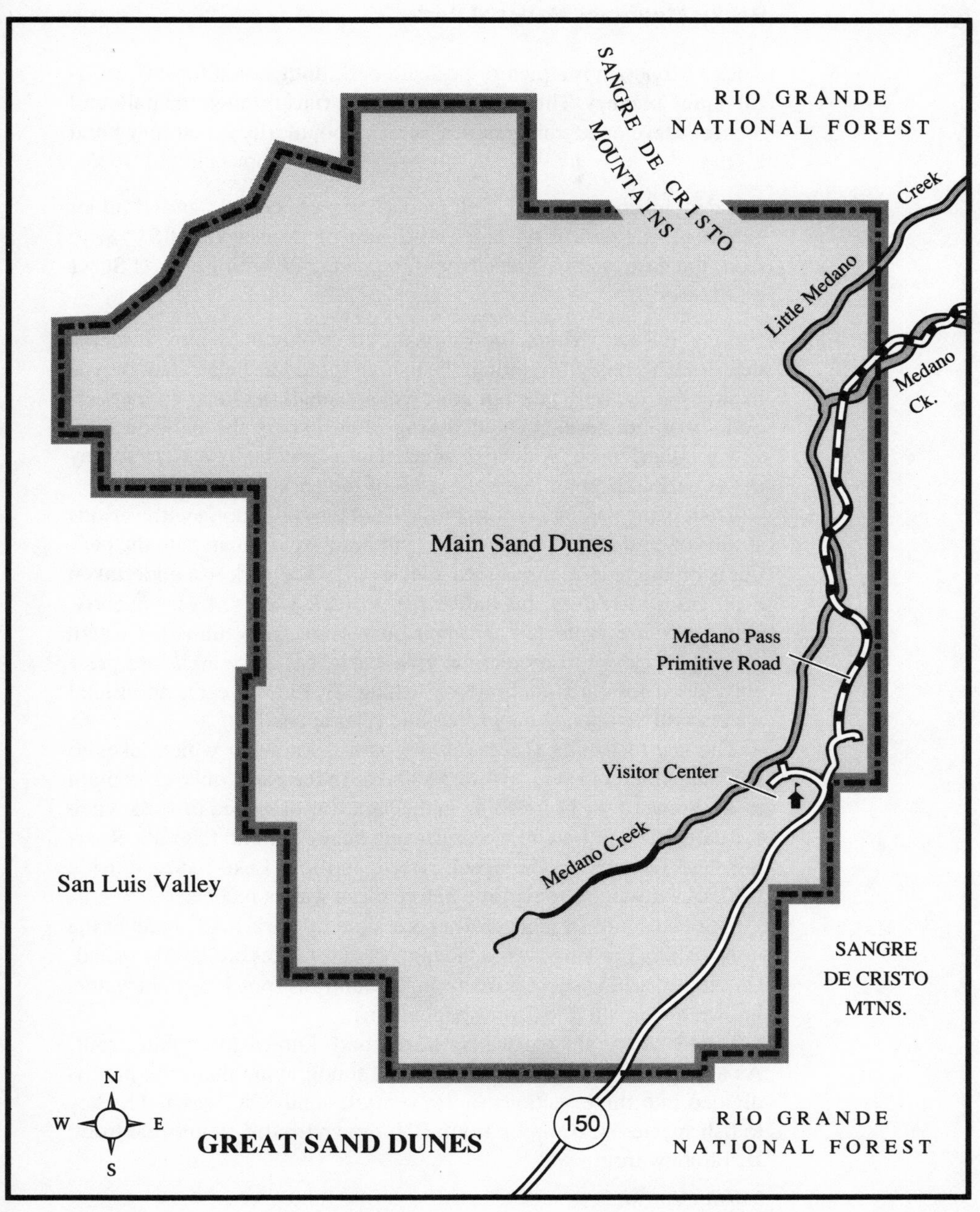
SANGRE DE CRISTO MOUNTAINS
RIO GRANDE NATIONAL FOREST
Creek
Little Medano
Medano Ck.
Main Sand Dunes
Medano Pass Primitive Road
Visitor Center
Medano Creek
San Luis Valley
SANGRE DE CRISTO MTNS.
N
W
E
S
150
GREAT SAND DUNES
RIO GRANDE NATIONAL FOREST

Rocky Mountain National Park

Rocky Mountain is a picture-postcard park, long noted for its beautiful alpine scenery. The Continental Divide runs through the park and the well-developed trail system assures its popularity for climbing and hiking.

Access Located in north central Colorado (Larimer, Grand, and Boulder counties), the park is 65 miles northwest of Denver via U.S. 34/36 from the east, and 91 miles from Cheyenne, Wyoming, via U.S. 34 on the west.

Fishing Fishing in Rocky Mountain National Park is only mediocre. It seems that in such a beautiful setting, the fishing should be better. Not only is fishing success only fair, but most fish are small (less that 12 inches). Folks who are serious about fishing often bypass the park on their way to other, more productive areas. This is proven by a 1976 survey in the park indicating that only 1.7% of the park visitors fished.

Trout in the park are brook, brown, and rainbow, along with various strains of cutthroat. The greenback cutthroat trout is native to the park but is on the federal threatened-species list. The park has undertaken a program to restore this native fish to park waters. Consequently, these trout are protected and their possession is prohibited. Certain waters are closed to protect the greenback, but three areas are presently open for catch-and-release fishing. In future years, additional waters will be opened on a catch-and-release basis.

The key to fishing success in the park is knowing which lakes to fish and which to avoid. Of the 147 lakes in the park, only 42 contain trout. Some of the best fishing in the park was damaged in 1982 when the dam failed at Lawn Lake, releasing heavy silt into the Fall, Roaring, and Lower Big Thompson rivers, and into Lake Estes, outside the park. It will be some time before these waters recover.

The lakes and streams easily accessible by park roads receive the most fishing pressure, while the high-country lakes are lightly fished. Generally, fishing success in this high country is spotty, even in waters known to contain good trout populations.

Listed below are the waters in the park known to contain trout. As a help in locating these waters on a topographic map, the park is divided into three sections (north central, southeast, west). The key to fish species is: **B,** brook trout; **BN,** brown trout; **C,** cutthroat trout; **R,** rainbow trout.

North Central

Cache La Poudre River—**B**
Cascade Creek—**B,BN**
Lost Lake—**B,C**
Mirror Lake—**BN,R**

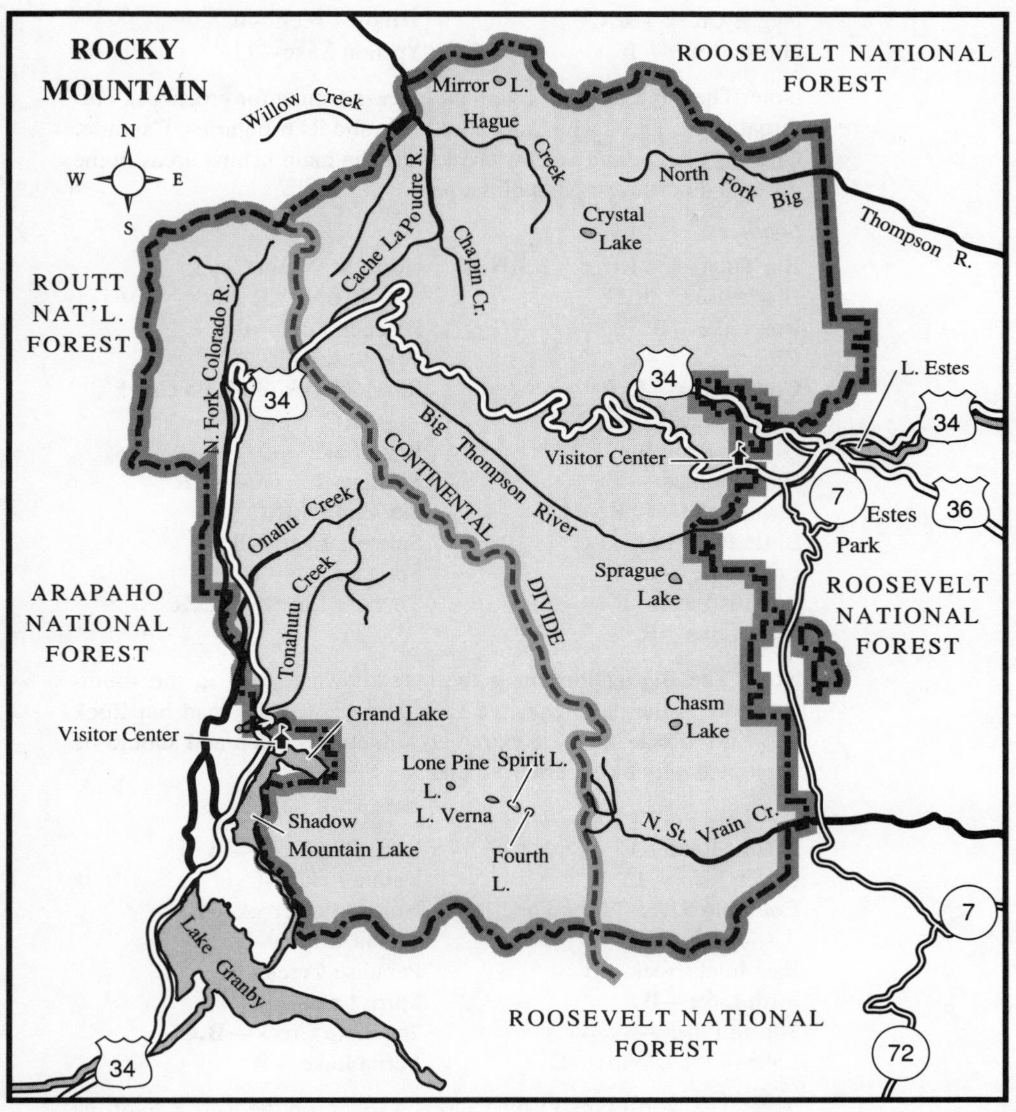
ROCKY MOUNTAIN
ROOSEVELT NATIONAL FOREST
N
W
E
S
Willow Creek
Mirror L.
Hague
Creek
North Fork Big
Thompson R.
Crystal Lake
Cache La Poudre R.
Chapin Cr.
ROUTT NAT'L. FOREST
N. Fork Colorado R.
34
34
L. Estes
34
Big Thompson River
CONTINENTAL DIVIDE
Visitor Center
7
Estes Park
36
Onahu Creek
Tonahutu Creek
Sprague Lake
ARAPAHO NATIONAL FOREST
ROOSEVELT NATIONAL FOREST
Chasm Lake
Grand Lake
Visitor Center
Lone Pine L.
Spirit L.
L. Verna
Fourth L.
N. St. Vrain Cr.
Shadow Mountain Lake
Lake Granby
7
ROOSEVELT NATIONAL FOREST
72
34

Chapin Creek—**B**
Crystal Lake—**C**
Fay Lakes—**C**
Hague Creek—**B,C**
Husted Lake—**B**
North Fork Thompson River —**B,C**
Poudre Lake—**B**
Willow Creek—**B**
Ypsilon Lake—**C**

Note: The Fay Lakes are catch-and-release fishing for greenback cutthroat trout. The Cache La Poudre River and its tributaries, Cascade, Chapin, Hague, and Willow creeks, are the main fishing areas in the north and northwest parts of the park.

Southeast

Big Thompson River—**B,BN,R**
Black Lake—**B,C**
Box Lake—**B**
Chasm Lake—**C**
Cony Creek—**C,R**
Glacier Creek—**C,R**
Glass Lake—**B,C**
Haiyaha Lake—**C**
Jewel Lake—**C,R**
Little Rock Lake—**C**
Loch Vale—**C,R**
Loomis Lake—**B**
Mills Lake—**R**
North St. Vrain Creek —**B,BN,C,R**
Peacock Pool—**B,C**
Pear Reservoir—**C**
Roaring Fork of Cabin Creek —**B,C**
Rock Lake—**C**
Sandbeach Lake—**C,R**
Sky Pond—**B,C**
Sprague Lake—**B**
Spruce Lake—**R**
Thunder Lake—**B,C,R**

Note: The Big Thompson is the best known fishery in the southeast part of the park. Sprague Lake is accessible by road but Rock and Little Rock lakes are extremely difficult to reach and should be attempted only by experienced hikers.

West

Adams Lake—**C**
Bench Lake—**C**
Colorado River (North Fork) —**B,BN,R**
East Inlet Creek—**B**
Fifth Lake—**B**
Fourth Lake—**B**
Lake of the Clouds—**C**
Lone Pine Lake—**B**
Nanita Lake—**C**
North Inlet Creek—**B**
Onahu Creek—**B**
Paradise Creek—**C**
Spirit Lake—**B**
Tonahutu Creek—**B,C**
Verna Lake—**B**

Note: The North Fork of the Colorado River, on the west side of the park, is good for brooks, browns, and rainbows.

Fishing in the park is permitted year-round, except in a few locations. Most lakes are frozen over in winter. Inquire at the park office.

Dream Lake, nestled below Hallett Peak, is a beautiful but fishless high-country lake. *—National Park Service photo by George Grant*

Generally in Colorado, stream fishing is best after late July. During May, June, and July, runoff and muddy water hamper stream fishing. If you plan to go into high country but are not experienced or properly equipped, horseback pack trips can be arranged by a park concessioner. Contact the park for a list of concessioners.

Outside the southwestern part of the park are Grand Lake, Shadow Mountain Lake, and Lake Granby. All have marinas and boat rentals and all contain kokanee salmon, and brown, rainbow, and lake trout.

Estes Lake is just outside the eastern entrance to the park. As mentioned, the lake was damaged by heavy silt after the collapse of the Lawn Lake Dam in 1982 and required dredging. The state annually stocks rainbow trout in the lake.

License A Colorado fishing license is required. Also, be sure to check park fishing regulations to find out which waters may be closed to protect the greenback trout. In addition, some waters have special regulations.

Camping The park has five roadside campgrounds: Aspenglen (56 spaces), Glacier Basin (152 spaces), Longs Peak (28 spaces), Moraine Park (250 spaces), and Timber Creek (100 spaces). In addition, there are approximately 250 trail-side campsites throughout the park.

A permit is required for all overnight trips into the back country. Reservations for permits may be made any time after January 1. Telephone requests are accepted only from October to May; during other months, requests should be made in writing or in person.

Maps There is a special USGS map of the entire park ("Rocky Mountain National Park") that you will need for back-country trips.

Park Address
Rocky Mountain NP
Estes Park, CO 80517
phone: (303) 586-2371

Chamber of Commerce
Estes Park C.C.
P.O. Box 3050
Estes Park, CO 80517
phone: (303) 586-4431
toll free: 1-800-443-7837

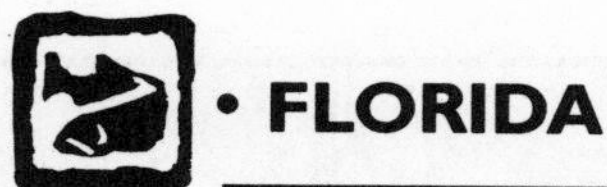

• FLORIDA

Big Cypress National Preserve

Big Cypress and the Big Thicket National Preserve were established in 1974 as the first preserves in the national parks system. Big Cypress is a large swamp (570,000 acres) adjoining the northwest section of Everglades National Park and is a crucial supplier of fresh water to the Everglades.

Unlike its neighboring park, Big Cypress is primarily a forested area of interesting and unusual plant communities, such as cypress stands and sloughs, mixed hardwood stands, cypress prairies, and pine islands. The preserve is about one-third covered with cypress trees.

Access The preserve is in southwestern Florida (Collier, Monroe, and Dade counties). Two major highways cross the preserve, Florida Highway 84 (Alligator Alley) crosses the north part and U.S. 41 (Tamiami Trail) crosses the south. They are connected by Florida Highway 29 to the west of the preserve boundary and a lime-rock road, Turner River Road (Florida Highway 839), inside Big Cypress.

Fishing Fishing is limited to man-made excavations, such as canals and borrow pits that create deep-water habitats for game fish. Most of these are found along the roadways and are easily accessible. Natural ponds deep enough to support game fish are rare and inaccessible.

As a rule, brackish water exists in the canals and ponds south of U.S. Highway 41 and fishing is for tarpon, snook, mullet, and pompano. North of U.S. 41 is fresh water where you will find largemouth bass and an array of sunfish and catfish.

License A Florida license is required for freshwater fishing.

Camping There is one privately owned campground in the preserve at Ochopee. Other campgrounds are nearby at Everglades City and at Collier-Seminole State Park. There are a few primitive campsites in the preserve such as Monument Lake, Midway Lake, and Bear Island.

Maps The preserve brochure map may suffice. It shows the limited-entry points into the preserve interior, including Florida Trail, a marked trail between Alligator Alley and the Tamiami Trail. Some of the

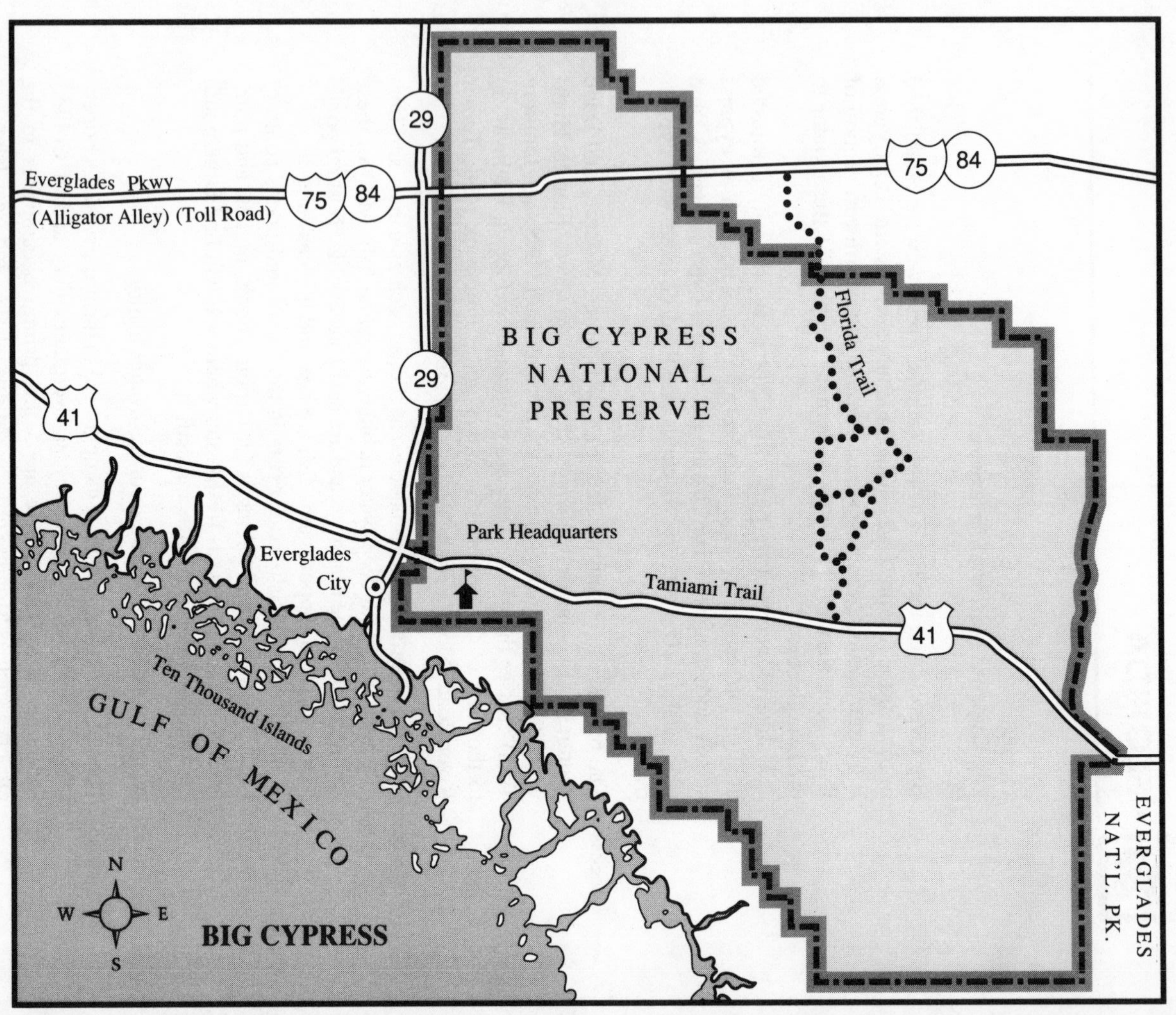
Everglades Pkwy
(Alligator Alley) (Toll Road)
75
84
29
41
BIG CYPRESS
NATIONAL
PRESERVE
Florida Trail
Park Headquarters
Everglades
City
Tamiami Trail
Ten Thousand Islands
GULF OF MEXICO
N
W
E
S
BIG CYPRESS
EVERGLADES
NAT'L. PK.

preserve remains in private ownership, so check with a park ranger before beginning a hike or an off-road vehicle trip.

Park Address
Big Cypress NP
Star Route Box 110
Ochopee, FL 33943
phone: (813) 695-2000

Chambers of Commerce
Naples Area C.C.
1700 N. Tamiami Trail
Naples, FL 33940
phone: (813) 262-6141

Everglades Area C.C.
P.O. Box 130
Everglades, FL 33929
phone: (813) 695-3941

Biscayne National Park

Biscayne National Park is a park of reefs and water off Florida's southeastern coast. There is very little land in the park, and that is in the form of reefs or low islands known as keys. The approximately 36 keys in the park form an almost continuous north-south chain. Because the park is mostly water, boating and fishing are the most popular activities.

Access The park is off the southeast coast of Florida, south of Miami and immediately north of Key Largo. Access to the park is by boat. Round trips to Elliott Key are offered by a park concessioner.

Fishing Biscayne Bay, which extends from the park north almost to Miami, is the northernmost range for bonefish, one of Florida's most highly prized sport fish. The bonefish is not valued for its edibility but is one of the wariest and best fighting fish that can be caught with light tackle. Biscayne Bay holds some of the largest bonefish in Florida, weighing up to 10 pounds. Light spinning tackle or fly rods are generally used to pursue this elusive quarry.

Bonefish roam the shallow flat-water areas to feed, usually in water less than 3 feet deep. These flats are scattered throughout Biscayne Bay and bonefish are often taken in view of the Miami skyline. In the park, prime bonefish areas are around Stiltsville, the Arsenicker Keys, and in Jones Lagoon between Totten Key and Old Rhodes Key.

Bonefish are extremely spooky and must be approached with stealth and caution. A guide is recommended if you have never fished for this species. Guides know where to go under the various tide, wind, and water conditions, and can teach the proper techniques for fishing the flats. A technique to try if you don't have a guide, is to fish a flat

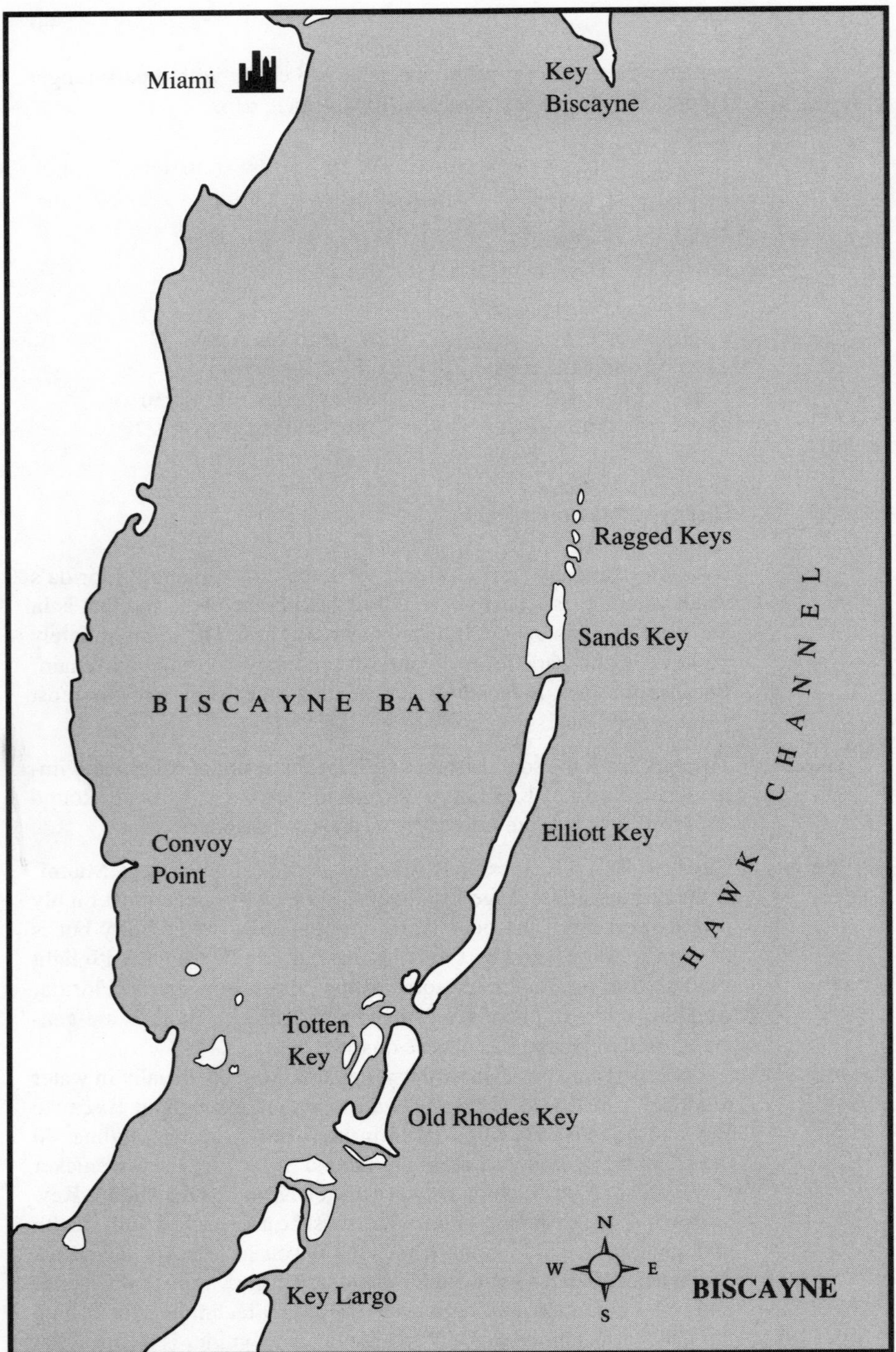
Miami
Key Biscayne
Ragged Keys
Sands Key
BISCAYNE BAY
HAWK CHANNEL
Elliott Key
Convoy Point
Totten Key
Old Rhodes Key
Key Largo
N
W
E
S
BISCAYNE

as the tide starts to flood it, working higher on the flat as the water continues to come in. Usually you can see the fish tailing as they feed right behind the advancing water.

Large numbers of bonefish are present all year in park waters, but the spring and summer months are the most productive. During the summer, bonefish are normally on the flats continuously. Throughout the year, they will be on or near the flats as long as the water temperature there remains above 70 degrees. If cold fronts cause water temperatures to drop below 70, the bonefish seek refuge in the deeper cuts.

Besides bonefish, there are almost 200 species of sport fish available in park waters. Dolphin, grouper, snapper, and jack crevalle, along with the spiny lobster, are all very popular targets for fishing in Biscayne Bay. During the winter, the cooler water on the flats attracts schools of barracudas. In the deeper channels of the bay and in Hawk Channel outside the bay, schools of jack crevalle abound.

Permit move onto the flats sometime in March. Fishing for permit improves as the spring progresses into summer. July and August are the prime months.

Also in the spring and summer, look for sea trout around the grassy areas. Tarpon make occasional appearances along the outer edges of the flats. Shark fishing improves in the summer and a variety of fish are taken from the deeper channels. This is also the time when dolphin fishing is best in the Gulf Stream, beyond the eastern park boundary.

Fall fishing is very good and October is one of the best fishing months of the year. As the water cools off, fish move inshore and become more active.

License A license is required for saltwater fishing in Florida. Check the regulations carefully because additional stamps are required for snook and spiny lobster.

Camping There are undeveloped campgrounds on Boca Chita Key and on Elliott Key at the harbor. The harbor also offers 66 free boat slips (no utilities) on a first-come, first-served basis.

Maps Nautical charts #11451 and #11463 are essential for safe boating in park waters.

Park Address	*Chamber of Commerce*
Biscayne NP	Homestead/Florida City C.C.
P.O. Box 1369	650 Homestead Blvd.
Homestead, FL 33030	Homestead, FL 33030
phone: (305) 247-2044	phone: (305) 247-2332

Additional Information The *Florida Outdoor Guide* is an annual publication covering fishing, boating, and camping, with details on where to go, boat ramps, and much more. This book is an essential timesaver and planning aid for fishing in Florida. It is available at newsstands throughout Florida or from: Miami Herald Publishing Company, 1 Herald Plaza, Miami, FL. 33132; phone: (305) 376-2614.

For information about fishing guides in the Biscayne Bay area, contact the Homestead/Florida City Chamber of Commerce at the above address.

Canaveral National Seashore

Canaveral National Seashore is a 24-mile stretch of beach in the central part of Florida's east coast. Behind this barrier-island beach is Merritt Island, part of which is designated as Merritt Island National Wildlife Refuge. Canaveral National Seashore is one of the few remaining wilderness beaches on Florida's highly developed Atlantic Coast.

Access The park is in central Florida (Brevard County) about 20 miles south of Daytona Beach and just north of the Kennedy Space Center at Cape Canaveral. The park is readily accessible via U.S. 1, and Interstates 95, 4, and 75. Florida Highway A1A is the northern access point and Florida Highway 402 is the southern access point.

Fishing Canaveral National Seashore encompasses nearly 40,000 acres of saltwater, including an area of ocean and the south part of Mosquito Lagoon behind the beach. The number of fish species available to the angler in the lagoon and surf is enormous.

Surf fishing is popular all along the beach. Bluefish, Spanish mackerel, whiting, pompano, and channel bass (redfish or red drum) are frequently caught. You can also catch cobia, shark, tarpon, flounder, ladyfish, and many others.

Mosquito Lagoon is a brackish body of water averaging less than 2 miles wide and 4 to 5 feet deep. The lagoon also has a variety of fish. Nearly all the fish caught on the surf side can be caught in the lagoon. The usual catch in the lagoon is sea trout, snook, sheepshead, catfish, channel bass, whiting, and an occasional grouper.

The beach is divided into three sections: Apollo Beach is the northern section, Klondike Beach is the middle section, and Playalinda Beach is the southern section. Klondike Beach is accessible only by foot and is rarely fished because of the considerable effort involved.

For surf fishing, pompano are caught along the beach year-round,

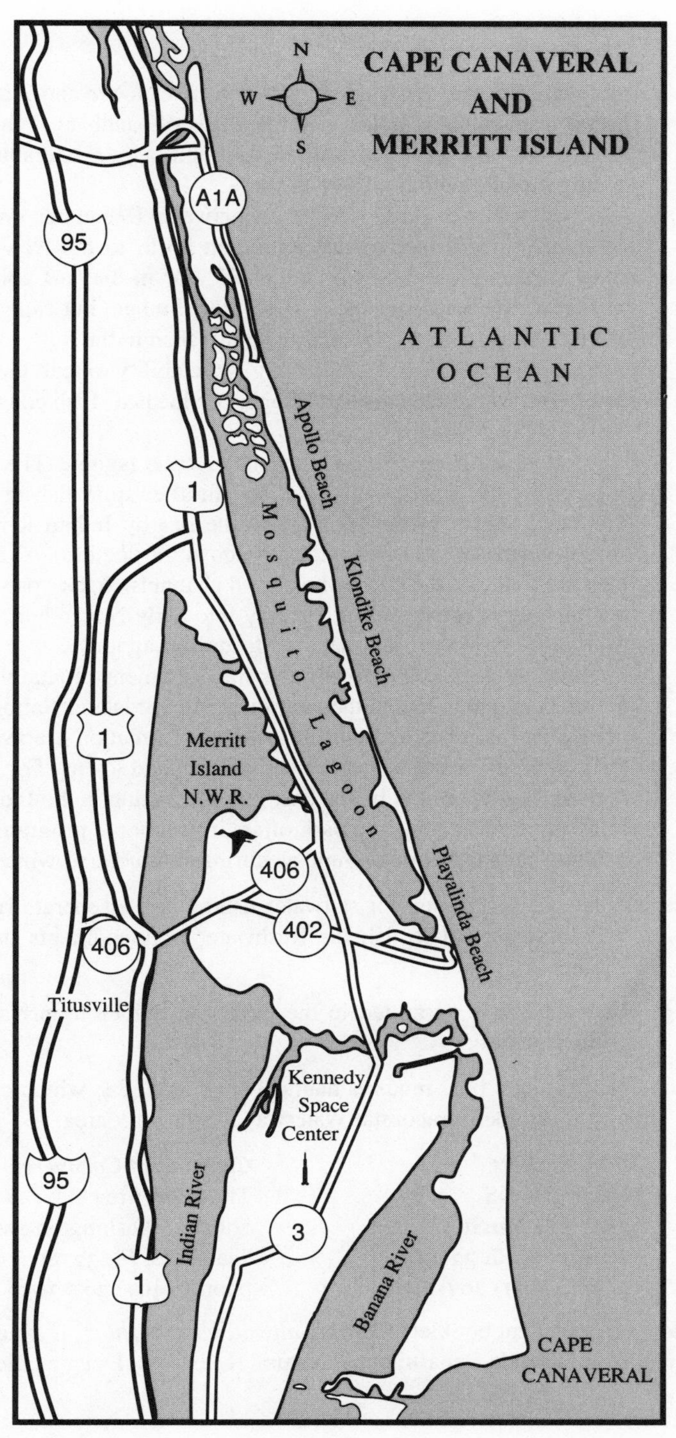
CAPE CANAVERAL
AND
MERRITT ISLAND
N
W
E
S
A1A
95
ATLANTIC
OCEAN
Apollo Beach
1
Mosquito Lagoon
Klondike Beach
1
Merritt
Island
N.W.R.
406
Playalinda Beach
402
406
Titusville
Kennedy
Space
Center
95
Indian River
3
Banana River
1
CAPE
CANAVERAL

although they are most common between October and April. They prefer deep troughs, holes, and the edges of sandbars. Whiting, the most commonly caught fish in the surf and lagoon, are abundant all year, generally within 30 feet of shore.

Bluefish occur along the beach between December and March when they begin their return migration north to the New England coast. Channel bass are also found all year in the surf and lagoon. These fish are usually in the 5-to-20-pound range, but can go as high as 80 pounds, with the larger fish being taken in the fall.

The key to successful surf fishing is the ability to read the surf and determine where the cuts and sloughs are located. Fish congregate in these cuts and sloughs to feed.

Spotted sea trout are found throughout the lagoon. The sea trout is probably the most popular and sought-after sport fish in the area. The trout spawn in the lagoon and the nearby Indian River in the spring when the estuaries warm to above 78 degrees. At this time, they are found in the deeper holes and channels. After spawning, the best fishing is usually from late July into early November, when the trout move onto the grass flats in Mosquito Lagoon.

There also are a few freshwater impoundments containing largemouth bass and bream in the interior of Merritt Island National Wildlife Refuge. Guides and current fishing information are available at the numerous tackle shops in nearby cities and towns. For the uninformed, a guide might be the best idea for fishing in the Indian River or Mosquito Lagoon. The park offers instructional programs on surf fishing Thursday through Sunday, during summer and winter.

License A license is required for saltwater fishing and a separate freshwater license is needed to fish the freshwater impoundments on Merritt Island.

Camping No camping is permitted in the park, but numerous private campgrounds are nearby.

Maps Navigating a boat requires nautical chart #11484, which covers the ocean and the Intracoastal Waterway for the park area.

Park Address
Canaveral NS
2532 Garden St.
Titusville, FL 32796
phone: (407) 267-1110

Chamber of Commerce
Titusville Area C.C.
2000 S. Washington Ave.
Titusville, FL 32780
phone: (407) 267-3036

Additional Information An excellent booklet, *Florida Saltwater Sportfishing*, is available free from: Florida Department of Natural Resources, Douglas Bldg., 3900

Commonwealth Blvd., Tallahassee, FL, 32303, phone: (904) 487-3122.

Everglades National Park

Everglades National Park is a large (1.4 million acres), sprawling wilderness established in 1947 to preserve this rich biological area of unique plant and animal communities. In 1982, the park was dedicated as an International Biosphere Reserve and a World Heritage Site, recognized by UNESCO (United Nations Educational, Scientific and Cultural Organization) and by conservation and scientific organizations around the world as a truly unique resource.

Access The park encompasses the southern tip of Florida (Collier, Monroe, and Dade counties). Florida Highway 27 is the main access to the park from the east while Florida Highway 29 provides access to the northwest park area (Ten Thousand Islands area) from Everglades City.

Fishing Everglades National Park is among the richest and most productive sport fisheries in the entire United States. The Florida Bay area on the south and the Ten Thousand Islands area on the west are renowned for snook, sea trout, redfish, snapper, and tarpon. In addition, there is unexplored freshwater fishing for largemouth bass and panfish in the freshwater sections of the park. The park is popular for light-tackle and fly-fishing.

While fine fishing still exists, the last decade has seen a decline in fish populations, a situation the park staff is attempting to rectify. The actual extent and cause of the decline of fish populations is unknown, but most experts agree that changes in inland watershed management may have reduced the productivity of the Everglades estuaries.

The entire park ecosystem, both freshwater and saltwater environments, depends on freshwater flow from land areas north of the park. Increased urbanization and levee construction in the north have impounded freshwater destined for Everglades National Park. The freshwater is crucial to the reproductive needs of many saltwater fish, since the freshwater decreases salinity where it meets saltwater and provides an ideal nursery habitat for young saltwater species, which predators cannot tolerate, allowing the young fish to thrive and grow. When diminished freshwater flows allow salinity levels to rise and saltwater to intrude further inland, significant drops in the populations of redfish, snook, sea trout, and other species may occur.

In addition to the decrease in freshwater flows, commercial and

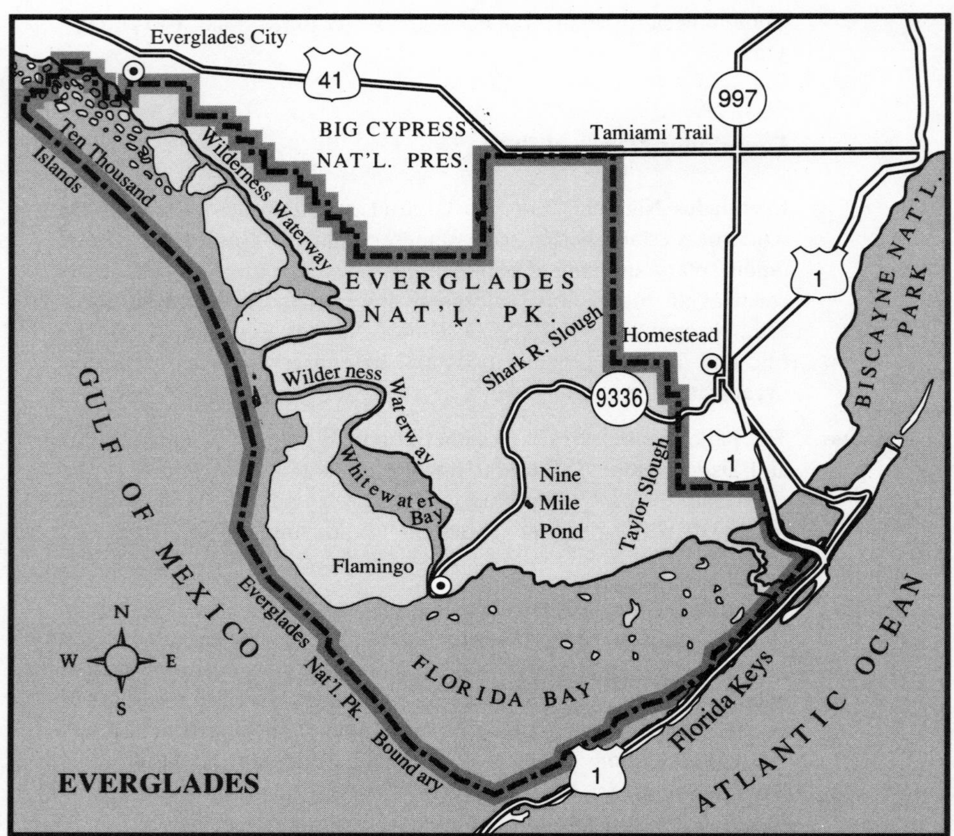

recreational fishing has taken a toll on the fish. To counter this, special bag limits have been established for all species of fish. The State of Florida, alarmed by the decline of snook populations, has also established special regulations for snook throughout Florida.

Commercial fishing was phased out of park waters. Other actions to help the fish populations recover include the construction of pumping stations outside the park to raise freshwater levels and restore the nursery areas to their former low salinity, and the plugging of canals to retain freshwater.

Flamingo is the center for fishing Florida Bay, while Everglades City is the starting point for the Ten Thousand Islands area. Guides, boat rentals, maps, and information are all available at both places. Anyone unfamiliar with this area would be well advised to hire a guide for the first trip out. The myriad channels, mud flats, oyster banks, sloughs, and canals can be confusing.

The Wilderness Waterway, a marked 99-mile inland water route connecting Flamingo to Everglades City, is popular with canoeists but is wide enough for houseboats. Five other marked canoe routes of shorter length all begin near Flamingo. The best months to canoe in the Everglades are October through March. Summertime is either too rainy, too hot, or too thick with mosquitoes. The park provides a brochure about canoe outfitters operating in the park and a canoe information sheet describing the canoe trails.

Freshwater Fishing

Very good freshwater fishing is available in the canals, creeks, sloughs, and borrow pits in the upper sections of the park. Largemouth bass and panfish, collectively called bream (pronounced brim) are abundant. A year-round food supply and the lack of a cold season enable bass and bream to grow rapidly. In times of periodic drought when water levels drop, the fish become heavily concentrated in the canals that crisscross the Everglades.

Taylor Slough and the Shark River Slough are important freshwater supply routes to the park and provide good fishing. The headwaters of the Harney and Broad rivers are also good areas for bass and bream. Other popular freshwater fishing areas in the park include: Nine Mile Pond, Paurotis Pond, Ficus Pond, Pine Glades Lake, Sisal Pond, and Sweet Bay Pond, all accessible from the main park road. Boats with motors are not allowed on freshwater lakes and creeks. During the winter, particularly in February and March, the canals along the Tamiami Trail (U.S. 41) are loaded with spawning bass and bream.

A major source of the park's freshwater supply comes from three large conservation areas to the north of the park, known as Conservation Areas 1, 2, and 3. Within these three areas are three recreation areas, known as Loxahatchee Recreation Area (Area 1), Sawgrass Recreation Park (Area 2), and Everglades Holiday Park (Area 3). The three areas are similar to park freshwater areas with heavy sawgrass and numerous canals. They are also superb for bass fishing.

Further information on the three conservation areas is available by contacting: Public Information Office, South Florida Water Management District, 3301 Gun Club Road, P.O. Box 24680, West Palm Beach, FL, 33416-4680; phone: (407) 686-8800.

Saltwater Fishing

Snook, redfish, bonefish, sea trout, and tarpon are the mainstays of Everglades fishing. Numerous other species, including grouper, jack crevalle, mangrove snappers, and ladyfish, are prevalent throughout park waters.

The two major saltwater areas in the park are the Ten Thousand

One of nature's fishermen, an Anhinga snares a bluegill.—*National Park Service*

Islands area in the west and southwest and Florida Bay on the southern tip of Florida. The Florida Keys are just outside the park boundary but a large part of the Keys fishing water is in the park, so the Florida Keys are also discussed under Florida Bay.

Ten Thousand Islands The Ten Thousand Islands area can seem as remote as any area on earth. Everglades City is the starting point for excursions into the Ten Thousand Islands. Soon after leaving the dock in Everglades City, you are in a wilderness of numerous mangrove islands intersected by small creeks and narrow waterways. A guide is highly recommended for this area, not only to keep you from getting lost, but a guide's knowledge of tides, seasonal fish movements and locations, and lure preferences may spell the difference between success and failure.

Snook frequent the creeks and rivers around mangrove roots, underneath dense foliage, and along edges of the oyster bars near river mouths. Snook can be taken all year but the biggest are found in the spring and early summer. Snook are particularly sensitive to cold weather and move into the deeper holes and become concentrated during a cold front. After the cold moderates, they return to the shallow, mud-lined bays.

Tarpon also are found year-round in the Ten Thousand Islands area, although some periods are better than others. Small tarpon are always around the mangroves and deeper channels, but the large, migratory tarpon usually move into the creeks in March, April, and May. Creek mouths, passes, and outside channels are prime tarpon hangouts. After mid-June, most of the migratory tarpon have moved out. In the fall, smaller tarpon return to the creeks. Tarpon fishing is good from October until the water turns cold in December. During the fall, the tarpon are further back into the creeks than in the spring when the mouth areas of creeks are more productive.

Properly fishing the tides is important for taking both snook and tarpon. In the bays, the best time is from high tide through the start of the falling tide. As the tide drops, move into the channels and passes, since both snook and tarpon line up to feed on bait fish which are being swept out of the shallows. Creek junctions are natural fish holes because the bait fish move into these areas.

Other good spots are the deep holes in main channels where relatively shallow water drops off over rocky bottoms. Grouper and snapper will stack up to feed in these places on the outflow. Knowledge of these tides and fish holes enable good guides to earn their money.

Fishing for redfish is best from September to November. Redfish prefer the shallow mud flats of the numerous bays and sloughs, where they root in the bottom for small crustaceans. From January through March, school-size redfish are found around oyster bars, channel edges, runoffs, and outside rock points.

Redfish action slows in the spring but they can occasionally be found in the bays around oyster bars on a rising tide and at river points on a falling tide. Action picks up again in the summer and peaks in the fall. Although September and October are the best months, redfish can be found on the flats along the Gulf Coast from spring through fall.

Fishing for sea trout is best in March and April. Look for grassy bottom areas and fish the tide, starting outside and moving in as the water rises. At other times, sea trout are found with redfish on the shallow mud flats and in channels. During the late fall and winter months, sea trout will be concentrated over grass flats, but, like snook, will move into deeper water quickly when temperatures drop.

Finally, ladyfish and jack crevalle abound in nearly all the deep channels and river mouths.

Florida Bay Florida Bay is a shallow body of water between the tip of the mainland and the string of highway-connected islands known as the Florida Keys. The bay is dotted with hundreds of mangrove islands and is locally known as the "back country." The extensive sections of shallow water are known as "the flats" and contain some of the world's best fishing grounds for sea trout, redfish, snook, tarpon, permit, and bonefish.

Most of Florida Bay is within the park boundary. Flamingo and the Florida Keys are the access points. The town of Islamorada on Upper Matecumbe Key is a fishing center just outside the park.

Bonefish are available all year on the flats, but during winter cold spells they tend to move to deep water for several days. As the weather warms, bonefish action improves and is best from April through June.

In the spring, the outer areas of Florida Bay provide excellent fishing for mackerel and ladyfish. In April, the large migratory tarpon begin to appear and snook move into the back country and along the coastal sloughs and rivers of the Everglades. May and June are best for large tarpon, sea trout, and redfish, which are plentiful on the flats.

During July, August, and September, fishing is usually slow in the bay. The summer heat wears out most people and limits fishing to very early or very late in the day. Redfish commonly are found on the flats in the summer, and bonefish action there can also be good.

Excellent fishing is found in the bay throughout the fall months. October is the best month. Bonefish, permit, and redfish are on the flats. The first cold fronts occur during November. As the weather begins to chill, bonefish retreat from the back country flats toward the oceanside flats. As the weather changes, look for snook and redfish in potholes and grass banks on the flats around Flamingo. Offshore, southward of the Keys, heavy concentrations of cobia, mackerel, and tuna occur in December. December is also the peak month for sailfish from Islamorada to Key West.

License Freshwater and saltwater fishing require separate Florida licenses. Be sure to check the state and special park regulations along with the special bag limits. Some freshwater and saltwater areas are closed to fishing.

Camping The park has two major developed campgrounds, Long Pine Key (107 spaces) and Flamingo (300 spaces). Primitive campsites at a limited number of Keys in Florida Bay and the back country are accessible only by water. A camping permit is required at these primitive sites. For your safety, it is recommended that you file a float plan if you intend to boat in the park.

Maps The following nautical charts cover the Everglades National Park fishing areas and are available at most marinas and tackle shops in the area. Nautical chart #11430 covers Lostmans River to Wiggins Pass on the west side in the Ten Thousand Islands area; nautical chart #11432, for Shark River to Lostmans River; nautical chart #11433, Whitewater Bay near Flamingo; and nautical chart #11451 covers the area from Miami to Marathon and details the Flamingo and Florida Bay area including the Florida Keys.

Park Address
Everglades NP
P.O. Box 279
Homestead, FL 33030
Phone: (305) 247-6211

Chambers of Commerce
Everglades Area C.C.
P.O. Drawer 130
Everglades City, FL 33929
Phone: (813) 695-3941

Florida Upper Keys C.C.
103400 Overseas Highway
235
Key Largo, FL 33037
Phone: (305) 451-1414

Additional Information An inexpensive, paperback book, *Fishing in the Florida Keys and Flamingo,* by Stu Apte, covers in detail much of the park area and describes fishing techniques along with a wealth of information about tides, marinas, and guides. The book is available from: Windward Publishing Inc., P.O. Box 371005, Miami, FL, 33137; phone: (305) 576-6232.

Park Ranger William Truesdell has written *A Guide to the Wilderness Waterway*, which describes and maps the 100-mile inland water route in the park. Before setting out on the Wilderness Waterway you should obtain and study this book. It is available from: Everglades Natural History Association Inc., P.O. Box 279, Homestead, FL, 33030. Ask for their catalog of publications. They also sell nautical charts for the park.

Fish-locating charts, indicating prime fishing areas, are available from: Wixtrom Publishing Co., 5901 SW 74th St., Miami, FL, 33143; phone: (305) 661-4222. Chart #702 covers Florida Bay and the Upper Keys; Chart #704 covers Everglades National Park.

Fort Jefferson National Monument

Fort Jefferson is the largest all-masonry fortification in the Western world. It is in the Dry Tortugas Islands, 68 miles west of Key West. It was originally constructed (1846–1876) as part of a chain of seacoast defenses from Maine to Texas, but construction was never completed and the fort never saw action. It was used as a prison during and after the Civil War. Dr. Samuel Mudd, the doctor who treated John Wilkes Booth, was once imprisoned at the fort.

Access The fort is accessible only by boat (private or charter) or seaplane. The Key West Chamber of Commerce provides information on charter boats and flights.

Fishing Fort Jefferson and the Dry Tortugas host some of the best saltwater fishing in the U.S. The Dry Tortugas are a group of small, low islands with sparse vegetation, surrounded by miles of shoals and reefs that abound with barracuda, snapper, grouper, jack crevalle, amberjack, yellowtail, cobia, and king mackerel. A few flats also attract bonefish, tarpon, and permit when the water temperature reaches 66 degrees or above. Of the more than five hundred species of fish in the area, snapper (gray and yellowtail) are the fish most frequently caught.

After traveling the 68 miles from Key West to Fort Jefferson, a boat will be needed to fish in the area. You may wish to visit the area in your own boat, arrange to have a skiff towed over, or even pack an inflatable boat on the seaplane. Whatever the arrangement, remember that there aren't any fuel docks, stores, or fresh water in the Dry Tortugas. Everything must be brought with you and all trash must be carried out.

If boating over from Key West, it is essential to pay close attention to the weather. A good radio is mandatory. January through March are months to avoid because of frequent cold fronts and high winds. The weather for this trip is best during May through October.

It is also practical to carry ample fuel for the round trip and fishing. Your boat should be powered by twin engines just in case one engine quits. If you don't have a boat, guides and multiple-day trips can be arranged from charter boat operators out of Key West.

Once there, you rarely see other groups fishing. The Tortugas do not receive much fishing pressure and fishing is consistently good throughout the area. Within a mile of the fort is enough good water to keep anyone content. Fishing can really be exciting with only light tackle or even fly rods.

License A saltwater fishing license is required.

Camping Camping is permitted in the grassed picnic area near the fort. There are no accommodations in the park itself. Remember, all food, water, and supplies must be brought from the mainland.

Maps If you are piloting a boat, nautical charts #11434 and #11438 are indispensible for safe boating from Key West to the Dry Tortugas. Chart #11434 is used for navigation from Key West, while chart #11438 details the monument area. The park brochure map points out good fishing areas and good scuba diving areas.

Park Address
Fort Jefferson NM
c/o U.S.C.G. Base
Key West, FL 33040
Phone: (305) 247-6211

Chamber of Commerce
Greater Key West C.C.
402 Wall St.
P.O. Box 984
Key West, FL 33040
phone: (305) 294-2587

Fort Matanzas National Monument

Fort Matanzas was built by the Spanish during 1740–1742 to keep the British from controlling Matanzas Inlet. The British regarded the inlet as the key to capturing the city of St. Augustine, to the north.

Access The park is on the northeast coast of Florida (St. Johns County), 14 miles south of St. Augustine via Florida Highway A1A.

Fishing Saltwater fishing is available on the Matanzas River at the Matanzas Inlet, and in the Atlantic Ocean off Anastasia Island. A variety of fish are caught all year in the river and the ocean, including bluefish, flounder, red and black drum, whiting, croaker, grunt, sheepshead, and sea trout. A few tarpon are taken when the water warms above 66 degrees.

Large red and black drum are taken around the inlet from late February into early May. The best times for flounder are early spring and early fall. Grunts (also known as pigfish) are plentiful but not avidly sought. They are common in estuaries, inlets, and along ocean beaches. Sheepshead hang around rock walls and jetties and are caught right along the fort walls.

Small croaker are taken all year in the Matanzas River. Larger croaker move inshore during the spring when the waters warm. Sea trout are prevalent throughout the river and the Intracoastal Waterway.

License A saltwater license is required. Be sure to check the special Florida regulations.

Camping No camping is available in the park. However, Anastasia State Park, just south of St. Augustine, permits camping.

Maps To navigate this section of the Matanzas River, which is part of the

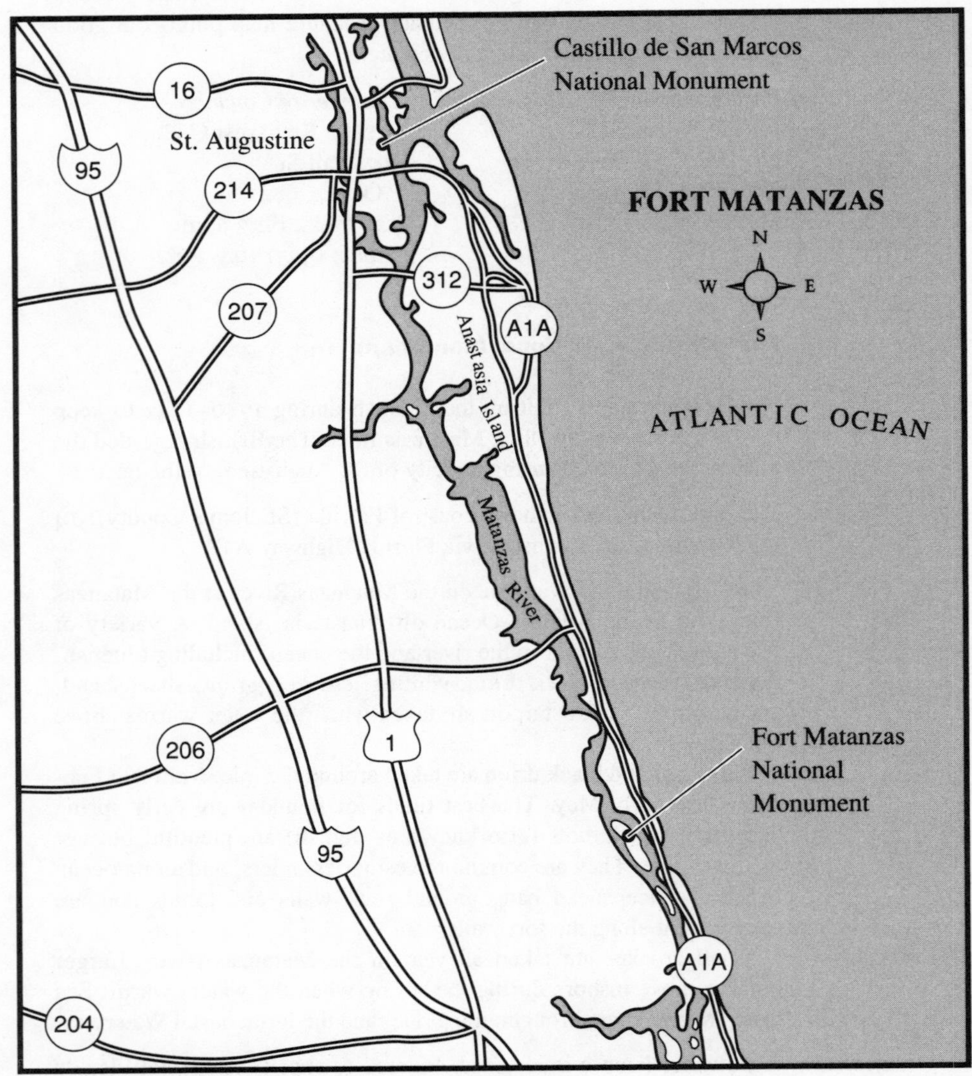
Castillo de San Marcos
National Monument
16
St. Augustine
95
214
FORT MATANZAS
N
W
E
S
312
207
A1A
Anastasia Island
ATLANTIC OCEAN
Matanzas River
1
206
Fort Matanzas
National
Monument
95
A1A
204

Intracoastal Waterway, requires nautical chart #11485. For offshore fishing, you will need nautical chart #11486.

Park Address
Fort Matanzas NM
c/o Castillo De San Marcos NM
1 Castillo Dr.
St. Augustine, FL 32084
phone: (904) 471-0116

Chamber of Commerce
St.Augustine-St.Johns County C.C.
P.O. Drawer 0
St. Augustine, FL 32085
phone: (904) 829-5681

Gulf Islands National Seashore

Gulf Islands National Seashore is a 150-mile-long string of offshore islands and keys stretching intermittently from Fort Walton Beach, Florida, to Gulfport, Mississippi, in the Gulf of Mexico. The park consists of separate units in Florida and Mississippi. The Mississippi unit includes Davis Bayou on the mainland and Ship, Petit Bois, and Horn islands offshore in Mississippi Sound. The Florida area is comprised of Santa Rosa Island, three historic forts in the Pensacola Naval Air Station, Perdido Key, and the Naval Live Oaks Plantation.

Access The seashore is on the southeast coast of Mississippi and the northwest coast of Florida, in the Gulf of Mexico. In Mississippi, the mainland section at Ocean Springs is reached via Park Road off U.S. 90, but the offshore islands are reached only by boat.

The Florida sections of the park are near Pensacola and Fort Walton Beach and are accessible by car. The park brochure contains complete details for reaching each park section in both states.

Fishing Fishing is big business along the Gulf Coast and is one of the many attractions at the park. Surf fishing, pier and bridge fishing, and offshore fishing are possible in the various sections of the park.

The Gulf of Mexico, Mississippi Sound, Pensacola Bay, and Santa Rosa Sound are the main fishing areas, hosting a wide variety of saltwater fish. Bluefish, pompano, cobia, and king mackerel predominate in the Gulf, while sea trout (spotted and white), flounder, whiting, croaker, and channel bass (redfish or red drum) are prevalent in the bay and sounds.

Fishing is a year-round activity in the Gulf of Mexico but the best and most comfortable months are from April into November. The northern Gulf Coast is subject to winter cold fronts that discourage most fishermen and send the fish seeking shelter from high winds and rough waters.

Channel bass, spotted sea trout, and white trout are found near

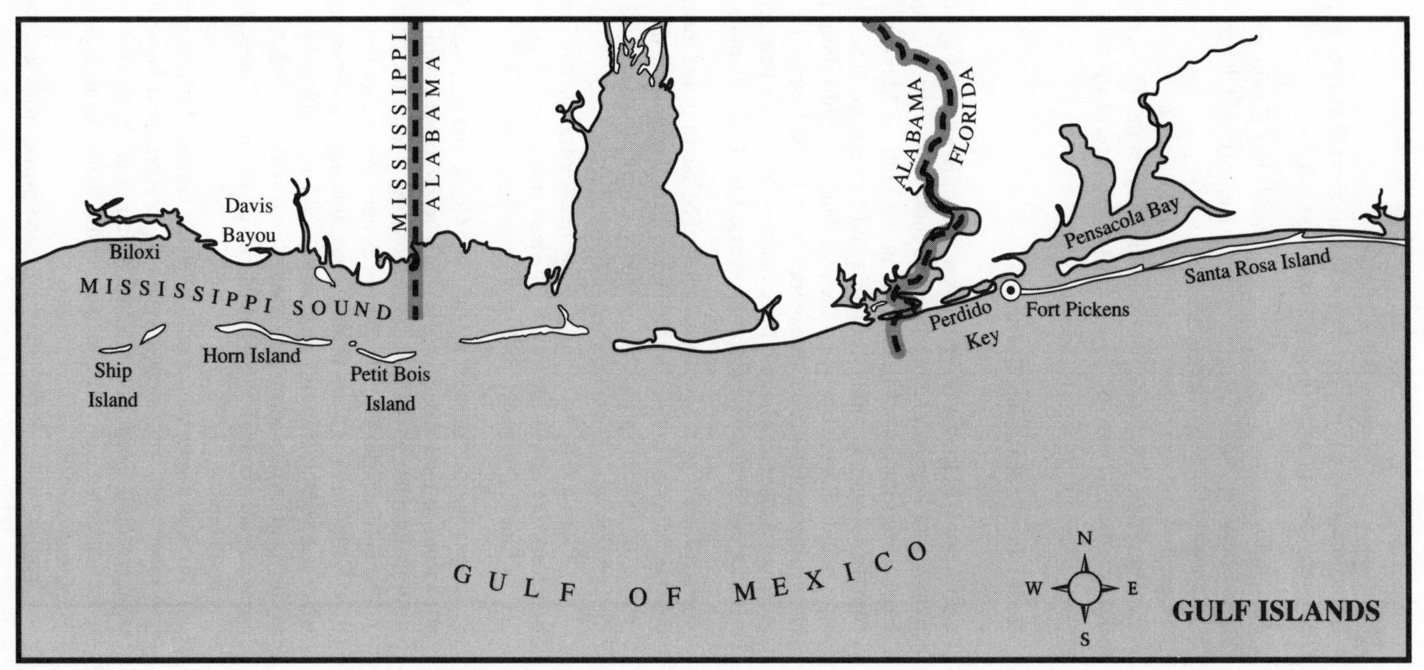
MISSISSIPPI
ALABAMA
ALABAMA
FLORIDA
Davis
Bayou
Biloxi
Pensacola Bay
Santa Rosa Island
MISSISSIPPI SOUND
Perdido
Key
Fort Pickens
Ship
Island
Horn Island
Petit Bois
Island
N
W
E
S
GULF OF MEXICO
GULF ISLANDS

shore and around the islands throughout the year. The peak fishing period is from mid-April to mid-June for trout and again in the fall when trout and channel bass move into the tidal rivers and creeks. In the summer, look for trout on the grass flats. Hordes of Spanish mackerel start migrating in March and can be caught in the surf but are heavily concentrated off the eastern end of Horn Island.

Cobia usually arrive with the Spanish mackerel in the spring. King mackerel are probably the most popular offshore species and are most plentiful in the Gulf from July through October. Fishing for both Spanish and king mackerel is very good around the artificial reefs constructed by the Mississippi Game and Fish Commission. The construction of these reefs has helped maintain productive fishing in the Gulf.

Starting in June, offshore trolling for marlin and sailfish attracts folks who want to fish for big game. October is one of the best months for marlin and sailfish as they move closer toward shore and remain until the cool water drives them south. Shore fishing from the bridges and piers usually yields croaker, trout, whiting, and channel bass.

Fishing charters and guides are found all along the Gulf Coast and current fishing information is readily available at the local tackle-and-bait shops. Excursion boats out of Gulfport and Biloxi, Mississippi, make regular trips to Ship Island where surf and shore fishing is usually good. These excursion boats are not fishing boats, but they will take you to the island at a very reasonable price.

License A saltwater fishing license is required in Florida but not in Mississippi.

Camping Developed campgrounds are available in Mississippi at Davis Bayou (51 spaces) and in Florida at Fort Pickens (200 spaces) on Santa Rosa Island. Primitive camping on the three Mississippi islands is another possibility.

Maps The park brochure map is good at showing access points and boat ramps. Fishing offshore will require nautical charts #11373 (Mississippi), and #11382 (Florida), or small craft charts 874-SC and 876-SC in Mississippi and 872-SC in Florida. There is also a very good chart, "Mississippi Sound and Approaches," available locally in Mississippi.

Park Address

Gulf Islands NS
P.O. Box 100
Gulf Breeze, FL 32561
phone: (904) 932-6316

Gulf Islands NS
3500 Park Road
Ocean Springs, MS 39564
phone: (601) 875-9057

Chambers of Commerce

Greater Gulf Breeze Area C.C.
P.O. Box 337
Gulf Breeze, FL 32561
phone: (904) 932-7888

Biloxi C.C.
Box 1928
Biloxi, MS, 39533
phone: (601) 374-2717

Greater Fort Walton Beach C.C.
34 Miracle Strip Pkwy. S.E.
Fort Walton Beach, FL 32548
phone: (904) 244-8191

Gulfport Area C.C.
1401 20th Ave.
P.O. Box FF
Gulfport, MS 39502
phone: (601) 863-2933

Pensacola Area C.C.
P.O. Box 550
Pensacola, FL 32593-0550
phone: (904) 438-4081

Ocean Springs C.C.
P.O. Box 187
Ocean Springs, MS 39564
phone: (601) 875-4424

Additional Information

For a detailed month-by-month description of saltwater fishing in northwest Florida, write for a copy of *Florida Saltwater Sportfishing* from: Florida Department of Natural Resources, Douglas Bldg., 3900 Commonwealth Blvd., Tallahassee, FL, 32303; phone: (904) 487-3122.

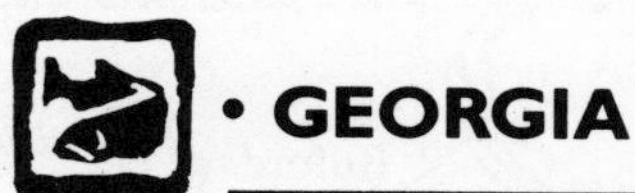

• GEORGIA

Chattahoochee River National Recreation Area

Established in 1978, Chattahoochee River NRA is a string of parklands along a 48-mile stretch of the Chattahoochee River. The park begins at Buford Dam, which forms Lake Sidney Lanier, and extends downstream to Atlanta, where the Chattahoochee acts as the city's northwestern boundary. The park receives intensive recreational use from the heavily populated Atlanta area. Canoeing, rafting, fishing, hiking, and picnicking are all popular activities in the park.

Access The river is accessible from a number of state and county roads that cross or parallel it as it flows through parts of Gwinnett, Forsyth, Fulton, and Cobb counties.

Fishing Trout fishing is a major attraction in the park. The entire 48-mile stretch of the Chattahoochee River in the park contains trout. Originally, this area did not hold trout. The cold water releases during power generation periods at Buford Dam, however, have made a viable trout fishery possible. Because of fluctuating water levels, people fishing here must always exercise caution because of the possibility of rising water. Trips should be planned to coincide with low-water periods, since those are the only times the river can be safely waded and fished. Normally, weekday mornings and weekend afternoons are low-water periods.

The low temperature of the water released from the dam, the favorable pool-to-riffle ratio, and an abundance of food makes for good trout habitat. However, there is virtually no trout reproduction in this section of the river because of heavy fishing pressure and the lack of suitable spawning habitat. Brook, brown, and rainbow trout are stocked annually by the state between Buford Dam and Peachtree Creek. As a consequence, all the trout caught are stocked fish. Typical of tail-water trout, they grow rapidly and reach trophy size in a relatively short time. Most trout average 11 to 13 inches, but many over 5 pounds are taken, even within the Atlanta city limits.

The Chattahoochee is "big water" in fishing lingo. It can be either floated or waded. If waded, felt soles or studs are recommended because the bottom is slick.

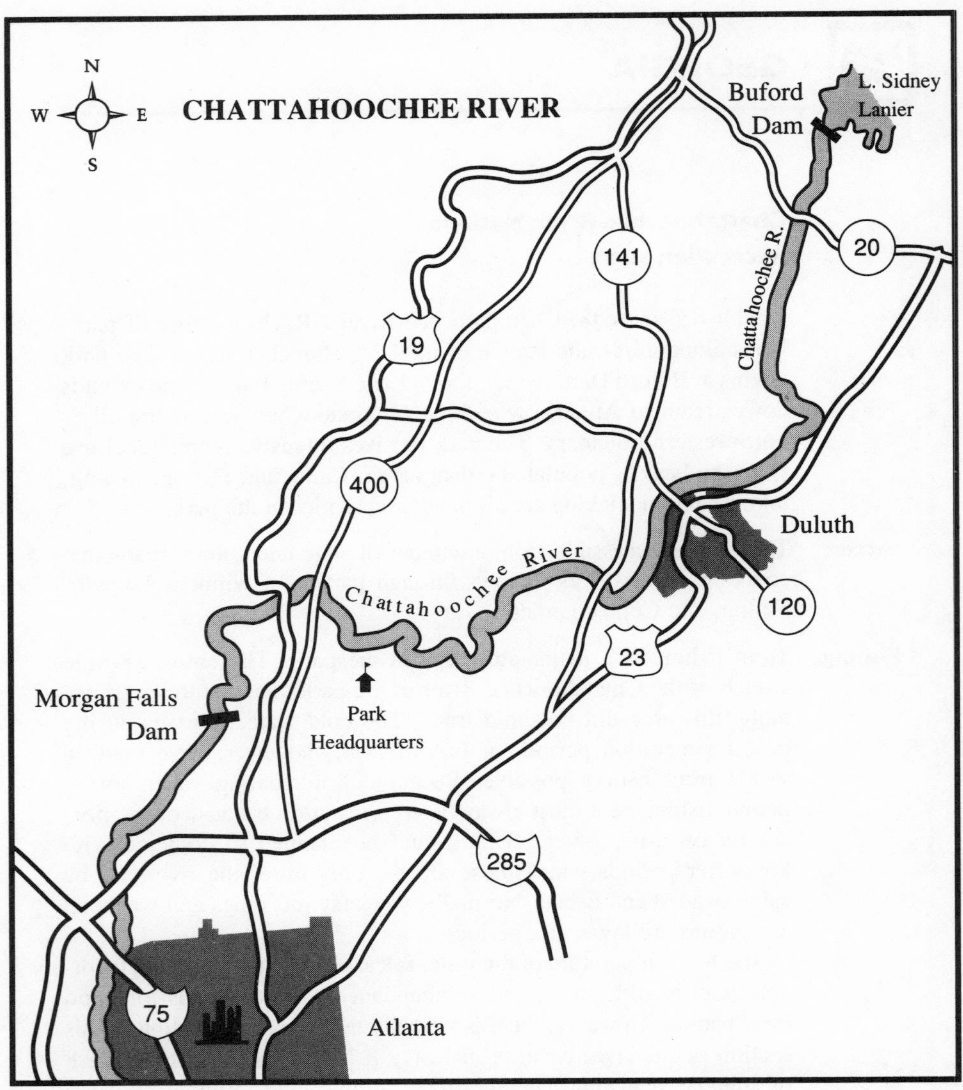

Fly-fishing or spin-fishing are the usual methods for catching trout. Most of the big trout are caught on spinners or lures imitating a bait fish or small trout. Float fishing with spinning gear is one of the more effective and popular ways of fishing on the Chattahoochee.

Fly-fishing can go quite well on the river. The shoal and riffle areas support many aquatic insects, including large caddis popula-

Trout are stocked regularly in the Chattahoochee River. Most trout average 11 to 13 inches. This nice brown is 15 inches.—*John Fiorini*

tions, especially the *Hydropsyche caddis*. Trout feed heavily on the green-bodied larvae of this insect.

Early in the year (late February to mid-April) large stoneflies occur in great quantity. Other species of caddis, mayflies, and midges hatch all year-round. Standard patterns to try are Adams, Royal Wulff and Light Cahill (dry flies), along with caddis pupa, stonefly, and the Gold-Ribbed Hares Ear (nymphs).

Terrestrials are important in the summer, particularly along river stretches with a sandy bottom that do not provide good habitat for aquatic insects. Japanese beetles are common along the river at times, but most properly presented terrestrial patterns produce.

Trout season runs from the last Saturday in March through October on most of the river. However, the 12-mile stretch from Morgan Falls Dam downstream to the Atlanta and Cobb County sewage treatment plant near Marietta Boulevard is open all year.

Some largemouth bass, bluegills, yellow perch, catfish, and crappie are also caught in the river, in addition to trout. These warm-water fish come from Lake Sidney Lanier and enter the river during water releases at Buford Dam. These fish cannot spawn in the cold water of the Chattahoochee, but they still provide a substantial fishery.

License A Georgia fishing license is required.

Camping There are no campground facilities in the park at this time. Primitive camping is possible along the river during overnight float trips. Camping permits are required for such trips. Apply to the park well in advance of the proposed trip.

Maps The park brochure map is excellent. It identifies private property to help assure that visitors do not trespass. This map also lists public access points and the distance and float time between points. Topographic maps are not needed.

Park Address
Chattahoochee River NRA
1978 Island Ford Parkway
Dunwoody, GA 30350
phone: (404) 394-7912

Chamber of Commerce
Georgia Dept. of Industry and Trade
Tourist Division
P.O. Box 1776
Atlanta, GA 30301
phone: (404) 656-3590

Additional Information You would be wise to check flow conditions before planning a trip to the Chattahoochee. Daily hours of generation at Buford Dam can be obtained by calling (404) 945-1466.

The Flint River Chapter of Trout Unlimited has published *The Georgia Trout Guide,* Vol.2, with four pages devoted to the Chattahoochee tail water, plus descriptions of numerous other Georgia trout waters. This book is available for $4.95 postpaid from: Flint River Chapter TU, P.O. Box 90204, East Point, GA, 30364.

Cumberland Island National Seashore

Cumberland Island was added to the park system in 1972 to preserve the unspoiled beaches, dunes, and marshes of the largest and most southerly island off the coast of Georgia. Most of the island is still in its natural condition. It was formerly a retreat for wealthy families and some individuals remain as year-round residents.

Access The island is in southeastern Georgia (Camden County). Access is by a National Park Service passenger ferry from St. Marys, Georgia. To reach St. Marys, take Georgia Highway 40 east from Interstate 95 near Kingsland. Cars cannot be ferried to the island; the only cars on the island are owned by a few residents, so once you arrive, you must depend on your feet. The park brochure contains the ferry schedule.

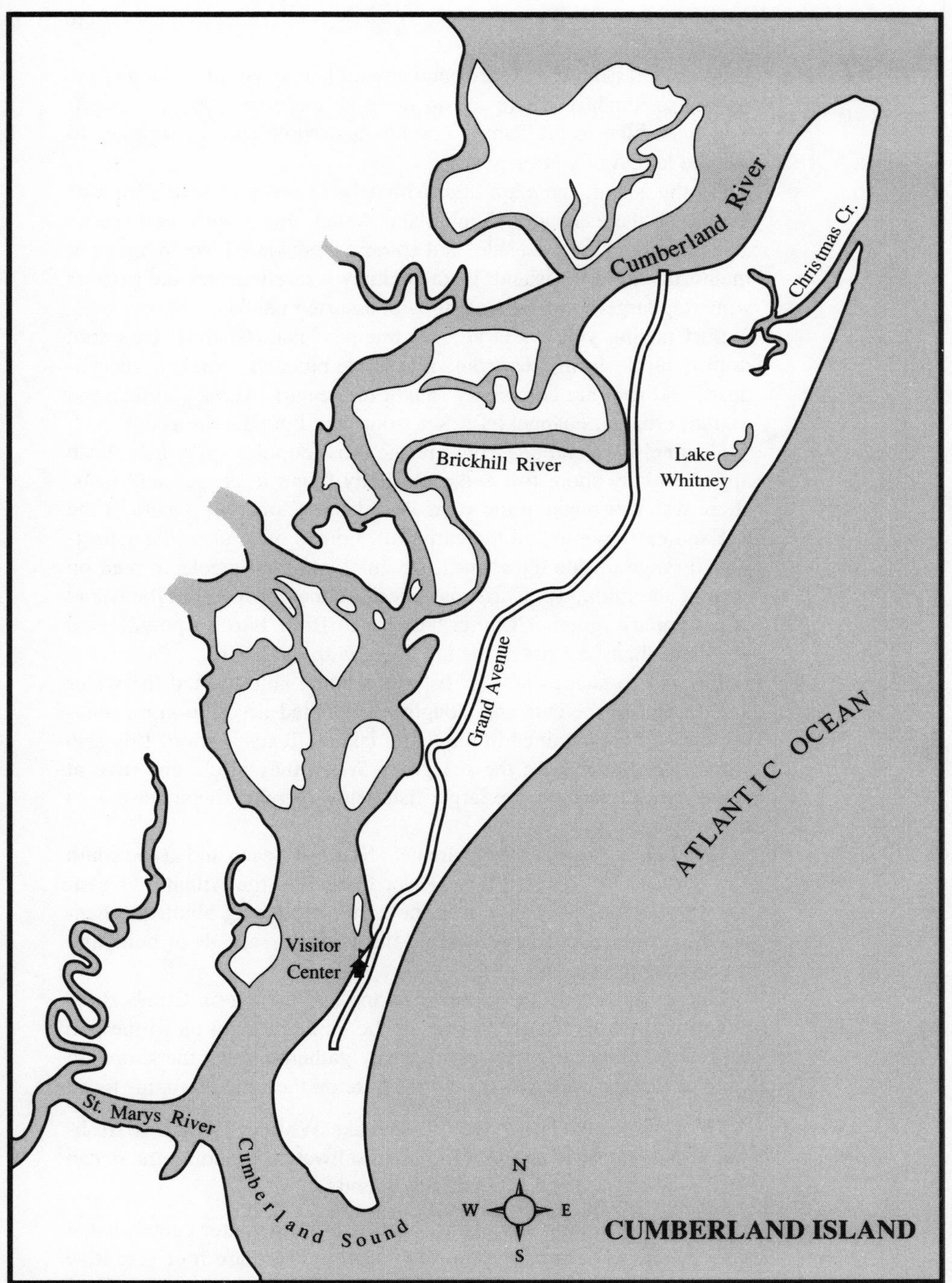
Cumberland River
Christmas Cr.
Brickhill River
Lake Whitney
Grand Avenue
ATLANTIC OCEAN
Visitor Center
St. Marys River
Cumberland Sound
N
W
E
S
CUMBERLAND ISLAND

Fishing Cumberland Island is a year-round coastal fishing paradise for anyone willing to rough it. There are no stores or motorized transportation. You must hike to the fishing grounds and carry enough supplies to last the length of your stay.

On the island, there are approximately 18 miles of beach for surf fishing on the east side, Cumberland Sound, along with tidal creeks and streams on the west side, and 40-acre freshwater Lake Whitney at the north end of the island. Lake Whitney is rarely fished and harbors some big largemouth bass along with assorted panfish.

Surf fishing yields a large assortment of fish. Channel bass (red drum), black drum, sea trout, mackerel, bluefish, croaker, sheepshead, and spot are commonly caught in the surf. Along Cumberland Sound, croaker, channel bass, sea trout, and flounder are taken.

Channel bass and sea trout are the most popular sport fish. Both are essentially shore fish and are usually found in coastal and nearshore water throughout the year. Peak fishing for trout occurs in the fall and early winter. In the early fall, hordes of trout in the 1-to-3-pound range invade the sounds, streams, and tidal creeks to feed on shrimp and minnows. Christmas Creek on the north end of the island is particularly good. Channel bass range from 1 to 40 pounds and also have their best run in the fall along with the trout.

The key to successful surf fishing is being able to read the water and recognize the cuts and sloughs. A detailed description on reading the surf is contained in the Padre Island, Texas section. It is also worthwhile to observe the sea gulls. When they circle and dive at small fish, often there are larger fish below, driving the small fish to the surface.

Good areas for surf fishing are near Stafford Beach and at the south end jetty where the St. Marys River flows into the Atlantic Ocean. The tidal pools in both areas are noted for producing bluefish, channel bass, trout, and sheepshead. In the summer, schools of pompano cruise near the beach.

One of the attractions of backpacking and fishing on Cumberland Island is the opportunity to live off the land. In addition to the fish you catch, clams and oysters are easily gathered along the shore. In spite of these attractions, fishing pressure on the island remains light.

License A Georgia license is needed to fish Lake Whitney, which is freshwater. No license is required to fish in saltwater, including the ocean surf, tidal creeks, and Cumberland Sound.

Camping Sea Camp Beach (16 spaces) near the Sea Camp visitor center, is the only developed campground on the island. There are four primitive campsites on the island. Back-country camping permits are required and may be obtained at the island visitor centers.

Maps Topographic maps aren't necessary. The park brochure map combined with the hiking-trail map from the park is enough. Offshore boating and fishing requires nautical chart #11502.

For fishing, it is advisable to obtain a copy of the *Guide to Coastal Fishing in Georgia, Camden County.* This detailed map and guide identifies fishing locations, species, fish camps, and much more. The map is available for $1 from: University of Georgia, Marine Extension Station, P.O. Box Z, Brunswick, GA, 31523; phone: (912) 264-7268.

Park Address
Cumberland Island NS
P.O. Box 806
St. Marys, GA 31558
phone: (912) 882-4337

Chamber of Commerce
Brunswick–Golden Isles C.C.
4 Glynn Avenue
Brunswick, GA 31520
phone: (912) 265-0620

Fort Frederica National Monument

Fort Frederica was built by British General James Oglethorpe in 1736–1748 during the Anglo-Spanish struggle for control of southeastern coastal lands. Oglethorpe scored a decisive victory over a Spanish invasion force in 1742.

Access The fort is in southeastern Georgia on St. Simons Island (Glynn County), 12 miles northeast of Brunswick via the Brunswick–St. Simons toll causeway.

Fishing Fishing is the park is limited to a short stretch of the Frederica River on the western boundary. Spotted sea trout, flounder, mullet, drum, and spot-tail bass are the usual fare from the river. Fishing pressure in the park is light, with most people fishing in the fall when the spotted sea trout are abundant in the river.

The spotted sea trout is the most popular game fish in the area. Its wide distribution in protected creeks and small tidal rivers make it available for fishing with smaller boats that are unable to navigate the periodic rough water in the open sounds.

Fishing the Frederica River is definitely worthwhile, but access from the park can be difficult. The park riverbank has been stabilized by filling eroded sections with sand and peat and planting marsh grasses. The grasses may impede the retrieval of lines and lures.

License No fishing license is required, but Georgia regulations apply.

Camping There are no camping facilities at the park. Jekyll Island State Park

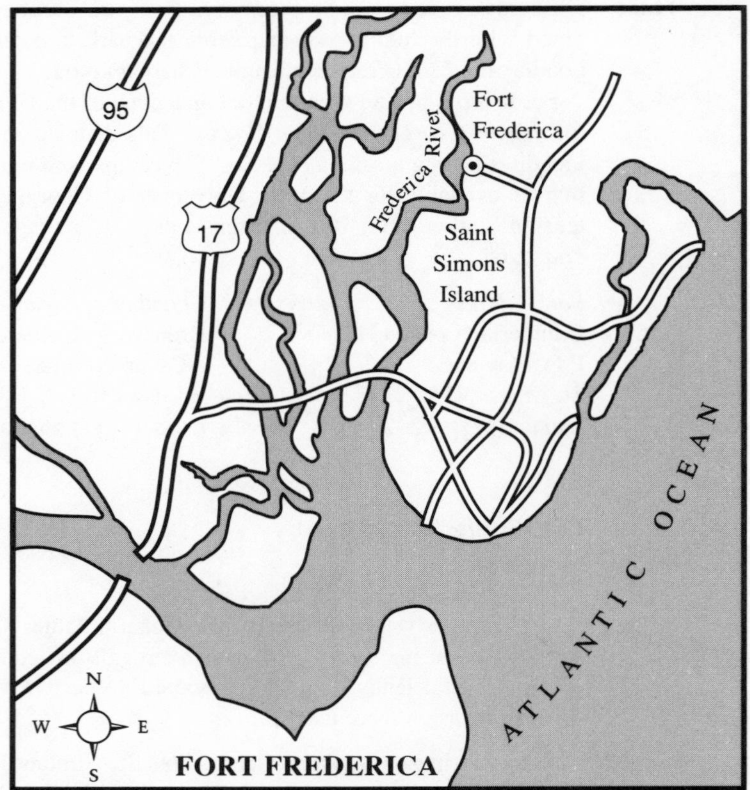

offers camping about 13 miles southeast of Brunswick via Georgia Highway 50.

Maps Nautical chart #11507 is part of the series for the Intracoastal Waterway and includes the area around St. Simons Island.

Park Address	*Chamber of Commerce*
Fort Frederica NM	Brunswick–Golden Isles C.C.
Route 4, Box 286-C	4 Glynn Avenue
St. Simons Island, GA 31522	Brunswick, GA 31520
phone: (912) 638-3639	phone: (912) 265-0620

Additional Information The Georgia Sea Grant College Program and the University of Georgia Marine and Extension Service have prepared a series of fishing guides and maps for Georgia's coast. The guides list marina locations and facilities, public ramps, piers, fishing methods, and more. The cost is $1 per guide for postage and handling from: University of Georgia, Marine Extension Service, P.O. Box Z, Brunswick, GA, 31523; phone: (912) 264-7268. Ask for the *Guide to Coastal Fishing in Georgia, Glynn County.*

Fort Pulaski National Monument

Fort Pulaski is a massive masonry fort surrounded by a moat. The fort was built (1829–1847) as part of a coastal defense system begun after the War of 1812. During the Civil War, the fort was considered invulnerable by the Confederates, but it was easily captured by the Union Army with the help of a new weapon, the rifled cannon.

Access The fort is in southeastern Georgia (Chatham County) on Cockspur Island at the mouth of the Savannah River. It is 17 miles east of Savannah via U.S. 80.

Fishing The park is on the end of Cockspur Island with the north channel of the Savannah River on the north, the south channel on the south, and Savannah Sound on the east. Bank fishing in the Savannah River is popular for spotted sea trout, kingfish, croaker, sheepshead, drum, and spot-tail bass. There are also boat ramps in the area for access to the waters of McQueens Island, which is also part of the park. This area of the Georgia coast is a labyrinth of estuaries, creeks, rivers, sounds, and bays with good fishing all along the coast.

The sea trout are found all year throughout the area, with spring and fall the peak seasons. In the spring, the lower reaches of the large rivers and the open sounds are very good. Live shrimp fished off the bottom near rock jetties, submerged sand bars, and oyster-shell beds is usually productive.

From mid-September to late December, schools of sea trout migrate up the tidal rivers and creeks. By late fall, the fish are concentrated in relatively shallow creeks and rivers and are very aggressive. Most are in the 1-to-2-pound range, but fish up to 4 pounds are not uncommon.

License No fishing license is required but Georgia regulations apply.

Camping There are no camping facilities in the park. Skidaway Island State Park, southeast of Savannah, has a campground. Limited camping is also available at private campgrounds on Tybee Island, 4 miles east of the park.

Maps Nautical chart #11512 is needed to navigate the area, including Savannah Sound.

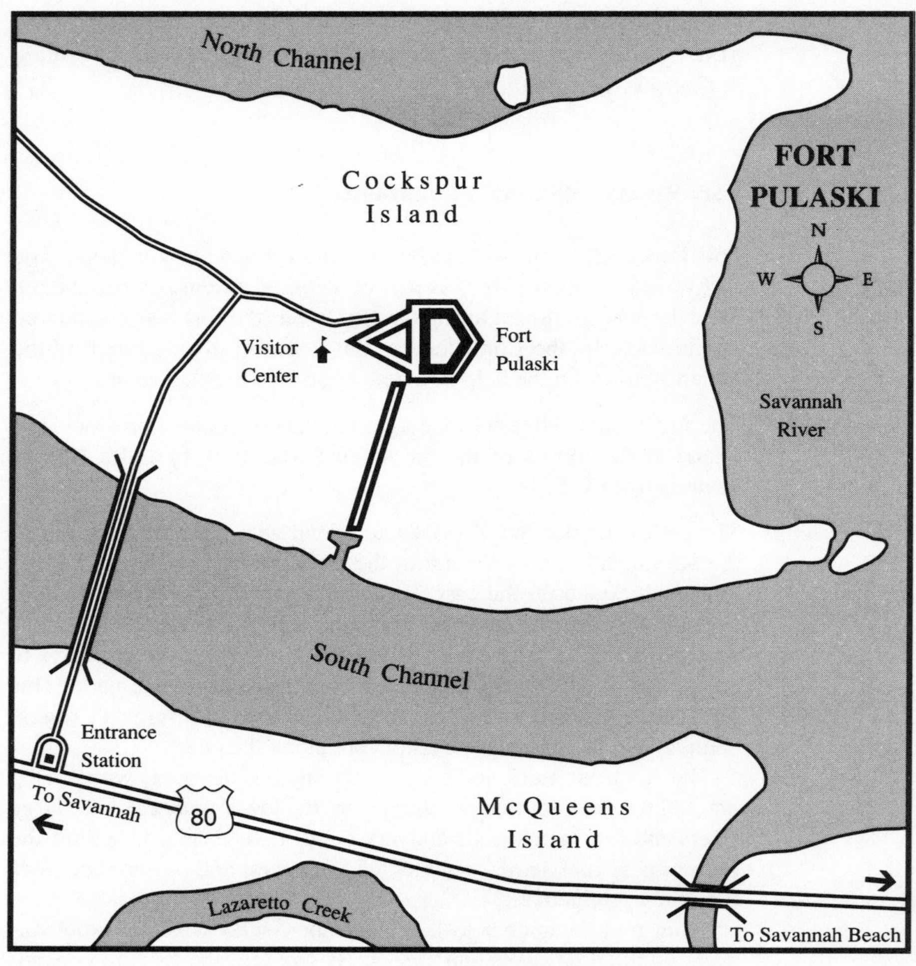

Park Address	*Chamber of Commerce*
Fort Pulaski NM	Savannah Area C.C.
P.O. Box 98	222 W. Oglethorpe Ave.
Tybee Island, GA 31328	Savannah, GA 31499
phone: (912) 786-5787	phone: (912) 944-0444

Additional Information Excellent county fishing maps and guides of the Georgia coast are available for $1 from: University of Georgia, Marine Extension Station, Box Z, Brunswick, GA, 31523; phone: (912) 264-7268. Ask for the *Guide to Coastal Fishing in Georgia, Chatham County.*

Ocmulgee National Monument

Ocmulgee National Monument, in central Georgia near Macon, was established to preserve the traces of the cultural evolution of southeastern Indian civilizations and includes the remains of large Indian ceremonial mounds. Traces of ten thousand years of Indian history up to the Creek Indians of the 18th century are preserved at Ocmulgee.

Access The monument is situated on the east edge of Macon (in Bibb County). Main access is from Interstate 16 east off Interstate 75. Take the first or second exit off Interstate 16 and follow the signs approximately a mile to the park entrance.

Fishing There are three bodies of water in the monument: the Ocmulgee

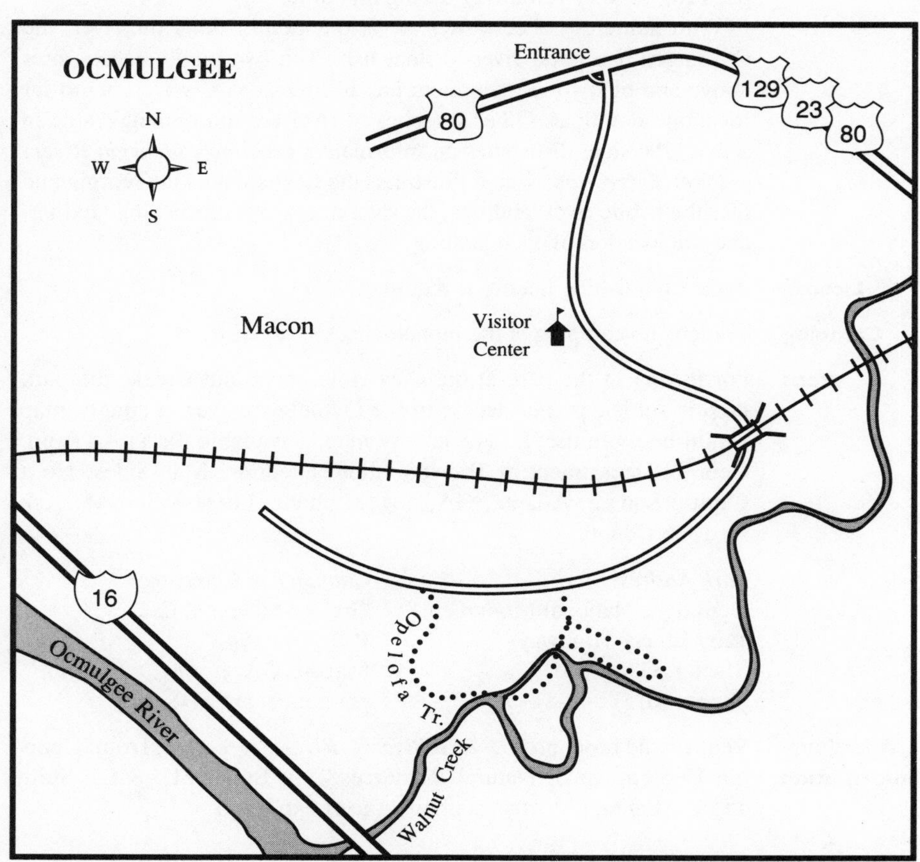

River, Walnut Creek, and a small pond near the Opelofa Nature Trail known as the Clay Hole. The Clay Hole contains bluegill and crappie. Largemouth bass and bluegill are the main species in Walnut Creek. The Ocmulgee River is accessible from the park by a trail, but heavy undergrowth along the river makes casting and fishing difficult.

The Ocmulgee River is one of the many large rivers in Georgia featuring good fishing for big largemouth bass. The section of river near Macon is especially noted for large bass. The river also ranks high for channel catfish. Fishing is also good for bluegill, white perch, and other panfish collectively known in the South as bream.

Spring fishing can be productive but the river is usually muddy in spring and the turbidity can be troublesome. Throughout the year, the shoal areas and backwaters are good. Bass fishing is best in the late summer and fall when the water is clearer. A fly rod and some bass bugs can be very rewarding during this time.

With numerous access sites at various points along the river, the Ocmulgee is a good river to float fish. The two public access sites above and below the monument are 28 miles apart, which is too far for a one-day float. Other stretches of river are more manageable in a day. The state distributes an informative brochure, *Georgia Rivers —River Recreation,* which illustrates the float streams in Georgia and lists the public river landings, the river miles to the following landing, and the location of each landing.

License A Georgia fishing license is required.

Camping There is no camping at the monument.

Maps For fishing in the park at the Clay Hole or Walnut Creek, the park map is sufficient. For access to the Ocmulgee River, a county map would be more useful. The county map is available for $1.50 from: Georgia Department of Transportation, attention: Map Sales, No.2 Capitol Square, Atlanta, GA, 30334; phone: (404) 656-5336. Ask for Bibb County.

Park Address
Ocmulgee National Monument
1207 Emery Highway
Macon, GA 31201
phone: (912) 752-8257

Chamber of Commerce
Greater Macon C.C.
P.O. Box 169
Macon, GA 31298
phone: (912) 741-8000

Additional Information Request the brochure *Georgia Rivers—River Recreation,* from: Georgia Department of Natural Resources, 205 Butler St., S.E., Suite 1258, Atlanta, GA 30334; phone: (404) 656-3530.

HAWAII

Hawaii is comprised of five major islands. From east to west, they are: Hawaii, Maui, Molokai, Oahu, and Kauai. The state takes its name from Hawaii, the largest of the islands.

The National Park Service manages four parks in Hawaii. Three are on the island of Hawaii: Hawaii Volcanoes National Park; Puukohola Heiau National Historic Site; and Pu'uhonua O Honaunau National Historical Park. The final park, Haleakala National Park, is located on the island of Maui.

None of the four parks feature sport fishing. There are no freshwater streams or ponds that contain fish, and neither Hawaii Volcanoes nor Haleakala has ocean frontage considered safe for fishing. Only Puukohola Heiau and Pu'uhonua O Honaunau have ocean frontage suitable for fishing. Pu'uhonua O Honaunau is considered a good place to fish because it offers access to the beach in an area where access is very limited. Most sport fishing in Hawaii takes place offshore in charters or via beach access at places other than the parks.

For offshore fishing, charters are available from all five of the islands. For charter information, contact: Hawaii Visitors Bureau, P.O. Box 8527, Honolulu, HI, 96815; phone: (808) 923-1811.

Pu'uhonau O Honaunau National Historical Park

Pu'uhonua O Honaunau means "place of refuge of Honaunau." The area was a sanctuary for Hawaiian tribes. Defeated warriors, *kapu* (taboo) breakers, or battle noncombatants escaped death by reaching the refuge ahead of their pursuers. A ceremony of absolution was performed by the *kahuna pule* (priest) and the offender could then return home safely without fear of reprisal.

Access The park is in the southwest section of the island of Hawaii, approximately 20 miles south of Kailua-Kona via Highway 11 to west Route 16.

Fishing Fishing is popular at the park because access is limited along other parts of the southwest coast. Fishing is best in the summer and fish-

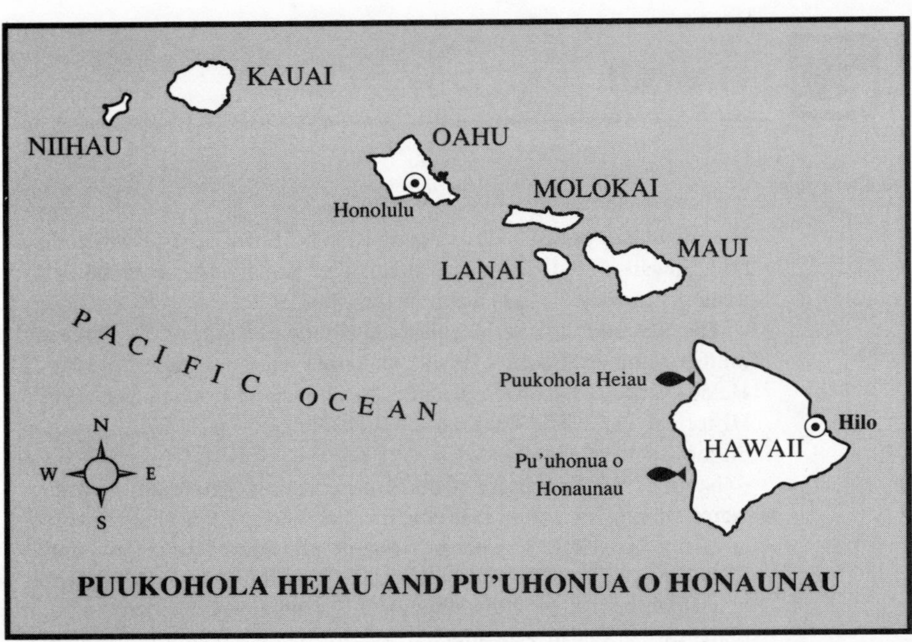

ing pressure can be heavy. The catch is usually *papio* (young jacks), *manini* (convict tang), *hinalea* (wrasse), and an occasional *kahala* (amberjack). Offshore charters are available at Kailua-Kona or Keauhau for *ahi* (yellowfin tuna), marlin, snapper, *opelu* (mackerel scad), and *ono* (wahoo).

License No license is required for fishing from shore within the park boundary; however, state fishing regulations are enforced by park rangers.

Camping No camping is provided in the park.

Maps Not needed. Offshore fishing requires nautical chart #19320.

Park Address
Pu'uhonua O Honaunau NHP
P.O. Box 129
Honaunau, Kona, HI 96726
phone: (808) 328-2326

Chamber of Commerce
Kona-Kohala C.C.
75-5737 Kaukini Hwy. #206
Kona, HI 96740
phone: (808) 329-1758

Puukohola Heiau National Historic Site

Puukohola Heiau was established in 1972 to preserve the remains of the last major temple of the ancient Hawaiian culture.

Access The park is on the northwestern part of the island of Hawaii and is 12 miles from Waimea-Kohala via State Route 27.

Fishing Both the historic site and Samuel Spencer County Park (immediately south of the historic site) are located on the protected side of the island (Kona Coast) where the fishing is good all year but best in the summer. The county park provides better access to the ocean than does the historic site.

Fishing from shore is mainly for *papio* (young jacks), *manini* (convict tang), or *weke* (spot goatfish), which swarm in shallow sandy areas during the summer. The *akule* (mackerel bigeye scad) is a popular fish that can be caught close to shore from July to December.

Offshore charters are available at Kawaihae for marlin, *ahi* (yellowfin tuna), dolphin, and *ono* (wahoo).

License A state fishing license is required. Check state regulations regarding size limits and equipment.

Camping No camping is available in the park. Camping is provided at nearby Samuel Spencer County Park.

Maps Not needed. Offshore fishing requires nautical chart #19327 or #19320, which covers the entire island of Hawaii.

Park Address
Puukohola Heiau NHS
P.O. Box 4963
Kawaihae, HI 96743
phone: (808) 882-7218

Chamber of Commerce
Hawaii Island C.C.
180 Kinoole St. # 18
Hilo, HI 96720
phone: (808) 935-7178

INDIANA

Indiana Dunes National Lakeshore

Located along the southern shore of Lake Michigan between Gary and Michigan City, Indiana Dunes National Lakeshore was established to preserve the remaining huge dunes, beaches, bogs, and marshes of the area. Although difficult to believe, this beautiful area exists within sight of some of the largest steel mills in the country.

Access The park is in northwestern Indiana in Porter County, about 60 miles east of Chicago. Access is via U.S. 12, U.S. 20, or Interstate 94.

Fishing With the introduction of salmon into the Great Lakes in the mid-1960s, a year-round sport fishery has developed along the Indiana shore of Lake Michigan. Since 1969, the state of Indiana has been stocking salmon and trout in Lake Michigan and in Trail Creek and the Little Calumet River. Trail Creek is just outside the park's eastern boundary. The Little Calumet River flows partially through the park into Lake Michigan at Burns Waterway (also known as Burns Ditch). Fishing in the area is for chinook and coho salmon, steelhead, brown and lake trout, and yellow perch. Indiana has also introduced a summer-run steelhead known as the Skamania-strain steelhead.

Michigan City is the headquarters for charter-boat activity on Lake Michigan, but fishing in the area is so good that shoreline and stream fishing are also worthwhile. Charter boats are also available out of Gary. Indiana has so little shoreline along Lake Michigan that all of Indiana's Great Lakes salmon and trout fishing takes place near these two cities.

Fishing is possible all year, but winter fishing is only for the diehard because of the severe cold. Large brown and rainbow trout may be caught during the winter wherever an industrial site is discharging warm water along the Lake Michigan shoreline. Limited access to warm-water-discharge areas is provided by the industrial plants. Also during winter, steelhead and some late-running coho and chinook salmon are found in Trail Creek and the Little Calumet River.

Some of Indiana's best fishing begins in the spring as soon as the ice leaves, usually in March. The southern part of the lake along Indiana and Illinois warms faster than the eastern and western shores

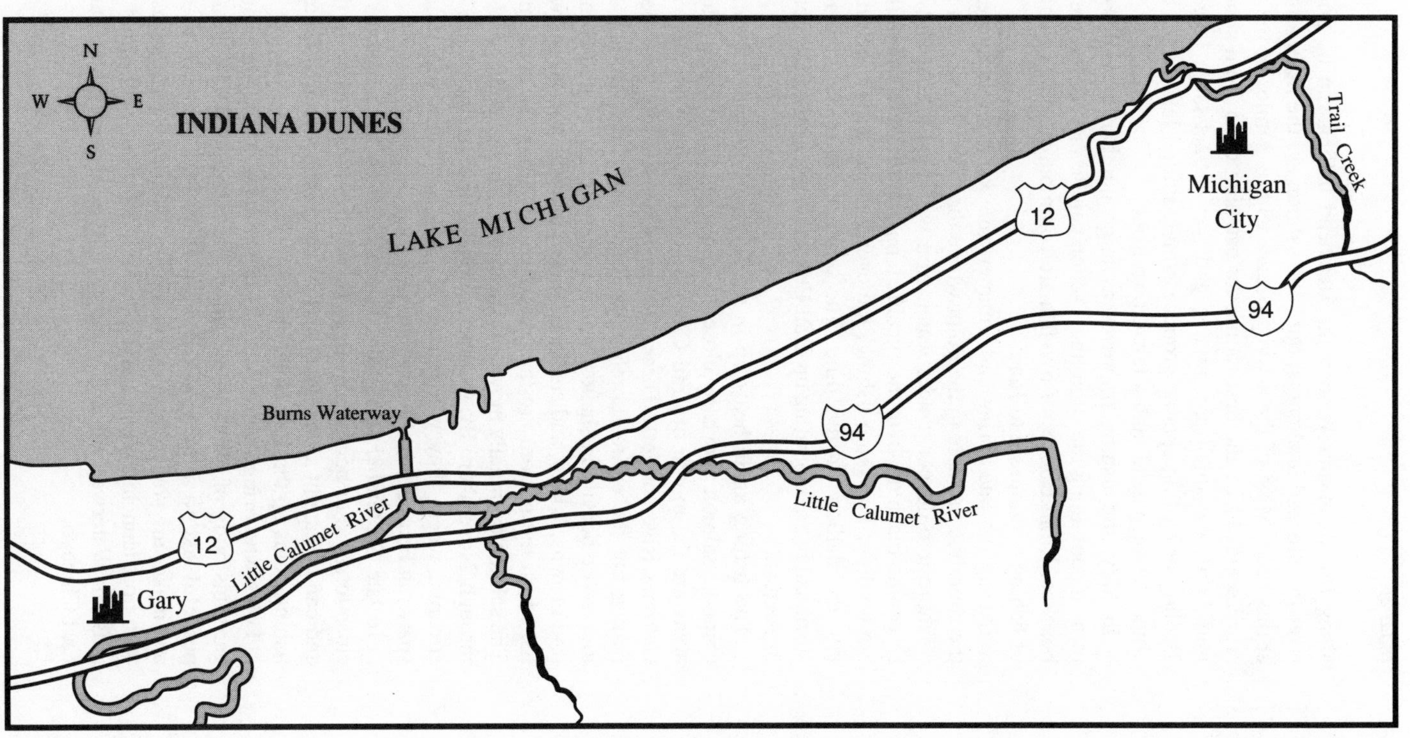

N
W
E
S
INDIANA DUNES
LAKE MICHIGAN
Michigan City
Trail Creek
12
94
Burns Waterway
94
Little Calumet River
12
Little Calumet River
Gary

along Michigan and Wisconsin. Steelhead fishing can be good off river mouths and in streams, but coho salmon are the main attraction at this time. Most of the activity occurs within 2 miles of the shore. April seems to be the best month for catching coho from shore. By mid-April, the smelt are running and they attract large lake trout. Trolling or casting spoons produces smelt-stuffed lake trout, cohos, chinooks, steelhead, and a few brown trout.

In May, the fishing improves as large numbers of salmon and trout school along the shoreline. Action can be fast off the piers and beaches. Limit catches of five fish are commonplace then. This type of fishing continues into June.

During the late spring and summer, the water temperatures near the shoreline increase to the point where the trout and salmon retreat offshore into deeper, colder water. You will need a boat and downriggers to reach down to the specific temperature zone where the fish are holding. For shore fishing, the ever-popular yellow perch move into the shallows at this time. The summer run of Skamania-strain steelhead begin migrating up Trail Creek and the Little Calumet River in August.

The fishing again heats up in the fall as thousands of coho and chinook salmon move in close to shore in September. The best areas are the mouth of Trail Creek and the Burns Waterway (Little Calumet River outlet). These two areas consistently provide good fishing but the entire shoreline can be worthwhile. Wading fishermen score heavily in shallow water at these locations and commonly find browns, lakers, and steelhead mixed in with salmon. Spawnbags fished on the bottom are the preferred bait along the river mouths. The salmon eventually move into the streams and provide good action through November. By October, most of the steelhead are in the streams, where they will remain for five to six months until they spawn in February or March.

In late September, lake-trout action picks up as the lakers move close to shore to begin spawning. Brown trout also spawn in the fall and can be caught along the shoreline and in the streams. Lake-trout fishing holds up through November.

Folks who bring their own boats to fish Lake Michigan should regard this body of water with caution—it can quickly change from a peaceful lake to a raging sea. Do not exceed the limits of your boat and make sure you are properly equipped. There are eight access sites with boat launching ramps along the Indiana shore, with three ramps at Burns Waterway, three at Michigan City, and one each at Gary and East Chicago.

License An Indiana fishing license along with a trout and salmon stamp is required. Lake Michigan is divided into state waters regulated by Michigan, Wisconsin, Illinois, and Indiana. For fishing in its waters, each state requires a license and the appropriate stamps. The proximity of the Michigan and Indiana state lines requires that those fishing offshore have licenses from both states.

Camping The only camping is at Indiana Dunes State Park, which is within the boundaries of the national lakeshore but is administered by the state. There are also commercial campgrounds nearby.

Maps The park brochure map is sufficient; there also is a special USGS map, entitled "Indiana Dunes National Lakeshore."

For offshore fishing, you'll need nautical chart #14926, a small-craft book chart for Chicago and the south shore of Lake Michigan.

Park Address
Indiana Dunes NL
1100 N. Mineral Springs Road
Porter, IN 46304
phone: (219) 926-7561

Chambers of Commerce

Michigan City C.C.
P.O. Box 9003
Michigan City, IN 46360
phone: (219) 874-6221

Greater Gary C.C.
504 Broadway
Suite 324
Gary, IN 46402
phone: (219) 885-7407

Portage C.C.
P.O. Box 98
Portage, IN 46368
phone: (219) 762-3300

Additional Information A useful and informative brochure is available free from the state, entitled *Indiana's Shoreline: A Recreation Guide*. Write to: Indiana Department of Natural Resources, 607 State Office Bldg., Indianapolis, IN, 46204; phone: (317) 232-4080.

Fort Larned National Historic Site

Fort Larned played a significant role in opening the West. The fort was built by the U.S. Army in 1859 to protect travelers and the mail from the Plains Indians. Subsequently, it became a base for military operations against the Indians, and was finally charged with guarding the construction crews building the Santa Fe Railroad west across the plains.

Access Located near the confluence of the Pawnee and Arkansas rivers in central Kansas (Pawnee County), Fort Larned is reached via Kansas Highway 156, approximately 6 miles west of the city of Larned.

Fishing Very little fishing occurs in the park area. Nearby in the Pawnee and Arkansas rivers, fishing for channel catfish is popular. Carp and black bullhead are also common and there are some sunfish and largemouth bass in the Arkansas River.

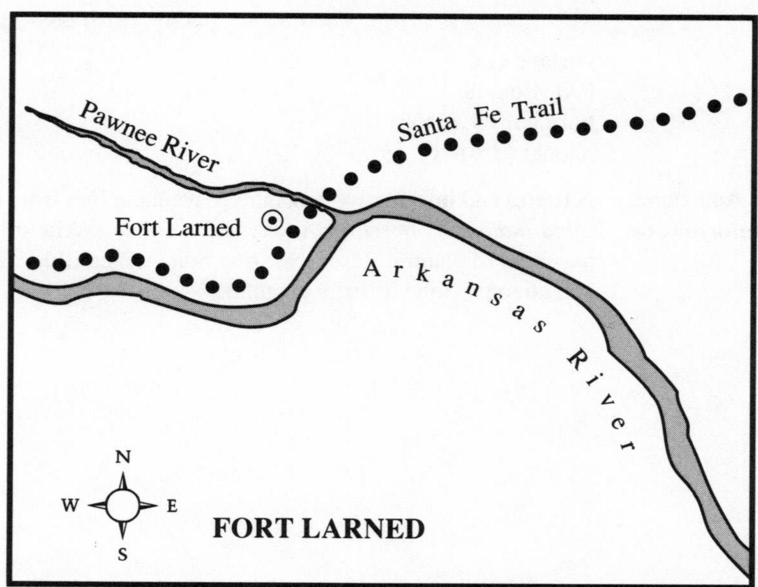

Most of the fishing is from a roadside picnic area off U.S. 156 that borders the north side of the Pawnee River. The best time to fish the Arkansas River is from March through June when river flows are adequate. The Arkansas River loses much of its water to irrigation demands upstream in Kansas and Colorado and the flows at Fort Larned are quite diminished through the summer and fall.

License A Kansas fishing license is required.

Camping None provided.

Maps Not needed.

Park Address
Fort Larned NHS
Route 3
Larned, KS 67550
phone: (316) 285-6911

Chamber of Commerce
Larned C.C.
502 Broadway
P.O. Box 240
Larned, KS 67550
phone: (316) 285-6916

• KENTUCKY

Cumberland Gap National Historical Park

Cumberland Gap was the mountain pass on the Wilderness Road that served as the main entrance for settlers through the Allegheny Mountains. The park contains more than 20,000 acres in Kentucky, Tennessee, and Virginia. Daniel Boone marked the trail to Kentucky along the gap.

Access The majority of the park is in the southeastern corner of Kentucky (Bell and Harlan counties), with parts of the park in Virginia (Lee County) and Tennessee (Claiborne County). The park is accessible via U.S. 25E from Kentucky and Tennessee or U.S. 58 from Virginia.

Fishing Cumberland Gap National Historical Park contains a unique plateau region drained by two main streams in Kentucky, Martins Fork and Shillalah Creek. Presently these are the only streams in the park with fishable populations of brook trout.

Martins Fork is the larger of the two streams and flows for 6 miles within the park. The stream is now populated with New England brook trout. Shillalah Creek has a total of 4.5 miles of stream within park boundaries and now contains Appalachian brook trout. Access to Martins Fork is via a 3-mile hike, while Shillalah Creek requires a 1-mile hike.

Prior to the damaging of each stream's water quality by improper timber cutting, both streams once contained native populations of brook trout. Brook trout were subsequently reintroduced into both streams, which were restocked in 1968 and closed until 1972. Since the initial stocking, natural reproduction has occurred. Due to heavy fishing pressure, each stream is checked in the spring to determine whether it should be open or closed for the season.

Yellow Creek near the visitor center is a children's fishing stream limited to children who are 14 years old or younger. The creek contains bluegill and channel catfish. It is very popular and heavily fished.

License A Kentucky fishing license and trout stamp are required. Check the special park regulations regarding seasons, size limits, and tackle.

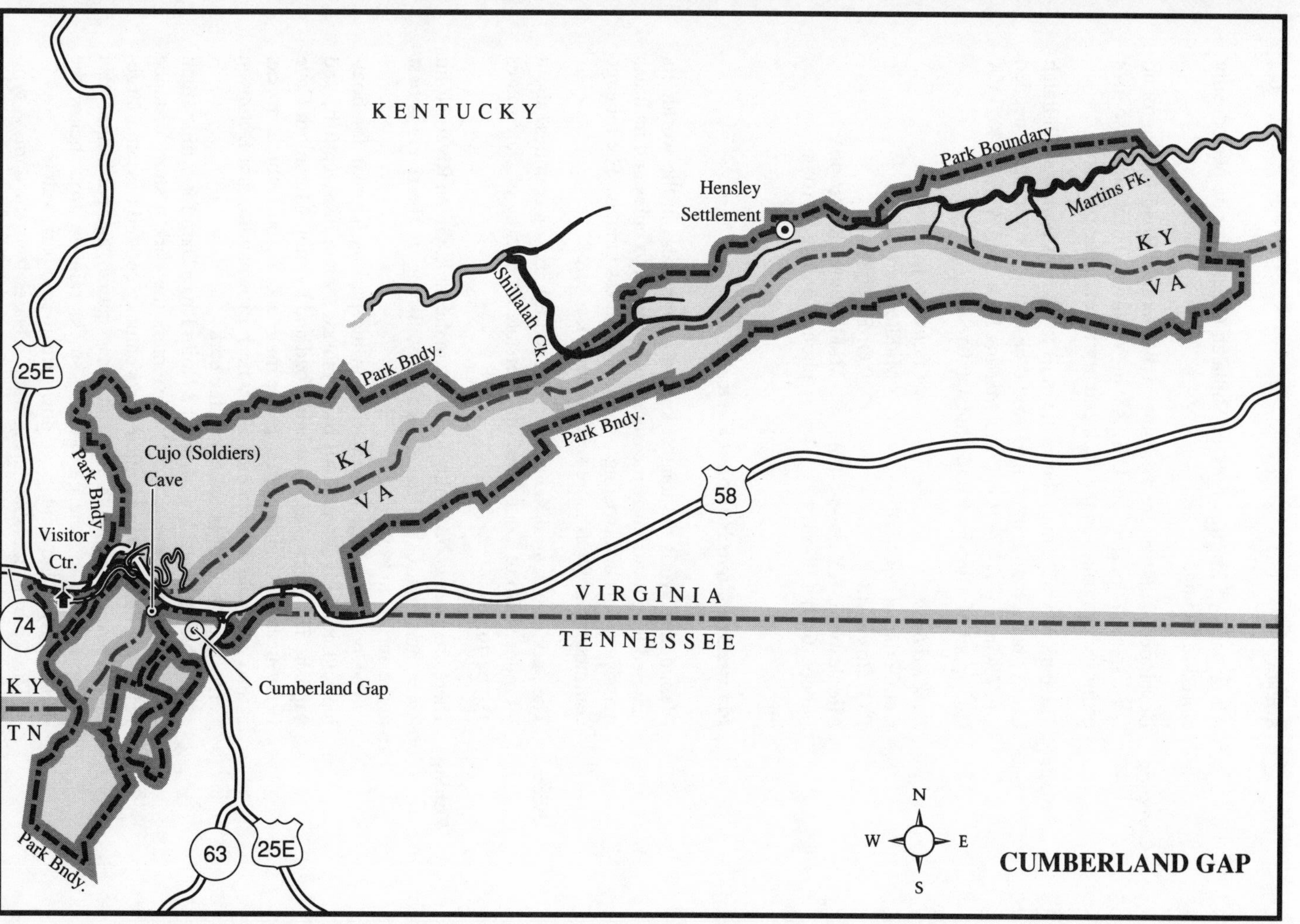

KENTUCKY
Park Boundary
Hensley
Settlement
Martins Fk.
KY
VA
Shillalah Ck.
25E
Park Bndy.
Park Bndy.
Cujo (Soldiers)
Cave
KY
VA
Park Bndy
Visitor
Ctr.
58
VIRGINIA
TENNESSEE
74
KY
TN
Cumberland Gap
N
W
E
S
63
25E
Park Bndy.
CUMBERLAND GAP

All or parts of Martins Fork or Shillalah Creek may be periodically closed to fishing.

Camping Developed facilities are available at Wilderness Road Campground (125 spaces) located on U.S. 58 in Virginia. There are also five primitive campsites in the back country that require permits.

Maps The park brochure map shows the trails to Martins Fork and Shillalah Creek, but a topographic map would be better. Quadrangles needed are: Ewing, KY-VA (for lower Martins Fork) and Varilla, KY-VA (for upper Martins Fork and Shillalah Creek).

Park Address
Cumberland Gap NHP
P.O. Box 1848
Middlesboro, KY 40965-1848
phone: (606) 248-2817

Chamber of Commerce
Middlesboro C.C.
P.O. Box 788
Middlesboro, KY 40965
phone: (606) 248-1075

Mammoth Cave National Park

Mammoth Cave is the longest known cave system in the world. Its mapped length currently measures more than 350 miles and includes massive rooms and twisting, seemingly endless tunnels. The mileage continues to grow as more sections are discovered.

Access The park is in central Kentucky (Hart and Edmonson counties) about 90 miles south of Louisville, off Interstate 65 by way of state routes 255 or 70.

Fishing There are three good fishing locations in the park, Green River, Nolin River, and First Creek Lake. Generally, fishing on the rivers is best in the spring and fall.

The portion of the Green River in the park is popular for floating and contains largemouth bass, muskie, white bass, catfish, and panfish. The river is accessible by road and by trail. Mammoth Cave Ferry near the visitor center is the main access, but vehicle access is also available at Houchins Ferry near Brownsville, and Dennison Ferry, near the east boundary of the park.

The Nolin River flows from the Nolin River Dam for 7 miles then joins the Green River. The Nolin enters the park a short distance below the dam and is excellent for Kentucky spotted bass and largemouth bass. Smallmouth and white bass, catfish, and panfish are also in the river. The state periodically stocks rainbow trout below the dam. Many of the trout move downstream into park waters.

The Nolin is floatable during water releases from the dam. A typi-

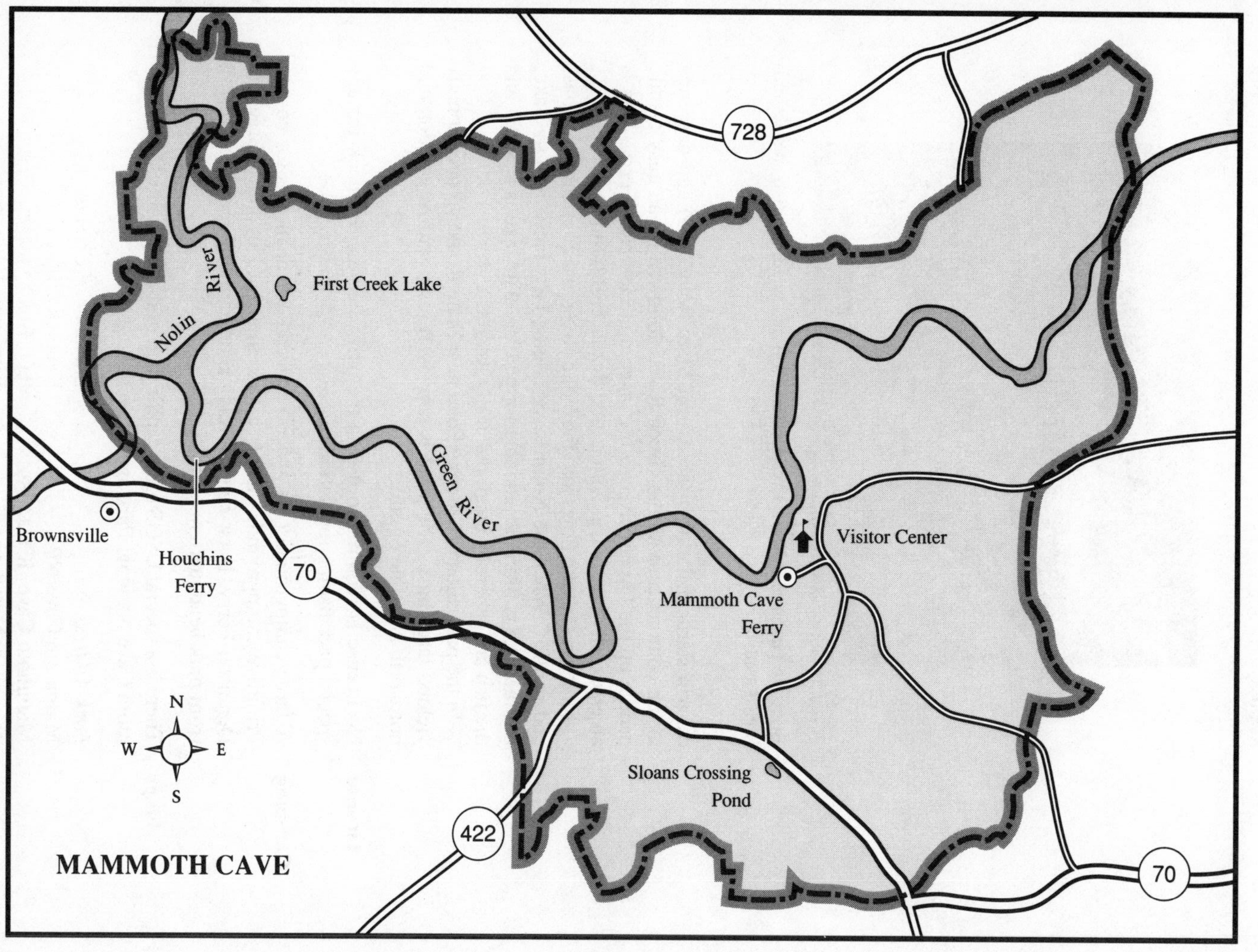
728
First Creek Lake
Nolin
River
Green River
Brownsville
Houchins
Ferry
70
Visitor Center
Mammoth Cave
Ferry
N
W
E
S
Sloans Crossing
Pond
422
70
MAMMOTH CAVE

Both the Green and Nolin Rivers offer good action for panfish, here a red-breast sunfish.—*Gene Hester*

cal trip starts at the dam (access off State Route 728) and descends to the confluence with the Green River, followed by an easy 2-mile paddle up the Green River to the takeout at Houchins Ferry. This is an especially scenic trip with a total distance of 9 miles.

First Creek Lake flows into the Nolin River and contains some bass and panfish. When the Nolin River floods, bass move into the lake, but the lake is more dependable for panfish. The lake is shallow and the fish are generally small but easily caught.

In the past, Sloans Crossing Pond near State Route 70 occasionally yielded large bass. The pond is now overgrown with vegetation and not worth any time or effort.

License No license is required to fish in the park. Be sure to check for any special park fishing regulations.

Camping A large campground (111 spaces) is located near the visitor center. Primitive campgrounds (about 12 spaces) are at Houchins Ferry and Dennison Ferry. Back-country and canoe camping require a permit from park headquarters.

Maps There is a special USGS topographic map of the area, entitled "Mammoth Cave National Park and Vicinity."

Park Address
Mammoth Cave NP
Mammoth Cave, KY 42259
phone: (502) 758-2251

Chamber of Commerce
Kentucky State C.C.
P.O. Box 817
Frankfort, KY 40601
phone: (502) 695-4700

Additional Information

A Fishing Guide to the Streams of Kentucky, by Bob Sehlinger and Win Underwood, contains details and maps on the Green and Nolin rivers, including floating information. The book is available from: Menasha Ridge Press, 2905 Kirkcaldy Lane, Birmingham, AL, 35243; phone: (toll free) 1-800-247-9437.

LOUISIANA

Jean Lafitte National Historical Park

Jean Lafitte National Historical Park is named for the pirate and adventurer who aided General Andrew Jackson at the Battle of New Orleans in the War of 1812. The park consists of four separate units—French Quarter, Chalmette, Barataria, and Big Oak Island—in the greater New Orleans area.

The French Quarter encompasses approximately 80 city blocks in the historic and cultural heart of New Orleans. The Chalmette commemorates the Battle of New Orleans, and Big Oak Island is an archeological site. The Barataria, with its numerous bayous and waterways, was home to Lafitte's extensive smuggling operations.

Access The Barataria (Jefferson Parish) is the only unit in which fishing is possible. It is about 20 miles south of New Orleans via Louisiana Highway 45.

Fishing Barataria is primarily a marsh environment, with numerous swamps, water courses, and ponds. The Salvador and Cataouatche lakes are adjacent to the park on the west. The unit is also crossed by several waterways, the natural bayous (Segnette, Barataria, and des Familles), and the Pipeline and Kenta canals, which were dug. These waterways are basically freshwater but there is some saltwater intrusion because the unit is at the upper limit of the Gulf's tidal influence.

The Barataria area is an extremely productive fishing area. Largemouth bass, blue and channel catfish, white perch, bowfin, gar, and bream are abundant throughout the area. The intertidal area yields weakfish and red snapper.

Fishing is possible all year but spring and fall are best, especially for bass and bream. Largemouth bass spawn in the early spring (February to April) when water temperatures reach 65 to 72 degrees. Fishing is limited in the summer because many of the backwater sites are closed by water hyacinth. Boat ramps are adjacent to the park unit.

License A Louisiana fishing license is required for both fresh and saltwater.

Camping None is available in the park.

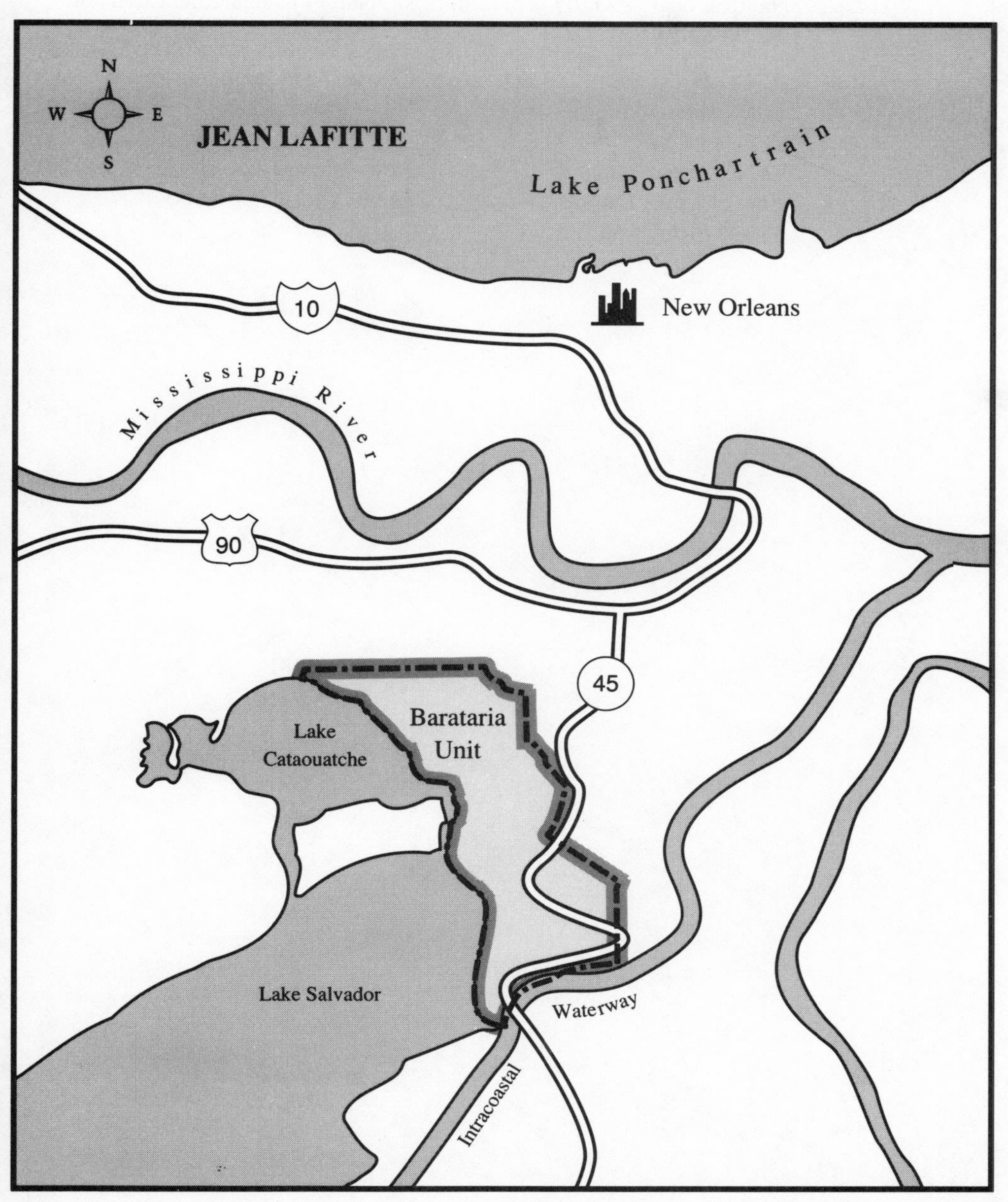
N
W
E
S
JEAN LAFITTE
Lake Ponchartrain
10
New Orleans
Mississippi River
90
45
Barataria
Unit
Lake
Cataouatche
Lake Salvador
Waterway
Intracoastal

Maps Nautical chart #11367 is helpful if you plan to navigate the canals of the Barataria Unit.

Park Address
Jean Lafitte NHP
423 Canal St.
Room 210
New Orleans, LA 70130-2341
phone: (504) 589-3882

Chamber of Commerce
New Orleans C.C.
P.O. Box 30240
New Orleans, LA 70190
phone: (504) 527-6900

• MAINE

Acadia National Park

Acadia, one of the most beautiful and interesting of the national parks, displays the natural beauty of Maine's coast, its coastal mountains, and its offshore islands. Acadia is a relatively small park (38,000 acres) with three separate parts, Mount Desert Island (highest elevation on the eastern seaboard), picturesque Schoodic Peninsula on the mainland, and Isle au Haut, which is reached by passenger ferry.

Access Located in Hancock County, Acadia is approximately 47 miles southeast of Bangor, Maine. Mount Desert Island is reached by car on Maine 3. Schoodic Peninsula is reached by Maine 186. Isle au Haut is reached by passenger ferry (no cars) from the town of Stonington, off Maine 15.

Fishing Acadia has been described as a three-or-four-hour diversion for people on their way to fish in other parts of Maine. Though it is not a fishing mecca, the rocky shorelines and the numerous lakes and ponds provide a variety of fishing opportunities. Most of the fishing is by local residents and fishing pressure is only light to moderate.

Saltwater Fishing Saltwater fishing in Maine is best from early spring to late fall, with the largest variety of species available during the summer months. The entire rocky coastline of Acadia provides good fishing opportunities. Within the bays and estuaries are striped bass, flounder, pollock, cod, and some mackerel. In recent years, bluefish have put in an appearance, moving farther north than they formerly were known to come. Striped bass are usually available from June through autumn. Inshore fishing reaps codfish and haddock along the rocks and beaches in the spring, and pollock during spring and fall.

Freshwater Fishing Freshwater fishing is available in a number of lakes and ponds ranging in size from 1.6 to 897 acres. Fish include landlocked salmon, brook and brown trout, lake trout (known as togue in Maine), smallmouth bass, pickerel, and panfish.

A major drawback to fishing in the park is the almost total absence of rental boats in the Acadia area. Because of this, the best time to fish the island waters is during May and June when the fish are in

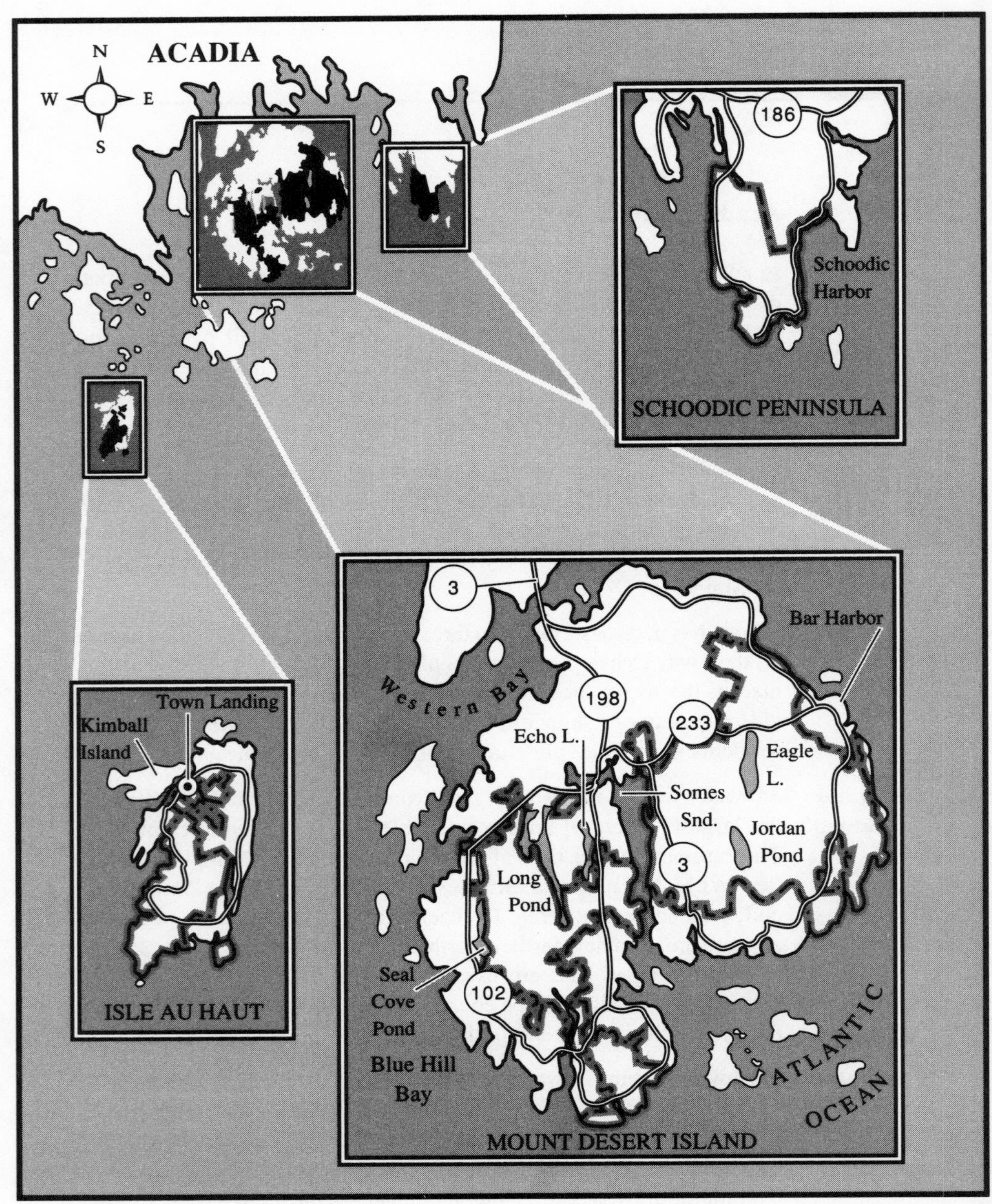
ACADIA
N
W
E
S
186
Schoodic
Harbor
SCHOODIC PENINSULA
Town Landing
Kimball
Island
ISLE AU HAUT
3
Western Bay
198
233
Bar Harbor
Echo L.
Eagle
L.
Somes
Snd.
Jordan
Pond
3
Long
Pond
Seal
Cove
Pond
102
Blue Hill
Bay
ATLANTIC
OCEAN
MOUNT DESERT ISLAND

close and can be caught from shore. At the height of the tourist season in July and August, the fish have retreated to deeper water. Specialized deep-water techniques, all of which require a boat, are needed to catch trout and salmon during the summer months.

A number of the waters in Acadia are governed by special regulations, so it is important to check the Hancock County section of the Maine fishing regulations.

The following is a summary of park waters:

Long Pond—located in Mount Desert and Southwest harbors, Long Pond consistently produces good catches of landlocked salmon. In the summer, the salmon are found at depths of 25 to 35 feet. Pickerel and smallmouth bass are also present, although the bass are small and grow slowly. This is the largest pond in the park.

Jordan Pond—offers good fishing for lake trout and salmon. The lake trout are at depths of 45 to 80 feet.

Eagle Lake—this picturesque lake surrounded by the mountains contains brook and lake trout and salmon.

Echo Lake—provides good brook trout and salmon fishing.

Witchole Pond—usually produces brook trout from 8 to 11 inches.

Upper Hadlock Pond—a good brown trout fishery. Small smelt are the main forage food for the browns. Streamer imitations can be effective. The pond drains into Lower Hadlock Pond.

Lower Hadlock Pond—also a good brown trout fishery. Trout growth is very good due to an abundant population of isopods, an aquatic crustacean. Brown trout up to 5 pounds have been caught here.

Long Pond—the second of three ponds with this name, this pond is on Isle au Haut and is the only natural body of freshwater on the island. It produces brook trout and an occasional landlocked salmon.

Bubble Pond—connects to the southern end of Eagle Lake and has mainly brook trout.

Hodgdon Pond—primarily a warm-water fishery with smallmouth bass and white perch.

Long Pond—the third pond of this name is outside the park, off Route 3, west of Seal Harbor. It is separated from the ocean by a narrow seawall and is connected to Jordan Pond by Jordan Stream. It contains brook trout.

Seal Cove Pond—inhabited mainly by smallmouth bass and white perch, with some brook and brown trout.

Round Pond—a warm-water fishery with smallmouth bass, pickerel, and sunfish.

There are a number of other ponds in or adjacent to the park but either their fishing value is rated low or information about them is sketchy. Boat launching facilities are provided at Seal Cove Pond, Jordan Pond, Eagle Lake, Echo Lake, and Long Pond (the big one).

License No license is required for saltwater fishing; however, a Maine license is needed for freshwater fishing and state regulations apply.

Camping There are only two campgrounds in the park, Blackwoods Campground (320 spaces) on the eastern side of Mount Desert Island, and Seawall Campground (214 spaces) on the western side. From June 15 to September 6, Blackwoods is on the Ticketron reservation system. Back-country camping is allowed from mid-May to mid-October at a site on Isle au Haut. There are a number of private campgrounds in the surrounding area.

Maps Topographic maps are not needed for fishing in the park. There is a special USGS map of the entire park, "Acadia National Park and Vicinity." Also available is a park trail map from the park.

For saltwater fishing, nautical chart #13312 is recommended. A number of more detailed nautical charts are available within the boundary of chart #13312. It would be best also to examine *Nautical Chart Catalog No. 1* to determine which charts you need.

Park Address
Acadia NP
P.O. Box 177
Bar Harbor, ME 04609
phone: (207) 288-9561

Chamber of Commerce
Bar Harbor C.C.
P.O. Box 158
Bar Harbor, ME 04609
phone: (207) 288-5103

MARYLAND

Antietam National Battlefield

Antietam Battlefield is the scene of one of the Civil War's most famous and bloodiest battles—a battle that brought to an end General Robert E. Lee's first northern invasion. The battle was fought on September 17, 1862 and a total of 23,110 soldiers on both sides were either killed or wounded.

Access The battlefield is in western Maryland (Washington County) off State Highway 65 about 12 miles south of Hagerstown. You can also get to the park from State Highway 34, which intersects Highway 65 at Sharpsburg. Both Highways 65 and 34 intersect either U.S. 40 or 40A and Interstate 70.

Fishing Antietam Creek contains sunfish and bass along with some carp and suckers. Occasionally trout will be caught that have moved into the stream from Little Antietam Creek (outside the park), which is stocked with trout. Antietam Creek is lightly fished. Folks prefer to fish the Potomac River, which is five minutes away. (See the section on the Chesapeake and Ohio Canal, Maryland, for a description of Potomac River fishing.)

License A Maryland fishing license is required. Be sure to check current state regulations.

Camping No camping is permitted in the park except for a group campground open from March through October. There are four sites for organized groups only. Camping is available along the C&O Canal nearby and at Greenbrier State Park, 15 miles northeast via Highways 34 and 40A.

Maps The map in the park brochure is adequate. If you want a topographic map, the Keedysville quad is the one to get.

Park Address
Antietam NB
P.O. Box 158
Sharpsburg, MD 21782
phone: (301) 432-5124

Chamber of Commerce
Hagerstown–Washington County C.C.
14 Public Square
Hagerstown, MD 21740
phone: (301) 739-2015

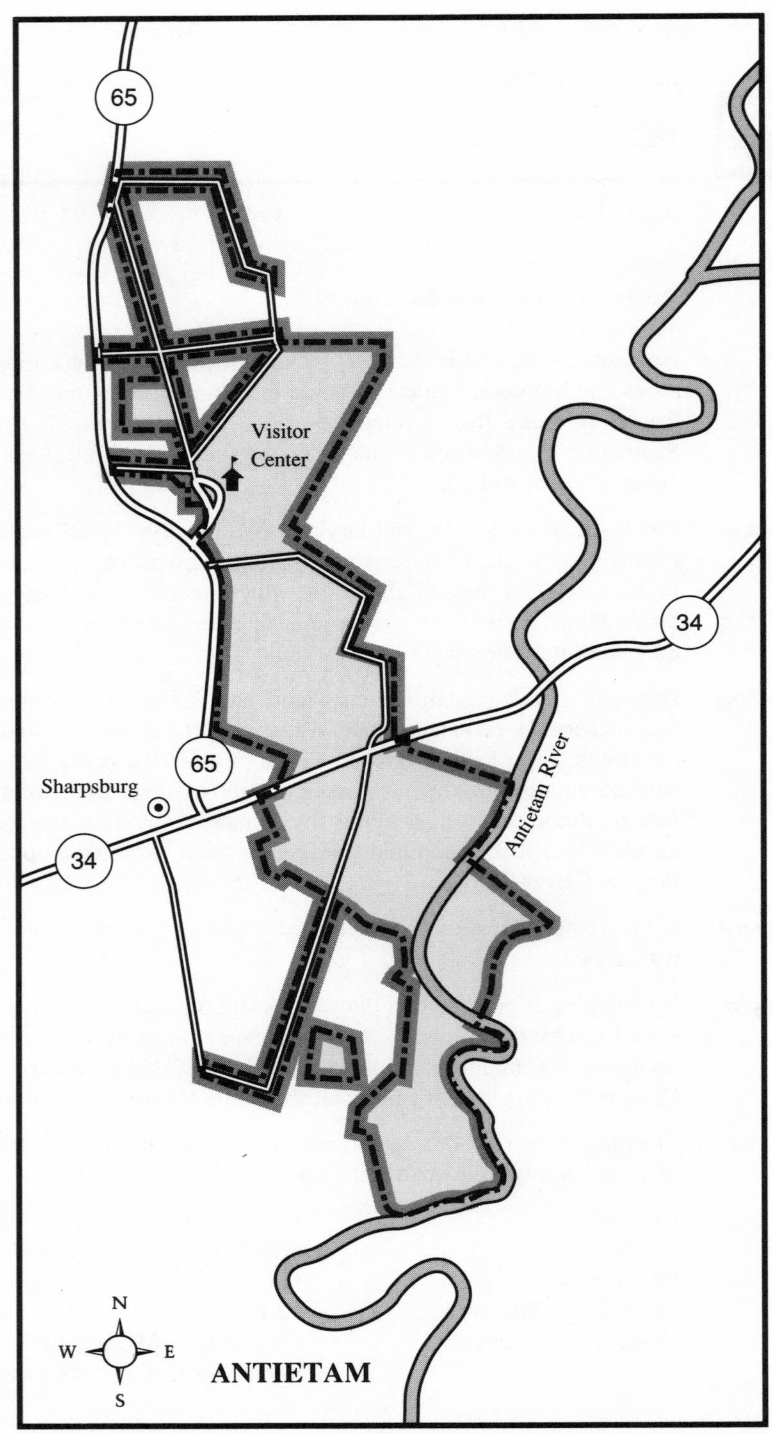
65
Visitor
Center
34
65
Sharpsburg
34
Antietam River
N
W
E
S
ANTIETAM

Assateague Island National Seashore

Assateague Island is a barrier island along the Maryland and Virginia coast. The park was established in 1965 to preserve and restore a 37-mile strip of coastal wilderness, including 19,000 acres of beach, sand dunes, and marsh. About half of the island is managed by the National Park Service. Assateague State Park, at the northern end of the island, is managed by the Maryland Park Service. Chincoteague National Wildlife Refuge to the south, including all of the Virginia portion of the island, is managed by the U.S. Fish and Wildlife Service.

Access The island is on the Atlantic coast of Maryland (Worcester County) and Virginia (Accomack County). Access is at either end—via Maryland Route 376 from Berlin to Route 611 at the north end, or via Virginia Route 175 to Chincoteague at the south end.

Fishing Assateague Island is a popular and productive area for surf fishing. Among the game fish along the island are flounder, bluefish, weakfish (sea trout), croaker (hardhead), whiting (kingfish), and sharks. Assateague is famous for sea trout, and it is the northernmost range for channel bass and black drum, which, along with striped bass, are becoming increasingly scarce.

Some of the best surf fishing is found just south of the NPS primitive campground south of Assateague State Park. A road leads to the park service campground and then ends. Only four-wheel-drive vehicles are allowed on the beach beyond the road. These vehicles must have a beach access permit to travel on the sand. The annual permits cost $30 and are available from park headquarters on Route 611. To qualify, a vehicle must be four-wheel drive or otherwise adapted for sand travel, equipped with a shovel, tire gauge, jack (with support), and tow ropes or chain.

Although some good fishing can be reached without resorting to an over-sand vehicle, most of the activity takes place along the roadless beach on the 14-mile stretch from the park service campground south to the Virginia line, which is the boundary for Chincoteague National Wildlife Refuge. The refuge can be entered only from Chincoteague and the refuge shoreline is a foot-access-only area, except for the southern hook of land enclosing the sheltered waters of Toms Cove, where over-sand vehicles are permitted. Another foot-access-only area is the 6-mile stretch of beach from the Route 611 bridge north to the Ocean City Inlet.

When fishing the surf, it is essential to be able to read the water

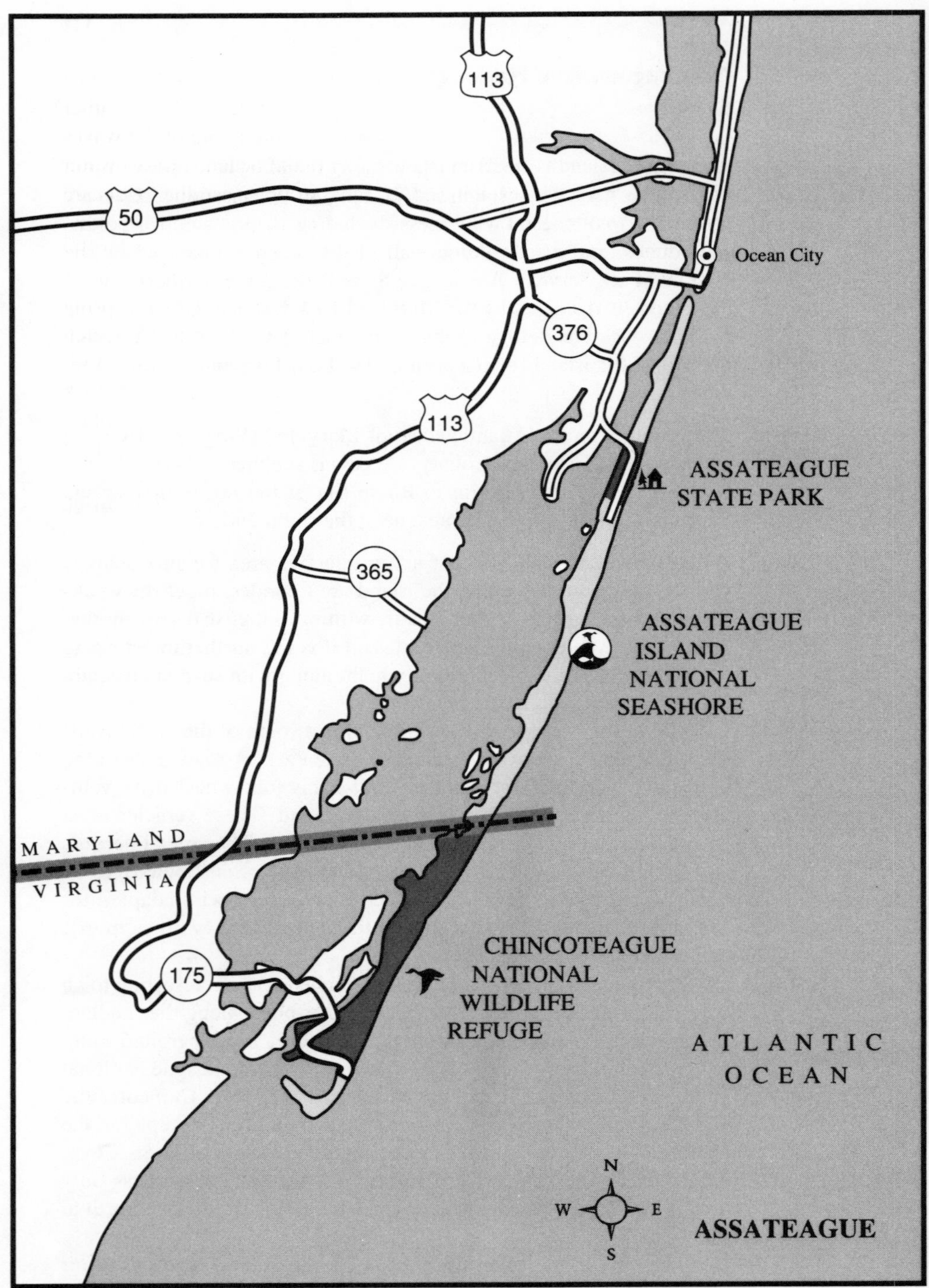
113
50
Ocean City
376
113
ASSATEAGUE
STATE PARK
365
ASSATEAGUE
ISLAND
NATIONAL
SEASHORE
MARYLAND
VIRGINIA
175
CHINCOTEAGUE
NATIONAL
WILDLIFE
REFUGE
ATLANTIC
OCEAN
N
W
E
S
ASSATEAGUE

and to recognize the places where waves break over sandbars. Just beyond and in front of the sandbars are troughs where the fish gather and feed. These troughs can be identified by a flattening of the waves and slightly darker water running parallel to the beach. Darker water perpendicular to the beach indicates a cut through a sandbar. Cuts are the best areas to fish because the fish use these to travel to the troughs. Also watch for large gatherings of sea gulls, which usually indicate feeding or schooling fish.

The best fishing takes place from April through November. Spring fishing usually starts in late April for whiting, which are easy to catch and range throughout the surf into October. Bluefish arrive in mid-May, but fishing success for them is inconsistent. Schools of bluefish move in close to shore then depart unexpectedly. At times, the bluefishing can be excellent. The best fishing for blues occurs from August through October.

Sea trout begin showing up in late May to early June and can be caught throughout the summer. Flounder and croaker are also taken in the surf all summer but the better flounder fishing is in Chincoteague Bay and Sinepuxent Bay between the island and the mainland.

Sharks move into the Assateague surf in early June and hang around through September. Hammerhead, tiger, dusky, sand tiger, lemon, black tip, and bull sharks are all in the area but are seldom caught

Four-wheel drive vehicles are needed to traverse the roadless beach at Assateague.—*National Park Service photo by Richard Frear*

in the surf. Dogfish and sandbar sharks account for 95 percent of the sharks taken in the surf.

Fall fishing can be good along Assateague, usually starting in late September. Whiting, bluefish, sea trout, and a few channel bass up to 50 pounds are taken in the surf. The best fall fishing lasts through November.

Charter boats, head boats, and guides are all available in the area. Check with local bait shops for the latest information on baits and techniques. Another alternative is fishing from canoes in Chincoteague and Sinepuxent Bays. Three canoe-in campsites have been developed in the Maryland section of the park. Canoeists should make reservations to use these campsites.

License No license is required to fish in the park. An overnight fishing permit is required in the Virginia portion of the park if you wish to fish after 10:00 P.M. Permits may be obtained at the Toms Cove visitor center.

Camping Assateague State Park operates a large modern campground. The National Park Service offers only primitive camping just south of the state park. There are private campgrounds on the mainland and further south on Chincoteague Island. The park service distributes a free booklet on camping at Assateague.

Maps The park brochure map is sufficient for beach fishing. For offshore fishing, nautical chart #12211 is needed. Tide tables are also helpful since surf fishing is best during high tide.

Topographic maps are helpful for canoeing and camping in the bays. The quads for the entire island are: Ocean City, Berlin, Tingles Island, Whittington Point, and Box Iron (all in Maryland) and Chincoteague East, Chincoteague West, and Wallops Island (in Virginia).

Park Address
Assateague Island National Seashore
Route 2, Box 294
Berlin, MD 21811
phone: (301) 641-1443

Chambers of Commerce

Salisbury C.C.
P.O. Box 510
Salisbury, MD 21801
phone: (301) 749-0144

Chincoteague C.C.
P.O. Box 258
Chincoteague, VA 23336
phone: (804) 336-6161

Ocean City C.C.
Route 1
Box 310A
Ocean City, MD 21842
phone: (301) 289-8559

Additional Information Chincoteague National Wildlife Refuge
Box 62
Chincoteague, VA 23336
phone: (804) 336-6122

Assateague State Park
Route 2, Box 293
Berlin, MD 21811
phone: (301) 641-2120

Fishing in Maryland and the Mid-Atlantic is an excellent publication that covers the entire state and includes maps, regulations, tide tables, and directories. It is available at most book stores or tackle shops in Maryland, or you can order it from: Fishing in Maryland Inc., P.O. Box 201, Phoenix, MD, 21131; phone: (301) 243-3413.

A complete guidebook, *Assateague Island National Seashore,* by William Amos and the National Park Service Division of Publications, is available for $6 from the Superintendent of Documents, U.S. Government Printing Office, Washington, D.C., 20402; phone: (202) 783-3238. Include the stock number: 024-005-00776-8.

Catoctin Mountain Park

Catoctin Mountain Park is the location of Camp David, the famous presidential retreat. The Camp David portion of the park is closed to the public, but the remainder of this forested park is open and popular for its numerous outdoor recreation possibilities. The park is adjacent to Cunningham Falls State Park and both parks are heavily visited by outdoor enthusiasts from the Baltimore and Washington D.C. areas. These two parks feature camping, picnicking, hiking, cross-country skiing, horseback riding, swimming, sailing, and fishing.

Access Located in Frederick County, Catoctin Mountain Park is accessible off U.S. Route 15 to Maryland Route 77. You can also reach Cunningham Falls State Park off Route 77, since that highway forms the boundary between the two parks. The main entrances to the parks are less than one-tenth mile apart.

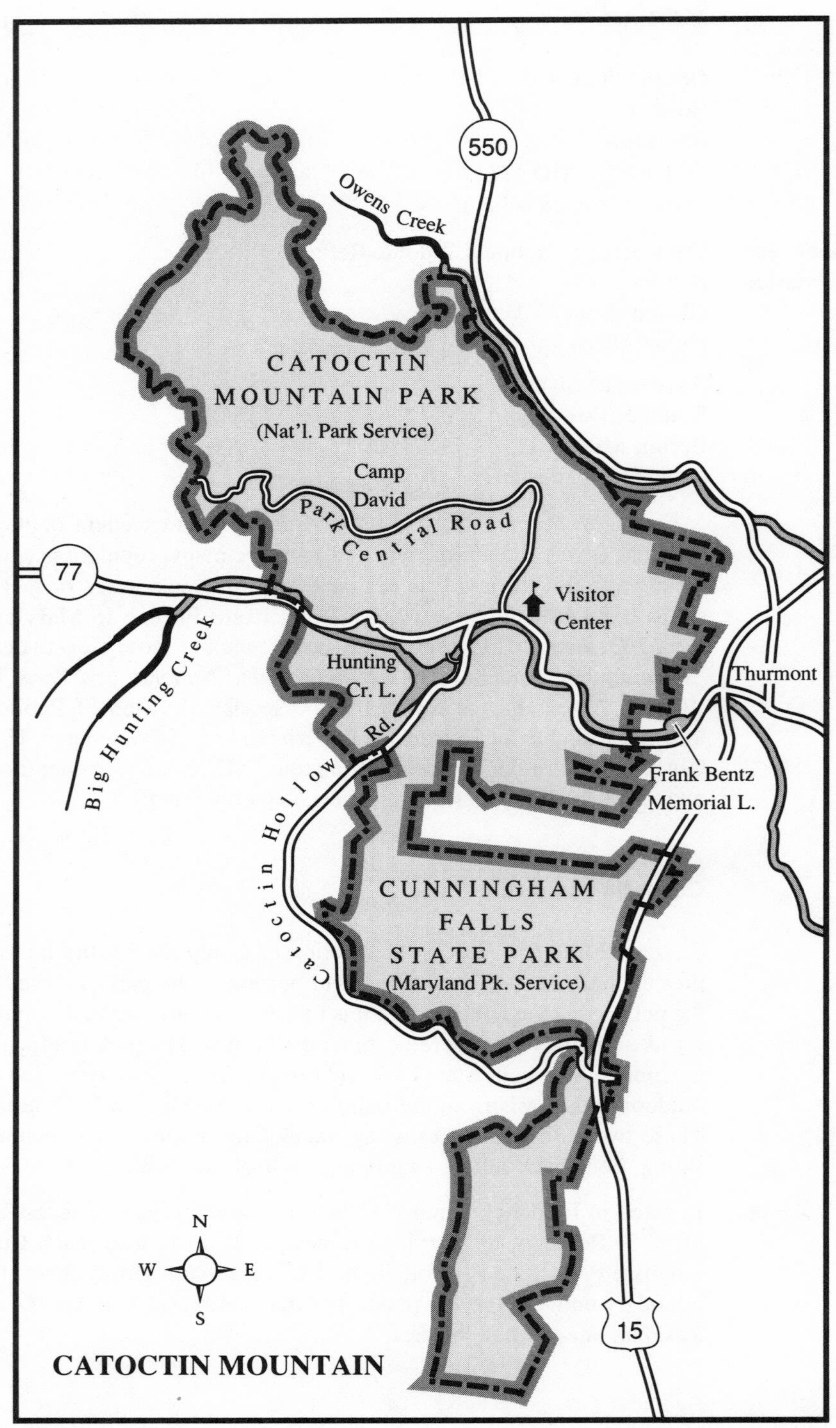
550
Owens Creek
CATOCTIN
MOUNTAIN PARK
(Nat'l. Park Service)
Camp
David
Park Central Road
77
Visitor
Center
Hunting
Cr. L.
Big Hunting Creek
Rd.
Thurmont
Frank Bentz
Memorial L.
Catoctin Hollow
CUNNINGHAM
FALLS
STATE PARK
(Maryland Pk. Service)
N
W
E
S
15
CATOCTIN MOUNTAIN

Fishing Trout fishing is the attraction in these parks. Big Hunting Creek and Owens Creek are the two main permanent streams that flow through the area. Both are small mountain streams subject to highly fluctuating flows. Big Hunting Creek and Hauver Branch were dammed to form Hunting Creek Lake in the state park. The lake is stocked with rainbow trout and also has largemouth bass.

Big Hunting Creek is one of the finest trout streams in Maryland. The creek supports wild brown trout and the state stocks rainbows every year. Currently the stream is open year-round and managed as a fly-fishing-only, catch-and-release, no-kill area. As a result of these regulations, fishing is good throughout the year, although it is difficult during the low water of summer.

For most of its distance, Big Hunting Creek parallels Route 77 and there are parking pull-offs along the stream. The stream originates from natural springs high in the Catoctin Mountains and is very small and difficult to fish above Hunting Creek Lake. Below the lake outlet, the stream is a series of pools, and interconnecting runs beneath a dense canopy of hardwoods and evergreens. Because of its small size (10 to 20 feet wide), only short casts are required. The pools should be approached cautiously to avoid spooking the trout. The most popular stretch of stream is from the lake outlet to the Frank Bentz Pond.

Owens Creek is accessible by following Route 550, 2 miles north from its junction with U.S. Route 15 at Thurmont, or along Foxville-Deerfield Road in the park. Only the headwaters of Owens Creek are in the park, but both roads parallel the stream. Owens Creek contains native brook trout and wild brown trout, and it is stocked with rainbows by the state. The creek has some hard-to-get-to pools with large browns for the anyone willing to make the effort. There are no special regulations for Owens Creek and it is managed as a put-and-take fishery with any type of bait and tackle allowed.

Both Big Hunting Creek and Owens Creek have good aquatic insect populations. Big Hunting Creek has large populations of stoneflies, mayflies, and caddis flies. For fly-fishing, the following information on fly hatches may be helpful.

1. Little Black Stonefly—very good hatch but you have to use very small flies in sizes 18–22. Late February to late March.
2. Blue Quill—sizes 16–18. Mid to late March.
3. Larger Stonefly—approximately April 15 to May 15.
   Hendrickson—approximately April 15 to May 15.
   Quill Gordon—approximately April 15 to May 15.
4. March Brown—early May to mid-May.
5. Light Cahill—mid-May to early June.

6. Caddis—very small flies and the majority are dark. April through May.
7. Terrestrials—late May through summer. Ants and beetles are best. Also use a small, bright green inchworm.

Additional information on fly-fishing is contained in a brochure available from the park, entitled *Fly Fisherman's Guide to Big Hunting Creek.*

License A Maryland license is required and state regulations apply. Anyone fishing must have a Maryland trout stamp to possess trout as well as to fish in the no-kill areas. Be sure to check the regulations for Owens Creek because it closes periodically (at different times each year) and the opening day for Owens Creek fluctuates yearly.

Camping In Catoctin, the Owens Creek Campground has 51 sites and is open from mid-April through the third weekend in November. Cunningham Falls has two campgrounds, William Houck (148 sites) and Manor (31 sites).

Maps The park brochure map is very good and is sufficient for most fishing. The topographic quad map for Catoctin Mountain Park is Blue Ridge Summit and the quad map for Cunningham Falls State Park is Catoctin Furnace.

Park Address
Catoctin Mountain Park
Thurmont, MD 21788
phone: (301) 663-9343

Chamber of Commerce
Frederick County C.C.
43A S. Market St.
Frederick, MD 21701
phone: (301) 662-4164

Chesapeake and Ohio Canal National Historical Park

The remains of the historic, 19th-century C&O Canal are preserved by a 185-mile-long strip of parkland along the Potomac River. The park stretches from downtown Georgetown in the District of Columbia, northward to Cumberland, Maryland. Most of the park is in Maryland and follows the Potomac River, which borders Virginia and West Virginia.

The canal was used (1850–1924) to transport goods and materials, including lumber and coal to the cities, from the Midwest to the East. Goods were transported by barges pulled by mules moving along an elevated trail paralleling the canal. The canal was rendered obsolete with the construction of the Baltimore & Ohio Railroad, and was

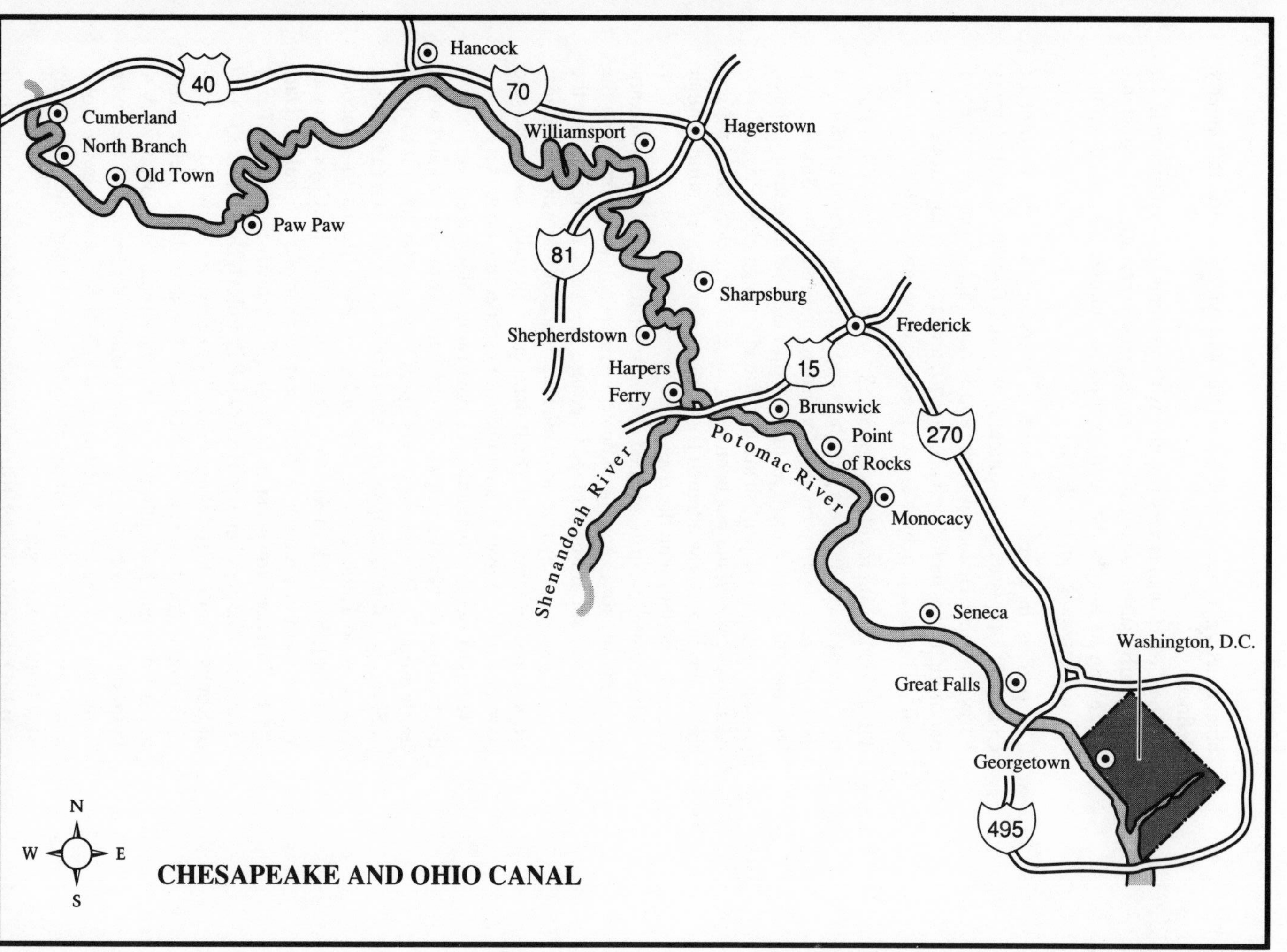
Hancock
40
70
Cumberland
North Branch
Old Town
Paw Paw
Williamsport
Hagerstown
81
Sharpsburg
Shepherdstown
Frederick
Harpers
Ferry
15
Brunswick
Point
of Rocks
270
Potomac River
Shenandoah River
Monocacy
Seneca
Washington, D.C.
Great Falls
Georgetown
495
N
W
E
S
CHESAPEAKE AND OHIO CANAL

abandoned in 1924. Both the towpath and the canal are still clearly defined.

The C&O Canal is very popular with residents of Washington D.C. and nearby suburban areas for the extensive recreational opportunities along its length. The park is used for hiking, biking, camping, fishing, canoeing, and jogging.

Access The park is in central and western Maryland and the District of Columbia. It passes near Antietam National Battlefield and Harpers Ferry National Historical Park, and is accessible from a number of major highways including U.S. 40, 70, and 270 and numerous lesser roads. The park brochure shows the myriad access points.

Fishing The C&O Canal provides access to 185 miles of the bass-filled Potomac River, in addition to a few short and widely separated sections of the canal that are deep enough for fishing and canoeing. Smallmouth bass are the main attraction in the Potomac, but largemouth bass, catfish, and various panfish are also found throughout the river. In recent years, Maryland has been stocking walleye below Dam #4 and the walleye have now attained legal size (14 inches), creating another exciting possibility on the river.

The Potomac can be floated for most of its length but is recommended only for experienced boaters (canoeists). All dams, even the small ones, should be portaged because the water plunging over the dams creates a dangerous hydraulic wave action that can hold a boat or person indefinitely. The small dams are especially dangerous and have claimed the lives of a number of unsuspecting boaters.

The park service maintains 14 boat ramps along the river, allowing for trips of various lengths. As the summer progresses and water levels drop, the Potomac above Harpers Ferry can be difficult to float.

Some possible float trips are: Cumberland to Oldtown (22 miles); Paw Paw to Little Orleans (22 miles); Little Orleans to Hancock (17 miles); Hancock to McCoys Ferry (14 miles); McCoys Ferry to Williamsport (14 miles); Williamsport to Dam #4 (16 miles); Dam #4 to Shepherdstown (11 miles); Shepherdstown to Harpers Ferry (11 miles); Harpers Ferry to Brunswick (7 miles); Brunswick to Point of Rocks (7 miles); and Point of Rocks to Seneca (27 miles).

Fishing is good everywhere along the Potomac River. Lefty Kreh, noted fisherman and author, considers the stretch from Brunswick to Point of Rocks to be the top trophy-smallmouth section of the river. Some parts of the canal's towpath provide better access to the Potomac than others, but by hiking along you can usually find a relatively easy route to the river.

It isn't difficult to catch fish in the Potomac. When fly-fishing, there is plenty of room for casting. Streamers and poppers are effective for smallmouth. Crayfish are a major food source for the bass, and any good crayfish or minnow imitation takes fish.

Most of the smallmouth average 9 to 12 inches and 100-fish days are not uncommon. As the river comes into the Seneca Rocks area near Washington D.C., more largemouth bass are found. Downstream from Seneca Rocks, the Potomac becomes slower, wider, and less rocky and begins to become affected by tidal influences from its Chesapeake Bay outlet.

Fishing is good throughout the spring, summer, and fall. In the spring, the bass are more concentrated in deep holes; in April they move into the shallows to spawn. In the summer, work the riffles and rapids around large rocks, underwater boulders, and ledges. Come fall, the bass are again schooling and locating in the deeper holes. Fall can be exceptional, since this is the time when the smallmouth bass feed heavily in the cooling water.

The sections of the canal that are deep enough for fishing or canoeing are located in downtown Georgetown; in the Widewater section (good fishing) near Washington; and upstream from Violets Lock at Big Pool, Little Pool, and Town Creek to Oldtown. The Little Pool and Oldtown sections are currently stocked with rainbow trout by Maryland. The trout-stocking practice by the state varies, and it may be discontinued. The Georgetown section is noted for lunchtime fishermen in three-piece suits, who fly-cast deerhair mulberry imitations to the carp that are prowling beneath overhanging mulberry bushes for the dropping berries.

License A Maryland license is required for fishing the Potomac from the Maryland side. The sections of the canal with water are also in Maryland. You need a license to fish in the District of Columbia. West Virginia, District of Columbia, and Virginia residents can purchase a special Potomac River license that is cheaper than a regular nonresident license and allows fishing in the Potomac River from either side.

Camping Primitive camping is permitted in five designated campgrounds (67 spaces) along the canal and at the 30 hiker-biker units, spaced at 5-mile intervals.

Maps The park brochure map along with a Maryland highway map should be sufficient. The park brochure details access sites, boat ramps, and park facilities.

Park Address
C&O Canal NHP
P.O. Box 4
Sharpsburg, MD 21782
phone: (301) 739-4200

Additional Information

The annual guidebook, *Fishing in Maryland,* maps the entire Potomac River, shows access sites and ramps, and notes the best areas for the various fish species in the river. The guidebook is available at most Maryland tackle shops and book stores, or can be obtained from: Fishing In Maryland Inc., P.O. Box 201, Phoenix, MD, 21131; phone: (301) 243-3413.

The book *Fishing the Upper Potomac River*, by Ken Penrod, provides a detailed description of 140 miles of the Potomac River from Paw Paw, West Virginia, to Great Falls near Washington, D.C. It is available ($21 postpaid) from PPC Publications, 13028 Ingleside Dr., Beltsville, MD, 20705; phone: (301) 572-5688.

Guides are available to float fish the upper Potomac. Contact: Outdoor Life Unlimited, 13028 Ingleside Dr., Beltsville, MD, 20705; phone: (301) 572-5688; or Mark Kovach, 737 Thayer Ave., Silver Spring, MD, 20910; phone: (301) 588-8472.

Check the West Virginia chapter of this book for a detailed description of the Harpers Ferry portion of the Potomac River.

• MASSACHUSETTS

Cape Cod National Seashore

Cape Cod National Seashore was established in 1961 to preserve the natural, cultural, and archeological features and historic scene of the cape that provided the Pilgrims with their first view of the New World. Today, its ocean beaches, dunes, marshes, ponds, and woodlands provide unlimited recreational opportunities. The seashore is very rich in plant life and popular with birdwatchers, since the different habitats attract a variety of birds.

Access The park is located in southeastern Massachusetts on the Cape Cod Peninsula (Barnstable County). It is accessible via U.S. 6.

Fishing Cape Cod is an area of excellent saltwater fishing. You can expect to find fish along the entire length of the seashore. The National Seashore runs 40 miles north and south along the arm of the Cape. The east shore of the Cape is comprised of relatively unspoiled and undeveloped beaches because the brutal winter storms discourage development. The result is clean, white beaches with ample surf-fishing opportunities.

Bluefish and striped bass are the main attractions of Cape surf fishing. Additionally, there are seasonal invasions of cod, flounder, whiting, mackerel, pollock, tautog, weakfish, bonito, and scup (porgy). Freshwater fishing takes a back seat to saltwater, but the entire Cape is dotted with freshwater ponds containing trout, largemouth and smallmouth bass, catfish, pickerel, and panfish.

The two major fishing areas along the seashore are the Province Lands area at the northern Cape (Race Point Beach) and Nauset Beach. The latter is accessible through and administered by the town of Orleans. Both areas require a four-wheel-drive vehicle to reach the best spots. Vehicles are required to stay on the designated over-sand vehicle routes. Nauset Beach is a grueling 12-mile stretch.

Annual permits are required for each area, with prices that vary in both locations. In 1989, the non-resident access permit to Nauset Beach cost $80. Permits for Nauset are available from the local police station in Orleans. Access permits to the Province Land beaches cost $30 and are available from the ranger station at Race Point Beach. Contact the park headquarters for current costs.

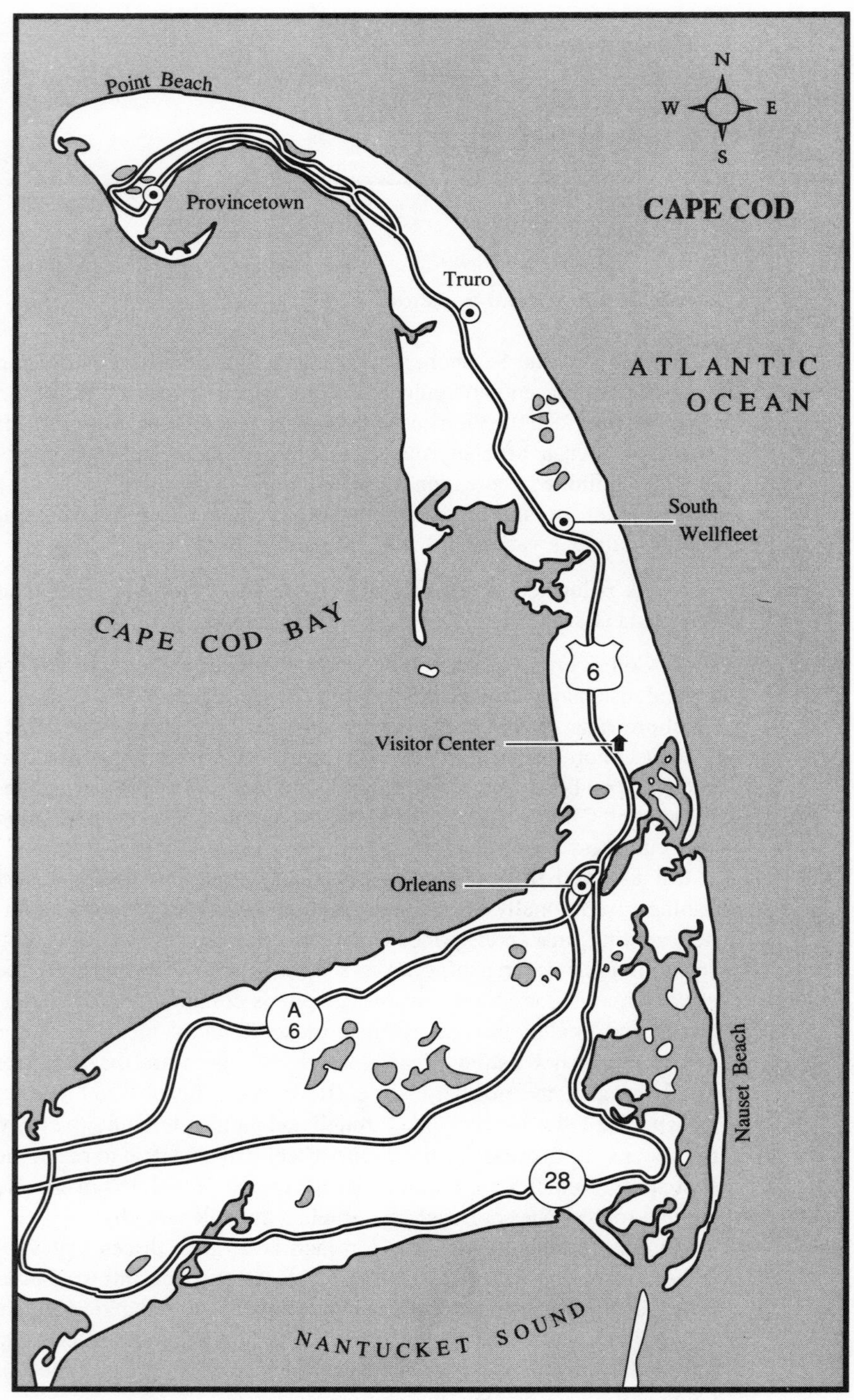
N
W
E
S
CAPE COD
Point Beach
Provincetown
Truro
ATLANTIC
OCEAN
South
Wellfleet
CAPE COD BAY
6
Visitor Center
Orleans
A
6
Nauset Beach
28
NANTUCKET SOUND

Surf fishing is best in the spring and fall with larger fish taken in the fall. Striped bass appear along the outer beaches in mid-May. Striped bass have been declining further south, from New York to North Carolina, but Cape Cod continues to attract good numbers of stripers, although not in the great numbers of former years. In 1984, the state enacted new regulations to reduce the bag limits for striped bass and help rebuild the striped bass populations. Be sure to check the current regulations.

Bluefish arrive in late May and stay into July. Blues and stripers reappear in late August and stay through October as they are grouping together for their southern migration. They feed heavily on menhaden in Cape waters prior to their departure for warmer waters.

The summer months, July and August particularly, are usually slow for surf fishing. Most of the summer catch is panfish, such as cod, flounder, whiting, and tautog. Small bluefish and small striped bass are also available. Early morning or late evening are the best times to be on the beach during the summer. When surf fishing slackens, fishing in Cape Cod Bay often remains fair to good. Some giant tuna are found in the Bay but they begin to move out about mid-September. The Provincetown area, at the tip of the Cape, is usually productive for tuna.

Check with local tackle stores for the latest information on fish locations and best baits. Rocky areas, jetties, inlets, and points are always good areas to fish. An arduous haul is required to reach the Chatham Inlet at the south end of Nauset Beach, but the effort may be worthwhile. The convergence of currents and resulting turbidity at the inlet attracts predators (bluefish and striped bass) in search of bait fish. Look for the cuts and sloughs along sandy beaches that often harbor panfish.

Other productive saltwater areas outside the park are Nantucket Sound, south of the Cape, and the 7.7-mile-long Cape Cod Canal, which connects Cape Cod and mainland Massachusetts.

As mentioned earlier, the Cape boasts good freshwater fishing. In the park area, try Great Pond, Gull Pond, and the Pamet River for brook, brown, and rainbow trout. Great and Gull ponds also contain smallmouth bass. A car-top boat is helpful on the ponds.

Outside the park area, Cape Cod has an excellent sea-run trout fishery with large brown trout, called salters, arriving in the fall to spawn. Most of the Cape salter streams are on the south side, except Scorton Creek in Sandwich, on the north. Some of the top streams are the Mashpee, Quashnet, Santuit, Childs, and Coonamessett. The Cape also contains a number of cranberry bogs that offer good fishing for largemouth bass.

License A Massachusetts license is required to fish the freshwater ponds or rivers. No license is required for saltwater fishing. Be sure to check the current state regulations for both fresh and saltwater fishing.

Camping There are no camping facilities on park service land, but Nickerson State Park in Brewster has developed campgrounds, and there are private campgrounds in the area. The Cape Cod Chamber of Commerce can provide a campground listing. Reservations are recommended.

Camping in self-contained vehicles is permitted in designated areas of Race Point in accordance with permit requirements.

Maps The park brochure map is a good general location map. The following USGS quad sheets are also helpful: Provincetown, North Truro, Wellfleet, Orleans, and Chatham. Offshore navigation requires nautical chart #13246.

The Chamber of Commerce offers a free map, "Sportsman's Guide to Cape Cod," that shows all the pond and stream fishing, boat ramps, and surf fishing access areas on the Cape.

Park Address	*Chamber of Commerce*
Cape Cod NS	Cape Cod C.C.
South Wellfleet, MA 02663	Hyannis, MA 02601
phone: (508) 349-3785	phone: (508) 362-3225

Additional Information The book *50 Trout Ponds in Massachusetts*, by Owen Flynn, describes ten trout ponds on Cape Cod and includes contour maps. The book is available from: New Hampshire Publishing Company, Somersworth, NH, 03878.

For a complete list of the trout and bass waters in Massachusetts, send a stamped, self-addressed envelope to: Division of Fisheries and Wildlife Field Headquarters, Route 135, Westboro, MA, 01581.

MICHIGAN

Isle Royale National Park

Isle Royale, in the northwest corner of Lake Superior, is famous for the beauty of its wilderness. The largest island in Lake Superior, it is approximately 45 miles long and 9 miles across at its widest point. The island is a sanctuary for wolves and moose, and wildlife scientists have used it to study the population dynamics that keep both species in balance. There are no roads on Isle Royale, only forests, lakes, wildlife, and scenic shores.

Access Transportation from the mainland (Michigan or Minnesota) is by boat or floatplane. Reservations are always required. There are no roads or cars on the island, only 176 miles of foot trails. A boat regularly circles the island and drops off and picks up passengers at various points. The park distributes a free brochure, *Getting There,* that lists rates, schedules, and contacts for both boats and seaplanes.

Fishing Where do you fish on an island surrounded by water and dotted with inland lakes and streams? Just about anywhere is good at Isle Royale. Of the 38 lakes scattered over the island, 31 are known to contain game fish. Most contain northern pike. Walleye are found in Whittlesey and Chickenbone lakes, while Siskiwit Lake (largest inland lake) contains brook trout and lake trout in addition to pike and yellow perch. The seven lakes without fish are: Hatchet, Lily, Newt, Sumner, Stickleback, Theresa, and Wallace.

The fishing on these 31 underfished lakes is excellent throughout the summer for those willing to venture inland. The only access is by canoe or foot trail. Canoes and small boats may be transported to the island on the passenger boats. Siskiwit Lake is only a half-mile portage from Malone Bay on the south side of the island. Other lakes may be reached by portaging from the east end of Siskiwit. Rather than bring your own boat, you can rent canoes, boats, and motors on the island. Motors are not allowed on inland lakes. The park also has a brochure showing the suggested canoeing routes.

The streams on the island contain mostly brook trout, with some rainbow trout. Washington Creek is one of the better streams for rainbow trout. Steelhead find their way into the island streams in

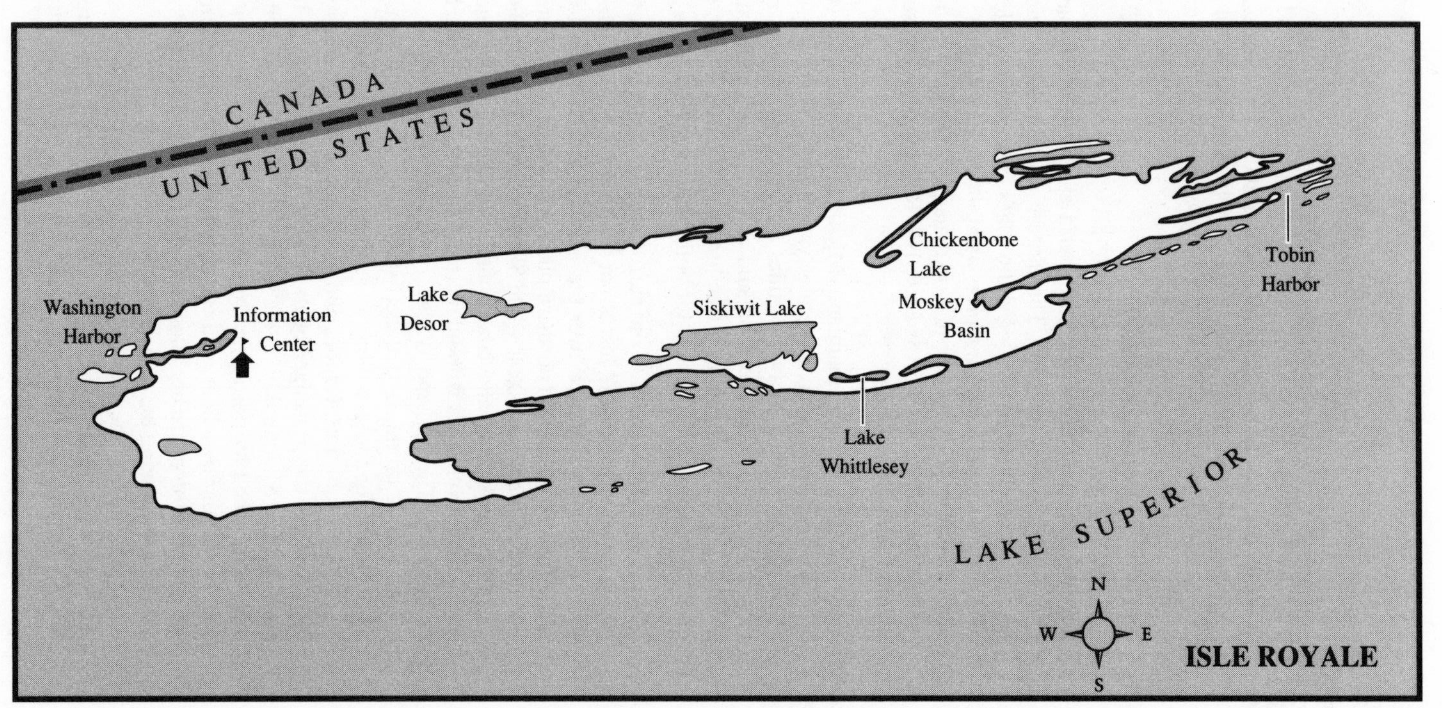
CANADA
UNITED STATES
Washington Harbor
Information Center
Lake Desor
Siskiwit Lake
Chickenbone Lake
Moskey Basin
Tobin Harbor
Lake Whittlesey
LAKE SUPERIOR
N
W
E
S
ISLE ROYALE

the spring and the fall. Not much is known about fishing the island streams for steelhead because there have been very few visitors during the steelhead runs. There are more dependable steelhead streams on the mainland in Michigan, Minnesota, and Wisconsin.

Rainbow trout fishing on the island is best in late April through May. The best brook and rainbow trout fishing is found off the mouths of the island streams. Tobin Harbor, Moskey Basin, and Washington Harbor are good areas.

Northern pike are found in most of the coves around the island but Lake Superior is usually fished for lake trout. The lake trout are of two varieties, one called lean trout, the other called fat or siscowet. The siscowet are good-sized, but poor table fare because of the high levels of fat or oil in their flesh. These fish are identified by their blocky appearance.

Lake trout fishing is best from July through August, when the fish are in shallow water near the island and can be caught using light tackle. During the remainder of the year, they are further off shore near rocky reefs or ledges in 100 to 200 feet of water, requiring heavy-duty trolling gear. Lake Superior charters equipped with trolling gear are available at the island.

License A Michigan license is required to fish in Lake Superior; however, you do not need a license to fish the inland lakes and streams. Michigan fishing regulations apply in both cases.

Camping There are 36 back-country camping areas on the island, with a total of 247 spaces. A camping permit is required and is available free from park headquarters or a ranger station. The camping season is from May through October; the island is closed from November 1 to April 15. The park distributes a free brochure, *Camping, Hiking, Boating,* that details complete camping information.

Maps There is a special USGS park map, entitled "Isle Royale National Park." For fishing or boating in Lake Superior, you should obtain nautical chart #14976.

Park Address
Isle Royale NP
87 North Ripley St.
Houghton, MI 49931
phone: (906) 482-0986

Chamber of Commerce
Keweenaw Peninsula C.C.
P.O. Box 336
Houghton, MI 49931
phone: (906) 482-5240

Additional Information A small book, *Fishes of Isle Royale,* is available for a reasonable price from the Isle Royale Natural History Association. The book describes the major sport fish of the island and contains a map of the park listing the fish species in each lake. Most of the research for this book was compiled some years ago, but the book has recently been updated and reprinted. Contact: Isle Royale Natural History Association, 87 N. Ripley St., Houghton, MI, 49931; phone: (906) 482-0986. Maps are also available from the Association. Ask for a catalog of park publications.

A good guide to the park is *Isle Royale National Park: Foot Trails and Water Routes,* by Jim DuFresne. This book describes hiking, camping, fishing spots, and the portage system as well as harbors and coves. Available from: The Mountaineers, 306 Second Avenue West, Seattle, WA, 98119; phone (toll free): 1-800-553-4453.

Pictured Rocks National Lakeshore

Located in Michigan's Upper Peninsula, along the Lake Superior shoreline between Munising and Grand Marais, Pictured Rocks is a little-known park that has something for everyone. The park offers beautiful scenery, waterfalls, forest, beaches, fishing, hiking, and camping. Pictured Rocks was established in 1966 as the first national lakeshore in the National Park System.

Access The park is in Alger County and can be reached either from Michigan 28 at Munising or Michigan 77 at Grand Marais. Other county and state roads lead directly into the park.

Fishing Fishing opportunities abound at Pictured Rocks. The park waters support a wide variety of fish including northern pike, largemouth and smallmouth bass, muskellunge, yellow perch, brook, brown, and lake trout, whitefish, and splake (a hybrid of brook and lake trout). Anadromous species include coho, chinook, and pink salmon, along with steelhead and smelt.

Because there is so much information, this section will first discuss Lake Superior, then the inland lakes, and finally the streams.

Lake Superior Because of its cold water, Lake Superior is not as fertile as the other Great Lakes and does not stratify. Large salmon and trout run throughout the lake, but these fish do not grow as large as the fish in the other Great Lakes. Nonetheless, the fishing is still good in the Pictured Rocks area from Munising to Grand Marais.

Fishing along the 35-mile Pictured Rocks shoreline is a sightseer's delight. Boating east out of Munising, you will see sheer rock cliffs of various shapes and colors in addition to waterfalls. The scenery is different west of Grand Marais, where the park encompasses the Grand Sable Dunes. At all times, boaters should be cautious and aware of

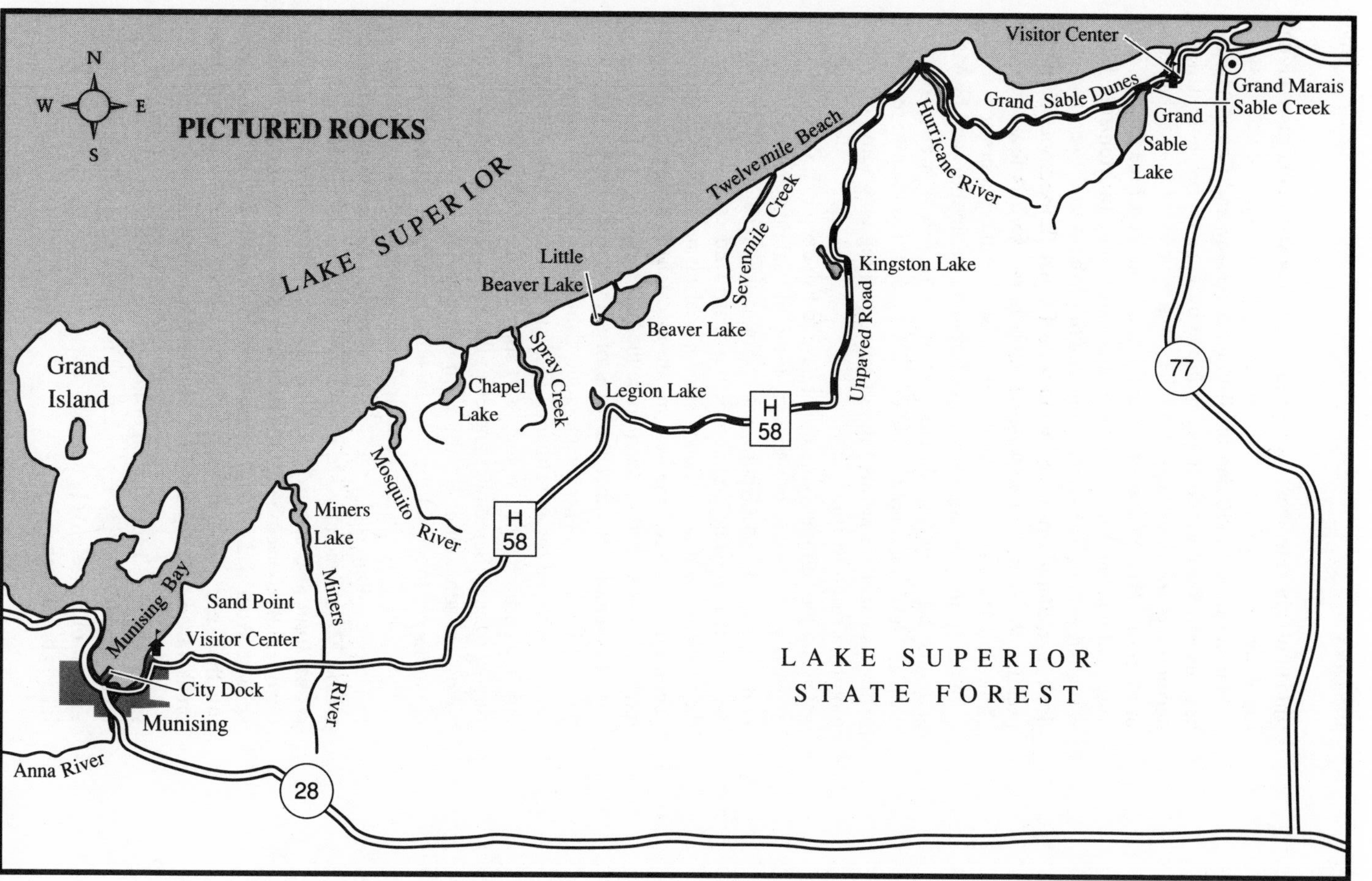
N
W
E
S
PICTURED ROCKS
LAKE SUPERIOR
Visitor Center
Grand Sable Dunes
Grand Marais
Sable Creek
Grand Sable Lake
Hurricane River
Twelvemile Beach
Sevenmile Creek
Kingston Lake
Unpaved Road
Little Beaver Lake
Beaver Lake
Grand Island
Chapel Lake
Spray Creek
Legion Lake
H 58
77
Mosquito River
Miners Lake
H 58
Miners River
Munising Bay
Sand Point
Visitor Center
City Dock
Munising
Anna River
28
LAKE SUPERIOR STATE FOREST

sudden weather changes, for there are very few safe anchorages along the shore.

Starting with winter and ice fishing, Munising and Grand Marais bays usually have a safe covering of ice by January, however, strong currents can create weak spots in the ice in the east and west channels of Munising Bay. Whitefish are the primary targets of ice fishing, but trout, salmon, and northern pike are also taken. In Munising Bay, whitefish angling is heavy off the mouth of the Anna River, the city dock, and Sand Point in 45 to 80 feet of water. Lake trout fishing is popular off Sand Point in water as deep as 100 feet. A few coho and chinook salmon are also caught off the Sand Point boathouse.

In the spring, steelhead are found around river mouths and by May and June all along the shoreline in 10 to 15 feet of water. Brown trout and lake trout, cohos, and chinooks are all found close to shore; fishing is excellent at this time of year. Trolling or wading off river mouths is often worthwhile.

During the summer, you do not have to fish deep in Lake Superior. Because the lake doesn't stratify, trout and salmon are often found in the upper 10 to 20 feet of water. You can also catch fish by going deep, if that is your preference, but it isn't necessary. By August, the chinooks and some cohos start appearing near shore. August is generally considered the best month to catch chinooks, and before daybreak and after dark seem to be the best times.

In September, the first fall runs of salmon show up in Lake Superior tributaries. This means good fishing off the river mouths as well as in the rivers and streams. In alternate years, pink salmon provide the earliest action as they start appearing in river mouths by late August or early September and enter the rivers shortly thereafter. The cohos and some chinooks follow in mid-September. Both cohos and chinooks are found off the river mouths throughout September.

Fall fishing is always good in Lake Superior. Lake trout spawn in October along rocky reefs. The islands near Munising and in the Grand Marais vicinity are good areas to try. Coho, steelhead, and brown trout also spawn in the fall and provide good action through October. By November, whitefish have moved into the shallows to spawn. Trout and salmon often intermingle with the whitefish, eating their eggs, and are caught along with whitefish. Fishing near breakwalls is usually good for whitefish at this time.

Inland Lakes There are eight inland lakes in the park with a total area of approximately 1,700 acres. Fish grow slowly in these lakes as a result of the relatively unproductive cold-water environment. Each lake is briefly reviewed.

Grand Sable Lake—features splake, rainbow and lake trout, northern pike, smallmouth bass, rock bass, and yellow perch. A picnic ground and launch site are on the northeast corner.

Trappers Lake—contains yellow perch, largemouth bass, and rock bass. The only access to this lake is by trail.

Beaver Lake and Little Beaver Lake—These lakes are connected by a short stream. Both contain northern pike, walleye, smallmouth bass, rock bass, yellow perch, and bullheads. Each spring, Beaver Lake gets a few steelhead via an outlet stream to Lake Superior. The best area for smallmouths on Beaver Lake is along the rocky southeast shore. Both lakes produce large pike—from 12 to 20 pounds—each year. There is a campground on Little Beaver Lake and access to Beaver Lake is via the connecting creek.

Chapel Lake—contains northern pike and yellow perch. The average size of the pike is relatively large with most fish weighing 25 to 30 pounds.

Legion Lake—contains yellow perch and splake, including some large splake. Fingerling brook trout were stocked in 1983. This lake is closed to winter fishing.

Kingston Lake—contains tiger muskie, largemouth and smallmouth bass, walleye, yellow perch, and bluegills. There are many bays with numerous fallen trees providing shoreline cover for bass and muskies. Walleyes are caught regularly in the immediate vicinity of the launch ramp. There is a state forest campground at the north end of the lake.

Miners Lake—a 30-acre lake containing yellow perch, northern pike, and white suckers. The Miners River flows through the lake. There is no direct access to the lake, but you can wade or canoe up the Miners River to it or walk in from the road. Fishing is fair to good for perch and pike, with an occasional good-sized brook or rainbow trout.

Streams Brook trout streams within the park are too numerous to list. Six of the major streams are discussed below. All are small and wadeable. Fly-fishing is hampered by the small size of the streams and the tag alder fringes that restrict fly casting.

Hurricane River—contains brook trout in the headwaters and beaver ponds. There are good steelhead runs in the spring and fall, and coho salmon run in the fall. The stream is only 15 to 20 feet wide and all fishing is done by wading. The best areas for steelhead and coho are off the river mouth in Lake Superior and below a low head falls just below County Road 700. There is a campground at the mouth.

Miners River—similar to the Hurricane River, it contains brook trout and has steelhead runs in spring and fall and a coho run in the fall.

Mosquito River—a difficult river for anglers to reach. Trails leading to the river are often impassable after heavy rains or during spring snow melt. The river has brook trout above Mosquito Falls and steelhead runs in the spring and fall below. The best brook trout fishing is in beaver ponds. Steelhead fishing is good around the river mouth as well as in the 3 miles of log-jammed river up to the falls.

Sable Creek—this creek has good runs of steelhead in the spring and pink salmon in the fall. Steelhead and coho salmon also run in the river in the fall. The fish can only go about one-quarter mile above the river mouth before waterfalls block their passage. Above the falls, the creek contains suckers and rock bass and is not worth your time.

Seven Mile Creek—contains brook trout, plus runs of steelhead in the spring and fall. Both species are found throughout the creek, which is noted as a consistent trout producer.

Spray Creek—same as Seven Mile Creek.

Although it is outside the park, the Anna River is worth a try. It is west of the park and flows into Munising Bay. The river is open to fishing all year and has the usual spring and fall runs of steelhead, plus a fall run of coho salmon. It is also good in the spring for brown trout entering from the lake. The river mouth is a consistent fish producer.

License A Michigan fishing license is required.

Camping There are three primitive camping areas accessible by car: Hurricane River (22 spaces), 12 Mile Beach (37 spaces) and Little Beaver Lake (8 spaces). There are also 13 back-country camping areas. These areas are open from May until November. Developed campgrounds are also available in nearby Hiawatha National Forest and Grand Sable State Forest.

Maps There is a topographic map of all of Pictured Rocks Lakeshore available from the park for a reasonable price. If any extensive exploring is planned, you should have this map.

Contour maps are available for Little Beaver, Beaver, Grand Sable, Legion, and Miners lakes from the Michigan United Conservation Clubs (MUCC). For a catalog and prices, contact: MUCC, P.O. Box 30235, Lansing, MI, 48909; phone: (517) 371-1041.

For fishing in Lake Superior, nautical chart #14963 is helpful.

Park Address
Pictured Rocks NL
P.O. Box 40
Munising, MI 49862
phone: (906) 387-2607

Chamber of Commerce
Alger C.C.
P.O. Box 405
Munising, MI, 49862
phone: (906) 387-2138

Additional Information A book available from the Michigan United Conservation Clubs, entitled *Trout Streams of Michigan,* Vol. 1, contains five pages of descriptive information on trout streams in Alger County. The book describes more than 30 streams in both the Upper and Lower Peninsulas. To order the book, write to the address given for the Michigan United Conservation Clubs in the map section above.

Available also is *Travel Service Directory to Michigan's Upper Peninsula*, free from: Upper Peninsula Travel and Recreation Association, P.O. Box 400, Iron Mountain, MI, 49801; phone: (906) 774-5480.

Sleeping Bear Dunes National Lakeshore

Sleeping Bear Dunes is a glacial-formed area located along Lake Michigan. It is fringed with massive coastal dunes and dotted with numerous clear lakes. Also included as part of the park are the offshore Manitou Islands. Mixed in with the dunes and the lakes are dense beech and maple forests and cedar-lined streams flowing into Lake Michigan. The park is extremely popular for a variety of recreational pursuits and the entire region attracts thousands of vacationers.

Access The park is on the northwestern shore of Michigan's lower peninsula (Benzie and Leelanau counties). The entire lakeshore within the park is accessible via Michigan Highway 22 (M22).

Fishing Sleeping Bear Dunes offers a cornucopia of opportunities for lake, river, and surf fishing. The entire region is renowned for great fishing, with salmon and steelhead attracting hordes of anglers. The park lakes and streams provide good fishing, but most of the attention is on Lake Michigan and the Platte River, which consistently yield large coho and chinook salmon and steelhead.

Lake Michigan Since coho salmon were introduced into the Platte River and Lake Michigan in the mid-1960s, they have spread to the other Great Lakes and completely revitalized the sport fishing industry in the surrounding Great Lake states and Canadian provinces. In addition to coho, chinook salmon were later introduced and experiments with Atlantic salmon are continuing in Michigan.

Fishing is good all along Lake Michigan in the park area, but Platte Bay is one of the most productive locations. Fishing in the Platte Bay area starts in April with the spring run of steelhead up the Platte River. The river mouth is the local hot spot and usually crowded.

There is a boat ramp at the river mouth (small boats only) and

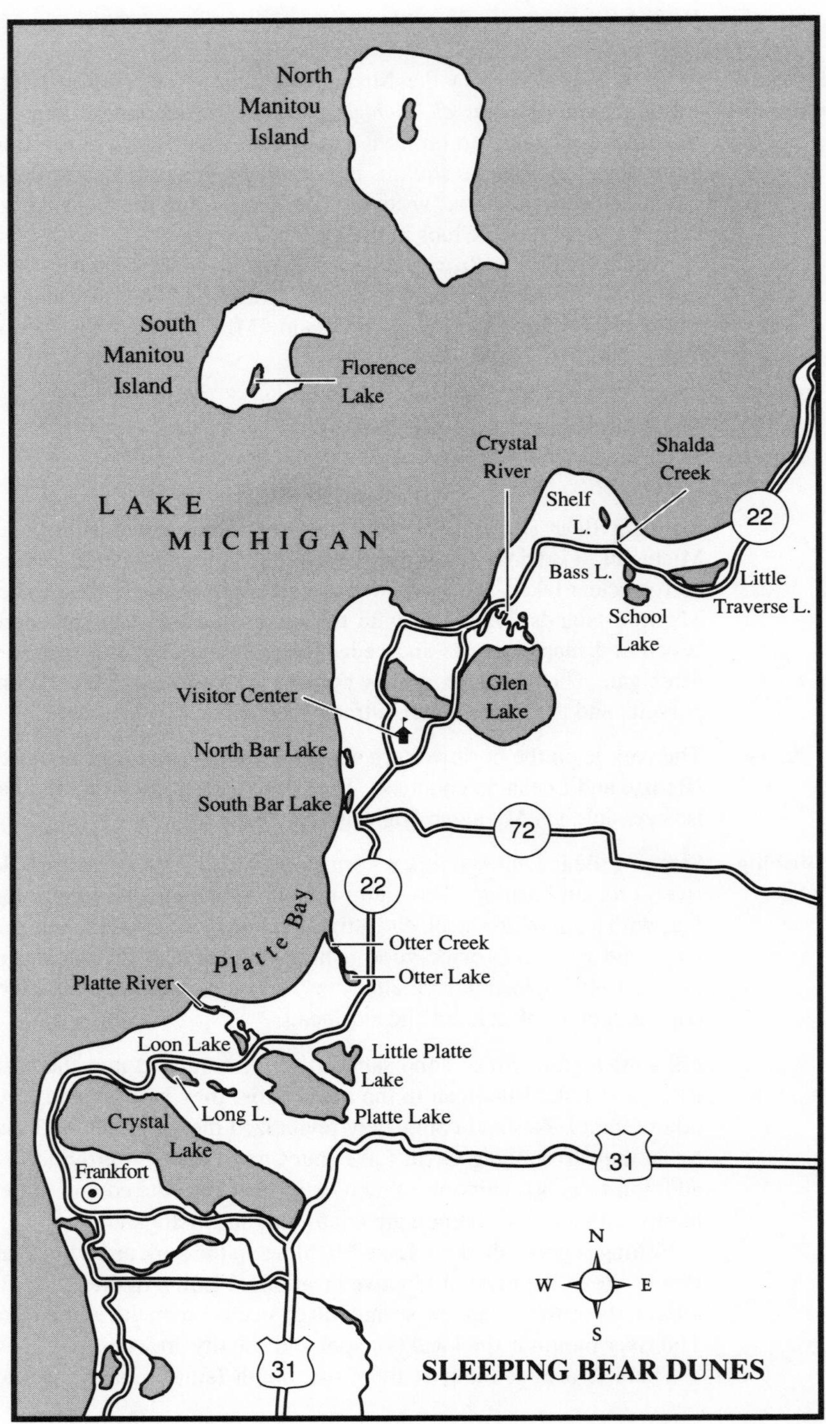
North Manitou Island
South Manitou Island
Florence Lake
LAKE MICHIGAN
Crystal River
Shalda Creek
Shelf L.
22
Bass L.
Little Traverse L.
School Lake
Glen Lake
Visitor Center
North Bar Lake
South Bar Lake
72
22
Platte Bay
Otter Creek
Otter Lake
Platte River
Loon Lake
Little Platte Lake
Long L.
Platte Lake
Crystal Lake
Frankfort
31
N
W
E
S
31
SLEEPING BEAR DUNES

A 12-pound brown trout taken from Platte Bay. Note the large "beer belly" typical of these lake-dwelling fish.—*Mike Osman*

folks fishing there troll throughout the bay and work the river with spawn sacs and steelhead flies. I have fly-cast at the river mouth in mid-April and watched in amazement as schools of steelhead rushed by my legs (ignoring my fly) into the Platte River. Surf fishing also gets good results with spawn sacs or spoons at this time all along the shoreline. An unexpected bonus is the possibility of catching the large brown trout that cruise the lake shallows close enough to be fished from shore. The browns are often referred to as footballs or beer bellies because of their shape. They are relatively short but very fat and heavy, similar to a football.

Just about all Lake Michigan tributaries within Michigan support good spring steelhead runs.

By May, brown and lake trout, along with coho and chinook salmon, have moved in along the shore. The coho average 2 to 5 pounds, and the chinook 10 to 20 pounds. This fishing lasts through June.

When July arrives, the salmon are farther offshore and a boat with specialized trolling equipment is required. The key to taking salmon is to locate 54-degree water and fish hard around alewife schools. Alewife, the main forage fish for salmon in the Great Lakes, allow the salmon to gain substantial amounts of weight in a relatively short time. A sonar or graph unit is indispensible in combination with a thermometer to locate the fish. The Manitou Islands are a hot spot for chinook salmon in the summer. Although the islands are a 20-mile run from the port of Leland, the fishing can be worth the extra time and effort.

July is also one of the finest months for large brown trout in Platte Bay. The browns are usually at 10- to 25-foot depths, but may hit at any depth when they are feeding.

As summer progresses, the salmon move farther out into the lake. August is considered the premier month for salmon fishing in Lake Michigan. The weather is usually beautiful and the salmon, after months of feeding on alewife, may top 30 pounds. Platte Bay probably produces more salmon during August than any other spot in the Great Lakes. September is just as productive, but the weather often isn't as pleasant. Chinook are found near shore at dawn and can be taken by surf fishing from piers. The pier at Frankfort is one of the best fishing piers on Lake Michigan.

In September, huge schools of coho and chinook gather off river mouths and small inland lakes tributary to Lake Michigan. Platte Bay harbors vast schools and the action is spectacular. Shoreline anglers score consistently at this time in the Platte river-mouth area. The fish are heading up the Platte River to spawn and by October most of the salmon are in the rivers. Lake trout and brown trout, along with immature coho and chinook salmon, move in close to shore in the fall. Browns enter the Platte River in September to spawn. In October, the browns go on a postspawn feeding spree in the bay and near the river mouth.

October and November can be excellent for surf fishing, providing the anglers can tough out the often miserable weather. Steelhead gather off river mouths to feed and to enter the rivers for their fall run. Lake trout fishing off the Frankfort pier is also good in November.

Platte River The Platte River is a beautiful, wooded, crystal-clear stream with a sand and gravel bottom, making it a perfect spawning river for salmon, steelhead, and brown trout. When coho salmon were first introduced into the Great Lakes, they were planted in the Platte River and nearby Bear Creek.

The main attractions of the Platte River are the spring and fall runs of steelhead and the fall run of coho salmon, along with a good population of resident brown trout. The coho are popular fly-fishing targets because of their willingness to take a fly. The best months for steelhead are April and November through December; coho fishing is best from late September into November. The salmon enter the river to spawn and die, not to feed, so repeated casts to the salmon are usually necessary.

The river is shallow enough for easy wading and so clear that you can spot the fish on their lies. The clarity of the water also works against fishing efforts, and a stealthy approach is demanded. The Platte also has a good population of native brown trout, which are difficult to catch because the river gets heavily fished throughout the year.

The Betsie River The Betsie River is also a noteworthy steelhead and salmon stream. The runs are similar to those in the Platte River. The river is a very popular fishing spot and can become quite crowded during the runs.

Other Waters Michigan justifiably bills itself as a Water Wonderland. There are rivers and lakes throughout the interior of the state, a number of them within or just outside the park boundaries. From north to south, they are:

Little Traverse Lake—a northern pike, muskellunge, bass, and panfish lake, just outside the park.

Shalda Creek—the outlet to Little Traverse Lake. It is a small stream with a few brook and brown trout present. It also receives a spring run of smelt.

Shell Lake—93 acres with a fair population of largemouth bass. It also contains pike, panfish, and yellow perch. There is an extensive shoal at the lake's perimeter.

Bass Lake—small, silty, and weedy. Don't bother.

School Lake—a shallow, 100-acre lake with largemouth bass, pike, and panfish.

Tucker Lake—a small, weedy lake with bass, pike, and panfish.

Crystal River—the outlet to Glen Lake. A small, clear stream with spring runs of smelt, steelhead, and smallmouth bass. It also has fall runs of steelhead, coho, chinook, and pink salmon.

Glen Lake—a large, clear, deep lake containing yellow perch, splake (a hybrid of brook and lake trout), lake trout, coho salmon, northern pike, and panfish. It has a very regular bottom contour and is connected to Little Glen Lake by a short channel. The same species are found in Little Glen, which is shallow with a sandy bottom.

North Bar Lake—a small lake with a modest population of bass and panfish.

South Bar Lake—a small lake with pike, bass, and panfish, just outside the park.

Otter Creek—a small stream with a small resident population of brook and brown trout. It receives spring runs of smelt and steelhead, and fall runs of salmon and steelhead. Surf fishing near the creek mouth is popular in the spring and fall for salmon and steelhead.

Otter, Bass, Deer lakes—these lakes form the headwaters of Otter Creek and contain moderate populations of panfish, bass, and pike. No motors are allowed on these lakes.

Loon Lake—the Platte River flows through the lake. It has resident populations of largemouth bass, northern pike, and panfish. In the spring, runs of steelhead and suckers enter the lake and in the fall, steelhead, coho and chinook salmon and brown trout are present.

Florence Lake—located on South Manitou Island. It contains perch, bass, and pike. It is easy to wade and fish from the shallows.

Crystal Lake—a picturesque, large, deep, clear lake just south of the park boundary. It is very good for lake trout especially during the winter, and also contains brown and rainbow trout, coho salmon, whitefish, yellow perch, smallmouth bass, and burbot.

With all the fishing and vacationing possibilities in the region, many tourists, including those who come to fish, are drawn to the park area and constitute a major part of the regional economy. Guides, charter boats, boat and canoe rentals, and lodging are readily available.

License A Michigan fishing license is required. Be sure to check the state regulations because some waters may be closed and a variety of special fishing regulations apply to the Platte River. Also check park regulations because several inland lakes in the park have motor restrictions.

Camping There are two developed campgrounds in the park, D. H. Day (93 spaces) and Platte River (160 spaces). Back-country camping (permit required) is allowed on the mainland and on South Manitou Island. Other private campgrounds and state forest campgrounds are available nearby.

Maps Topographic maps are useful for getting to some of the lakes and streams. The quad sheets needed are: Frankfort, Empire, Maple City, and North Manitou. These maps are in the 15-minute series. North Manitou is useful only if you plan to explore South Manitou Island.

Navigating around Lake Michigan requires nautical chart #14912, which includes the Manitou Islands and Platte Bay. From Platte Bay south, you will need nautical chart #14907.

Contour maps are available for South Bar and Glen Lakes in Leelanau County and for Crystal Lake in Benzie County. For a catalog of maps and publications, contact: Michigan United Conservation Clubs (MUCC), P.O. Box 30235, Lansing, MI, 48909; phone: (517) 371-1041. They also sell nautical charts.

Park Address
Sleeping Bear Dunes NL
P.O. Box 277
9922 Front St. (Hwy. M-72)
Empire, MI 49630
phone: (616) 326-5134

Chambers of Commerce

Benzie County C.C.
P.O. Box 505
Beulah, MI 49617
phone: (616) 882-5802

Western Michigan Tourist Assn.
136 Fulton E.
Grand Rapids, MI 49503
phone: (616) 456-8557

Additional Information

The Michigan Travel Bureau distributes a packet of information specifically about fishing in Michigan, including a charter boat directory for the Great Lakes. Write to: Michigan Travel Bureau, P.O. Box 30226, Lansing, MI, 48909; phone: (toll free) 1-800-543-2937.

A detailed description of the Platte and Betsie rivers is part of *Trout Streams of Michigan,* Vol. 2, by Janet Mehl. This book is available from the Michigan United Conservation Clubs. See their address in the map section above.

The Michigan Fishing Hotline, sponsored by the Michigan Department of Natural Resources, provides current fishing information about the Great Lakes. The line is operational from Memorial Day to Labor Day. Phone: (517) 373-0908.

MINNESOTA

Grand Portage National Monument

Grand Portage National Monument, on the site of the old North West Company depot on Lake Superior, recalls an era of trappers and fur traders. The Grand Portage area was part of the main route of explorers, Indians, fur traders, and missionaries into the northwest.

Access Grand Portage is in the northeastern tip of Minnesota in Cook County, 36 miles northeast of Grand Marais and 145 miles northeast of Duluth, off U.S. 61.

Fishing The park provides very limited fishing opportunities. Grand Portage Creek runs through the park and contains some steelhead, salmon, and trout. Steelhead are in the creek in the spring and fall and coho salmon appear in the fall.

The creek is regulated by the Chippewa Indians of Grand Portage, whose land surrounds the park. Other streams in the area are noted for receiving good runs of steelhead and salmon and Grand Portage Creek is not usually regarded as one of the better streams.

The Grand Portage Trail (8.5 miles) goes from the stockade to the site of Fort Charlotte on the Pigeon River. Northern pike fishing is generally good on the Pigeon River near Fort Charlotte.

License A Minnesota fishing license and a permit from the Grand Portage Chippewa Indians are required.

Camping Primitive back-country camping is available at Fort Charlotte on the Pigeon River. There are several small private campgrounds in the area. Judge Magney State Park Campground is 22 miles south on U.S. 61.

Maps Topographic maps are not necessary. The park brochure map will suffice.

Park Address
Grand Portage NM
P.O. Box 666
Grand Marais, MN 55604
phone: (218) 387-2788

Chamber of Commerce
Tip of the Arrowhead
Association
Grand Marais, MN 55604
phone: (218) 387-2524

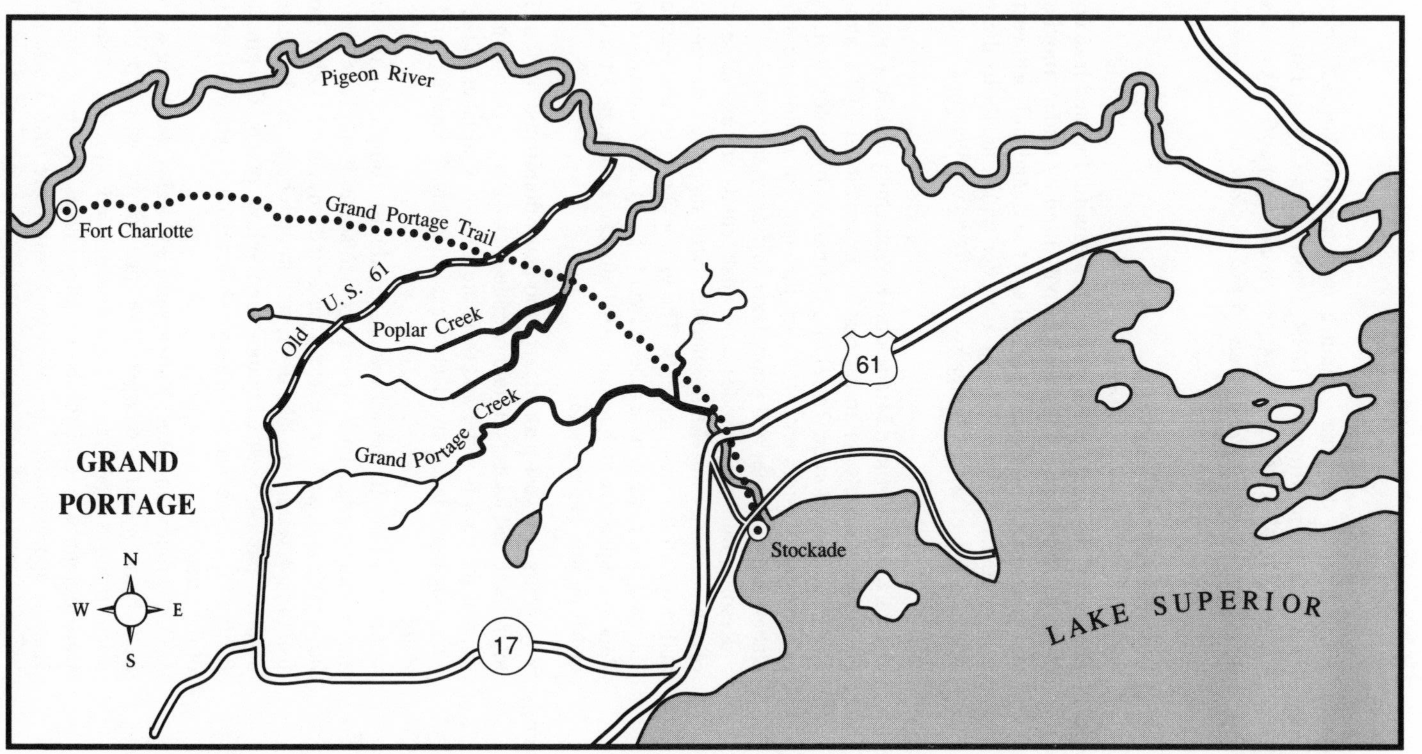
Pigeon River
Fort Charlotte
Grand Portage Trail
Old U.S. 61
Poplar Creek
Grand Portage Creek
GRAND PORTAGE
N
W
E
S
61
Stockade
17
LAKE SUPERIOR

Additional Information For fishing in the area, obtain a free copy of *North Shore Fishing Guide* from: Minnesota DNR, Information Center, Box 40, 500 Lafayette Rd., St.Paul, MN 55155; phone (612) 296-6157. Also ask for a copy of *Public Water Access for Cook County.*

Voyageurs National Park

Voyageurs National Park is part of the beautiful forested lake country of northern Minnesota that was heavily used by traders moving furs and other goods between Montreal and the Canadian Northwest. The park contains 30 lakes, shares a border with Canada to the north, and is adjacent to the better-known Boundary Waters Canoe Area (BWCA).

Access The park is in northern Minnesota (Koochiching and St. Louis counties) approximately 11 miles east of International Falls, along the U.S./Canadian border. Travel into the park is by motor boat, canoe, or airplane. Visitors enter the park through four main access points: Kabetogama, Crane, and Rainy lakes or from Ash River.

Resorts, outfitters, guides, and boat rentals are available at each of the access points. Many outfitters will supply all the equipment and make all the arrangements. The visitor center on the west end of Kabetogama Lake can be reached via U.S. 53 and County Road 122. Park headquarters at International Falls can be reached via U.S. 53 or Minnesota Highway 11.

Fishing Voyageurs is a vast park of 219,000 acres dominated by four large, interconnected lakes and innumerable rocky islands. More than one-third of the park is water and there are a total of 30 lakes in the park. The four main lakes are: Kabetogama, Rainy, Namakan, and Sand Point.

Sport fishing in the area focusses almost completely on walleye and northern pike. Park waters provide some of the best fishing for both pike and walleye that can be found anywhere. Other popular fish in park waters are lake trout, smallmouth bass, muskellunge, and assorted panfish such as crappie and yellow perch. Despite superb fishing for all species, the walleye (Minnesota's state fish), gets most of the attention.

Of the four main lakes, Kabetogama and Rainy are the best known. Lake Kabetogama, the largest lake, lies entirely within park boundaries. It has a total area of 25,000 acres and 78 miles of shoreline. Kabetogama is one of the best walleye lakes in the country. Rainy Lake is approximately 40 miles long with more than 4,000 miles of

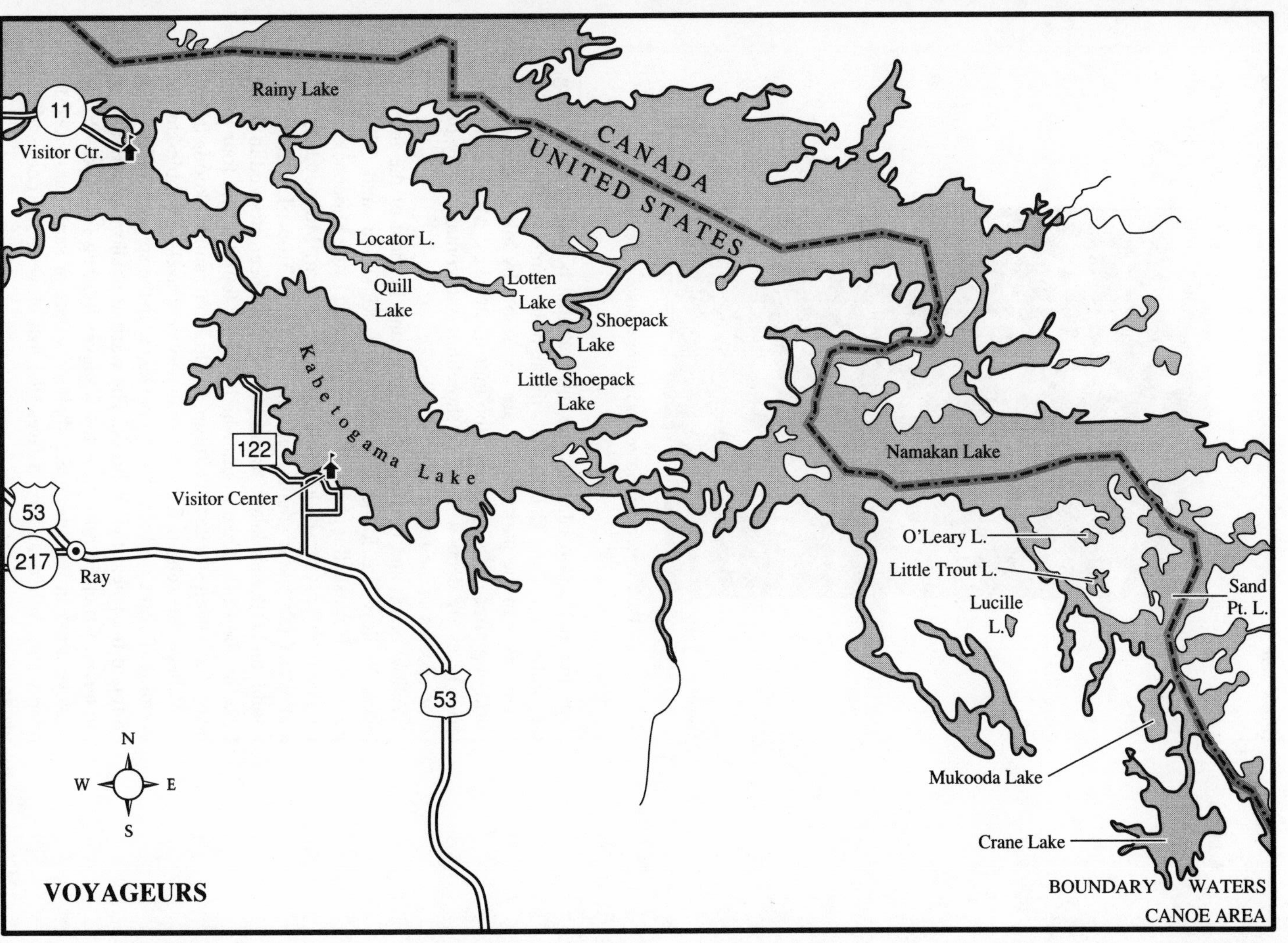

Rainy Lake
11
Visitor Ctr.
CANADA
UNITED STATES
Locator L.
Quill Lake
Lotten Lake
Shoepack Lake
Little Shoepack Lake
Kabetogama Lake
122
Visitor Center
53
217
Ray
Namakan Lake
O'Leary L.
Little Trout L.
Lucille L.
Sand Pt. L.
Mukooda Lake
Crane Lake
N
W
E
S
VOYAGEURS
BOUNDARY WATERS CANOE AREA

Park waters are noted for northern pike.—*Ken Alt*

shoreline and 1,600 islands. The international boundary separating the United States and Canada runs through the center of the lake.

The lakes in the park interior are accessible by hiking and canoe portaging after crossing one of the four main lakes. Most of the interior lakes are deep with rocky shorelines and contain many of the same species as the four major lakes.

Yellow perch and northern pike are found in most of the interior lakes. Walleye are found in Little Trout, Mukooda, and O'Leary lakes, while muskellunge inhabit Shoepack and Little Shoepack lakes. Largemouth bass are in Jorgens, Locator, Loiten, Mukooda, Quill, and War Club lakes; smallmouth bass in Little Trout, Lucille, Mukooda, and O'Leary lakes. Rainbow trout have been stocked in Beast Lake by the state. Lake trout, which are not found in the four main lakes, have been stocked in Cruiser, Little Trout, and Mukooda lakes.

Walleye are school fish and spawn over gravel or rubble-strewn bottoms after the ice breaks up on the lakes. In the spring, walleye can be found in or near the shallows. The warmer shallow waters attract minnows, which in turn draw the walleyes looking for food. Prime walleye areas in the spring are shallow waters or sand bars close to deep water. When summer arrives, the fish move to the cooler deep water.

Walleye and smallmouth bass share the same habitat. Both prefer gravel or rocky bottom areas, reefs, and dropoffs. Look for smallmouth around rocky points, near downed trees along the shoreline, and among pencil reeds between islands or off points. Smallmouth in the 2-to-3 pound range are common.

Northern pike are abundant throughout the park and fish over 10 pounds are not uncommon. Pike favor shallow weed beds and are particularly fond of weedy areas where flowing water enters a lake. From their weedy hideouts, the predaceous pike can easily ambush other fish.

Lake trout are found in the shallows during the spring, just after the ice goes out, and around rocky reefs in the fall when they spawn. During the summer, lakers are in deep water where the temperature is 42 to 45 degrees.

The best time for fishing and canoeing is in the early summer and early fall. Fishing is best during these times, the mosquitos aren't as bad, and the area is much less crowded.

License A Minnesota license is required. A Ontario license is required if fishing in Canadian waters.

Camping Approximately 100 primitive boat-in campsites are scattered throughout the park, mostly on islands or near the shore. Public camping facilities are available in nearby Kabetogama State Forest, while private campgrounds are found throughout the area.

Maps There is a special USGS map of the entire park, "Voyageurs National Park," which shows campsites and is helpful for anyone planning to explore the park. Nautical charts are available for Rainy Lake and canoe charts (which do not show lake depth) are available for Sand Point, Namakan, and Kabetogama. Maps and additional publications to help plan a Voyageurs trip can be purchased at park visitor centers and are available by mail from: Lake States Interpretive Association, Box 672, International Falls, MN, 56649; phone: (218) 283-9821.

Contour lake maps are available for the major lakes and most of the smaller lakes in the park. Write for the *Minnesota Outdoors Catalog* from: Minnesota State Documents Center, 117 University Avenue, Ford Bldg., St. Paul, MN, 55155; phone: (612) 297-3000. The catalog contains a wealth of information along with additional publications to help plan a Voyageurs trip.

A map of public water access sites and boat ramps is available for St. Louis County from: Minnesota Department of Natural Resources, Regional Headquarters, 1201 E. Highway 2, Grand Rapids, MN, 55744; phone: (218) 327-4455. Ask for the public water access map for St. Louis County, Sheet 3.

Park Address
Voyageurs NP
P.O. Box 50
International Falls, MN 56649
phone: (218) 283-9821

Chamber of Commerce
Greater International Falls C.C.
P.O. Box 169
International Falls, MN 56649
phone: (218) 283-9400

Additional Information

The Boundary Waters Canoe Area (BWCA), with over 1,500 miles of lakes and rivers, is just east of Voyageurs National Park and accessible from the park via Crane Lake. This wilderness area is so popular that entry is limited and motorized travel is forbidden on some of the lakes. For BWCA information, maps, and reservation forms, contact: Forest Supervisor, Superior National Forest, Box 338, Duluth, MN, 55801; phone: (218) 720-5322.

• MISSOURI

Ozark National Scenic Riverways

Located in the Ozark highlands of southeastern Missouri and comprised of the Current and Jacks Fork rivers, the Ozark National Scenic Riverways is a highly scenic and relatively undeveloped area of narrow, steep-sided valleys and impressive limestone bluffs. The Current and Jacks Fork rivers provide 134 miles of excellent fishing and canoeing.

The park contains some of the nation's largest and most significant springs and an extended cave system with more than 100 caves within the park boundaries. The park is one of Missouri's best tourist attractions, drawing over two million people a year.

Access The park is approximately 175 miles south of St. Louis and 250 miles southeast of Kansas City, Missouri, in Shannon, Carter, Texas, and Dent counties. A number of state and federal highways provide access to various parts of each river. Park headquarters is in the town of Van Buren, on U.S. 60.

Fishing Both the Current River and the Jacks Fork River are excellent for fishing. The Current has trout in its upper reaches, mainly smallmouth bass and rock bass in the middle stretches, and walleye in the lower area. The Jacks Fork is known for its good smallmouth fishing.

Canoeing is the most popular sport in the park and both rivers can get very crowded, especially on summer weekends when there seem to be bumper-to-bumper canoes on the water. Many fishermen have been driven off by the hordes of canoes. Consequently, the rivers are not getting fished as much as in former years and the fishing has improved. Those who are serious about fishing and want to avoid the crowds should either plan a mid-week trip, fish early or late in the day, or fish during the winter.

The Current River is formed by the confluence of Pigeon Creek and Montauk Springs in Montauk State Park, which is on the northern border of the Ozark Riverways. The Current, from the state park boundary down to Cedargrove, is stocked by the state with brown and rainbow trout and is managed as a trophy trout stream with a daily limit of three fish of 15 inches or longer. State record trout have come

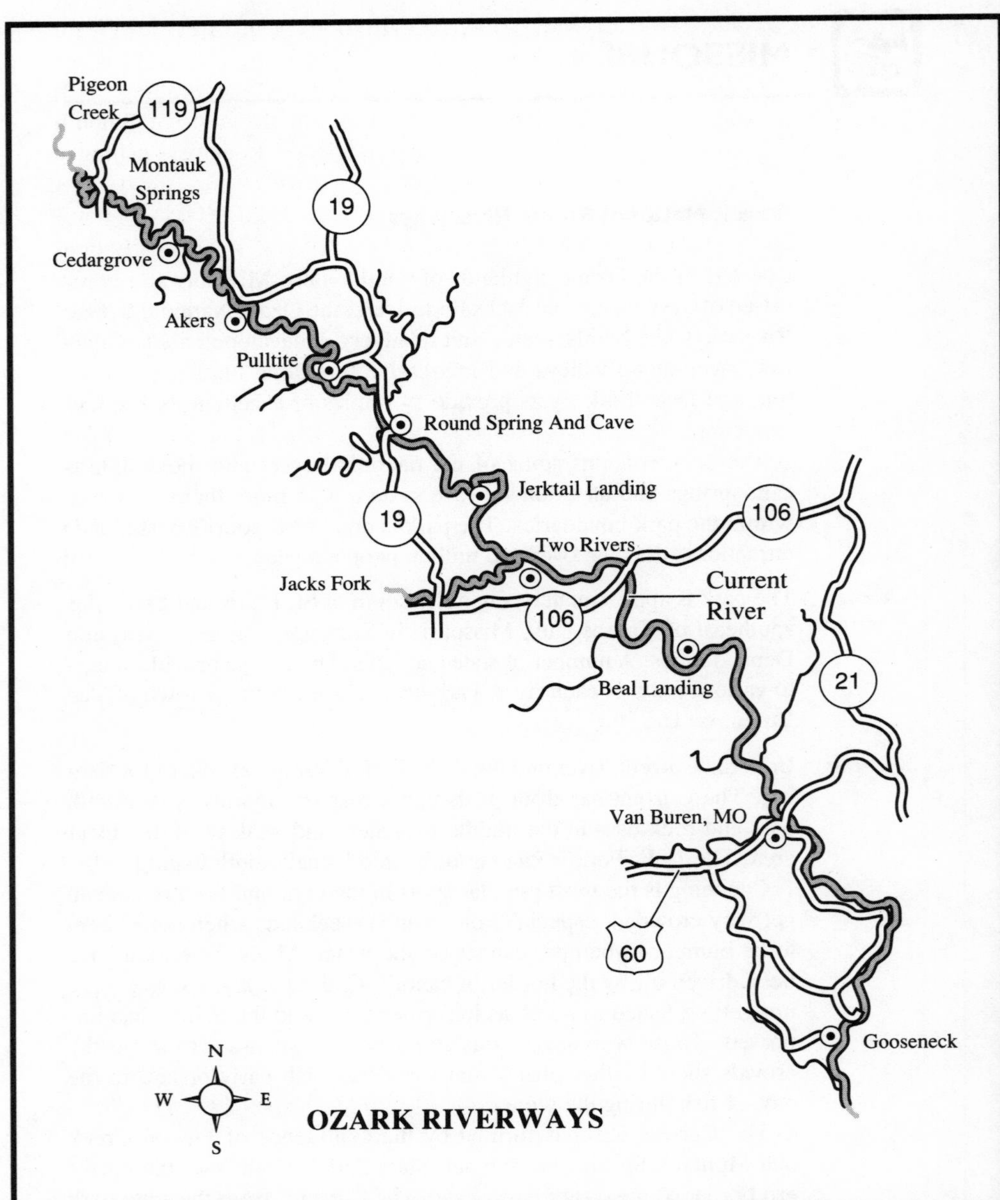
Pigeon Creek
119
Montauk Springs
19
Cedargrove
Akers
Pulltite
Round Spring And Cave
Jerktail Landing
19
106
Two Rivers
Jacks Fork
106
Current River
Beal Landing
21
Van Buren, MO
60
Gooseneck
N
W
E
S
OZARK RIVERWAYS

from this stretch of river. Trout water extends from Montauk about 20 miles downstream to the Akers access point. Only the stretch from Montauk to Cedargrove is managed as trophy water. The trout water is popular because of its clearness, large fish, and easy wading.

Below Akers, the Current becomes one of the best smallmouth bass rivers in the state, with bass up to 8 pounds. Rock bass fishing is also good, especially in April and May. Pools where tributary streams flow into the river are usually productive. Deep pools with large boulders on the bottom are found throughout the river and usually hold good-sized fish. Two particularly fine holes are Twin Rocks below Jerktail Landing and Quiet Pool below Beal Landing. Recommended two-day bass floats are from Round Spring to Powder Mill Ferry, and from Powder Mill Ferry to Van Buren.

Below the town of Van Buren in the lower stretches of the Current, huge walleyes up to 20 pounds inhabit the deep holes. Very few people fish for walleyes from Van Buren to the end of the park at Gooseneck Landing.

The Jacks Fork River is very good for smallmouth bass and rock bass and also has some largemouth bass and walleye. The Jacks Fork is lined with gravel bars, limestone cliffs, caves, and springs; it flows into the Current River at Two Rivers access point. Fishing is good throughout this river. Steep banks, undercut banks, root wads, logs, and boulders are the preferred smallmouth bass habitat. A noted hole is the Fish Trap Hole below Bay Creek Landing, which is one of the favorite deep holes on the river.

Canoe rentals are available at many points all along both rivers. If you have your own canoe, shuttle service is available at a reasonable fee. Johnboats with or without guides can also be rented. The Current can be floated year-round, as can the Jacks Fork, but the water above Alley Spring in the Jacks Fork is likely to be very low in the summer. Both rivers are susceptible to flash floods and river conditions should always be checked locally.

License A Missouri fishing license is required. Be sure to check the regulations for the trophy trout water.

Camping Campgrounds, both public and private, are plentiful along the river. The park service maintains ten campgrounds along the river. Primitive camping on riverbanks, gravel bars, and islands is also available, but campers should be aware of the danger of flash floods.

Maps The park brochure has a good map, but a better map is contained on an information brochure available from the park, entitled *Information on Ozark National Scenic Riverways*. This brochure lists campgrounds and available facilities, travel times by car and canoe between access points, and other general information. Topo maps are too numerous and too expensive and not really necessary for the fisherman.

Park Address
Ozark NSR
P.O. Box 490
Van Buren, MO 63965
phone: (314) 323-4236

Chamber of Commerce
Big Spring Area C.C.
P.O. Box 356
Van Buren, MO 63965
phone: (314) 323-4782

Additional Information

A *Missouri Travel Guide,* listing canoe rentals for Missouri rivers, is available from: Missouri Division of Tourism, P.O. Box 1055, Jefferson City, MO, 65102; phone: (314) 751-4133.

For the very low price of $1.50 (postage paid), you can get a book from the Missouri Conservation Department entitled *Missouri Ozark Waterways,* by Oz Hawksley. The book is a detailed guide to 37 major float streams in the Missouri Ozark highlands, including the Current and Jacks Fork rivers. There is a tremendous amount of information in this book. Although it is aimed more at the canoeist, fishing folks can also benefit from it. Contact: Outdoor Library, Missouri Department of Conservation, P.O. Box 180, Jefferson City, MO, 65102; phone: (314) 751-4115.

MONTANA

Big Hole National Battlefield

Big Hole National Battlefield is a memorial to the Nez Percé Indians, led by the famous Chief Joseph, and to the soldiers of the Seventh U.S. Infantry, who clashed at the Battle of the Big Hole on August 9–10, 1877. The battle was a military victory for the Nez Percé and the turning point in the Nez Percé War. The park is nationally significant as an example of Indian-White relations and it illustrates the human price of the westward expansion of the nation.

Access The park is in southwest Montana in Beaverhead County. It is 12 miles west of Wisdom, Montana, on Montana 43. From Butte, take Interstate 15 southwest to Divide, then Montana 43 to Wisdom.

Fishing The North Fork of the Big Hole River begins in the park with the joining of Trail Creek from the west and Ruby Creek from the south. The North Fork of the Big Hole winds through a maze of willow thickets and beaver ponds before merging with the nationally famous Big Hole River, 9 miles north of Wisdom.

The North Fork in the park is a slow, placid stream that consistently produces brook trout in the 8-to-10 inch range and a few rainbow trout and whitefish. Occasionally a grayling is caught, but grayling are more prevalent in the upper Big Hole River.

Ruby Creek and Trail Creek also produce smallish brook trout and some whitefish. Trail Creek also has some cutthroats and is more easily fished since it is accessible by Montana Highway 43 and Forest Road 106 for most of its length.

Fishing pressure in the park is moderate to light since the Big Hole River near Wisdom is far more popular.

License A Montana fishing license is required.

Camping No camping or overnight facilities are provided in the park, but several campgrounds are nearby.

Maps The best map for the area is the Beaverhead National Forest map. The map is available for a small fee by writing to: Forest Supervisor, Beaverhead National Forest, 610 N. Montana St., Dillon, MT, 59725; phone: (406) 683-3900.

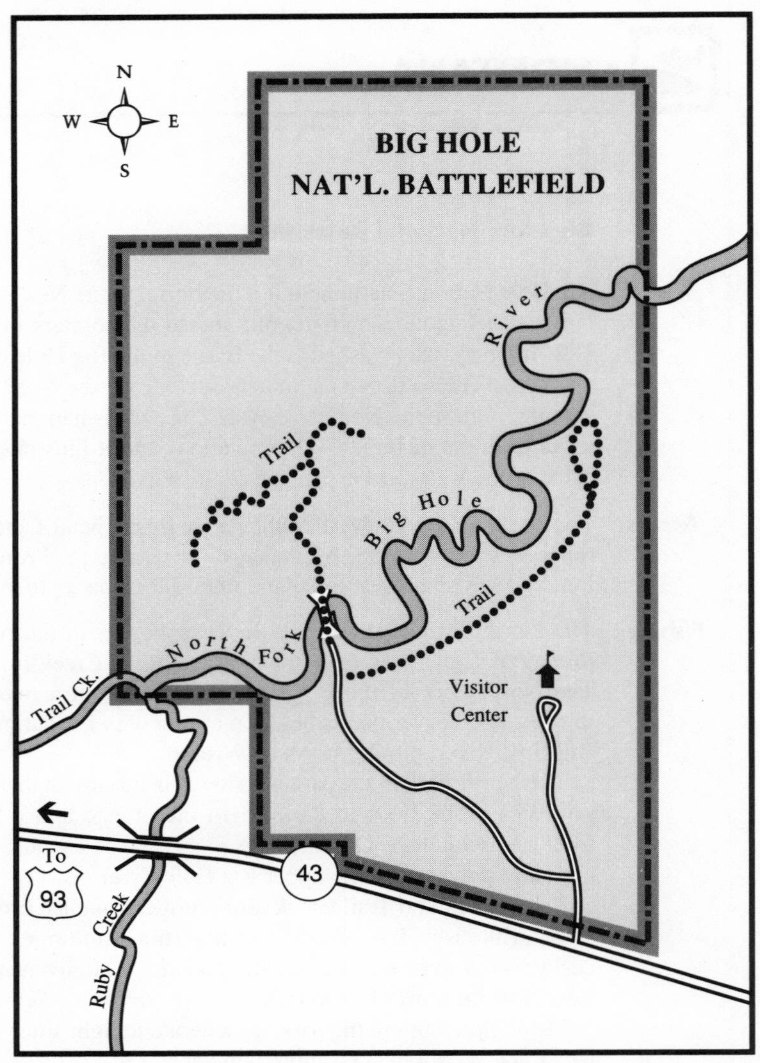

Park Address
Big Hole NB
P.O. Box 237
Wisdom, MT 59761
phone: (406) 689-3155

Chamber of Commerce
Beaverhead C.C.
P.O. Box 830
Dillon, MT 59725
phone: (406) 683-5511

Additional Information When you contact the Beaverhead National Forest for a map, also ask for a copy of their *Recreation Opportunity for the Wisdom Ranger*

District. This guide is a good source of camping, fishing, and hiking information.

Bighorn Canyon National Recreation Area

Bighorn Canyon NRA consists of Bighorn Lake in Wyoming and Montana, formed by the Yellowtail Dam on the Bighorn River, and a section of the Bighorn River below the dam. The Crow Indian Reservation surrounds a large part of the park. Yellowtail Dam was built by the Bureau of Reclamation, but the National Park Service administers the recreation facilities. Boating, fishing, waterskiing, and swimming are the main attractions.

Access The park is in north central Wyoming (Big Horn County) and southeastern Montana (Carbon and Big Horn counties). Access to this elongated park is limited. The southern part is reached via U.S. 14A and Wyoming State Road 37 about 3 miles east of Lovell, Wyoming. The northern part, including Yellowtail Dam and the Bighorn River, is reached via Montana Highway 313, about 43 miles south of Hardin, Montana.

Fishing Fishing is excellent in Bighorn Canyon NRA. There are a choice of locations for fishing: the 71-mile-long Bighorn Lake, the 2-mile-long Afterbay Reservoir below Bighorn Lake and Yellowtail Dam, or the approximately 12 miles of the Bighorn River below the Afterbay Reservoir.

Bighorn Lake Bighorn Lake—also referred to as Yellowtail Reservoir—is a deep, green-water lake extending into Wyoming. The lower 47 miles of the lake are within the spectacular, steep-walled, Bighorn Canyon. Lake levels are subject to fluctuations depending on a number of factors, including the amount of spring runoff and the amount of water needed for power generation and downstream irrigation.

The lake is managed as a warm-water fishery and is fair to good for walleye, which have been heavily stocked in the Wyoming portion. Fishing quality fluctuates from fair to excellent on a seasonal basis, with spring and fall being the best periods. Walleye are the primary game fish, but brown, rainbow, and lake trout are also caught along with channel catfish, sunfish, sauger, ling, and a few crappie.

Deep water trolling is the best method for consistently taking walleye, but jigging is also productive. During the summer, the fish are usually very deep and scatter among the canyon arms. Popular areas are Black Canyon, Devils Canyon, Bull Elk Basin, and Horseshoe Bend, which is also good for ice fishing.

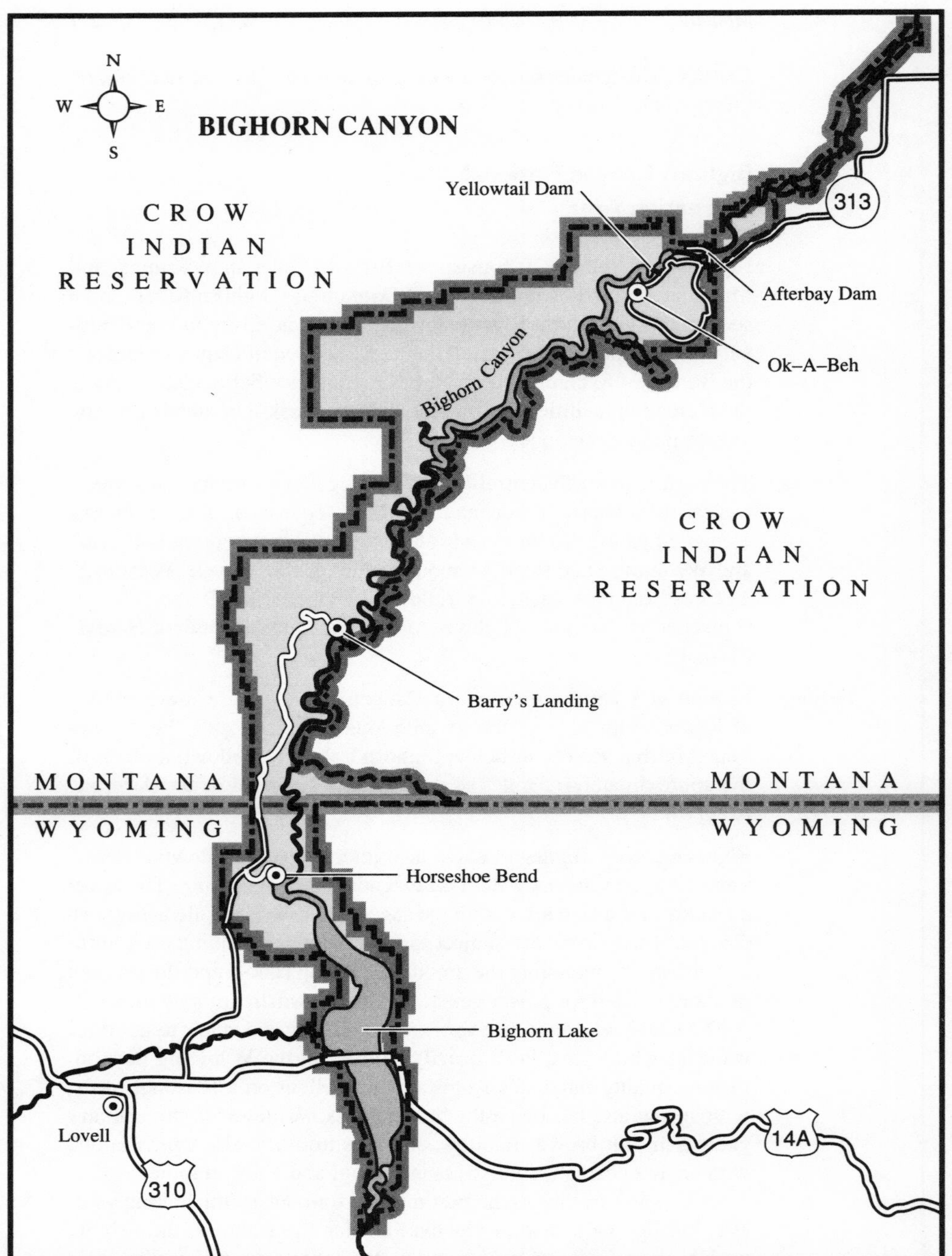
N
W
E
S
BIGHORN CANYON
CROW
INDIAN
RESERVATION
Yellowtail Dam
313
Afterbay Dam
Ok–A–Beh
Bighorn Canyon
CROW
INDIAN
RESERVATION
Barry's Landing
MONTANA
WYOMING
MONTANA
WYOMING
Horseshoe Bend
Bighorn Lake
Lovell
310
14A

A marina with boat rentals and ramp is available at Horseshoe Bend in Wyoming. Ramps are also located at OK-A-BEH near Yellowtail Dam and at Barry's Landing.

Afterbay Reservoir The Afterbay Reservoir is a 2-mile-long lake immediately below Yellowtail Dam. The Afterbay Dam was built to ensure a dependable, constant flow into the Bighorn River. Water releases from Yellowtail fluctuate according to power-generation demands. The Afterbay Reservoir stabilizes these fluctuating flows and releases a steady flow into the Bighorn River through the Afterbay Dam. Fishing is fair in the Afterbay Reservoir for hatchery-bred rainbow trout in the 1-to-6 pound range. A boat ramp and campground are located at Afterbay.

Bighorn River Since 1981 when it was reopened to the public, the Bighorn River has become nationally known as one of the best trout streams in the United States. It has been the subject of numerous magazine articles describing battles with trophy trout, and fly-fishing aficionados have flocked to the river for the chance to take large trout on the fly.

There is no doubt about it, the Bighorn River is a magnificent trout stream. Although the river contains many larger trout, the average trout will be in the 15-to-18 inch range. Wade Fredenberg, a state fisheries biologist, writing in *Montana Outdoors* (July-August 1983; reprinted in *Fly Fisherman,* March 1984), explains that many who came to fish the river were disappointed because large trout weren't taken on every cast. His advice is to visit the river with reasonable expectations and you won't be disappointed, since there are many trout in the 2-to-4-pound range and a few in the 5-to-6-pound class.

Below Afterbay Dam, the Bighorn River flows through the Crow Indian Reservation. In 1975, the Crows closed the river to fishing by non-Indians, claiming ownership of the river and its bed. The state of Montana also claimed ownership and the Crows sued the state. The river remained closed until August 1981, when the U.S. Supreme Court ruled that non-Indians could fish the Bighorn up to its normal high-water level.

The ruling means that visitors may fish the Bighorn, but they may not trespass on any land along the river above the high-water mark. Consequently, river access is almost entirely by watercraft and the river must be floated to be fished effectively. A number of outfitters now offer float trips on the Bighorn. A list of these guides is available from the park.

Float trips start below Afterbay Dam and usually go for 12 miles to the Bighorn Fishing Access Area. This is the most productive stretch and the one most popular for fly-fishing. A recently opened access, the National Park Service River Ranch Access, is only 3 miles below the Afterbay Dam and allows a more leisurely trip where you can beach the boat and wade to thoroughly fish an area.

Wild brown trout predominate in the river and outnumber the stocked rainbow trout. Though few in numbers, northern pike, walleye, whitefish, bullhead, and sunfish are also found in the river. The Bighorn is amazingly rich in nutrients, resulting in abundant vegetation and insect life. Mayflies, caddis flies, stoneflies, and scuds (small freshwater shrimp) multiply rapidly to provide a constant food source for the trout.

The river is open to fishing all year. After April, runoff hampers the fishing until July. The best fishing is in the fall, starting in September when the big browns begin to spawn. Because of the well-deserved publicity, fishing pressure on the Bighorn is very heavy and you are advised to make arrangements and book guides well in advance.

The following is a general guide to Bighorn River fly hatches. Up-to-date hatch information is obtained by contacting one of the river outfitters.

1. Midges—March through May. Sizes 16 to 22 in browns and grays. A Trico hatch starts in August and goes into mid-September.
2. Blue Wing Olives—mid-March through mid-May and mid-September through December, in grayish colors, sizes 18 and 20. In August and September is another hatch of pale to medium olive flies in sizes 18 to 24.
3. Pale Morning Duns—July to mid-September; use light olive imitations in sizes 14 to 18.
4. Yellow Stoneflies—July and August in sizes 12 to 16.
5. Caddis—July through mid-October in brown, speckled brown, and black, sizes 12 to 20.
6. Pale Olive Duns—mid-August through September in sizes 18 and 20.

Nymphing is probably the deadliest technique on the Bighorn. The San Juan Worm is lethal. Other nymphs you should have (sizes 6 to 20) are the Gold-Ribbed Hares Ear, Pheasant Tail, LaFontaine Caddis Pupa, Midge Pupae, and Orange, Pink, and Tan Scuds.

License Fishing in either Montana or Wyoming requires the appropriate state fishing license. Be sure to check Montana and Wyoming regulations for Bighorn Lake and the current regulations for the Bighorn River. Regulations on the river can be expected to change as Montana fishery biologists seek to optimize the fishery.

Camping There are three campgrounds in the park: Afterbay, Horseshoe Bend, and Barry's Landing. In addition, there are two campgrounds accessible only by boat: Medicine Creek and Black Canyon. Back-country permits (free) are required for camping in non-designated areas. More detailed information is available from the park.

Maps Maps available from the park include the park brochure map, a boater's map indicating navigational markers, and a map showing public access areas to the river.

Park Address
Bighorn Canyon NRA
P.O. Box 458
Fort Smith, MT 59035
phone: (406) 666-2412

Chambers of Commerce

North Big Horn Lovell C.C.
P.O. Box 302
Lovell, WY 82431
phone: (307) 548-7552

Billings Area C.C.
P.O. Box 2519
Billings, MT 59103
phone: (406) 245-4111

The town of Fort Smith is the headquarters for fishing the Bighorn River, but there is no Chamber of Commerce to provide lodging or guide information. Guides for the Bighorn are available in Billings, Livingston, and Hardin. At this time, guides are available in Fort Smith from Quill Gordon Fly Fishers, P.O. Box 597, Fort Smith, MT, 59035; phone: (406) 666-2253.

Additional Information George Anderson, a writer, river guide, and fly-shop owner in Livingston, has written a description of the Bighorn River and how to fish it, including the best time of year, equipment needed, fly hatches and recommended patterns, and local accommodations. For a free copy of this Bighorn River fact sheet, contact: George Anderson's Yellowstone Angler, 124 N. Main St., Livingston, MT, 59047; phone: (406) 222-7130.

Glacier National Park

Glacier National Park contains more than 1 million acres of the finest mountain scenery in the United States, including more more than 50 glaciers and 200 lakes in the park. The park abounds with wildlife and is one of the last refuges of the grizzly bear in the continental United States.

Immediately north of Glacier National Park, in Canada, is Water-

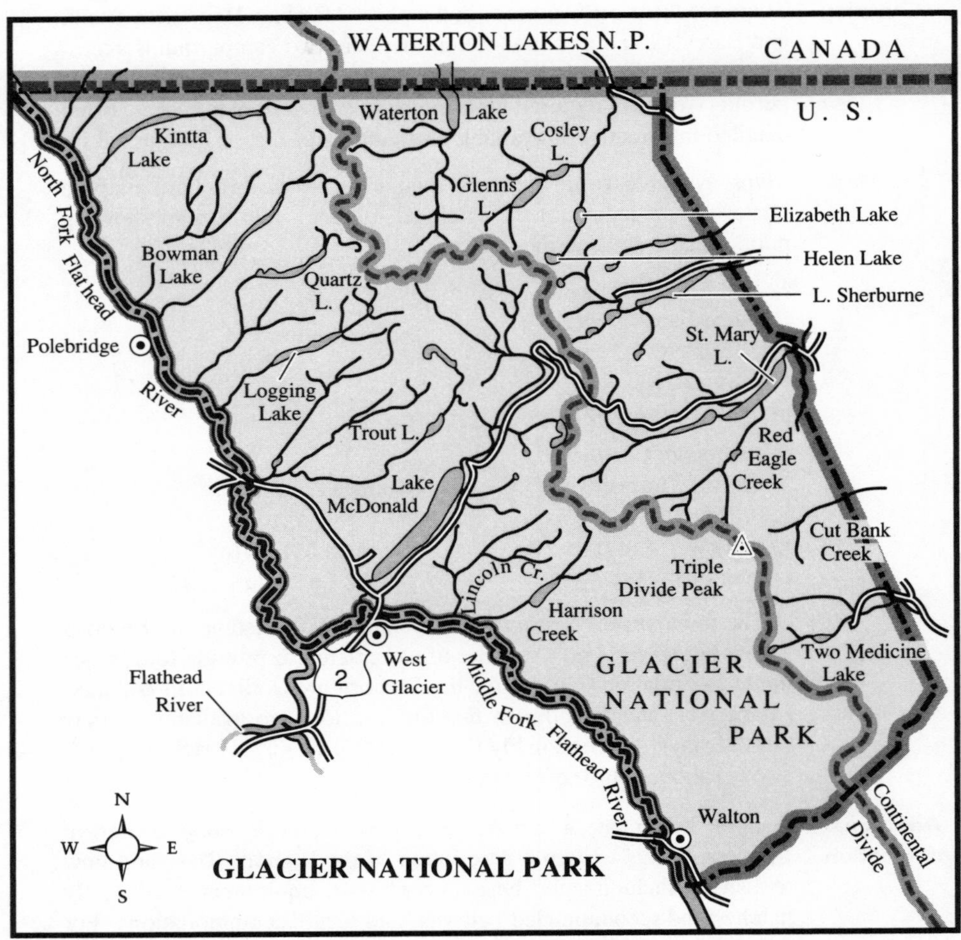

ton Lakes National Park, managed by Parks Canada. The official name of the combined parks is Waterton-Glacier International Peace Park.

Access The park is in northwestern Montana (Glacier and Flathead counties), next to the Canadian border and is reached via U.S. 2 and U.S. 89.

Fishing Glacier National Park may provide you with an unbelievably good fishing trip or with a dismal failure of a trip that leaves you swearing there isn't a fish in the park. I've had friends describe each experience, and indeed, it was the mixture of joys and disappointments in this area that sparked the idea for this book as a whole. The key to a successful trip in Glacier—as it is in so many spots—is knowing where to fish. There are more than 200 lakes in the park and the majority are barren of fish. This situation frustrates many people who hike to a beautiful high-country lake and can't believe the lake is totally devoid of fish. Believe it—there *are,* for reasons discussed in the first chapter of this book, many barren lakes in the high country.

In the park, most of the lakes are interconnected by an excellent 750-mile trail network, one of the finest in the entire park system. For best results, concentrate on the lakes that are proven fish producers along the trails.

The Continental Divide runs through the park, and lakes are commonly referred to as east-slope or west-slope lakes. The following list indicates which lakes are on each slope and the species contained in these lakes. There may be a few fish in other lakes, but the lakes listed are known to contain fish.

The key to fish species is: **B,** brook trout; **C,** cutthroat trout; **BT,** bull trout (sometimes called Dolly Varden, but the bull trout is actually a different species); **G,** grayling; **K,** kokanee salmon; **L,** lake trout; **P,** pike; **R,** rainbow trout; and **W,** whitefish. There are distinctions among the cutthroat trout between the west-slope cutthroat, which is native to the park, and the Yellowstone cutthroat, which was introduced to the area. There are also hybrids between the two along with cutthroat-rainbow hybrids. For simplicity, all the cutthroats and hybrids are listed as cutthroat, **C.**

East Slope Lakes	*Species*	*West Slope Lakes*	*Species*
Bullhead	**B**	Akokala	**BT,C**
Cosley	**B,L,W**	Arrow	**BT,C**
Cracker	**BT**	Avalanche	**C**
Elizabeth	**G,R**	Bowman	**BT,C,K**
Francis	**R**	Camas	**C**
Glenns	**B,L,W**	Ellen Wilson	**B**
Grinnell	**B**	Evangeline	**C**
Gunsight	**R**	Fish	**C**
Josephine	**B,K,R**	Grace	**C**
Katoya	**C**	Harrison	**B,BT, C,K**
Kootenai Lakes	**B**	Hidden	**C**
Lost	**B,R**	Howe	**C**
Medicine Grizzly	**R**	Isabel	**BT,C**
Mokowanis	**B**	Upper Isabel	**BT,C**
Morning Star	**C**	Kintla	**BT,C, K,L**

East Slope Lakes	*Species*	*West Slope Lakes*	*Species*
No Name	**B,R**	Upper Kintla	**BT**
Old Man	**C**	Lincoln	**B,BT,C**
Otokomi	**C**	Logging	**BT,C**
Pitamakin	**B**	McDonald	**BT,C, K,L,W**
Ptarmigan	**B**	Ole	**C**
Red Eagle	**C,R**	Quartz	**BT,C**
Red Rock	**B**	Lower Quartz	**BT,C**
St. Mary	**L,P,R,W**	Middle Quartz	**BT,C**
Sherburne	**B,P**	Rogers	**C**
Slide	**BT,C**	Snyder	**C**
Swiftcurrent	**B,K,R**	Trout	**BT,C**
Two Medicine	**B,R**		
Lower Two Medicine	**R**		
Upper Two Medicine	**B,R**		
Windmaker	**B**		
Waterton	**BT,L,P, R,W**		

Most of these lakes are accessible only by hikes of various length, except for Windmaker on the east slope and Evangeline on the west slope, which are not accessible by trail. In addition, Sherburne, St. Mary, Two Medicine, Lower Two Medicine, McDonald, Bowman, Waterton, and Kintla lakes are all accessible by road. Except for Kintla and Bowman, the road-accessible lakes also have boat rentals. Some of the better back-country lakes are: Quartz, Glenns, Elizabeth, Logging, Gunsight, and Old Man.

The lake trout in McDonald, Kintla, St. Mary, and Waterton are found near shore in spring and late fall. Fishing around creek mouths in these lakes in late May and early June is often productive. At other times, the lake trout are in deep water.

Rivers and Streams

The North Fork of the Flathead River flows along the western boundary and the Middle Fork of the Flathead along the southern boundary of the park. These rivers are components of the National Wild and Scenic River System. U.S. Highway 2 runs along the Middle Fork up to West Glacier and beyond. A gravel county road parallels the North Fork as far as the Canadian border. Both rivers are easily accessible from main and secondary roads and are popular with rafters. Commercial float trips are available locally.

Both are medium-sized rivers with large boulders, white-water, riffles, and long deep pools. Because of the spring runoff, fishing is best after June. The water is often high and roiled until July. If you plan to float either river, get advice locally because there are hazards to avoid.

Both rivers offer good fishing for cutthroat trout and bull trout. Whitefish are found throughout both rivers. Kokanee salmon are abundant only when they migrate from Flathead Lake up the two rivers to spawn in their tributaries in the fall.

As mentioned earlier, the bull trout is often mistakenly called a Dolly Varden trout. Actually this is not a trout, but a char in the same genus (*Salvelinus*) with Arctic char, brook trout, and lake trout. Dolly Varden (*Salvelinus malma*) are found along the coast of Alaska and Washington and are anadromous, maturing in saltwater but returning to freshwater to spawn. The bull trout live their entire lives in freshwater and are a distinct species (*Salvelinus confluentus*).

In the spring, the bull trout leave Flathead Lake, outside the park, and begin their long journey to the headwaters of the upper forks of the Flathead River. These fish are often large, exceeding 10 pounds, but most average 4 to 6 pounds. They spawn in September and October and then return downstream toward Flathead Lake. The best fishing for bull trout is from May through July, but some are found most of the year in the rivers.

There are four other rivers (Belly, St. Mary, Waterton, and Two Medicine) and numerous creeks in the park. Generally, these streams are lightly fished and contain wild trout averaging 9 inches. Although the average is 9 inches, many of the park streams yield larger trout in the 2-to-4 pound range. Some of the better streams are the Belly River, which also has grayling, St. Mary River, Cut Bank Creek, and Kennedy Creek.

One final bit of advice before going into the back country is to always remember that you are in grizzly bear territory. A pamphlet on minimizing bear contact is available from the park. Be sure to read it and take the proper precautions.

License A fishing license is not required to fish in the park, but a free permit is required and may be obtained on entering the park. A Montana license is required for the Middle Fork of the Flathead River and the North Fork of the Flathead from mid-channel to the west bank, which are outside the park.

Be sure to read the brochure detailing park fishing regulations; some waters are closed to protect spawning fish and there are special regulations (fly-fishing only, catch and release) on other waters.

Camping There are eight developed campgrounds accessible by paved road and seven less-developed campgrounds accessible by gravel roads. In addition, there are back-country campsites that require a permit. A digest of camping regulations is available from the park. Private campgrounds are located at St. Mary, West Glacier, and East Glacier.

Maps You definitely need good maps for the back country. There is a special USGS map, "Glacier National Park." Also request a hiking trail map from the park.

Park Address
Glacier National Park
West Glacier, MT 59936
phone: (406) 888-5441

Chamber of Commerce
Kalispell Area C.C.
15 Depot Loop
Kalispell, MT 59901
phone: (406) 752-6166

Additional Information *Fishing Glacier National Park,* by Paul M. Hintzen, is highly recommended. This book contains just about everything you need to know about fishing in the park, including means and difficulty of access, and a rating for each body of water. It is available from the Glacier Natural History Association, West Glacier, MT, 59936; phone: (406) 888-5441.

Also from the Glacier Natural History Association is *Three Forks of the Flathead,* a floater's guide to the North, Middle, and South Forks of the Flathead River. Maps and text are printed on waterproof paper.

Another good information source is *The Montanans' Fishing Guide,* Vol. 1, *Montana Waters West of the Continental Divide,* by Dale Burk. This guide contains a special section on waters in Glacier National Park. Contact: Mountain Press Publishing Co., P.O. Box 2399, Missoula, MT, 59806; phone: (406) 728-1900.

The Floaters Guide to Montana, by Hank Fischer, is a good information source for floating many of Montana's rivers. It contains sections on the North and Middle Forks of the Flathead River. While the book is written for floaters, it contains some good general fishing information, including maps showing roads and public access areas. Contact: Falcon Press, P.O. Box 1718, Helena, MT, 59624; phone: (toll free) 1-800-582-2665.

Grant-Kohrs Ranch National Historic Site

Grant-Kohrs was one of the largest and best-known range ranches during the 19th century. It illustrates the development of the northern plains cattle industry from the 1850s to recent times.

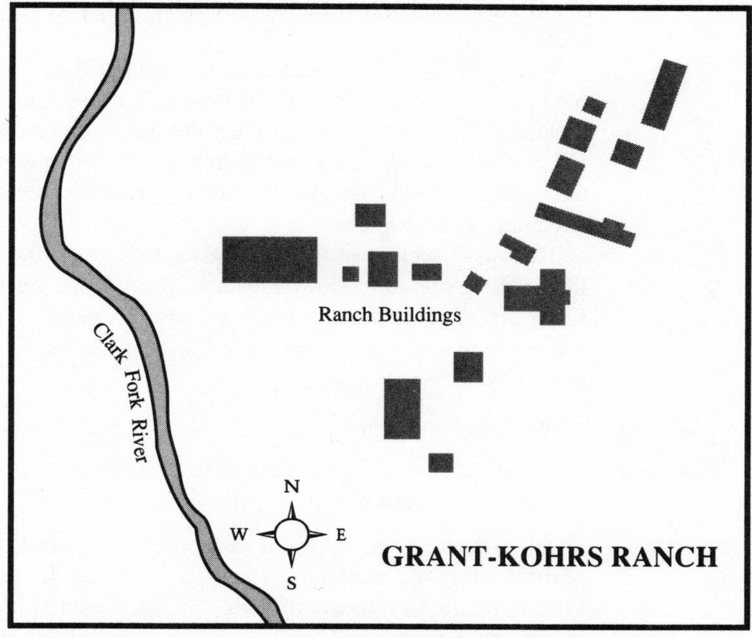

Access The ranch is in western Montana near the town of Deer Lodge (Powell County). Access is via Interstate 90 to U.S. 10 to the fairgrounds.

Fishing The Clark Fork River flows through the ranch and provides good trout fishing for brown trout, although little fishing is attempted in the park. The river is paralleled by Interstate 90 along most of its length, so it is accessible at county road bridges and public access sites.

This upper section of the Clark Fork is difficult to fish. The water is slow, the fish are predominantly brown trout, and the fly hatches are all caddis hatches. The river has made an amazing recovery from its acid pollution in the early 1970s, although there are still some problems with water quality. The uneven water quality accounts for the predominance of caddis flies, which are more tolerant to pollution than are mayflies.

Large brown trout are found throughout this upper section of the river. One of the first major caddis hatches to bring these large browns to the surface is the spotted sedge (*Hydropsyche caddis*), which occurs from June to mid-July. In late June and early July, the Western Grannom (*Brachycentrus*) is an important evening hatch. At other times, streamers such as the Muddler, Dark Edson Tiger, or Sculpin imitations are productive, as are weighted caddis pupa imitations and the Gold-Ribbed Hares Ear. A good dry fly pattern is the Elk Hair Caddis.

When the water is low and warm (mid to late summer), algae blooms may be a problem. Try fishing with a streamer on or near the surface. Use a strong leader so that the mossy algae can be snapped off the hook on the back casts. In the fall, the browns move into the open channels over gravel beds to spawn and are susceptible to streamers and bucktails.

The upper section of the Clark Fork River near the park receives little fishing pressure. Downstream sections of the river toward Missoula are more popular because the water quality improves below tributary streams such as the Little Blackfoot River, Flint Creek, and Rock Creek.

License A Montana fishing license is required.

Camping No camping is permitted at the ranch. Camping is available at nearby Deerlodge National Forest.

Maps Detailed maps are not essential since Interstate 90 follows along most of the river. If you want more detail, the best maps for the upper Clark Fork River are the Bureau of Land Management (BLM) maps showing the public lands in Montana. These are available at a reasonable price from the BLM state office in Billings. Ask for Granite (#21) and Avon (#22), which cover the entire upper river. Avon covers the ranch area. Write to: Bureau of Land Management, Federal Building, 222 N. 32nd St., P.O. Box 30157, Billings, MT 59107; phone: (406) 245-6462.

Park Address
Grant-Kohrs Ranch NHS
P.O. Box 790
Deer Lodge, MT 59722
phone: (406) 846-2070

Chambers of Commerce

Deer Lodge C.C.
84 East Side Rd.
Deer Lodge, MT 59722
phone: (406) 846-2094

Missoula C.C.
P.O. Box 7577
Missoula, MT 59807
phone: (406) 543-6623

Additional Information Information and maps for Deerlodge National Forest are available from: Forest Supervisor, Deerlodge National Forest, Federal Bldg., Box 400, Butte, MT, 59703; phone: (406) 496-3400.

• NEBRASKA

Agate Fossil Beds National Monument

Agate Fossil Beds is well known to scientists because of the numerous well-preserved mammal fossils found there. Fossils from the Miocene period (15 to 20 million years ago) are extremely abundant, with many complete skeletons. The fossil beds acquired their name from their proximity to rock formations containing agates.

Access Located in the panhandle section of Nebraska in Sioux County, the monument is 23 miles south of U.S. 20 at Harrison, via Nebraska 29, or 34 miles north of U.S. 26 at Mitchell, via Nebraska 29.

Fishing The Niobrara River flows east through the monument for 5 miles. The Niobrara and its tributaries include some of the best trout water in the state.

The section of river in the park is stocked with brown trout by the state each spring. Some rainbow trout are also present. Natural reproduction of trout is minimal because of fluctuating river flows.

Spring is the best time to fish because the river is badly dewatered by irrigation during the summer and fall. In the monument, the river is approximately 6 feet wide with an average depth of 18 inches. Fishing pressure in the monument is light. After early spring, visitors to the area should be wary of rattlesnakes.

License A Nebraska fishing license is required and state regulations apply.

Camping There are no camping facilities in the park.

Maps The park brochure map is adequate. The park road follows the river.

Park Address
Agate Fossil Beds NM
c/o Scotts Bluff NM
P.O. Box 427
Gering, NE 69341
phone: (308) 668-2211

Chamber of Commerce
Scottsbluff-Gering United C.C.
P.O. Box 1350
Scottsbluff, NE 69361
phone: (308) 632-2133

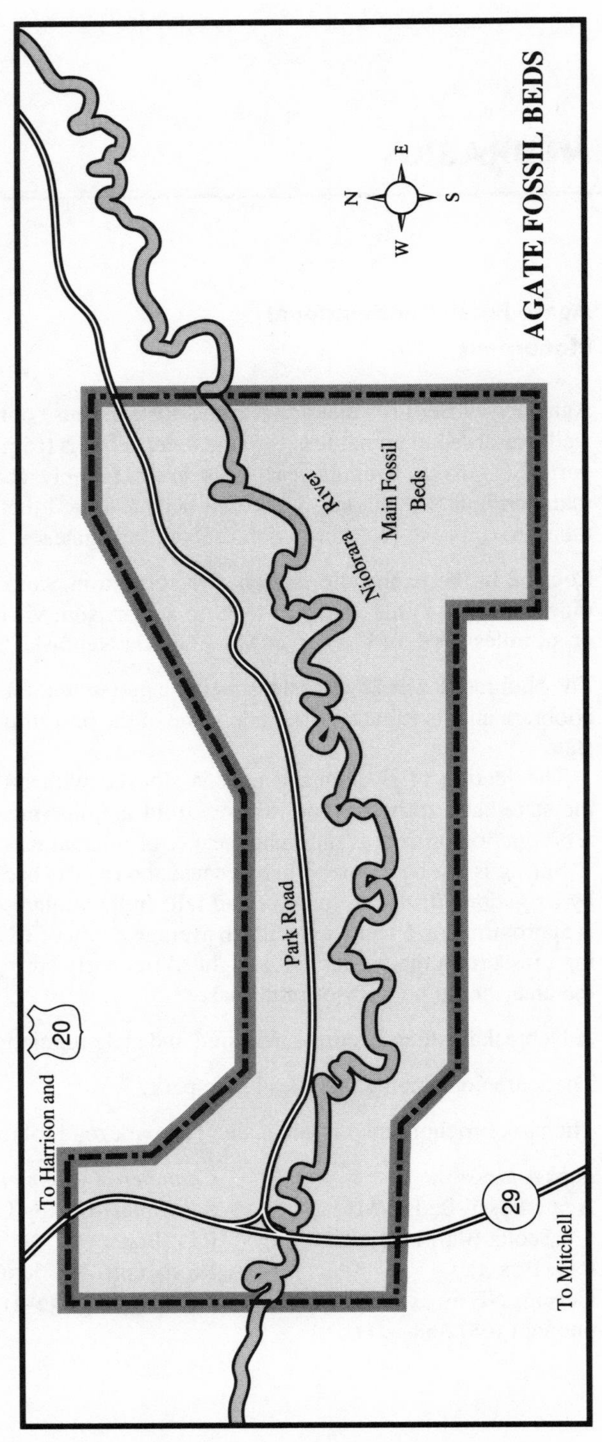
AGATE FOSSIL BEDS
N
E
S
W
Niobrara River
Main Fossil Beds
Park Road
To Harrison and
20
29
To Mitchell

NEVADA

Great Basin National Park

The nation's 49th national park (established October 27, 1986) and Nevada's first, encompasses 77,091 acres of sagebrush country with 13,063-foot Wheeler Peak as its centerpiece. The park offers high-elevation camping (one-third of the park is above 10,000 feet) amid the solitude of the South Snake Mountain Range and a wondrous display of alpine meadows, forests, and animals.

The park also features the spectacular underground beauty of Lehman Caves, a subterranean profusion of stalagmites, stalactites, crystals, and columns.

Access The park is near the Nevada-Utah border. Park headquarters are located at Lehman Caves. Take U.S. 50/6 to Nevada 487 (70 miles east of Ely, Nevada). Go south on 487 to Baker and take Nevada 488 west for 5 miles to the park entrance.

Fishing There are five lakes in the park, but only two contain fish. Baker Lake holds Lahontan cutthroat trout and Johnson Lake features brook trout. Both lakes are above 10,500 feet in elevation and consequently the fishing season is short. The lakes are usually ice-free from June through September.

Four creeks in the park are worth trying. Snake Creek has a small population of rainbow trout. Baker Creek contains brown and rainbow trout and Lehman Creek holds rainbow trout. Strawberry Creek features rainbows and Bonneville cutthroat trout, which are native to the area.

Camping The park has four minimally developed campgrounds suitable for tents or recreation vehicles. Lower Lehman Creek (11 spaces) is open all year. Baker Creek (32 spaces) and Upper Lehman Creek (24 spaces) are open from about May 15 through October. Wheeler Peak (37 spaces) is open from about May 15 to October 1; exact dates depend on snow conditions. Water is available at all campgrounds only from about May through September. To date, potable water exists only at Upper and Lower Lehman Creek campgrounds, where a $5 daily fee is charged. Back-country camping is permitted all year at designated sites and throughout much of the park.

License A Nevada fishing license and a separate Nevada trout stamp are required.

Maps The park brochure map is only a general location map. For exploring the park, you'll need USGS maps. The six quad sheets for the park are: Lehman Caves, Kious Basin, Arch Canyon, Wheeler Peak, Windy Peak, and Minerva Canyon.

Park Address
Great Basin NP
Baker, NV 89311
phone: (702) 234-7331

Lake Mead National Recreation Area

Lake Mead was created in the 1930s by the construction of Hoover Dam on the Colorado River. The lake is just downstream from the western boundary of Grand Canyon National Park. Below Hoover Dam, and part of the national recreation area, is Lake Mohave, created by Davis Dam. Both dams were built to provide flood control, irrigation, and hydroelectric power but the lakes are of major importance for the water-based recreation they provide in a desert environment.

Access The park is in southern Nevada (Clark County) and northwestern Arizona (Mohave County), about 30 miles east of Las Vegas. U.S. 93, from Las Vegas to Kingman, Arizona, is the main access to the visitor center. The park brochure map shows the numerous access roads to the marinas around both lakes.

Fishing Both well-publicized Lake Mead and the lesser-known Lake Mohave offer excellent fishing. Prior to the construction of Hoover and Davis dams, very little fishing occurred along the segment of river now occupied by the two reservoirs. Both lakes contain largemouth bass, crappie, bluegill, and channel catfish. Striped bass have proliferated in Lake Mead and below Davis Dam and have also spread to Lake Mohave.

Typical of large desert lakes, Mead and Mohave are very deep with many steep walled coves. Most of the shoreline in the two desert lakes consists of rock formations, with many points and fallen rock piles. A depth-finder or graph unit is essential if you are to be successful in locating the best fishing spots. It would be wise to hire a guide on your first visit to either lake. Guides can be recommended by the various marinas or you can get a list from the Chamber of Commerce or the

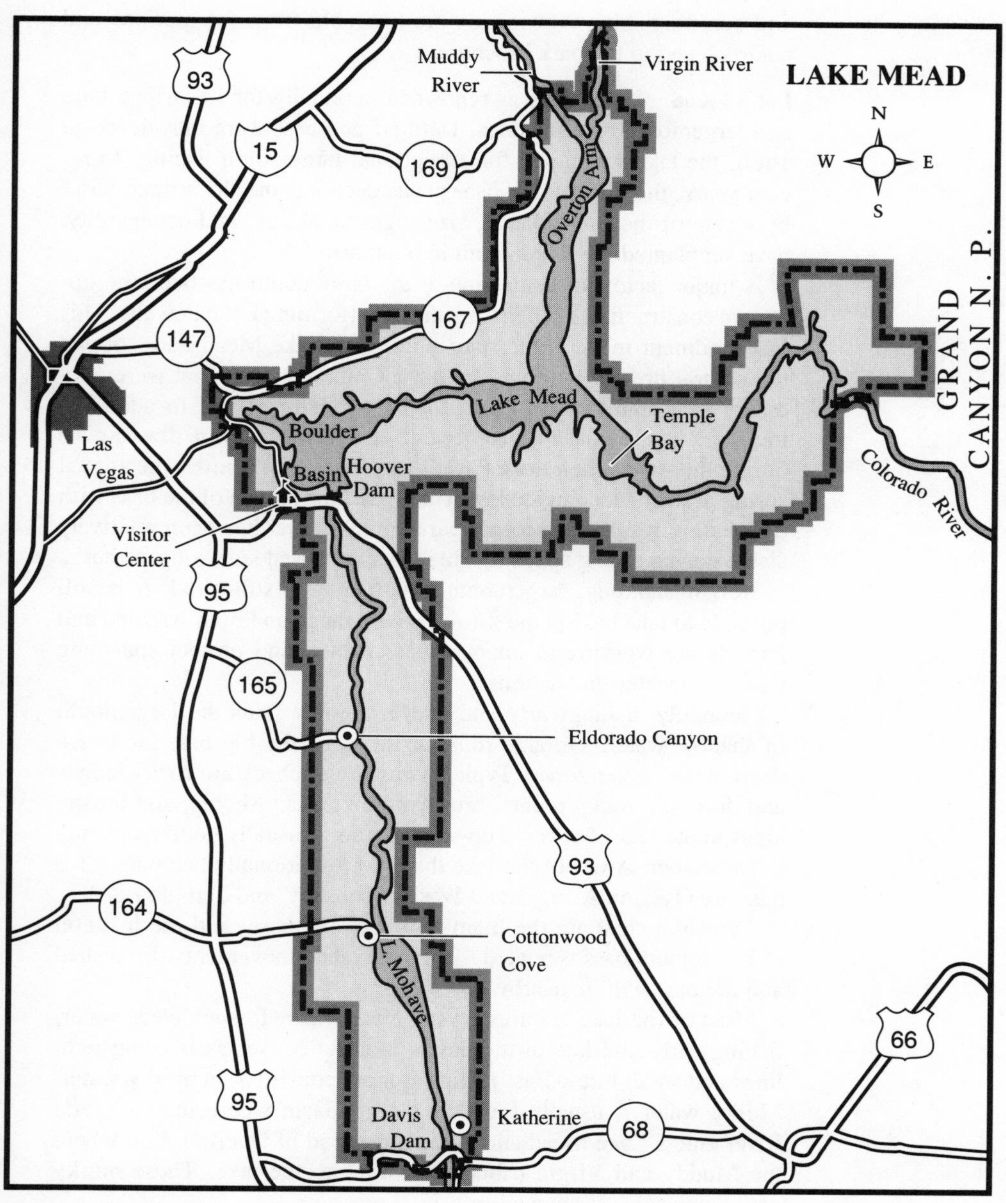
LAKE MEAD
N
S
E
W
Muddy River
Virgin River
93
15
169
Overton Arm
GRAND CANYON N. P.
167
147
Lake Mead
Temple Bay
Boulder Basin
Hoover Dam
Las Vegas
Visitor Center
Colorado River
95
165
Eldorado Canyon
93
164
Cottonwood Cove
L. Mohave
66
95
Davis Dam
Katherine
68

Nevada Department of Wildlife office in Las Vegas. Boats, motors, and current fishing information are available from the marinas and resorts listed in the park brochure.

Lake Mead Lake Mead is renowned nationally for its striped bass and largemouth bass fisheries. Until striped bass were introduced in 1969, the lake was noted for exceptional largemouth fishing. In recent years, the largemouth fishery has declined and the striped bass, by virtue of their abundance, size, fighting ability, and catchability, have supplanted the largemouth in popularity.

A major factor in the decline of the largemouth has been the upstream construction of Glen Canyon Dam (forming Lake Powell). This impoundment reduced the river flows into Lake Mead and stopped the natural flow of nutrients from the Colorado River that were necessary to sustain a food chain for the predatory bass. In addition, the water level at Lake Mead became erratic, with severe drawdowns during the years when Lake Powell was filling. Thereafter, the annual spring drawdown coincided with the spawning season of the bass with devastating results. In recent years the lake level has been relatively stable during spring spawns, which has improved spawning success.

Notwithstanding, largemouth bass fishing is still good. It is still possible to take bass in the 5-to-6-pound range and both Arizona and Nevada are working to improve bass habitat and protect spawning bass from water fluctuations.

Generally, fishing early and late in the day finds the largemouth in shallow water. Through most of the year, the big bass are down deep in the cooler zones. Typical structure to check are rocky ledges and dropoffs, rocky points, brushy points, rocky shores, and brushy areas in the rear of coves. Top-water action is usually good from July to December. Areas of the lake that have traditionally been good for bass are Overton Arm, Grand Wash, Echo Bay, and Temple Bar.

Threadfin shad are the main forage of the bass, and the location of largemouth bass is related to threadfin shad movements. Find shad and the bass will be nearby.

Most of the lake features crystal clear water. In such clear water, fishing early and late in the day is more effective, as is using light lines and small lures. Bass fishing is more consistent in murky water. Murky water is usually found in Gregg Basin where the Colorado River enters Lake Mead and in the upper end of Overton Arm where the Muddy and Virgin tributaries flow into the lake. These murky water areas also receive more fishing pressure.

In the spring, look for bass in the shallow flats of the major river arms in the main lake and in the shallow back sections of coves where they go to spawn and feed on threadfin shad. The bass will locate

Largemouth bass such as this one in Lake Mead are found near threadfin shad, their main food source.—*U.S. Fish and Wildlife Service photo by Brian Montague*

along brushy shoreline sections because of the rising lake levels from spring runoff. Spring fishing is best in the afternoon when water temperatures rise. Usually temperatures in the main lake will be in the mid-50s, but the river arms and coves will be in around 60 degrees.

From June through August, a significant segment of the bass population is in deep water (15 to 60 feet) near major points. Top-water lures are productive early in the morning and late in the evening. Small, soft plastic worms or jigs should be fished very slow, deep and tight to the major points and nearby dropoffs.

In the fall (late September through October) the bass follow the shad back into the river arms, shallow flats and backs of coves. Peak feeding times are often in the early morning and midafternoon.

During the winter (November through January), most of the bass move back into deep water, holding along major points and rock slides at 15-to-60-foot depths, depending on the shad location. Bass also suspend along sheer rock walls in 15 to 20 feet of water. When the afternoon temperatures warm the shallows, bass can occasionally be taken along shoreline stick-ups and bushes by slow-rolled spinnerbaits.

Striped bass are now found throughout the lake. The stripers grow rapidly in Lake Mead because of the abundance of threadfin shad as forage. Stripers are now established in the lake and natural reproduction is occurring. They average 2 to 5 pounds but a handful of large fish in the 30-to-40 pound class are caught each year.

The best time for stripers is March to late November. The fish can be caught all year but action can be slow in the winter months when the fish are in very deep water. Top-water action is good during the summer and fall when it's not unusual to see a school of stripers tearing up the water surface. If surface action isn't evident, concentrate on the points and try jigs or bait at the 20-to-50-foot level. When the fish are deep, a favorite method is to drift frozen anchovies (cut in two pieces) along the bottom.

The increase in striped bass popularity has had a beneficial impact on the largemouth bass. With more concentrated fishing for striped bass, the fishing pressure has lessened on the largemouth.

Channel catfish and bluegill are still abundant in the lake. Channel catfish are caught by bottom fishing with natural or prepared stink baits, while bluegill and an occasional crappie are caught along the canyon walls and in the coves.

Lake Mohave Lake Mohave is a narrow, 67-mile-long reservoir below Hoover Dam and Lake Mead. For most of its length, Lake Mohave is confined between the canyon walls of the old Colorado River channel. The fishing at Lake Mohave can be exceptional with largemouth bass and trout often running 3 pounds, and some trout going up to 10 pounds.

Lake Mohave is a clear, cold-water environment, ideally suited for trout. However, nutrient problems have caused trout fishing to decline in recent years. Large rainbow trout are occasionally taken in the river below Hoover Dam.

Trout are found in the cold water areas of the lake. The lake section from Hoover Dam to Eldorado Canyon always holds trout. In the rest of the lake, trout are found in the colder deep water. The stocking of rainbow trout has continued regularly in the lake, while cutthroat trout seem to be doing well after recent stockings.

Striped bass somehow found their way into Lake Mohave and are now established and reproducing. Although they are a great sport fish, because of their predaceous nature, striped bass may eventually have a detrimental effect on the trout.

From Eldorado Canyon south to Davis Dam, the lake is excellent for largemouth bass, channel catfish, and sunfish. The largemouth bass have done very well, especially since threadfin shad were stocked in the mid-1950s to serve as a food base for the bass. Bass fishing times and structure preferences are similar to those of Lake Mead. Cottonwood Cove and Katherine are noted bass areas.

License If you fish from shore, you will need a license from the appropriate state. Fishing from a boat requires a license from Arizona or Nevada along with a special-use stamp from the other state.

Camping There are ten campgrounds in the park in addition to trailer sites. Primitive camping is allowed on remote beaches and in the back country away from the developed areas.

Maps Topographic maps are not needed. Nautical chart #18687 is useful when boating on Lake Mead. Lake Mohave does not have a nautical chart. Also of help is the "Cove Name Map" for the two lakes. The chart and map are available from the park. Write for a publication list and prices.

Contour maps of Lake Mead and Lake Mohave are available from Fish-N-Map Co., 8535 W. 79th Ave., Arvada, CO, 80005; phone: (303) 421-5994.

Park Address
Lake Mead NRA
601 Nevada Highway
Boulder City, NV 89005
phone: (702) 293-8920

Chambers of Commerce

Boulder City C.C.
1497 Nevada Highway
Boulder City, NV 89005
phone: (702) 293-2034

Greater Las Vegas C.C.
2301 E. Sahara Ave.
Las Vegas, NV 89104
phone: (702) 457-4664

Additional Information The Nevada Department of Wildlife has an office in Las Vegas if you need additional information about Lake Mead NRA. Contact: Nevada Department of Wildlife, 4747 Vegas Drive, Las Vegas, NV 89108; phone: (702) 486-5127.

• NEW MEXICO

Gila Cliff Dwellings National Monument

Gila Cliff Dwellings National Monument preserves the ruins of homes built in natural caves more than 700 years ago. Around the end of the 13th century, people of the Mogollon Culture began constructing rooms in a south-facing cliff about 175 feet above the canyon floor. Abandoned by the mid-14th century, the dwellings have remained empty and silent. The national monument status was proclaimed in 1907.

The park is surrounded by Gila National Forest and adjoins the Gila Wilderness, the nation's first designated wilderness area. Although part of the National Park System, Gila Cliff Dwellings NM is administered by the U.S. Forest Service (Department of Agriculture).

Access The park is in southwest New Mexico (Catron County), 44 miles north of Silver City via State Highway 15.

Fishing A one-half-mile section of the West Fork of the Gila River flows through the park. The river is easily accessible since it parallels the park road. The West Fork is good for rainbow and brown trout, and an occasional cutthroat trout.

Rainbow trout are stocked throughout the year by the New Mexico Department of Game and Fish. Placed just below the park boundary, the trout migrate into park waters. Channel catfish are found downstream in the main Gila River, but sometimes surprise people fishing for trout, especially when the catfish are taken on flies.

By starting in the park, you can walk either upstream into the wilderness area, or downstream along the stocked section below the park. The Gila National Forest and Wilderness offer many additional fishing opportunities on a number of streams and lakes.

Normally, the flow of the Gila peaks during the April thaw. Thereafter, the flow depends on summer showers to maintain adequate levels. Without the added water, the Gila may be reduced to little more than a trickle. Most of the year, the river is characterized by a series of shallows, riffles, and pools, and is easily waded in most places.

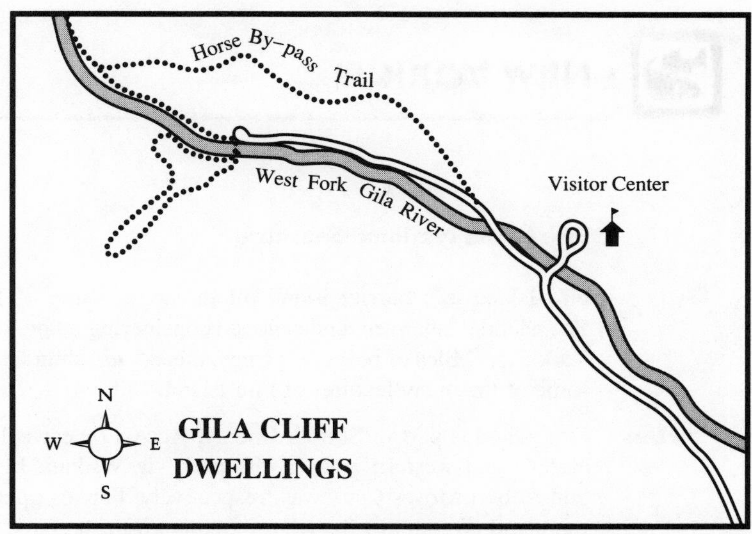

License A New Mexico fishing license is required.

Camping There are two Forest Service campgrounds adjacent to the park, Lower Scorpion (7 spaces) and Upper Scorpion (13 spaces). Additional campgrounds are found throughout the Gila National Forest. Back-country travel in the Gila Wilderness requires a permit from one of the Forest's district offices. A permit also may be obtained in advance by writing to the park address below.

Maps Topographic maps are of little value in the park. However, a map of the Gila National Forest opens up recreational opportunities throughout the entire region. The map is available from: Forest Supervisor, Gila National Forest, 2610 N. Silver St., Silver City, NM, 88061; phone: (505) 388-8201.

Park Address
Gila Cliff Dwellings NM
Box 100
Silver City, NM 88061
phone: (505) 536-9461

Chamber of Commerce
Silver City–Grant County C.C.
1103 N. Hudson
Silver City, NM 88061
phone: (505) 538-3785

NEW YORK

Fire Island National Seashore

Fire Island is a barrier island off the south shore of Long Island. The island is relatively undeveloped considering its proximity to New York City. Miles of beach, marshes, dunes, and abundant wildlife are some of the many features of Fire Island.

Access Fire Island is part of Suffolk County. Access by car is limited to the eastern and western ends of the park via William Floyd Parkway and Robert Moses Causeway, respectively. Ferries operate from the mainland (Bayshore, Sayville, Patchogue) to the park from May to November. The park brochure contains a detailed description of park access.

Fishing Fire Island offers a good diversity of fishing. Surf fishing can be done on the island's 32 miles of Atlantic Ocean beach. Fishing in Great South Bay and Moriches Bay requires a boat. Offshore fishing for large game fish is also popular, but requires large boats capable of navigating dangerous ocean inlets.

Surf Fishing Surf fishing on the ocean side is most productive from mid-September to mid-November, when the fish are concentrated closer to shore. Earlier in the year, surf fishing is slow because the fish are still too far out. Fall fishing is for bluefish, striped bass, and weakfish. Bluefish are the most common; striped bass and weakfish are less common but more highly prized. Popular surf fishing spots are Moriches Inlet and Fire Island Inlet which drain large shallow bays and serve as highways in and out of the bay system for the fish.

Fishing pressure in the surf substantially increases in the fall but with 32 miles of beach, there is ample room. For access to much of the beach, a four-wheel drive vehicle is required. Special permits required for these vehicles are available at the Smith Point Ranger Station at the terminus of the William Floyd Parkway on the east end of the island. Driving on the beach is permitted only from September 15 to December 31.

Bay Fishing Fishing in the Great South Bay and Moriches Bay picks up during April. Earlier in the year fishing is slow due to cold water and inactive fish. Blackback (winter) flounder are the first game fish to appear

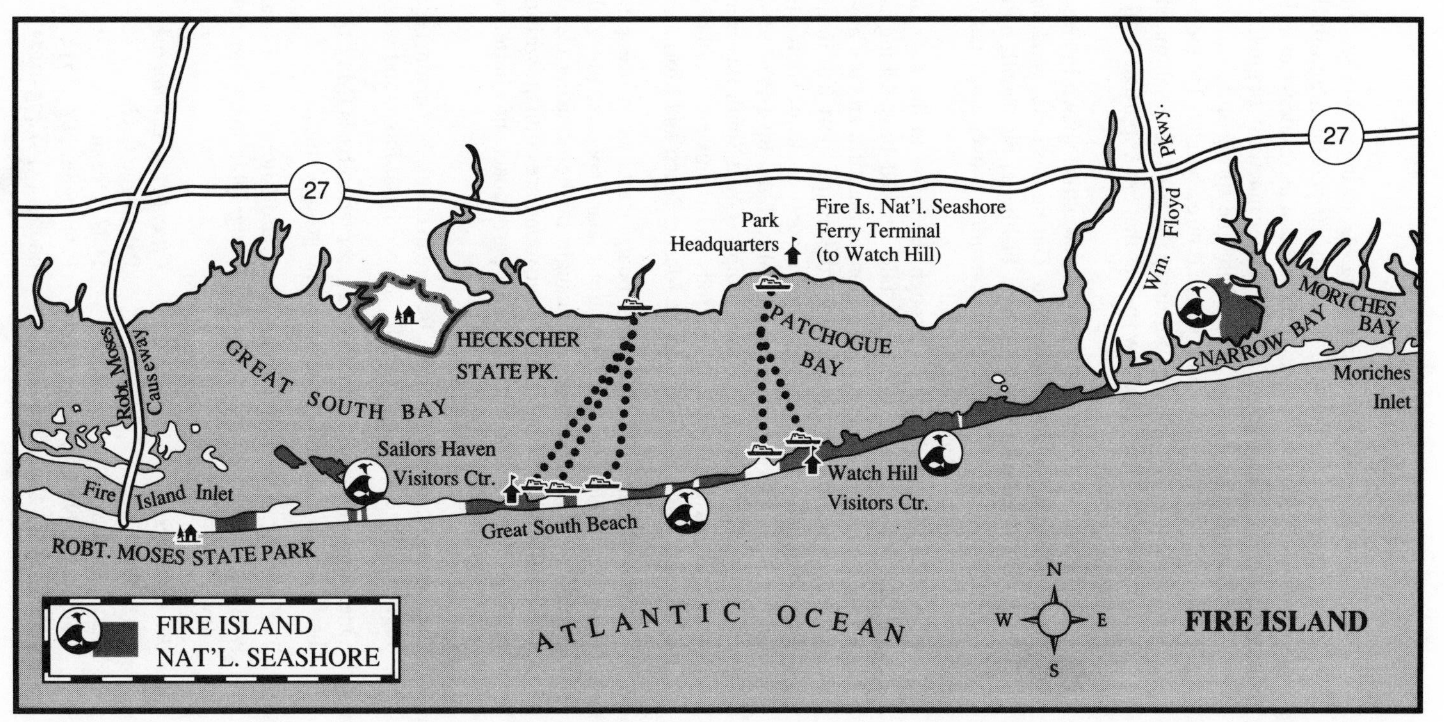
27
27
Robt. Moses Causeway
GREAT SOUTH BAY
HECKSCHER
STATE PK.
Park
Headquarters
Fire Is. Nat'l. Seashore
Ferry Terminal
(to Watch Hill)
PATCHOGUE
BAY
Wm. Floyd Pkwy.
MORICHES
BAY
NARROW BAY
Moriches
Inlet
Sailors Haven
Visitors Ctr.
Fire Island Inlet
Watch Hill
Visitors Ctr.
Great South Beach
ROBT. MOSES STATE PARK
FIRE ISLAND
NAT'L. SEASHORE
ATLANTIC OCEAN
N
W
E
S
FIRE ISLAND

and they feed heavily after spawning. As spring progresses into June, bluefish, blackfish (tautog), weakfish, striped bass, and fluke (summer flounder) arrive to spawn and remain as residents until late fall, when southern migrations start or winter inactivity begins.

Fish are drawn into the bays during the spring and summer by the availability of abundant food, which is directly related to the extensive and productive salt marshes adjoining the bays. The salt marshes provide habitat for many minnow species that are important food sources for the larger fish.

From late April into early May the weakfish spawn in Great South Bay, making it a prime fishing area. During this time, weakfish in the 12-to-15 pound range are common. Fishing at night with light tackle can be outstanding. By June the spawning is over and weakfish have moved to open water until the fall.

In mid-May, fluke move through the inlets to the bays and fishing for fluke remains good into fall. Striped bass fishing is in full swing by June. These fish are no longer plentiful and are now highly prized. By mid-June, bluefish are the major sport fish in the bays. Baby bluefish (snappers) are found around docks or shore structures and provide action to shorebound folks, but a boat is needed to fish the bays effectively. A free boat ramp to Great South Bay is available at Heckscher State Park. Numerous pay ramps are available on the south shore of Long Island in the Mastic Beach and Moriches area.

Offshore Fishing Offshore fishing, requiring large boats, starts when ocean temperatures reach the high 50s. Numerous shark species, tuna, albacore, bonita, sailfish, and marlin are caught offshore during the summer. Other offshore fish that remain year-round are codfish, whiting, ling, sea bass, porgy, and pollock. Large party boats and charter boats are available on Long Island.

License No fishing license is required. Be sure to check the current regulations regarding size and bag limits for striped bass, fluke, and weakfish.

Camping One campground is available on a reservation basis (May 15 to October 15) at Watch Hill (25 spaces, one group camp).

Maps For boating in the Great South Bay and offshore of Fire Island, you will need nautical chart #12352. Topographic maps are not necessary.

Park Address
Fire Island NS
120 Laurel St.
Patchogue, NY 11772
phone: (516) 289-4810

Chamber of Commerce
Patchogue C.C.
15 N. Ocean Ave.
Patchogue, NY 11713
phone: (516) 475-0121

Additional Information A free map detailing major marine sport fishing access areas in Suffolk County is available from: New York State, Department of Environmental Conservation, Finfish & Crustaceans, Bldg. 40–SUNY, Stony Brook, NY, 11794; phone: (516) 751-7900.

Gateway National Recreation Area

Gateway NRA was established in 1972 as one of the first urban parks in the National Park System. The park consists of three separate units in the New York City harbor area.

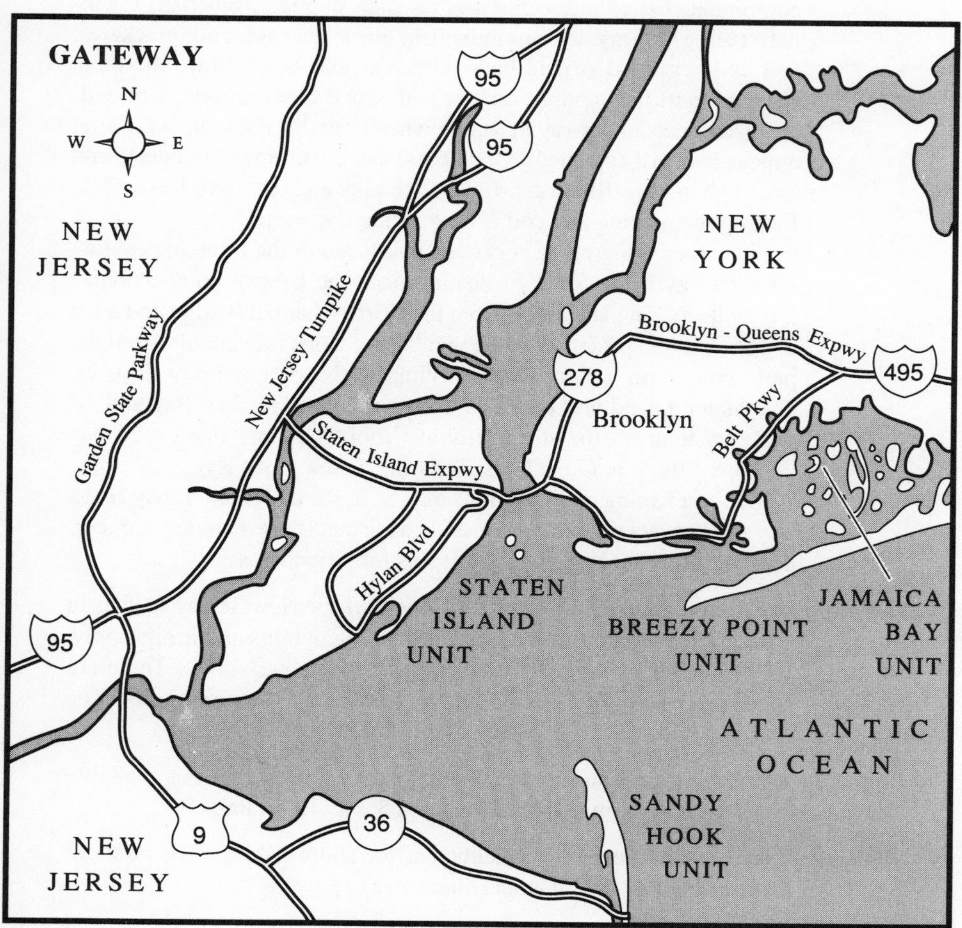

The Jamaica Bay–Breezy Point unit is a 17,000-acre wildlife and nature refuge. The Breezy Point District (part of the Jamaica Bay–Breezy Point unit) is on the Rockaway Peninsula in Brooklyn and the Staten Island unit is on Raritan Bay in Staten Island. The Sandy Hook unit is on a peninsula in the northwest corner of New Jersey. These three units provide a variety of recreational facilities and opportunities for New York City residents.

Access All units in the harbor area are accessible by bus, car, or subway. The park brochure contains a complete description of how to get to each unit.

Fishing The entire New York harbor area, including the three Gateway units, is heavily fished. Anglers throughout the bays utilize a variety of equipment, baits, and techniques to catch flounder, bluefish, blackfish (tautog), porgy, whiting, kingfish, black sea bass, cod, mackerel, and an occasional striped bass. Flounder and bluefish are the most popular sport fish, and the rare striped bass is the most highly prized.

Fishing gets underway in March when flounder show up. Mackerel appear in April followed by sea bass, fluke (summer flounder), and blackfish in May. Bluefish arrive in late May and stay until December. Fishing for whiting and cod is best during the winter.

Fishermen congregate at certain points along the three park units. Jamaica Bay is the focus for fishing from the Breezy Point–Jamaica Bay unit. Fishing is popular from the North Channel Bridge and a list of fish species, preferred baits, and best seasons is available from the park along with a pamphlet on fishing in the Breezy Point District. The Staten Island unit provides fishing access to Raritan Bay and includes fishing off the stone jetty at Crooke's Point, along with bay and surf fishing in Great Kills Harbor and New York Bay.

The best fishing of all the units may be at Sandy Hook. Sandy Hook Bay is an especially productive and consistent shore-fishing producer. Sandy Hook is one of the prime spots for striped bass.

License No license is required in either New York or New Jersey to fish in saltwater, although the appropriate state regulations and limits apply. Be sure to check the regulations in each of the park units. There are special permits or passes needed to park or fish at some units. The park brochure contains the details.

Camping A few primitive campsites for organized youth groups are available by reservation at the Jamaica Bay and Sandy Hook units.

Maps The park brochure map is sufficient for shore fishing. For offshore fishing you will need nautical chart #12327.

Park Address
Gateway NRA
Floyd Bennett Field
Bldg. 69
Brooklyn, NY 11234
phone: (718) 338-3338

Chamber of Commerce
Brooklyn C.C.
333 Atlantic Ave.
Brooklyn, NY 11201
phone: (718) 875-1000

Additional Information For a copy of the book *Saltwater Fishing in New York Waters,* by Nick Karas, contact: Karmapsco, Box 194, St. James, NY, 11780.

The New Jersey Saltwater Fishing Guide, by Pete Barrett, is available from: The Fisherman Library, 1620 Beaver Dam Rd., Point Pleasant, NJ, 08742; phone: (201) 295-1370.

Upper Delaware National Scenic and Recreational River

The Upper Delaware National Scenic and Recreational River flows for 73 miles, forming the border between Pennsylvania and New York from Hancock, New York, downstream to Sparrow Bush, just above Port Jervis, New York. The Delaware is created by the confluence of the East and West Branches of the Delaware at Hancock and eventually empties into the sea at Delaware Bay after flowing 255 miles through major population centers and industrial areas in four states. The establishment of the park in 1978 preserves the upper portion of the river, which remains relatively uninhabited and undeveloped.

Access The river is in northeast Pennsylvania (Wayne and Pike counties) and south central New York (Delaware, Sullivan, and Orange counties). New York Highway 97 parallels the river on the east. In Pennsylvania, Highway 191 parallels about 10 miles of river below Hancock. The remaining river sections can be reached by a variety of state and county roads.

Public access to the river is limited to eight public access areas (five in Pennsylvania; three in New York) and to several bridge crossings. Almost all the land along the river is privately owned. Ask permission before crossing someone's property, because area residents are very strict with trespassers. Some of the 13 canoe liveries that own access points to the river can accommodate people there to fish.

Fishing The upper Delaware is one of the finest rivers I have ever fished. The river is amazingly rich with fish and insect life, but its large size intimidates many who are new to it. In size, the Delaware is typical of many western rivers, with 50-to-100-yard widths and long deep pools and riffles.

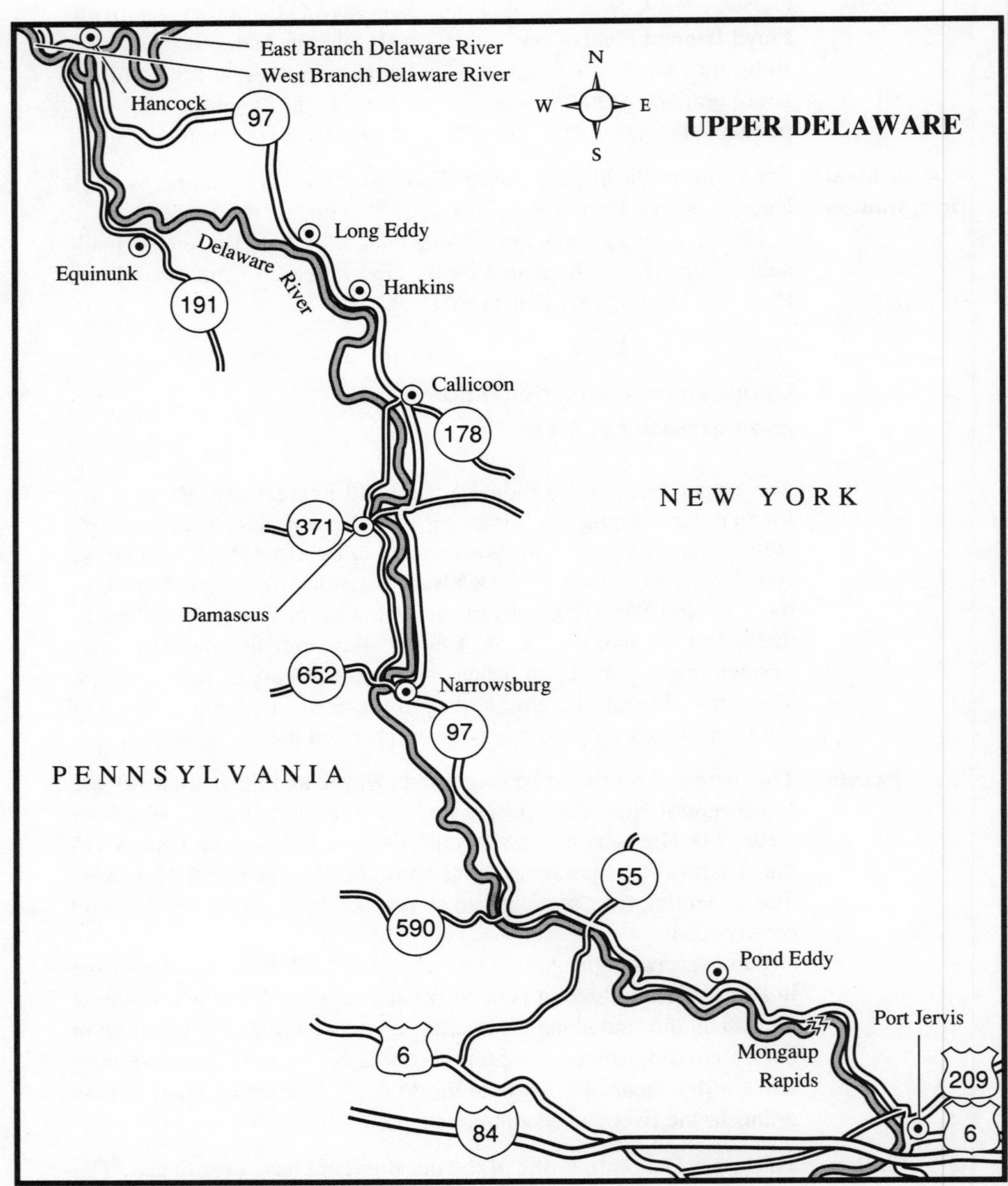
UPPER DELAWARE
N
W
E
S
East Branch Delaware River
West Branch Delaware River
Hancock
97
Long Eddy
Delaware River
Equinunk
Hankins
191
Callicoon
178
NEW YORK
371
Damascus
652
Narrowsburg
97
PENNSYLVANIA
55
590
Pond Eddy
Port Jervis
6
Mongaup Rapids
209
84
6

Unless you are with someone who knows the river, floating is the best way to reach productive fishing spots. The Delaware is relatively easy to float, with an occasional Class II rapid, which most canoeists can easily handle. Besides the superb fishing, this is a beautifully scenic river to float.

The first 28.2 miles, from Hancock to Callicoon, contains good populations of wild brown and rainbow trout, including many trophy-size fish. In addition are smallmouth bass, walleye, pickerel, panfish, and American shad at certain times of the year. Below Callicoon, trout fishing falls off with an occasional trout taken at the mouths of tributary streams that bring cooler water into the river.

Actually, the Delaware River is a tail-water fishery and the quality of trout fishing down to Callicoon depends on cold-water releases from Cannonsville Reservoir on the West Branch and Pepacton Reservoir on the East Branch. Both reservoirs are part of the New York City water supply system. In past years, water temperatures in the river have soared above 70 degrees, dangerously affecting trout survival. A schedule of water releases is currently in effect to maintain water levels and temperatures ideal for trout and aquatic insect survival and growth.

The best trout fishing occurs from mid-May through June, and again from late summer until the season ends on September 30, when water temperatures range between 55 and 65 degrees. Trout can be taken throughout the summer as long as water temperatures stay below 70 degrees. Trout fishing slows when temperatures exceed 70. Even during the prime time in spring, the trout are never easy to catch and you must work for your fish. Rainbow and brown trout are the dominant species. Studies have indicated that the brown is the more dominant of the two; however, the rainbow shows up more often in the angler's creel. An occasional brook trout is caught, usually around a tributary stream, but generally, water temperatures are too high for brooks.

Rainbow and brown trout thrive in the Delaware because the river is an extraordinary insect factory. There are so many different hatches of mayflies, caddis flies, and stoneflies that I first found it unbelievable. Fishing near Hankins one evening in late May, I identified Sulphurs, March Browns, Green Drakes, Brown Drakes, Grey Foxes, and three types of caddis. Fish were rising everywhere. Surprisingly, they were ignoring the large Green Drakes, floating downstream like overloaded barges, but were instead concentrating on a small tan caddis.

The upper 28.2 miles provide an outstanding piece of fly-fishing water. You can try to match the hatch, but many knowledgeable Delaware anglers find that an Adams, Ausable Wulff, White Wulff, or

Elk-hair Caddis (sizes 8 to 16), along with some spinner patterns (sizes 12 to 22) for after the hatch, and a Pheasant Tail Midge (sizes 20 to 26) will suffice. With so many hatches, dry fly-fishing is an effective way to fish the river.

Among the nymph patterns, it's hard to beat the Gold Ribbed Hares Ear and stoneflies. Some folks resort to wet flies in the riffle areas. Productive wet patterns are the March Brown, Light or Dark Cahills, Hares Ear, and Lead-wing Coachman.

My favorite way to fish the Delaware down to Callicoon is to wade and fly-fish near camp in the morning. About mid-morning I hop in a canoe and float downstream for several hours, fishing with spinning tackle. I always take a fly rod when canoeing and often am able to beach the canoe and fish a mid-day hatch. During the evening, I'll return with the fly rod to wade an especially productive or attractive section of river.

Below Callicoon, the water has warmed and smallmouth bass fishing picks up. A few trout are taken but smallmouth are now the main fish, along with shad, walleye, and an occasional pickerel.

Smallmouth are found in the same riffles, eddies, and pools that trout prefer and hit the same flies and lures used for trout. Crayfish imitations are especially good since smallmouth avidly feed on crayfish. Hellgrammites are another excellent bait.

Walleyes are found on the bottom in deep pools generally just below the riffles. I have often spotted walleyes on the bottom and canoed back upstream to drift over the spot again with nightcrawlers or lamprey eels (excellent walleye bait). Look for pickerel in the weedy shallows.

In the spring, American shad migrate up the Delaware River from the ocean to spawn. The annual shad run attracts a fishing crowd. The fish average 3 to 6 pounds, with occasional 7-to-8-pound fish taken. The shad gradually work upstream to the Hancock area. By mid-May they have moved past Port Jervis and into park waters. By late May, they are well above the Callicoon area. Good shad fishing is possible through June.

Shad prefer the deeper pools and eddies and are found in schools of varying sizes. They tend to follow the deeper water of the river channel during their upstream migration. The same spots are usually productive year after year. A famous shad hole is the Zane Grey Pool, where the Lackawaxen River enters the Delaware. A small lead jig, known as a shad dart, is the best and most popular lure.

Throughout the Delaware River, fallfish, a large chub often reaching 16 inches or more, are often caught—like many others, you might think you have a trout or bass and be disappointed. Fallfish hit the same lures and bait that trout and bass do and they fight well. On slow days, they are better than nothing.

Float trips on the Delaware (as on any river) should be carefully planned. There are numerous canoe liveries along the river. For additional information about Delaware River fishing, refer to the Delaware Water Gap section in the Pennsylvania chapter of this book. The Delaware Water Gap starts immediately downstream from Port Jervis and continues downstream for an additional 37 miles to Slateford Creek in Pennsylvania.

License To fish the river, you must have either a Pennsylvania or a New York license. Regulations for the river are standard for each state, except that there is a difference in shad creel limits.

Camping There are no public campgrounds but several private campgrounds are found along the river. For fly-fishing, the Red Barn Campground in Hankins, New York, is hard to beat. The section of river in the Hankins area is excellent and the consistently productive Kellams Bridge area is just a short drive upstream. Canoes and shuttle service are available. For information or reservations, contact: Red Barn Campground, P.O. Box 159, Hankins, NY, 12741; phone: (914) 887-4995. Another good campground and canoe rental on a prime stretch of river is the Riverside Campground, Equinunk, PA, 18417; phone: (717) 224-6410.

Maps The park has a free set of river guides that break the 73 miles into canoeable stretches. Access sites and rapids are noted. The guides also list the topographic map for each stretch. Topographic maps aren't necessary, but sometimes the additional detail is helpful.

The Delaware River Basin Commission publishes a set of river recreation maps for the Delaware River. For price and ordering information, contact: DRBC, P.O. Box 7360, West Trenton, NJ, 08628; phone: (609) 883-9500.

Park Address
Upper Delaware NSRR
P.O. Box C
Narrowsburg, NY 12764-0159
phone: (717) 729-7135

Chambers of Commerce

Wayne County C.C.
742 Main St.
Honesdale, PA 18431
phone: (717) 253-1960

Port Jervis/Tri-States C.C.
P.O. Box 121
Port Jervis, NY 11050
phone: (914) 856-6695

Additional Information

A small and relatively inexpensive book, *Fishing and Canoeing on the Upper Delaware River,* by John Punola, describes the river and its fishing, along with camping and canoe rental information. This book also describes nearby fishing opportunities and has guided me to good fishing when heavy rains and subsequent high water kept me off the Delaware. It is available from: Pathfinder Publications, 210 Central Avenue, Madison, NJ, 07940; phone: (201) 822-2395.

For additional reference materials, refer to the Additional Information section under the Delaware Water Gap National Recreation Area in Pennsylvania.

• NORTH CAROLINA

Blue Ridge Parkway

The Blue Ridge Parkway follows the crest of the Blue Ridge Mountains, extending 469 miles through the southern Appalachians. The parkway links Shenandoah National Park in Virginia with Great Smoky Mountains National Park in North Carolina and Tennessee.

As the first national parkway, Blue Ridge was designed for automobile-oriented recreation. The two-lane highway is relatively uncrowded. Commercial vehicles and billboards are prohibited. The entire route is beautifully scenic and 230 overlooks enable travelers to stop frequently and enjoy the view.

Access The parkway is in western North Carolina and Virginia. It is intersected by numerous roads in both states. Interstate 81 parallels the Virginia section on the west at varying distances.

Fishing The Blue Ridge Parkway contains approximately 62 miles of streams and 88 acres of lakes in which you may fish for brook, brown, and rainbow trout, and panfish, along with smallmouth and largemouth bass. Fishing pressure is heavy on the relatively small amount of available water.

The generally high elevations of most streams and the narrow confines of the parkway (an average of 1,000 feet wide) limits fishing within the parkway. The headwaters of some streams lie within the parkway, and others meander in and out. One of the main benefits of the parkway is that it provides excellent access to adjacent streams, many of which are on national forest lands. The Jefferson and George Washington National Forests in Virginia and the Pisgah and Nantahala National Forests in North Carolina all contain a number of good streams.

The following list of the primary fishing streams and lakes starts in Virginia at Milepost 58 and extends south to Milepost 340 in North Carolina. The parkway crosses from Virginia into North Carolina at Milepost 216.9. The key to fish species in the list is: **B,** Brook Trout; **BN,** Brown Trout; **R,** Rainbow Trout; **T,** Trout; and bass and panfish are listed as **WW,** for Warm-water Species.

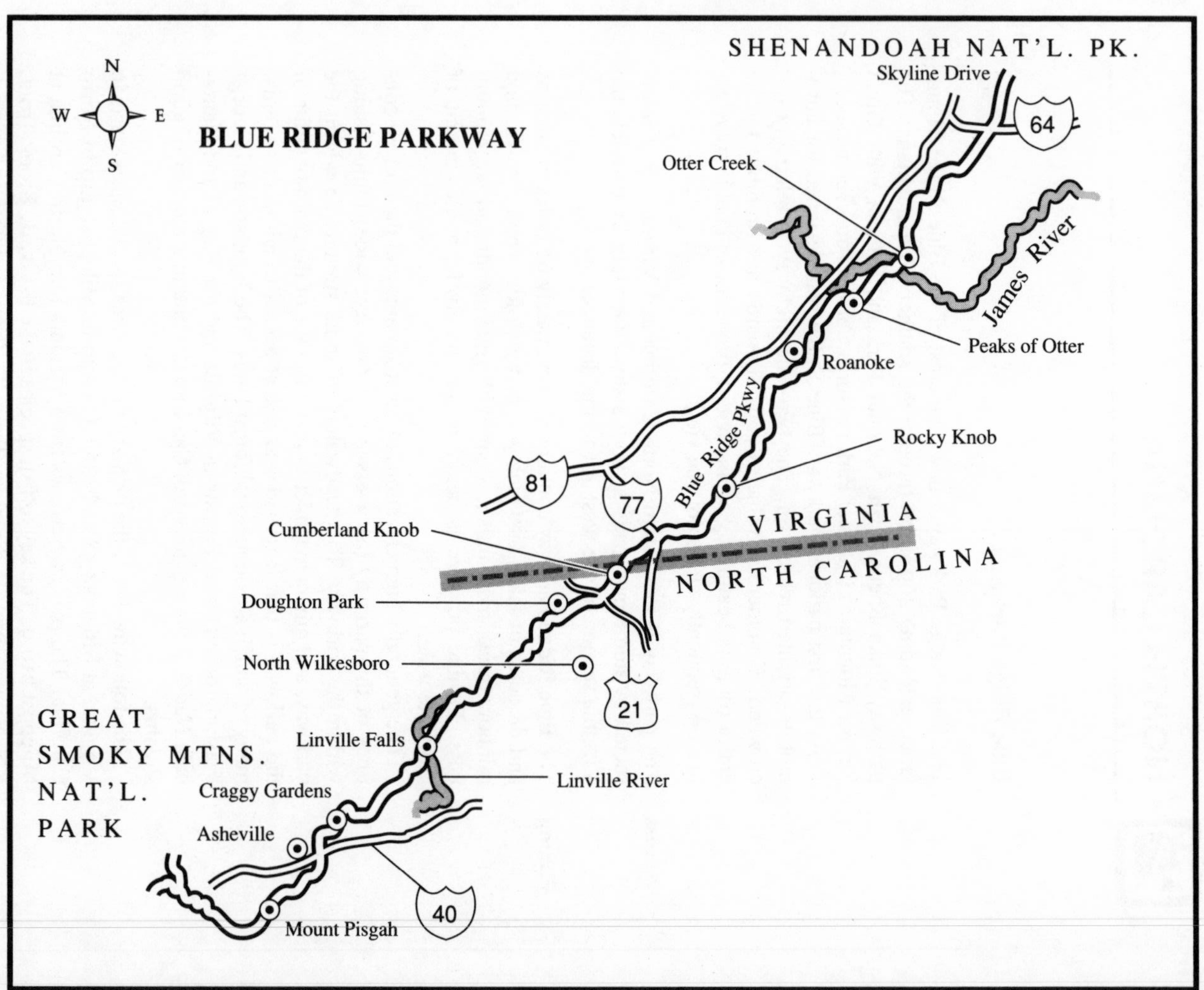

N
W
E
S
BLUE RIDGE PARKWAY
SHENANDOAH NAT'L. PK.
Skyline Drive
64
Otter Creek
James River
Peaks of Otter
Roanoke
Blue Ridge Pkwy
Rocky Knob
81
77
VIRGINIA
NORTH CAROLINA
Cumberland Knob
Doughton Park
North Wilkesboro
21
GREAT
SMOKY MTNS.
NAT'L.
PARK
Linville Falls
Linville River
Craggy Gardens
Asheville
Mount Pisgah
40

Name	*Milepost*	*Fish Species*
Otter Creek	58–64	**WW**
Otter Lake	63	**WW**
Battery Creek	64–65	**WW**
Abbott Lake (Peaks of Otter Lake)	86	**BN,R**
Big Stoney Creek	86	**B**
Little Stoney Creek	86	**B**
Smart View Pond	154	**WW**
Dodds Creek	162	**WW**
Rakes Mill Pond	162	**WW**
Upper Rock Castle Creek	167–174	**B,R**
Lower Rock Castle Creek	167–174	**B,R**
Little Rock Castle Creek	167–174	**B,R**
Laurel Creek	173–175	**T**
Laurel Fork Creek	174	**T**
Crooked Creek (Round Meadow Creek)	179–180	**T**
Hunted Creek (Mabry Creek)	180–181	**T**

Mabry Mill along the Blue Ridge Parkway in Virginia is probably the most photographed mill in the United States.—*National Park Service*

Name	*Milepost*	*Fish Species*
Pine Creek	187–188	**B,BN**
Chestnut Creek	215–217	**B**
Saddle Mountain Creek	218	**B**
Big Pine Creek	221–225	**B**
Hare Mill Pond	225	**B**
Brush Creek	227–228	**B,R**
Little Glade Creek	228–231	**B**
Little Glade Mill Pond	230	**WW**
Basin Creek	238–244	**B,R**
Cove Creek	238–244	**B,R**
Meadow Fork	246–249	**B**
Laurel Creek	250	**B**
Goshen Creek	286	**B**
Middle Fork	292	**BN**
Bass Lake	293	**WW**
Little Trout Lake	293	**B,BN,R**
Trout Lake	294	**B,BN,R**
Henley Branch	294	**B,BN,R**
Sims Lake (Pond)	296	**B,BN,R**
Price Lake	297	**B,BN,R**
Boone Fork	297–303	**B,BN,R**
Laurel Creek	297	**B,BN,R**
Moody's Mill Creek	297	**B**
Cold Prong	298	**B,BN,R**
Ashe Bear Pen Lake (Pond)	301	**B,BN,R**
Camp Creek	315–318	**B,BN**
Linville River	317	**B,BN,R**
Crabtree Creek	340	**B**

License A state fishing license is required for parkway waters; however, a special trout license is not required. Request a copy of the fishing regulations for parkway waters in each state, since some waters are managed as "special waters" with lure restrictions. A few lakes and streams may be closed for management and research purposes.

Camping There are nine developed campgrounds along the parkway with a total of 1,070 spaces. There are four campgrounds in Virginia at mileposts 60.9, 86, 120.5, and 167.1, and five in North Carolina at mileposts 241.1, 297.1, 316.3, 339.5, and 408.6.

Maps Because of the narrow width of the parkway, topographic maps are of little assistance for fishing. The park brochure contains a good, general location map. Road and trail maps showing lake and stream access are available (free) from the park office for the Rocky Knob, Peaks of Otter, Moses Cone, Julian Price, Doughton Pond, and Linville Falls areas.

Park Address
Blue Ridge Parkway
700 BBT Building
One Pack Square
Asheville, NC 28801
Phone: (704) 259-0718

Additional Information A series of four parkway guides, along with maps, brochures, and other publications, are available from the Eastern National Park and Monument Association. Request a catalog from: ENPMA, Blue Ridge Parkway, Box 9098, Asheville, NC, 28815; phone: (704) 257-4200.

Maps and information for Jefferson National Forest are available from: Forest Supervisor, Jefferson National Forest, 210 Franklin Rd. SW, Caller Service 2900, Roanoke, VA, 24001; phone: (703) 982-6270. For George Washington National Forest, contact: Forest Supervisor, George Washington National Forest, P.O. Box 233, Harrison Plaza, Harrisonburg, VA, 22801; phone: (703) 433-2491. For the Pisgah and Nantahala National Forests, contact: Forest Supervisor, National Forests in North Carolina, Box 2750, Asheville, NC, 28802; phone: (704) 257-4200.

A good information source for trout streams in and near the parkway is the book *Trout Fishing the Southern Appalachians,* by J. Wayne Fears. The book contains descriptions of the eight southern Appalachian states (Kentucky, Tennessee, Alabama, Georgia, South Carolina, North Carolina, Virginia, and West Virginia). The book is available from: Globe Pequot Press, Box Q, Chester, CT, 06412; phone: (toll free) 1-800-243-0495.

Cape Hatteras National Seashore

Cape Hatteras National Seashore, a slender, 70-mile-long strand of barrier island beaches that forms part of North Carolina's famous Outer Banks, was established in 1937 as the nation's first national seashore. The Outer Banks are a line of barrier islands extending 175 miles from Cape Henry, Virginia, to Cape Fear, North Carolina. Included within the park but administered by the U.S. Fish and Wildlife Service is the 5,915-acre Pea Island National Wildlife Refuge.

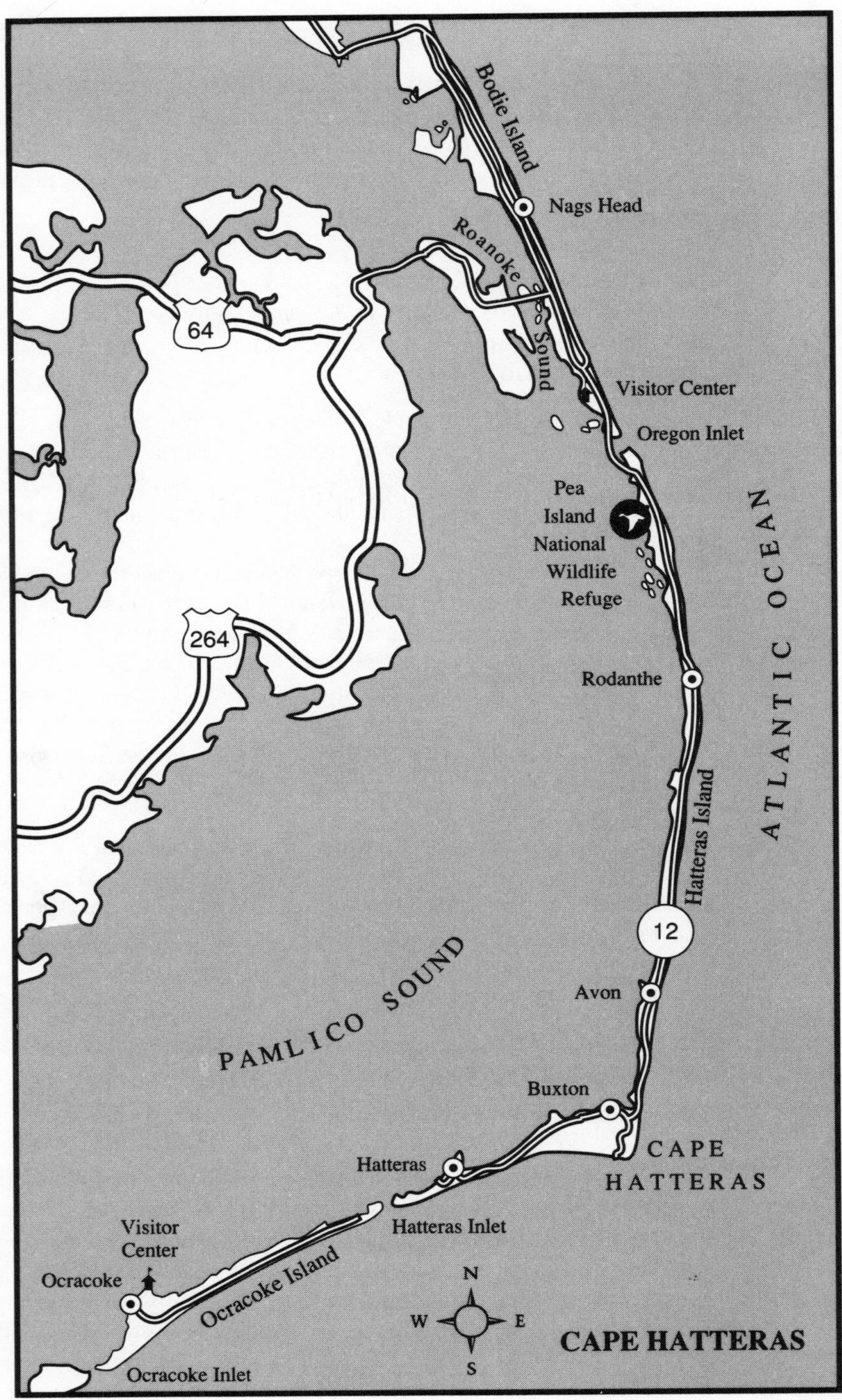
Bodie Island
Nags Head
Roanoke Sound
64
Visitor Center
Oregon Inlet
Pea Island National Wildlife Refuge
ATLANTIC OCEAN
264
Rodanthe
Hatteras Island
12
Avon
PAMLICO SOUND
Buxton
CAPE HATTERAS
Hatteras
Hatteras Inlet
Visitor Center
Ocracoke
Ocracoke Island
N
W
E
S
Ocracoke Inlet
CAPE HATTERAS

Access Cape Hatteras is on North Carolina's coast. The park is reached via U.S. 64 from the west, 264 from the south, and 158 from the north. North Carolina Highway 12 runs along the entire length of the park, connected by bridge to Hatteras Island and by free ferry to Ocracoke Island.

Fishing The entire Outer Banks are justifiably celebrated as an angling mecca. Surf, pier, and offshore fishing opportunities abound all along the park from South Nags Head on Bodie Island, through Hatteras Island on to the southern end of Ocracoke Island. Cape Hatteras, on Hatteras Island, is the easternmost tip of the Outer Banks. To the west of the park is Pamlico Sound, which is protected from the pounding surf by the barrier islands.

The name, Cape Hatteras, conjures visions of surf fishing for large bluefish and channel bass (also known as redfish or red drum). These two fish are the most popular and sought-after fish on the coast, attracting large crowds in the spring and fall.

Offshore from Cape Hatteras, the warm Gulf Stream waters meet the colder northern currents. This junction produces an incredible diversity of game fish. Depending on the time of year, fishing is done offshore for blue marlin, sailfish, dolphin, and wahoo, or in the surf, piers, and Pamlico Sound for channel bass, bluefish, sea trout, flounder, mackerel, and a variety of other fish.

The best fishing is in the spring and fall. Spring brings an influx of people fishing for channel bass, some of which top 60 pounds. The peak period is from late March through May. Fishing for channel bass tapers off after May then picks up again in October and peaks in November. At these times, the fish are in the surf feeding on schools of mullet.

Channel bass are especially active at night. If you don't care for surf fishing at night, early morning and later evening are usually productive. Generally, the fish are larger in the fall. The best and most dependable areas to fish are the inlets, especially Ocracoke and Oregon inlets.

Bluefish also run in the spring and fall. Spring fishing is especially good. Bluefish appear in late March as the waters begin to warm and fishing peaks in May. Small bluefish, up to 3 pounds, are called snappers; they usually remain within surf-casting distance throughout the summer. The larger blues return in October and remain until January. November is the best month to catch blues in the 15-to-20-pound class.

The sight of bluefish in the surf is an unforgettable experience. Schools of bluefish chase bait fish, such as menhaden, over shallow bars to trap them in the surf. Hundreds of blues boil the water as they

Cape Hatteras is famous for its surf fishing. The historic Cape Hatteras Lighthouse is in the background.—*National Park Service photo by Cecil Stoughton*

go into a feeding frenzy and tear into the bait fish. This is known as a "bluefish blitz" and is the time when they can be taken on every cast. A good tipoff to a blitz is to watch the sea gulls. If gulls are swirling and diving wildly, they are feeding on the bait fish remains, a signal that a blitz is in progress. Blitzes are unpredictable, but during a blitz artificial lures are best. Spoons, jigs, and plugs are taken indiscriminately by the frenzied blues.

For both channel bass and bluefish, long surf rods work best, since they maximize casting distance to reach the schools. Serious fishing often means cruising the beach in four-wheel drive vehicles, exchanging information over CB radios, and watching for the gulls to pinpoint the action. Generally, the best fishing areas are near the island inlets that serve as migration routes in and out of Pamlico Sound, and also at Cape Point, the tip of Cape Hatteras.

Cape Hatteras was formerly a haven for striped bass (also known as rockfish or rock). Over the years, stripers have become increasingly rare all along the Atlantic Coast, to the point that some eastern seaboard states have place restrictions on striper fishing. Winter is the time when striped bass appear in the surf along the Outer Banks.

Sea trout and flounder are staples along the Outer Banks. Sea trout are taken in the surf from October through the winter and into May. By late May, they move back into the shallow waters of Pamlico Sound. One of the best surf areas is from Avon to Frisco on Hatteras Island. Flounder are taken year-round. They are plentiful but small in the spring months of April, May, and June. Fishing drops off in the summer but improves in September and October. Another popular fish is the Spanish mackerel. They are in the surf from late spring through the early fall, peaking in August.

Generally, summer fishing is poor except for Spanish mackerel. Summer is the peak of the tourist season, but serious fishing takes place in the spring and fall. Small bluefish, whiting, and flounder are the usual summer catch.

Successful surf fishing requires mobility and four-wheel drive vehicles with low pressure (12 to 15 pounds), wide tires are popular. Anything less may get you in trouble. Experienced drivers stay on the harder packed sand as much as possible as they cruise the beach in search of offshore activity. Driving on the fragile dunes is prohibited and certain portions of the park beaches may be closed to vehicles. Access to the beach from the road is at marked ramps only.

Pamlico Sound, inside the park beaches, is an important nursery ground for coastal migratory fish. The best fishing periods in the sound correspond to the peak surf-fishing periods. Large numbers of channel bass are taken from the sound from April to mid-June and again in October and November. Sea trout move from the surf into the sound in May and stay until October. Cobia (also known as ling or lemonfish) are best in June and July. Cobia are bottom feeders, prowling the sound in search of blue crabs, and are often taken at the edge of a deep channel flowing through shallow water.

Trolling is the usual method of fishing in the sound. Pamlico Sound waters are well protected by the Outer Banks, allowing fishing in the area on most days.

In addition to the surf and the sound, three piers extend out 1,000 feet or more from the beach on Hatteras Island at Rodanthe, Avon, and Frisco. The same species taken in the surf can be caught from piers, as can sheepshead, which favor pier pilings. The world all-tackle record channel bass was caught from a Hatteras Island pier. It weighed 90 pounds.

Offshore fishing from Hatteras Island for blue marlin is very popular. Because of the proximity of the Gulf Stream, fishing is also excellent for sailfish, dolphin, and white marlin. The blue marlin run begins in June, and most charter boats are booked months in advance. The major big-game fleets are based at Hatteras Village and Oregon Inlet.

Sport fishing is a major industry along the Outer Banks. Guides, charter boats, tackle rentals, fishing information, and accommodations are available throughout the area. The Chamber of Commerce can provide a packet of helpful information.

To continue fishing south of Cape Hatteras along the Outer Banks, refer to the following section on Cape Lookout National Seashore. Cape Lookout starts at the southern boundary of Cape Hatteras National Seashore.

License No license is required for saltwater fishing in North Carolina.

Camping There are five campgrounds in the park with a total of 714 spaces. Developed campgrounds are available from approximately April 1 until the Monday after Thanksgiving at Cape Point (202 spaces), Oregon Inlet (120 spaces), and Ocracoke (136 spaces). Campgrounds at Salvo (130 spaces) and Frisco (124 spaces) are open only from Memorial Day to Labor Day. Reservations through Ticketron are recommended for Ocracoke Campground.

Maps The park brochure contains a general location map which is sufficient for most purposes. Tide tables are beneficial and are available locally. Navigating a boat offshore and in Pamlico Sound requires nautical charts #12204 and #11555.

Park Address
Cape Hatteras NS
Route 1, Box 675
Manteo, NC 27954
phone: (919) 473-2111.

Chambers of Commerce

Outer Banks C.C.
P.O. Box 1757
Kill Devil Hills, NC 27949
phone: (919) 441-8144

Dare County Tourist Bureau
P.O. Box 399
Manteo, NC 27954
phone: (919) 473-2138

Additional Information A wealth of information is available from the State Division of Travel and Tourism. Ask for the booklet *Fishing in North Carolina,* along with *Fishing Information Bulletin,* No. 102, *Outer Banks Surf Fishing,* and the *North Carolina Camping and Outdoors Directory.* Contact: North Carolina Travel and Tourism Division, Dept. 867, 430 North Salisbury St., Raleigh, NC, 27611; phone: (toll free) 1-800-847-4862.

Fishing location maps with Loran C coordinates for Oregon Inlet and Pamlico Sound are available for a nominal fee from: UNC Sea Grant, 105 1911 Building, North Carolina State University, Raleigh, NC, 27650; phone: (919) 737-2454.

Cape Lookout National Seashore

Cape Lookout is a 55-mile series of low, sandy, barrier islands running from the Ocracoke Inlet on the northeast to Beaufort Inlet on the southwest. Cape Lookout is part of North Carolina's Outer Banks.

Extending south from the southern boundary of Cape Hatteras National Seashore, the islands of Cape Lookout comprise a relatively undisturbed area featuring extensive beaches and salt marshes, low dunes, and historic Portsmouth, a former seaport.

Access Cape Lookout is on the southeast coast of North Carolina (Carteret County). No part of the park is connected to the mainland. All access is by toll ferry or private boat; some of the ferries are equipped to transport four-wheel drive vehicles. The park brochure contains more detailed information about ferries and the park office can send you a list of the ferry operators servicing Cape Lookout. There are no maintained roads in the park.

Fishing The fishing at Cape Lookout National Seashore is much like that at Cape Hatteras, with similar fish species and seasons. I suggest you read the description of fishing at Cape Hatteras National Seashore for more detail.

The prime fishing periods are spring and fall with fall attracting more folks because the fish are usually larger then. Because of the lack of easy access, Cape Lookout receives only a small fraction of the fishing pressure experienced at popular Cape Hatteras National Seashore.

Visitors who come to Cape Lookout for the fishing either leave their cars on the mainland, take a ferry to the park, and walk along the beaches looking for a likely spot, or they ferry over their four-wheel drive vehicles to cruise the beaches in search of fish activity. A free permit, available from the park office or ferry operators, is required to drive a vehicle in the park.

Channel bass (redfish or red drum) fishing is best in late April through May and again in late September through November. Small channel bass are available throughout the summer, along with flounder, bluefish, and sharks. Most of the fishing activity is from the Ocracoke Inlet–Portsmouth Village area south 22 miles to Drum Inlet.

Drum Inlet divides the Core Banks into the northern section, including Portsmouth Island, and the southern section, including Lookout Point. A shoal extends seaward from Lookout Point, and fishing the point area is usually productive. Lookout Point is a dependable spot for spring bluefish, which winter near the shipwrecks off Cape Lookout. Inlets often provide your best fishing. Beaufort and Barden inlets leading to Back Sound are good bets.

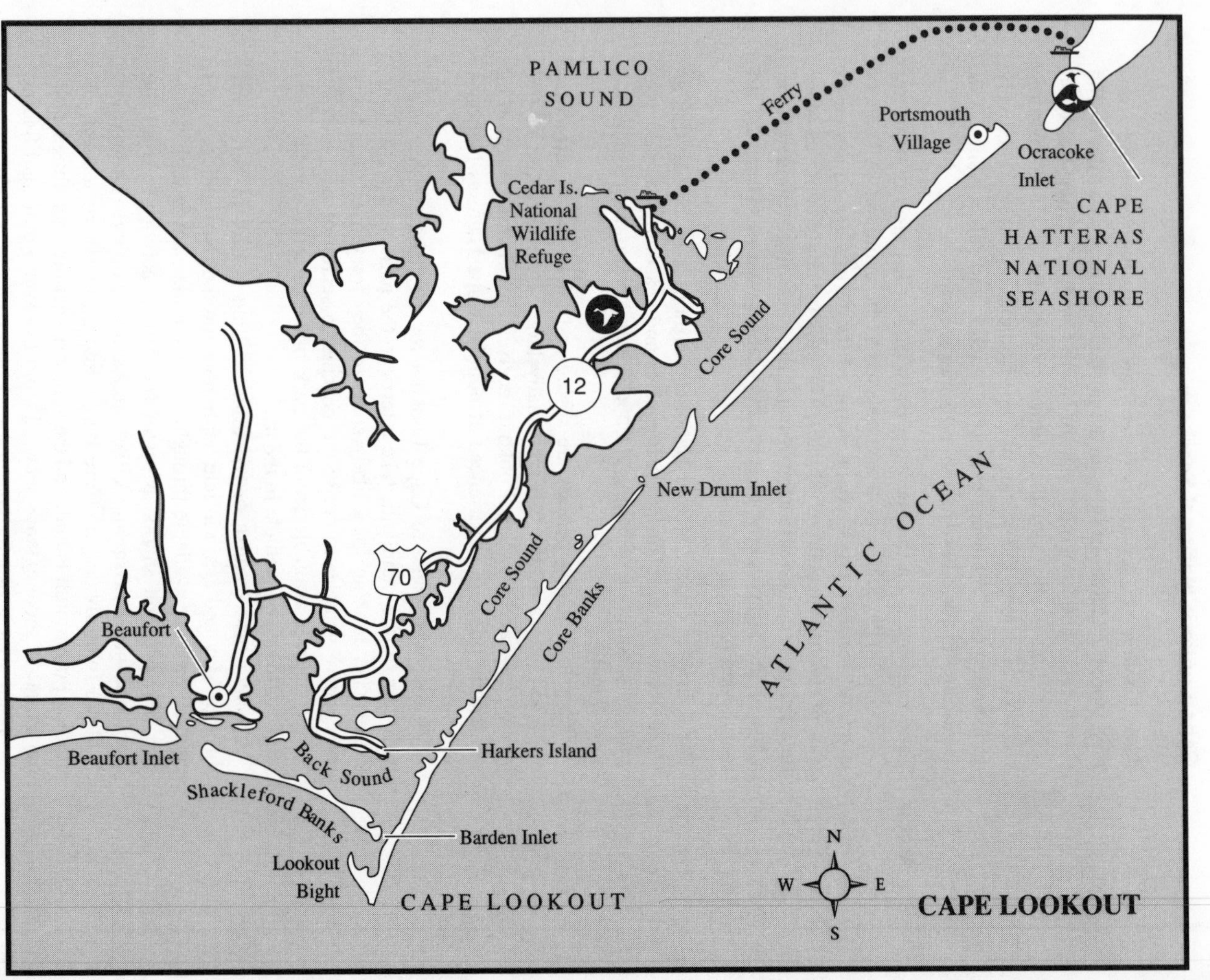
PAMLICO SOUND
Ferry
Portsmouth Village
Ocracoke Inlet
CAPE HATTERAS NATIONAL SEASHORE
Cedar Is. National Wildlife Refuge
Core Sound
12
New Drum Inlet
ATLANTIC OCEAN
70
Core Sound
Core Banks
Beaufort
Beaufort Inlet
Back Sound
Harkers Island
Shackleford Banks
Barden Inlet
Lookout Bight
CAPE LOOKOUT
N
W
E
S
CAPE LOOKOUT

The Lookout Bight area between Lookout Point and the Shackleford Banks is another productive area. Kingfish and cobia are abundant in the Bight area in June, and Back Sound harbors gray sea trout and flounder. Harkers Island, accessible from U.S. 70, is the launching point for fishing in Back Sound, Barden Inlet, and Lookout Bight.

License No license is required for saltwater fishing in North Carolina.

Camping The park is undeveloped, and there are no designated camping facilities. Primitive camping is allowed throughout the park, with only a few restrictions. A brochure discussing camping and park conditions is available from the park office.

Maps Topographic maps are of little use. The park brochure map is a general location map and should suffice. Tide tables, available locally, are helpful.

To navigate the sounds or offshore requires nautical charts #11550 and #11545.

Park Address
Cape Lookout NS
P.O. Box 690
Beaufort, NC 28516
phone: (919) 728-2121

Chamber of Commerce
Carteret County C.C.
Box 1198
Morehead City, NC 28557
phone: (919) 726-6831

Additional Information See the references for Cape Hatteras National Seashore. *The Surf Fishing Information Bulletin,* No. 102, available from the North Carolina Travel and Tourism Division, lists guides and offers advice on tackle, clothing, and fishing seasons. The UNC Sea Grant Maps show fishing locations in the Beaufort Inlet area.

NORTH DAKOTA

Knife River Indian Villages National Historic Site

Knife River Indian Villages NHS preserves remnants of the historic and prehistoric Indian villages that were last occupied by the Hidatsa Indians in 1845. The Lewis and Clark expedition stopped at the three Hidatsa villages on the Knife River in 1804.

Access The park is in west central North Dakota (Mercer County), approximately 3 miles north of Stanton via County Highway 37.

Fishing The Knife River runs through the 1,300-acre park and flows into the Missouri River on the park's east boundary. Walleye, sauger, northern pike, and channel catfish are the common fish species caught.

Walleye fishing is best in the spring when the walleye spawn over gravel or rubble-strewn areas. When walleye are not spawning, look for them at the edges of weed beds or at the intersection of shallow and deep waters. Northern pike favor weedy areas. Catfish are bottom feeders and are taken throughout the year.

Fishing pressure is moderate in the park, with the spring and fall fishing attracting the most people.

License A North Dakota fishing license is required.

Camping No facilities exist in the park, but private campgrounds are located nearby.

Maps The park brochure contains a general location map that is sufficient.

Park Address
Knife River Indian Villages NHS
RR #1, Box 168
Stanton, ND 58571
phone: (701) 745-3309

Chamber of Commerce
North Dakota State C.C.
P.O. Box 2467
Fargo, ND 58108
phone: (701) 237-9461

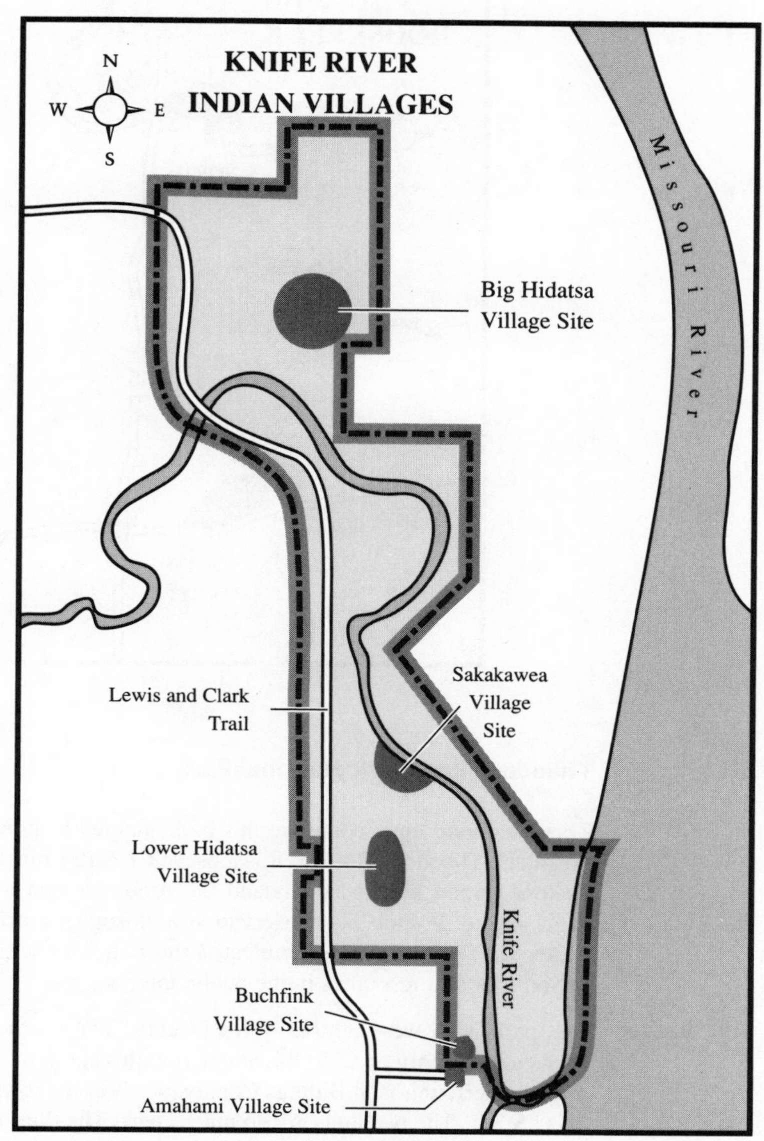
KNIFE RIVER
INDIAN VILLAGES
N
W
E
S
Missouri River
Big Hidatsa
Village Site
Sakakawea
Village
Site
Lewis and Clark
Trail
Lower Hidatsa
Village Site
Knife River
Buchfink
Village Site
Amahami Village Site

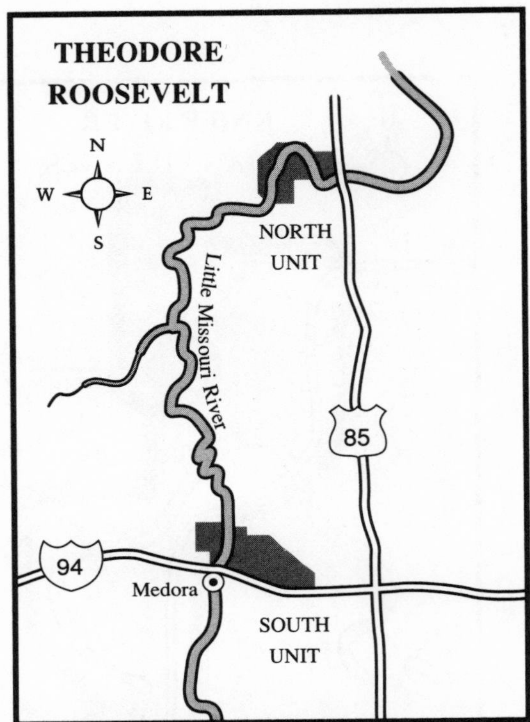

Theodore Roosevelt National Park

Three separate units comprise this park, named in honor of former president Theodore Roosevelt. Roosevelt's cattle ranches in North Dakota helped him to understand the problems and settlers of the West and to develop his conservation philosophy. During his presidency (1901–1909), he promulgated the policy of wisely using the nation's natural resources in the public interest.

Access The park is in west central North Dakota. The northern unit is in McKenzie County on U.S. 85, about 17 miles south of Watford City. The southern unit is in Billings County, north of the town of Medora, off U.S. 94. The two units are 50 miles apart. The third unit, Elkhorn Ranch, is accessible by dirt road (20 miles) from the south unit.

Fishing The Little Missouri River, a tributary of the Missouri River, flows through both the north and south units of the park. Little fishing occurs in park waters, mostly in May and June for channel catfish.

Fishing success depends on water flows. In years of good flows and increased water depths, spawning catfish move further upstream from the river's mouth, which is approximately 170 miles downstream from park headquarters at Medora. In some years, if the flow is fairly high and the silt load relatively low, northern pike may move upstream to river sections within the park.

The Little Missouri is typical of rivers in the northern and western plains. It usually has a very high sediment load during the spring runoff and a very low flow during the rest of the year. As a result, good fishing conditions are restricted to a short period in the spring, when fish species tolerant to high, silty flows are caught.

License A North Dakota fishing license is required.

Camping In the south unit, Cottonwood Campground has 78 spaces; Squaw Creek Campground in the north unit has 50 spaces. A group campground is available in each unit and requires a reservation.

Maps The park brochure map is sufficient since it shows the access points to the river in both units.

Park Address
Theodore Roosevelt NP
P.O. Box 7
Medora, ND 58645
phone: (701) 623-4466

Chamber of Commerce
North Dakota State C.C.
P.O. Box 2467
Fargo, ND 58108
phone: (701) 237-9461

• OHIO

Cuyahoga Valley National Recreation Area

Cuyahoga Valley NRA is a 32,000-acre park along 22 miles of the Cuyahoga River between Cleveland and Akron. Congress created the park in 1974 to preserve a pastoral river valley amidst a region of continuing urbanization.

Access The park is located along the Cuyahoga River in northeastern Ohio (Cuyahoga and Summit counties). The park is paralleled by Interstate 77 on the west and by State Highway 8 on the east.

Fishing Fishing in the park is not a major activity. Generally, Cuyahoga Valley NRA is a place to go picnicking and let the kids fish. Because of its poor water quality, fishing is marginal in the Cuyahoga River and its tributaries, Furnace Run and Tinkers Creek. There are a few smallmouth bass, rock bass, and northern pike, amidst numerous carp and suckers.

Approximately 104 ponds and small lakes are found within the park boundaries, but not all are owned by the park service. Only 7 are recommended for fishing. They are:

Fawn Pond—3.9 acres
Horseshoe Pond—3.4 acres
Goosefeather Pond—2.3 acres
Sylvan Pond—4.7 acres
Meadow Edge Pond—2 acres
Indigo Lake—9.8 acres
Kendall Lake—11.9 acres

The fish species found in the different ponds and lakes do not vary much. Based on park sampling, they include largemouth bass, catfish, bluegill, sunfish, crappie (only in Fawn Pond), carp, and suckers.

License An Ohio license is required. Some of the ponds and lakes may be temporarily closed for management purposes. Check with park rangers about special park fishing regulations.

Camping No camping facilities exist in the park, but private campgrounds are located nearby.

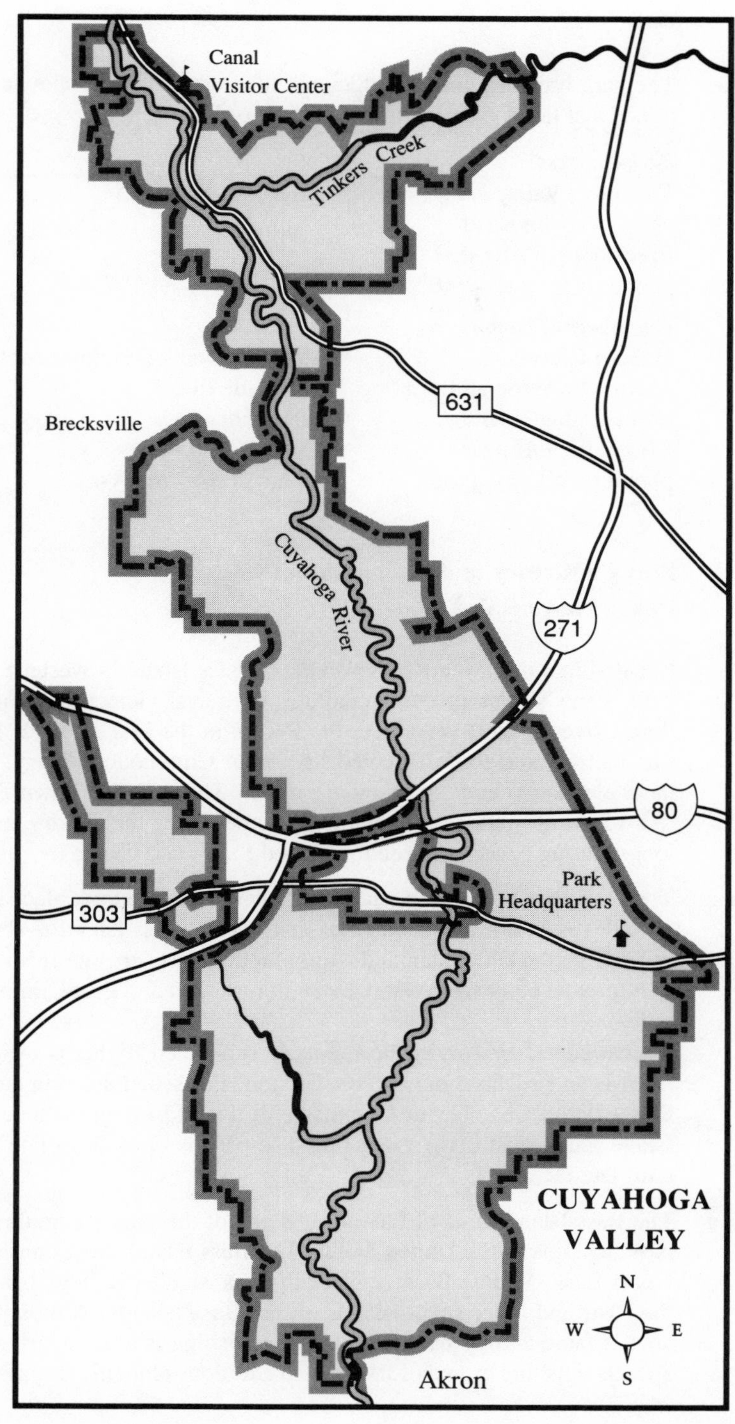
Canal
Visitor Center
Tinkers Creek
631
Brecksville
Cuyahoga River
271
80
303
Park
Headquarters
CUYAHOGA
VALLEY
N
W
E
S
Akron

Maps The park brochure map is sufficient, although it doesn't show all the ponds and lakes. Topographic maps are of little benefit.

Park Address
Cuyahoga Valley NRA
15610 Vaughn Road
Brecksville, OH 44141
phone: (216) 526-5256

Chambers of Commerce

Greater Cleveland
Growth Association
690 Huntington Bldg.
Cleveland, OH 44115
phone: (216) 621-3300

Akron Regional Development Board
1 Cascade Plaza
Suite 800
Akron, OH 44308
phone: (216) 376-5550

Perry's Victory and International Peace Memorial

Located in northwestern Ohio on South Bass Island in western Lake Erie, Perry's Victory commemorates the naval victory of Commodore Oliver Hazard Perry over the British in the War of 1812. From this battle came the oft-quoted line from Commodore Perry: "We have met the enemy and they are ours." The park is known for its 352-foot-high pink granite memorial symbolizing the victory and the longstanding peace between the United States and Canada.

Access The park is on South Bass Island, although the battle took place about 10 miles west-northwest on Lake Erie. South Bass Island is about 4 miles from the Ohio mainland. Automobile ferries operate from April to mid-November from Catawba Point (4 miles) and Port Clinton (14 miles).

Year-round air service on regularly scheduled flights is available from Island Airlines out of Port Clinton. For schedules, contact the Port Clinton Chamber of Commerce at the address given below, or Island Airlines at (419) 734-3149. The park is open from late April until late October.

Fishing The Bass Islands area of Lake Erie is one of the greatest smallmouth bass fisheries in the United States. The Bass Islands area consists of North Bass, Middle Bass, and South Bass islands, Kelleys Island to the east, and other small islands off the Bass Islands. Although this area is famous for smallmouth, walleye fishing is also superb and it attracts a fishing crowd of its own. In addition, bluegill, crappie, and

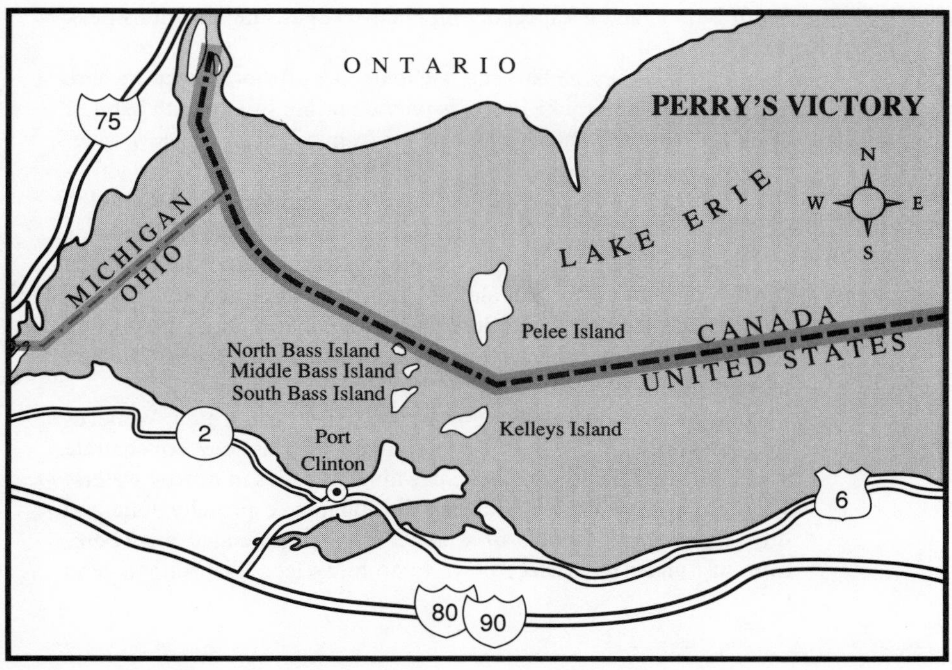

yellow perch can be taken all year. Surprisingly, yellow perch are the most popular game fish in Lake Erie. Channel catfish, pike, largemouth bass, white bass, and freshwater drum are also caught in the area.

The island park is surrounded by Lake Erie, but there are no waters inside the park itself. Fishing is allowed from the sea walls. For the best fishing, however, a boat is necessary. Guides and rental boats are available but are at a premium early in the season. If you use your own boat, remember that Lake Erie is big water and can be dangerous. A boat in the 16-to-18-foot range is recommended. The water around the Bass Islands is fairly shallow, averaging 30 feet deep, and may churn up quickly even in a light breeze. The shallow waters contain numerous shoals and reefs that form the major fish attracting areas. Fishing pressure is heavy, since western Lake Erie provides some of the best fishing in the Great Lakes.

Smallmouth bass fishing heats up in May after water temperatures rise above 55 degrees. This is the spawning period for smallmouth. From mid-May to mid-June or later, smallmouth are found in the near-shore shallows off the islands. The shallow, rocky shoreline of

South Bass Island is especially productive. Spawning activities peak in June.

After spawning, the bass migrate to deeper offshore waters, where bottom rubble and rocky dropoffs provide prime smallmouth habitat. Look for reefs and shoals that drop off from relatively shallow water to deeper water in the open areas of the lake. By July, spawning activities have been completed and the bass have regrouped and schooled on the reefs and shoals. These schools of bass often contain hundreds of fish and last into September. Anchoring over a dropoff and using a crayfish or minnow for bait almost guarantees some action.

In the fall, the bass move close to shore again and good bass fishing continues into November, as long as the weather cooperates. The east shore of South Bass Island can be very productive then.

Walleyes provide the other major sport fishery in the area. Walleyes are found west of the Bass Islands in late May as they concentrate around the reefs following their spawning activities in nearby waters. The best walleye fishing is during the summer, especially June and July. By August, schools of walleye can be suspended anywhere, from just under the surface down to 20 to 25 feet. The schools tend

The Bass Islands area of Lake Erie produces some of the best smallmouth bass fishing in the country.—*Ohio Department of Natural Resources photo by Ron Keil*

to break up and the fish migrate east in August, but good fishing is still possible around the reefs and shoals.

The primary tactic for walleye fishing is drifting with the wind over known walleye areas using a June Bug-type spinner and a night crawler. This technique also produces an occasional channel catfish, although night fishing in the summer is the preferred method for catfish. Yellow perch are also a big attraction and can be caught all year around the Bass Islands, with fall the best time.

Ice fishing is extremely popular and attracts hundreds of people to the Bass Islands. Yellow perch, walleyes, and white bass are the principal species, and South Bass Island is the hub of island ice-fishing activity.

Ice-fishing guides may be hired. The guide will arrange transportation via Island Airlines to and from Put-In-Bay Airport on South Bass Island and provide a heated shanty along with bait and tackle. Information on guides and facilities can be obtained by contacting Island Airlines at (419) 734-3149.

License An Ohio fishing license is required and Ohio regulations apply. At the present time, smallmouth bass and walleye can be fished all year, but be sure to check current regulations.

Camping There are no camping facilities in the park. Limited camping facilities are available at South Bass Island State Park. Contact the Chamber of Commerce for accommodations.

Maps To avoid running aground on one of Lake Erie's many shallow reefs, you will need nautical chart #14830 for the west end of Lake Erie. This map is available at marine stores in the area or from the National Ocean Survey in Maryland.

You should also have the *Guide to Fishing Reefs in Western Lake Erie,* which consists of maps pinpointing all the major fishing areas of the Western Basin of the lake. The guide is available for $2.00 (postpaid) from: Ohio Sea Grant Program, Ohio State University, 1541 Research Center, 1314 Kinnear Rd., Columbus, OH, 43212; phone: (614) 292-8949.

Park Address
Perry's Victory and International Peace Memorial
P.O. Box 549
Put-In-Bay, OH 43456
phone: (419) 285-2184

Chambers of Commerce

The Port Clinton Area Chamber of Commerce has a complete packet of fishing information listing charter boats, camping, accommodations, ferry service, airline service, and restaurants. You should also inquire of the Put-In-Bay Chamber of Commerce on South Bass Island.

Port Clinton Area C.C.
130 Jefferson St. #1B
Port Clinton, OH 43452
phone: (419) 734-5503

Put-In-Bay C.C.
P.O. Box 250
Put-In-Bay, OH 43456
phone: (419) 285-2832

Additional Information

Western Lake Erie, a free publication from the Ohio Department of Natural Resources, contains a map of the area showing some contours around the Bass Islands and discusses the fish in the area, the best times of the year, and techniques. Contact: Publications, Ohio Department of Natural Resources, Fountain Square, Columbus, OH, 43224; phone: (614) 265-6606.

OKLAHOMA

Chickasaw National Recreation Area

Chickasaw NRA was created in 1976 by combining Platt National Park and Arbuckle National Recreation Area. The former Platt National Park is now known as the Travertine District of Chickasaw and is noted for its freshwater and mineral springs. Eight miles southwest of Travertine is Lake of the Arbuckles, created by Arbuckle Dam at the confluence of Buckhorn, Guy Sandy, and Rock creeks.

Access The park is in south central Oklahoma in Murray County, near Sulphur, just east of Interstate 35, which connects Oklahoma City and Dallas–Fort Worth.

Fishing Lake of the Arbuckles is a 2,350-acre reservoir with 36 miles of shoreline nestled in the canyons of the Arbuckle Mountains. The lake is noted for its natural scenic beauty and exceptionally good water quality. The shoreline includes a series of deep coves and rocky points that are good fishing areas.

Largemouth bass, spotted bass, crappie, white bass, bream, and catfish comprise the major sport fishery. An occasional walleye is also taken. The best fishing months are February to May. Fishing slows during the hot summer period from June through September. Boat ramps are located at the three major access areas: Guy Sandy, the Point, and Buckhorn. As might be expected, largemouth bass are the most sought-after game fish.

The largemouth has been the subject of considerable research in the Lake of the Arbuckles. The Oklahoma Department of Wildlife Conservation, noting that the largemouth fishery had declined in recent years, placed a 13-to-16-inch-length limit to protect largemouth and spotted bass. This is known as a slot length limit; all bass in the 13-to-16-inch slot must be returned immediately to the lake. This regulation is designed to provide a quality fishery in the future by allowing more bass to grow to larger sizes.

Peak fishing for largemouth is from late March through May, when they move into shallow water to spawn. Crankbaits, worms, and jig and eel combinations are all productive. Good top-water action can be had in May and June. The three arms of the lake where the creeks come in are all good areas, especially the Buckhorn Creek channel.

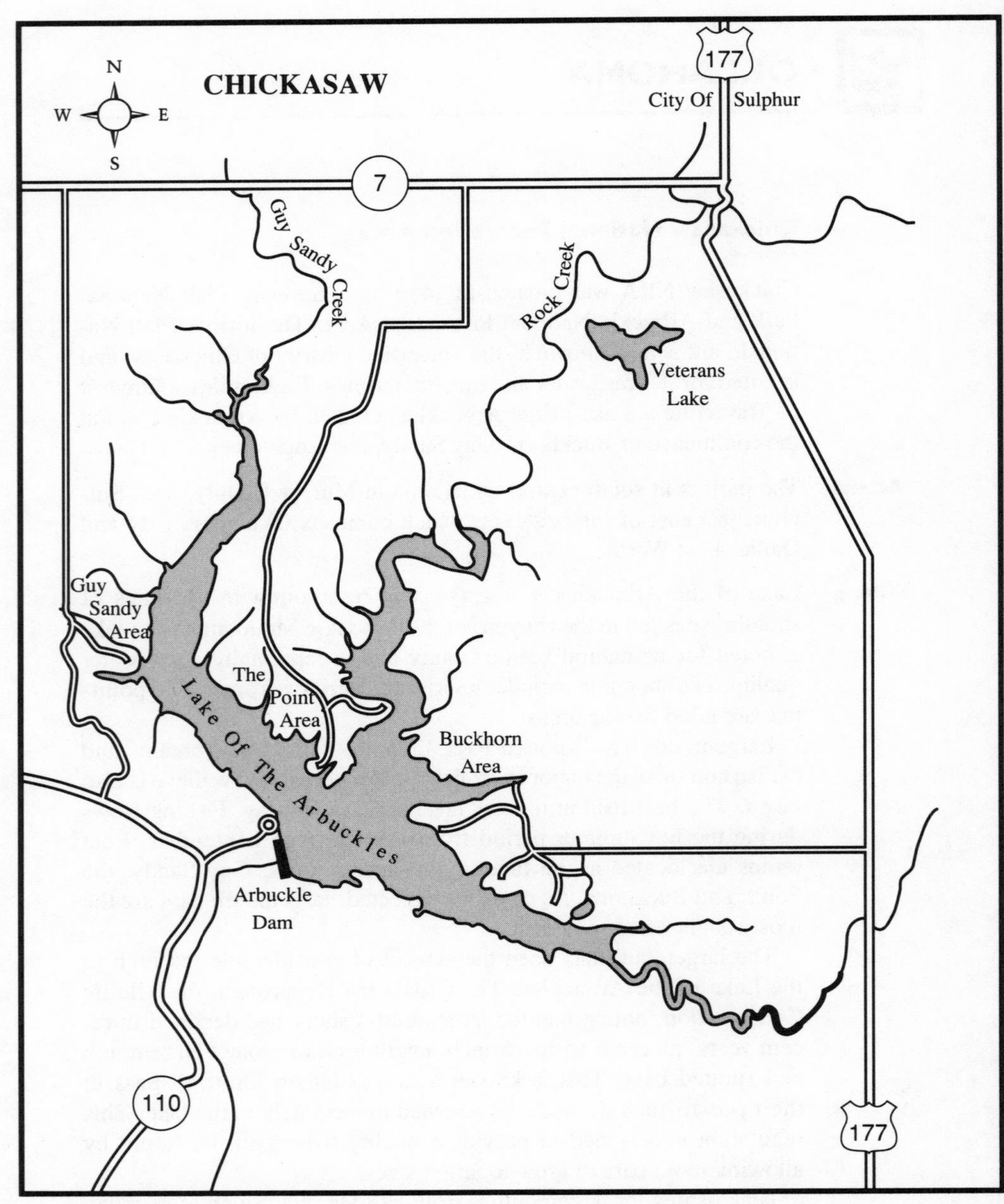
CHICKASAW
N
W
E
S
177
City Of Sulphur
7
Guy Sandy Creek
Rock Creek
Veterans Lake
Guy Sandy Area
The Point Area
Lake Of The Arbuckles
Buckhorn Area
Arbuckle Dam
110
177

Fishing is good for both black and white crappie. As is typical of crappie, most angler success occurs in areas that have sunken trees or brush. Because natural crappie habitat was limited, marked brush shelters were placed near the three major access areas to concentrate the crappie for anglers; these shelters are marked so they can be located.

Walleye were first stocked in 1971, but only limited reproduction occurred. The state is attempting additional management strategies to enhance the walleye fishery.

The three tributary streams into the lake, Buckhorn, Guy Sandy, and Rock creeks, are not large. They flow through private property with limited access. These streams have a few good holes but do not have substantial fish populations.

Veterans Lake is a small lake (67 acres) near the south edge of Sulphur City but within the Travertine District. The lake contains bass, bream, crappie, and catfish.

License An Oklahoma fishing license is required. Be sure to check the regulations for Lake of the Arbuckles.

Camping There are five campgrounds (444 spaces) and four group campgrounds in the park.

Maps Contour maps are unavailable for Lake of the Arbuckles, and topographic maps aren't needed. The map on the park brochure is adequate.

Park Address
Chickasaw NRA
P.O. Box 201
Sulphur, OK 73086
phone: (405) 622-3161

Chamber of Commerce
Oklahoma State C.C.
4020 N. Lincoln Blvd.
Oklahoma City, OK 73105
phone: (405) 424-4003

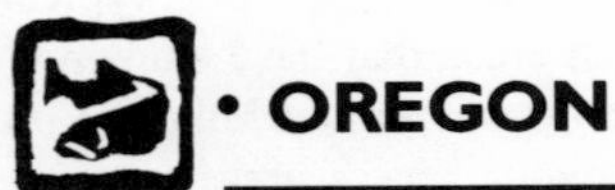

• OREGON

Crater Lake National Park

Crater Lake is the deepest lake (1,932 feet) in the United States. It was formed 6,000 years ago when Mount Mazama, a huge volcano, collapsed to form an immense basin. Over the centuries, the basin filled with water from rain and snow to form Crater Lake. The lake is noted for its brilliant blue color, caused by the reflection from its depths of the rays of the sun.

Access The park is in southern Oregon (Klamath County), approximately 47 miles north of Klamath Falls. It can be reached from the north by Oregon Highway 138 and from the south by Oregon Highway 62, which runs through the southwest corner of the park.

Fishing Fishing in Crater Lake and in park streams is only marginal. Consequently, fewer than 1 percent of all park visitors fish. Crater Lake was originally devoid of fish, but was stocked repeatedly from 1910 until 1939 with a variety of salmon and trout. Today, there are naturally reproducing populations of kokanee salmon, rainbow trout, and brown trout. The kokanee are relatively abundant and average 9 to 18 inches. Rainbow trout are less common, but some grow to 24 inches. Brown trout are rarely caught.

Boats are not allowed on the lake, and fishing is possible only from shore. The lakeshore is accessible only via the Cleetwood Cove Trail on the north side of the lake. Fishing is also possible from Wizard Island, which is reached by regularly scheduled boat tours.

There are 34 streams within the park, 10 of which were stocked with trout in the 1930s. These 10 are the major streams in the park and the only ones with fishable populations. They are: Sand, Sun, Munson, Lost, Annie, Middle Fork Annie, Patton, Castle, Trapper, and Bybee. The remaining 24 streams have only seasonal flows and do not support fishable populations.

The streams were originally stocked with brook trout and rainbow trout. The brook trout are now more abundant. Dolly Varden, found only in Sun Creek, is considered the only native trout in the park.

The fishing season is May 20 through October 31. Snow may cover the ground well into the fishing season and prevent access to many park waters. A fishing brochure is available from the park.

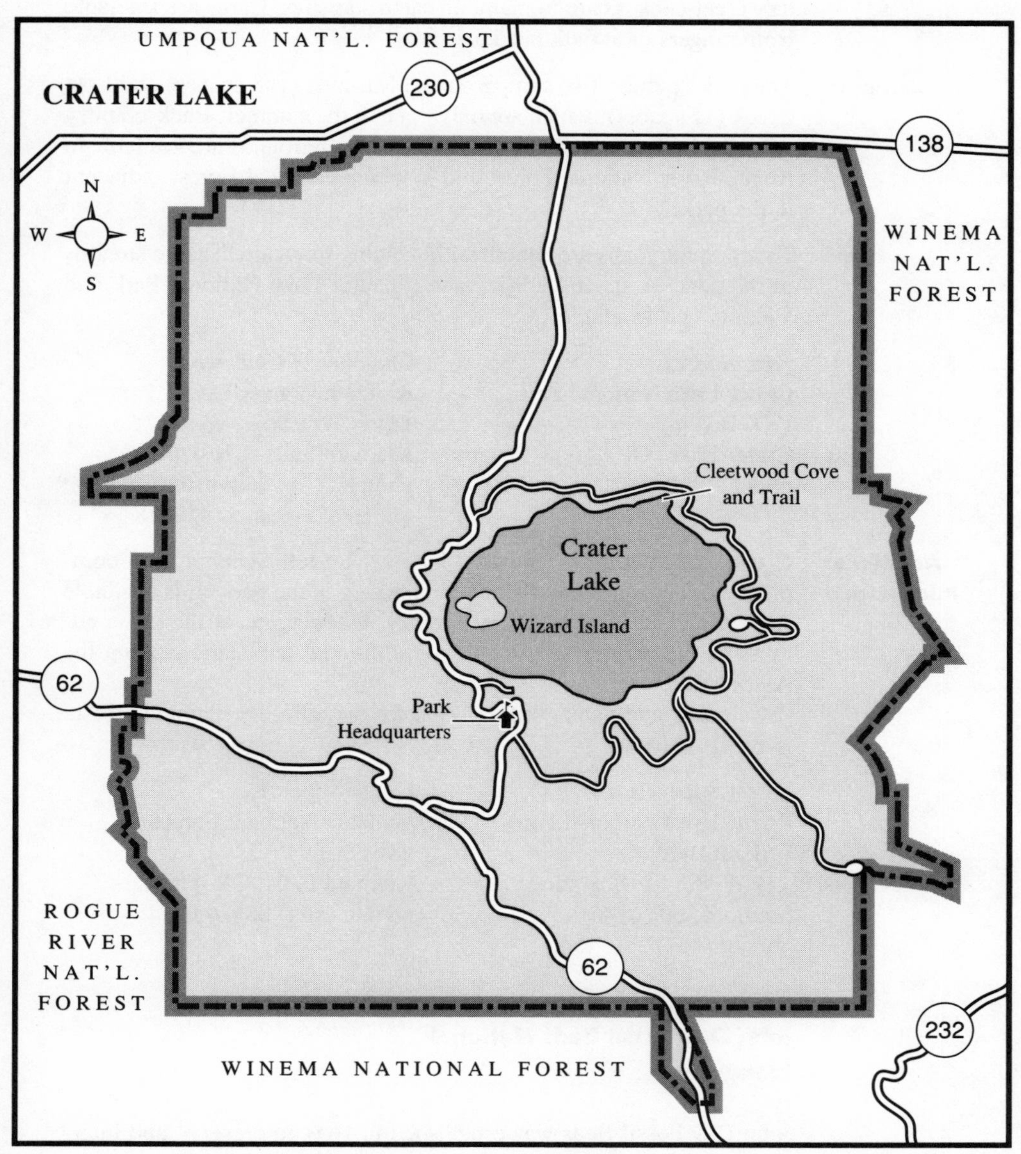
UMPQUA NAT'L. FOREST
CRATER LAKE
230
138
N
W
E
S
WINEMA
NAT'L.
FOREST
Cleetwood Cove
and Trail
Crater
Lake
Wizard Island
62
Park
Headquarters
ROGUE
RIVER
NAT'L.
FOREST
62
232
WINEMA NATIONAL FOREST

License No fishing license is required in the park. The park uses a voluntary creel-census card to maintain catch statistics. Cards are available from rangers or at park headquarters.

Camping The park operates two campgrounds, Mazama (198 spaces) and Lost Creek (12 spaces), which are only open in the summer. Back-country camping is allowed with a permit. Other campgrounds are available in Rogue River National Forest and Winema National Forest, adjacent to the park.

Maps Topographic maps are beneficial in helping to locate fishable streams in the park. A special USGS map ("Crater Lake National Park and Vicinity") is available.

Park Address
Crater Lake National Park
P.O. Box 7
Crater Lake, OR 97604
phone: (503) 594-2211

Chamber of Commerce
Klamath County C.C.
125 N. 8th St.
Klamath Falls, OR 97601
phone: (503) 884-5193
toll free: 1-800-445-6728

Additional Information *Crater Lake National Park and Vicinity,* by Jeff Schaffer, is a complete guide to camping, fishing, and hiking in the park. It is available from the Crater Lake Natural History Association, at the same address as the park. Request a list of additional publications from the Association.

Camping and fishing information for the adjacent national forests is available from:

Forest Supervisor
Rogue River National Forest
Federal Bldg.
333 W. 8th St, Box 520
Medford, OR 97501
phone: (503) 776-3600

Forest Supervisor
Winema National Forest
2819 Dahlia
Klamath Falls, OR 97601
phone: (503) 883-6714

John Day Fossil Beds National Monument

John Day Fossil Beds was established in 1975 to preserve and interpret a fossil record extending back 40 million years. A major part of the Age of Mammals record derives from this area. The park is composed of three separate sections, Sheep Rock, Painted Hills, and Clarno, all within the John Day River Valley. Distances of 40 miles or more separate each unit from the others.

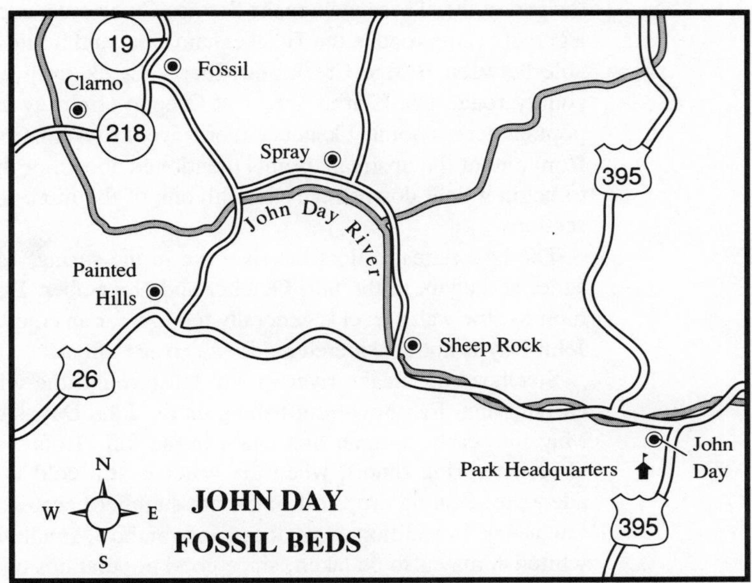

Access The park is in north central Oregon (Grant and Wheeler counties). The main access roads to the area are U.S. 395 (north-south) and U.S. 26 (east-west). The Sheep Rock Unit is 5 miles northwest of Dayville via U.S. 26 and Oregon Highway 19. The Painted Hills Unit is near Mitchell off U.S. 26. The Clarno Unit is on Oregon Highway 218, about 20 miles west of Fossil.

Fishing The park has two streams that contain sport fish. The John Day River flows through the Sheep Rock Unit for approximately 5 miles and is known for its fine steelhead fishing. Another stream, Bridge Creek, lies adjacent to the Painted Hills Unit. The lower reaches of Bridge Creek contain a few rainbow trout. However, a combination of warm water and heavy silt preclude the existence of a reliable trout population.

The John Day River is popular for river floating as well as fishing. Most of the fishing for steelhead is done from shore or by wading. U.S. 26 and Oregon Highway 19 run along the river in the Sheep Rock Unit and provide good access.

Most land along other sections of the John Day is privately owned and river access is limited, making the Sheep Rock Unit a popular spot for fishing. Along the 160-mile stretch from Service Creek to Oregon Highway 207, there are a number of public access sites for floaters to enter or leave the water, most within a few miles of one of the park units. These include the Service Creek area, access by way of a gravel county road in the Twickenham area, and limited access available between Bridge Creek and Cherry Creek from another gravel county road. The Clarno access at Oregon Highway 218 is another popular access point. Floaters either leave the river here after floating from one of the upstream points mentioned above, or they enter here to begin a float downstream through one of the more remote canyon sections.

The best times to float the river are in the spring, March through June, and again in the fall, October and November. During summer months, the water level is generally too low for an enjoyable trip. The John Day is not considered a difficult river to float.

Steelhead are in the river in late fall through the winter and into early spring. Rainbow-trout fishing on the John Day is best from late May into early summer and again in the fall. Trout fishing is good after the spring runoff, when the water is still cold and the flow is adequate. Fishing drops off in the hot summer because of the warm, low water. In addition to steelhead and rainbow, smallmouth bass and whitefish may also be taken, since good populations of these fish are found in various reaches of the river.

License An Oregon fishing license is required, along with a special Salmon-Steelhead license if you are fishing for steelhead. Check the regulations and seasons for steelhead and trout.

Camping There is no camping in the park. Private and public campgrounds are located in the surrounding area.

Maps Topographic maps are not necessary. The best maps are Bureau of Land Management (BLM) river maps, which may be purchased from: BLM, 185 East 4th Street, P.O. Box 550, Prineville, OR, 97754; phone: (503) 447-4115.

Park Address	*Chamber of Commerce*
John Day Fossil Beds NM	Grant County C.C.
420 West Main St.	281 West Main St.
John Day, OR 97845	John Day, OR 97845
phone: (503) 575-0721	phone: (503) 575-0547

Additional Information *The John Day River Drift and Historical Guide,* by Arthur Campbell, should be read before you float the river. It contains drift times between access points and detailed information on rapids, campsites, and fishing. The book is available from Frank Amato Publications, P.O. Box 02112, Portland, OR, 97202; phone: (503) 236-2305.

• PENNSYLVANIA

Delaware Water Gap National Recreation Area

The Delaware Water Gap NRA encompasses a 37-mile stretch of the Delaware River and the adjoining lands along the narrow Delaware Valley, which separates New Jersey's Kittatinny Mountains on the east from Pennsylvania's Pocono Mountains on the west. This gap in the mountains is one of the nation's most distinctive natural landmarks. The Delaware River forms the boundary between Pennsylvania and New Jersey.

Canoeing, fishing, and hiking are major attractions of this popular recreation area. The Appalachian Trail bisects the southern and eastern portions of the park.

Access The park is in northeast Pennsylvania (Pike and Monroe counties) and northwest New Jersey (Sussex and Warren counties), just south of Port Jervis, New York. Access is from U.S. 209, which parallels the river on the Pennsylvania side, and from various county roads on the New Jersey side. Interstate 84 crosses the river just north of the park, and Interstate 80 crosses at the south end.

Actual access to the river is limited to the designated access sites on each side of the river or by permission from the private landowners. There are seven access sites from just north of the park at Matamoras, Pennsylvania, down to Interstate 80. The sites and their descriptions are listed on a brochure from the park, *Canoeing and Boating on the Delaware River*.

Fishing This section of the Delaware River is a magnificent fishery. Smallmouth bass, walleye, and muskellunge are the usual quarry, except in the spring, when the American shad move up the river to spawn. The shad run has improved in recent years as the formerly polluted downstream river sections were cleaned up. The shad had been devastated by industrial pollution near the mouth and by domestic pollution in the upper estuary.

There are also some good tributary trout streams such as the Big Flatbrook and Van Campens Brook in New Jersey and the Big Bushkill, Little Bushkill, Toms Creek, and Broadhead Creek in Pennsyl-

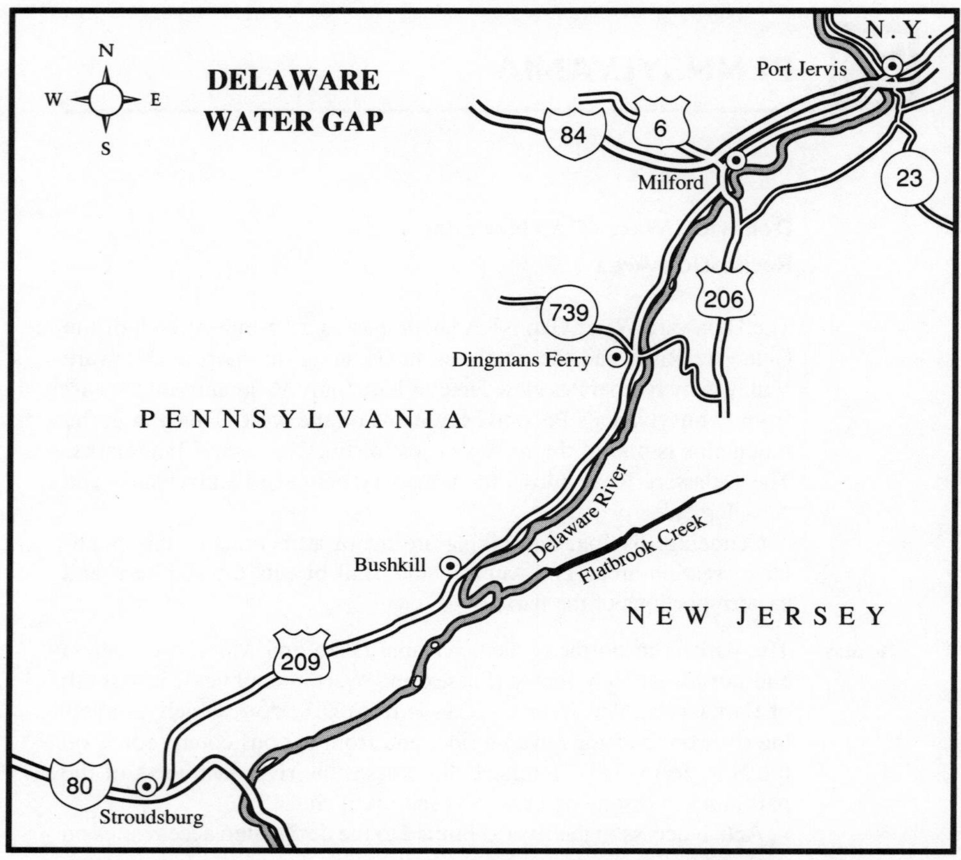

vania. In addition, a number of small lakes and ponds within the park contain bass, pickerel, and panfish.

Shad move into lower park waters in early April and by late April have reached the park waters around the Water Gap, Bushkill, Dingmans Ferry, and Milford Beach, where they provide an outstanding fishery. When the water temperature reaches 55 degrees, the shad begin to strike. Schools of shad congregate in the deeper pools in the main river channel. Fishing is best in the early morning or late evening, and cloudy days are better than sunny days because the shad are light sensitive and generally not inclined to hit under bright conditions.

Besides deep holes, shad are found at the edges of heavy currents and behind large rocks or other obstructions. They also like the long

This fisherman is unhooking a nice-sized American shad taken during the annual spring shad run. Most shad average between 3 to 6 pounds.—*Richard Gross*

runs between the deeper pools and the riffles. Before spawning, they readily strike small lead jigs known as shad darts. Once spawning begins, usually by mid-May, shad stop striking.

Buck shad (males) average 3 to 5 pounds and roe shad (females) 4 to 6 pounds, with some up to 8 pounds. The Water Gap is a prime spawning area for shad as they work their way upstream from the Delaware Bay. Some of the better river sections for shad are near the Milford Beach, Dingmans Ferry, and Smithfield Beach access sites.

The Water Gap section of the Delaware is one of the finest smallmouth bass areas in the eastern United States. The river consistently provides bass in the 2-pound class and occasional 4-to-5-pound bass also show up. Fishing is good all year, but best in late May to early June and late August to early September. Smallmouth can be taken regularly during the summer by fishing very early or very late, mostly with live bait.

Large brown trout make infrequent appearances in the park section of the Delaware; when they do appear, they are usually taken in the riffles and near the mouths of tributary streams. Casting spinners or fishing with live crayfish near the inflowing tributaries can produce browns up to 6 pounds. Browns are even known to hit shad darts. Spring and fall are the best times.

Look for walleyes on the bottom in big pools and slow sections. Drift live bait along the bottom for best results, especially at night, since walleye are nocturnal feeders.

Muskellunge fry were first stocked in 1965, and in 1972 purebred and tiger muskie fingerlings were stocked. Muskie thrive in the Delaware and are now found above the Port Jervis area. Drifting with bait through long eddies is the accepted technique in spring and fall. During the summer, muskie are taken on surface plugs. Few people fishing the river are experienced or knowledgeable about muskie, so most muskies are taken only incidentally.

The Delaware River within the park also holds catfish, yellow perch, pickerel, and sunfish. Look for crappie near bridge abutments. Other than during the shad run, the Delaware is virtually unfished. It is popular with canoeists, but largely ignored by fishing folks.

The 37-mile stretch of river in the park is canoeable, but there are some Class III rapids to navigate. Riverbed configuration and river depth generally limit motor boats to three areas: Milford Beach, Smithfield Beach, and Kittatinny Point.

On the New Jersey side of the park, the Big Flatbrook is regarded as one of the best trout streams in the state. A stream of assorted riffles, glides, deep holes, and pocket water, it harbors some good-sized trout. The river is stocked weekly in the spring and, as expected, is heavily fished. Avoid spring weekends, if possible, when there often is someone fishing about every 10 yards along the river.

Bait fishing produces good results on this stream, but there is a 4-mile stretch restricted to fly-fishing (from the Route 206 concrete bridge downstream to Roy Bridge). May is the best month for fly-fishing, with consistent hatches of March Browns, Grey Foxes, some Green Drakes, and Tan Caddis. Isonychia, Sulphurs, and Light Cahills all appear in June. After June, terrestrials are steady fish takers.

Van Campens Brook, a small stream in New Jersey in the Watergate area of the park, contains brook, brown, and rainbow trout. The stream is better suited for light spinning tackle because the stream sides are very brushy and difficult for fly-fishing. The stream is remote, with good water quality and a healthy trout population. A portion of the brook has been designated by New Jersey as a Natural Trout Fishing Area.

There are several other good trout-water tributaries in the park. In Pennsylvania, Broadhead Creek in the lower portion of the park and the Big Bushkill River near the park headquarters are well known. Broadhead Creek comes into the Delaware near the Water Gap and the Big Bushkill River crosses Route 209 in the town of Bushkill. A small paved road (T-301) parallels the Big Bushkill for 2 miles before doubling back to Route 209. There is a 6-mile fly-fishing-only stretch on the Ressica Falls Boy Scout Reservation, accessible from Route 402. A free permit is required from scout headquarters on Route 402.

The Big Bushkill is regularly stocked by the state until summer. Standard dry fly patterns, along with Muddler Minnows and brown stonefly nymphs, are popular for fly-fishing. Bait and spin fishing in the stream also gets generous results in the spring during the regular stockings.

Several other excellent trout streams are found on the Pennsylvania side of the park. The Little Bushkill, where it is stocked, affords some good back-country fishing. Toms Creek has substantial trout reproduction (brooks and browns) and offers fine fishing for wild trout.

For information about Delaware River fishing upstream from the Delaware Water Gap NRA, refer to the section on the Upper Delaware National Scenic and Recreational River in the New York chapter.

License If you are fishing the Delaware River from a boat, a single license from either Pennsylvania, New York, or New Jersey suffices. If fishing or wading the Delaware from shore, along the river section shared by Pennsylvania and New Jersey, you must have a license from the state in which you entered the water; where Pennsylvania and New York share the river, a license from either state allows you to fish from either shore.

Inland waters in each state require the appropriate state license. Special interstate regulations standardize seasons, size, and creel limits for the Delaware River. State regulations apply for the inland streams, lakes, and ponds.

Camping Dingmans Campground (107 spaces) and two group campgrounds are open from April through October. State and private campgrounds are also found nearby. Canoeists and float-fishing folks are allowed to camp for one night only on the following islands: Mashipacong, Minisink, Namonock, Shapnock, Buck, Depew, Tocks, and Labar islands, as well as at several designated shore areas.

Maps The park brochure map is very good. Also, the Delaware River Basin Commission publishes a detailed and extensive set of river recreation maps, available at a reasonable price. Contact: DRBC, P.O. Box 7360, West Trenton, NJ, 08628; phone: (609) 883-9500.

Park Address
Delaware Water Gap NRA
Bushkill, PA 18324
phone: (717) 588-2435

Chamber of Commerce
Pike County C.C.
P.O. Box 883
Milford, PA 18337
phone: (717) 296-8700

Additional Information The Delaware River Shad Fishermens Association publishes a detailed, comprehensive pamphlet about shad fishing in the Delaware River. For a free copy, send a self-addressed stamped envelope to: DRSFA, 501 Magnolia Road, Hellertown, PA, 18055.

See the Additional Information section under the Upper Delaware National Scenic and Recreational River in New York for more reference materials.

Valley Forge National Historical Park

Valley Forge is the site of the 1777–1778 winter encampment of George Washington and the Continental Army. Valley Forge derives its name from an iron forge built along Valley Creek in the 1740s. Interpretive programs at the park describe the miserable conditions the army had to endure and the significance of the events associated with the winter encampment.

Access The park is approximately 20 miles northwest of Philadelphia via Interstate 76 and State Highway 363 north. From the Pennsylvania Turnpike, take exit 24 to 363 north.

Fishing Valley Creek and the Schuylkill River are the two streams in the park, and both provide good fishing.

Valley Creek is a fine brown-trout stream. Only the lower 2 miles are inside the park. The creek has a native population of brown trout, supplemented by state-stocked rainbow trout. You may also catch an occasional brook trout.

Studies have revealed that polychlorinated biphenyls (PCBs) are present in the creek and in some of the fish. The PCBs are found in the native and holdover trout rather than recently stocked fish, because it takes time for PCB concentrations to build up in fish. Testing has shown that the native or holdover trout have about 1.75 parts per million (PPM) of PCB in them, but this is still well below the danger level of 5.0 PPM. Although the Pennsylvania Department of Environmental Resources does not believe that eating these fish poses a health hazard, you may wish to return all trout to the stream.

Pennsylvania Route 252 parallels the stream in the park. Parking areas are available near the junction of routes 252 and 23 and along the stream.

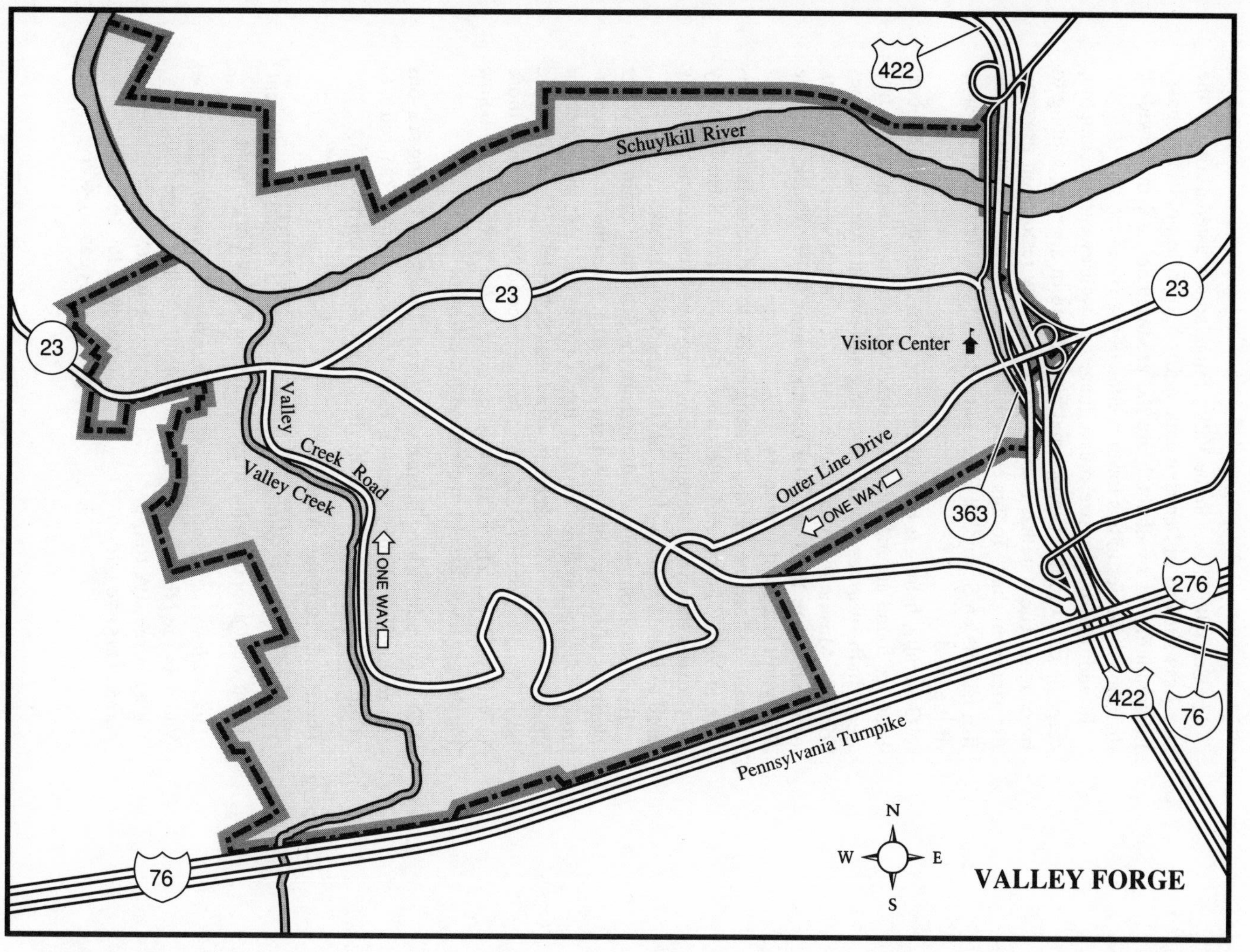
422
Schuylkill River
23
23
23
Visitor Center
Valley Creek Road
Valley Creek
Outer Line Drive
ONE WAY
ONE WAY
363
276
422
76
Pennsylvania Turnpike
76
N
W
E
S
VALLEY FORGE

The Schuylkill River in the Valley Forge area is listed as one of the best bass streams in Pennsylvania and is known to hold large bass. Largemouth and smallmouth are the predominant and most widely distributed species in this lower section of the river.

In addition, trophy-size muskellunge, as well as catfish, crappie, carp, perch, walleye, sunfish, and bluegill are in the river waiting to be caught. The state has also undertaken a new restoration program for American shad. To this end, the Fish Commission is constructing fish ladders on Schuylkill River dams to allow the upstream passage of the shad.

Generally, fishing is best on the river from April through October. Bass are found around rocks and other obstructions such as downed trees. In the warmer months, morning and evening are the best times for bass. Muskie roam the river but are often caught wherever a creek or canal enters the river. The confluence of Valley Creek with the Schuylkill is a good spot to try.

Besides shoreline fishing, boating access to the Schuylkill is available at Valley Forge Park–Betzwood Access, where State Highway 363 crosses the river. The ramp, which has a parking area, is primarily used to launch shallow-draft, lightweight fishing boats.

Because of silt problems throughout the Schuylkill drainage, water clarity is often a problem. A hard rain usually results in turbid conditions for two to three days. A major storm may roil the water for up to five days. Also, keep in mind that Schuylkill River fish have been found to contain PCBs, and in higher concentrations than those in Valley Creek. The PCB levels recorded in the river are still below the danger level, except in carp and American eel.

License A Pennsylvania fishing license is required. Check the fishing seasons and regulations. Valley Creek is closed for a short time (March 1 to about mid-April), but the Schuylkill River is open all year.

Camping There is no camping in the park.

Maps The park brochure contains a good map, which should be sufficient. If you want a topographic map, obtain the Valley Forge quad.

Park Address
Valley Forge NHP
Valley Forge, PA 19481
phone: (215) 783-1000

Chamber of Commerce
Greater Valley Forge C.C.
73 E. Main St.
Norristown, PA 19401
phone: (215) 277-9500

SOUTH CAROLINA

Congaree Swamp National Monument

Congaree Swamp National Monument was established in 1976 to protect the last significant tract (15,000 acres) of old-growth southern bottom-land hardwoods in the southeastern U.S.

Access Congaree Swamp is in south central South Carolina (Richland County), 20 miles southeast of Columbia near State Highway 48.

Fishing Congaree Swamp is a network of creeks and oxbow lakes, providing fair fishing for largemouth bass, yellow perch, crappie, and several species of sunfish. At present, there is an overabundance of nongame species, including bowfin, carp, and longnose gar.

Fishing is limited to accessible reaches of Cedar Creek and Toms Creek and a few oxbow lakes; there is a trail to Cedar Creek.

The Congaree River is adjacent to parts of the park's southern border and is the primary fishery of the area. The river periodically overflows into the park, and there is a question whether frequent flooding naturally stocks game fish within the park. The Congaree River is a popular spot in the spring, when the white bass ascend the river to spawn.

License A South Carolina fishing license is required. Park waters may be closed to fishing for short periods in order to study and monitor fish populations.

Camping None within the park at the present time.

Maps This is all swamp country. If you intend to wander around in the swamp, you should have the Gadsden and Wateree quad sheets.

Park Address
Congaree Swamp NM
P.O. Box 11938
Columbia, SC 29211
phone: (803) 765-5571

Chamber of Commerce
South Carolina State C.C.
P.O. Box 11278
Columbia, SC 29211
phone: (803) 799-4601

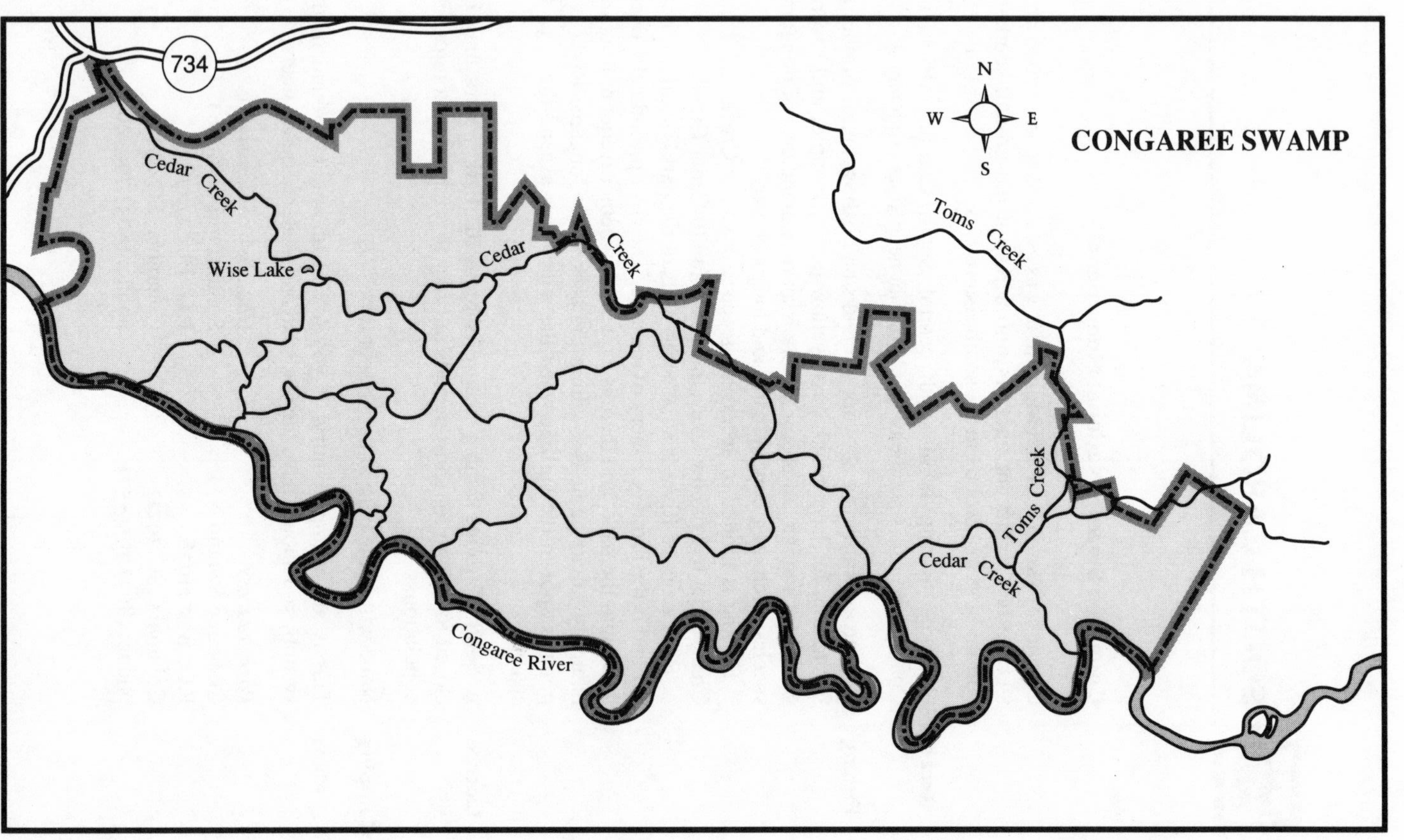
CONGAREE SWAMP
N
W
E
S
734
Cedar Creek
Wise Lake
Cedar
Creek
Toms Creek
Toms Creek
Cedar Creek
Congaree River

Ninety Six National Historic Site

Ninety Six was a frontier settlement and British military post during the Revolutionary War. It was besieged by General Nathanael Greene and the Continental Army in 1781, but the attack failed. The park was established in 1976 and is currently in the development stage.

Access The park is in western South Carolina (Greenwood County), 2 miles south of the town of Ninety Six off State Highway 248.

Fishing The park contains a 27-acre impoundment locally known as "the reservoir." Several small streams were dammed to form the reservoir, and it is also spring fed. The reservoir has largemouth bass, crappie, bluegill, and catfish and is only lightly fished by local residents. With such major reservoirs as Clark Hill, Hartwell, Richard Russell, and Santee-Cooper nearby, few outsiders come here to fish.

License A South Carolina fishing license is required.

Camping None in the park. The nearest lodgings are in the town of Greenwood, 10 miles to the west.

Maps The park brochure map is sufficient.

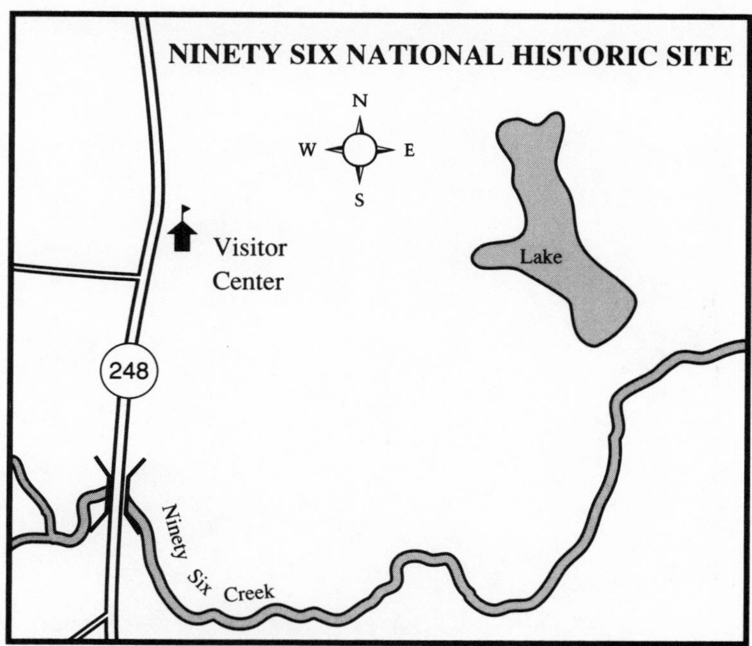

Park Address
Ninety Six NHS
P.O. Box 496
Ninety Six, SC 29666
phone: (803) 543-4068

Chamber of Commerce
Ninety Six C.C.
P.O. Box 8
Ninety Six, SC 29666
phone: (803) 543-2900

• SOUTH DAKOTA

Wind Cave National Park

Wind Cave is a lightly visited park along the southeastern flank of South Dakota's Black Hills. Wind Cave is a limestone cavern featuring a series of subterranean passages and rooms. Strong air currents alternately blow in and out of the cave, giving the cave its name. Above ground is an original prairie grassland complete with buffalo and prairie dogs.

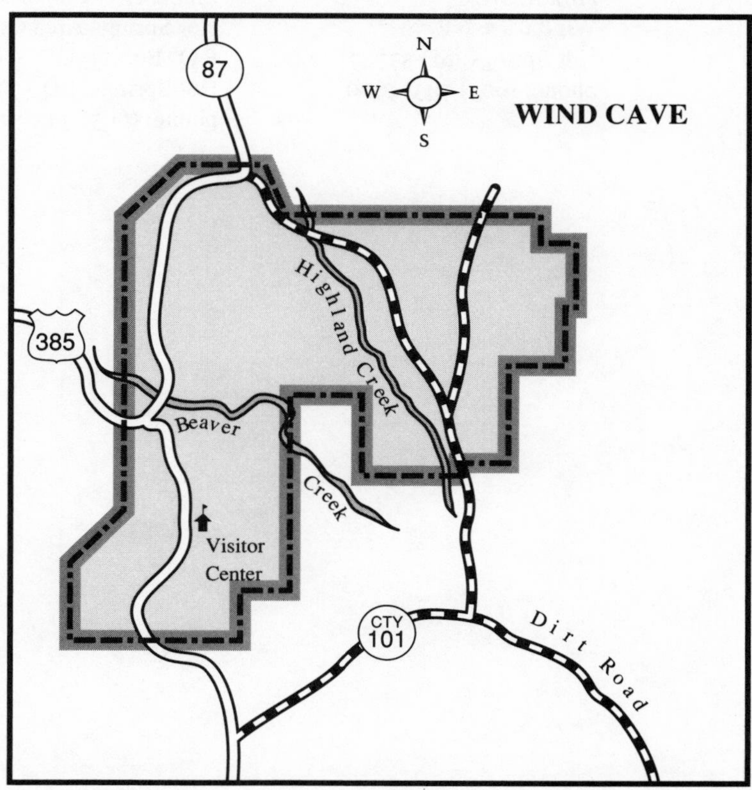

Access The park is in southwestern South Dakota (Custer County), approximately 60 miles south of Rapid City via U.S 16 and 385.

Fishing Very little fishing occurs in the park. Beaver Creek and Highland Creek are small streams flowing through the park, and each contains small brook and rainbow trout in the 6-to-8-inch range. Both streams are stocked outside the park, and any fish in park waters have migrated from the outside stockings. Most of the fishing activity is by park personnel.

License A South Dakota license is required.

Camping Elk Mountain campground (100 spaces) is open from May 15 to September. Custer State Park, to the north, also provides camping.

Maps The park brochure map should be enough, even though it doesn't show the streams. The topographic quad map of the park is Wind Cave.

Park Address
Wind Cave NP
Hot Springs, SD 57747
phone: (605) 745-4600

Chamber of Commerce
Hot Springs Area C.C.
P.O. Box 1158
Hot Springs, SD 57747
phone: (605) 745-5165

• TENNESSEE

Big South Fork National River and Recreation Area

Big South Fork refers to the Big South Fork of the Cumberland River in Tennessee and Kentucky. The park was established in 1974 to preserve the natural and historic features of 123,000 acres of scenic gorges and valleys. The Big South Fork and its two tributaries, the Clear Fork and the New River, are popular with white-water boaters.

The park is a combination of a national river and a national recreation area. The U.S. Army Corps of Engineers coordinates the park planning, land acquisition, and development, and the National Park Service is in charge of park operation and maintenance.

Access The park is in northeastern Tennessee (Scott, Fentress, Pickett, and Morgan counties) and southeastern Kentucky (McCreary County). Park headquarters are 9 miles west of Oneida, Tennessee, on Leatherwood Ford Road. U.S. 27 runs through Oneida and along the eastern part of the park.

Fishing The Big South Fork basin is noted for its good fishing with Lake Cumberland as the main attraction. Most of the lake lies outside the park in Kentucky; only the headwaters of the lake are in the park. Fishing in the park is usually by local people who are familiar with the river and know the local access points. Access is limited at this time, but trails and additional river access are being created as the park is developed.

Sport fish in the rivers and streams are largemouth, smallmouth, and spotted bass, crappie, rock bass, walleye, white bass, rainbow and brown trout, and catfish. The Big South Fork of the Cumberland River is the principal fishery in the park. The Big South Fork is formed in Tennessee by the junction of the Clear Fork and the New River, and it flows for 46 miles before entering Lake Cumberland in Kentucky.

The river attracts numerous white-water paddlers from November into June. If you want to float and fish this river, you should have white-water experience and the trip should be carefully planned, because certain river sections can be dangerous and access points are

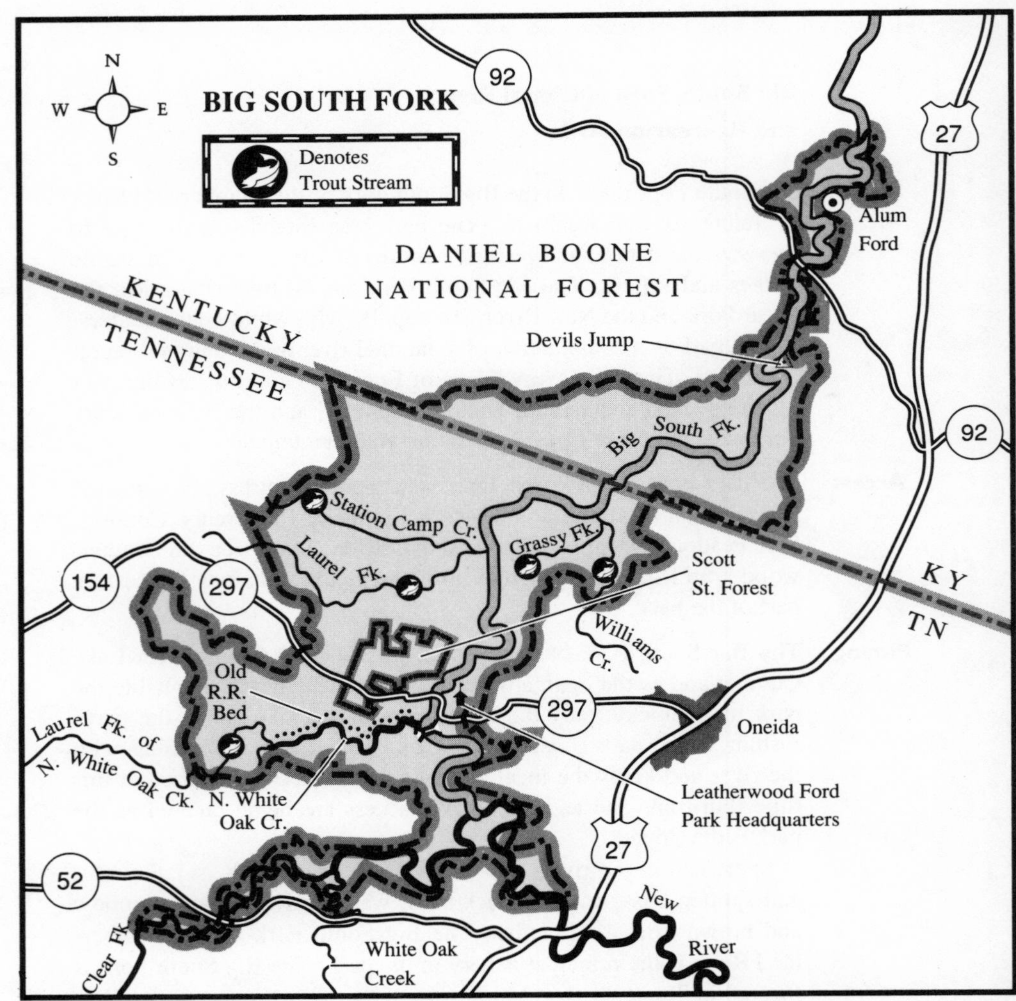
N
W
E
S
BIG SOUTH FORK
Denotes
Trout Stream
92
27
Alum
Ford
DANIEL BOONE
NATIONAL FOREST
KENTUCKY
TENNESSEE
Devils Jump
Big South Fk.
92
Station Camp Cr.
Laurel Fk.
Grassy Fk.
Scott
St. Forest
KY
TN
154
297
Williams
Cr.
Old
R.R.
Bed
297
Oneida
Laurel Fk. of
N. White Oak Ck.
N. White
Oak Cr.
Leatherwood Ford
Park Headquarters
27
52
New
River
White Oak
Creek
Clear Fk.

few. Generally, the river from Leatherwood Ford north can be floated all year except during dry summers. Powerboats are permissible from just below Devils Jump to the north park boundary, otherwise only nonmotorized craft are allowed. The park can supply a list of concessioners who run the river and may serve as guides.

Floating and fishing is productive because the Big South Fork receives little fishing pressure. Fishing for smallmouth bass can be very good, especially within the gorge along the Kentucky–Tennessee border. Crowds are drawn to certain sections of the river every year by the spring walleye run. From mid-February to mid-April, big runs of spawning walleye move into the river from Lake Cumberland. The upper river in Kentucky receives most of the run, and Alum Ford is the principal access during the run. Walleye begin moving into the river when the water temperature reaches the mid-40s.

Jigging is a popular technique because the walleye are usually on or very close to the bottom around rocky banks where they spawn. White bass also spawn in the spring, and their run may overlap part of the walleye run. Fish the shoals and sand bars near the current edge for white bass. The Clear Fork is excellent for panfish and largemouth bass, and the New River offers some good walleye fishing.

Trout are stocked in a few tributary streams in the Tennessee part of the park. Williams Creek and Laurel Fork of Station Camp Creek contain brown and rainbow trout. The trout are reproducing in these creeks and establishing wild populations. In Kentucky, Rock Creek, just west of the park boundary in Daniel Boone National Forest, is a popular rainbow trout stream.

License Fishing in Tennessee or Kentucky requires the appropriate state license. Be sure to check the state regulations. Muskellunge are present in park waters but are protected and may not be kept.

Camping Alum Ford Campground (10 spaces) is open all year. Bandy Creek (150 spaces) and Blue Heron (49 spaces) are open from early April to early December.

Maps The park brochure map provides a good overview but topographic maps are needed if you plan to explore the park or float the river. The USGS quad sheets required are: Barthell S.W., Honey Creek, Sharp Place, Rugby, Oneida North, Oneida South, (Tennessee); Barthell and Nevelsville (Kentucky).

The park can also send information sheets that describe river sections and show access areas and the distances between them.

Park Address
Big South Fork NRRA
P.O. Drawer 630
Oneida, TN 37841
phone: (615) 879-4890

Chambers of Commerce

Scott County C.C.
P.O. Box 442
Oneida, TN 37841
phone: (615) 569-6900

McCreary County C.C.
P.O. Box 478
Whitley City, KY 42653
phone: (606) 376-5004

Additional Information The Kentucky portion of the park is surrounded by the Daniel Boone National Forest, which has approximately 18 streams containing rainbow trout. To obtain a forest map and fishing information, contact: Forest Supervisor, Daniel Boone National Forest, 100 Vaught Rd., Winchester, KY, 40391; phone: (606) 745-3100.

A good description of the Big South Fork is contained in *A Fishing Guide to the Streams of Kentucky,* by Bob Sehlinger and Win Underwood. Order the book from: Menasha Ridge Press, 2905 Kirkcaldy Lane, Birmingham, AL, 35243; phone: (toll free) 1-800-247-9437.

Fort Donelson National Battlefield

Fort Donelson was the site of the first major victory for the Union Army in the Civil War. The Union Army was led by Ulysses Grant, then a little-known brigadier general. Grant's superior forces surrounded the fort and forced the surrender of nearly 13,000 Confederate troops after a fierce battle. The victory opened a path into the heartland of the Confederacy.

Access The park is in northwest Tennessee (Stewart County), 1 mile west of Dover and 3 miles east of Land Between the Lakes on U.S. 79.

Fishing The park borders Lake Barkley (Cumberland River) which, along with Kentucky Lake, is part of the popular Land Between the Lakes recreation area managed by the Tennessee Valley Authority (TVA). This part of Tennessee has an abundance of fishing waters, and Lake Barkley is one of the most popular in the state.

Lake Barkley is a noted producer of large crappie, catfish, and largemouth bass. Most of the fishing in the area is by boat. Some bank-fishing occurs in the park on the lake and in Hickman Creek on the west boundary.

Fishing from the park itself is light, but the lake is heavily fished, especially in the spring for spawning crappie. Both Lake Barkley and

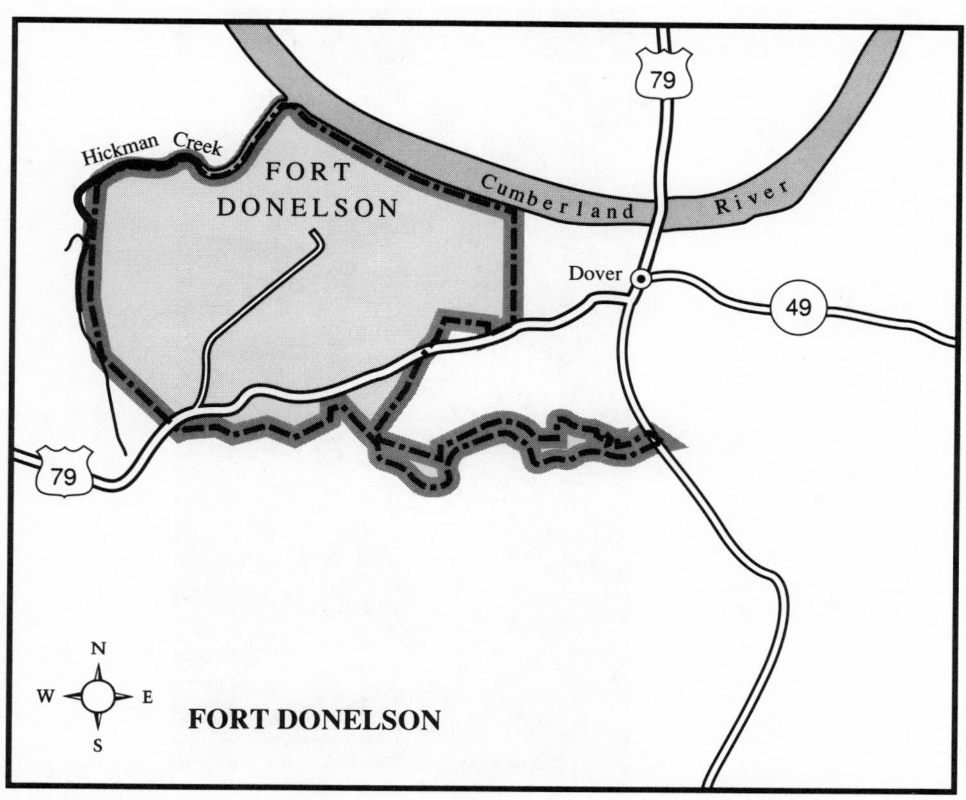

Kentucky Lake are nationally famous for their crappie fishing. Crappie and largemouth bass fishing is best from March into June and again in the fall during September and October. Hickman Creek is full of crappie in the spring and has enough cover to hold some fish all year.

Lake Barkley is also one of the best lakes for sauger in the southeast United States. Sauger can be hard to find, since they frequent deep-water dropoffs and the lake bottom. Local residents fishing here depend on their knowledge of the waters and past experience in being able to locate the various hot spots throughout the lake. A guide may be advisable for your first time on the lake. Guides, boat rentals, and equipment are available.

License A Tennessee fishing license is required.

Camping No camping is permitted in the park. The nearby Land Between the Lakes is a major recreation area and has fully developed camp-

A crappie caught on a rubber jig.—*Gene Hester*

grounds. Piney Campground is 9 miles west of Fort Donelson on U.S. 79.

Maps The Corps of Engineers has a set of Lake Barkley Navigation Charts (8 maps) showing lake depths and contours. The maps come in two sizes, are reasonably priced, and may be ordered from: U.S. Army Corps of Engineers, Maps and Charts Section, P.O. Box 1070, Nashville, TN, 37202-1070; phone: (615) 736-5641.

A waterproof contour fishing map is available from local tackle shops or from: Lakes Illustrated, 315 East South St., Mt. Vernon, MO, 65712; phone: (417) 466-7136.

Park Address
Fort Donelson NB
P.O. Box 434
Dover, TN 37058-0434
phone: (615) 232-5348

Chamber of Commerce
Clarksville Area C.C.
P.O. Box 883
Clarksville, TN 37041-0883
phone: (615) 647-2331

Additional Information Land Between the Lakes is a national recreation demonstration area developed and managed by the TVA. Several maps and brochures are available about camping and fishing from: Land Between the Lakes, TVA, Golden Pond, KY, 42231; phone: (502) 924-5602.

Great Smoky Mountains National Park

One of the most popular and scenic parks in the National Park System, Great Smoky Mountains encompasses more than 500,000 acres of majestic forested mountains along the Tennessee–North Carolina border. The park gets its name from the seemingly ever present smokelike haze enveloping the mountains. Rich soil and abundant rainfall contribute to the existence of a world-renowned variety of flora in the park.

Great Smoky Mountains is popular because it is within a day's drive of most of the major population centers in the East and because it provides a variety of recreational opportunities in a beautiful natural setting. For hikers, the Appalachian Trail threads the crest of the Smokies for approximately 70 miles.

Access The park is in southeastern Tennessee (Blount, Sevier, and Cocke counties) and southwestern North Carolina (Swain and Haywood counties). U.S. 441 bisects the park and connects Gatlinburg, Tennessee, with Cherokee, North Carolina.

Fishing There are 330 trout streams totaling over 700 miles in Great Smoky Mountains National Park. Most of these streams are rarely fished, even though the park receives such heavy use. Reaching most of the park streams requires a hike, which discourages all but the avid individual. The majority of tourists rarely venture into the park interior and are content to view the park from their cars, occasionally stopping at the overlooks, visitor centers, and restored historic structures.

Excellent fishing is available in the roadless back country. Some of the streams are only a short hike from a campsite or roadside, whereas others may take hours to reach. Typically, the more remote the stream, the better the fishing. However, even the streams along roadsides may provide good action.

Reproducing populations of brook, brown, and rainbow trout, smallmouth bass, and rock bass (redeye) are found in park streams. Trout average 9 to 14 inches with fish up to 20 inches in the lower reaches. Rainbow trout are now the most abundant species in the park.

Brook trout, the only trout native to the area, are found in the higher elevation streams (above 3,000 feet). Formerly more wide-

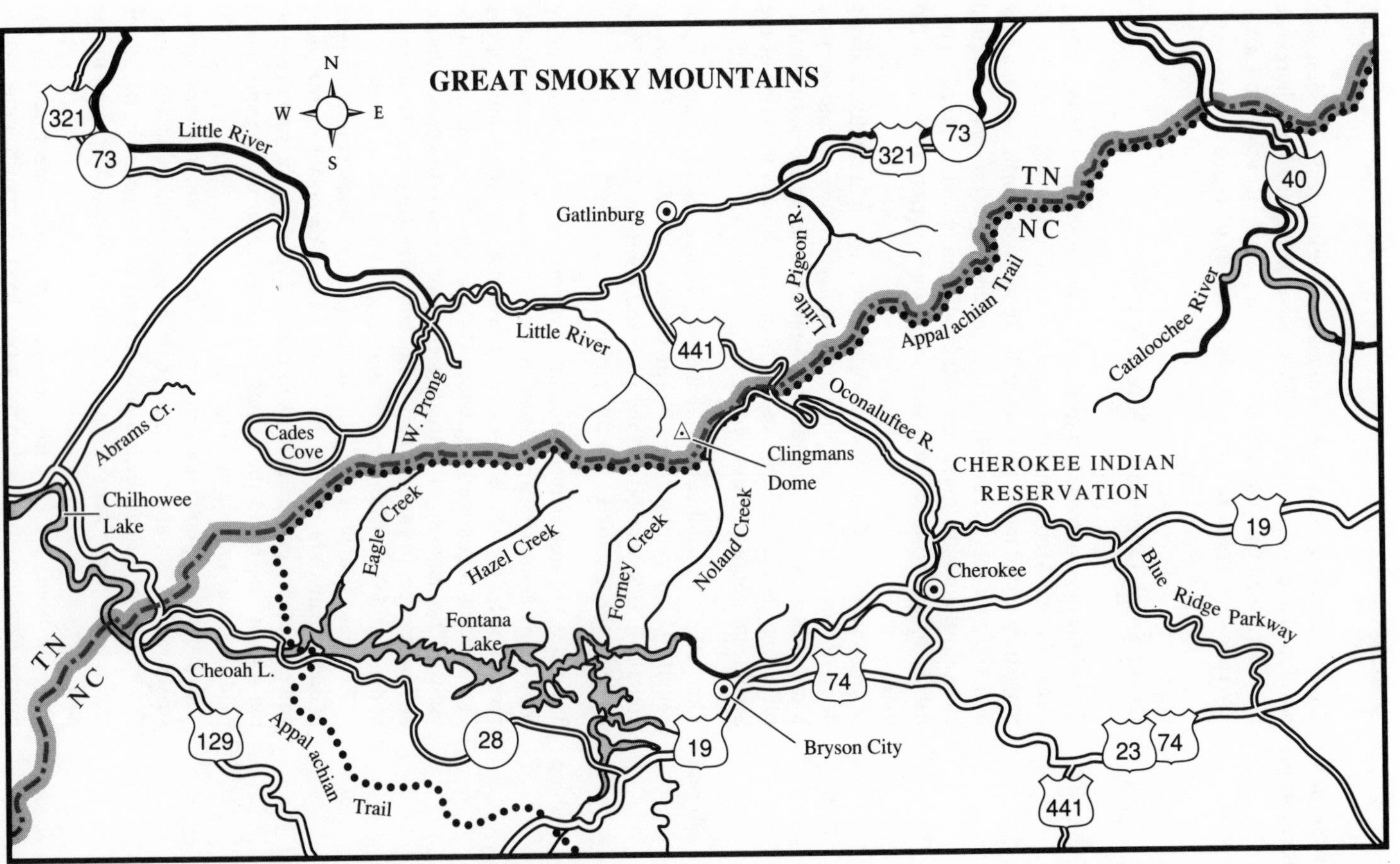
GREAT SMOKY MOUNTAINS
N
W
E
S
321
73
Little River
321
73
40
TN
NC
Gatlinburg
Little Pigeon R.
Appalachian Trail
Cataloochee River
Little River
441
Oconaluftee R.
Abrams Cr.
W. Prong
Cades Cove
Clingmans Dome
CHEROKEE INDIAN RESERVATION
Chilhowee Lake
Eagle Creek
Hazel Creek
Forney Creek
Noland Creek
19
Cherokee
Blue Ridge Parkway
Fontana Lake
TN
NC
Cheoah L.
74
129
Appalachian Trail
28
19
Bryson City
23
74
441

spread, the brook trout has seen its range shrink drastically as a result of changes in stream quality from logging, fires, the introduction of rainbow trout, and overfishing. Today, brook trout are protected in the park and fishing for, or possession of, a brook trout is prohibited. If a brook trout is caught, it must be released. Several streams, including most of the higher elevation streams, are closed to fishing in an effort to protect the species.

Smallmouth bass and rock bass are found in a few of the streams at the lower elevations. Brown trout inhabit the same streams as the rainbows but are not as widespread.

Some of the better park streams are: Abrams Creek, Little River, Cataloochee River, West Prong of the Little Pigeon River, Oconaluftee River, Raven Fork, and Eagle, Hazel, and Forney creeks. Most park streams average 10 to 30 feet in width. They are clear and swift, and canopied by trees and brush. In the higher elevations, the streams are steep and boulder strewn, tumbling downhill in stair-step arrangements. As the streams flow downhill, the gradient lessens and they are characterized by large pools and deep water runs.

Because of a lack of nutrients in the water, most park streams are poor producers of aquatic insects. Abrams Creek in the Cades Cove area is an exception. It flows over a limestone bedrock and produces amazing quantities of mayflies, caddis flies, and stoneflies.

Standard fly patterns produce consistently on park streams despite the paucity of aquatic insects. Dry flies (size 10 to 18) such as the Adams, Quill Gordon, Light and Dark Cahill, Elk-hair Caddis, and Royal Wulff, take fish all year. Most fly hatches occur during late spring and early summer. As the summer progresses, switch to such terrestrial patterns as ants, beetles, grasshoppers, and bees. Nymphs (sizes 8 to 14) worth trying are the Gold-Ribbed Hares Ear and Tellico, along with mayfly, caddis, and stonefly patterns. Wet-fly patterns with yellow in the body are effective, and the Lead-wing Coachman is a favorite.

Park streams demand a quiet approach; the fish are extremely skittish in the clear waters. Fishing is best in the spring and early summer, when water levels and fly hatches are optimum. As summer progresses and water levels drop, fishing becomes more demanding and more work is required for each fish. Then, stealth, light leaders, and accurate fly presentation are in order. Fall fishing is still difficult but can be rewarding as the brown trout begin to spawn.

On the park's southern boundary, in North Carolina, is Fontana Lake. The lake was created and is managed by the Tennessee Valley Authority. Fontana is a well-known producer of good-sized smallmouth bass, walleye, crappie, and rainbow trout. Beginning in 1973,

North Carolina began to develop a winter steelhead fishery in Fontana. Now, strong winter runs of steelhead in the 5-to-10-pound range are caught in Fontana's tributaries starting in December. The mouths of Eagle, Hazel, and Forney creeks are good areas to try for steelhead.

Outside the park along the southeast boundary is the Cherokee Indian Reservation. Many of the park streams flow into the reservation. The Cherokees have opened up approximately 30 miles of stream to public fishing, for a fee. Trout are regularly stocked in these tribal waters and catching fish isn't difficult, even for beginners. Permits are available in the town of Cherokee.

As a precautionary note, be sure to make the proper preparations when venturing into the back-country. The park is home to black bears, wild boars, and poisonous snakes. Some of the hikes can be very steep and taxing. Summer thunderstorms are a regular occurrence, so be properly equipped whether you plan a day trip or an extended overnight stay.

License A Tennessee or a North Carolina license is required. Either license allows you to fish anywhere in the park. Be sure to check the special park fishing regulations. Currently only flies or single-hook artificials are allowed (no bait). Remember, all brook trout must be released.

Camping There are nine campgrounds in the park with a total of 920 spaces and seven group campgrounds. In addition there are 14 trail shelters along the Appalachian Trail, plus 116 back-country campsites (permit required). Due to heavy visitation, the campgrounds fill up quickly. Elkmont, Cades Cove, and Smokemont campgrounds are on the Ticketron reservation system, while the others are first come-first served.

Both Gatlinburg and Cherokee have private campgrounds and lodging. Additional public campgrounds are available in nearby Cherokee, Nantahala, and Pisgah national forests.

Maps A park trail map is available from park headquarters. The well-developed and well-marked park trail system can take you wherever in the park you wish to fish. There is also a special USGS map of the park, "Great Smoky Mountains National Park and Vicinity."

Park Address
Great Smoky Mountains NP
Gatlinburg, TN 37738
phone: (615) 436-1201

Chambers of Commerce

Gatlinburg C.C.
P.O. Box 527
Gatlinburg, TN 37738
phone: (615) 436-4178
toll free 1-800-822-1998

Cherokee C.C.
P.O. Box 465
Cherokee, NC 28719
phone: (704) 497-9195
in-state: 1-800-222-6157
out of state: 1-800-438-1601

Additional Information The park is bounded on the northeast by the Cherokee National Forest, on the south by the Nantahala National Forest, and on the southeast by the Pisgah National Forest. Good fishing is available in each. For fishing information and maps about the Cherokee National Forest, contact: Forest Supervisor, Cherokee National Forest, 2800 N. Ocoee St., Box 2010, Cleveland, TN, 37320; phone: (615) 476-9700.

Both Nantahala and Pisgah National Forests are managed by the North Carolina Forests Office in Asheville. Contact: U.S. Forest Service, Plateau Bldg., Box 2750, Asheville, NC, 28802; phone: (704) 257-4200.

Fontana Lake along the southern park boundary is managed by the TVA. It is not part of the Great Smoky Mountains National Park. Contour and navigation maps of the lake are available from: TVA Mapping Services Branch, Room 101, Haney Bldg., Chattanooga, TN, 37401; phone: (615) 751-6277.

A fishing information brochure and map for the Cherokee Indian waters is available from the Cherokee Chamber of Commerce.

Smoky Mountains Trout Fishing Guide, by Don Kirk, provides additional detail on the park streams. The book is available from: Menasha Ridge Press, 2905 Kirkcaldy Lane, Birmingham, AL, 35243; phone: (toll free) 1-800-247-9437.

Obed Wild and Scenic River

The Obed Wild and Scenic River (WSR) consists of sections of four different streams with lengths totaling 100 miles: the Obed River (34 miles), Daddys Creek (34.5 miles), Clear Creek (29.5 miles), and the Emory River (2 miles). The Obed WSR was added to the National Park System in 1976 and is managed jointly by the park service and the Tennessee Wildlife Resources Agency. Part of the river flows through the Catoosa Wildlife Management Area, which is managed by the state.

Access The Obed WSR is in central east Tennessee (Fentress, Morgan, and Cumberland counties) near the towns of Crossville and Wartburg.

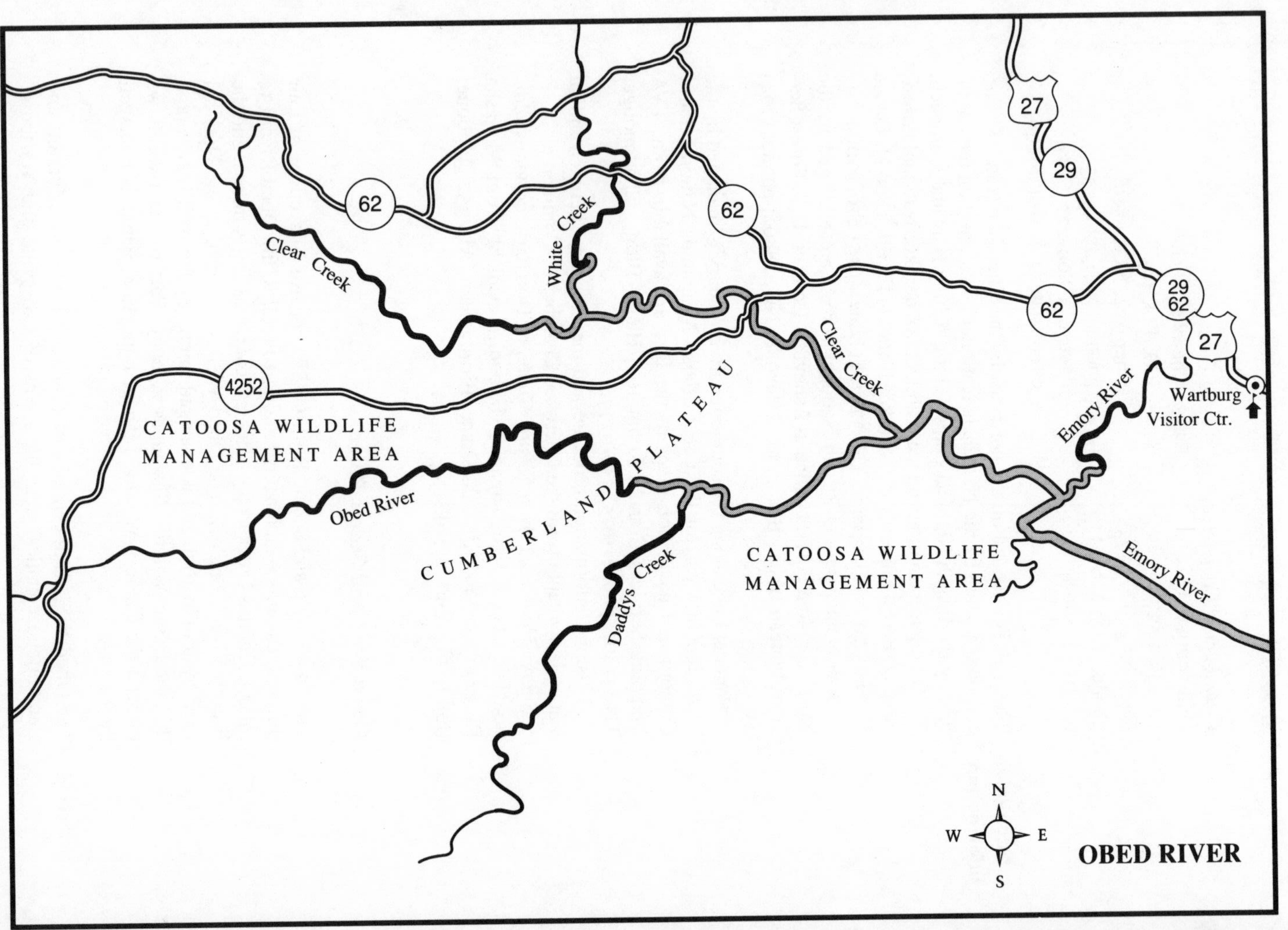
27
29
62
62
62
29
62
27
4252
Clear Creek
White Creek
Clear Creek
Wartburg
Visitor Ctr.
Emory River
CATOOSA WILDLIFE
MANAGEMENT AREA
PLATEAU
CUMBERLAND
Obed River
Daddys Creek
CATOOSA WILDLIFE
MANAGEMENT AREA
Emory River
N
W
E
S
OBED RIVER

U.S. 27 and 127 run north and south and connect with Tennessee Highway 62, which skirts the northern edge of the area.

Fishing The fish habitat of the Obed River area is among the best in the state. The streams contain largemouth, smallmouth, and rock bass, sunfish, flathead catfish, and buffalo. The Obed River and Daddys Creek are also the southernmost range for native muskellunge. Previously, muskie fishing was prohibited in park waters but the waters are now open for muskie.

The rivers are popular with canoeists because of their wilderness character and relative inaccessibility, particularly the gorge section of the Obed River. The rivers are difficult to float and require experienced canoeists. Daddys Creek and Clear Creek are tributaries of the Obed River. These three streams usually cannot be floated from July into October unless there has been sufficient rainfall.

The area is lightly fished due to inaccessibility and the low population of the surrounding area. Canoeists fish while floating on the calmer stream sections, and local residents hike in to fish isolated areas. Most of the fishing occurs at the points where roads provide access.

License A Tennessee fishing license is required.

Camping There are no developed facilities along the river at this time. Camping is available at nearby Frozen Head State Park (primitive facilities) and Cumberland Mountain State Park (developed facilities).

Maps The park brochure map is very good because it shows the access areas and contains a river chart with the distances between access sites and the degree of floating difficulty. Topographic maps are helpful, but too many would be required for the entire Obed WSR. Determine the river sections you plan to float and order the appropriate quad maps by using the Tennessee Map Index.

The following quad sheets show the sections of the Obed River, Daddys Creek, Clear Creek, and the Emory River that have been included in the wild and scenic river: Fox Creek, Hebbertsburg, Jones Knob, Lancing, Pilot Mountain, and Twin Bridges.

The best general map of the Obed area is the "Emory River Watershed Map." It is available from: TVA Mapping Services, Room 101, Haney Bldg., Chattanooga, TN, 37401; phone: (615) 751-6277.

Park Address
Obed WSR
P.O. 429
Wartburg, TN 37887
phone: (615) 346-6294

Chamber of Commerce
Greater Cumberland County C.C.
P.O. Box 453
Crossville, TN 38557
phone: (615) 484-8444

Additional Information

Additional fishing information is available from: Manager, Catoosa Wildlife Management Area, 216 East Penfield, Crossville, TN, 38555; phone: (615) 484-9571.

A Paddler's Guide to the Obed/Emory Watershed, by Monte Smith, is a very informative and readable guidebook about the area and is useful for planning a river trip. It is available from Menasha Ridge Press, 2905 Kirkcaldy Lane, Birmingham, AL, 35243; phone (toll free): 1-800-247-9437.

• TEXAS

Amistad National Recreation Area

Lake Amistad, in the semidesert area of southwest Texas, is a 67,000-acre reservoir on the Texas-Mexico border. Amistad is Spanish for "friendship," and the lake is a joint project built by the United States and the Republic of Mexico on the Rio Grande. The lake is managed by the International Boundary Water Commission (I.B.W.C.). The National Park Service is responsible for the recreation facilities and programs on the U.S. side of the reservoir.

Access Lake Amistad is 12 miles north and west of Del Rio, Texas, (Val Verde County) and approximately 180 miles west of San Antonio. U.S. 277 and U.S. 90 both cross the lake and access areas are reachable from both highways. Cuidad Acuna in Mexico can be reached by bridge.

Fishing Lake Amistad has long been known for its superb largemouth bass fishing, but it is also one of the best striped bass lakes in Texas. Amistad also provides good fishing for walleye and smallmouth bass and for large catfish (channel, flathead, and blue), sunfish, crappie, and white bass.

The lake can be intimidating and frustrating to the first timer. The long, narrow lake, which runs mainly east and west, is characterized by deep, clear water in a setting of steep, dry, rocky hills. A guide is almost mandatory for the inexperienced.

Largemouth bass get the most attention in Amistad. March and April are two of the best months for largemouth fishing. As spawning time beckons and the water warms, the bass move to the tops of ledges and nearby shallow areas. Amistad is known for its excellent top-water fishing, and top-water lures are very productive during these months.

As summer progresses, the largemouth return to deeper water near the ledges, moving back to the shallow water to feed only in the late afternoon. Activity increases in October and November as the bass spend more time on the ledges and in the shallows. During the winter months, the bass are near dropoffs and ledges at depths of 20 to 30 feet. The more productive ledges are located in the main channels of arroyos entering the lake.

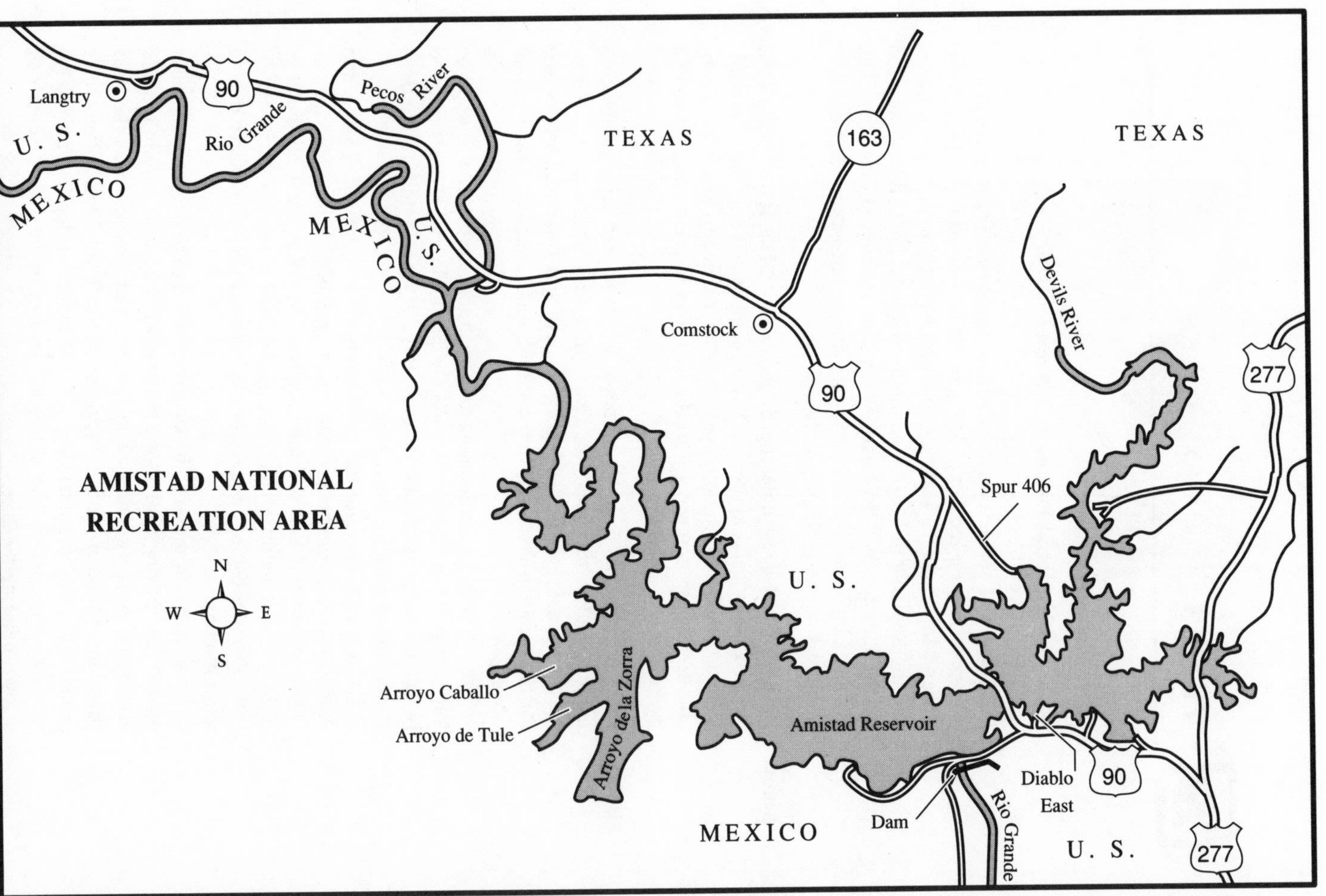
AMISTAD NATIONAL
RECREATION AREA
Langtry
90
Pecos River
Rio Grande
U. S.
MEXICO
MEXICO
U.S.
TEXAS
163
TEXAS
Comstock
90
Devils River
277
Spur 406
U. S.
Arroyo Caballo
Arroyo de Tule
Arroyo de la Zorra
Amistad Reservoir
Diablo
East
90
Dam
Rio Grande
MEXICO
U. S.
277
N
W
E
S

Amistad is one of the best largemouth bass lakes in Texas. This nice largemouth was fooled by a spinnerbait.—*Ken Penrod*

Striped bass fishing is remarkably good. The state stocks these fish and they have flourished in this deep-water environment. Striped bass hybrids are also in the lake. The best catches are made in April and May, but those with experience catch them all year long.

Striped bass and their hybrids are often found in the same locations as largemouth bass, as well as in deeper water. Some stripers migrate up the rivers in the spring to spawn. During summer and fall, they are in deeper water and in winter they locate over ledges and dropoffs near main river channels in 30 to 60 feet of water.

November and December are the best months for catching large striped bass weighing 20 pounds or more. These fish are in shallow water at the back ends of major canyons early and late in the day. If the weather is overcast, they stay shallow all day. The best spots are off brushy points. Bait fish congregate near the brush and striped bass go in after them. The best areas include the back ends of Zorro, Tule, Caballo, and Burro canyons on the Rio Grande arm of the lake and San Pedro and Castle canyons on the Devils River arm.

In November, also watch for stripers schooling on the surface chasing shad. Circling and diving sea gulls can help you locate the schools. The gulls are feeding on dead or crippled shad.

Smallmouth bass and walleye have been stocked and are now reproducing and beginning to appear regularly on the stringer. White bass are plentiful and spawn in the rivers in the spring. Trot-line fishing for catfish is also very popular. Trot lines are usually fished near points and along coves in depths of 20 to 50 feet.

Because most of the game fish in Amistad prefer the same habitat, stringers of mixed species are common. Some of the best fishing for all species is in three canyons on the Mexican side of the western end of the lake. Caballo, Tule, and Zorro canyons all extend 6 to 10 miles into Mexico and are fed by springs and clear streams.

Two important factors to remember when fishing Amistad are the wind and the sun. Wind can pick up quickly and create heavy wave action, calling for a large, powerful boat with the proper safety equipment. The hot sun and high temperatures in the summer can be devastating to the unprepared.

There are four major boat ramps—Pecos, Diablo East, Cow Creek, and Rough Canyon—and unimproved boat ramps at several other points. You can drive to the water's edge only at designated sites. Currently, the park service operates two marinas on the lake. One is Diablo East, near the U.S. 90 bridge, and the other is the Rough Canyon marina, off U.S. 277-377.

License A Texas license is required and also a Mexican license, if you plan to fish in Mexican waters. Buoys mark the international border. A Mexican fishing license for Amistad is available from Anglers Lodge, (512) 775-1586), or Amistad Lodge, (512) 775-8591. Both lodges are on Highway 90 near the lake.

Camping Primitive camping facilities are available at 63 designated sites.

Maps Topo maps are not needed. A contoured depth map of Amistad Lake is published by A.I.D. Associates, P.O. Box 811454, Dallas, TX, 75381; phone: (214) 386-6277.

A.I.D. publishes these sports-oriented maps for most of the major lakes in Texas. The maps are revised regularly to show the most up-to-date navigation markers, road systems, access points, and public areas, including marinas and bait shops.

Park Address
Amistad NRA
P.O. Box 420367
Del Rio, TX 78842
phone: (512) 775-7491

Chamber of Commerce
Del Rio C.C.
1915 Avenue F
Del Rio, TX 78840
phone: (512) 775-3551

Big Bend National Park/ Rio Grande Wild and Scenic River

Big Bend National Park includes more than 740,000 acres of mountain scenery and Chihuahua desert and is the only national park to contain an entire mountain range, the Chisos Mountains. "Big Bend" refers to the large *U*-turn by the Rio Grande, which forms the border between Texas and Mexico. The park combines spectacular scenery and geologic features with an outstanding array of southwestern flora and fauna.

Part of the Rio Grande (196 miles) was designated in 1978 as a Wild and Scenic River (WSR). The Rio Grande forms the southern boundary of Big Bend, but only a portion of the river in the park is designated as wild and scenic. The wild and scenic designation starts at Mariscal Canyon and extends outside the park down to the Terrell–Val Verde County line, just west of the town of Langtry.

Access Big Bend National Park and the Rio Grande Wild and Scenic River are located in southwest Texas (Brewster County). Both areas are long distances from major population centers, 410 miles from San Antonio and 323 miles from El Paso. Big Bend is reached via U.S. 385, south of Marathon, or via Texas Highway 118, south of Alpine. The Rio Grande WSR is reached by various roads (mostly unimproved) that interlace the river valley and provide limited access to the river.

Fishing From the western park boundary near Lajitas, through numerous canyons to the end of the designated wild-and-scenic river at Val Verde County, the Rio Grande winds for 234 miles. Although this portion of the river does contain some largemouth bass and sunfish, it is primarily noted for good populations of blue, flathead, and channel catfish. The river also has good numbers of rough fish such as carp, plus an occasional large gar. No other permanent fishing streams exist in the park.

The best fishing is outside the park in the wild and scenic river section, especially for catfish. When turbidity levels are low, the deeper parts of the river are the most productive. However, the river is often too muddy or too low for good fishing. Consequently, fishing pressure is low, both in the park and along the WSR extension.

Although fishing is a year-round activity, the summer is the favorite time because then the water is lower and the deep pools are better defined. Fishing is also good when the catfish are spawning (May to July). Then they are found in the depressions and sheltered nooks along the river banks and canyon cliffs.

River access is limited in both the park and the WSR. The Black

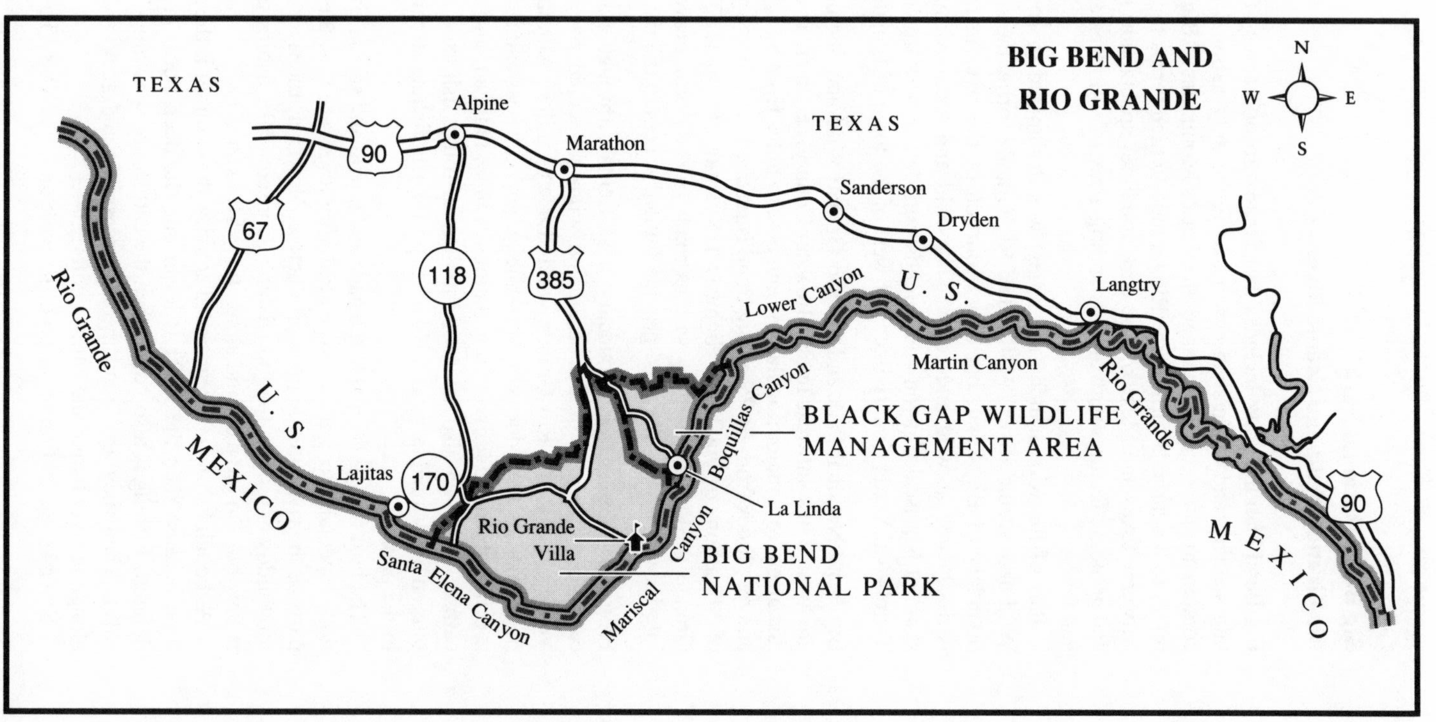
BIG BEND AND
RIO GRANDE
N
W
E
S
TEXAS
TEXAS
Alpine
Marathon
Sanderson
Dryden
Langtry
90
67
118
385
170
90
Lajitas
Rio Grande
U. S.
MEXICO
Lower Canyon
U. S.
Martin Canyon
Boquillas Canyon
BLACK GAP WILDLIFE
MANAGEMENT AREA
Rio Grande
La Linda
Rio Grande
Villa
BIG BEND
NATIONAL PARK
Canyon
Mariscal
Santa Elena Canyon
MEXICO

Gap Wildlife Management Area, managed by the state, is located along the WSR just outside the park's northeastern boundary. It affords more access than any other river segment. Enter the management area from Ranch Road 2627. Visitors must check in and out at headquarters. Black Gap has 22 miles of riverfront for fishing. Approximately 250 miles of unimproved roads traverse the area, touching the river at various places.

The Rio Grande is becoming increasingly popular with river runners. Trips of various lengths are possible. If you float the river on your own, I would recommend a detailed study of a river segment before you float. I have floated and fished some of the canyons of the Rio Grande and can verify that, although the river looks placid, it can be dangerous. The Rio Grande is subject to flash floods and contains stretches for experts only. The park can provide additional information, including a list of guides.

License No license is required to fish the Rio Grande within the park. Once you leave the park boundary, a Texas license is required along the remaining 127 miles of the Rio Grande WSR.

Camping The park has three campgrounds: Chisos Basin (63 spaces), in the center of the park; Cottonwood (35 spaces), near Castolon, at the western edge of the park; and Rio Grande Village (300 spaces), including a concessioner-operated trailer park at the eastern edge of the park. Permits (free) are required if you plan to camp overnight along the river.

Maps Topographic maps for the river in the park are not necessary. The park brochure map is adequate, since it shows the river access points. There is a special USGS map of the park, "Big Bend National Park and Vicinity."

For the 127 miles of the Rio Grande WSR outside the park, topographic maps are useful to show river access points. From the park boundary down to the Terrell–Val Verde County line, the following quads (in order) are needed: Reagan Canyon, Bullis Gap, Indian Wells, Dryden Crossing, and Malvado.

Much of the land along the WSR is in private ownership, so be sure to check with a park ranger to ensure that you are not trespassing. Another option is to ask permission from landowners.

Park Address
Big Bend NP
Big Bend National Park,
TX 79834
phone: (915) 477-2251

Chamber of Commerce
Alpine C.C.
P.O. Box 209
Alpine, TX 79831
phone: (915) 837-2326

Additional Information A set of guides for the Rio Grande are available from the Big Bend Natural History Association. The guides are designed for river runners and printed on waterproof paper. They contain topographic strip maps, labeled rapids, major topographic features, useful telephone numbers, and put-in/take-out information. For more information and a list of publications, contact: Big Bend Natural History Association, Box 68, Big Bend National Park, TX, 79834; phone: (915) 477-2236.

Big Thicket National Preserve

Big Thicket is a unique biological area combining segments of a once extensive area composed of virgin pine, cypress forest, hardwood forest, meadow, and blackwater swamp. Noted for its large variety of plant and animal species, the park was established in 1974. The park, which totals 84,550 acres, is composed of 12 units in parts of seven Texas counties.

Access Big Thicket is in southeast Texas in parts of Polk, Tyler, Jasper, Hardin, Orange, Jefferson, and Liberty counties. Numerous roads cross through the region, providing access to the various park units. U.S. 69/287 and Texas Highway 92 are the main north-south routes, while U.S. 190 is the main east-west route. Towns in the area include Beaumont, Kountze, Silsbee, Woodville, Saratoga, and Lumberton.

Fishing Big Thicket contains a number of streams. Quality fishing is found in the Neches River below Lake Steinhagen (also known as Dam B), the lower reaches of Pine Island Bayou, and in Village Creek. The Neches River contains good populations of largemouth and spotted bass, crappie, white bass, sunfish, and catfish (flathead and channel), plus substantial numbers of hybrid striped bass, which move downstream from Lake Steinhagen.

Pine Island Bayou and Village Creek provide good fishing throughout much of the year for bass, catfish, and crappie.

Fishing is a year-round sport in the region, but most of the activity occurs in the spring and fall. Crappie and white bass spawning are the attraction in the spring and usually fishing pressure is light. Nearby, Livingston, Rayburn, and Toledo Bend lakes are famous for bass and crappie and they draw visitors from all over Texas and Louisiana. Lake Steinhagen, just north of the park, is not as famous but is also good, especially for crappie.

The Neches River flows through mile after mile of remote bottomland hardwood and pine. Access is from various highway crossings along the river. The Neches can be floated, but downed trees and

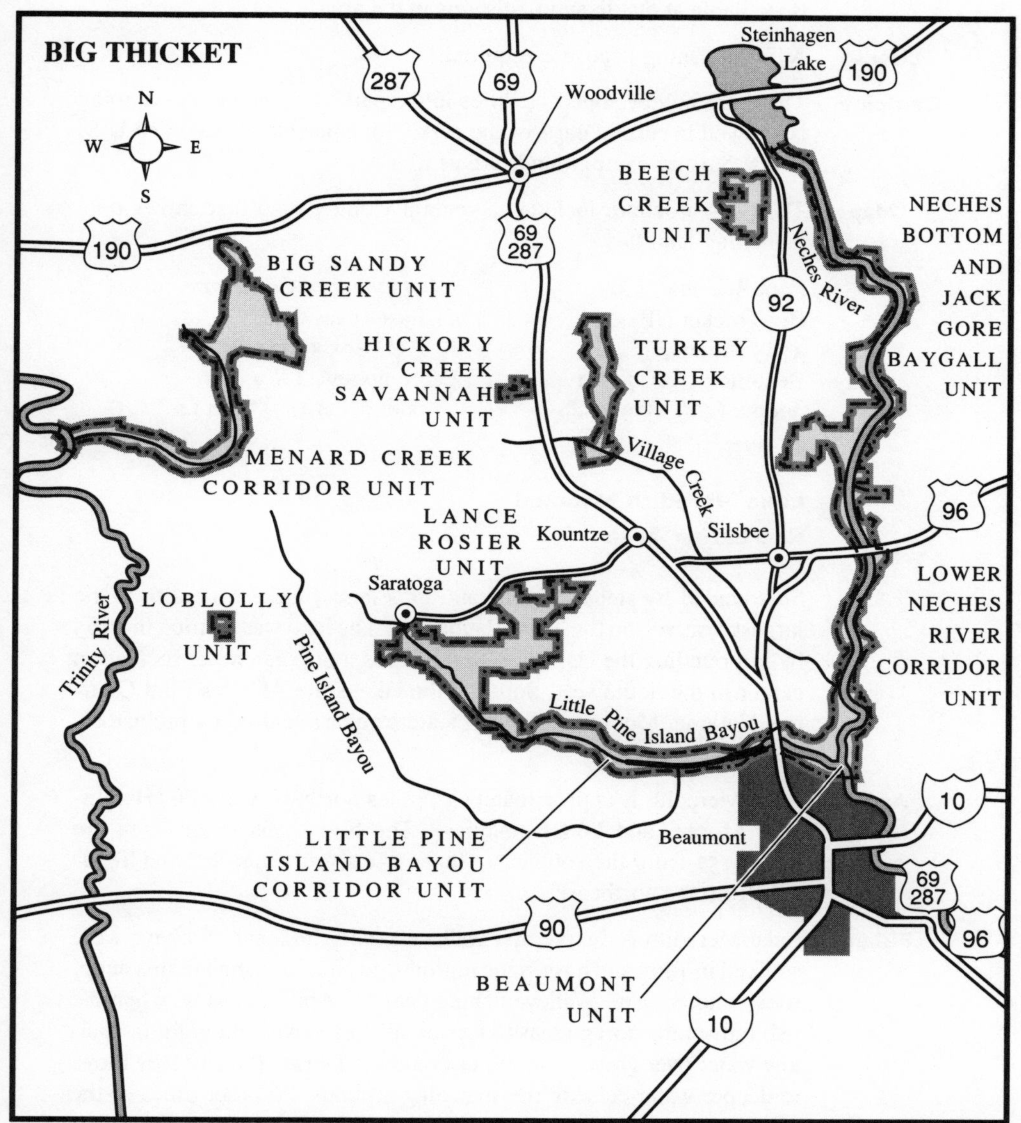
BIG THICKET
N
W
E
S
287
69
Woodville
Steinhagen
Lake
190
BEECH
CREEK
UNIT
NECHES
BOTTOM
AND
JACK
GORE
BAYGALL
UNIT
69
287
190
BIG SANDY
CREEK UNIT
Neches River
92
HICKORY
CREEK
SAVANNAH
UNIT
TURKEY
CREEK
UNIT
Village
Creek
MENARD CREEK
CORRIDOR UNIT
96
LANCE
ROSIER
UNIT
Kountze
Silsbee
LOWER
NECHES
RIVER
CORRIDOR
UNIT
Saratoga
LOBLOLLY
UNIT
Trinity River
Pine Island Bayou
Little Pine Island Bayou
10
LITTLE PINE
ISLAND BAYOU
CORRIDOR UNIT
Beaumont
69
287
90
96
BEAUMONT
UNIT
10

limbs occasionally present hazards in the river, in Village Creek, and in Pine Island Bayou. Current information on fishing and water levels is available at tackle and bait shops in the area.

License A Texas fishing license is required.

Camping There are no developed facilities in the park. Back-country camping is allowed in certain parts of the park with a permit. Private and U.S. Forest Service campgrounds are nearby.

Maps The park brochure includes a general vicinity map that shows boat launching facilities.

Park Address
Big Thicket NP
3785 Milam
Beaumont, TX 77701
phone: (409) 839-2689

Chamber of Commerce
East Texas C.C.
P.O. Box 1592
Longview, TX 75606
phone: (214) 757-4444

Lake Meredith National Recreation Area

Surrounded by steep canyons and grasslands, Lake Meredith is the largest reservoir in the Texas Panhandle. The lake was formed in 1965 by impounding the Canadian River and is a popular water recreation center in the Southwest. South of the lake is the Alibates Flint Quarries National Monument, which features quarries used by prehistoric people.

Access Lake Meredith is approximately 35 miles north of Amarillo (Hutchison, Moore, and Potter counties). The best roads to the area are Texas 152 from the southeast, Texas 136 from Amarillo, and Texas 207 from the northeast.

Fishing Lake Meredith is the premier walleye fishery in Texas. Walleye were stocked in 1965 and have since reproduced and flourished in this deep, rocky-shored lake. Walleye fishing peaks in April and May, when the fish move into riprap areas to spawn. Walleye spawn at night in shallow water over gravel, rubble, or boulders. During the day they move to deeper water close to the spawning grounds. At other times of the year, walleye are found over boulders, reefs, and rubble in water 15 to 40 feet deep.

Other sport fish in the lake are catfish, smallmouth bass, white bass, some largemouth bass, and white crappie. Gizzard shad are the most important forage fish.

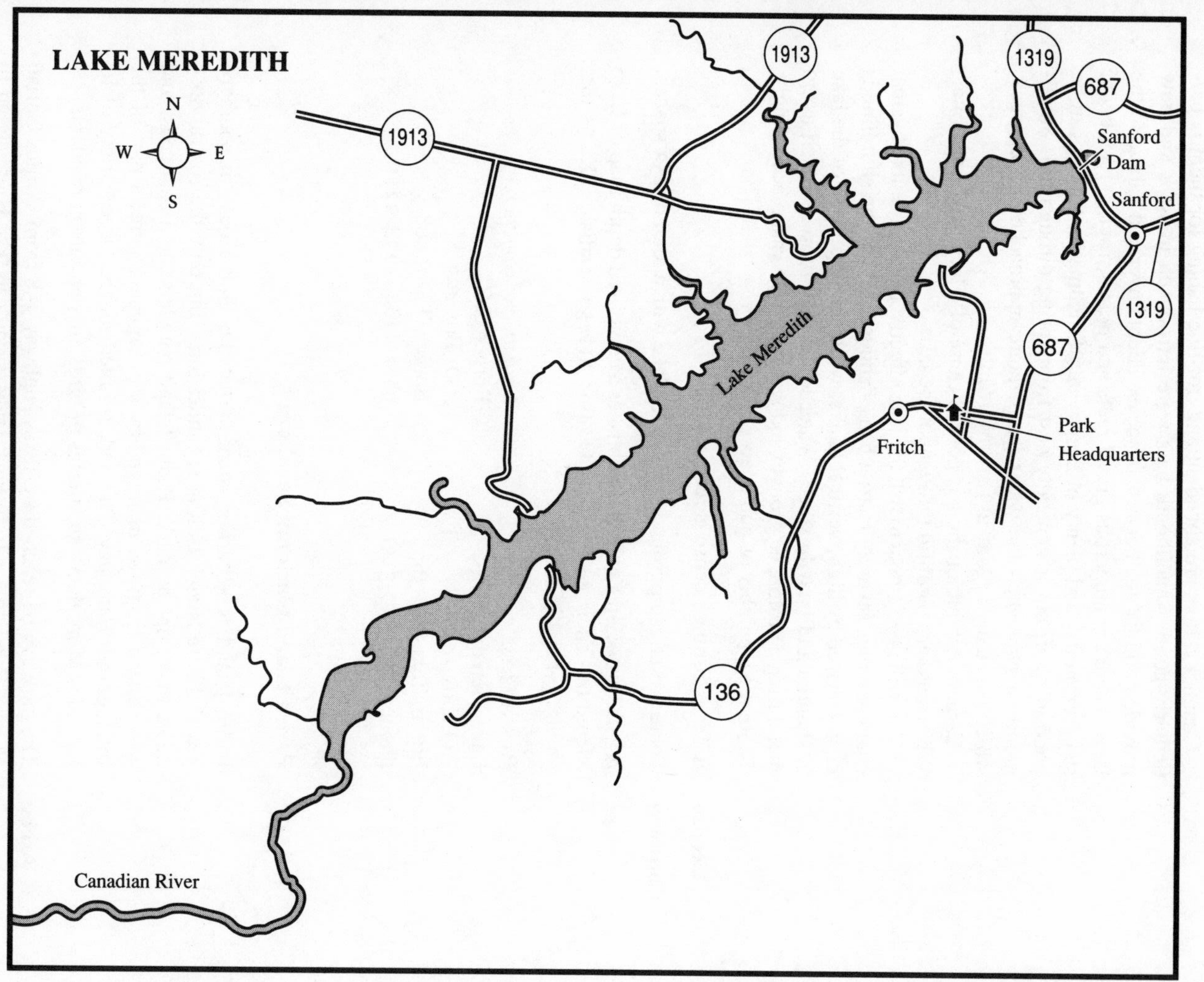
LAKE MEREDITH
N
W
E
S
1913
1913
1319
687
Sanford
Dam
Sanford
1319
687
Lake Meredith
Fritch
Park
Headquarters
136
Canadian River

Channel catfish are abundant and trot-line fishing for them is particularly good. Smallmouth bass were introduced in 1974 and now provide good fishing because of the excellent cover and habitat in the lake. There are numerous gravel reefs and points, rocky creek beds, steep dropoffs, and plenty of deep water. Smallmouth fishing can be good all year, but is generally best from spring through fall. Smallmouth spawn when the water temperature approaches 60 degrees, which is usually in May at Lake Meredith.

Largemouth bass fishing is poor because of a lack of good habitat. White bass are plentiful throughout the lake.

You will need a boat to fish the lake effectively, because its physical characteristics severely restrict bank fishing. Most of the shoreline is characterized by high, vertical banks, while the upper end of the lake is shallow and heavily silted. Water levels may drop as much as 40 feet during a prolonged drought and water acreage varies accordingly. There are a number of public access sites.

License A Texas fishing license is required.

Camping There are 12 campgrounds around the lake with a total of 253 spaces.

Maps A.I.D. Associates in Dallas publishes a contoured depth map of Lake Meredith. Their address is P.O. Box 811454, Dallas, TX, 75381; phone: (512) 386-6277.

Park Address
Lake Meredith NRA
P.O. Box 1438
Fritch, Texas 79036
phone: (806) 857-3151

Chamber of Commerce
Borger C.C.
P.O. Box 490
Borger, TX 79008
phone: (806) 274-2211

Padre Island National Seashore

Padre Island is a barrier island along the Gulf Coast in southern Texas. Padre Island itself is 113 miles long, but only the central 80.5 miles make up the park. Padre Island parallels the Texas coast and is separated from the mainland by the Laguna Madre, a part of the Intracoastal Waterway. The park is noted for the large variety of its bird life. More than 350 species of birds are permanent residents.

Access The park can be reached by Texas Highway 358 from Corpus Christi to Park Road 22, or from Port Aransas you can take Highway 53 to Park Road 22. A car can travel only 14 miles into the park because of the soft sands. The first 8.5 miles are on a hard-surfaced road, and

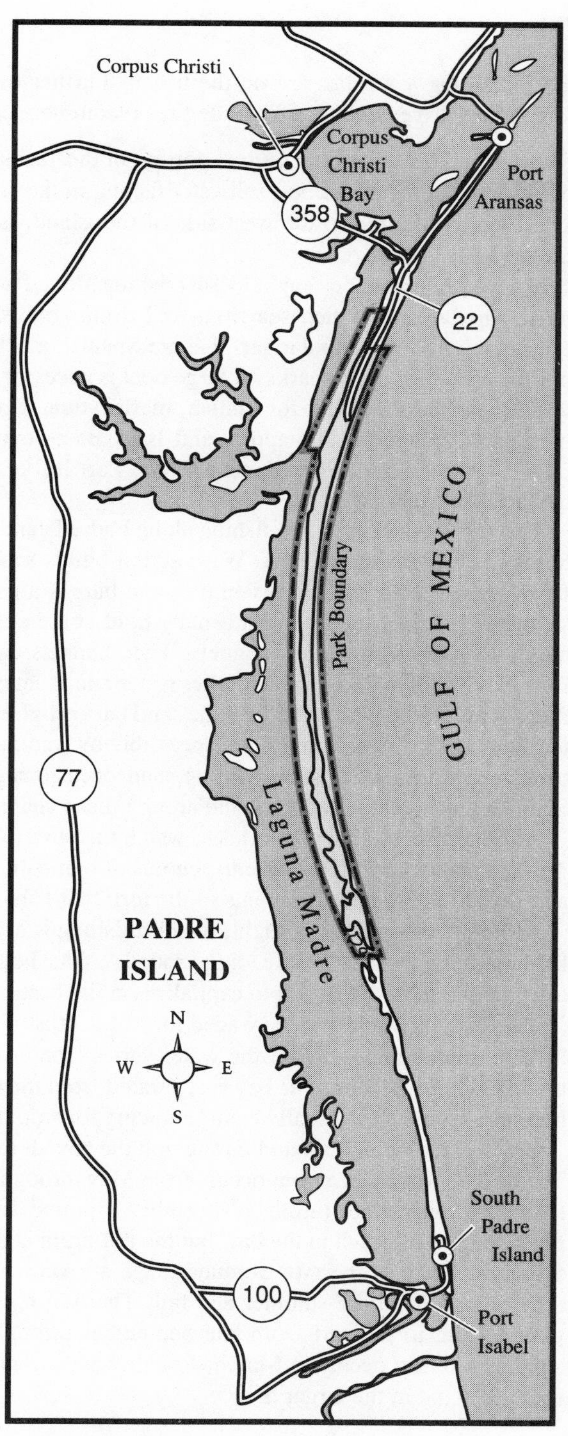
Corpus Christi
Corpus Christi Bay
Port Aransas
358
22
Park Boundary
GULF OF MEXICO
77
Laguna Madre
PADRE ISLAND
N
W
E
S
South Padre Island
100
Port Isabel

the remaining 5.5 miles are on the beach. Further travel requires a four-wheel drive vehicle, with wide tires recommended.

Fishing Padre Island occupies only a small portion of the Texas Gulf coastline but it offers some of the best saltwater fishing in the Gulf of Mexico. The Laguna Madre, on the west side of the island, is especially renowned.

Many species can be caught by surf fishing along Padre Island. The most popular are spotted sea trout, red drum (redfish), and southern flounder. Other popular surf fish are Spanish mackerel, bluefish, pompano, tarpon, and sharks. A large boat is necessary if you plan to go further out in the Gulf for sailfish, marlin, tuna, Spanish and king mackerel, grouper, red snapper, and ling. Boats may be chartered from Corpus Christi, Port Mansfield, and Port Isabel for all types of bay and Gulf fishing.

The key to successful surf fishing along Padre Island is to locate the hot spots by reading the surf. Wave action builds sand bars at regular intervals in the surf. Between the sand bars is a parallel channel, known as a trough or gut. Fish usually hold at the edges of the sand bars and often feed in the channels. The channels can be identified from the beach by looking for darker water and recurring stretches of flat, foamy water. The water over the sand bars is lighter. Usually only the first two or three channels are accessible by wading. Speckled sea trout, red drum, pompano, whiting, and occasionally bluefish and Spanish mackerel are found in and around these channels.

Another fish-finding method is to watch the birds. As bluefish, red drum, or other sport fish tear into schools of bait fish, the birds circle and dive to feed on the remnants of the torn bait fish.

Although tidal action is slight, the best fishing is at high tide as the fish come in closer to new feeding grounds. You should always keep a set of tide tables with you to capitalize on the best times.

The Laguna Madre can be waded for miles. It is fairly shallow and hard bottomed and much of the water varies from a few inches to 3 to 4 feet deep. Because this bay is separated from the Gulf of Mexico by Padre Island, it is usually calm, allowing for safe fishing.

Spotted sea trout are found throughout the bay all through the year. The best fishing for sea trout occurs from May through July, and again from late September through November. Spotted sea trout are the most sought-after fish in the bay, but the red drum is the most prized. Small red drum in the 1-to-2-pound range are known as rat reds and may be caught in the summer and fall. The bull reds (larger than 8 pounds) run in the surf from late September through December. A smaller run also occurs in March. Rough weather and pounding surf seem to bring in the larger fish.

Southern flounder are common in the bay from May through November. They are found along channel edges and on sand flats. In December they migrate to the Gulf to spawn but return to the bay in March. Flounder may be caught using artificial and natural baits. The most popular method, however, is gigging at night using a lantern to spot the fish.

License A Texas fishing license is required and Texas regulations apply.

Camping The only developed campground in the park is Malaquite Beach Campground with 42 spaces. Primitive camping is allowed on the beaches and at Bird Island Basin. Public campgrounds are available on Padre Island outside the park at Nueces County Park north of the park and at Cameron County Park south of the park near Port Isabel.

Maps Nautical charts are beneficial at Padre Island. Nautical chart #11307 encompasses Aransas Pass to Baffin Bay; chart #11304 covers the northern part of Laguna Madre and chart #11301 covers the southern part. The above charts include the Gulf of Mexico side of the park. If you are only interested in Laguna Madre proper, then use small-craft charts #11306 and #11308, which cover the Intracoastal Waterway.

Park Address
Padre Island NS
9405 South Padre Island Drive
Corpus Christi, TX 78418
phone: (512) 937-2621

Chambers of Commerce

Corpus Christi Area Convention and Tourist Bureau
1201 N. Shoreline
P.O. Box 640
Corpus Christi, TX 78403
phone: (512) 882-6161

South Padre Island Tourist Development Bureau
Box 2098
South Padre Island, TX 78597
phone: (512) 943-3112

Additional Information A free publication, entitled *Fishing the Texas Surf,* by Tony Fedler, is available from Texas A&M University. This booklet is a guide to surf, wade, and pier fishing on the Texas coast. It includes tackle and techniques, fish species, and the best times of year for each species. Write to: Sea Grant College Program, Marine Information Service, Texas A&M University, College Station, TX, 77843; phone: (409) 845-3984.

The Texas Parks and Wildlife Department publishes three brochures that are also free and provide valuable information: *The Southern Flounder in Texas*; *The Red Drum in Texas*; and *The Black Drum in Texas*. For these publications, contact: Texas Parks and Wildlife Department, 4200 Smith School Road, Austin, TX, 78744; phone: (512) 389-4566.

The Corpus Christi Area Convention and Tourist Bureau (address above) publishes the *Corpus Christi Area Sport Fishing Guide*.

• UTAH

Canyonlands National Park

Canyonlands is a wonderland of rock arches, towering spires, needles, and mesas. One of the park spectacles is the confluence of the Green and Colorado rivers amid colorful, deep, winding gorges.

Access The park is in southeast Utah (Wayne, San Juan, and Garfield counties) about 50 miles northwest of Monticello, via Utah Highway 211, and a few miles southwest of Moab via Utah Highway 279.

Fishing Ninety miles of the Colorado and Green rivers flow through the park. Channel catfish are the predominant game fish. Both rivers are accessible only by boat. The only fishing in the park is by an occasional boater.

Both rivers are popular with white-water boaters, but the Colorado is used by more river parties. Cataract Canyon, below the confluence of the two rivers, contains 22 rapids and includes some of the wildest white water in the U.S.

This isn't a park that one visits for the fishing. The float trips are a major attraction, and a list of concessioners providing guided trips can be obtained from the park.

License A Utah fishing license is required.

Camping There are two campgrounds in the park, Squaw Flat (26 spaces) and Willow Flat (12 spaces), in addition to primitive camping in areas accessible by four-wheel drive vehicles.

Maps There is a special USGS map of the park, "Canyonlands National Park and Vicinity," although maps are not needed for fishing.

Park Address
Canyonlands NP
125 West 200 South
Moab, UT 84532
phone: (801) 259-7164

Chamber of Commerce
Moab C.C.
59 South Main St.
Moab, UT 84532
phone: (801) 259-7531

Additional Information *Canyonlands River Guide,* available from Westwater Books, contains maps, pictures, and river descriptions. This book concentrates on

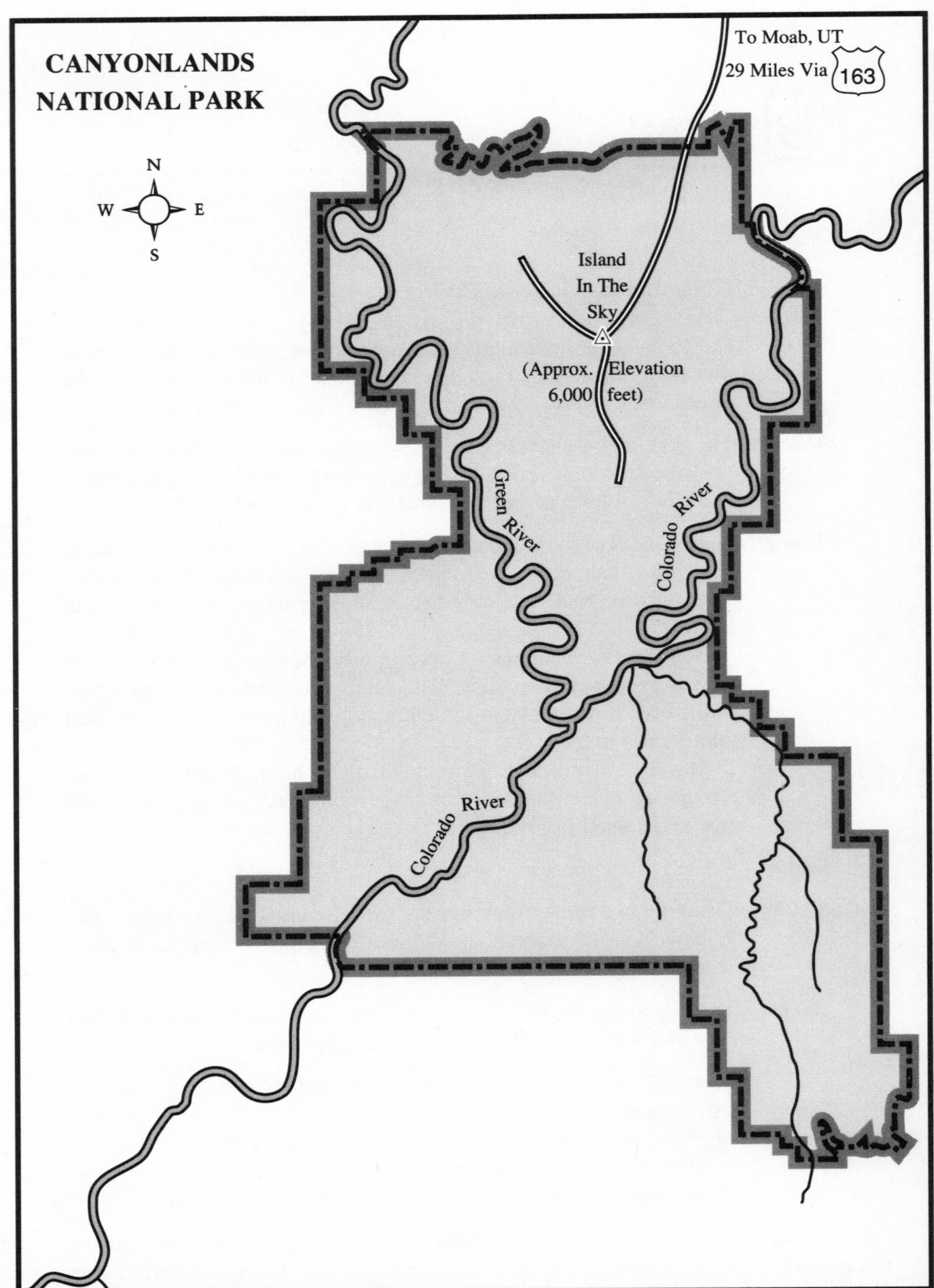
CANYONLANDS
NATIONAL PARK
N
W
E
S
To Moab, UT
29 Miles Via
163
Island
In The
Sky
(Approx. Elevation
6,000 feet)
Green River
Colorado River
Colorado River

boating rather than fishing. Contact: Westwater Books, P.O. Box 2560, Evergreen, CO, 80439; phone: (303) 674-5410.

Capitol Reef National Park

Capitol Reef features a 60-mile uplift of sandstone cliffs with highly colored sedimentary rock formations. The park name comes from a huge dome-shaped whitecap rock along the Fremont River.

Access The park is in south central Utah (Wayne and Garfield counties) and is reached via Utah Highway 24.

Fishing The Fremont River and Pleasant Creek flow through the park and contain trout. There are brown and rainbow trout in the Fremont. Pleasant Creek holds rainbow and cutthroat trout. Some surprisingly large trout are taken from the Fremont River, but there are many trout in the 2-pound class.

Pleasant Creek is subject to periodic floods, which basically eliminate the fishery in the creek for a year or two. The Fremont River is more reliable. The best section of the Fremont is along the west boundary of the park. The headwaters area has never been very productive.

Because the park is relatively isolated, fishing pressure is light. Fishing is possible all year, but the best times are spring and fall. At other times the waters are often subject to flash floods, or can be muddy from summer thunderstorms or frozen over in winter.

License A Utah fishing license is required.

Camping Fruita Campground has 70 spaces. Cathedral Valley and Cedar Mesa campgrounds each have 5 spaces and are accessible via dirt roads. Contact the park for up-to-date road conditions. A permit is required for overnight stays in the back country.

Maps The park brochure map is sufficient. It shows access to Pleasant Creek and the Fremont River.

Park Address
Capitol Reef NP
Torrey, UT 84775
phone: (801) 425-3791

Additional Information Fish Lake National Forest and Dixie National Forest border the park on the west and offer additional fishing and camping options. The Fremont River in the Bicknell area (Fish Lake National Forest) is

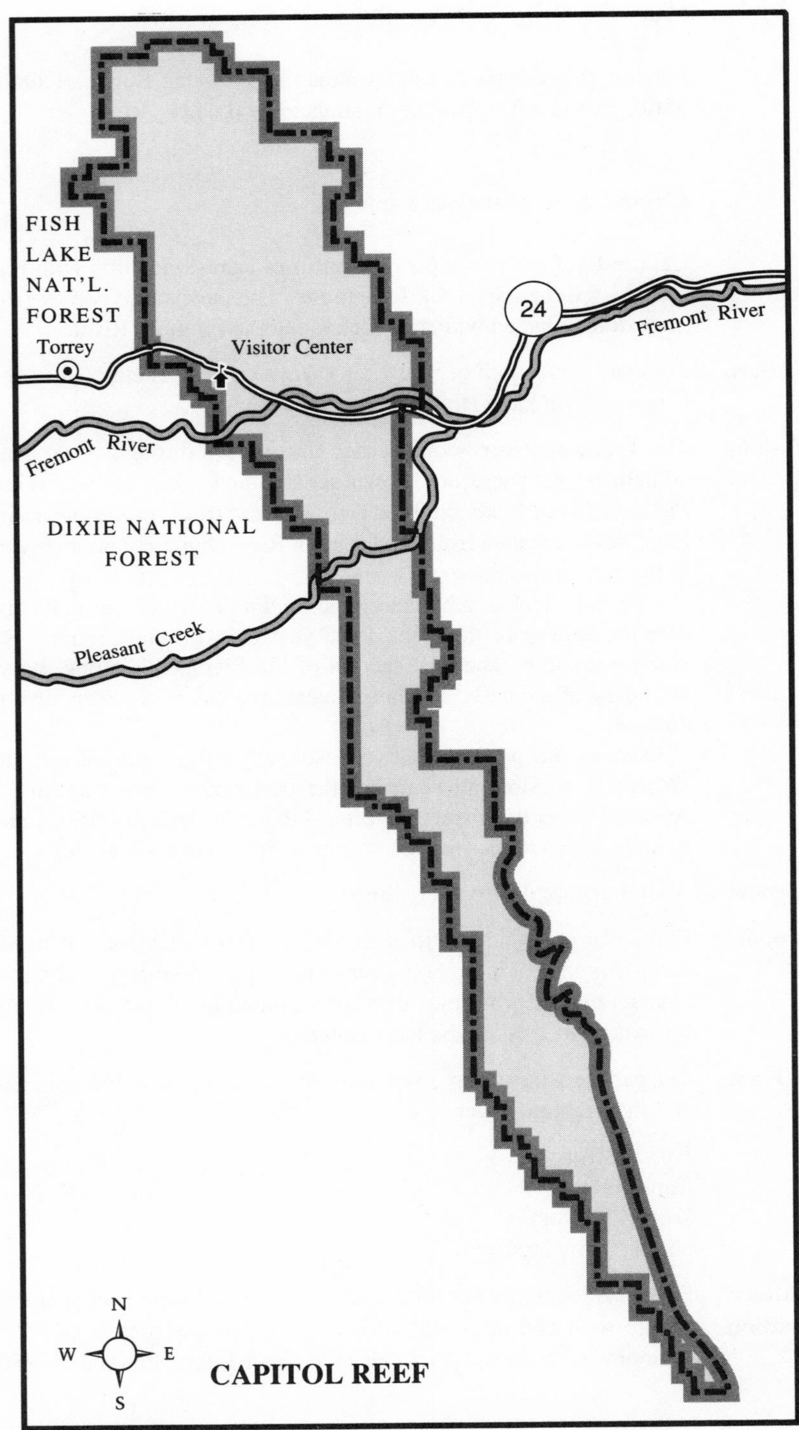
FISH
LAKE
NAT'L.
FOREST
Torrey
Visitor Center
24
Fremont River
Fremont River
DIXIE NATIONAL
FOREST
Pleasant Creek
N
W
E
S
CAPITOL REEF

noted for large brown trout. Maps and information can be obtained from:

Forest Supervisor
Fish Lake National Forest
115 East 900 North
Richfield, UT 84701
phone: (801) 896-4491

Forest Supervisor
Dixie National Forest
82 North 100 East
P.O. Box 580
Cedar City, UT 84720
phone: (801) 586-2421

Timpanogos Cave National Monument

Timpanogos Cave, on the north side of Mount Timpanogos, is a colorful limestone cavern noted for its helictites, which are water-created

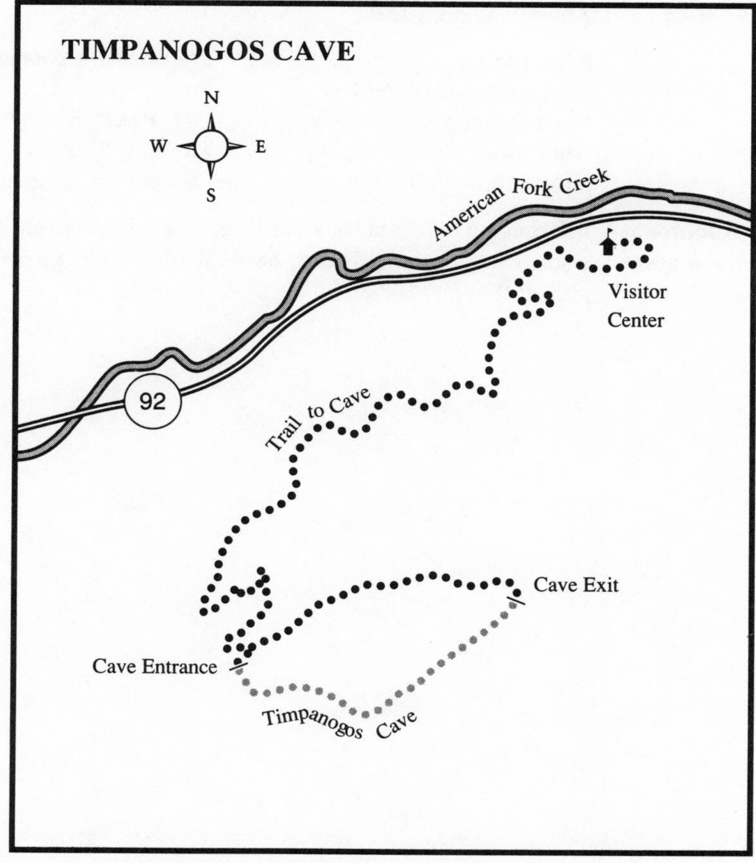

formations that grow in all directions. Middle Cave and Hansen Cave are also part of the park; tunnels have been dug connecting them to Timpanogos Cave.

Access The park is in northeast Utah (Utah County) about 30 miles south of Salt Lake City and 25 miles north of Provo. It is reached by Utah Highway 92, 7 miles east of American Fork, Utah.

Fishing American Fork Creek flows through the park and is accessible by road and trail. The stream is considered good for brown and rainbow trout.

Further upstream, the North and South Fork tributaries of American Fork Creek, and Silver Creek, also provide good fishing.

License A Utah fishing license is required.

Camping There is no camping in the park, but camping is available at nearby Uinta National Forest.

Maps The park brochure map shows the road and trail access points to American Fork Creek.

Park Address
Timpanogos Cave NM
Rural Route 3, Box 200
American Fork, UT 84003
phone: (801) 756-5238

Chamber of Commerce
Provo Area C.C.
P.O. Box 738
Provo, UT 84603
phone: (801) 224-3636

Additional Information Information on Uinta National Forest is available from: Forest Supervisor, Uinta National Forest, 88 West 100 North, Provo, UT, 84601; phone: (801) 377-5780.

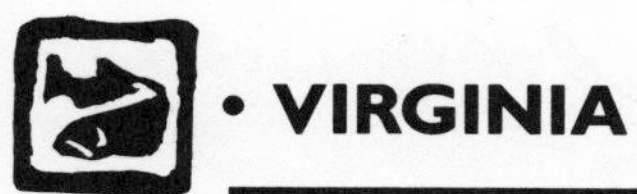

• VIRGINIA

Colonial National Historical Park

Colonial National Historical Park is composed of two separate parks (Jamestown and Yorktown) connected by a parkway. Jamestown, the site of the first permanent English settlement in North America, is a short drive from Yorktown, the site of the decisive battle of the Revolutionary War.

Access The parks are in southeastern Virginia (York and James City counties). Jamestown is on the James River, and Yorktown is on the York River. They are connected by the Colonial Parkway, which also passes through the historic town of Williamsburg.

Fishing Both the James and York rivers flow into Chesapeake Bay and provide very good estuarine fishing. The most commonly caught fish in the York River are sea trout, spot, croaker, flounder, and small bluefish; the most common in the James River are channel catfish, spot, croaker, and small blues. Nearby tidal creeks contain largemouth bass, bluegills, crappie, and catfish.

Both rivers will yield a few striped bass, usually from March to early June and again in October and November. Flounder move close to shore in March and concentrate near sandy areas, where they spawn. Flounder fishing holds up all summer in the York River.

Spot and croaker are found in the rivers during summer and fall. Fishing for sea trout is best from mid-March through May, while July through September is best for spot and croaker. Current fishing information, along with charters, boat ramps, and rentals, are available locally. Launching or landing boats in the park is prohibited.

License No license is required for saltwater fishing in Virginia. A license is required for freshwater fishing.

Camping There are no camping facilities in the parks, but private campgrounds are nearby.

Maps For navigating a boat, you will need nautical chart #12248 for the James River and #12238 and #12243 for the York River.

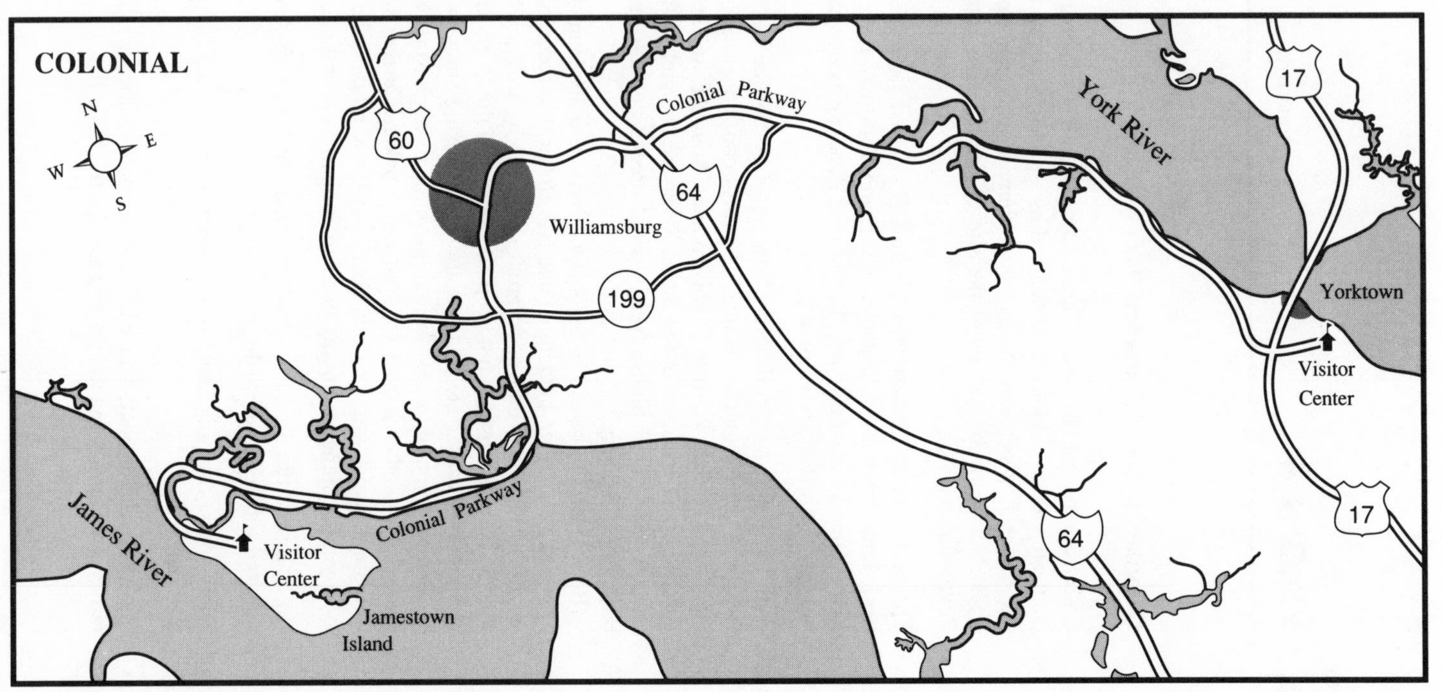
COLONIAL
N
E
S
W
60
Colonial Parkway
64
Williamsburg
199
York River
17
Yorktown
Visitor
Center
17
64
Colonial Parkway
James River
Visitor
Center
Jamestown
Island

Park Address
Colonial NHP
P.O. Box 210
Yorktown, VA 23690
phone: (804) 898-3400

Chamber of Commerce
Williamsburg Area C.C.
901 Richmond Rd.
P.O. Box HG
Williamsburg, VA 23185
phone: (804) 229-6511

George Washington Memorial Parkway

George Washington Memorial Parkway traverses the natural beauty and scenery of the Potomac River and connects George Washington's Mount Vernon home, south of Washington D.C., with the Great Falls of the Potomac, to the north of the city. Although it is used as a commuter route during weekday rush hours, the parkway is much more than just a highway. Scenic and historic sites are located along its entire length. The parkway links a group of parks that provide a variety of recreational, natural, and historical experiences to more than 9 million people each year.

Access The parkway is in northeastern Virginia (Fairfax County) and a small section is in Maryland (Montgomery County), where it connects Great Falls with Chain Bridge in the Georgetown section of Washington D.C.

Fishing With a wide variety of fish-producing habitat, the Potomac River in the Washington D.C. area is a veritable fish factory. In former years, this river section of the Potomac was badly polluted and considered a national embarrassment. The river has been cleaned and rejuvenated and is now an excellent fishery. In fact, the river is getting crowded with fishing folks and recreational boaters.

The parkway consists of a number of sites along its length that provide access to the Potomac River for fishing and boating. Boat ramps are available at four parkway sites and fishing at eight sites.

Starting in the north, the fishing sites are:

1. Great Falls Park
2. Theodore Roosevelt Island, across the river from the John F. Kennedy Center for the Performing Arts
3. Gravelly Point, near Washington National Airport
4. Roaches Run Waterfowl Sanctuary, also near the airport
5. Jones Point Lighthouse, just south of Wilson Bridge connecting Virginia and Maryland
6. Belle Haven, just south of Wilson Bridge

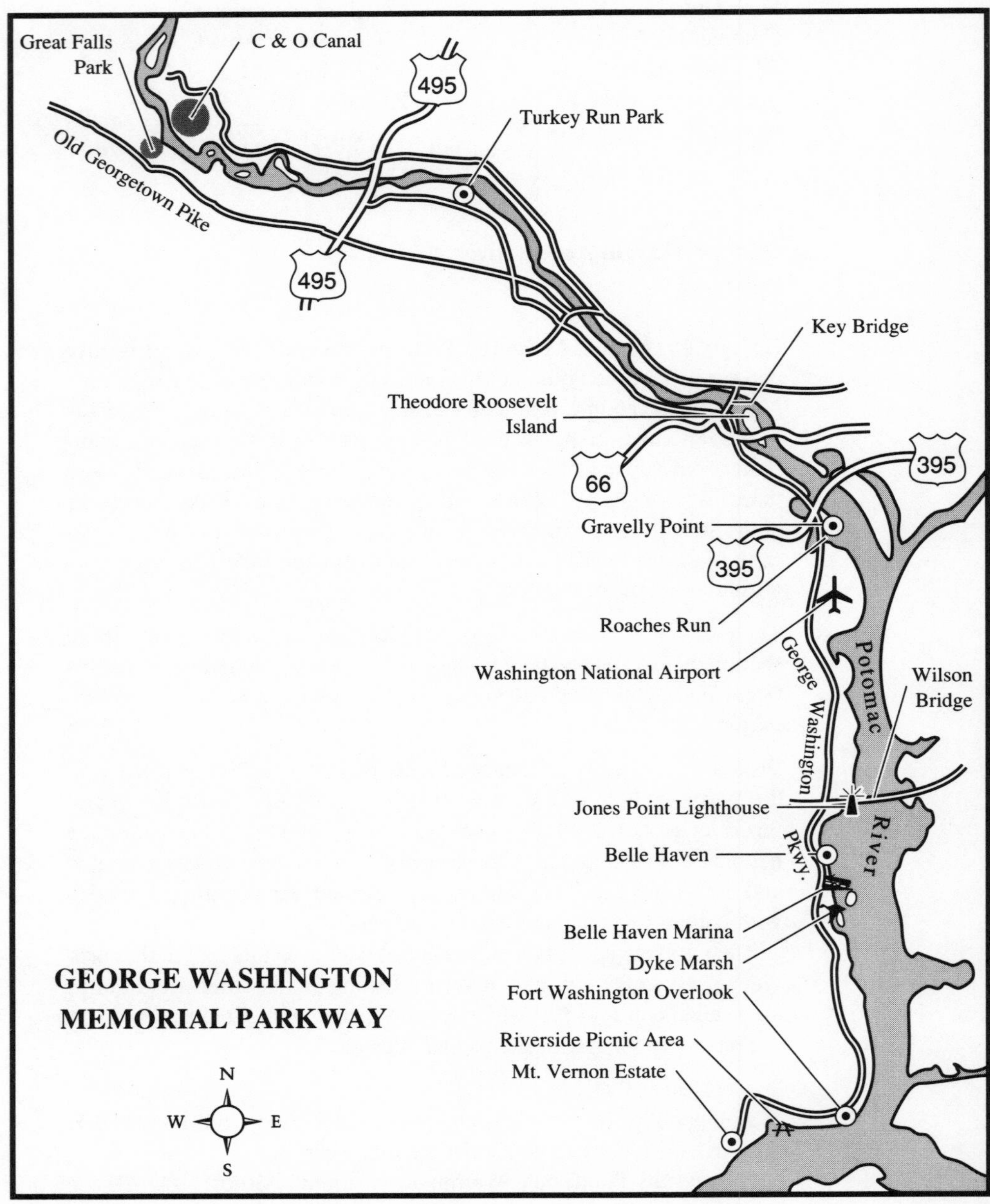
Great Falls Park
C & O Canal
495
Turkey Run Park
Old Georgetown Pike
495
Key Bridge
Theodore Roosevelt Island
66
395
Gravelly Point
395
Roaches Run
Washington National Airport
George Washington Pkwy.
Potomac River
Wilson Bridge
Jones Point Lighthouse
Belle Haven
Belle Haven Marina
Dyke Marsh
Fort Washington Overlook
Riverside Picnic Area
Mt. Vernon Estate
GEORGE WASHINGTON MEMORIAL PARKWAY
N
W
E
S

7. Dyke Marsh, also just south of Wilson Bridge
8. Riverside Picnic Area, near George Washington's Mount Vernon estate.

The first of these, Great Falls Park, offers good fishing for smallmouth bass in the spring and fall. The river current is very strong in this section of the Potomac, and wading is prohibited. Immediately upstream from Great Falls Park is Riverbend Park, which has a marina and is administered by the Fairfax County Park Authority.

The other seven fishing areas south of Washington D.C. also are affected by tides, so be aware of the tide schedules if you launch a boat at one of the boat ramps. Some of the best fishing is during the first couple hours of an incoming tide and during the last hours of the outgoing tide.

Roosevelt Island has a footbridge connecting the island to the Virginia shore and many shoreline clearings on the island are good for fishing. Roaches Run is wadeable at low tide and popular for fly-fishing. It is also a good area to catch spawning largemouth bass in the spring. Dyke Marsh is also wadeable in spots. The remaining sites provide bank fishing.

Downstream from Great Falls, largemouth bass, striped bass, shad, crappie, and catfish are the main attractions in the river. Fishing is usually best in the spring and fall, but largemouth can be taken consistently during the summer.

The yellow perch run begins in late February when water temperatures reach 42 to 45 degrees. Striped bass begin moving into the river to spawn in April; May is the best month for stripers, and that is also the time when herring, a favorite bait for the striped bass, are spawning. The outlet of Roaches Run at Gravelly Point is a good spot for striped bass in the spring. There is a boat ramp at Gravelly Point, but it can't be used at low tide. Hickory shad also run in the Potomac during April and May.

Largemouth-bass fishing is best in the spring, particularly April when water temperatures move above 50 degrees. The bass migrate into the creeks and large coves in preparation for spawning. Look for shallow spawning flats in the backs of the creeks and coves. A key is the hydrilla and milfoil weed-beds that are submerged in the spring. The spawning beds will often be located in the submerged hydrilla. Fish the outside edges of the hydrilla in slightly deeper water, using crankbaits, spinnerbaits, and plastic worms. When fishing plastic worms, try small (5-inch) rib worms in motor oil/chartreuse, black/chartreuse, and red bloodline. Good areas to try are the Washington Channel and Aquia, Mattawoman, and Swan creeks. Also try fishing around the marinas; the water there retains heat well and attracts bass.

The formerly polluted Potomac River is now clean, and consistently produces bass in the 3- to-5-pound range.—*Ken Penrod*

Summer bass fishing is excellent. After spawning, the bass move toward the main river channel and around the hydrilla beds in the main river. Buzzbaits produce in weedy areas and spinnerbaits and plastic worms worked along the channel and weed bed edges also account for many bass. The largest concentration of hydrilla is from Pohick Bay (Virginia side) to the Woodrow Wilson Bridge. The hydrilla attracts bass like a magnet and this area is consistently productive.

Fall fishing begins in mid-September and continues through November. The bass are on the deeper edges of the grass beds in 8 to 12 feet of water and can be taken by spinnerbaits fished along the weed edges. Another good technique is to fish buzzbaits on the surface early and late in the day. Once water temperatures drop into the low 60s, crankbaits become less effective and the slower jig-and-pig becomes more effective.

Winter is the slowest time for bass. They get sluggish when the water temperature is below 50 degrees, avoid the main current, and move into coves and bays, staying at 5- to 10-foot depths. The Spoils area and the rocks and dropoffs around the Woodrow Wilson Bridge are good areas to try. Try a jigging spoon along the sea walls and bridge pilings along the river.

License You need a Virginia license to fish from the Virginia side, a Maryland license to fish from Maryland, or a District of Columbia license to fish in District waters of the Potomac. The District started requiring licenses in 1988. They are available throughout Washington at various outlets. For a list of license vendors, contact: DCRA, Fisheries Division, 5010 Overlook Ave., SW, Washington, D.C., 20036; phone: (202) 767-8422.

Camping There are no camping facilities along the parkway. The parkway is mainly used by residents of the Washington D.C. area. There is very little camping in the area.

Maps The park brochure map is excellent as a general location map. A Potomac River Fishing Map is available from: Alexandria Drafting Company, 6440 General Green Way, Alexandria, VA, 22312; phone: (703) 750-0510.

Park Address
George Washington MPKY
Turkey Run Park
McLean, VA 22101
phone: (703) 285-2600

Chamber of Commerce
Fairfax County C.C.
8391 Old Courthouse #300
Vienna, VA 22180
phone: (703) 749-0400

Washington Convention and Visitors Association
1575 Eye St. NW
Suite 250
Washington, D.C. 20005
phone: (202) 789-7000

Additional Information Information about Riverbend Park is available from: Fairfax County Park Authority, 3701 Pender Dr., Fairfax, VA, 22030; phone: (703) 246-5700.

The Potomac River can increase its volume and rise very quickly. The National Weather Service has a 24-hour recorded telephone message that gives the tides, current, and predicted water level, along with warnings of high water, high winds, and other conditions that could be dangerous to anyone fishing or boating. Phone: (301) 899-3210. The information is updated twice a day.

A guide is recommended to introduce you to this tidal river and its underfished bass waters. There are two places you might contact: Outdoor Life Unlimited, 13028 Ingleside Dr., Beltsville, MD,

20705; phone: (301) 572-5688; or Glenn Peacock, 2025 Glen Ross Rd., Silver Spring, MD, 20910; phone: (301) 589-1644.

Ken Penrod, one of the owners of Outdoor Life Unlimited, has written a book, *Fishing the Tidal Potomac River*. This detailed text covers more than 60 miles of the Potomac River between Chain Bridge and Port Tobacco. It is available ($23 postpaid) from PPC Publications, 13028 Ingleside Dr., Beltsville, MD, 20705; phone: (301) 572-5688.

You can rent a rowboat (no motors) and get a D.C. license at Fletcher's Boathouse in the District. Located at 4940 Canal Rd., NW; phone: (202) 244-0461. Fletcher's can also provide current fishing information.

Manassas National Battlefield Park

Manassas is the site of two major Confederate victories in the Civil War. The battles are named First Manassas (July 1861) and Second Manassas (August 1862). They are better known as the Battles of Bull Run, named for the stream flowing through the battlefield.

Access The park is in northern Virginia (Prince William County) about 26 miles southwest of Washington D.C., near the intersection of Interstate 66 and Virginia Highway 234.

Fishing Bull Run is a small, quiet creek flowing through parts of the park. Largemouth and smallmouth bass, crappie, and bluegill are found throughout the creek. The stream is rarely fished but can be surprisingly good. Only local residents fish here. Bull Run is too small to float. It is wadeable in places, but most fishing is from shore.

Fishing is best in the spring and fall, when the fish are active or spawning. Summers in this part of Virginia find both fish and people sluggish and uninterested.

License A Virginia fishing license is required.

Camping No camping is available in the park, but private campgrounds are nearby.

Maps None needed. The creek runs along part of Virginia Highway 234 and is accessible from the road.

Park Address
Manassas NBP
6511 Sudley Rd.
Manassas, VA 22110
phone: (703) 754-7107

Chamber of Commerce
Greater Manassas C.C.
P.O. Box 495
Manassas, VA 22110
phone: (703) 368-4813

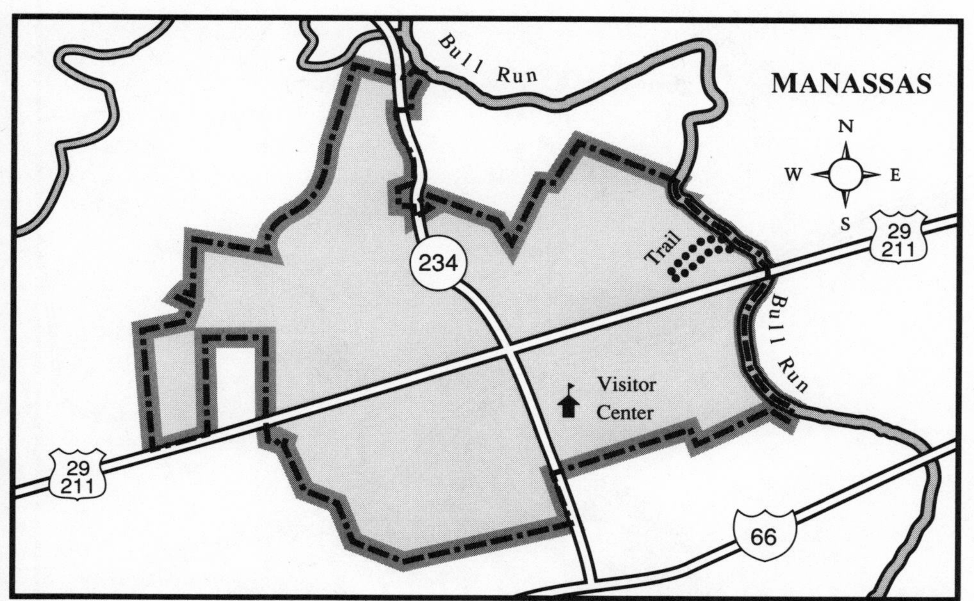

Prince William Forest Park

Prince William Forest Park is an 18,571-acre forest community of Virginia pine trees and other pine-forest flora. The park is only 35 miles southwest of Washington, D.C., and is popular for hiking, camping, picnicking, and fishing.

Access The park is in northeastern Virginia (Prince William County) in Triangle and is easily accessible from Interstate 95. The park entrance is at Interstate 95 and Virginia State Route 619.

Fishing Within the park boundary is the Quantico Creek watershed. The park contains 15 miles of streams and two lakes that are open to fishing.

The North and South Branches of Quantico Creek flow through the park and contain warm-water species such as largemouth bass, catfish, and bluegill.

The two lakes are stocked with largemouth and smallmouth bass, catfish, bluegill, and pickerel.

Fishing areas are accessible by trail from parking areas along park roads. Park waters are open all year.

License A Virginia fishing license is required, and state regulations apply. Special park regulations are listed in the *Angler's Guide,* available at park headquarters or the nature center.

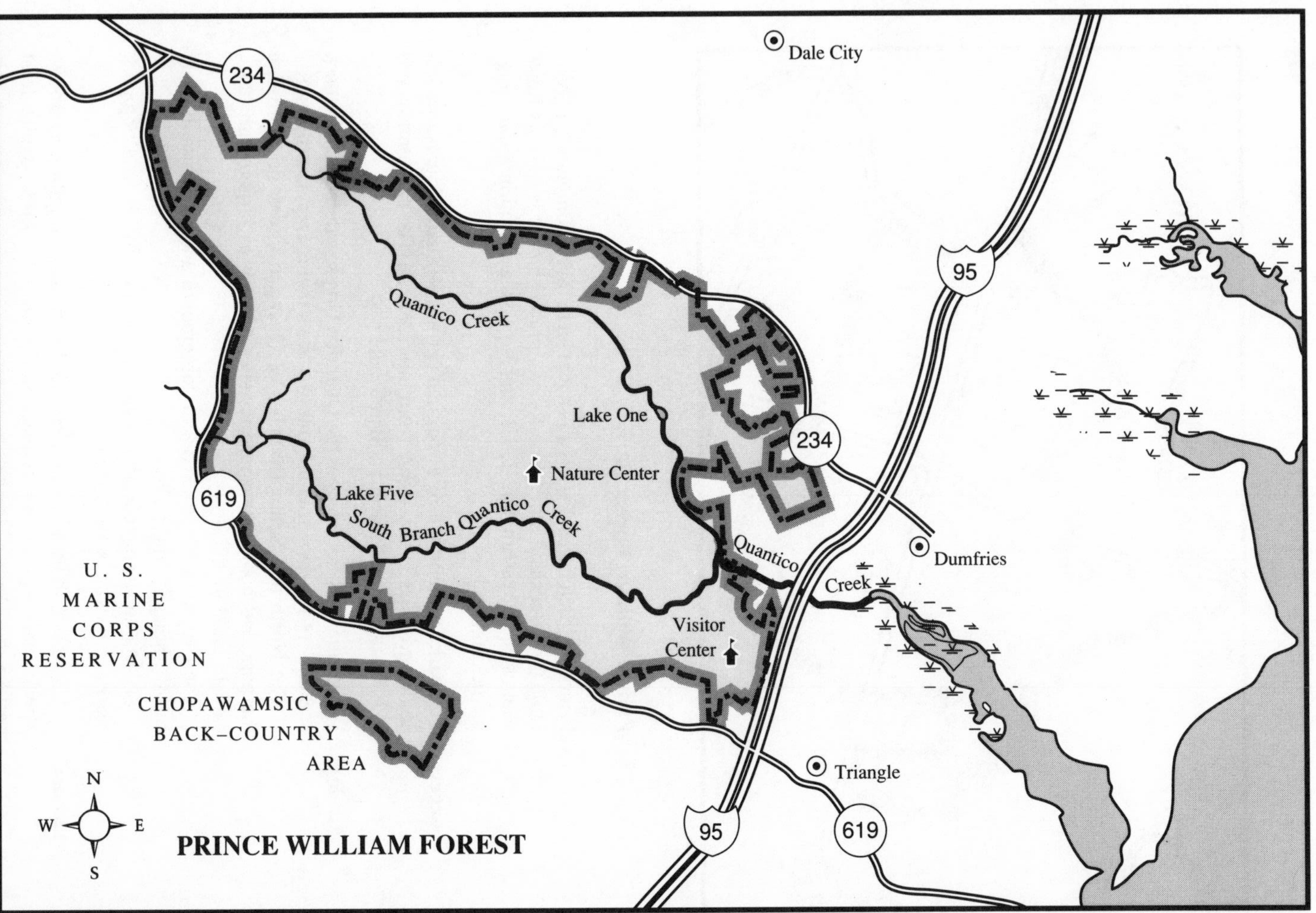

Dale City
234
95
Quantico Creek
Lake One
234
Nature Center
Lake Five
619
South Branch Quantico Creek
Quantico
Creek
Dumfries
Visitor Center
U. S.
MARINE
CORPS
RESERVATION
CHOPAWAMSIC
BACK-COUNTRY
AREA
Triangle
N
W
E
S
PRINCE WILLIAM FOREST
95
619

Camping A variety of camping is available. Oak Ridge Campground is 6 miles from the park entrance and contains 80 tent sites. The Travel Trailer Village is located on Virginia State Route 234. This concession-operated campground has 79 sites with water, electric, and sewer hook-ups available. Call: (703) 221-2474 for more information on the Travel Trailer Village.

Tent camping is available for groups. There are also group cabin camps available for groups of 50 or more. Reservations are required for both areas. Primitive camping is available with a permit. For group reservations or permits, contact the park headquarters.

Maps The park brochure map shows the roads and the well-marked trails in the park.

Park Address
Prince William Forest Park
Box 208
Triangle, VA 22172
phone: (703) 221-7181

Chamber of Commerce
Prince William County C.C.
4320 Ridgewood Center
Woodbridge, VA 22192
phone: (703) 590-5000

Shenandoah National Park

Lying along an 80-mile stretch of the Blue Ridge Mountains, beautiful Shenandoah National Park is rightly regarded as one of the most scenically enjoyable areas in the National Park System.

Skyline Drive runs along the Blue Ridge through the length of the park, providing magnificent vistas of the Shenandoah Valley and the nearby Massanutten Mountains. The park is extremely popular for a variety of outdoor activities including fishing, camping, and hiking. The Appalachian Trail extends through the park.

Access Shenandoah National Park is in parts of nine counties in northwestern Virginia. Interstate 66 crosses just north of the park at Front Royal, and Interstate 64 crosses below the southern boundary, west of Charlottesville. Skyline Drive runs through the park and connects to the Blue Ridge Parkway. The park is about 60 miles west of Washington, D.C.

Fishing Shenandoah National Park features 42 mountain trout streams, all containing wild brook trout. The park is one of the few remaining bastions of native brook trout in the southeastern United States. Park streams are all somewhat similar in that they have steep gradients with alternating rapids and pools, host modest fly hatches, and are remote, requiring hikes of various lengths. The reward for your effort

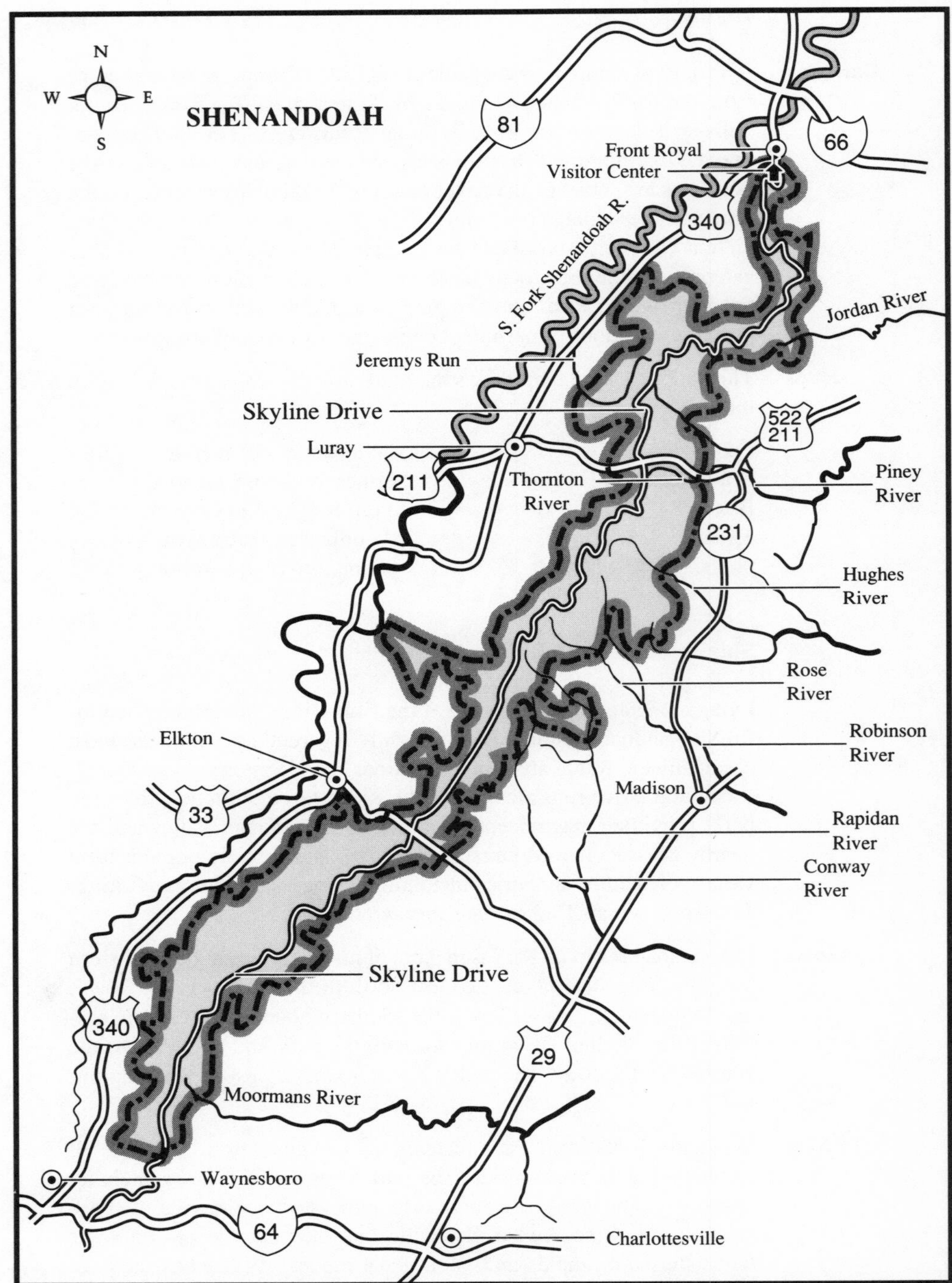
N
W
E
S
SHENANDOAH
81
66
Front Royal
Visitor Center
340
S. Fork Shenandoah R.
Jordan River
Jeremys Run
Skyline Drive
522
211
Luray
211
Thornton
River
Piney
River
231
Hughes
River
Rose
River
Elkton
Robinson
River
33
Madison
Rapidan
River
Conway
River
Skyline Drive
340
29
Moormans River
Waynesboro
64
Charlottesville

is uncrowded fishing, in a beautiful setting, for colorful native brook trout.

Typical of any fishery, the more effort required to reach a stream, the less fishing pressure. Some of the park streams require fairly strenuous hikes of one to three hours. Other streams are more easily reached. Most of the time, you will be fishing alone, especially after June.

Spring thaws draw many people to the park to fish, since the fishing season begins on the first Saturday in April. With the streams in good condition (bank full, clear, 50 to 60 degrees), it's not uncommon to catch 30 to 40 fish in a day. Most are small, but some reach quite a respectable size.

Park fishing is restricted to single-hook artificial lures. Small ultralight spinning lures such as Mepps, Colorado spinners, Rooster Tails, and Panther Martins are consistent producers. However, the majority of those fishing in the park use flies. Fly visibility and buoyancy are more important than pattern in these tumbling mountain streams where trout feed opportunistically rather than selectively. Hair-wing patterns such as the Royal Wulff or the local Mr. Rapidan are best. Other standard dry flies (sizes 12–18) are the Adams, Quill Gordon, and caddis patterns.

Nymphs (sizes 10–12) are good in the early season. The Gold-Ribbed Hares Ear, Quill Gordon, Dark Stonefly, and Olive Caddis Pupa should cover your needs. If the water is high and discolored, streamers are effective. Try the Olive Woolly Bugger or the Black-Nosed Dace in sizes 8–10.

After May, the fishing becomes tougher as stream levels drop. During summer, the low, clear pools demand long, light leaders and flawless presentation. Terrestrials (ants, beetles) are your main choices in the summer.

For those fly-fishers who enjoy matching the hatch, there are seven major insect hatches on the park streams. Listed below are the seven insects and their approximate emergence dates. The dates can vary each year due to changing weather and water conditions.

Insect	*Emergence Dates*
Quill Gordon (*Epeorus pleuralis*)	February 20–May 10
Dark Blue Quill (*Paraleptophlebia adoptiva*)	February 20–May 15
March Brown (*Stenonema vicarium*)	April 5–May 20
Grey Fox (*Stenonema fuscum*)	April 20–May 15
Light Cahill (*Stenonema canadense*)	April 20–May 20

Insect	*Emergence Dates*
Little Yellow Stonefly (*Isoperla bilineata*)	April 15–July 20
Giant Dark Stonefly (*Pteronarcys californica*)	April 10–July 25

At all times, stealth and accurate presentation are the keys to taking fish. The trout are very wary and demand a quiet approach. Noisily walking up to the water's edge will encourage the trout to do their disappearing act. Standard fishing tactics on park streams include crouching behind rocks and trees and crawling on hands and knees.

The streams are small and brushy, so light tackle is recommended. Fly rods should be from 6 to 7.5 feet long, carrying 3-to-5-weight lines. Ultralight spinning rods from 4.5 to 5 feet are best, equipped with 2- or 4-pound line.

The 42 trout streams in the park are listed below according to park district (north, central, south), the side of the park where located (east or west), and the access to the stream (road or trail). Some of the better-known streams are the Rapidan, Staunton, Rose, Hughes, Conway, and Thornton rivers, along with Hawksbill Creek, Big Run, Jeremys Run, and Ivy Creek.

Stream	*Side of Park*	*Access*
North District		
Gooney Run	West (top)	County Road #631
Jeremys Run	West (bottom)	County Road #611
Jordan River, South Fork	East (top)	County Road #629
Piney Run	East (bottom)	NPS Fire Road
Thornton River, North Fork	East (bottom)	County Road #612
Central District		
Brokenback Run	East (top)	NPS Fire Road
Cedar Run	East (middle)	NPS Trail
Conway River	East (bottom)	NPS Fire Road
Dry Run, North Fork	West (top)	County Road #669
Dry Run, South Fork	West (top)	County Road #696
Hawksbill Creek	West (top)	County Road #629
Hazel River	East (top)	Trail
Hogcamp Branch	East (middle)	NPS Trail
Hughes River	East (top)	NPS Trail
Little Hawksbill Creek	West (middle)	County Road #611

Stream	*Side of Park*	*Access*
Naked Creek, East Branch	West (bottom)	County Road #759
Naked Creek, West Branch	West (bottom)	County Road #607
Pass Run	West (top)	U.S. 211
Pocosin Hollow Run	East (bottom)	Trail
Ragged Run	East (top)	Trail
Rapidan River	East (middle)	NPS Fire Road
Rose River	East (middle)	County Road #670
Shaver Hollow Run	West (top)	NPS Trail
South River	East (bottom)	NPS Trail
Staunton River	East (middle)	NPS Trail
Thornton River, South Fork	East (top)	U.S. 211
Whiteoak Canyon Run	East (middle)	NPS Fire Road
South District		
Big Run	West (top)	NPS Fire Road
Hawksbill Creek	West (top)	County Road #628
Ivy Creek	East (top)	Trail
Lewis Run, Upper	West (middle)	NPS Fire Road
Lewis Run, Lower	West (middle)	NPS Fire Road
Madison Run	West (middle)	NPS Fire Road
Moorman River, North Fork	East (bottom)	NPS Fire Road
Moorman River, South Fork	East (bottom)	NPS Fire Road
One-Mile Run	West (top)	County Road #892
Paine Run	West (middle)	NPS Fire Road
Pond Ridge Brook	East (bottom)	NPS Fire Road
Rip Rap Hollow Run	West (bottom)	NPS Fire Road
Rocky Mountain Run	West (top)	NPS Fire Road
Two Mile Run	West (top)	County Road #649
Turk Branch	East (bottom)	NPS Fire Road

The Rapidan River is probably the most famous river in the park. Former president Herbert Hoover maintained a camp on the river and fished there frequently. The Rapidan and Staunton rivers are open all year under special regulations as fish-for-fun streams. The Rapidan boasts an outstanding population of native brook trout. It is an extremely popular stream, especially in the spring when the Quill Gordons begin hatching in March. Access to the Rapidan is also easier than for most other streams. It is near the town of Madison, off Route 29.

License A Virginia fishing license is required. Be sure to check the special park regulations. The park conducts annual stream surveys and may close some streams to protect the brook-trout population. In 1989, of the 42 park streams, 28 were open for fishing. Check each year to see which streams are open.

Camping There are four developed campgrounds (665 spaces) and one group camp. Most of the park is open to back-country camping, with a permit. The Big Meadows Campground (227 spaces) is on the Ticketron reservation system.

Maps You will need topographic maps to find the trout streams scattered throughout the park. There are three maps (north, central, south) of the park in the 15-minute series, published and updated by the Potomac Appalachian Trail Club. The maps are available from the Shenandoah Natural History Association at the park address.

A special map and description of the Rapidan Wildlife Management Area has detailed directions to the Rapidan River. The map is free from: Virginia Commission of Game and Inland Fisheries, 4010 West Broad St., Richmond, VA, 23230; phone: (804) 367-1000.

Park Address
Shenandoah NP
Route 4, Box 292
Luray, VA 22835
phone: (703) 999-2243

Chamber of Commerce
Luray-Page County C.C.
46 E. Main St.
Luray, VA 22835
phone: (703) 743-3915

Additional Information The best source of information about park streams, fly hatches, and water levels is Edinburg pharmacist, author, and fishing guide, Harry Murray. Harry knows the park streams intimately and can direct you or guide you to the best streams at the time. He operates a fly shop in the Peoples Drugstore in Edinburg, Virginia, just off Interstate 81, west of the park. His book, *Trout Fishing in the Shenandoah National Park,* provides information on the locations and access points to park streams and explains his various successful angling techniques in the park. His free fly shop catalog contains a description of the book and a hatch chart of the major aquatic insects in the park. He can also supply you with topographic maps. Contact: Harry Murray, Box 156, Edinburg, VA, 22824; phone: (703) 984-4212 (days) or 984-8126 (evenings).

The Mr. Rapidan dry fly was created specifically for Shenandoah Park trout streams by Harry Murray. This high-floating, visible fly is intended to present the brook trout with something similar to what they see in the early season (Quill Gordon) and to take advantage of the large March Browns that follow. Harry's pattern for the Mr. Rapidan is:

Hook: Mustad 94845 (Barbless), or 94840, sizes 12–18
Thread: 6/0 Prewaxed Herb Howard – Tan
Wing: Yellow Calf Tail
Tail: Dark Moose Body Hair
Body: Blend of 50% of Flyrite #34 (Quill Gordon/Brown Yellow Drake) and 50% of Flyrite #30 (March Brown).
Hackle: One medium brown and one grizzly hackle.

An excellent source of information about fishing in Virginia is *Fresh Water Fishing and Hunting in Virginia*. It contains descriptions and maps of fishing waters throughout Virginia. It is available from: Alexandria Drafting Company, 6440 General Green Way, Alexandria, VA, 22312; phone: (703) 750-0510.

• VIRGIN ISLANDS

Virgin Islands National Park

Located on St. John Island, the smallest of the three major U.S. Virgin Islands, the park preserves an area of clear tropical seas, white sandy beaches, quiet coves, and colorful coral reefs. Included in the park are most of the islands just offshore from St. John. Hiking, swimming, and snorkeling are the main activities in this beautiful park.

Access To reach the park, it is necessary to fly to St. Thomas Island, 1,200 miles southeast of Miami, and then take one of the daily ferry runs from Red Hook on St. Thomas to St. John.

Fishing The waters surrounding the U.S. Virgin Islands are a major vacation attraction. Part of the lure of big game fishing is the opportunity to set a world record for blue marlin. Nine International Game Fish Association world records have been set for blue marlin in the past 18 years, along with world records for kingfish, cobia, wahoo, and tuna.

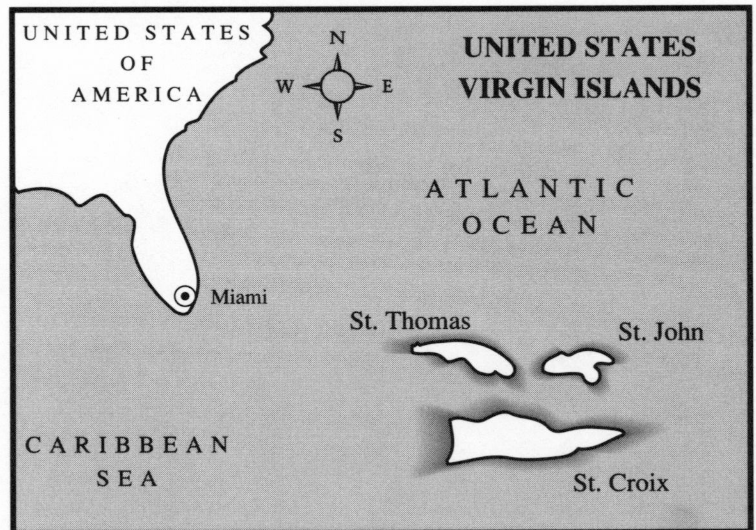

Saltwater fishing is good all year. Boats for deep sea fishing or inshore drifting and trolling may be chartered at St. John or St. Thomas. Most of the fishing fleet is headquartered at the St. Thomas marinas, since there is more fishing activity on St. Thomas than St. John. The latter is more of a haven for swimming, sailing, snorkeling, and scuba diving, although shore fishing is permitted away from public swimming or snorkeling beaches.

Blue marlin average 350 pounds and are taken throughout the year by offshore charter boats. The largest fish are taken from July to October. The smaller white marlin are also present all year, as are Allison tuna. Spring and fall are the best times for these fish.

Sailfish move inshore and are frequently taken from December through March. Kingfish, wahoo, bonita, mackerel, and blackfin tuna may can be caught all year but are sought mostly during the winter months. A variety of other species, including barracuda and bonefish, are found at various times of the year throughout Virgin Island waters.

License No fishing license is required.

Camping Cinnamon Bay Campground has 40 rental cottages and also rents tents and tent sites. Reservations must be made well in advance. For information and reservations, contact: Cinnamon Bay Campground, P.O. Box 720, Cruz Bay, St. John, VI, 00830; phone: (809) 776-6330. In lieu of camping, luxury resorts and hotels are found on St. Thomas.

Maps Navigating in the vicinity of St. John Island requires nautical chart #25641.

Park Address
Virgin Islands NP
P.O. Box 7789
St. Thomas, VI 00801
phone: (809) 775-6238

Chamber of Commerce
St. Thomas–St. John C.C.
P.O. Box 324
St. Thomas, VI, 00801
phone: (809) 776-0100

WASHINGTON

Coulee Dam National Recreation Area

Grand Coulee Dam is the largest concrete structure in the world. The dam was built on the Columbia River by the Bureau of Reclamation for irrigation, power generation, and flood control. Franklin D. Roosevelt Lake, the reservoir created by the dam, extends 150 miles north and east to the Canadian border and up the Spokane River, a tributary of the Columbia River. As might be expected, water-oriented sports are the main attractions in the NRA.

Access Grand Coulee Dam and Franklin D. Roosevelt Lake are in northeast Washington (Stevens, Ferry, and Lincoln counties). The dam and lake are accessible via a number of highways. Park headquarters are near the dam off Washington Highway 174. Washington Highway 25 parallels the eastern side of the lake.

Fishing With 79,000 acres and 660 miles of shoreline, Franklin D. Roosevelt Lake is the largest body of water in the state. Although not considered a premier fishery, the lake does host a wide variety of fish including Dolly Varden, brook, brown, rainbow, and cutthroat trout, chinook and kokanee salmon, largemouth and smallmouth bass, walleye, sturgeon, and panfish. The best fishing areas are generally at the mouths of the numerous streams flowing into the lake.

The walleye is the main sport fish in both Roosevelt Lake and the lower Spokane River. Over the past several years, these waters have provided some of the best walleye fishing in the entire Columbia River system. Because of the increasing fishing pressure on walleye, the state is considering tightening the fishing regulations to protect and improve the walleye fishery.

Fishing is a year-round activity on the lake, but spring (March to June) and fall (September to November) are the peak periods for most fish species. Walleye spawn in the spring and are easily found as they congregate over shallow rock piles and gravel bars. After spawning, they move to deeper water and are more difficult to locate. Remember that walleye travel in schools, and if you catch one there is a good chance that additional fish may taken in the same area.

On a lake as large as Roosevelt, knowing where, when, and how

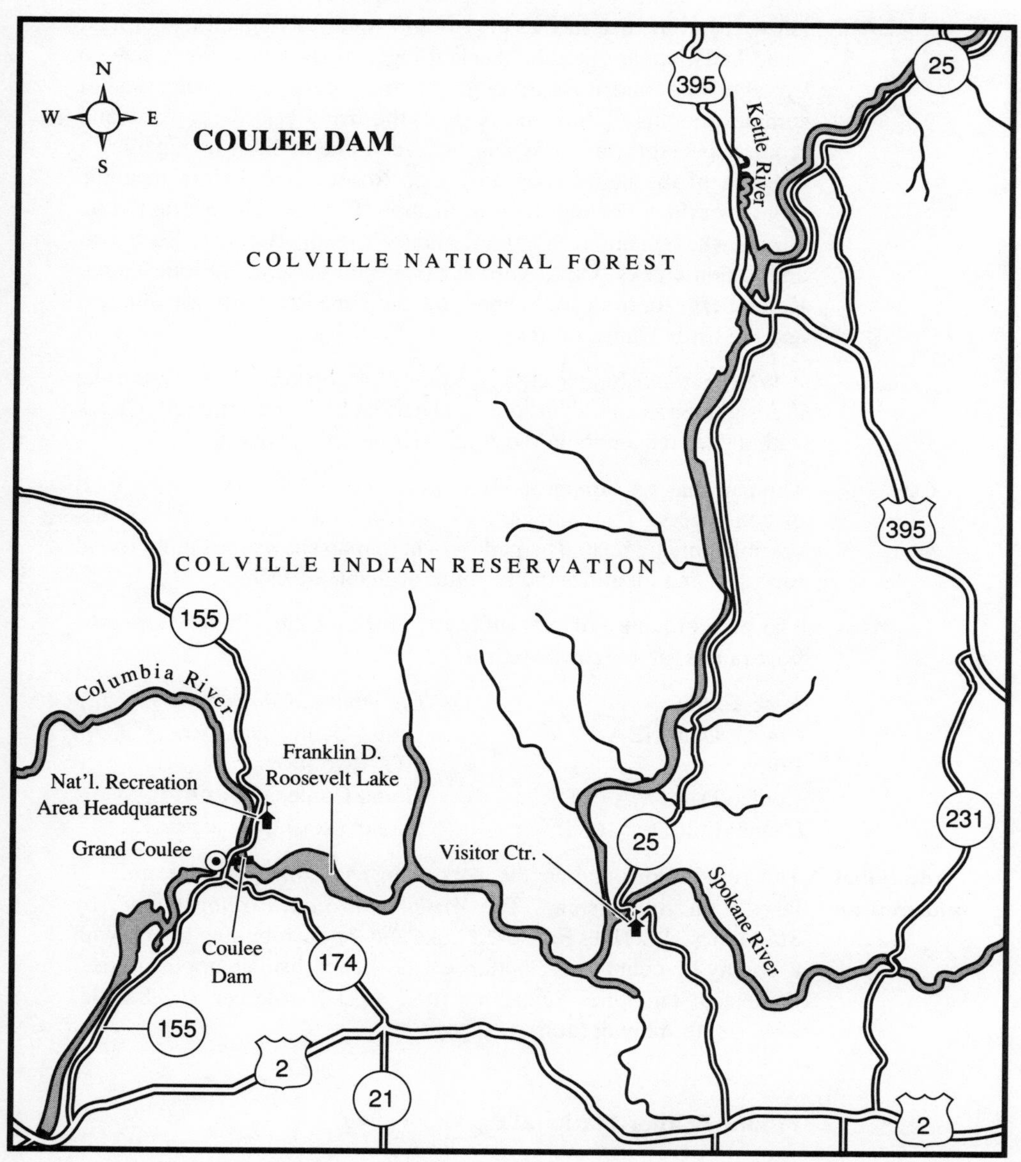
COULEE DAM
N
W
E
S
COLVILLE NATIONAL FOREST
COLVILLE INDIAN RESERVATION
395
25
Kettle River
395
155
Columbia River
Franklin D.
Roosevelt Lake
Nat'l. Recreation
Area Headquarters
Grand Coulee
Coulee
Dam
Visitor Ctr.
25
231
Spokane River
174
155
2
21
2

to fish can be difficult. Fishing is often best early and late in the day, and trolling is the most popular method. Concentrate on areas known to attract fish such as the bases of waterfalls and cliffs, springs, weed beds, stream mouths, sunken logs, rocky areas, areas shaded by vegetation, and along the edges of strong currents. During the hot summer months of July and August, the fish are in deep water and require special techniques, such as leaded line and down-riggers.

Some of the better spots to try on Roosevelt Lake are near the mouths of the following streams: Sanpoil, Colville, and Kettle rivers, and Hawk, Ninemile, Wilmont, Hunter's, Hall, Barnaby, Sherman, and Onion creeks. Other good areas are the base of the bluffs near Keller Ferry for trout and salmon, the Spokane River arm for walleye, and the Little Dalles for trout.

License A Washington fishing license is required. A portion of Roosevelt Lake is designated as an Indian zone, and a tribal license is required. Check with a park ranger about the zones and the tribal license.

Camping The park has 25 campgrounds scattered around the lake with a total of 624 spaces. The campgrounds vary in facilities and some are accessible only by boat. The park brochure map shows the campground locations and identifies the facilities available at each.

Maps The park brochure map is sufficient; it shows the tributary streams, boat ramps, and highway access.

Park Address
Coulee Dam NRA
Box 37
Coulee Dam, WA 99116
Phone: (509) 633-0881

Chamber of Commerce
Grand Coulee Dam Area C.C.
P.O. Box 760
Grand Coulee, WA 99133
phone: (509) 633-3074

Additional Information The region surrounding the park area has numerous streams and lakes with good fishing. The *Washington State Fishing Guide*, by Stan Jones, describes Roosevelt Lake and the surrounding region with a county-by-county description of the better fishing opportunities. Write to: Stan Jones Publishing Inc., 3421 E. Mercer St., Seattle, WA, 98112; phone: (206) 323-3970.

Mount Rainier National Park

Mount Rainier National Park was established in 1899 as the nation's fifth national park. Mount Rainier, one of the most photographed mountains in the country, is a volcano presently in a dormant stage. The park contains numerous glaciers and other alpine features, with

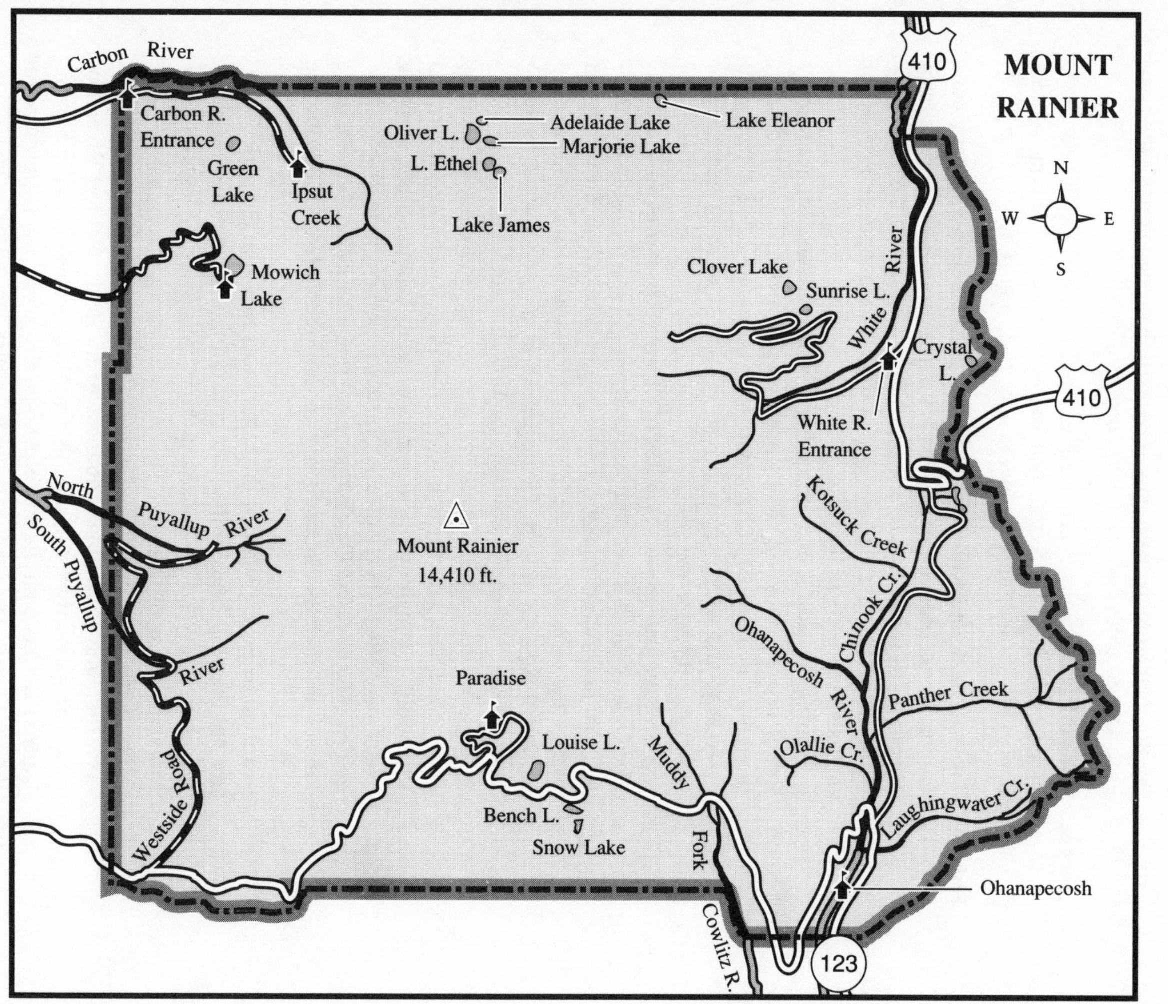

MOUNT RAINIER
N
W
E
S
410
410
123
Carbon River
Carbon R. Entrance
Green Lake
Ipsut Creek
Mowich Lake
Oliver L.
L. Ethel
Lake James
Adelaide Lake
Marjorie Lake
Lake Eleanor
Clover Lake
Sunrise L.
White River
Crystal L.
White R. Entrance
Kotsuck Creek
Chinook Cr.
Ohanapecosh River
Panther Creek
Olallie Cr.
Laughingwater Cr.
Ohanapecosh
Cowlitz R.
Muddy Fork
Mount Rainier 14,410 ft.
Paradise
Louise L.
Bench L.
Snow Lake
North Puyallup River
South Puyallup
River
Westside Road

hundreds of miles of foot trails, and is very popular with mountain climbers and hikers. A forest of Douglas fir, red cedar, and western hemlock encircle the mountain. Over 2 million people visit the park each year to enjoy its recreational opportunities.

Access The park is in southwestern Washington (Pierce and Lewis counties), 95 miles southeast of Seattle and 103 miles west of Yakima. Access is via U.S. 12 and State Highways 410, 706, and 165.

Fishing The park is dotted with alpine lakes and glacial streams, many containing brook, brown, rainbow, and cutthroat trout. Fishing requires a hike to reach these lakes or streams, most of which are far from park roads. However, the well-developed trail system extends to most of the fishable waters in the park.

Fishing pressure is considered light. Many streams are not heavily fished because they are cloudy with glacial melt most of the time, though a few regularly flow clear. Most lakes are not ice-free until early July, and heavy snowfall restricts access to most waters from November through May.

There are only about 35 miles of clearwater streams in the park. The Ohanapecosh River and its tributaries (Chinook, Kotsuck, Olallie, Panther, Boulder, and Laughingwater creeks), in the southeast part of the park, are the main clear-water streams and are managed as fly-fishing-only waters. Ohanapecosh is an Indian word meaning "clear water." The river contains rainbow and cutthroat trout.

Some of the better streams to fish, if you find them in a clear-water condition, are: Carbon River, Puyallup River (both north and south forks), and the White River, along with Tahoma, Fish, Rushing Water, and Huckleberry creeks. Such well-known rivers as the Nisqually, Puyallup, and Cowlitz originate in the park, but they are more famous for their steelhead fishing in the lower stretches outside the park.

Listed below are some of the better lakes to fish in the park. These are not the only lakes in the park containing fish, but over the years they have provided dependable fishing. Access is by back-country trails of varying difficulty.

For purposes of this book, I have divided the park into four sections corresponding to the four entrances to the park: Carbon River Entrance on the northwest; Nisqually Entrance on the southwest; Stevens Canyon Entrance on the southeast; and the White River Entrance on the northeast. The lakes are placed under the entrance you would normally take to begin hiking to the particular lake. The key to fish species in each lake is: **B,** brook trout: **C,** cutthroat trout; and **R,** rainbow trout.

Carbon River Entrance

Adelaide Lake—**R**
Chenuis Lake—**C**
Ethel Lake—**R**
Green Lake—**C**
James Lake—**R**
Marjorie Lake—**R**
Mowich Lake—**B,C,R**
Mystic Lake—**C**
Oliver Lake—**R**

Mowich Lake can be reached by road in late July after the snow has melted.

Nisqually Entrance

Golden Lakes—**B**

Stevens Canyon Entrance

Bench Lake—**B,C**
Louise Lake—**B**
Snow Lake—**C**

White River Entrance

Bear Park Lake—**C**
Clover Lake—**B,C,R**
Crystal Lakes—**C**
Deadwood Lakes—**C**
Eleanor Lake—**R**
Green Park Lakes—**C**
Hidden Lake—**B,R**
Lost Lake—**B**
Palisade Lakes—**R**
Sunrise Lake—**B,C,R**

License No fishing license is required in the park but state regulations apply. Be sure to check the special park regulations and note the list of closed waters.

Camping There are five developed campgrounds in the park with a total of 596 spaces. In addition, there are numerous back-country trailside camps. Back-country hiking and camping requires a permit from one of the park ranger stations. The park publishes the *Backcountry Trip Planner*, which has an excellent map and valuable information on back-country camping.

Maps There is a special USGS map of the park, "Mt. Rainier National Park and Vicinity," which is helpful for traveling to the back-country lakes.

The *Backcountry Trip Planner,* mentioned above, shows the more than 300 miles of trails in the park and the lakes accessible from the trails, as does the park brochure map. Both are good general location maps but are not suitable for longer hikes. For such hikes, topographic maps should be obtained.

Park Address
Mt. Rainier NP
Tahoma Woods, Star Route
Ashford, WA 98304-9801
phone: (206) 569-2211

Chamber of Commerce
Puyallup Valley C.C.
2823 E. Main St.
Puyallup, WA 98372
phone: (206) 845-6755

Additional Information

A concise guide to the park, *Exploring Mt. Rainier,* is available from: Pacific Northwest National Parks and Forests Association, 83 S. King St., Room 212, Seattle, WA, 98104; phone: (206) 442-7958. Ask for their catalog, which also contains USGS topographic maps for the park.

A detailed description of the lakes and streams in Mt. Rainier National Park is contained in *The Washington State Fishing Guide,* available from: Stan Jones Publishing Inc., 3421 E. Mercer St., Seattle, WA, 98102; phone: (206) 323-3970.

The North Cascades National Park Service Complex

The North Cascades National Park Service Complex consists of three units: North Cascades National Park, Ross Lake National Recreation Area, and Lake Chelan National Recreation Area. These three separate but adjoining units in north central Washington were all added to the National Park System on the same day, October 2, 1968. The three units together encompass 1,053 square miles of magnificent alpine scenery. Few were aware of the scope and grandeur of this area before the park was established. The superintendent of North Cascades National Park manages the complex from headquarters in Sedro Woolley, west of the area.

The North Cascades Complex is popular with hikers and backpackers. Approximately 300 miles of trails offer access to more than 600,000 acres of wilderness. The complex includes many natural lakes and streams, with the lakes ranging in character from shallow ponds to relatively deep alpine lakes. Many are accessible for only a short season. Most of the high elevation lakes are not free of ice and snow until July to late August, depending on the severity of the previous winter and spring.

The lakes accessible by road or trail experience light to moderate fishing pressure. Some waters receive locally heavy pressure on opening dates, weekends, and holidays. Virtually all the high elevation lakes were once devoid of fish life because of natural barriers to fish migration in their outlet streams, and although many were stocked prior to park establishment, some have reverted to a fishless

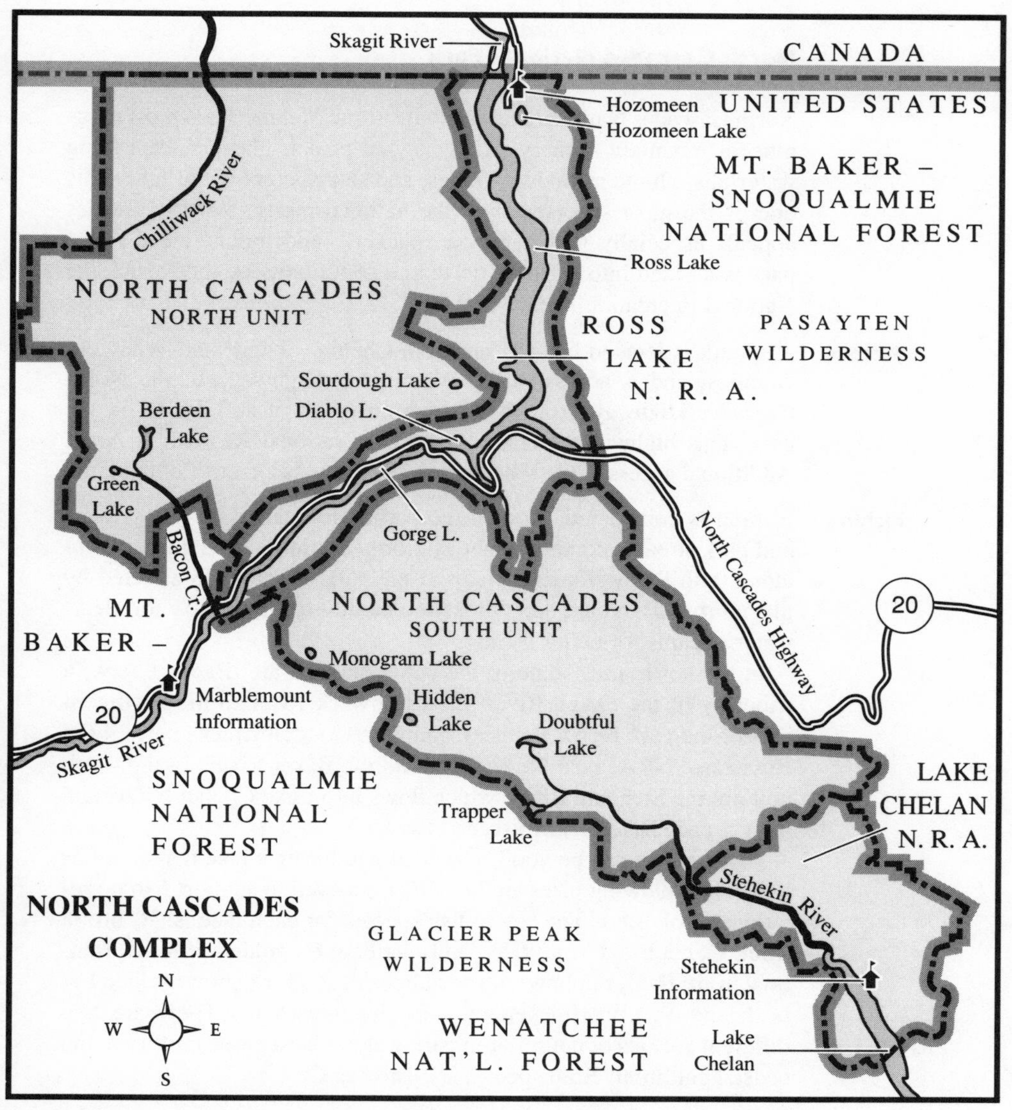
Skagit River
CANADA
UNITED STATES
Hozomeen
Hozomeen Lake
MT. BAKER –
SNOQUALMIE
NATIONAL FOREST
Chilliwack River
Ross Lake
NORTH CASCADES
NORTH UNIT
ROSS
LAKE
N. R. A.
PASAYTEN
WILDERNESS
Sourdough Lake
Berdeen
Lake
Diablo L.
Green
Lake
Gorge L.
Bacon Cr.
North Cascades Highway
MT.
BAKER –
NORTH CASCADES
SOUTH UNIT
20
Monogram Lake
Marblemount
Information
Hidden
Lake
Doubtful
Lake
20
Skagit River
SNOQUALMIE
NATIONAL
FOREST
Trapper
Lake
LAKE
CHELAN
N. R. A.
Stehekin River
NORTH CASCADES
COMPLEX
GLACIER PEAK
WILDERNESS
N
W
E
S
Stehekin
Information
WENATCHEE
NAT'L. FOREST
Lake
Chelan

state. A list of the major fishing waters in each unit follows. The park headquarters office can provide you with additional information.

North Cascades National Park

North Cascades National Park contains some of America's most magnificent mountain scenery. High, jagged peaks, glaciers, cascading waterfalls, alpine meadows, ridges, and slopes combine to make this one of the most spectacular of the national parks. North Cascades appeals especially to hikers, backpackers, and mountaineers. The park is divided into separate north and south units by the Ross Lake National Recreation Area.

Access The park is located below Canada in Chelan, Skagit, and Whatcom counties, and is accessible by Washington Highway 20, the North Cascades Highway, from Burlington on the west and Twisp on the east. This highway traverses Ross Lake National Recreation Area. Additional access is via Washington Highway 542 from Bellingham.

Fishing Fishing is considered good in the park. Mountain and valley lakes and park streams contain rainbow, brook, cutthroat, and golden trout along with Dolly Varden. Many of the park streams are affected by glacial runoff and are sometimes too cloudy to fish. Look for clear-water streams for better fishing.

In the north unit, some of the better streams are: Bacon Creek, a tributary of the Skagit River; the Chilliwack River in the northwest part of the park below British Columbia; Goodell Creek, partially in Ross Lake NRA, near Newhalem; and the Baker River. In the south unit are the Stehekin River, which flows into Lake Chelan NRA, and the Cascade River near Cascade Pass.

Lake fishing can be good, provided you locate a lake that contains fish. The following lakes are known or believed to support fish populations as of 1989. The key to fish species for each lake is: **B,** brook trout; **C,** cutthroat trout; **DV,** Dolly Varden; **G,** golden trout; **R,** rainbow trout; **R/C,** rainbow/cutthroat hybrid; **R/G,** rainbow/golden hybrid; and **T,** trout (in general—species uncertain). There are two different species of cutthroat in park waters, west-slope cutthroat and coastal cutthroat. Both species are listed as **C.**

North Unit Lakes

Bear Lake—**C**
Berdeen Lake—**C**
Blum Lakes (lower 2 lakes)—**B**
Copper Lake—**C**
Ipsoot Lake—**C**
Jeanita Lake—**G**
Kwahnesum Lake—**R**
No Name Lake—**R**

Diobsud Lakes—**C**
Firn Lake—**R**
Green Lake—**C,R,R/C**
Hanging Lake—**T**
Hi-Yu Lake—**R**
Skymo Lake—**T**
Sourdough Lake—**B**
Lower Thornton Lake—**C**
Middle Thornton Lake—**G**
Triumph Lake—**R**

Note: Diobsud, Firn, Hi-Yu, Kwahnesum, and Triumph lakes are locally named lakes. Other lake names appear on USGS topographic maps. There are also some unnamed lakes or beaver ponds containing fish in the north unit. The Chilliwack beaver ponds contain coho salmon and cutthroat trout, as do the Baker River beaver ponds, along with brook trout. The lake below Berdeen Lake has cutthroat trout, and the ponds below No Name Lake contain rainbow trout. The major fishing lakes in the north unit are Copper, Sourdough, and Lower Thornton.

South Unit Lakes

Dagger Lake—**C**
Doubtful Lake—**C**
Hidden Lake—**R**
Kettling Lake—**C,R,R/C**
Lily Lake—**C,R**
Monogram Lake—**C**
Sandy Lake—**R**
Sourpuss Lake—**R**
Stiletto Lake—**C**
Stout Lake—**C**
Sweet Pea Lake—**R**
Torment Lake—**R**
Trapper Lake—**C**
Vulcan Lake—**R**

Notes: Lily, Torment, Sandy, Stiletto, Sweet Pea, Sourpuss, and Vulcan are all locally named. Other lake names appear on the USGS topographic maps. Unnamed lakes containing fish in the south unit are the pond below Stout Lake, which has cutthroat trout, and the lake above Bouck Lake (in Ross Lake NRA), with golden trout. The major fishing lakes in the south unit are: Hidden, Monogram, Doubtful, Trapper, Dagger, and Stiletto. These lakes are at least partially accessible by trail.

License A Washington fishing license is required.

Camping Back-country campsites are available in both units. A back-country permit is required. Camping is prohibited on the fragile alpine or subalpine meadows except at designated sites.

Maps A special USGS topographic map, "North Cascades National Park," is helpful for reaching back-country lakes. This map should be used in conjunction with the park trail map, "Main Trails and Back-country Camp Areas, North Cascades Complex, Washington," available free from park headquarters.

Park Address	*Chamber of Commerce*
North Cascades NP	Sedro Woolley C.C.
2105 Highway 20	714 Metcalf St.
Sedro Woolley, WA 98284	Sedro Woolley, WA 98284
phone: (206) 855-1331	phone: (206) 855-1841

Lake Chelan National Recreation Area

Lake Chelan is the largest natural lake in Washington. It is also one of the most scenic lakes in the United States. Lake Chelan NRA borders the south unit of North Cascades National Park.

Chelan is a fjordlike lake. It is situated in a precipitous glacial trough in mountains that reach more than 8,000 feet from lake bottom to valley crest. Chelan is 55 miles long and averages only about 1 mile wide. It is hemmed in by the Chelan Mountain Range on the southwest and the Sawtooth Mountains on the northeast. Only the northerly 5 miles and 2,000 acres of Lake Chelan are included in the national recreation area. Much of the lake is part of the Wenatchee National Forest.

Access Lake Chelan NRA is in Chelan County, and is accessible either by plane, by a 55-mile boat trip from the town of Chelan to Stehekin, an isolated village at the head of Lake Chelan, or by trail. There is no road access. The town of Chelan is outside the park, at the foot of the lake, and accessible via U.S. 97. Floatplanes may be chartered in the town of Chelan.

Fishing Lake Chelan, one of the nation's deepest lakes, is dammed at the town of Chelan, where it joins the Columbia River. Even though it is dammed, Lake Chelan is a natural lake. The dam was built in 1927 and raised the existing lake level 21 feet to increase power production. The shape of the lake has been described as "just a widening of the river."

Because of its large size and difficult access, Lake Chelan is not heavily fished. Most of the fishing pressure is south of the park area, near the town of Chelan. Lake Chelan provides good fishing for cutthroat and rainbow trout, along with kokanee salmon (known as silver trout), chinook salmon, burbot (ling), and an occasional brook trout. On this huge lake, the most dependable areas to fish are at the mouths of the numerous feeder creeks.

The entire region is dotted with lakes and streams. Within the park interior, the Stehekin River, which flows into Lake Chelan, is the principal fishery and contains rainbow and cutthroat trout. Stehekin

Road parallels the river, providing easy access. The road is used by residents of the village who have ferried cars to their homes. The Stehekin River extends upstream from the High Bridge area into North Cascades National Park.

Boulder, Bridge, Company, and Rainbow creeks are tributaries of the Stehekin River. These four streams are accessible by trail and contain a mixture of rainbow, cutthroat, and brook trout. Coon, McAlester, and the two small Triplet lakes all contain cutthroat trout, while Rainbow Lake, appropriately enough, contains rainbow trout, as does Battalion Lake.

The low elevation trails in Lake Chelan NRA are usually accessible from early April through late November. The higher trails are not free of snow until mid or late July. Accommodations and boat rentals are available at the North Cascades Lodge at Stehekin.

License A Washington fishing license is required. Be sure to check the state regulations. The lake is open to fishing all year, but Dolly Varden are a protected species and may not be kept.

Camping Primitive camping is available at a number of back-country sites and lakeshore camps.

Maps There is a special USGS map, "North Cascades National Park," that covers Lake Chelan NRA and is useful for back-country travel.

Park Address
Lake Chelan NRA
P.O. Box 7
Stehekin, WA 98852
phone: (509) 682-4404

Chamber of Commerce
Lake Chelan C.C.
P.O. Box 216
Lake Chelan, WA 98816
phone: (509) 682-2022 or (toll free in-state) 1-800-424-3526

Additional Information A map of the Wenatchee National Forest, covering part of Lake Chelan, is available from: Forest Supervisor, Wenatchee National Forest, Box 811, Wenatchee, WA, 98801; phone: (509) 662-4335.

Ross Lake National Recreation Area

Ross Lake NRA separates the north and south units of North Cascades National Park. The NRA consists of three lakes—Ross, Diablo, and Gorge—that were formed by damming the Skagit River to provide electrical power for Seattle. Ross Lake is the largest of the three. It is 24 miles long, extending into Canada, and 2 miles across at its widest point. Ross Lake has 12,000 surface acres, while the smaller Diablo and Gorge have 910 and 210 acres respectively. The lakes are managed to minimize drawdown in the summer and offer numerous recreation opportunities.

Access Ross Lake NRA is in Whatcom County. Access is via Washington Highway 20, the North Cascades Highway. Gorge and Diablo lakes are accessible by vehicle from the North Cascades Highway. Vehicle access to the extreme upper end of Ross Lake is by unimproved road from Canada. There is no other road access to Ross Lake, itself. The North Cascades Highway is closed part of the year because of heavy snows; it is generally open from May through mid-November, but those dates vary according to weather and avalanche conditions.

Fishing Ross, Diablo, and Gorge lakes all contain Dolly Varden, rainbow, brook, and cutthroat trout. Diablo and Gorge lakes are stocked periodically by the state. Ross Lake has naturally reproducing rainbow trout and Dolly Varden. The trout spawn in the tributary streams and in the Skagit River in British Columbia, north of the park. Rainbow move into the upper Skagit and Ross lakes' tributaries from mid-May to late June to spawn in the gravel riffles. Dolly Varden spawn in the fall in these same gravel areas.

Ross Lake is a large lake and contains rainbow trout up to 5 pounds. The best fishing is near the mouths of tributary streams. Diablo and Gorge lakes receive more fishing pressure than Ross Lake because they are more readily accessible.

Road access to the Hozomeen Campground on Ross Lake, which has a boat launch, is from British Columbia. The Ross Lake Resort, which also rents boats, is at the south end of the lake and reached only by trail. Both Diablo and Gorge lakes have launch ramps, and the Diablo Lake Resort has rental boats.

Other small lakes within the NRA that have trout are: Thunder, Bouck, the Hozomeen lakes, and the Panther Potholes.

The Skagit River below Gorge Dam flows for 10 miles within the park. Once it leaves the park boundary, it is designated as part of the National Wild and Scenic River System. The Skagit is nationally renowned for its steelhead fishing. Within the park area, the Skagit has resident rainbow trout. It also contains Dolly Varden, cutthroat trout, and steelhead. The lower sections of the river, near Puget Sound, receive heavy salmon runs.

Steelhead fishing in the Skagit is best during February through April. Some shoreline areas are wadeable but the river is best fished from a boat. Guides are available in Sedro Woolley and elsewhere in Washington. Productive steelhead fly patterns for the upper Skagit are: Silver Hilton, Skunk, Fall Favorite, Golden Demon, and marabou streamer patterns. The North Cascades Highway parallels the river, providing good access.

The Skagit River is best fished from a boat or by canoeing and stopping at prime areas to wade fish.—*Stanford Young*

License A Washington fishing license is required. Be sure to check the state regulations because some creek mouth areas on Ross Lake are closed.

Camping There are 6 campgrounds with a total of 459 spaces, accessible by road. The Colonial Creek, Goodell Creek, Diablo Lake Resort, Gorge Lake, and Newhalem Creek campgrounds are along the North Cascades Highway, while Hozomeen Campground is reached by Canada Highway 3. In addition, there are 17 small campgrounds on Ross Lake and 3 on Diablo accessible only by boat or trail.

Maps A special USGS map, "North Cascades National Park," is useful for back-country travel. The park office can also provide you with a map of the main trails and back-country camp areas in the North Cascades Complex.

Park Address
Ross Lake NRA
c/o North Cascades NP
800 State St.
Sedro Woolley, WA 98284
phone: (206) 873-4500

Chamber of Commerce
Sedro Woolley C.C.
714 Metcalf St.
Sedro Woolley, WA 98284
phone: (206) 855-1841

Olympic National Park

Olympic National Park occupies about 900,000 acres in the center of northwest Washington's Olympic Peninsula as well as a narrow coastal strip along the western margin of the peninsula. This mountain wilderness contains active glaciers, 50 miles of scenic ocean shore, the finest existing remnant of Pacific Northwest rain forest, and the rare Roosevelt elk.

Access The park is on the Olympic Peninsula (Clallam, Jefferson, and Grays Harbor counties) and is reached via U.S. Highway 101 and numerous side roads off 101. Few roads go very far into the park.

Fishing The Olympic Peninsula is noted for its many beautiful coastal streams and numerous high-country lakes. Fishing in Olympic National Park is seldom publicized, and the rivers and lakes are uncrowded. The headwaters and upper reaches of nearly all the peninsula's important river systems supporting steelhead and salmon are in the park. Rivers such as the Hoh, Queets, Bogachiel, and Soleduck originate in the wilderness of the park and offer some of the best fishing in the Northwest for salmon and steelhead. Because the park is about a three-hour drive from Seattle and Tacoma, it doesn't get the fishing pressure found on rivers closer to those population centers.

Generally the west and north drainages and a few of the east drainages support anadromous salmon and steelhead populations. The popular species in these waters are chinook (king) and coho (silver) salmon, steelhead (sea-run rainbow trout), and sea-run cutthroat trout. Many of the park streams also have resident populations of rainbow, cutthroat, and Dolly Varden trout, along with whitefish.

The little angling pressure that exists in the park is on the better-known streams, leaving lesser-known streams neglected and unfished. Park streams such as Big, Buckinghorse, Graves, and Tshletshy creeks are virtual strangers to fishing.

Roads do not extend far into the park, and it is possible to find isolated fishing only a short distance from the roads. Olympic National Park boasts a fine trail system, and wilderness fishing possibilities are endless to those willing to hike and explore.

It is important to know the many regulations governing fishing, not only in the park but on the entire peninsula. Most of the major rivers flow through an often confusing array of federal, state, and Indian tribal jurisdictions. The lower reaches of two of the major rivers (Hoh and Quillayute) are in the detached coastal strip of the park and thus are in the unusual position of being under park control at both ends but not in the middle.

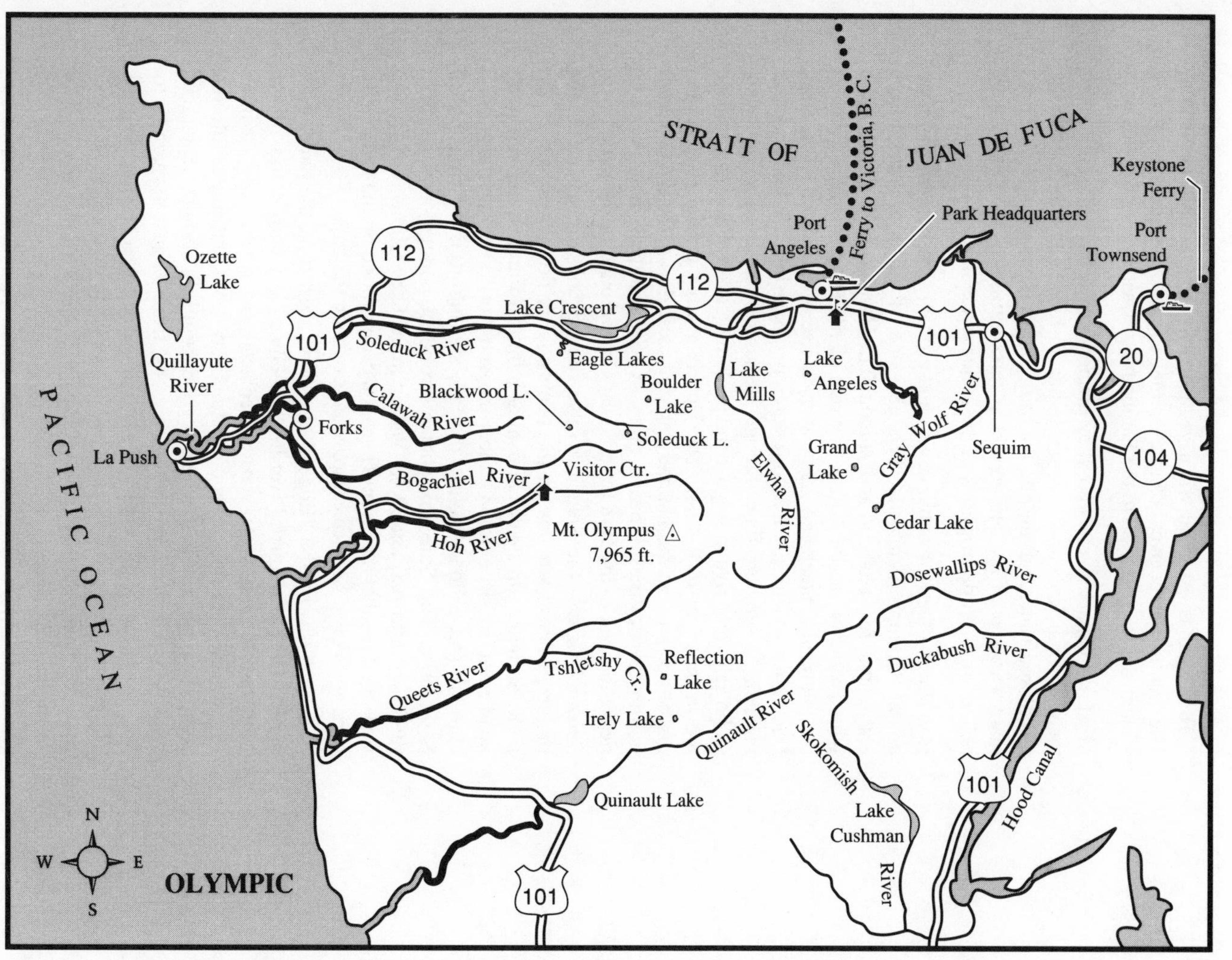
STRAIT OF
JUAN DE FUCA
Ferry to Victoria, B. C.
Keystone Ferry
Port Angeles
Park Headquarters
Port Townsend
112
112
Ozette Lake
Lake Crescent
101
Soleduck River
Eagle Lakes
Boulder Lake
Lake Mills
Lake Angeles
101
Sequim
20
104
Quillayute River
Calawah River
Blackwood L.
Soleduck L.
Forks
La Push
Grand Lake
Gray Wolf River
Bogachiel River
Visitor Ctr.
Elwha River
Hoh River
Mt. Olympus
7,965 ft.
Cedar Lake
PACIFIC OCEAN
Dosewallips River
Duckabush River
Tshletshy Cr.
Reflection Lake
Queets River
Irely Lake
Quinault River
Skokomish
101
Hood Canal
Quinault Lake
Lake Cushman
River
N
W
E
S
OLYMPIC
101

Rain gear is essential when venturing to the Olympic Peninsula. The peninsula receives a large annual rainfall, particularly during winter, the rainy season in the Pacific Northwest.

Rivers Most of the park rivers are fed by glaciers and often run milky when the runoff quickens up in warm weather. Fishing can be difficult in the discolored water, but despite the milky appearance of glacial rivers, many varieties of fish are present at certain times of the year. Listed below are short descriptions of the major rivers in the park:

Hoh River—the Hoh is the largest and probably the best-known river on the Olympic Peninsula. It is also one of the best rivers in the entire state for steelhead and salmon. The Hoh has both summer and winter runs of steelhead, hosting one of the biggest winter runs on the peninsula. Steelhead arrive at each rise of the water level, from December into spring. Chinook salmon appear in April and continue through November. June through September is best for chinooks. Coho salmon arrive in August and peak in October. Sea-run cutthroat are in the river in the fall. The Hoh is a large glacial river and is discolored most of the summer, but runs clear during the cold weather months except during heavy rains. A road parallels the river from near the coast to the Hoh Rain Forest Campground in the park.

Soleduck River—the Soleduck (also spelled Sol Duc) is one of the major steelhead streams on the peninsula. It flows west out of the park. Summer-run steelhead fishing is best in June; winter-run steelhead enter the river from October through April. The river also hosts chinook and coho salmon in the fall, starting after the first rain of September. The Soleduck contains resident populations of brook, rainbow, cutthroat, and Dolly Varden trout. U.S. Highway 101 and a park road parallel the river. There is a campground on the river in the park and Forest Service campgrounds outside the park.

Bogachiel River—the "Bogey" also flows west from the park and is similar to the Soleduck River in its steelhead and salmon runs. It has both summer and winter runs of steelhead, but is primarily a winter-run stream with fish arriving continuously from December into late April. Sea-run cutthroat fishing is good from July through September, while chinook and coho salmon are best from August through October. In the park, the river and its north fork are accessible by trail. Outside the park, the river is reached by U.S. 101 and an unpaved road. Bogachiel State Park is on U.S. 101, about 6 miles south of the town of Forks.

Quillayute River—this large, short stream (4 miles) is formed by the confluence of the Soleduck and Bogachiel rivers. The Quillayute flows into the coastal strip of the park where it enters the ocean at the

Indian town of La Push. The Quillayute hosts both summer and winter runs of steelhead with heavy winter runs from December into late April. Chinook salmon enter the river in August and coho salmon in September. Both are taken into October. The Quillayute is a beautiful river of broad, slow reaches and riffles. One of the best stretches to fish is the long riffle below the confluence of the Bogachiel and Soleduck rivers (outside the park). The Quillayute is accessible by road in spots, and there is a park service campground near the river mouth opposite the Indian village of Mora.

Calawah River—the Calawah is a tributary of the Bogachiel River on the western side of the park. Fishing here is similar to that in the Bogachiel. The river is more accessible outside the park where U.S. 101 crosses it, just north of Forks. In the park, the south fork of the Calawah is reached by trail. Fishing in the park is excellent, but the trail traverses rough country.

Queets River—the Queets flows southwest out of the park and is one of the best rivers in the state. It receives large runs of both summer and winter steelhead. July and August are best for summer steelhead in the 5-pound class, while December through April is best for larger winter steelhead. Winter-run fish in the 15-to-20-pound range are occasionally taken, with March the most productive month. Chinook salmon arrive in April and continue through November. Sea-run cutthroat make their way into the river by August, and good-sized Dolly Varden are always around. Fishing is good year-round, with August providing perhaps the best variety of fishing.

The Queets is glacier fed and seldom really clear. When the Queets is highly discolored, try the mouths of the clear tributary streams. An unpaved road off U.S. 101 parallels the river and leads to Queets Campground. Two large clay-bank areas just above and below the campground add a cement-gray color to the river during rains. Go above the upper clay bank to find clearer water.

Salmon River—a major tributary of the Queets River, only a short portion of the Salmon is in the park. It is crossed by the road leading to Queets Campground. The Salmon has some steelhead and salmon fishing similar to the runs on the Queets, but is best known for sea-run cutthroat trout from July through October.

Quinault River—the upper river is in the park and flows into the east end of Quinault Lake. The entire lower Quinault River below the lake is within the Quinault Indian Reservation and requires an Indian guide. Contact the resorts around Quinault Lake if you wish to fish the lower river.

The Quinault has a good summer run of steelhead from July through September. Winter-run steelhead action is best from Decem-

The Olympic Peninsula is noted for high-quality steelhead fishing. Fishermen are encouraged to release all wild steelhead as this angler is about to do.—*Stanford Young*

ber through March. Some of the biggest fish are taken during March. The north and east forks have excellent fishing for rainbow, brook, cutthroat, and Dolly Varden trout, with an occasional coho or sockeye salmon. Unpaved roads run up each fork and lead to campgrounds. The east fork, around Graves Creek, is good for summer steelhead. As a glacial stream, the Quinault is often discolored in the summer but clear in the winter.

Duckabush River—the Duckabush flows east into the Hood Canal and receives a good run of summer steelhead during May and June. Winter steelheading is best from November through February. Most of the good steelhead action is outside the park. Inside the park, the river is accessible by trail through brushy country and contains rainbow trout throughout the river to the headwaters.

Skokomish River—located in the southeast park area, the Skokomish River is not to be confused with the more widely known Skykomish and Snohomish rivers east of Seattle. The north fork is in the park above Lake Cushman and contains rainbow trout. An unpaved road along Lake Cushman leads to Staircase Campground on the river. From the campground, the river is accessible by trail.

Dosewallips River—this river flows out of the southeast park area into Hood Canal at the town of Brinnon on U.S. 101. The Dosewallips is a winter-run steelhead river, with January and February as the best months. In the park, an unpaved road leads to the Dosewallips Campground. There are no steelhead upstream from the campground because a falls blocks their migration. The river is reached by trail, and it branches about a mile and a half above the campground. The west fork contains rainbow trout, and the main branch holds rainbow, brook, and a few cutthroat trout.

Elwha River—located in the northeast part of the park, the Elwha is noted as an excellent stream in which to fly-fish for rainbow and Dolly Varden trout. The Elwha flows into and out of Lake Mills and is accessible by road to Whiskey Bend Campground, south of the lake, where trails follow the river for 28 miles. Major tributaries, which also provide good fishing and are accessible by trail, are the Lillian, Goldie, Long, and Hayes rivers.

Gray Wolf River—this major tributary of the Dungeness River (outside the park) offers good fishing for rainbow, brook, and Dolly Varden trout and some salmon. The confluence of Cameron and Grand creeks with the Gray Wolf is a good fishing area. The Gray Wolf is reached by trail.

Others—the entire park is laced with excellent fishing streams that rarely see a hook because of the hike required to get to them. Why hike when roads put you next to good water? For those willing to hike, some of the better streams in the park are listed below. The major rivers and lakes to which the streams are tributary are noted in parentheses.

Big Creek (Quinault River)
Boulder Creek (Lake Mills)
Buckinghorse Creek (Elwha River)
Cameron Creek (Gray Wolf River)
Cat Creek (Lake Mills)
Godkin Creek (Elwha River)
Grand Creek (Gray Wolf River)
Graves Creek (East Fork Quinault)
Pelton Creek (Queets River)
Rustler Creek (North Fork Quinault)
Tom Creek (Hoh River)
Tshletshy Creek (Queets River)

Lakes There are five major lakes in or along the park, all accessible by road.

Lake Crescent—in the northwest corner, Crescent is the largest lake in the park. Lake Crescent is unbelievably beautiful and noted for large rainbow and cutthroat trout. It has a long history of good fishing.

Lake Mills—formed by a dam on the Elwha River in the north central part of the park, Mills covers 451 acres and contains rainbow, brook, cutthroat, and Dolly Varden trout. An unpaved road to Whiskey Bend parallels the eastern side of the lake. A boat ramp is at the lower west end. A good spot to try is the upper end of the lake where the Elwha River flows in.

Lake Cushman—this lake touches the southeast boundary and contains rainbow, cutthroat, Dolly Varden, and kokanee salmon (locally known as silver trout). May and June are the best months for kokanee. The large Dolly Varden stay deep in the lake except when they ascend the feeder streams in the fall to spawn. Coastal cutthroat trout were planted by the state because of their tendency to cruise the shoreline, making them accessible to bank fishing.

Quinault Lake—located along the southwest park boundary on the Quinault Indian Reservation, it contains cutthroat, Dolly Varden, and steelhead, along with several species of salmon. Fishing is regulated by the Indians and requires a permit, available from the resorts at Amanda Park or along the south shore.

Ozette Lake—the third largest natural lake in the state, Ozette lies within the northern strip of coastal parkland. It drains into the Pacific Ocean via the Ozette River. Steelhead, sockeye salmon, and cutthroat trout are the major species. Most of the big fish are taken from the south end of the lake by trolling. A campground at Ericksons Bay is accessible only by boat.

Crescent, Cushman, and Quinault lakes all have resorts, boat rentals, and ramps. Ozette Lake is relatively undeveloped but does have a boat ramp, as does Lake Mills.

The park also has more than 200 high-country lakes (above 3500 feet elevation), but the majority are barren of fish. At one time, trout were stocked in most of the high lakes. Stocking was discontinued in 1973, and since then trout populations either have disappeared or are sustaining themselves at differing levels.

The entire park is crisscrossed with trails that provide access to many of these isolated mountain lakes. The best hiking and fishing is from midsummer (late June to early July) into the fall when the lakes are usually free of ice and snow drifts no longer block trails. Generally, lakes with western or southern exposures lose their ice first. Streams running into and out of lakes hasten the thaw.

Some of the better lakes are listed below. For convenience, the park is divided into four quadrants. None of the lakes are in the coastal section of the park. The key to fish species is: **B,** brook trout; **C,** cutthroat trout; **DV,** Dolly Varden; and **R,** rainbow trout.

Northwest Quadrant

Blackwood Lake—**B**
Bogachiel Lake—**B**
Boulder Lake—**B,R**
Clear Lake—**B,R**
Eagle Lakes—**B**
Elk Lake—**B**
Happy Lake—**B**
Hoh Lake—**B,R**
Lake #8—**B, R**
Long Lake—**B,R**
Lunch Lake—**B,R**
Mink Lake—**B,R**
Morganroth Lake—**B,R**
No Name Lake—**B,R**
Round Lake—**B,R**
Royal Lake—**B**
Soleduck Lake—**B,R**

Northeast Quadrant

Angeles Lake—**B,R**
Cedar Lake—**R**
Deer Lakes—**B,R**
Gladys Lake—**B,R**
Grand Lake—**B,R**
May Lake—**B,R**
Moose Lake—**B,R**

Southwest Quadrant

Irely Lake—**C,R**
Reflection Lake—**B**

Southeast Quadrant

Constance Lake—**B,R**
Flapjack Lakes—**B,R**
Hart Lake—**R**
Lena (Upper) Lake—**R**
Milk Lake—**B**
Scout Lake—**R**
Smith Lake—**B,R**
Sundown Lake—**R**
Wildcat Lake—**B**

License No license is required to fish in the park. To fish for salmon or steelhead, you are required to carry a state punch card for salmon and steelhead. State regulations require that you use the punch cards to account for all salmon and steelhead kept. A state fishing license is required to fish the lakes that are not entirely in the park (Ozette, Cushman, and Quinault) and to fish in Olympic National Forest.

Be sure to check the current park and state fishing regulations. Some rivers may be closed to fishing during certain months, and park regulations may change from year to year because of fluctuating numbers of fish.

You are encouraged to release all wild steelhead and keep only the hatchery fish. The illustration on p. 378 notes the differences between wild fish and hatchery fish.

Camping The park has 15 developed campgrounds accessible by car (total 918 spaces). Nine of these campgrounds are open all year. Permits are required for overnight trips in the back country. There are many other campgrounds outside the park in state parks, the Olympic National Forest, and on private lands owned by timber companies.

Maps There is a special USGS map of the park, "Olympic National Park and Vicinity," which is helpful for fishing excursions. Another useful map

HATCHERY FISH

DORSAL FIN RAYS bent, or crooked, less than 2.0 inches high fully extended. Other fins may also contain crooked rays or have "clipped" appearance.

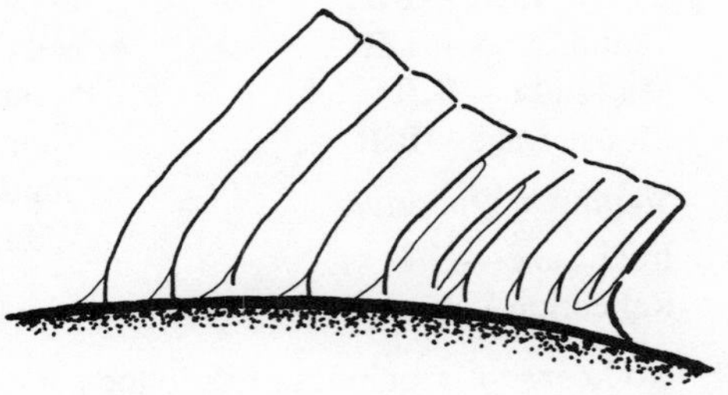

WILD FISH

DORSAL FIN RAYS are not bent or crooked; generally more than 2.0 inches high when fully extended. All other fins with straight, branched fin rays.

is the "Olympic National Forest/Olympic National Park Recreational Map," which details boundaries, hiking trails, roads, and campgrounds. Both maps are available from: Pacific Northwest National Parks and Forests Association, 83 S. King St., Room 212, Seattle, WA, 98104; phone: (206) 442-7958.

Park Address
Olympic NP
600 East Park Avenue
Port Angeles, WA 98362
phone: (206) 452-4501

Chamber of Commerce
Port Angeles C.C.
121 East Railroad Ave.
Port Angeles, WA 98362
phone: (206) 452-2363

Additional Information

A special map, "Steelhead Map of Washington and Oregon," shows the steelhead streams in both states and differentiates between the streams hosting winter runs, summer runs, and both summer and winter runs. The map also contains monthly catch statistics for each stream and is valuable in determining where and when to fish. The Steelhead Map is available from: Frank Amato Publications, P.O. Box 02112, Portland, OR, 97202; phone: (503) 236-2305.

A variety of motels, lodges, and cabins are available inside and outside the park on the Olympic Peninsula. Guides can often be booked at the lodges. For information, write: Resort and Hotel Association, Seattle Ferry Terminal, Seattle, WA, 98104.

The *Washington State Fishing Guide,* by Stan Jones, provides detailed information on rivers and lakes throughout the state. Included are six pages about Olympic National Park describing the park waters with notes on access, campsites, and fishing tips. The book is available from: Stan Jones Publications, 3421 E. Mercer St., Seattle, WA, 98112; phone: (206) 323-3970.

A detailed map of Olympic National Forest is available for a small fee from: Forest Supervisor, Olympic National Forest, Box 2288, Olympia, WA, 98507; phone: (206) 753-9534.

• WEST VIRGINIA

Harpers Ferry National Historical Park

Harpers Ferry is a small town located at the confluence of the Shenandoah and Potomac rivers in West Virginia. The town is famous as the site of John Brown's raid and takeover of the U.S. Armory in 1859. Harpers Ferry was also the scene of continual Civil War activity.

Access The park is in the northeast corner of West Virginia (Jefferson County) and is reached by U.S. 340. The park is about 70 miles northwest of Washington, D.C., and 22 miles southwest of Frederick, Maryland.

Fishing The Shenandoah and Potomac rivers are two of the finest smallmouth bass rivers in the United States. The Shenandoah flows into the Potomac at Harpers Ferry. Both rivers in the Harpers Ferry area are popular for fishing and canoeing.

These rivers combine fast runs, rock ledges, gravel shallows, and slow currents to provide prime habitat for smallmouth. Both rivers contain large numbers of smallmouth that grow fat and big on a diet of minnows, crayfish, and hellgrammites. Most smallmouths average 8 to 12 inches, but the Potomac has a good number of fish in the 3-to-5-pound range.

Fishing gets started in April, when the bass are on their spawning beds. By late April or early May, they are off the beds and actively prowling the shorelines for minnows and crayfish. Working the willow grass beds where minnows hide can be very effective. Water is often high and roily from spring rains during April and May.

By June, the rivers are back to normal and fishing really picks up. Smallmouth are found in the riffles and pools and aren't difficult to catch. The heat of the summer is the time of abundant insect hatches that bring smallmouth to the surface. The white-fly hatch occurs in July, attracting numbers of fly-fishers. A heavily dressed white fly (size 8) such as the White Wulff or Light Cahill is all that is needed for fast dry-fly action. While waiting for a hatch to start, I have often used nymphs on a fly rod to take good-sized smallmouth and channel catfish.

The fall is your best time to catch big bass, usually from late

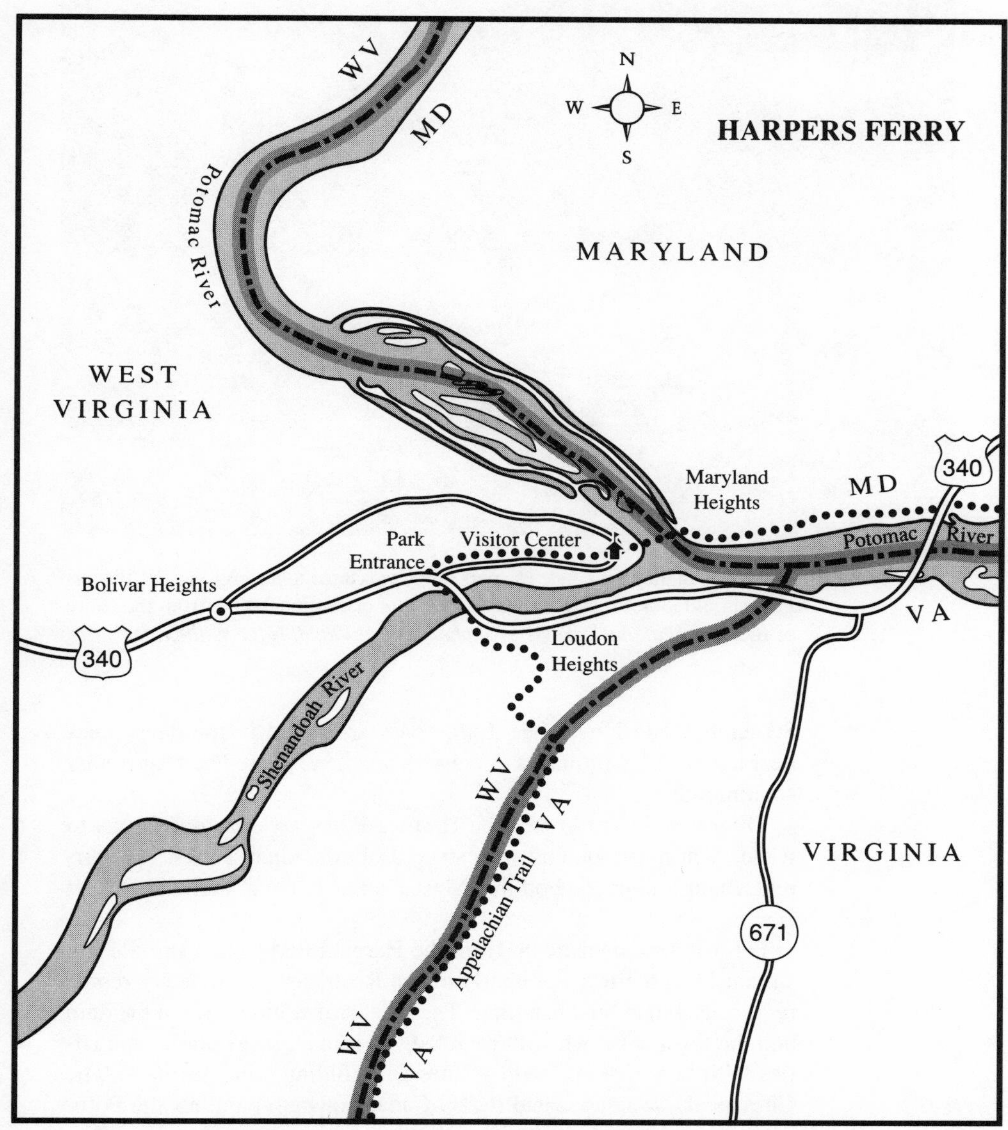
HARPERS FERRY
N
W
E
S
WV
MD
Potomac River
MARYLAND
WEST
VIRGINIA
Maryland
Heights
340
MD
Potomac
River
Park
Entrance
Visitor Center
Bolivar Heights
340
VA
Loudon
Heights
Shenandoah River
WV
VA
Appalachian Trail
VIRGINIA
671
WV
VA

The rivers in the immediate Harpers Ferry area are dangerous to wade. Fishermen should look for safe wadeable stretches or cautiously fish from the shore or rocks.—*National Park Service photo by M. Woodbridge Williams*

September into November. Large bass are found in the deep holes near ledges. Live minnows or crayfish are the preferred bait for trophy smallmouth.

The rivers in the immediate Harpers Ferry area are dangerous to wade. You must contend with steep dropoffs, sharp rocks, fast currents, and a slippery bottom. Most fishing is from shore or raft or canoe.

For 3 miles downstream from the Harpers Ferry Dam (a mile upstream from the town on the Potomac River) are some heavy rapids requiring skilled boat handling. The stretch of water between the dam and the town is strewn with rock ledges, rapids, short pools, and riffles with hundreds of feeding lanes and holding areas for bass. The Chesapeake & Ohio Canal (C&O Canal) towpath parallels the Potomac River. You can hike along the towpath to get to the river. The Harpers Ferry Dam is a Potomac hot spot, especially in the spring.

Upstream from Harpers Ferry on the Shenandoah River is a section of river known as the Stairsteps, which are wadeable and harbor many smallmouth.

My advice is to fish these waters wherever you can get to them. Bait fishing (minnows, crayfish, hellgrammites), jigs, spinners, crankbaits, and flies are all productive. Both rivers are custom-made for fly-fishing. There is plenty of room to fly-cast in a beautiful setting to a river full of cooperative fish. Streamers imitating crayfish, sculpins, and minnows rarely fail, along with a Gold-Ribbed Hares Ear nymph, a dry Adams or Light Cahill, and terrestrials such as a grasshopper or ant.

License With three states bordering the park, the license requirements can be confusing. To fish the Shenandoah, you need a West Virginia license. A Maryland license allows you to fish the Potomac from either the Maryland or West Virginia bank. A Virginia license allows you to fish the Potomac from either the Virginia or Maryland bank. Maryland sells a special Potomac River license to residents of Virginia, West Virginia, and the District of Columbia, allowing them to fish the entire Potomac River from Maryland.

Request a copy of the fishing regulations from the park. The regulations contain a complete description of the license requirements and also a list of the locations in the three states where licenses may be purchased.

Camping There is no camping in the park, but a private campground is nearby.

Maps The park brochure map should suffice.

Park Address
Harpers Ferry NHP
P.O. Box 65
Harpers Ferry, WV 25425
phone: (304) 535-6371

Chamber of Commerce
West Virginia State C.C.
P.O. Box 2789
Charleston, WV 25301
phone: (304) 342-1115

Additional Information The National Park Service office at the C&O Canal provides a free map of the Potomac from Cumberland, Maryland, to Washington, D.C., showing boat ramps and access sites. You should also read the section on the C&O Canal in the Maryland chapter. Contact: C&O Canal NHP, Box 4, Sharpsburg, MD, 21782; phone: (301) 739-4200.

If you are interested in float fishing the upper Potomac and need a fishing guide, see the Additional Information section of the Chesapeake and Ohio Canal National Historical Park, Maryland.

New River Gorge National River

The New River is one of the best and most popular white-water rafting rivers in the East. The park entails a 50-mile stretch of river from below Bluestone Dam at Hinton to just north of the world-famous New River Gorge Bridge on U.S. 19 near Fayetteville.

Access The park is in southern West Virginia (Summers, Raleigh, and Fayette counties) about 55 miles southeast of Charleston. It is accessible by road at a number of places along its 50-mile length. The West Virginia Turnpike/I-77 and U.S. 19 are both major north-south travel routes. U.S. 60 is the primary route for east-west travelers. Another popular road is State Route 3 to Hinton, which is heavily used in the summer by vacationers and especially by folks going to and from Bluestone Lake and the tail waters of the dam.

Fishing The New River is one of West Virginia's best warm-water fisheries. At least six state-record fish have been taken from the New in recent years. Practically every species of warm-water fish found in West Virginia exists in the New, including largemouth, smallmouth, and spotted bass, crappie, walleye, sunfish, channel catfish, and muskellunge.

This is a large river and a difficult one to fish. The fish-catching part is easy, but navigating the river requires special skills. The U.S. Army Corps of Engineers operates Bluestone Dam and regulates the water releases to the New River.

The best flows for boat fishing and wading are between 1,500 and 3,000 cubic feet per second (cfs). During heavy rains, the Corps releases more water and the Greenbrier River (which joins the New below Bluestone Dam) makes an additional contribution. When the flows exceed 3,000 cfs, the current is too swift and dangerous for fishing. Water flow information is available from the Corps office in Hinton; phone: (304) 466-0156.

The area below Bluestone Dam at Hinton is popular with wading anglers in search of trophy smallmouth bass. The Corps has built launch ramps on State Highways 3 and 20 on both sides of the river. The 11-mile stretch from the dam to Sandstone Falls is a good segment to float by raft, johnboat, or canoe since much of it is shallow and wadeable. This is a one-day float trip. A word of caution: only experienced boaters should attempt to float-fish the New.

Sandstone Falls, on Highway 26, is a local hot spot. This area is very good for smallmouth below the falls. Floating from Sandstone downstream 12 miles to Prince is another popular trip, although some portaging is necessary.

The 12-mile section from Prince to Thurmond is for intermediate and advanced canoeists and rafters. Below Thurmond, you enter the Gorge and exit at Fayette Station below U.S. 19. This river segment is for expert boaters only and was known as the River of Death by

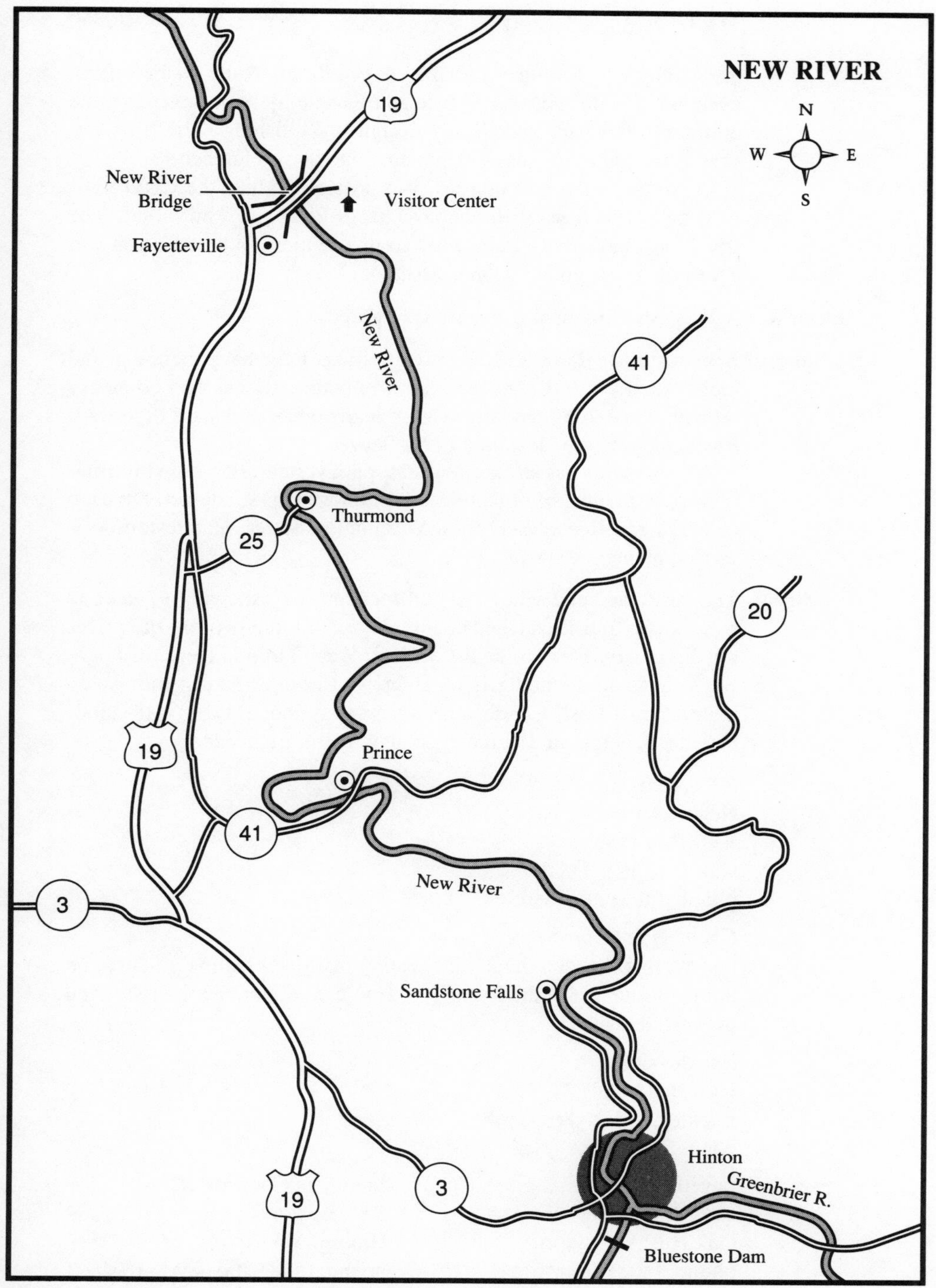
NEW RIVER
N
W
E
S
19
New River
Bridge
Visitor Center
Fayetteville
New River
41
Thurmond
25
20
19
Prince
41
New River
3
Sandstone Falls
Hinton
Greenbrier R.
3
19
Bluestone Dam

the Conoy and Mohican Indians. A significant white-water rafting business operates between Prince and Fayette Station. Several of the outfitters offer trips specifically designed for fishing. The trips can vary from one to five days, depending on your preference.

If you are really adventurous, it is possible to hike the C&O Railroad bed, which parallels the river from Prince to Thurmond. The tracks still have daily train runs, so use caution. Wherever you can get to the river, good action is assured.

License A West Virginia fishing license is required.

Camping Babcock State Park and Grandview State Park have camping and lodge facilities. Both state parks are within the national river boundary but are operated by the state. Other nearby state parks are Pipestem, Bluestone, Hawks Nest, and Little Beaver.

West Virginia has an excellent state park system. For more information, reservations, or brochures on the above parks, contact: Division of Parks and Recreation, 1900 Washington Street, Charleston, WV 25305; phone: (304) 348-2764.

Maps The park can send you a general location map showing towns and river access areas. Detailed county maps are more helpful; the prices for these vary. For a price list contact: West Virginia Dept. of Highways, Systems Planning Div., Bldg. 5, Room A-824, 1900 Washington Street East, Charleston, WV 25305; phone: (304) 348-2868. Fayette, Raleigh, and Summers county maps are needed.

Park Address
New River Gorge NR
P.O. Box 1189
Oak Hill, WV 25901
phone: (304) 465-0508

Chambers of Commerce
For overnight accommodations, eating facilities, fishing guides, and points of interest in the New River Gorge area, contact the following organizations:

Beckley/Raleigh C.C.
P.O. Box 1798
Beckley, WV 25802-1798
phone: (304) 252-7328

Fayette Plateau C.C.
214 Main Street
Oak Hill, WV 25901
phone: (304) 465-5617

Summers County C.C.
P.O. Box 309
Hinton, WV 25951
phone: (304) 466-5332

Additional Information The "West Virginia Stream Map" is available from: Department of Natural Resources, Wildlife Division, 1800 Washington Street East, Charleston, WV, 25305; phone: (304) 348-2771. This map contains a wealth of information for the entire state. Also request the *West Virginia Trout Fishing Guide*.

• WISCONSIN

Apostle Islands National Lakeshore

The Apostle Islands are a group of 22 islands off of the tip of the northern Wisconsin mainland in Lake Superior. Twenty of the 22 islands, and a 12-mile section of mainland shoreline on the Bayfield Peninsula, comprise the National Lakeshore.

Access The Bayfield Peninsula is approximately 71 miles northeast of Duluth, Minnesota, via Wisconsin Highway 13.

Fishing The Apostle Islands area is one of the best fish-producing habitats in Lake Superior. Fishing near the islands is good for steelhead, lake and brown trout, coho, chinook, and pink salmon, and splake (brook trout–lake trout hybrid), with some northern pike and smallmouth bass. Stream fishing for trout is good on the Sand River within the park on the Bayfield Peninsula, which has a number of fine trout streams.

Fishing is good much of the year at the Apostle Islands, with spring through early fall the most productive and popular time. In the spring, the river mouths and shoreline along the peninsula are hot spots for brown and lake trout, coho salmon, steelhead, and splake. Splake are stocked regularly in Chequamenon Bay and usually provide good fall fishing. Steelhead move into the Sand River in April.

Smallmouth bass fishing starts up in mid-May, and smallmouth are found along the peninsula bays and shorelines until they finish spawning and move to the reefs and rocky dropoffs.

From June through September, lake trout are the favorites. The islands have plenty of shoreline and shoals for trolling. Two of the best areas for lake trout are in the vicinity of Eagle Island, northeast of Cornucopia, and in the South Channel on the south side of Madeline Island, where the water is from 80 to more than 100 feet deep. The South Channel is always a good spot to try for lake trout but deep-water gear is necessary after inshore water temperatures rise.

The inner islands are good for northern pike but not until midsummer, when the waters have warmed and the weed beds have grown to provide pike habitat. Brown trout enter the streams in mid-August through November, and fishing is again good at the river mouths. Look for lake trout in the fall off island points and rock bars.

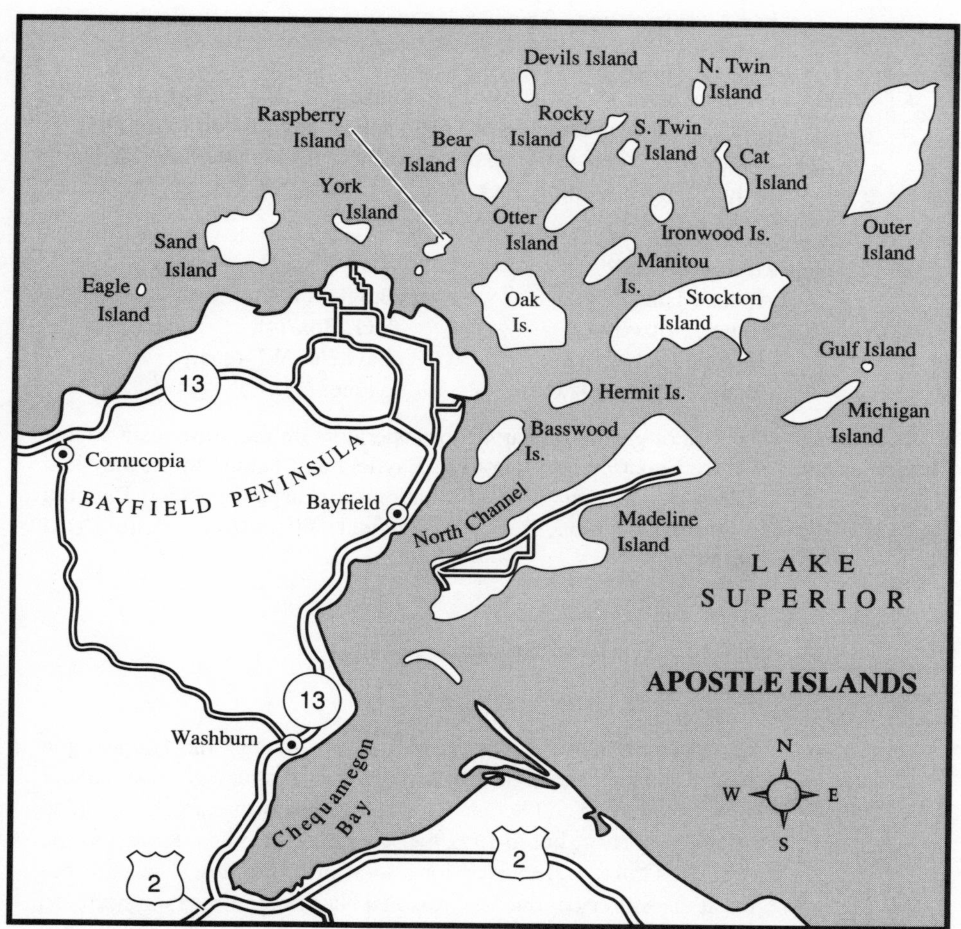

License A Wisconsin fishing license is required. Be sure to check regulations and seasons. At the present time, the lake trout season ends on September 30. If you fish the Sand River, be aware that a portion of the river is located on the Red Cliff Indian Reservation and is closed to fishing to the general public.

Camping Camping is permitted at designated campsites on Raspberry, Basswood, Devils, South Twin, Sand, Oak, and Rocky islands. Camping permits are required for these sites and may be obtained at information or ranger stations. Back-country camping is also permitted.

There are two campgrounds on Stockton Island, one of which is a group campground. Big Bay State Park on Madeline Island also has a campground. Commercial campgrounds are available on the peninsula.

Maps Nautical chart #14973, covering Apostle Islands, is helpful. A Bayfield County map is needed for fishing the many streams in the county. For an order blank and map prices, contact: Document Sales, Department of Transportation, P.O. Box 7713, Madison, WI, 53707; phone: (608) 246-3265.

Park Address
Apostle Islands NL
Route 1, Box 4
Bayfield, WI 54814
phone: (715) 779-3397

Chamber of Commerce
Bayfield C.C.
P.O. Box 138
Bayfield, WI 54814
phone: (715) 779-3335

Additional Information The largest group of charter boat operators on the Wisconsin shores of Lake Superior operate out of Bayfield and belong to the Bayfield Trollers Association. For information on charters, contact: Bayfield Trollers Association, Box 406, Bayfield, WI, 54814; phone: (715) 779-3330.

St. Croix National Scenic Riverway

The upper St. Croix River, including its tributary the Namekagon River, was established in 1968 as one of the original eight rivers under the National Wild and Scenic Rivers Act. The original park included 200 miles of river, but in 1972 the remaining 52 miles, known as the lower St. Croix, were added for a total of 252 miles. The park begins at the sources of the St. Croix and Namekagon rivers in northern Wisconsin and extends to where the St. Croix joins the Mississippi River at Prescott, Wisconsin. The riverway is an important recreation outlet for residents of the Minneapolis–St. Paul metropolitan area, as well as attracting visitors from across the country.

Access The upper Namekagon River portion of the park is in northwestern Wisconsin (Bayfield, Sawyer, Burnett, and Washburn counties) and is accessible via U.S. 63 from Trego upstream to its source at Namekagon Lake. The remaining portions of the St. Croix and Namekagon rivers are accessible by a variety of public roads in each state. For 141 miles, the St. Croix River forms the border between the two states.

Fishing The St. Croix (meaning Holy Cross; it was named by French voyageurs and explorers) and the Namekagon (meaning River of Sturgeon, named by the Ojibway Indians) are both excellent and relatively

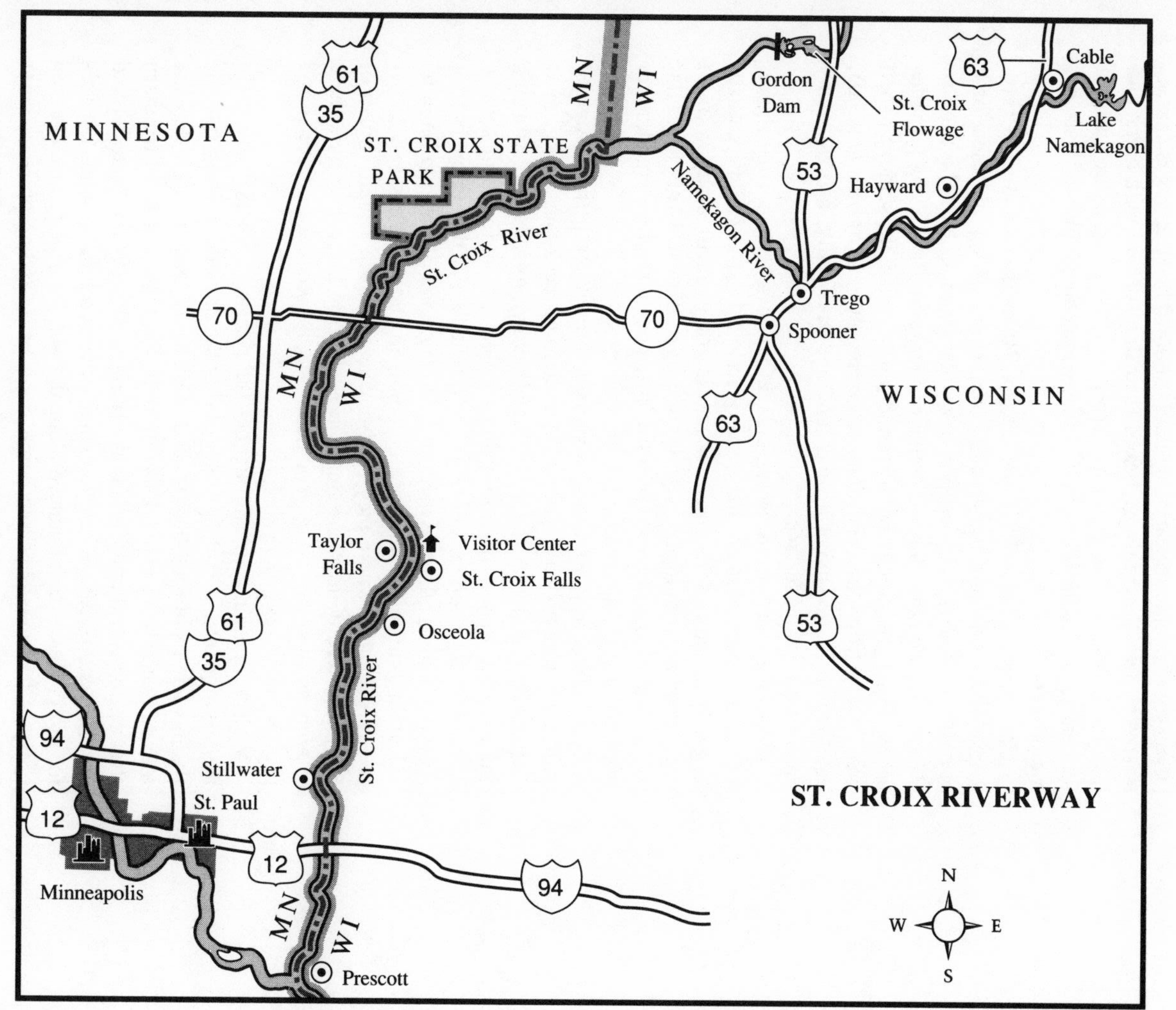
ST. CROIX RIVERWAY
MINNESOTA
WISCONSIN
ST. CROIX STATE PARK
MN
WI
St. Croix River
Namekagon River
Gordon Dam
St. Croix Flowage
Cable
Lake Namekagon
Hayward
Trego
Spooner
Taylor Falls
Visitor Center
St. Croix Falls
Osceola
Stillwater
St. Paul
Minneapolis
Prescott
61
35
70
53
63
94
12
N
S
E
W

underfished rivers. The rivers total 252 miles of fish-filled water, but attract more people for canoeing than fishing. The riverway is characterized by free-flowing stretches of river interspersed with dams and lakelike flowages. The upper St. Croix and Namekagon are suitable for canoes, while the lower St. Croix is wide enough for sailboats and motorboats.

The upper stretch of the Namekagon River, from Cable to Hayward, offers excellent brown and brook trout fishing and most of it is easily wadeable. This section is regularly stocked by the state of Wisconsin and holds a good number of large trout. U.S. 63 provides access along this stretch, but by canoe you can reach the seldom-fished areas away from the road. The large mayfly (*Hexagenia limbata*), hatching in the evenings in mid-June and early July, brings trophy brown trout to the surface.

Below Hayward, trout fishing tails off, and walleye, northern pike, and smallmouth bass are the main quarry. Mixed in will be catfish, largemouth bass, and numerous species of panfish, along with an occasional muskellunge, sturgeon, or sauger. The St. Croix is similar to the Namekagon below Hayward. It is one of the best smallmouth bass rivers in the United States.

Smallmouth bass are widely dispersed throughout the riverway and can reach weights to 6 pounds. Smallmouth seek out rocky areas and can be found near steep banks and below rapids. In the morning and evening, they move into shallow riffle areas and will hit surface lures. Fly-rod poppers and bugs are productive at this time, but for everyday fishing, the crayfish is the favorite food of the smallmouth.

Largemouth bass are more common in the flowages and larger bodies of water, where they seek out heavy cover, usually brush or lily pads. Weedy areas are home to northern pike, which hide there to ambush their prey. Jigs, spinners, and spoons are traditional and proven pike lures.

Walleye are abundant throughout the riverway. Walleye are night feeders, remaining in deep water during the day and moving into the shallow sand and rock bars to feed at night. During the day, they are found in deep holes at the ends of rapids, near the mouths of tributary streams, on river bends, and under bridges. Walleye are bottom feeders and school fish. When you catch one, continue to work the area for more. Jigs or bait bounced along the bottom usually produce.

Bluegill, sunfish, yellow perch, rock bass, and crappie are common throughout the riverway. Their numbers and the ease with which they can be caught will ensure their continued popularity.

Fishing is good throughout the season but is better in the fall, when the rivers are lower and the fish are concentrated in the holes. The riverway can be floated by canoe any time during the fishing season. The park brochure map indicates rapids in both rivers and should be checked before floating. The park provides a list of commercial canoe outfitters along the river.

In the winter, ice fishing is extremely popular on both rivers, particularly along the wider, slower sections of the St. Croix.

License A Wisconsin license is needed to fish the Namekagon River and the 25 miles of the St. Croix River solely in Wisconsin. Along the 141 miles where the St. Croix is the border between the two states, a license from either state suffices when fishing from a boat. Fishing from the shore of either state requires the appropriate state license. Check each state's regulations.

Camping Primitive campgrounds are located along the entire riverway. Developed campgrounds are found in five Minnesota and two Wisconsin state parks along the river. Minnesota state parks are: St. Croix, Interstate, St. Croix Wild River, William O'Brien, and Afton. The Wisconsin parks are Interstate and Kinnichinnic. Accommodations and supplies are available in communities near the riverway.

Maps The park brochure map is sufficient because it shows the numerous access points along the entire riverway. The park can provide photocopied map-and-information sheets of specific river segments for both the Namekagon and St. Croix rivers. These sheets list access points, mileages, canoe information, and more, and are invaluable for trip planning.

A set of five St. Croix canoe route maps from Trego, Wisconsin, on the Namekagon River down to the Mississippi River can be ordered from: Minnesota DNR, Information Unit, Box 40, 500 Lafayette Rd., St. Paul, MN, 55155; phone: (612) 296-6699.

Park Address
St. Croix NSR
P.O. Box 708
St. Croix Falls, WI 54024
phone: (715) 483-3284

Chamber of Commerce
St. Croix C.C.
P.O. Box 178
St. Croix Falls, WI 54024

Additional Information Two spiral-bound river guides are available for the St. Croix River from Danbury, Wisconsin, to the confluence with the Mississippi River. For a catalog and order form, contact: Minnesota Documents Center, 117 University Ave., St. Paul, MN, 55155; phone: (612) 297-3000.

WYOMING

Devils Tower National Monument

Devils Tower is a massive 865-foot tower of columnar rock created by volcanic activity. The park was established in 1906 as the nation's first national monument. It is familiar as the site of the alien landing in the movie *Close Encounters of the Third Kind.*

Access The park is in the northeast corner of Wyoming (Crook County). The park entrance is on Wyoming Highway 24, 7 miles north of U.S. 14.

Fishing The Belle Fourche (pronounced Bell Foosh) River flows through the park for approximately one-half mile. The Belle Fourche is a scenic and attractive river and contains channel catfish, some sauger, and smallmouth bass.

The river is subject to fluctuating flows from water releases at Keyhole Reservoir upstream. Although fishing for channel catfish can be excellent, fishing pressure is light because other nearby waters (Sand Creek, Keyhole Reservoir) are far better.

License A Wyoming fishing license is required.

Camping The park has one campground with 51 spaces.

Maps The map on the park brochure will suffice, although there is a special USGS map, "Devils Tower National Monument."

Park Address
Devils Tower NM
Devils Tower, WY 82714
phone: (307) 467-5370

Chamber of Commerce
Wyoming Travel Commission
I-25 and College Dr.
Cheyenne, WY 82002-0660
phone: (307) 777-7777, or
(toll free out-of-state)
1-800-225-5996

Fort Laramie National Historic Site

From 1834 until 1890, Fort Laramie was an important frontier center located on the Oregon Trail, the main pioneer route west. At various

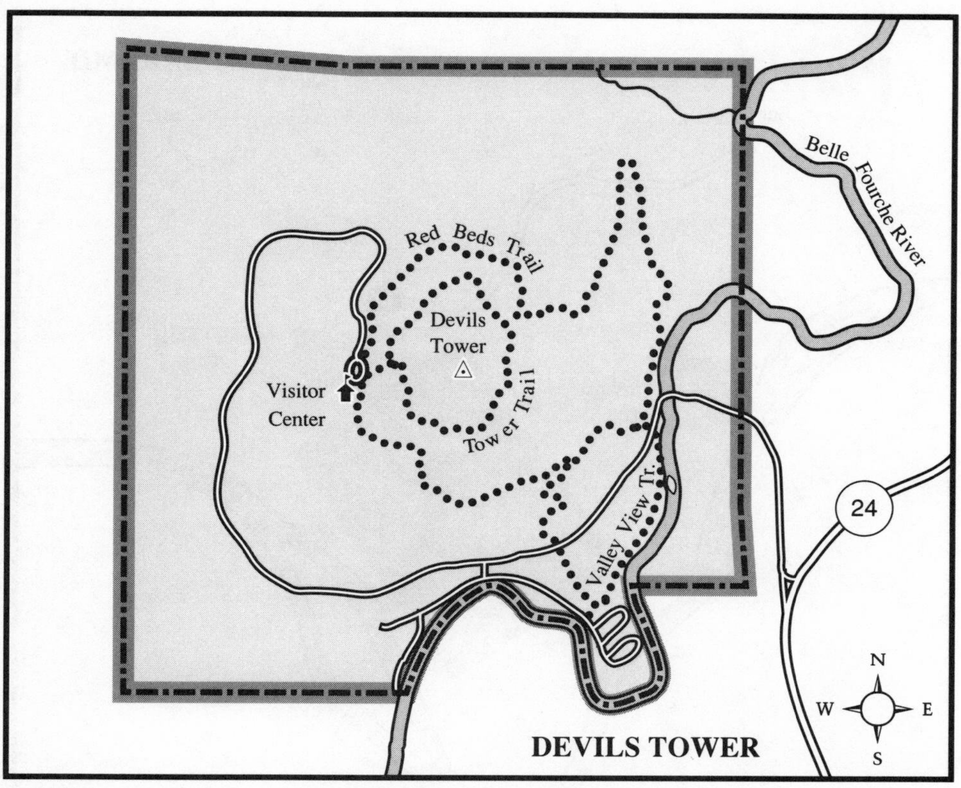

times it was a major trading post, a station for the pony express, and a staging area for military campaigns against the Indians.

Access The park is in eastern Wyoming (Goshen County), 3 miles southwest of the town of Fort Laramie, on U.S. 26.

Fishing The park is located at the junction of the North Platte River and the Laramie River. Two miles of the North Platte River are along the eastern boundary, and 3 miles of the Laramie River are along the southwest part of the park.

The North Platte River in this area is a marginal fishery. River flows are subject to irrigation demands and the main sport fish that has been stocked here is channel catfish. Further upstream, rainbow trout are found below the Glendo Dam.

The Laramie River is noted for its brown trout fishing. The better fishing is upstream, outside the park, although some trout are caught in the park. Most of the river upstream from the park is on

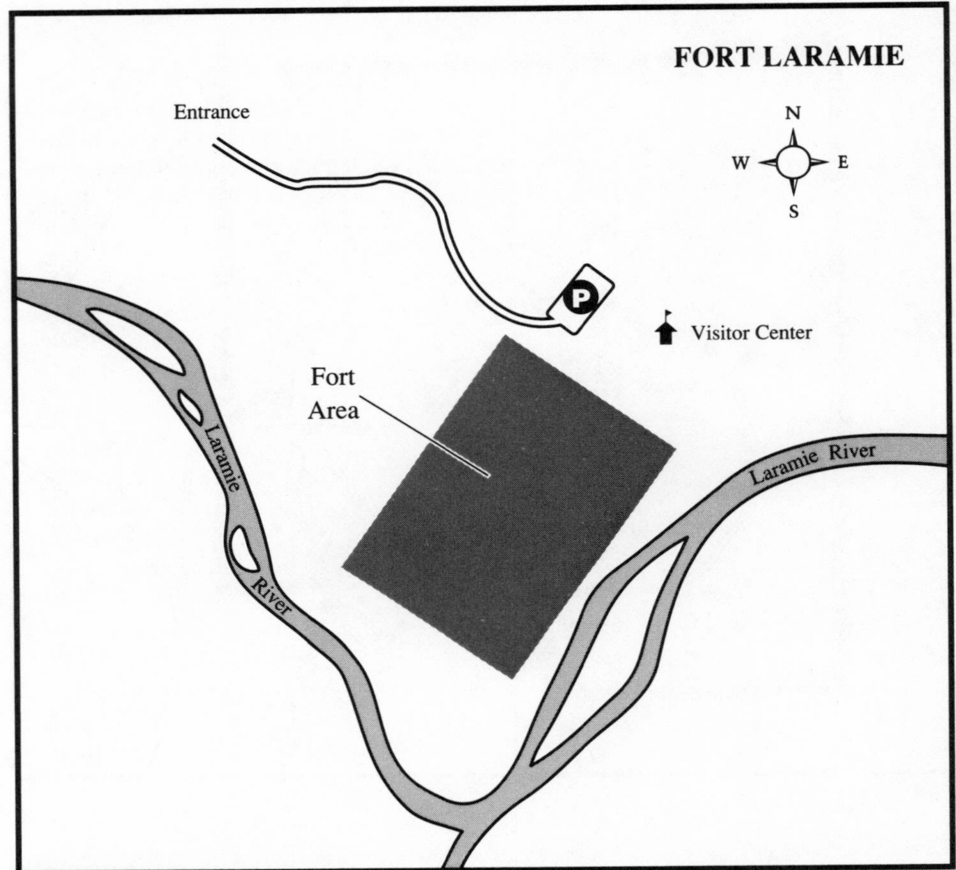

private property and you must obtain access permission from the landowners. The river is accessible along Wyoming Route 230, out of Fort Laramie.

License A Wyoming fishing license is required.

Camping There is no camping in the park, but camping is available in the town of Fort Laramie.

Maps No map is needed.

Park Address
Fort Laramie NHS
Fort Laramie, WY 82212
phone: (307) 837-2221

Chamber of Commerce
Laramie Area C.C.
P.O. Box 1166
Laramie, WY 82070
phone: (307) 745-7339

Grand Teton National Park

The Grand Tetons are a cluster of jagged peaks, rising abruptly without benefit of foothills and totally dominating the landscape. The park is one of the crown jewels of the national park system. It is an exceptional wildlife sanctuary and is part of an immense outdoor recreation region that includes nearby Yellowstone National Park and the Teton, Shoshone, and Targhee national forests.

Access The park is in the northwest corner of Wyoming (Teton County), directly south of Yellowstone National Park. The town of Jackson is the gateway to the park. Highway access to Jackson is via U.S. 26/89/189/191 from the south, Wyoming Highway 22 from the west, and U.S. 26/89/287 from the north.

Fishing There is an abundance of good fishing water in the park. Park waters contain cutthroat, brook, brown, rainbow, and lake trout and whitefish. The Snake River receives the most publicity and is one of the most popular fishing rivers in the country. In addition to the Snake, there are a number of other lakes and streams in the park with good fishing.

The Wyoming Game and Fish Department manages the fishery resources in the park and has developed an outstanding cutthroat fishery in the Snake River, including a specific species, the Snake River cutthroat, that is found only in the upper Snake River watershed. It is identified by bright red slash marks under the throat and small black spots on the yellow-bronze body.

Snake River The Snake River flows south out of Yellowstone Park through the John D. Rockefeller Memorial Parkway area and into Jackson Lake in Grand Teton National Park. The Snake River was dammed in 1916 to form Jackson Lake. The Snake emerges from Jackson Lake to become a major northwestern river as it flows south around the Tetons on the long westward journey to the Columbia River and the Pacific Ocean.

Below Jackson Lake, the usual catch is cutthroat trout, although whitefish are plentiful and there are some brook, brown, and rainbow trout. This park section of the Snake offers some of the finest fishing in the country for cutthroat ranging from 11 to 20 inches.

The Snake River opens for trout on April 1. Early fishing is unpredictable. The Snake gets a heavy snow runoff, and the river remains high and roily until late July or early August. Before the runoff starts, fly-fishing can be good with weighted nymphs and sculpin patterns. Occasionally hatches of small caddis and snowflies provide early dry fly action.

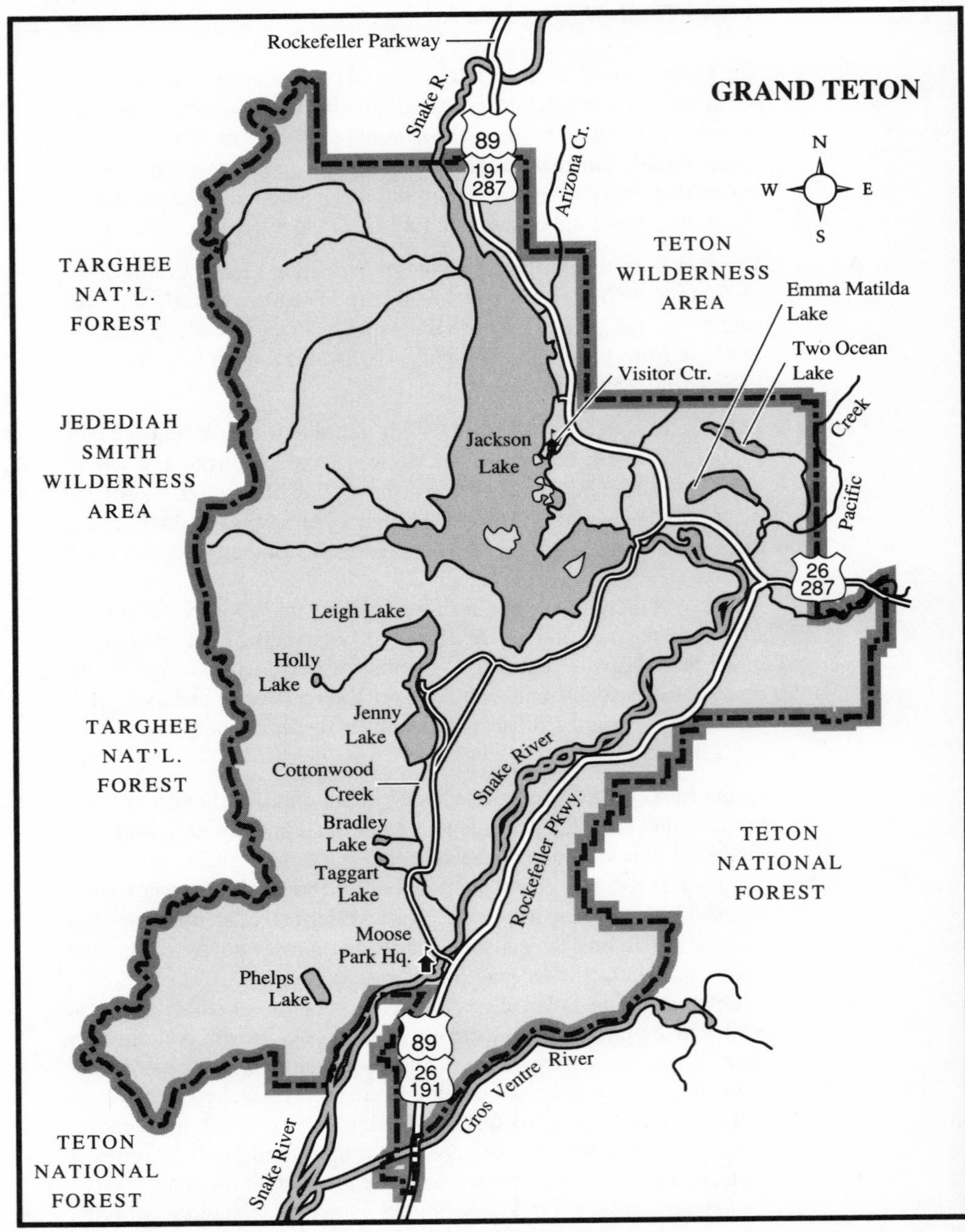
GRAND TETON
Rockefeller Parkway
Snake R.
89
191
287
Arizona Cr.
N
W
E
S
TARGHEE
NAT'L.
FOREST
TETON
WILDERNESS
AREA
Emma Matilda
Lake
Two Ocean
Lake
Visitor Ctr.
JEDEDIAH
SMITH
WILDERNESS
AREA
Jackson
Lake
Creek
Pacific
26
287
Leigh Lake
Holly
Lake
Jenny
Lake
TARGHEE
NAT'L.
FOREST
Cottonwood
Creek
Snake River
Bradley
Lake
Taggart
Lake
Rockefeller Pkwy.
TETON
NATIONAL
FOREST
Moose
Park Hq.
Phelps
Lake
89
26
191
Gros Ventre River
TETON
NATIONAL
FOREST
Snake River

The tributary streams in the park are often clear enough by June to provide some fishing, but from June to early July the Snake is unfishable in the Jackson Hole area. By early August, the river should be in good shape and is best fished with large streamers, weighted nymphs, or spinners. Dry-fly-fishing excels in late August through September. Effective patterns include the Royal Wulff, Yellow or Green Humpy, and grasshopper imitations, along with the standard caddis and mayfly patterns.

One of the most productive ways to fish the Snake is to float it. The river is swift and difficult in places and should be attempted only by experienced boaters. Float-fishing trips are available from a number of guides in the area. If you plan to float the river yourself, a boat permit (free) is required from the park.

Lakes The park lakes offering the best fishing are Jackson, Jenny, Leigh, and Phelps. Most of the high-country lakes in the park are sterile and do not contain fish. Of the remaining lakes, the best bets are Bradley, Taggart, Holly, Surprise, and Lake Solitude. Most of the lakes are ice-covered into July.

Jackson Lake is very good for lake trout and cutthroat trout. It also contains brook and brown trout and whitefish. Jackson has produced lake trout in the 30-to-40-pound range. Fishing near shore and at inlets is good when the ice breaks up in the spring. By July, the fish are in deep water and are taken by trolling, but they return closer to shore in the fall. There are three marinas with boat and motor rentals on the east side of the lake.

Beautiful Jenny Lake is more popular for photography than for fishing. Jenny Lake contains lake and cutthroat trout, whitefish, and a few brook trout. The best fishing is in June and July along shoreline dropoffs.

Leigh Lake has a fish population similar to that of Jenny Lake. Leigh Lake requires a mile hike, or it can be reached by canoe from String Lake.

Phelps Lake is another little-fished lake requiring a hike. It lies southwest of Moose and is accessible only by foot. Fishing is for brook, cutthroat, and lake trout.

Two Ocean and Emma Matilda lakes, on the east side of the park, were formerly popular, but they have declined. Environmental conditions in both lakes are marginal for trout.

Stream Fishing The lower reaches of major tributary streams have the same species as the Snake River. Cottonwood, Upper BC Spring, and Blacktail Spring creeks don't open until August 1 because they are important spawning areas. Cutthroat and brook trout are most abundant.

Wherever you fish in the park, the magnificent Teton Mountains will be your background.—*National Park Service photo by Cecil Stoughton*

The Buffalo Fork River joins the Snake below Moran Junction and has some good fishing for cutthroat in its upper reaches. Pacific and Pilgrim creeks, north of Moran Junction, are marginal for cutthroat. The upstream sections of these creeks, outside the park, are far better but require a long hike. Arizona Creek enters Jackson Lake on the upper east side and is fair for cutthroat and brook trout.

License A Wyoming fishing license is required. Be sure to check park regulations.

Camping The park service operates five campgrounds (908 spaces) from May 15 to October 15, weather permitting. There is also a concessioner-operated trailer village at Colter Bay. Permits are required for overnight trips into the back country. More than a dozen Forest Service and commercial campgrounds are located near the park.

Maps There is a special USGS map of the park, "Grand Teton National Park." Topographic maps are of limited value unless you plan a trip into the back country and are not needed if you confine your fishing to the Snake River and Jackson Lake.

Park Address
Grand Teton NP
P.O. Drawer 170
Moose, WY 83012
phone: (307) 733-2880

Chamber of Commerce
Tourism is the lifeblood of Jackson's economy. The Chamber of Commerce provides a listing of guides, guest ranches, fly shops, and tackle shops, each of which will book your entire trip or provide current fishing information.

Jackson Hole Area C.C.
532 N. Cache Ave.
P.O. Box E
Jackson, WY 83001
phone: (307) 733-3316

Additional Information The *Snake River Guide* provides a detailed description of the Snake River, along with historical notes and maps, all the way from the south entrance of Yellowstone National Park, through Grand Teton National Park, and down to Alpine Junction at the end of the Grand Canyon of the Snake. Available from: Westwater Books, P.O. Box 2560, Evergreen, CO, 80439; phone: (303) 674-5410.

The Wyoming Fishing Guide, by Ken Knapp, describes the fishing opportunities in each county and contains information about both

Grand Teton and Yellowstone National Parks. It is available ($6.95 postpaid) from: Rising Trout Publishing Co., P.O. Box 725, Sheridan, WY, 82801.

John D. Rockefeller Jr. Memorial Parkway

This 82-mile scenic highway starts in Grand Teton National Park and ends in Yellowstone National Park. The distance between the two parks is only 8 miles.

The parkway was named after John D. Rockefeller, Jr., in recognition of his many significant contributions to the cause of conservation in the United States. Grand Teton National Park was made possible through his efforts and generosity.

Access The parkway (U.S. 89) is in northwestern Wyoming (Teton and Park counties).

Fishing The Snake River flows adjacent to the parkway along the 8-mile span between the two parks. The Snake is famous as an excellent river for native cutthroat trout. It has become a popular float stream, particularly the stretch between Yellowstone and Flagg Ranch. Flagg Ranch is a lodge about 2 miles below the Yellowstone boundary. Float trips of varying lengths can be arranged in Jackson, Wyoming.

License A Wyoming fishing license is required.

Camping There are two campgrounds (174 spaces) and one trailer village (175 spaces) along the parkway.

Maps A highway map is sufficient. You can pull the car off the road and walk to the river at a number of points.

Park Address
John D. Rockefeller Jr. MPKY
c/o Grand Teton National Park
P.O. Drawer 170
Moose, WY 83012
phone: (307) 733-2880

Yellowstone National Park

Probably the most famous and most popular park in the United States, if not the world, Yellowstone was established in 1872 as our first

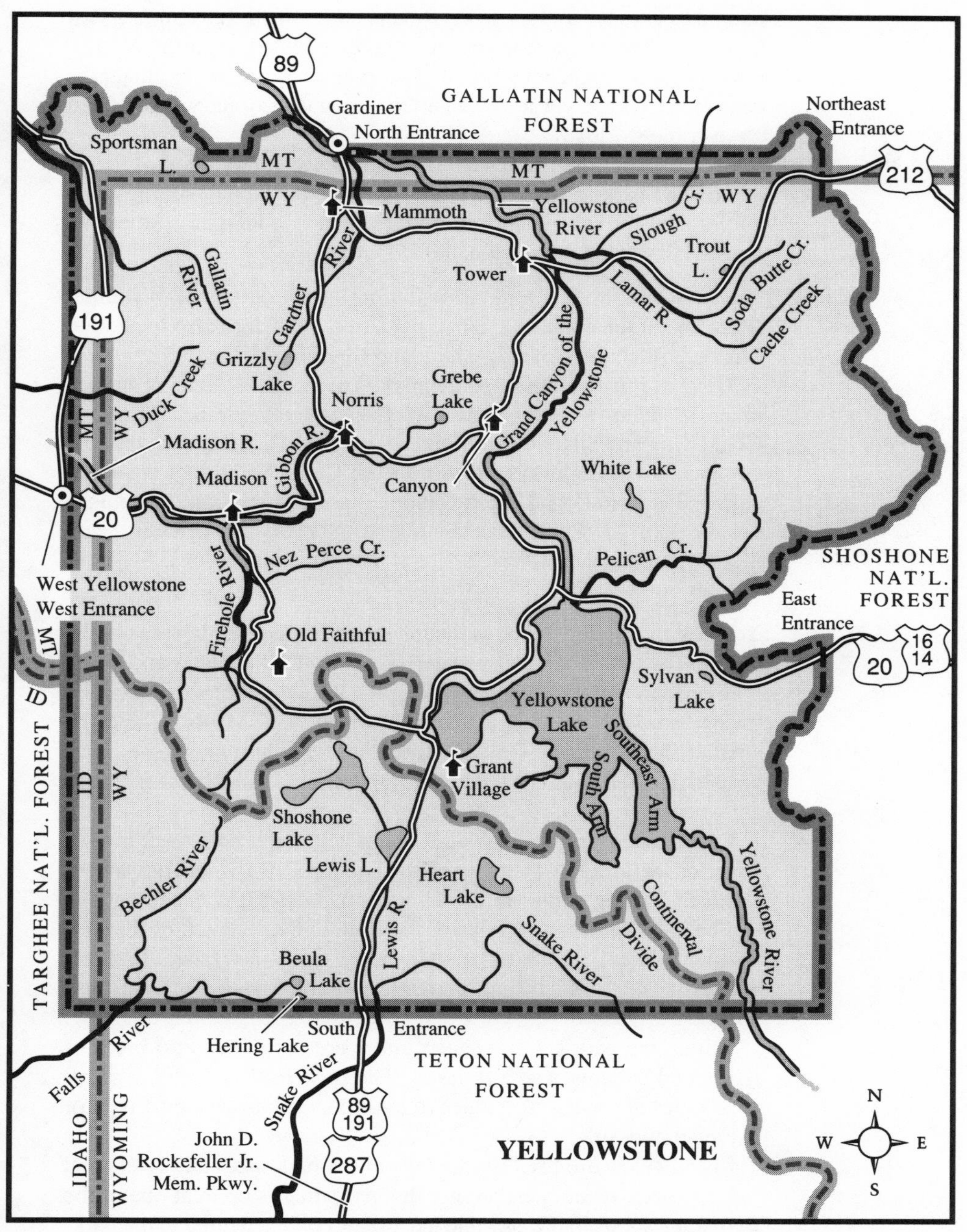
89
GALLATIN NATIONAL FOREST
Gardiner
North Entrance
Northeast Entrance
Sportsman L.
MT
WY
MT
WY
212
Mammoth
Yellowstone River
Slough Cr.
Trout L.
Gallatin River
Gardner River
Tower
Lamar R.
Soda Butte Cr.
Cache Creek
191
Grizzly Lake
Grand Canyon of the Yellowstone
Grebe Lake
Norris
Duck Creek
MT
WY
Madison R.
Gibbon R.
Madison
Canyon
White Lake
20
Nez Perce Cr.
Pelican Cr.
SHOSHONE NAT'L. FOREST
West Yellowstone
West Entrance
Firehole River
East Entrance
Old Faithful
20
16
14
MT
ID
Sylvan Lake
Yellowstone Lake
Southeast Arm
South Arm
TARGHEE NAT'L. FOREST
ID
WY
Grant Village
Shoshone Lake
Bechler River
Lewis L.
Heart Lake
Continental Divide
Yellowstone River
Lewis R.
Snake River
Beula Lake
Hering Lake
South Entrance
River
Falls
TETON NATIONAL FOREST
Snake River
89
191
IDAHO
WYOMING
John D. Rockefeller Jr. Mem. Pkwy.
287
YELLOWSTONE
N
W
E
S

national park. It covers 2,221,773 acres and offers the visitor a vast and unique collection of natural features unequalled on earth. Wilderness, geysers, abundant wildlife, mud pots, thermal basins, magnificent scenery, and a water wonderland annually attract visitors from all over the world.

Until Yellowstone was established, there was no tradition of federally owned parks anywhere in the world; the practice of setting aside public land for conservation and enjoyment is a uniquely American idea. Yellowstone is truly a national treasure.

Access Yellowstone National Park is in the northwest corner of Wyoming (Park and Teton counties). Small parts of the park are also located in Montana (Gallatin County), and Idaho (Fremont County).

There are five entrances to the park. The north entrance is at Gardiner, Montana, on U.S Highway 89; the northeast entrance is through Cooke City and Silver Gate, Montana, on U.S. Highway 212; the east entrance is via Highways 14/16/20 from Cody, Wyoming; the south entrance is from Grand Teton National Park and Jackson, Wyoming, via the John D. Rockefeller Jr. Memorial Parkway (U.S. 89); and the west entrance is at West Yellowstone, Montana, from U.S. Highway 20.

Fishing Yellowstone National Park is the finest public trout-fishing area in the world. The park is a water wonderland of trout-filled lakes and rivers with enough variety for anyone's angling tastes. It offers a choice between broad rivers, such as the Yellowstone and Madison, and the smaller, back-country streams. Lakes abound throughout the park, headed by Yellowstone Lake, one of the best fishing lakes found anywhere.

Experienced anglers may seek the placid waters of the Firehole River or the meadow stretches of the Gibbon River where advanced, technical fishing skills are often required. Less experienced anglers can head to Yellowstone Lake or the Buffalo Ford stretch of the Yellowstone River for cutthroat trout in the 16-to-18-inch range. In short, whatever your trout fishing preference, Yellowstone National Park has it.

Within the park's 3,400 square miles are more than 800 miles of rivers and streams, and 175 lakes. The park road and trail systems (400 miles of road; 1,200 miles of trail) take you to whatever type of fishing you desire.

Listed below are brief discussions of the park lakes and rivers and fishing tackle recommendations. Before fishing, stop in at one of the fly-fishing shops in the area and get a report on the fishing in the park. These people are experts on the area. They can give you information on river conditions and fly hatches and can recommend current hot spots.

Lakes The park is dotted with 175 lakes, most of them in the back country. Not all contain fish, and with the exception of Yellowstone, Lewis, and Sylvan lakes, which are accessible by road, hikes of varying distances are required. Yellowstone, Lewis, and Shoshone lakes are the largest and probably the most popular fishing lakes in the park.

The best fishing on most of the lakes is in June and July and again from September into early October. Motorboats are allowed on Lewis Lake and most of Yellowstone Lake but are not allowed on the back-country lakes.

Yellowstone Lake For consistent action for cutthroat in the 15-to-17-inch range, it's hard to beat Yellowstone Lake, in the middle of the park. This 89,000-acre lake has miles and miles of shoreline to explore. The north and west shores are accessible in places by road, but the remainder can be reached only by boat or on foot.

Because the lake depth averages 140 feet, most of the trout feed near the shore, enabling shoreline anglers to catch fish regularly. It is not necessary to wade, since trout cruise the shoreline within casting distance. For those who prefer to boat, there are launch ramps and a marina on the lake; however, caution should be foremost on this large lake, because rapid weather changes can make boating dangerous.

Some of the best fishing is around inlet streams, especially in June when the trout move out of the lake to spawn. Dry flies (small caddis or mayflies, size 14–16) are productive if the fish are rising; otherwise, wet-fly-fishing is usually good. The cutthroats are not particularly selective, and most wet-fly patterns will work.

Lewis Lake Located about 10 miles south of Yellowstone Lake, Lewis Lake is the third largest lake in the park. Lewis mainly contains brown trout, with some lake trout and a small number of brook trout. Roadside access, a boat launching ramp, and a lake-side campground encourage fishing pressure. The brown trout make fishing a bit more challenging. Rising fish are common in the mornings and evenings.

Lewis Lake is best fished from a boat since the larger trout seem to prefer the shore opposite the road. The lake along the road has a gently sloping bottom and attracts small brown trout. Exercise caution when using a boat; storms come up quickly, just as on Yellowstone Lake.

Shoshone Lake Shoshone Lake is the second largest lake in the park (over 80,000 acres) and is accessible by trail (3- to-4-mile hike) or by boat or canoe from Lewis Lake. The 4-mile-long Lewis River connects the two lakes and can be paddled (no motors allowed) from Lewis to Shoshone. There is less fishing pressure on Shoshone due to the more difficult access.

The lake hosts large brown and lake trout along with some good-sized brook and cutthroat trout. Lake trout and browns are caught near shore early in the season after the ice goes out. In summer, the lake trout move to deeper water; however, there are enough brown trout to keep you busy fishing the shoreline.

Fall (September and October) is the best time to fish. The lake trout come into shallow water to spawn, and the channel between Lewis and Shoshone lakes is filled with spawning brown trout. Other streams flowing into Shoshone Lake also have spawning browns.

Other Lakes Other popular lakes are Grebe, Wolf, and Cascade, which contain grayling. Sylvan Lake, a 28-acre lake off East Entrance Road, is popular because of easy access, but the fishing for cutthroat trout is only fair. Trout Lake, a small 12-acre lake in the northeast corner of the park, contains rainbow trout, some up to 5 pounds. Trout Lake is reached by a short hike from the highway near the northeast entrance. Heart Lake, an 8-mile hike from South Entrance Road, yielded a park-record, 43-pound lake trout.

Listed below are all the lakes in the park that contain fish. The key to fish species is: **B,** brook trout; **BN,** brown trout; **C,** cutthroat trout; **G,** grayling; **L,** lake trout; **R,** rainbow trout; and **W,** mountain whitefish.

Alder Lake—**C**
Basin Creek Lake—**B,C**
Beaver Lake—**B**
Beula Lake—**C**
Blacktail Lake—**B,C**
Buck Lake—**C**
Cascade Lake—**C,G**
Fawn Lake—**B**
Fern Lake—**C**
Goose Lake—**R**
Grebe Lake—**G,R**
Grizzly Lake—**B**
Heart Lake—**C,L,W**
Hering Lake—**C**
High Lake—**C**
Indian Pond—**C**
Joffe Lake—**B**
Lewis Lake—**B,BN, L**
Mammoth Reservoir—**B**
Mariposa Lake—**C**
McBride Lake—**C**
Outlet Lake—**C**
Pocket Lake—**C**
Ribbon Lake—**R**
Sheridan Lake—**C**
Shoshone Lake—**B,BN,C,L**
Sportsman Lake—**C**
Sylvan Lake—**C**
Trail Lake—**C**
Trilobite Lake—**B**
Trout Lake—**C,R**
Unnamed Lake #2041—**C,W**
White Lake—**C**
Wolf Lake—**G,R**
Yellowstone Lake—**C**

Rivers The rivers of Yellowstone belong on a list of top trout waters in the country and are the greatest attraction to the majority of fishing visitors to the park. Rivers such as the Madison, Firehole, Yellowstone, Gallatin, and Gibbon are classic western trout waters that have been extolled for decades in numerous sporting publications. The famous rivers draw most of the crowds, but the park contains many less-publicized rivers and streams that also offer excellent fishing. Described below are some of the top fishing rivers and streams in the park.

Yellowstone River The most popular river in the park and one of the great wild trout fisheries in the country, the Yellowstone River contains cutthroat trout from the southeast corner of the park throughout its length to its exit from the park at Gardiner, Montana. The river is renowned for healthy cutthroat trout averaging 16 to 18 inches and 1 to 2 pounds. They are a delightful fly-fishing target because they are not picky about what they eat, although they show a preference for caddis flies, which abound in the river.

The upper reaches of the river, above Yellowstone Lake (southeast corner area), hold large populations of native cutthroat trout. These reaches are in a seldom-traveled wilderness and rarely see any fishing. The fishing is outstanding for trout averaging 17 inches. Access is by trail or by boat to the river outlet in the southeast arm of Yellowstone Lake, and then by trail.

For a mile below Yellowstone Lake the river is closed to fishing. From there, it flows placidly for 6 miles down to Sulphur Caldron. This is the most popular stretch of the Yellowstone River because here the road parallels the river and fishing is excellent. Within this stretch is the Buffalo Ford access, where catches of 50 to 60 trout a day are not uncommon in the early season; this section opens on July 15.

Buffalo Ford is a good area for novices because cutthroat trout are everywhere and come readily to the fly. Four or five fish may feed almost at your feet while you fish, eating the nymphs that your wading has dislodged. Later in the season, the fishing gets a bit tougher, but terrestrial patterns often produce during the day and caddis patterns in the evening. Try a Prince nymph or a fly with peacock herl in it. This section can be easily waded with a little caution.

Below Sulphur Caldron to Alum Creek, the river is a wildlife study area and closed to fishing. Moose, elk, deer, buffalo, and otter are commonly viewed along this stretch.

The Grand Canyon of the Yellowstone, below the upper and lower falls, is a fine stretch and produces some great fishing. This area is for strong hikers; the trek down into the canyon is difficult enough, but the climb out is downright brutal. Entrance is from the Canyon

The popular Buffalo Ford section of the Yellowstone River consistently produces fine cutthroat trout fishing.—*Suzanne Mingo*

area on the south or Tower from the north. The Seven Mile Hole from Canyon and the Quartz Creek area from Tower are always productive, but the entire stretch contains deep, rarely fished pools full of cutthroat.

The last section in the park is Black Canyon, which flows for 20 miles westward across the north side of the park from Tower to Gardiner. Several trails lead to the river from the Tower-Gardiner Road, and a trail follows along the river's edge. This section is rarely fished for the fat cutthroat, rainbow, and brown trout it contains. Fishing is good from mid-July into the fall. This is predominantly stonefly water, and fishing can be outstanding during the heavy stonefly hatch in July, which local residents call the salmonfly hatch.

Lamar River Located in the northeast corner, the Lamar River flows for 66 miles through the park before joining the Yellowstone River near Tower. The upper stretches and tributaries are accessible by trail and hold small cutthroats. The Lamar parallels the road along its

The author plays a cutthroat trout on the Lamar River.—*Robert Ritsch*

lower reaches from the junction of Soda Butte Creek to Tower. From Cache Creek (just upstream from Soda Butte Creek and accessible by trail) to the Yellowstone River, the Lamar features catch-and-release fishing for cutthroats and rainbows with a very high success rate. The Lamar can be moody. Move around until you find fish. Ignore the riffles and concentrate on the holes and runs.

The Lamar is one of the last streams to clear from spring runoff and it muddies easily after heavy rains. Fishing is usually best later in the summer. Tributaries worth a try are the Little Lamar River, along with Cache, South Cache, Soda Butte, Amphitheater, Flint, Calfee, Cold, and Miller creeks. Soda Butte Creek is especially popular because a road follows it for most of its length. It provides good fishing for cutthroats and rainbows.

Slough Creek Also located in the northeast corner of the park, Slough Creek flows through the park for 16 miles before emptying into the Lamar River, east of Tower. A campground is located on Slough Creek about 4 miles upstream from the Lamar River, but the best fishing for native cutthroat trout requires a hike upstream from the campground to the meadow areas. Fishing is on a catch-and-release basis in Slough Creek.

The section from the campground downstream to the Lamar River is a series of cascades and riffles. Rainbows and rainbow-cutthroat hybrids predominate. By following the trail upstream from the campground, you come to First Meadow (about an hour's hike) and then Second Meadow (a three-hour hike). As expected, First Meadow receives more fishing pressure, but it consistently provides good action for cutthroat averaging 14 inches.

At low water, Slough Creek is wadeable except at the deep pools. However, wading is not necessary in the meadow sections (high grass along the banks), and there isn't any need to haul waders with you on the hike. On the lower cascade-riffle sections, stoneflies are abundant and large stonefly nymphs can be deadly as can black Woolly Worms. Small caddis and mayflies are plentiful (sizes 14–20), and grasshopper patterns can be very effective (especially in the meadows) beginning in late July. Fishing is often slow in June because of spring runoff, but it picks up by July.

Gardner River The Gardner, in the northwestern park area near Mammoth Hot Springs, flows into the Yellowstone River near the north entrance at Gardiner. Osprey Falls divides the river into two distinct sections. The section above the falls is 23 miles long and accessible only by trail. It contains mostly brook trout, many in the 9-to-10-inch range. The 8-mile section below the falls is characterized by swiftly flowing pocket water that holds brown and rainbow trout.

This lower stretch is reached by road (North Entrance Road and Grand Loop Road) and trail. High-floating flies or large weighted nymphs are effective on this fast water. During the fall spawning season, large brown trout move up out of the Yellowstone River into this lower section.

Tributary creeks—Indian, Obsidian, Panther, and Glen—all contain small brook trout. Indian Creek is near a campground and receives more pressure than the others, but it also offers the best fishing.

Gibbon River Another famous and popular river, the Gibbon, flows for 38 miles from Grebe Lake to its confluence with the Firehole

River at Madison Junction, where the two rivers join to form the Madison River. The Gibbon is accessible by road along most of its length. From Gibbon Falls downstream to the Firehole, the river is restricted to fly-fishing. Wary browns and rainbows, including some large fish, inhabit this stretch.

This lower stretch, as well as the river above the falls, has many meadow sections. These sections can prove difficult, for the water is placid and clear. The meadow stretches are best fished during a hatch or with a terrestrial pattern (ants and grasshoppers) using light leaders and small flies. Many prefer the broken-water sections, which are less demanding and allow the use of nymphs or high-floating dry flies (Humpies or Wulff patterns).

The upper river, from Grebe Lake to Elk Park at Norris Geyser Basin, contains numerous small brook trout and some rarely-caught grayling. Brown and rainbow replace the brooks from Elk Park on downstream. Fishing the Gibbon is best in June and July and September and October.

Firehole River The legendary Firehole is restricted to fly-fishing and can be very demanding for all but the most experienced fly-fisher. The order of the day is long leaders, light tippets, small flies, and a delicate approach.

Unlike most of the other park and area streams, which are high and muddy until late June or July, the Firehole is in top fishing condition by the time the general fishing season opens in the park on May 28. The Firehole is fed by thermal springs, and the waters seldom rise or become unfishable. In summer the fishing may drop off because the thermal springs raise the water temperatures to the point where the fish become sluggish and indifferent. July and August are good months to avoid the Firehole. Fishing action picks up again in September.

The Firehole, in the southwestern section of the park, flows past Old Faithful and other less famous geysers. It is a scenic, placid stream for most of its length and easy to wade, but beware of wading too close to hot thermal inlets. The Loop Road follows portions of the river, so access is no problem.

Most of the fish are 11- to-12-inch rainbow and brown trout. Larger fish are found in the Biscuit Basin Meadows river section (14 miles from Madison Junction), but this section also receives the most fishing pressure. Two tributaries are worth fishing near Biscuit Basin. The Little Firehole River joins the Firehole below the bridge, and Iron Spring Creek enters above the bridge. Both contain brooks, browns, and rainbows in the 9- to-11-inch range, but the Little Firehole offers consistently better fishing. During the summer, larger trout move into

Iron Spring Creek from the Firehole to seek the cooler waters, but these trout are very wary and difficult to catch.

Other popular areas to fish on the Firehole include Goose Lake Meadows, Muleshoe Bend just off the road above Midway Geyser Basin, and the section just below Nez Perce Creek. Mayfly and caddis imitations in sizes 14 to 20 are standard, along with small midges. During the summer, grasshopper imitations are effective.

Madison River One of the most famous trout streams in the country, the Madison is formed by the confluence of the Gibbon and Firehole rivers at Madison Junction and flows for 14 miles before leaving the park near West Yellowstone. The river is paralleled by the entrance road from West Yellowstone and receives heavy fishing pressure. The result is that Madison River trout are difficult for the inexperienced to catch.

The Madison deserves its reputation as a great trout stream. The river contains mostly brown trout, along with rainbows. Most of the river within the park is similar to a meadow stream, with smooth flows and deep holes. The Madison is restricted in the park to fly-fishing. Dry flies are effective, with caddis hatches occurring regularly in the evening and grasshoppers abundant in July and August. In broken-water stretches, large stonefly nymphs and streamers are your best bets.

In the fall, large brown trout move out of Hebgen Lake into the park to spawn. Hebgen Lake is just outside the park near West Yellowstone. Most of the tourists are gone after Labor Day, and fall fishing can be exceptional. Outside the park, the river flows into Hebgen and Quake lakes and has been described as "one long riffle." Guided float trips are popular outside the park and can be easily arranged at the fly shops in West Yellowstone.

Gallatin River The gentle, meandering Gallatin River flows for 31 miles in the northwest corner. The upper reaches are accessible by trail and the lower reaches are off U.S. Highway 191. Fishing the highway stretch is fair for cutthroat, rainbow, and brown trout. As expected, most of the fishing occurs along the highway. Better fishing is found in the upper reaches, which require a hike.

The Gallatin has continuous riffles of varying depths. The lack of pools precludes the presence of large fish, and most of the trout average 12 to 13 inches. It is a popular river for fly-fishing because it is wadeable and can be easily covered from shore to shore with a fly rod. Small mayflies and caddis abound in the riffles, and the famed salmonfly hatch (large stoneflies) usually peaks during the last week of June.

Because of late runoff and cold water temperatures from its mountain origins, the Gallatin is most productive from August into late fall. Fishing during a bright, sunny day can be effective.

Lewis River The Lewis River flows south for 4 miles from Shoshone Lake to Lewis Lake. From Lewis Lake, the river continues south for 1 mile to Lewis Falls and then through Lewis Canyon to its confluence with the Snake River near the south entrance. Below the falls, the river is catch-and-release water.

The 4-mile channel between Shoshone and Lewis lakes is only fair during the summer, but in the fall becomes good for large brown trout, which move out of the lakes to spawn. Mixed in with the browns are some lake trout. They usually spawn in the fall in lakes but for some reason also show up in this section of the river. Fishing with large streamers or small spinners and spoons will take both browns and lakers averaging 18 inches. The channel requires a hike of 3 to 4 miles from various starting points, or you can paddle across Lewis Lake to reach it.

Once the river leaves Lewis Lake, it is paralleled by South Entrance Road. The short section between the lake and Lewis Falls is similar to the channel. During most of the season it holds only average size fish, but in the fall, large browns and lake trout move out of Lewis Lake to spawn. This is a fast-flowing, rocky stretch of river, and large stonefly nymphs or streamers (Sculpin, Zonker) usually take fish.

Below the falls, the river becomes a slow-moving meadow stream before entering Lewis Canyon. Rainbows, brooks, and cutthroats are caught, along with the brown trout. Fish the banks with a grasshopper or drift high-floating flies over the riffle areas. When the river enters Lewis Canyon, it becomes inaccessible down to its confluence with the Snake River.

Pelican Creek A popular stream because of the high success rate, Pelican Creek flows into the north end of Yellowstone Lake. This is a major spawning stream for cutthroat trout from the lake and a prolific producer along much of its 52-mile length (fishing is rare above Raven Creek). Pelican Creek is protected by catch-and-release regulations and provides fast action for trout averaging 16 inches. Access is by a trail just east of Fishing Bridge. Be sure to check the regulations as sections of the stream may be closed to fishing.

Bechler River The Bechler River is in the remote southwest corner of the park, an area noted for its outstanding fishing and backpacking. The Bechler is a tributary of the Falls River, which eventually flows into the Henry's Fork of the Snake. Only the mouth of the Bechler is accessible by road. The 20 miles of river in the park are reached only by trail.

The Bechler contains mostly rainbow trout, along with cutthroats. The larger fish are found in its lower stretches. Boundary Creek, a tributary stream, also offers good fishing. The trail in this area is usually wet and soft, and the flies and mosquitoes can be maddening in the summer, so be prepared.

Falls River The Falls River flows for 31 miles out of Beula Lake in the remote southwest corner. The numerous waterfalls and cascades along the river provide its name. The Falls is good for cutthroat and rainbow trout, with fishing success improving as you move further upstream. Trout average 10 to 12 inches, but larger trout are found in the deep pools below the waterfalls. The river is regarded as an excellent fly-fishing stream. Access is by trail or by the old Reclamation Road, a primitive, poorly maintained, dirt road.

Snake River This is the same famous river that flows through Grand Teton National Park further south. The Snake winds for approximately 40 miles through the southern section of the park. Access is limited to lengthy hikes, effectively reducing fishing pressure.

The river contains mainly cutthroat trout and whitefish and a scattering of brook, brown, lake, and rainbow trout. The Snake is more accessible from the John D. Rockefeller Jr. Memorial Parkway, which connects Yellowstone and Grand Teton national parks.

Other Streams The park has too many smaller streams to list and discuss, many tributary to the larger waters discussed above. Listed below are some of the better ones in the park, where you usually can count on catching pan-size trout. During the spawning season, many of these streams receive runs of larger trout, but during the regular season the larger fish are usually found only in the lower sections near the confluence with a major river. The park trail system leads to many of these streams. The major rivers and lakes to which the streams are tributary are noted in parentheses.

Amphitheater Creek (Soda Butte Creek)
Basin Creek (Snake River)
Beaver Creek (Heart Lake)
Blacktail Deer Creek (Yellowstone River)
Boundary Creek (Bechler River)
Cache Creek (Lamar River)
Calfee Creek (Lamar River)
Clear Creek (Yellowstone Lake)
Cold Creek (Lamar River)

Daly Creek (Gallatin River)
DeLacy Creek (Shoshone Lake)
Duck Creek (Madison River)
Fan Creek (Gallatin River)
Grayling Creek (Hebgen Lake)
Heart River (Snake River)
Hellroaring Creek (Yellowstone River)
Indian Creek (Gardner River)
Lava Creek (Gardner River)
Maple Creek (Madison River)
Moose Creek (Shoshone Lake)
Mountain Ash Creek (Falls River)
Pebble Creek (Soda Butte Creek)
Richards Creek (Duck Creek)
Soda Butte Creek (Lamar River)
South Cache Creek (Cache Creek)
Specimen Creek (Gallatin River)
Straight Creek (Winter Creek)
Thorofare Creek (Yellowstone River)
Tower Creek (Yellowstone River)
Winter Creek (Obsidian Creek)

Flies and Tackle The variety of streams in the park calls for fly rod outfits in weights ranging from 4 to 8. A 6-weight outfit is the usual compromise. Long, light tippets to 5x (occasionally smaller) are needed on sections of the Gibbon, Firehole, and upper Madison.

Check with area fly-fishing shops about the fly hatches on specific rivers. Generally, you should carry the following flies: dry flies needed are Wulff patterns, Coachman Trude, Elk Hair Caddis, Adams, Humpies, Pale Morning Dun, Blue-Winged Olive, along with midge and terrestrial patterns (grasshoppers and ants). Nymphs should include the ubiquitous Gold-Ribbed Hare's Ear, Caddis Pupa, Zug Bug, Woolly Worms, and various Stonefly imitations. For streamers, its hard to beat Zonkers, Woolly Buggers, Sculpins, and Muddler Minnows.

Spinning equipment is also popular. Ultralight spinning rods of 5.5 to 7 feet equipped with fast-retrieving reels are effective. The usual assortment of spinners (Mepps, Panther-Martin, Roostertail) and spoons will produce.

License No state fishing license is required to fish in the park. However, a free permit is required, obtainable at all entrance stations, visitor centers, ranger stations, and area fishing tackle shops. Be sure to review the special park fishing regulations, which divide the park into six zones. Some rivers or river sections are restricted to fly-fishing, and other sections may be closed for management purposes.

No boats are permitted on park rivers. No live bait is allowed anywhere in the park and all grayling are protected and may be fished only on a catch-and-release basis. The park fishing season is normally from May 28 to October 31, but some popular rivers near main roads now open earlier and close later.

Camping There are 12 campgrounds in the park, with a total of 2,161 spaces and a recreation vehicle campground with 358 spaces. Only Mammoth Campground is open all year. Bridge Bay Campground (420 spaces) is on the Ticketron reservation system; otherwise, camping is on a first come-first served basis and can be a problem during the summer because of the heavy demand for campsites. By noon, most campgrounds are full. Check the information boards at each entrance to see which campgrounds still have available sites.

A permit is required for overnight trips into the back country. There are numerous private campgrounds outside the park in the West Yellowstone area. In addition, there are numerous Forest Service campgrounds near the park.

Whether you are an experienced angler or a beginner, Yellowstone has trout waters to suit your skills.—*Suzanne Mingo*

Maps There is a special USGS map of the park, "Yellowstone National Park," but some of the information depicted on this map is from the 1950s and no longer accurate. A more current "Trails Illustrated" map is available in a waterproof edition. This map may be obtained from: Yellowstone Library and Museum Association, P.O. Box 117, Yellowstone National Park, WY, 82190; phone: (307) 344-7381.

The park brochure map is very good as a general location map. If you don't plan on backpacking into remote areas, the park brochure map should be sufficient.

Park Address
Yellowstone NP
P.O. Box 168
Yellowstone NP, WY 82190
phone: (307) 344-7381

Chamber of Commerce
West Yellowstone C.C.
P.O. Box 458
West Yellowstone, MT 59758
phone: (406) 646-7701

The park can send a complete packet of information that includes, if specifically requested, a list of area fishing and outdoor guides and outfitters, along with a list of chambers of commerce for the areas surrounding the park.

Additional Information There is no shortage of information about the Yellowstone Park area. Some of the better sources that I have found useful are noted below.

The Yellowstone Fishing Guide, by Robert Charlton, is a comprehensive guide to all the lakes and streams in the park. This spiral-bound, modestly priced book discusses the waters in each park zone (same zones as park regulations) and identifies the best access to each lake or stream. This dependable guide is available from: Robert Charlton, 49 North 6 East, St. Anthony, ID, 83445; phone: (208) 624-4116.

A superb book, *Freshwater Wilderness,* by John Varley and Paul Schullery, is of interest to serious students of park waters. This is not a how-to or where-to tome but instead describes the fish of Yellowstone Park and their history, management, distribution, habitat, spawning habits, and growth rates. It also contains a chapter on fishing in the park, describing the best places and seasons to fish, along with tackle recommendations. In the back is an appendix listing all the park's waters and the species of fish found in them. This book is available from the Yellowstone Library and Museum Association, P.O. Box 117, Yellowstone National Park, WY, 82190; phone: (307) 344-7381.

The late fly-fishing author Charles Brooks wrote a number of books about the trout waters in and around the park. His *Fishing Yellowstone Waters* is a guide containing detailed descriptions of area rivers (both inside and outside the park), effective fishing techniques, and the best flies to use and when to use them. He also wrote *The Living River,* a history and description of the Madison River. His other books, *Nymph Fishing for Larger Trout*; *The Trout and the Stream*; and *Larger Trout for the Western Fly Fisherman,* are how-to books that detail fishing techniques, but they also contain quite a bit of information about park rivers.

Many area fly-fishing shops have catalogs that contain descriptions of the fishing opportunities in the area, recommendations for tackle and clothing, and fly hatch charts. These shops also provide guide and float services (no floating in the park). The park or a chamber of commerce can send you a list of outfitters and fly shops in the area. From this list, request catalogs or phone them for current fishing conditions.

A map of the fly hatches in Yellowstone country is available from Dan Bailey's Fly Shop for $2, postpaid. The map includes tackle and fly recommendations for a number of rivers in the park and surrounding area. I highly recommend this map. Contact: Dan Bailey Flies & Tackle, 209 West Park St., Box 1019, Livingston, MT, 59047; phone: (toll free) 1-800-356-4052.

The Lakes of Yellowstone, by Steve Pierce, is a detailed guidebook describing 49 lakes accessible by car or day-hike and short descriptions of 44 other lakes. Information on each lake includes location, access, source of waters, fish types, thermal features, and individual history. This fine book is available from: The Mountaineers, 306 Second Avenue West, Seattle, WA, 98119; phone: (toll free) 1-800-553-4453.

One of the best discussions of the great fishing in the park is found in the March, 1981 issue of *Fly Fisherman,* in the article "Great Waters—Yellowstone Park." Check local libraries for this back issue or borrow it from a friend.

Write for a free Montana *Vacation Information Guide,* which contains hunting and fishing information, from: Travel Montana, Room 835, Deerlodge, MT, 59722; phone: (406) 444-2654. Out of state, call toll free 1-800-541-1447.

The *Wyoming Family Water Sports* booklet is free and contains information on Wyoming guides and fishing. Contact: Wyoming Travel Commission, I-25 and College Dr., Cheyenne, WY, 82002-0660; phone: (307) 777-7777. Out of state, call toll free 1-800-225-5996.

Information and maps of the adjacent national forests may be obtained from:

Forest Supervisor
Shoshone National Forest
Box 2140
Cody, WY 82414
phone: (307) 527-6241

Forest Supervisor
Gallatin National Forest
Box 130
Bozeman, MT 59771
phone: (406) 587-6701

Forest Supervisor
Bridger-Teton National Forest
Box 1888
Jackson, WY 83001
phone: (307) 733-2752

Forest Supervisor
Targhee National Forest
P.O. Box 208
St. Anthony, ID 83445
phone: (208) 624-3151

• APPENDIX I
Concession Facilities

Listed below are the parks in this book that have concessioner-operated lodging facilities and other services, such as sightseeing tours, raft or pack horse trips, and boat rentals. The park office can usually provide a list of lodging facilities within the park.

The best information source is a book, *National Parks Visitor Facilities and Services,* published by the Conference of Natural Park Concessioners. The book lists each park in the entire national park system that has a concession operation and describes the facilities available, prices, and the necessary addresses and phone numbers. The book can be purchased for $4.15 (postpaid) from: Conference of National Park Concessioners, c/o G.B. Hanson, Mammoth Cave, KY, 42259; phone: (502) 773-2191.

Park List/State

Acadia National Park—Maine
Amistad National Recreation Area—Texas
Apostle Islands National Lakeshore—Wisconsin
Big Bend National Park—Texas
Bighorn Canyon National Recreation Area—Montana/Wyoming
Biscayne National Park—Florida
Black Canyon of the Gunnison National Monument—Colorado
Blue Ridge Parkway—North Carolina/Virginia
Buffalo National River—Arkansas
Canyonlands National Park—Utah
Cape Cod National Seashore—Massachusetts
Cape Hatteras National Seashore—North Carolina
Cape Lookout National Seashore—North Carolina
Capital Reef National Park—Utah
Channel Islands National Park—California
Chattahoochee River National Recreation Area—Georgia
Chesapeake and Ohio Canal National Historical Park—Maryland
Chickasaw National Recreation Area—Oklahoma
Colonial National Historic Site—Virginia
Coulee Dam National Recreation Area—Washington
Crater Lake National Park—Oregon

Cumberland Island National Seashore—Georgia
Curecanti National Recreation Area—Colorado
Denali National Park and Preserve—Alaska
Dinosaur National Monument—Colorado
Everglades National Park—Florida
Fire Island National Seashore—New York
Fort Laramie National Historic Site—Wyoming
Gates of the Arctic National Park and Preserve—Alaska
Gateway National Recreation Area—New York/New Jersey
George Washington Memorial Parkway—Virginia
Glacier Bay National Park and Preserve—Alaska
Glacier National Park—Montana
Glen Canyon National Recreation Area—Arizona/Utah
Golden Gate National Recreation Area—California
Grand Canyon National Park—Arizona
Grand Portage National Monument—Minnesota
Grand Teton National Park—Wyoming
Great Sand Dunes National Monument—Colorado
Great Smoky Mountains National Park—Tennessee
Gulf Islands National Seashore—Florida/Mississippi
Indiana Dunes National Lakeshore—Indiana
Isle Royale National Park—Michigan
Katmai National Park and Preserve—Alaska
Kenai Fjords National Park and Preserve—Alaska
Lake Mead National Recreation Area—Nevada/Arizona
Lake Meredith National Recreation Area—Texas
Lassen Volcanic National Park—California
Mammoth Cave National Park—Kentucky
Mount Rainier National Park—Washington
North Cascades National Park—Washington
Olympic National Park—Washington
Ozark National Scenic Riverways—Missouri
Padre Island National Seashore—Texas
Point Reyes National Seashore—California
Prince William Forest Park—Virginia
Rocky Mountain National Park—Colorado
Sequoia and Kings Canyon National Parks—California
Shenandoah National Park—Virginia
Sleeping Bear Dunes National Lakeshore—Michigan
Theodore Roosevelt National Park—North Dakota
Timpanogos Cave National Monument—Utah
Valley Forge National Historical Park—Pennsylvania
Virgin Islands National Park—Virgin Islands

Voyageurs National Park—Minnesota
Whiskeytown National Recreation Area—California
Wind Cave National Park—South Dakota
Wrangell–St. Elias National Park and Preserve—Alaska
Yellowstone National Park—Wyoming/Montana
Yosemite National Park—California

• APPENDIX 2
State Tourism Offices

As an additional planning aid, you may want to contact the tourism office for a particular state. Listed below are the tourism offices for all 50 states, including phone numbers and toll-free 800 numbers for some states. The toll-free, out-of-state numbers are only for the continental United States.

Alabama Bureau of Tourism and Travel
532 South Perry St.
Montgomery, AL 36104-4614
(205) 832-5510
toll free, in state:
1-800-392-8096
toll free, out-of-state:
1-800-252-2262

Alaska Division of Tourism
Pouch E, TIA
Juneau, AK 99811
(907) 465-2010

Arizona Office of Tourism
1100 West Washington Ave.
1100-A
Phoenix, AZ 85007
(602) 255-4764

Arkansas Tourism Office
One Capitol Mall
Little Rock, AR 72201
(501) 682-7777
toll free, in state:
1-800-482-8999
toll free, out-of-state:
1-800-643-8383

California Office of Tourism
1121 L St.
Suite 103, Dept. TIA
Sacramento, CA 95814
(916) 322-2881
toll free: 1-800-862-2543

Colorado Tourism Board
1625 Broadway
Suite 1700, COLO #1
Denver, CO 80202
(303) 592-5410
toll free: 1-800-433-2656

Connecticut Tourism Division
210 Washington St.
Room 900
Hartford, CT 06106
(203) 566-3948
toll free, in state:
1-800-842-7492
toll free, out-of-state (Maine to Virginia) 1-800-243-1685

Delaware Tourism Office
99 Kings Highway
Box 1401, Dept. TIA
Dover, DE 19903
(302) 736-4254
toll free, in state:
1-800-282-8667
toll free, out-of-state:
1-800-441-8846

Washington DC Convention and Visitors Association
1575 "I" St. NW, 88 STD
Washington, DC 20005
(202) 789-7000

Florida Division of Tourism
126 Van Buren St.
FLDA
Tallahassee, FL 32399-2000
(904) 487-1462

Georgia Tourist Division
PO Box 1776
Atlanta, GA 30301
(404) 656-3590

Hawaii Visitors Bureau
P.O. Box 8527
HVB
Honolulu, HI 96815
(808) 923-1811

Idaho Travel Council
Statehouse Mail Dept. C
Boise, ID 83720
(208) 334-2470
toll free, out-of-state:
1-800-635-7820

Illinois Tourist Information Center
310 S. Michigan
Dept. IOT, Suite 108
Chicago, IL 60604
(312) 793-2094
toll free: 1-800-223-0121

Indiana Tourism Development Division
One North Capitol
Suite 700, IN-DA
Indianapolis, IN 46204
(317) 232-8860
toll free: 1-800-292-6337

Iowa Bureau of Tourism and Visitors
200 East Grand
P.O. Box 6127, TIA
Des Moines, IA 50309
(515) 281-3100
toll free: 1-800-345-4692

Kansas Travel and Tourism Division
400 West 8th
Dept. DIS, 5th Floor
Topeka, KS 66603
(913) 296-2009

Kentucky Department of Travel Development
2200 Capital Plaza Tower, Dept. DA
Frankfort, KY 40601
(502) 564-4930
toll free: 1-800-225-8747

Louisiana Office of Tourism
PO Box 94291, LOT
Baton Rouge, LA 70804-9291
(504) 925-3860
toll free, out-of-state:
1-800-334-8626

Maine Publicity Bureau
97 Winthrop Street
Hollwell, ME 04347-2300
(207) 289-2423
toll free: (September to April, East Coast United States)
1-800-533-9595

Maryland Office of Tourism Development
45 Calvert St., Dept. A
Annapolis, MD 21401
(301) 974-3519
toll free: 1-800-331-1750, operator 250

Massachusetts Office of Travel and Tourism
100 Cambridge Street, 13th Floor
Boston, MA 02202
(617) 727-3201/3202
toll free: (for vacation kit) 1-800-942-6277, ext. TIA)

Michigan Travel Bureau
P.O. Box 30226
Lansing, MI 48909
(517) 373-0670
toll free: 1-800-543-2937

Minnesota Office of Tourism
375 Jackson St., Dept. 21
250 Skyway Level
St. Paul, MN 55101
(612) 296-5029
toll free, in state: 1-800-652-9747
toll free, out-of-state: 1-800-328-1461

Mississippi Division of Tourism
PO Box 22825, Dept. T
Jackson, MS 39205
(601) 359-3426
toll free: 1-800-647-2290

Missouri Division of Tourism
PO Box 1055
Jefferson City, MO 65102
(314) 751-4133

Travel Montana
Room 835
Deerlodge, MT 59722
(406) 444-2654
toll free, out-of-state: 1-800-541-1447

Nebraska Division of Travel and Tourism
PO Box 94666
Room 88937
Lincoln, NE 68509-4666
(402) 471-3794
toll free, in state: 1-800-742-7595
toll free, out-of-state: 1-800-228-4307

Nevada Commission on Tourism
State Capitol Complex
Dept. TIA
Carson City, NV 89710
(702) 885-3636
toll free, out-of-state: 1-800-638-2328

New Hampshire Office of Vacation Travel
105 Loudon Rd.
PO Box 856 DA
Concord, NH 03301
(603) 271-2665

New Jersey Division of Travel and Tourism
20 West State St., CN 826, TIA
Trenton, NJ 08625
(609) 292-2470
toll free: 1-800-537-7397

New Mexico Tourism and Travel Division
1100 M. Montoya Bldg.
Room 777
Santa Fe, NM 887503
(505) 827-0291
toll free: 1-800-545-2040

New York State Commerce Department
Operator 3
One Commerce Plaza
Albany, NY 12245
(518) 474-4116
toll free: 1-800-225-5697

North Carolina Travel and Tourism Division
430 N. Salisbury Street, Dept. 867
Raleigh, NC 27611
(919) 733-4171
toll free: 1-800-847-4862

North Dakota Tourism Promotion
Room 250
Liberty Memorial Bldg.
Capitol Grounds
Bismarck, ND 58505
(701) 224-2525
toll free, in state: 1-800-472-2100
toll free, out-of-state: 1-800-437-2077
in Canada: 1-800-537-8879

Ohio Division of Travel and Tourism
PO Box 1001
Columbus, OH 43266-0101
(614) 466-8844
toll free: 1-800-282-5393

Oklahoma Tourism and Recreation
Marketing Services Division
500 Will Rogers Building, DA 88
Oklahoma City, OK 73105
(405) 521-2406
toll free: 1-800-652-6552

Oregon Tourism Division
595 Cottage St. NE
Salem, OR 97310
(503) 378-3451
toll free, in state: 1-800-233-3306
toll free, out-of-state: 1-800-547-7842

Pennsylvania Bureau of Travel Development
416 Forum Building, Dept. PR 901
Harrisburg, PA 17120
(717) 787-5453
toll free: 1-800-847-4872

Rhode Island Department of Economic Development
Tourism and Promotion
7 Jackson Walkway
Providence, RI 02903
(401) 277-2601

South Carolina Division of Tourism
Box 71
Room 902
Columbia, SC 29202
(803) 734-0122

South Dakota Department of Tourism
Room TIA
Capitol Lake Plaza
711 Wells Ave.
Pierre, SD 57501
(605) 773-3301
toll free, in state: 1-800-952-3625 or 2217
toll free, out-of-state: 1-800-843-8000

Tennessee Department of Tourist Development
PO Box 23170, TNDA
Nashville, TN 37202
(615) 741-2158

Texas Tourist Development Agency
Box 12008
Austin, TX 78711
(512) 462-9191

Utah Travel Council
Council Hall
Capitol Hill
Salt Lake City, UT 84114
(801) 533-5681

Vermont Travel Division
134 State St.
Montpelier, VT 05602
(802) 828-3236

Virgin Islands Division of Tourism
Box 6400, VITIA
Charlotte Amalie, St. Thomas, USVI 00801
(809) 774-8784
toll free: 1-800-372-8784

Virginia Division of Tourism
202 North 9th St.
Suite 500, Dept. VT
Richmond, VA 23219
(804) 786-2051
toll free: 1-800-847-4882

Washington State Tourism Development Division
101 General Administration Bldg.
MSAX-13, WASH
Olympia, WA 98504-0613
(206) 753-5600
toll free: 1-800-544-1800

West Virginia Marketing/ Tourism Division
2101 Washington Street, East
Charleston, WV 25305
(304) 384-2286
toll free: 1-800-225-5982

Wisconsin Division of Tourism Development
P.O. Box 7606
Madison, WI 53707
(608) 266-2161
toll free: 1-800-432-8747 (except Nebraska, Hawaii, and Alaska)

Wyoming Travel Commission
I-25 and College Drive
Cheyenne, WY 82002-0660
(307) 777-7777
toll free, out-of-state: 1-800-225-5996

• APPENDIX 3
State Fish and Wildlife Departments

Listed below are the addresses and phone numbers for all 50 states, the District of Columbia and the Virgin Islands.

Alabama Dept. of Game and Fish
64 N. Union St.
Montgomery, AL 36104
phone: (205) 832-6300

Alaska Dept. of Fish and Game
P.O. Box 3-2000
Juneau, AK 99802
phone: (907) 465-4100

Arizona Game and Fish Dept.
2222 West Greenway Rd.
Phoenix, AZ 85023
phone: (602) 942-3000

Arkansas Game and Fish Commission
#2 Natural Resources Dr.
Little Rock, AR 72205
phone: (501) 223-6300

California Dept. Fish and Game
1416 9th St.
Sacramento, CA 95814
phone: (916) 445-3531

Colorado Division of Wildlife
6060 Broadway
Denver, CO 80216
phone: (303) 297-1192

Connecticut Dept. Environmental Protection
State Office Bldg.
165 Capitol Ave.
Hartford, CT 06115
phone: (203) 566-5599

Delaware Division of Fish and Wildlife
P.O. Box 1401
Dover, DE 19901
phone: (302) 736-4431

District of Columbia Department of Conservation and Regulatory Affairs
Environmental Control Division/Fisheries
5010 Overlook Ave. SW
Washington, D.C. 20032
phone: (202) 767-7370

Florida Game and Freshwater Fish Commission
620 S. Meridian St.
Tallahassee, FL 32301
phone: (904) 488-1960

Florida Division of Marine Resources
Dept. Natural Resources
Douglas Bldg.
Tallahassee, FL 32303
phone: (904) 488-1554

Georgia State Game and Fish Division
Floyd Towers East
Suite 1366
205 Butler St. SE
Atlanta, GA 30334
phone: (404) 656-3530

Hawaii Division of Aquatic Resources
1151 Punchbowl St.
Honolulu, HI 96813
phone: (808) 548-4000

Idaho Fish and Game Dept.
600 S. Walnut St.
Box 25
Boise, ID 83707
phone: (208) 334-5159

Illinois Dept. Conservation
Fish and Wildlife Resources Division
Lincoln Tower Plaza
524 South Second St.
Springfield, IL 62706
phone: (217) 782-6302

Indiana Dept. Natural Resources
Division Fish and Wildlife
607 State Office Bldg.
Indianapolis, IN 46204
phone: (317) 232-4080

Iowa Depart. Natural Resources
Wallace State Office Bldg.
Des Moines, IA
phone: (515) 281-5385

Kansas Fish and Game Commission
Box 54A, RR 2
Pratt, KS 67124
phone: (316) 672-5911

Kentucky Dept. Fish and Wildlife Resources
#1 Game Farm Rd.
Frankfort, KY 40601
phone: (502) 564-3400

Louisiana Dept. Wildlife and Fisheries
P.O. Box 15570
Baton Rouge, LA 70895
phone: (504) 925-3617

Maine Dept. Inland Fisheries and Wildlife
284 State St.
Station #41
Augusta, ME 04333
phone: (207) 289-3371

Maine Dept. Marine Resources
State House Station #21
Augusta, ME 04333
phone: (207) 289-2291

Maryland Dept. Natural Resources
Tawes State Office Bldg.
Annapolis, MD 21401
phone: (301) 974-7947

Massachusetts Division Fisheries and Wildlife
100 Cambridge St.
Boston, MA 02202
phone: (617) 727-3151

Michigan Dept. Natural Resources
Box 30028
Lansing, MI 48909
phone: (517) 373-1220

Minnesota Dept. Natural Resources
Section of Fisheries
500 Lafayette Rd.
St. Paul, MN 55155-4020
phone: (612) 296-6157

Mississippi Dept. Wildlife Conservation
P.O. Box 451
Jackson, MS 39205
phone: (601) 961-5315

Missouri Dept. Conservation
2901 N. Ten Mile Dr.
Jefferson City, MO 65102
phone: (314) 751-4115

Montana Dept. Fish, Wildlife, and Parks
Fisheries Division
1420 East Sixth Ave.
Helena, MT 59620
phone: (406) 449-3186

Nebraska Game and Parks Commission
Box 30370
Lincoln, NB 68503
phone: (402) 464-0641

Nevada Dept. Wildlife
Box 10678
Reno, NV 89520
phone: (702) 784-6214

New Hampshire Fish and Game Dept.
34 Bridge St.
Concord, NH 03301
phone: (603) 271-3421

New Jersey Division Fish, Game, and Wildlife
CN 400
Trenton, NJ 08625
phone: (609) 292-9410

New Mexico Game and Fish Dept.
Villagra Bldg.
Santa Fe, NM 87503
phone: (505) 827-7835

New York Division Fish and Wildlife
50 Wolf Rd.
Albany, NY 12233
phone: (518) 457-5690

North Carolina Wildlife Resources Commission
Archdale Bldg.
512 N. Salisbury St.
Raleigh, NC 27611
phone: (919) 733-3391

North Dakota Game and Fish Dept.
100 North Bismarck Expressway
Bismarck, ND 58501
phone: (701) 224-2180

Ohio Division of Wildlife
Fountain Square
Columbus, OH 43224
phone: (614) 265-6300

Oklahoma Dept. Wildlife Conservation
1801 N. Lincoln Blvd.
P.O. Box 53465
Oklahoma City, OK 73152
phone: (405) 521-3851

Oregon Dept. Fish and Wildlife
Box 59
Portland, OR 97207
phone: (503) 229-5551

Pennsylvania Fish Commission
Box 1673
Harrisburg, PA 17105
phone: (717) 787-6593

Rhode Island Div. Fish and Wildlife
Washington County Government Center
Tower Hill
Wakefield, RI 02879
phone: (401) 789-3094

South Carolina Wildlife and Marine Resources Dept.
Box 167
Columbia, SC 29202
phone: (803) 758-0020

South Dakota Dept. Game, Fish, and Parks
445 East Capitol
Pierre, SD 57501-3185
phone: (605) 773-3387

Tennessee Wildlife Resources Agency
Fish Management Division
Ellington Agriculture Center
P.O. Box 40747
Nashville, TN 37204
phone: (615) 741-1431

Texas Parks and Wildlife Dept.
4200 Smith School Rd.
Austin, TX 78744
phone: (512) 479-4800

Utah Division of Wildlife Resources
1596 W. North Temple
Salt Lake City, UT 84116
phone: (801) 533-9333

Vermont Fish and Game Dept.
103 S. Main St.
10 South
Waterbury, VT 05676
phone: (802) 828-3371

Virgin Islands Dept. Conservation
P.O. Box 4399
St. Thomas, VI 00801
phone: (809) 774-3320

Virginia Dept. of Game and Inland Fisheries
Box 11104
4010 W. Broad St.
Richmond, VA 23230
phone: (804) 257-1000

Washington Dept. of Fisheries
115 General Administration Blvd.
Olympia, WA 98504
phone: (206) 753-6623

West Virginia Division Wildlife Resources
1800 Washington St. East
Charleston, WV 25305
phone: (304) 348-2771

Wisconsin Dept. Natural Resources
Bureau Fish Management
Box 7921
Madison, WI 53707
phone: (608) 266-2121

Wyoming Game and Fish Dept.
5400 Bishop Blvd.
Cheyenne, WY 82002
phone: (307) 777-7631

• APPENDIX 4
National Park Service Regional Offices

North Atlantic Regional Office
National Park Service
15 State St.
Boston, MA 02109
phone: (617) 565-8800
Jurisdiction: Maine, Vermont, New Hampshire, New York, Massachusetts, Connecticut, Rhode Island, New Jersey.

Mid-Atlantic Regional Office
National Park Service
143 South Third St.
Philadelphia, PA 19106
phone: (215) 597-7013
Jurisdiction: Pennsylvania, West Virginia, Delaware, Maryland, Virginia.

National Capital Region
National Park Service
1100 Ohio Drive SW
Washington, D.C. 20242
phone: (202) 655-4000
Jurisdiction: Washington, D.C., and some parks in Maryland, Virginia, and West Virginia.

Southeast Regional Office
National Park Service
75 Spring St. S.W.
Atlanta, GA 30303
phone: (404) 331-5185
Jurisdiction: Kentucky, Tennessee, Mississippi, Alabama, Florida, Virgin Islands, Puerto Rico, Georgia, South Carolina, North Carolina.

Midwest Regional Office
National Park Service
1709 Jackson St.
Omaha, NE 68102
phone: (402) 221-3431
Jurisdiction: Nebraska, Kansas, Missouri, Illinois, Iowa, Minnesota, Wisconsin, Indiana, Michigan, Ohio.

Rocky Mountain Region
National Park Service
12795 West Alameda Parkway
P.O. Box 25287
Denver, CO 80225-0287
phone: (303) 969-2500
Jurisdiction: Colorado, Montana, North Dakota, South Dakota, Wyoming, Utah.

Southwest Regional Office
National Park Service
P.O. Box 728
Santa Fe, NM 87504-0728
phone: (505) 988-6781
Jurisdiction: New Mexico, part of Arizona, Texas, Oklahoma, Arkansas, Louisiana.

Western Region
National Park Service
450 Golden Gate Avenue
Box 36063
San Francisco, CA 94102
phone: (415) 556-4196

Jurisdiction: California, Hawaii, Guam, Nevada, most of Arizona.

Pacific Northwest Region
National Park Service
83 South King Street
Suite 212
Seattle, WA 98104
phone: (206) 442-5565
Jurisdiction: Washington, Oregon, Idaho.

Alaska Region
National Park Service
2525 Gambell St., Room 107
Anchorage, AK 99503
phone: (907) 261-2690
Jurisdiction: All the Alaska parks.

• APPENDIX 5
National Park Service Location Map

Legend to map pp. 436–37

Alabama

1. Horseshoe Bend Nat'l. Military Park

Alaska

1. Aniakchak Nat'l. Monument and Preserve
2. Bering Land Bridge Nat'l. Preserve
3. Cape Krusenstern Nat'l. Monument
4. Denali (Mount McKinley) Nat'l. Park and Preserve
5. Gates of the Arctic Nat'l. Park and Preserve
6. Glacier Bay Nat'l. Park and Preserve
7. Katmai Nat'l. Park and Preserve
8. Kenai Fjords Nat'l. Park
9. Kobuk Valley Nat'l. Park
10. Lake Clark Nat'l. Park and Preserve
11. Noatak Nat'l. Preserve
12. Sitka Nat'l. Historical Park
13. Wrangell-St. Elias Nat'l. Park and Preserve
14. Yukon-Charley Rivers Nat'l. Preserve

Arizona

1. Glen Canyon Nat'l. Recreation Area
2. Grand Canyon Nat'l. Park

Arkansas

1. Arkansas Post Nat'l. Memorial
2. Buffalo Nat'l. River

California

1. Cabrillo Nat'l. Monument
2. Channel Islands Nat'l. Park
3. Devils Postpile Nat'l. Monument
4. Fort Point Nat'l. Historic Site
5. Golden Gate Nat'l. Recreation Area
6. Lassen Volcanic Nat'l. Park
7. Point Reyes Nat'l. Seashore
8. Redwood Nat'l. Park
9. Sequoia/Kings Canyon Nat'l. Parks
10. Whiskeytown-Shasta-Trinity Nat'l. Recreation Area
11. Yosemite Nat'l. Park

Colorado

1. Black Canyon of the Gunnison Nat'l. Monument
2. Curecanti Nat'l. Recreation Area
3. Dinosaur Nat'l. Monument
4. Great Sand Dunes Nat'l. Monument
5. Rocky Mountain Nat'l. Park

Florida

1. Big Cypress Nat'l. Preserve
2. Biscayne Nat'l. Park
3. Canaveral Nat'l. Seashore
4. Everglades Nat'l. Park
5. Fort Jefferson Nat'l. Monument
6. Fort Matanzas Nat'l. Monument
7. Gulf Islands Nat'l. Seashore

Georgia

1. Chattahoochee River Nat'l. Recreation Area
2. Cumberland Island Nat'l. Seashore
3. Fort Frederica Nat'l. Monument
4. Fort Pulaski Nat'l. Monument
5. Ocmulgee Nat'l. Monument

Hawaii

1. Pu'uhonua o Honaunau Nat'l. Historical Park
2. Puukohola Heiau Nat'l. Historic Site

Indiana

1. Indiana Dunes Nat'l. Lakeshore

Kansas

1. Fort Larned Nat'l. Historic Site

Kentucky

1. Cumberland Gap Nat'l. Historical Park
2. Mammoth Cave Nat'l. Park

Louisiana

1. Jean Lafitte Nat'l. Historical Park

Maine

1. Acadia Nat'l. Park

Maryland

1. Antietam Nat'l. Battlefield
2. Assateague Island Nat'l. Seashore
3. Catoctin Mountain Park
4. Chesapeake and Ohio Canal Nat'l. Historical Park

Massachusetts

1. Cape Cod Nat'l. Seashore

(*legend continued on p. 438*)

WASHINGTON
MONTANA
NORTH DAKOTA
OREGON
IDAHO
SOUTH DAKOTA
WYOMING
NEBRASKA
NEVADA
UTAH
COLORADO
KANSAS
CALIFORNIA
ARIZONA
NEW MEXICO
OKLA
TEXAS
ALASKA

ESOTA
WISCONSIN
MI
MI
VA
ILLINOIS
IN
OHIO
MISSOURI
KY
ARKANSAS
TENNESSEE
MS
AL
GEORGIA
LOUISIANA
FL
SC
NORTH CAROLINA
VIRGINIA
WV
MD
PA
NEW YORK
VT
NH
MAINE
MA
RI
CT
New York
NJ
DE
Maryland
Virginia
HAWAII
U.S. VIRGIN ISLANDS

Michigan
1. Isle Royale Nat'l. Park
2. Pictured Rocks Nat'l. Lakeshore
3. Sleeping Bear Dunes Nat'l. Lakeshore

Minnesota
1. Grand Portage Nat'l. Monument
2. Voyageurs Nat'l. Park

Missouri
1. Ozark Nat'l. Scenic Riverways

Montana
1. Big Hole Nat'l. Battlefield
2. Bighorn Canyon Nat'l. Recreation Area
3. Glacier Nat'l. Park
4. Grant-Kohrs Ranch Nat'l. Historic Site

Nebraska
1. Agate Fossil Beds Nat'l. Monument

Nevada
1. Great Basin Nat'l. Park
2. Lake Mead Nat'l. Recreation Area

New Mexico
1. Gila Cliff Dwellings Nat'l. Monument

New York
1. Fire Island Nat'l. Seashore
2. Gateway Nat'l. Recreation Area
3. Upper Delaware Nat'l. Scenic and Recreational River

North Carolina
1. Blue Ridge Parkway
2. Cape Hatteras Nat'l. Seashore
3. Cape Lookout Nat'l. Seashore

North Dakota
1. Knife River Indian Villages Nat'l. Historic Site
2. Theodore Roosevelt Nat'l. Park

Ohio
1. Cuyahoga Valley Nat'l. Recreation Area
2. Perry's Victory and International Peace Memorial

Oklahoma
1. Chickasaw Nat'l. Recreation Area

Oregon
1. Crater Lake Nat'l. Park
2. John Day Fossil Beds Nat'l. Monument

Pennsylvania
1. Delaware Water Gap Nat'l. Recreation Area
2. Valley Forge Nat'l. Historical Park

South Carolina
1. Congaree Swamp Nat'l. Monument
2. Ninety Six Nat'l. Historic Site

South Dakota
1. Wind Cave Nat'l. Park

Tennessee
1. Big South Fork Nat'l. River and Recreation Area
2. Fort Donelson Nat'l. Battlefield
3. Great Smoky Mountains Nat'l. Park
4. Obed Wild and Scenic River

Texas
1. Amistad Nat'l. Recreation Area
2. Big Bend Nat'l. Park/Rio Grande Wild and Scenic River
3. Big Thicket Nat'l. Preserve
4. Lake Meredith Nat'l. Recreation Area
5. Padre Island Nat'l. Seashore

Utah
1. Canyonlands Nat'l. Park
2. Capitol Reef Nat'l. Park
3. Timpanogos Cave Nat'l. Monument

Virginia
1. Colonial Nat'l. Historical Park
2. George Washington Memorial Parkway
3. Manassas Nat'l. Battlefield Park
4. Prince William Forest Park
5. Shenandoah Nat'l. Park

Virgin Islands
1. Virgin Islands Nat'l. Park

Washington
1. Coulee Dam Nat'l. Recreation Area
2. Mount Rainier Nat'l. Park
3. North Cascades Nat'l. Park Service Complex
4. North Cascades Nat'l. Park
5. Lake Chelan Nat'l. Recreation Area
6. Ross Lake Nat'l. Recreation Area
7. Olympic Nat'l. Park

West Virginia
1. Harpers Ferry Nat'l. Historical Park
2. New River Gorge Nat'l. River

Wisconsin
1. Apostle Islands Nat'l. Lakeshore
2. St. Croix Nat'l. Scenic Riverway

Wyoming
1. Devils Tower Nat'l. Monument
2. Fort Laramie Nat'l. Historic Site
3. Grand Teton Nat'l. Park
4. John D. Rockefeller Jr. Memorial Parkway
5. Yellowstone Nat'l. Park

• INDEX

Bob Gartner is a native of Detroit, Michigan, and has a bachelor's degree from Michigan State University and a master's degree from Texas A&M University in Natural Resource Management. He formerly worked as a park planner with the U.S. Army Corps of Engineers in Fort Worth, Texas, and Savannah, Georgia. He has been with the National Park Service since 1978 in their headquarters office in Washington, D.C. With the park service, he has worked on the following programs: Wild and Scenic Rivers, National Trails, Wilderness, Grazing, Fire, Fisheries, Endangered Species, and Planning.

He currently resides with his wife, Sally, and daughter, Amy, in Burke, Virginia, outside of Washington, D.C. Bob is an avid and well-traveled fisherman, active in Trout Unlimited, the Federation of Flyfishers, and the Bass Anglers Sportsman Society (BASS). Besides fishing, his favorite pastimes are reading and canoeing.